1000

BEST-EVER RECIPES
FROM AWW

THE AUSTRALIAN
Women's Weekly

1000
BEST-EVER RECIPES
FROM AWW

acp books

CONTENTS

It was Ellen Sinclair (Food Editor of *The Australian Women's Weekly* 1968 to 1984) who first started using the words "Best Ever" to describe recipes we'd developed and tested over and over again, until the whole Test Kitchen team thought we had an absolute winner of a recipe on our hands.

The Best Ever title wasn't won easily, I remember many a discussion – sometimes heated ones – over whether a recipe was worthy or not of the title. When the first Australian Women's Weekly soft-covered cookbook was released in 1976, it was called *Best Ever Recipes* – a compilation of wonderful recipes from the Weekly. It sold out completely in a matter of days and went on to be reprinted countless times. Many Australian cooks still use this much-loved cookbook (now out of print) with the roast turkey on the cover.

Thirty-plus years on, we have many more "best ever" recipes, all triple-tested in *The Australian Women's Weekly* Test Kitchen, the standard is just as high now as it was years ago. You can be confident that these recipes will work for you the first time you make them.

Pamela Clark, Director, AWW Test Kitchen

RISE & SHINE

orange, carrot and celery juice

1 large orange (300g), peeled, quartered
1 large carrot (180g), chopped coarsely
1 trimmed celery stalk (100g), chopped coarsely

1   Push ingredients through juice extractor into glass; stir to combine.

preparation time *10 minutes* serves *1*
nutritional count per serving *0.5g total fat; (0g saturated fat); 573kJ (137 cal); 28.6g carbohydrate; 4.2g protein; 1.3g fibre*

watercress, beetroot and celery juice

1 trimmed celery stalk (100g), chopped coarsely
3 baby beetroots (75g), cut into wedges
50g watercress, trimmed
½ cup (125ml) water

1   Push celery, beetroot and watercress through juice extractor into glass; stir in the water.

preparation time *10 minutes* serves *1*
nutritional count per serving *0.4g total fat; (0g saturated fat); 222kJ (53 cal); 8.9g carbohydrate; 3.5g protein; 6g fibre*

silver beet, apple and celery juice

1 trimmed silver beet leaf (80g), chopped coarsely
1 large apple (200g), cut into wedges
1 trimmed celery stalk (100g), chopped coarsely

1   Push ingredients through juice extractor into glass; stir to combine.

preparation time *10 minutes* serves *1*
nutritional count per serving *0.5g total fat; (0g saturated fat); 60kJ (110 cal); 24.6g carbohydrate; 2.4g protein; 7.8g fibre*

raspberry and peach juice

1 large peach (220g), chopped coarsely
¼ cup (35g) raspberries
½ cup (125ml) water

1   Blend or process peach and raspberry until smooth; pour into glass. Stir in the water.

preparation time *10 minutes* serves *1*
nutritional count per serving *0.3g total fat; (0g saturated fat); 301kJ (72 cal); 14.1g carbohydrate; 2.1g protein; 4.5g fibre*

beetroot, carrot and spinach juice

1 small beetroot (100g), cut into wedges
1 small carrot (70g), chopped coarsely
20g baby spinach leaves
½ cup (125ml) water

1   Push beetroot, carrot and spinach through juice extractor into glass. Stir in the water.

preparation time *10 minutes* serves *1*
nutritional count per serving *0.2g total fat (0g saturated fat); 238kJ (57 cal); 11.2g carbohydrate; 2.7g protein; 5.3g fibre*

pineapple, orange and strawberry juice

1 small orange (180g), peeled, quartered
150g pineapple, chopped coarsely
2 strawberries (40g)
¼ cup (60ml) water

1   Push orange, pineapple and strawberries through juice extractor into glass; stir in the water.

preparation time *10 minutes* serves *1*
nutritional count per serving *0.3g total fat; (0g saturated fat); 468kJ (112 cal); 23.2g carbohydrate; 3.5g protein; 6.6g fibre*

watermelon and mint juice

450g watermelon flesh, chopped coarsely
4 mint leaves

1 Blend ingredients until smooth.

preparation time *5 minutes* makes *1 cup (250ml)*
nutritional count per 250ml *1g total fat (0g
saturated fat); 447kJ (107 cal); 22.9g carbohydrate;
1.5g protein; 3.1g fibre*

rosemary mint camomile tea

5cm piece fresh rosemary
¼ cup loosely packed fresh peppermint leaves
4 camomile teabags
5cm strip lemon rind
1 tablespoon honey
1 litre (4 cups) boiling water

1 Combine ingredients in large heatproof jug; stand
3 minutes before straining into cups or tea glasses.

preparation time *5 minutes* serves *4*
nutritional count per serving *0g total fat (0g
saturated fat); 105kJ (25 cal); 6.1g carbohydrate;
0.1g protein; 0.3g fibre*

spiced rosehip and hibiscus tea

2 rosehip and hibiscus teabags
2 x 10cm strips orange rind
1 cinnamon stick
1 litre (4 cups) boiling water

1 Combine ingredients in large heatproof jug; stand
2 minutes. Strain into another large heatproof jug.

preparation time *5 minutes*
cooking time *2 minutes* serves *4*
nutritional count per serving *0g total fat (0g
saturated fat); 13kJ (3 cal); 0.7g carbohydrate;
0.1g protein; 0.2g fibre*

iced mocha

1 tablespoon instant coffee powder
1 tablespoon boiling water
2 tablespoons chocolate-flavoured topping
1½ cups (375ml) cold milk
4 scoops (500ml) vanilla ice-cream
½ cup (125ml) cream, whipped
1 teaspoon drinking chocolate

1 Combine coffee and the water in large heatproof
jug; stir until dissolved. Stir in chocolate-flavoured
topping and milk.
2 Pour mocha into two large glasses and top each
with 2 scoops ice-cream and cream.
3 Sprinkle with sifted drinking chocolate and
serve immediately.

preparation time *10 minutes* serves *2*
nutritional count per serving *49.4g total fat (32.4g
saturated fat); 2985kJ (714 cal); 54.9g carbohydrate;
13.1g protein; 0.4g fibre*

real hot chocolate

1 litre (4 cups) milk
200g milk eating chocolate, chopped
100g dark eating chocolate, chopped

1 Stir milk and both chocolates in medium saucepan
over low heat until chocolate is melted. Do not boil milk.
2 Divide milk among heatproof serving glasses.

preparation time *10 minutes*
cooking time *2 minutes* serves *6*
nutritional count per serving *20.7g total fat (14.5g
saturated fat); 1576kJ (377 cal); 38.2g carbohydrate;
9.1g protein; 1g fibre*

hot mocha

2 cups (500ml) milk
100g dark eating chocolate, chopped coarsely
2 cups (500ml) hot black coffee
1 teaspoon cocoa powder

1   Heat milk in medium saucepan, without boiling.
2   Meanwhile, divide chocolate among four 1¼-cup
(310ml) glasses.
3   Stir coffee into milk then pour mixture into glasses.
Dust with sifted cocoa powder before serving.

preparation time *5 minutes*
cooking time *5 minutes* serves *4*
nutritional count per 250ml *12.1g total fat (7.5g*
saturated fat); 920kJ (220 cal); 21.9g carbohydrate;
5.7g protein; 0.4g fibre

pineapple and rockmelon frappé

1 small pineapple (900g), chopped coarsely
½ small rockmelon (650g), chopped coarsely
40 ice cubes, crushed
2 tablespoons finely chopped fresh mint

1   Blend or process pineapple and rockmelon,
in batches, until smooth; transfer to large jug.
2   Stir in ice and mint; pour into serving glasses.
Serve with fresh mint leaves, if you like.

preparation time *10 minutes* makes *1.5 litres (6 cups)*
nutritional count per 250ml *0.2g total fat (0g*
saturated fat); 213kJ (51 cal); 9.9g carbohydrate;
1.2g protein; 2.5g fibre

indian chai

5 cardamom pods, bruised
10 cloves
1 cinnamon stick
1cm piece fresh ginger (5g), sliced thickly
2 teaspoons fennel seeds
1 teaspoon vanilla extract
3 cups (750ml) water
4 darjeeling teabags
2 cups (500ml) milk
⅓ cup (90g) grated palm sugar

1   Bring cardamom, cloves, cinnamon, ginger, fennel,
extract and the water to the boil in medium saucepan.
Simmer, covered, 5 minutes. Remove from heat; stand,
covered, 10 minutes.
2   Return spice mixture to the boil, add teabags;
remove from heat. Stand 5 minutes.
3   Meanwhile, heat milk in medium saucepan without
boiling. Pour milk into tea mixture; add sugar, stir until
sugar dissolves.

preparation time *5 minutes*
cooking time *10 minutes* makes *1 litre (4 cups)*
nutritional count per 250ml *4.9g total fat (3.2g*
saturated fat); 727kJ (174 cal); 27.9g carbohydrate;
4.3g protein; 0g fibre

mixed berry smoothie

2 cups (300g) frozen mixed berries
1¾ cups (480g) vanilla yogurt
2½ cups (625ml) milk
2 tablespoons honey

1   Blend or process ingredients until smooth.
2   Pour into glasses; serve sprinkled with extra frozen
mixed berries, if you like.

preparation time *5 minutes* makes *1.5 litres (6 cups)*
nutritional count per 250ml *6.8g total fat (4.4g*
saturated fat); 711kJ (170 cal); 18.2g carbohydrate;
8.2g protein; 1.2g fibre

banana smoothie

2 cups (500ml) low-fat milk
2 medium bananas (400g), chopped coarsely
½ cup (140g) low-fat yogurt
1 tablespoon honey
1 tablespoon wheat germ
¼ teaspoon ground cinnamon

1 Blend ingredients until smooth. Serve immediately.

preparation time *5 minutes* makes *1 litre (4 cups)*
nutritional count per 250ml *0.4g total fat (0.2g
saturated fat); 648kJ (155 cal); 28.3g carbohydrate;
8.3g protein; 1.8g fibre*

banana passionfruit
soy smoothie

½ cup (125ml) passionfruit pulp
2 medium ripe bananas (400g), chopped coarsely
2 cups (500ml) soy milk

1 Strain passionfruit pulp through sieve into small bowl;
reserve liquid and seeds.
2 Blend passionfruit liquid, banana and milk, in batches,
until smooth. Pour into large jug; stir in reserved seeds.

preparation time *10 minutes* makes *1 litre (4 cups)*
nutritional count per 250ml *4.7g total fat (0.5g
saturated fat); 702kJ (168 cal); 21.5g carbohydrate;
6.6g protein; 6.5g fibre*

pear and grape juice

1 medium pear (230g), cut into wedges
175g seedless red grapes

1 Push ingredients through juice extractor into glass;
stir to combine.

preparation time *10 minutes* serves *1*
nutritional count per serving *0.4g total fat (0g
saturated fat); 55.6g carbohydrate; 953kJ (228 cal);
2.8g protein; 7.3g fibre*

spiced iced coffee milkshake

¼ cup (20g) ground espresso coffee
¾ cup (180ml) boiling water
2 cardamom pods, bruised
¼ teaspoon ground cinnamon
1 tablespoon brown sugar
3 scoops (375ml) low-fat vanilla ice-cream
2½ cups (625ml) no-fat milk

1 Place coffee then the water in coffee plunger;
stand 2 minutes before plunging. Pour coffee into
small heatproof bowl with cardamom, cinnamon and
sugar; stir to dissolve sugar then cool 10 minutes.
2 Strain coffee mixture through fine sieve into blender
or processor; process with ice-cream and milk until
smooth. Serve immediately.

preparation time *10 minutes* makes *1 litre (4 cups)*
nutritional count per 250ml *1.6g total fat (1.1g
saturated fat); 556kJ (133 cal); 20.4g carbohydrate;
8.6g protein; 0.8g fibre*

vanilla caffé latte

⅓ cup (30g) coarsely ground coffee beans
500ml (2 cups) milk
1 teaspoon vanilla extract

1 Stir ingredients in medium saucepan over low heat
until heated through, but not boiling.
2 Pour through fine strainer into heatproof serving glasses.

preparation time *5 minutes*
cooking time *2 minutes* serves *2*
nutritional count per serving *9.8g total fat (6.4g
saturated fat); 715kJ (171 cal); 12.1g carbohydrate;
8.5g protein; 0g fibre*

strawberry and papaya juice

4 strawberries (80g)
80g papaya (red-fleshed Hawaiian)
½ cup (125ml) water

1 Blend or process ingredients until smooth.

preparation time *10 minutes* serves *1*
nutritional count per serving *0.2g total fat (0g saturated fat); 163kJ (39 cal); 7.7g carbohydrate; 1.7g protein; 3.6g fibre*

coconut mango thickshake

3 medium mangoes (1.3kg)
200ml can coconut milk
1½ cups (375ml) milk
500ml vanilla ice-cream, chopped

1 Cut mango flesh from both sides of the seed. Remove the skin and freeze mango for several hours or until firm.
2 Blend milks, mango and ice-cream, in two batches, until smooth. Serve immediately.

preparation time *10 minutes (plus freezing time)*
makes *2 litres (8 cups)*
nutritional count per serving *11g total fat (8.2g saturated fat); 915kJ (219 cal); 24.7g carbohydrate; 4.5g protein; 2.2g fibre*

fruity vegetable juice

2 medium beetroot (600g), trimmed, quartered
3 trimmed celery sticks (300g)
3 medium carrots (360g), halved lengthways
2 small apples (260g), quartered
2 medium oranges (480g), peeled, quartered

1 Push through juice extractor into jug. Stir to combine.

preparation time *10 minutes* makes *1 litre (4 cups)*
nutritional count per 250ml *0.4g total fat (0g saturated fat); 656kJ (157 cal); 28.3g carbohydrate; 4.6g protein; 10.3g fibre*

tropical delight

1 small pineapple (800g), peeled, chopped coarsely
4 medium apples (600g), chopped coarsely
2 medium oranges (480g), peeled, chopped coarsely

1 Push fruit through juice extractor. Stir to combine.

preparation time *10 minutes* makes *1 litre (4 cups)*
nutritional count per 250ml *0.3g total fat (0g saturated fat); 656kJ (157 cal); 34.5g carbohydrate; 2.3g protein; 6.5g fibre*

mango and grapefruit juice

½ medium mango (215g), skinned, chopped coarsely
1 small grapefruit (350g), juiced
¼ cup (60ml) water

1 Blend ingredients until smooth.

preparation time *5 minutes* makes *1 cup (250ml)*
nutritional count per 250ml *0.9g total fat (0g saturated fat); 782kJ (187 cal); 37.8g carbohydrate; 4.2g protein; 4.6g fibre*

pineapple, orange and passionfruit frappé

½ cup (125ml) passionfruit pulp
1 medium pineapple (1.25kg), chopped coarsely
¾ cup (180ml) fresh orange juice
1 teaspoon finely grated orange rind
2 cups crushed ice

1 Strain passionfruit pulp through sieve into small bowl; reserve seeds and liquid.
2 Blend or process pineapple, orange juice and reserved passionfruit liquid, in batches, until smooth. Add rind and ice; pulse until combined. Stir in seeds.

preparation time *10 minutes* makes *1.5 litres (6 cups)*
nutritional count per 250ml *0.2g total fat (0g saturated fat); 284kJ (68 cal); 11.6g carbohydrate; 1.8g protein; 5g fibre*

minted tomato, rhubarb and lime frappé

4 cups (440g) chopped rhubarb
¼ cup (55g) sugar
¼ cup (60ml) water
4 medium tomatoes (760g), peeled, seeded, chopped
2½ tablespoons lime juice
3 cups ice cubes
2 tablespoons chopped fresh mint

1   Combine rhubarb, sugar and the water in medium saucepan; simmer, covered, about 10 minutes or until rhubarb is tender. Cool.
2   Blend or process rhubarb mixture with remaining ingredients until smooth; serve immediately.

preparation time *10 minutes*
cooking time *12 minutes (plus cooling time)*
makes *1.25 litres (5 cups)*
nutritional count per 250ml *0.4g total fat (0g saturated fat); 368kJ (88 cal); 15.6g carbohydrate; 3.0g protein; 4.8g fibre*

fresh berry frappé

300g blueberries
250g raspberries
4 cups crushed ice
1 cup (250ml) fresh orange juice

1   Blend berries until just smooth. Push puree through fine sieve into large bowl; discard solids in sieve.
2   Stir in ice and juice and spoon into serving glasses; serve immediately.

preparation time *10 minutes* makes *1 litre (4 cups)*
nutritional count per 250ml *0.4g total fat (0g saturated fat); 322kJ (77 cal); 14.6g carbohydrate; 1.4g protein; 4.8g fibre*

peach, apple and strawberry juice

1 medium peach (150g), cut into wedges
1 medium apple (150g), cut into wedges
2 strawberries (40g)

1   Push ingredients through juice extractor into glass; stir to combine.

preparation time *10 minutes* serves *1*
nutritional count per serving *0.3g total fat (0g saturated fat); 451kJ (108 cal); 24.3g carbohydrate; 2.2g protein; 5.1g fibre*

citrus compote

2 large limes (160g)
3 large oranges (900g)
2 medium pink grapefruit (850g)
2 teaspoons sugar
½ vanilla bean, split
1 tablespoon small fresh mint leaves

1   Grate the rind of 1 lime and 1 orange finely; reserve grated rind. Peel remaining lime, remaining oranges, and grapefruit.
2   Segment all citrus over a large bowl to save juice, removing and discarding membrane from each segment. Add segments to bowl with sugar, vanilla bean and reserved rind; stir gently to combine.
3   Stand, covered, at room temperature 5 minutes; sprinkle with mint leaves.

preparation time *20 minutes (plus standing time)*
serves *4*
nutritional count per serving *0.7g total fat (0g saturated fat); 685kJ (164 cal); 33.3g carbohydrate; 4.7g protein; 6.7g fibre*

bircher muesli

2 cups (180g) rolled oats
1¼ cups (310ml) apple juice
1 cup (280g) yogurt
2 medium green apples (300g)
¼ cup (35g) roasted slivered almonds
¼ cup (40g) dried currants
¼ cup (20g) toasted shredded coconut
1 teaspoon ground cinnamon
½ cup (140g) yogurt, extra

1 Combine oats, juice and yogurt in medium bowl.
Cover; refrigerate overnight.
2 Peel, core and coarsely grate one apple; stir into oat
mixture with nuts, currants, coconut and cinnamon.
3 Core and thinly slice remaining apple. Serve muesli
topped with extra yogurt and apple slices.

preparation time *10 minutes (plus refrigeration time)*
serves *6*
nutritional count per serving *9.2g total fat (3g
saturated fat); 1120kJ (268 cal); 36.1g carbohydrate;
8.1g protein; 3.9g fibre*

untoasted muesli

2 cups (180g) rolled oats
½ cup (35g) All-Bran
1 tablespoon sunflower seeds
⅓ cup (55g) sultanas
¼ cup (35g) finely chopped dried apricots
½ cup (80g) finely chopped dried dates
3 cups (750ml) no-fat milk
½ cup (140g) low-fat yogurt

1 Combine rolled oats, All-Bran, sunflower seeds and
dried fruit in large bowl.
2 Divide muesli and milk among bowls. Top with yogurt.

preparation time *10 minutes* serves *6*
nutritional count per serving *4.1g total fat (0.7g
saturated fat); 1132kJ (270 cal); 47.3g carbohydrate;
11.3g protein; 6.2g fibre*

ricotta and banana toasts

8 x 1cm-thick slices fruit bread, toasted
1 cup (240g) ricotta cheese
2 large bananas (460g), sliced thickly
2 tablespoons honey

1 Top toast with cheese and banana; drizzle with honey.

preparation time *5 minutes* serves *4*
nutritional count per serving *10.7g total fat (5g
saturated fat); 2199kJ (526 cal); 87.1g carbohydrate;
15.8g protein; 6.6g fibre*

bircher muesli with figs and pistachios

1½ cups (135g) rolled oats
¼ cup (30g) oat bran
¼ cup (15g) natural bran flakes
¾ cup (180ml) milk
¾ cup (180ml) orange juice
¾ cup (200g) low-fat greek-style yogurt
½ cup (100g) finely chopped dried figs
½ teaspoon ground cinnamon
½ cup (70g) roasted pistachios, chopped coarsely
1 large orange (300g), segmented

1 Combine rolled oats, oat bran, bran flakes, milk,
juice, yogurt, figs and cinnamon in large bowl.
Cover; refrigerate overnight. Stir in half the nuts.
2 Divide muesli among serving bowls; top with orange
segments and remaining nuts.

preparation time *10 minutes (plus refrigeration time)*
cooking time *5 minutes* serves *4*
nutritional count per serving *14.5g total fat (2.9g
saturated fat); 1818kJ (435 cal); 56.1g carbohydrate;
15.1g protein; 10.4g fibre*

pancakes with three toppings

1 cup (150g) self-raising flour
¼ cup (55g) caster sugar
2 eggs
1 cup (250ml) milk

1   Sift flour and sugar into medium bowl; gradually whisk in combined eggs and milk until batter is smooth.
2   Pour ¼ cup batter into heated greased medium frying pan; cook pancake until bubbles begin to appear on surface. Turn pancake; cook until browned lightly. Cover to keep warm. Repeat with remaining batter.
3   Serve pancakes with your choice of topping.

preparation time *5 minutes*
cooking time *20 minutes* serves *4*
nutritional count per pancake *1.4g total fat (0.8g saturated fat); 502kJ (120 cal); 21.7g carbohydrate; 4.4g protein; 0.7g fibre*

TOPPINGS

RHUBARB AND PEAR Bring 2 cups coarsely chopped rhubarb, 1 coarsely chopped medium pear, ¼ cup caster sugar, 2 tablespoons water and 1 teaspoon mixed spice in medium saucepan to the boil. Reduce heat; simmer, stirring occasionally, 5 minutes or until fruit softens slightly.

nutritional count per serving *0.2g total fat (0g saturated fat); 380kJ (91 cal); 19.8g carbohydrate; 1g protein; 2.7g fibre*

ORANGE-GLAZED STRAWBERRIES Stir ¼ cup caster sugar and ¼ cup water in small saucepan over low heat until sugar dissolves. Bring to the boil; boil, uncovered, about 3 minutes or until syrup thickens slightly. Stir in 2 teaspoons finely grated orange rind and 1 tablespoon orange juice; cool. Stir in 250g quartered strawberries and ¼ cup coarsely chopped fresh mint.

nutritional count per serving *0.1g total fat (0g saturated fat); 301kJ (72 cal); 15.5g carbohydrate; 1.2g protein; 1.7g fibre*

CHOCOLATE, BANANA AND HAZELNUT Stir 100g coarsely chopped milk eating chocolate, 10g butter and ½ cup cream in small saucepan over low heat until smooth; drizzle over pancakes. Top with 2 thinly sliced bananas and ¼ cup coarsely chopped roasted hazelnuts.

nutritional count per serving *27.8g total fat (14.7g saturated fat); 1588kJ (380 cal); 29.9g carbohydrate; 4.9g protein; 2.3g fibre*

banana coconut pancakes

1¼ cups (185g) self-raising flour
1½ tablespoons caster sugar
1 egg
1½ cups (375ml) milk

BANANA COCONUT FILLING

90g butter
¾ cup (165g) firmly packed brown sugar
¾ cup (180ml) cream
½ cup (120g) sour cream
4 medium bananas, sliced
2 tablespoons shredded coconut, toasted

CREAM TOPPING

⅓ cup (80g) sour cream
2 tablespoons cream
2 teaspoons icing sugar
2 tablespoons underproof dark rum

1   Sift flour and sugar into medium bowl; gradually whisk in combined egg and milk until batter is smooth. Cover; stand 30 minutes.
2   Pour 2 tablespoons of the batter into heated greased heavy-based medium frying pan; cook pancake until bubbles begin to appear on surface. Turn pancake; cook until browned lightly. Cover to keep warm. Repeat with remaining batter to make a total of six pancakes.
3   Meanwhile, make banana coconut filling.
4   Combine ingredients for cream topping in small bowl.
5   Divide filling among pancakes, fold pancakes over; serve with cream topping.

BANANA COCONUT FILLING Melt butter in frying pan; stir in brown sugar over medium heat 1 minute or until dissolved. Stir in creams then banana and coconut.

preparation time *25 minutes (plus standing time)*
cooking time *15 minutes* serves *6*
nutritional count per serving *47.6g total fat (31.1g saturated fat); 2809kJ (672 cal); 50.1g carbohydrate; 9.4g protein; 3.4g fibre*

buttermilk pancakes with glazed strawberries

4 eggs
2 tablespoons caster sugar
1½ cups (375ml) buttermilk
100g butter, melted
1½ cups (225g) self-raising flour

GLAZED STRAWBERRIES

½ cup (170g) marmalade
1 tablespoon caster sugar
2 tablespoons lemon juice
⅓ cup (80ml) water
250g strawberries, quartered

1   Beat eggs and sugar in small bowl with electric mixer until thick; stir in buttermilk and half of the butter.
2   Sift flour into large bowl; whisk egg mixture gradually into flour until batter is smooth.
3   Heat heavy-based medium frying pan; brush pan with a little of the remaining butter. Pour ¼ cup of the batter into pan; cook pancake until bubbles appear on surface. Turn pancake; cook until browned lightly. Remove from pan; cover to keep warm. Repeat with remaining butter and batter.
4   Meanwhile, make glazed strawberries.
5   Serve pancakes with glazed strawberries.

GLAZED STRAWBERRIES Bring marmalade, sugar, juice and the water to the boil in small saucepan. Add strawberries, reduce heat; simmer, uncovered, about 2 minutes or until strawberries are hot.

preparation time *15 minutes*
cooking time *15 minutes* serves *4*
nutritional count per serving *28.5g total fat (16.5g saturated fat); 2867kJ (686 cal); 87.7g carbohydrate; 17.6g protein; 3.9g fibre*

oatcakes with honeyed ricotta and blueberries

Oatmeal, also sold as oatmeal flour, is made from milled oat kernels; it is not the same product as rolled oats or oat bran. It is available at health food stores.

⅔ cup (100g) wholemeal self-raising flour
1½ teaspoons baking powder
½ teaspoon ground cinnamon
½ cup (70g) oatmeal
2 egg whites
¾ cup (180ml) buttermilk
2 tablespoons honey
20g butter, melted
⅓ cup (60g) fresh blueberries

HONEYED RICOTTA

⅔ cup (130g) ricotta cheese
1 teaspoon finely grated lemon rind
2 tablespoons honey

1 Make honeyed ricotta.
2 Sift flour, baking powder and cinnamon into medium bowl; stir in oatmeal. Gradually whisk in combined egg whites, buttermilk and honey; stir in butter.
3 Pour ¼ cup batter into heated greased small frying pan; cook oatcake about 2 minutes or until bubbles appear on surface. Turn oatcake; cook until browned lightly. Repeat with remaining batter.
4 Serve oatcakes with honeyed ricotta and blueberries.

HONEYED RICOTTA Combine ingredients in small bowl.

preparation time *15 minutes*
cooking time *15 minutes serves 4*
nutritional count per serving *11.1g total fat (6.4g saturated fat); 1547kJ (370 cal); 51.8g carbohydrate; 13.9g protein; 5.5g fibre*

blueberry buttermilk pancakes with bacon

2 cups (300g) self-raising flour
¼ cup (55g) caster sugar
2 eggs
600ml buttermilk
50g butter, melted
1 cup (150g) fresh blueberries
cooking-oil spray
12 thin rindless bacon rashers (360g)
½ cup (125ml) maple syrup

1 Sift flour and sugar into large bowl. Whisk eggs, buttermilk and butter in large jug. Gradually whisk egg mixture into flour mixture until smooth; stir in berries. Pour batter into large jug.
2 Spray large heavy-based frying pan with cooking oil. Pour ¼-cup batter for each pancake into heated pan (you can cook four at a time); cook pancakes until bubbles appear on the surface. Turn pancakes; cook until browned lightly. Cover to keep warm.
3 Repeat process using cooking oil and remaining batter, wiping out pan between batches, to make 14 more pancakes.
4 Meanwhile, heat oiled large frying pan; cook bacon until crisp.
5 Drizzle pancakes with syrup; serve with bacon.

preparation time *10 minutes*
cooking time *25 minutes serves 6*
nutritional count per serving *15.4g total fat (7.7g saturated fat); 2224kJ (532 cal); 71.8g carbohydrate; 24.5g protein; 2.4g fibre*

bacon and corn soufflé omelettes

3 rindless bacon rashers (195g), chopped finely
1 clove garlic, crushed
½ medium red capsicum (100g), chopped finely
3 green onions, chopped finely
125g can corn kernels, drained
6 eggs, separated
1 tablespoon water
20g butter
½ cup (60g) grated gruyère or cheddar cheese

1 Cook bacon in medium non-stick frying pan until crisp. Add garlic, capsicum, onion and corn; cook, stirring, until softened. Remove from heat; cover to keep warm.
2 Lightly beat egg yolks with the water in large bowl until combined.
3 Beat egg whites in large bowl with an electric mixer until soft peaks form. Fold egg whites into egg yolk mixture in two batches.
4 Preheat grill.
5 Melt half of the butter in pan. Pour half of the egg mixture into pan, smooth top. Cook over medium heat until browned underneath. If necessary, cover pan handle with foil, then place pan under hot grill until top is just set.
6 Spoon half of the corn mixture over omelette, sprinkle with half of the cheese. Fold omelette over and slide onto serving plate. Repeat with remaining butter, egg, corn mixture and cheese.

preparation time *15 minutes*
cooking time *15 minutes* serves *2*
nutritional count per serving *41.7g total fat (19.2g saturated fat); 2483kJ (594 cal); 11.8g carbohydrate; 44g protein; 2.5g fibre*

creamy scrambled eggs on brioche with crispy bacon

250g cherry tomatoes
1 tablespoon olive oil
8 slices rindless shortcut bacon (280g)
8 eggs
½ cup (125ml) cream
2 tablespoons finely chopped fresh chives
30g butter
4 slices brioche, toasted

1 Preheat grill.
2 Toss tomatoes in oil. Cook bacon and tomato under grill until bacon is crisp and tomato skins start to split. Cover to keep warm.
3 Meanwhile, place eggs, cream and chives in medium bowl; beat lightly with fork.
4 Heat butter in large non-stick frying pan over medium heat. Add egg mixture, wait a few seconds, then use a wide spatula to gently scrape the set egg mixture along the base of the pan; cook until creamy and just set.
5 Serve brioche topped with egg, bacon and tomatoes.

preparation time *10 minutes*
cooking time *10 minutes* serves *4*
nutritional count per serving *52g total fat (23.9g saturated fat); 3223kJ (771 cal); 40g carbohydrate; 37.6g protein; 2.5g fibre*

1 BACON AND CORN SOUFFLE OMELETTES
2 CREAMY SCRAMBLED EGGS ON BRIOCHE WITH CRISPY BACON
3 SPINACH SCRAMBLED EGGS [P 24] 4 BREAKFAST BURRITO [P 24]

RISE & SHINE 23

spinach scrambled eggs

20g butter
75g spinach leaves
8 slices pancetta (120g)
8 eggs
½ cup (125ml) light cream
4 slices crusty bread

1 Preheat grill.
2 Heat half of the butter in large non-stick frying pan.
Add spinach; cook until spinach just wilts. Drain on
absorbent paper; cover to keep warm.
3 Grill pancetta until crisp; cover to keep warm.
4 Whisk eggs and cream in medium bowl until
combined.
5 Heat remaining butter in same cleaned pan over
medium heat. Add egg mixture; wait a few seconds,
then, using a wide spatula, gently scrape the set egg
mixture along the base of the pan; cook until creamy
and just set.
6 Meanwhile, toast bread.
7 Serve toast topped with pancetta, scrambled eggs
and spinach.

preparation time *10 minutes*
cooking time *10 minutes* serves *4*
nutritional count per serving *25.7g total fat (11.7g
saturated fat); 1559kJ (373 cal); 14.4g carbohydrate;
21.7g protein; 1.1g fibre*

breakfast burrito

250g cherry tomatoes
2 teaspoons olive oil
420g can kidney beans, rinsed, drained
⅓ cup coarsely chopped fresh flat-leaf parsley
1 tablespoon coarsely chopped
    pickled jalapeño chilli
1 tablespoon lime juice
1 large avocado (320g)
8 corn tortillas, warmed
50g baby spinach leaves
1 cup (120g) coarsely grated cheddar cheese

1 Preheat grill.
2 Combine tomatoes and oil in small shallow flameproof
dish; grill about 15 minutes or until tomatoes soften.
3 Combine beans, parsley, chilli and half the juice in
medium bowl with tomatoes.
4 Mash avocado in small bowl with remaining juice.
5 Serve warmed tortillas topped with bean mixture,
avocado, spinach leaves and cheese.

preparation time *25 minutes*
cooking time *20 minutes* serves *4*
nutritional count per serving *26.6g total fat (9.7g
saturated fat); 1810kJ (433 cal); 27.7g carbohydrate;
16.3g protein; 9.1g fibre*

pancetta and eggs

8 slices pancetta (120g)
2 green onions, chopped coarsely
4 eggs
4 thick slices white bread

1 Preheat oven to 200°C/180°C fan-forced.
Oil four holes of 12-hole (⅓ cup/80ml) muffin pan.
2 Line each pan hole with two slices of the pancetta,
overlapping to form cup shape. Divide onion among
pancetta cups; break one egg into each pancetta cup.
3 Bake, uncovered, about 10 minutes or until eggs
are just cooked and pancetta is crisp around edges.
Remove from pan carefully. Serve on toasted bread.

preparation time *10 minutes*
cooking time *10 minutes* serves *4*
nutritional count per serving *10.1g total fat (3.3g
saturated fat); 853kJ (204 cal); 13.1g carbohydrate;
14.9g protein; 0.9g fibre*

baked eggs with herbs and fetta

1 tablespoon finely chopped fresh flat-leaf parsley
1 tablespoon finely chopped fresh mint
1 green onion, sliced thinly
8 eggs
100g firm fetta cheese, crumbled
⅓ cup (40g) coarsely grated cheddar cheese

1 Preheat oven to 180°C/160°C fan-forced.
Oil four ¾-cup (180ml) shallow ovenproof dishes.
2 Divide herbs and onion among dishes; break two
eggs into each dish, sprinkle with combined cheeses.
3 Bake, uncovered, about 10 minutes or until eggs
are just set.

preparation time *10 minutes*
cooking time *10 minutes* serves *4*
nutritional count per serving *19.7g total fat (9.2g
saturated fat); 1083kJ (259 cal); 0.6g carbohydrate;
20.4g protein; 0.2g fibre*

french toast with berry compote

4 eggs
½ cup (125ml) cream
¼ cup (60ml) milk
1 teaspoon finely grated orange rind
1 teaspoon ground cinnamon
¼ cup (85g) honey
100g butter, melted
8 thick slices sourdough bread (320g)
¼ cup (40g) icing sugar

BERRY COMPOTE

1 teaspoon arrowroot
⅓ cup (80ml) water
2 cups (300g) frozen mixed berries
2 tablespoons caster sugar
1 tablespoon finely grated orange rind

1 Whisk eggs into medium bowl; whisk in cream,
milk, rind, cinnamon and honey.
2 Heat a quarter of the butter in medium frying pan.
Dip two bread slices into egg mixture, one at a time;
cook, uncovered, until browned both sides. Remove
from pan; cover to keep warm. Repeat with remaining
butter, bread slices and egg mixture.
3 Meanwhile, make berry compote.
4 Dust french toast with icing sugar; serve with
warm berry compote.

BERRY COMPOTE Blend arrowroot with the water in small
saucepan until smooth; stir in remaining ingredients.
Cook until mixture almost boils and thickens slightly.

preparation time *15 minutes*
cooking time *10 minutes* serves *4*
nutritional count per serving *43.7g total fat (25g
saturated fat); 3825kJ (915 cal); 104.8g carbohydrate;
20.9g protein; 9.9g fibre*

pumpkin, ricotta and parmesan frittata

1 tablespoon olive oil
600g butternut pumpkin, peeled, cut into small cubes
1 medium red onion (170g), cut into thin wedges
1 clove garlic, crushed
6 eggs
2 tablespoons milk
¼ cup finely chopped fresh chives
200g ricotta cheese
¾ cup (60g) finely grated parmesan cheese

1   Heat oil in non-stick medium frying pan (20cm base); cook pumpkin and onion, covered, stirring occasionally, 15 minutes or until tender. Add garlic; cook until fragrant.
2   Lightly beat eggs in large jug; beat in milk and half of the chives. Pour mixture into pan. Drop spoonfuls of ricotta over top; sprinkle with parmesan. Cook over low heat, uncovered, about 5 minutes or until edges are set.
3   Place under preheated grill until frittata sets and top is browned lightly. Sprinkle with remaining chives.

preparation *10 minutes*
cooking *25 minutes* serves *4*
nutritional count per serving *23.9g total fat (10.4g saturated fat); 1513kJ (362 cal); 11.7g carbohydrate; 24.6g protein; 2.2g fibre*

potato frittata with smoked salmon

You will need a medium ovenproof frying pan with a 17cm base for this recipe.

20g butter
1 tablespoon olive oil
2 medium potatoes (400g), cut into 1cm pieces
1 green onion, chopped finely
8 eggs
¼ cup (60ml) cream
⅓ cup (25g) finely grated parmesan cheese
1 tablespoon finely chopped fresh dill
200g smoked salmon
2 tablespoons sour cream

1   Preheat oven to 220°C/200°C fan-forced.
2   Heat butter and oil in medium frying pan; cook potato, stirring occasionally, until browned and tender. Add onion; cook, stirring gently, 1 minute.
3   Meanwhile, whisk eggs, cream, cheese and dill in medium jug. Pour into pan; stir gently. Cook frittata over medium heat, about 2 minutes or until bottom sets. Place pan in oven; cook, uncovered, about 10 minutes or until frittata sets.
4   Slide frittata onto serving plate; serve topped with salmon, sour cream and some extra dill, if you like.

preparation time *20 minutes*
cooking time *25 minutes* serves *4*
nutritional count per serving *34.1g total fat (15.2g saturated fat); 2031kJ (486 cal); 14.3g carbohydrate; 30.2g protein; 2.1g fibre*

mini onion and cheese frittatas

2 tablespoons olive oil
3 medium brown onions (450g), sliced thinly
1 medium red capsicum (200g), sliced thinly
8 eggs
½ cup (125ml) thickened cream
200g provolone cheese, cut into 1cm cubes

1 Preheat oven to 200°C/180°C fan-forced. Oil 12-hole (⅓-cup/80ml) muffin pan.
2 Heat oil in large frying pan; cook onion and capsicum, stirring occasionally, 15 minutes or until onion is soft.
3 Beat eggs and cream in medium bowl. Divide egg mixture among pan holes; top with onion mixture and cheese. Bake about 15 minutes or until just cooked.

preparation time *10 minutes*
cooking time *30 minutes* makes *12*
nutritional count per frittata *15.6g total fat (7.2g saturated fat); 807kJ (193 cal); 3g carbohydrate; 10.6g protein; 0.7g fibre*

morning trifles

⅓ cup (20g) All-Bran
⅓ cup (20g) Special K
⅓ cup (20g) puffed wheat
250g strawberries, hulled
1 cup (280g) low-fat vanilla yogurt
⅓ cup (80ml) passionfruit pulp

1 Combine cereals in small bowl.
2 Cut six strawberries in half; reserve. Slice remaining strawberries thinly.
3 Divide half of the cereal mixture among four 1-cup (250ml) serving bowls; divide half of the yogurt, all the strawberry slices and half of the passionfruit pulp among bowls. Continue layering with remaining cereal and yogurt; top with reserved strawberry halves and remaining passionfruit pulp.

preparation time *20 minutes* serves *4*
nutritional count per serving *0.7g total fat (0.1g saturated fat); 527kJ (126 cal); 20.4g carbohydrate; 8.1g protein; 6.4g fibre*

corn fritters with cucumber salad

1 cup (150g) self-raising flour
½ teaspoon bicarbonate of soda
1 teaspoon ground cumin
¾ cup (180ml) milk
2 eggs, separated
2 cups (330g) fresh corn kernels
2 green onions, sliced thinly
2 tablespoons finely chopped fresh coriander

CUCUMBER SALAD

2 lebanese cucumbers (260g), sliced thinly
1 small red onion (100g), sliced thinly
1 fresh long red chilli, sliced thinly
⅓ cup loosely packed fresh coriander leaves
2 tablespoons sweet chilli sauce
1 tablespoon fish sauce
1 tablespoon lime juice

1 Sift flour, soda and cumin into medium bowl. Gradually whisk in milk and egg yolks until batter is smooth.
2 Beat egg whites in small bowl with electric mixer until soft peaks form. Stir corn, onion and coriander into batter; fold in egg whites.
3 Pour 2 tablespoons of the batter into heated oiled large frying pan; using metal spatula, spread batter into round shape. Cook fritters, about 2 minutes each side or until cooked through. Remove from pan; cover to keep warm. Repeat process, wiping pan between batches and oiling if necessary, to make a total of 18 fritters.
4 Meanwhile, make cucumber salad.
5 Serve fritters topped with salad.

CUCUMBER SALAD Combine cucumber, onion, chilli and coriander in medium bowl. Place remaining ingredients in screw-top jar; shake well. Drizzle dressing over cucumber mixture; toss gently to combine.

preparation time *20 minutes*
cooking time *20 minutes* serves *6*
nutritional count per serving *4.2g total fat (1.5g saturated fat); 882kJ (211 cal); 31.8g carbohydrate; 9g protein; 4.7g fibre*

strawberries and cream on brioche

3 eggs
⅓ cup (80ml) milk
1 teaspoon vanilla extract
1 tablespoon caster sugar
6 small brioche (600g), halved
40g unsalted butter
250g strawberries, sliced thinly
⅔ cup (160ml) thickened cream

1   Combine eggs, milk, extract and sugar in large shallow bowl. Dip brioche in egg mixture.
2   Melt half the butter in large frying pan; cook half the brioche until browned both sides. Remove from pan; cover to keep warm. Repeat process with remaining butter and brioche.
3   Serve brioche with strawberries and cream.

preparation time *10 minutes*
cooking time *10 minutes* serves *6*
nutritional count per serving *30.5g total fat (16.5g saturated fat); 2286kJ (547 cal); 53.5g carbohydrate; 13.4g protein; 2.8g fibre*

eggs and smoked salmon on blini

8 eggs
200g sliced smoked salmon
2 tablespoons sour cream
1 tablespoon coarsely chopped fresh chives
BLINI
⅓ cup (50g) buckwheat flour
2 tablespoons plain flour
1 teaspoon baking powder
1 egg
½ cup (125ml) buttermilk
30g butter, melted

1   Make blini.
2   Half-fill a large frying pan with water; bring to the boil. Break one egg into cup then slide into pan. Working quickly, repeat process with three more eggs. When all four eggs are in pan, return water to the boil. Cover pan, turn off heat; stand about 4 minutes or until a light film of white sets over each yolk. Using a slotted spoon, remove eggs one at a time from pan; place on absorbent-paper-lined saucer to blot up poaching liquid. Repeat process to poach remaining eggs.
3   Serve blini topped with eggs, salmon, sour cream and chives.

BLINI Sift flours and baking powder into medium bowl; gradually whisk in combined egg and buttermilk until mixture is smooth. Stir in butter. Cook blini, in batches, by dropping 1 tablespoon of the batter into heated oiled large frying pan. Cook blini until browned both sides; you will have 12 blini. Cover to keep warm.

preparation time *10 minutes*
cooking time *20 minutes* serves *4*
nutritional count per serving *25.9g total fat (11.3g saturated fat); 1731kJ (414 cal); 14.1g carbohydrate; 31.5g protein; 1.6g fibre*

huevos rancheros

"Ranch-style eggs" is a Mexican standard that has become popular all over the world. For an extra bite, serve this dish with Tabasco, a fiery sauce made from hot red chillies.

3 chorizo sausages (500g), sliced thickly
8 eggs
½ cup (125ml) cream
20g butter
4 x 15cm flour tortillas
1 cup (120g) coarsely grated cheddar cheese
FRESH TOMATO SALSA
2 small tomatoes (180g), chopped finely
½ small red onion (50g), chopped finely
1 tablespoon red wine vinegar
1 tablespoon olive oil
¼ cup coarsely chopped fresh coriander

1 Preheat oven to 160°C/140°C fan-forced.
2 Make fresh tomato salsa.
3 Cook chorizo on heated oiled grill plate (or grill or barbecue) until well browned. Drain on absorbent paper; cover to keep warm.
4 Whisk eggs and cream in medium bowl. Melt butter in medium frying pan; cook egg mixture over low heat, stirring gently, until creamy.
5 Meanwhile, place tortillas on oven tray, sprinkle with cheese; warm in oven until cheese melts.
6 Divide tortillas among serving plates; top with egg, chorizo and salsa.

FRESH TOMATO SALSA Combine tomatoes, onion, vinegar and oil in small bowl; cover, stand 15 minutes. Stir in coriander just before serving.

preparation time *10 minutes*
cooking time *10 minutes* serves *4*
nutritional count per serving *81.7g total fat (35.8g saturated fat); 4126kJ (987 cal); 16.2g carbohydrate; 48.2g protein; 1.9g fibre*

stewed prunes with orange

½ cup (85g) seeded dried prunes
¼ cup (60ml) fresh orange juice
¼ cup (60ml) water
5cm strip orange rind, sliced thinly
1 cinnamon stick
2 cardamon pods, bruised

1 Bring ingredients to the boil in small saucepan. Reduce heat; simmer, covered, 10 minutes.
2 Serve stewed prunes with sheep milk yogurt, if you like.

preparation time *5 minutes*
cooking time *15 minutes* serves *1*
nutritional count per serving *0.4g total fat (0g saturated fat); 660kJ (158 cal); 32.5g carbohydrate; 2.3g protein; 6.8g fibre*

caramelised banana and hazelnut waffles

4 packaged belgian-style waffles
40g butter
4 ripe bananas (800g), sliced thickly
2 tablespoons brown sugar
½ cup (75g) roasted hazelnuts, chopped coarsely
⅓ cup (80ml) maple syrup

1 Preheat oven to 160°C/140°C fan-forced.
2 Place waffles, in single layer, on oven tray; heat, uncovered, in oven about 8 minutes.
3 Meanwhile, melt butter in medium frying pan; cook banana, stirring, about 2 minutes or until hot. Add sugar; cook, uncovered, over low heat, about 2 minutes or until banana is caramelised lightly.
4 Divide waffles among serving plates; top with banana mixture, nuts and syrup.

preparation time *10 minutes*
cooking time *15 minutes* serves *4*
nutritional count per serving *33.9g total fat (12g saturated fat); 2980kJ (713 cal); 85.6g carbohydrate; 13.1g protein; 6.4g fibre*

prosciutto and fontina croissants

4 croissants (320g)
2 teaspoons olive oil
8 slices prosciutto (120g)
½ cup (50g) coarsely grated fontina cheese
100g semi-dried tomatoes, drained, sliced thinly
30g baby rocket leaves

1 Preheat oven to 160°C/140°C fan-forced
2 Split croissants in half horizontally, without separating; place on oven tray. Heat in oven about 5 minutes.
3 Meanwhile, heat oil in small frying pan; cook prosciutto about 5 minutes or until crisp. Drain on absorbent paper.
4 Place equal amounts of cheese inside croissants; cook, uncovered, in oven about 5 minutes or until cheese melts. Fill croissants with prosciutto, tomato and rocket. Serve immediately.

preparation time *10 minutes*
cooking time *10 minutes* serves *4*
nutritional count per serving *30.2g total fat (15.2g saturated fat); 2566kJ (542 cal); 43.9g carbohydrate; 21g protein; 6.4g fibre*

blt on croissant

12 slices rindless shortcut bacon (420g)
4 large croissants (320g)
2 small tomatoes (180g), sliced thinly
8 large butter lettuce leaves

AIOLI

½ cup (150g) mayonnaise
1 clove garlic, crushed
1 tablespoon finely chopped fresh flat-leaf parsley

1 Preheat grill.
2 Cook bacon in large frying pan until crisp.
3 Meanwhile, make aïoli.
4 Toast croissants under grill about 30 seconds. Split croissants in half; spread aïoli over one half of each croissant then top with bacon, tomato, lettuce and remaining croissant half.

AIOLI Combine ingredients in small bowl.

preparation time *10 minutes*
cooking time *5 minutes* serves *4*
nutritional count per serving *36.8g total fat (13.9g saturated fat); 2592kJ (620 cal); 39.5g carbohydrate; 31.4g protein; 3.8g fibre*

chocolate hazelnut croissants

2 sheets ready-rolled puff pastry
⅓ cup (110g) chocolate hazelnut spread
30g dark chocolate, grated finely
25g butter, melted
1 tablespoon icing sugar

1 Preheat oven to 240°C/220°C fan-forced. Grease two oven trays.
2 Cut pastry sheets diagonally to make four triangles. Spread hazelnut spread over triangles, leaving a 1cm border; sprinkle each evenly with chocolate.
3 Roll triangles, starting at one wide end; place 3cm apart on trays with the tips tucked under and the ends slightly curved in to form a crescent shape. Brush with melted butter.
4 Bake croissants about 12 minutes or until browned lightly and cooked through. Dust with icing sugar and serve warm or at room temperature.

preparation time *15 minutes*
cooking time *15 minutes* makes *8*
nutritional count per croissant *17.7g total fat (4.8g saturated fat); 1166kJ (279 cal); 26.4g carbohydrate; 3.4g protein; 0.9g fibre*

fetta, avocado and roasted tomato toastie

8 x 1cm-thick slices walnut bread, toasted
250g fetta cheese, crumbled
30g baby rocket leaves
1 medium avocado (250g), sliced thinly

ROASTED TOMATO

2 tablespoons balsamic vinegar
2 tablespoons olive oil
2 cloves garlic, crushed
8 medium egg tomatoes (600g), halved

1 Make roasted tomato.
2 Top toast with cheese, rocket, roasted tomato and avocado then drizzle with pan juices.

ROASTED TOMATO Preheat oven to 240°C/220°C fan-forced. Combine vinegar, oil and garlic in small bowl. Place tomatoes, cut-side up, in medium baking dish; drizzle with vinegar mixture. Roast about 25 minutes.

preparation time *15 minutes*
cooking time *25 minutes* serves *4*
nutritional count per serving *41.5g total fat (13.8g saturated fat); 2546kJ (609 cal); 37.1g carbohydrate; 19.5g protein; 6.2g fibre*

figs with sheep milk yogurt and honey

2 medium fresh figs (120g), chopped coarsely
¼ cup (70g) sheep milk yogurt
4 medium fresh figs (240g), halved
1 teaspoon honey

1 Combine chopped figs and yogurt in small bowl.
2 Place halved figs on serving plate; drizzle with honey.
3 Serve figs with yogurt mixture.

preparation time *5 minutes serves 1*
nutritional count per serving *5.2g total fat (0g saturated fat); 932kJ (223 cal); 35.2g carbohydrate; 7.5g protein; 6.8g fibre*

maple rice pudding with pecans and dates

1½ litres (6 cups) milk
2 cups (500ml) cream
⅔ cup (160ml) maple syrup
¼ teaspoon ground cinnamon
⅔ cup (130g) medium-grain white rice
½ cup (85g) coarsely chopped seeded dates
½ cup (70g) roasted pecans, chopped coarsely

1 Bring milk, cream, syrup and cinnamon to the boil in large saucepan, stirring occasionally.
2 Gradually stir in rice; cook, uncovered, over low heat, stirring occasionally, 40 minutes or until rice is tender.
3 Serve rice with combined dates and nuts; drizzle with a little more maple syrup, if you like.

preparation time *10 minutes*
cook time *40 minutes serves 8*
nutritional count per serving *41.1g total fat (23.3g saturated fat); 2420kJ (579 cal); 45.4g carbohydrate; 9.6g protein; 1.4g fibre*

rice porridge with raisins

½ cup (100g) doongara rice
½ cup (125ml) water
2 cups (500ml) low-fat milk
1 tablespoon brown sugar
¼ cup (40g) raisins
pinch nutmeg
⅔ cup (160ml) low-fat milk, warmed, extra

1 Bring rice and the water to the boil in small saucepan. Reduce heat; simmer, uncovered, until liquid is absorbed.
2 Add milk, sugar and raisins; simmer 20 minutes or until rice is tender, stirring occasionally.
3 Stir in nutmeg; serve warm with extra milk.

preparation time *10 minutes*
cooking time *30 minutes serves 4*
nutritional count per serving *0.4g total fat (0.2g saturated fat); 789kJ (188 cal); 38.6g carbohydrate; 9.8g protein; 0.7g fibre*

almond, date and cinnamon couscous

1 cup (250ml) apple juice
½ cup (100g) couscous
2 tablespoons roasted slivered almonds
¾ cup (105g) coarsely chopped dried dates
1 cup (280g) low-fat vanilla yogurt
¼ teaspoon ground cinnamon
2 medium oranges (480g), segmented

1 Bring juice to the boil in small saucepan. Remove from heat.
2 Stir couscous into juice, cover; stand about 5 minutes or until juice is absorbed, fluffing with fork occasionally.
3 Stir nuts and dates into couscous.
4 Serve couscous topped with yogurt. Sprinkle with cinnamon then top with orange segments.

preparation time *10 minutes (plus cooling time)*
cooking time *5 minutes* serves *4*
nutritional count per serving *3.5g total fat (0.3g saturated fat); 1313kJ (314 cal); 57.9g carbohydrate; 9.9g protein; 4.8g fibre*

asian-spiced fruit salad

1 tablespoon grated palm sugar
2cm piece fresh ginger (10g), grated
1 star anise
1 cup (250ml) water
1 small pineapple (900g), chopped coarsely
1 small honeydew melon (1.3kg), chopped coarsely
1 small papaya (650g), chopped coarsely
2 small mangoes (600g), chopped coarsely
3 medium kiwifruits (255g), chopped coarsely
565g can lychees, drained, halved
¼ cup (60ml) lime juice
2 tablespoons passionfruit pulp
1 teaspoon finely grated whole nutmeg

1 Stir sugar, ginger, star anise and the water in small saucepan over heat, without boiling, until sugar dissolves. Bring to the boil; reduce heat, simmer, uncovered, without stirring, about 10 minutes or until syrup thickens slightly. Cool.
2 Meanwhile, combine pineapple, melon, papaya, mango, kiwifruit and lychees in large bowl.
3 Combine juice, pulp and nutmeg in medium jug; stir in syrup. Pour syrup mixture over fruit. Cover; refrigerate 20 minutes before serving.

preparation time *20 minutes (plus refrigeration time)*
cooking time *10 minutes* serves *6*
nutritional count per serving *0.9g total fat (0g saturated fat); 920kJ (220 cal); 44.3g carbohydrate; 3.9g protein; 8.7g fibre*

honey-roasted muesli

¾ cup (60g) rolled oats
½ cup (55g) rolled rye
½ cup (55g) rolled rice
¼ cup (15g) unprocessed wheat bran
½ cup (175g) honey
1 tablespoon vegetable oil
⅓ cup (40g) coarsely chopped walnuts
¼ cup (40g) pepitas
1 teaspoon ground cinnamon
⅓ cup (50g) coarsely chopped dried apricots
⅓ cup (30g) coarsely chopped dried apples
¼ cup (40g) raisins

1 Preheat oven to 180°C/160°C fan-forced.
2 Combine oats, rye, rice and bran in medium baking dish; drizzle evenly with honey and oil. Roast, uncovered, 5 minutes. Stir ingredients together in dish; roast, uncovered, further 10 minutes.
3 Remove dish from oven; stir in remaining ingredients.
4 Serve muesli with milk or yogurt.

preparation time *10 minutes*
cooking time *15 minutes* serves *4*
nutritional count per serving *21.1g total fat (2.7g saturated fat); 2320kJ (555 cal); 75.4g carbohydrate; 10.7g protein; 12.1g fibre*

scrambled eggs with chorizo

250g chorizo, sliced thickly
8 eggs
¾ cup (180ml) cream
2 tablespoons coarsely chopped fresh chives
10g butter

1 Cook chorizo, in batches, on heated grill plate
(or grill or barbecue) until browned both sides;
cover to keep warm.
2 Whisk eggs in medium bowl; whisk in cream
and half of the chives.
3 Melt butter in medium frying pan over low heat;
cook egg mixture, stirring gently constantly, until
egg mixture just begins to set.
4 Serve scrambled eggs, sprinkled with remaining
chives, and chorizo on slices of the toasted bread
of your choice.

preparation time *10 minutes*
cooking time *10 minutes* serves *4*
nutritional count per serving *50.8g total fat (24.2g
saturated fat); 2378kJ (569 cal); 3.3g carbohydrate;
26.3g protein; 0.3g fibre*

egg-white omelette

12 egg whites
4 green onions, chopped finely
¼ cup finely chopped fresh chives
¼ cup finely chopped fresh chervil
½ cup finely chopped fresh flat-leaf parsley
½ cup (60g) coarsely grated cheddar cheese
½ cup (50g) coarsely grated mozzarella cheese

1 Preheat grill.
2 Beat a quarter of the egg white in small bowl with
electric mixer until soft peaks form; fold in a quarter of
the combined onion and herbs.
3 Pour mixture into heated oiled 20cm non-stick frying
pan; cook over low heat until omelette is just browned
lightly on the bottom.
4 Sprinkle a quarter of the combined cheeses on
half of the omelette. Place pan under grill until cheese
begins to melt and omelette sets; fold omelette over to
completely cover cheese. Carefully slide onto serving
plate; cover to keep warm.
5 Repeat process three times with remaining egg
white, onion and herb mixture, and cheeses.

preparation time *25 minutes*
cooking time *20 minutes* serves *4*
nutritional count per serving *7.9g total fat (5g
saturated fat); 620kJ (148 cal); 1.1g carbohydrate;
18.2g protein; 0.7g fibre*

1 SCRAMBLED EGGS WITH CHORIZO 2 EGG-WHITE OMELETTE
3 BAKED EGGS WITH PROSCIUTTO AND BRIE [P 36]
4 POACHED EGGS WITH PANCETTA AND ASPARAGUS [P 36]

1

2

3

4

baked eggs with prosciutto and brie

1 tablespoon olive oil
100g prosciutto, chopped finely
100g button mushrooms, chopped finely
4 green onions, chopped finely
100g slightly underripe brie cheese,
    chopped coarsely
8 eggs

1 Preheat oven to 200°C/180°C fan-forced.
Oil four ¾-cup (180ml) shallow ovenproof dishes.
2 Heat oil in medium frying pan; cook prosciutto
and mushrooms, stirring, until mushrooms soften.
3 Add onion; cook, stirring, until onion softens.
Remove pan from heat; stir in half of the cheese.
4 Divide prosciutto mixture among dishes; break
two eggs into each dish.
5 Bake, uncovered, 5 minutes. Increase oven to
220°C/200°C fan-forced. Sprinkle wtih remaining
cheese; bake, uncovered, a further 5 minutes or until
eggs set and cheese melts. Serve immediately.

preparation time *10 minutes*
cooking time *15 minutes* serves *4*
nutritional count per serving *25.3g total fat (9.5g
saturated fat); 1388kJ (332 cal); 1.3g carbohydrate;
25.6g protein; 0.9g fibre*

poached eggs with pancetta and asparagus

4 slices pancetta
400g asparagus
¼ cup (60ml) white vinegar
4 eggs
30g butter, melted
¼ cup (20g) shaved parmesan cheese

1 Preheat grill.
2 Cook pancetta under grill until crisp.
3 Meanwhile, boil, steam or microwave asparagus
until just tender; drain.
4 Fill deep frying pan with 10cm water, add vinegar;
bring to a boil. Crack one egg into a cup, pour egg
carefully into boiling water; repeat with remaining eggs.
5 Lower heat to a gentle simmer; cook eggs,
uncovered, about 4 minutes or until cooked as desired.
Remove eggs, one at a time, using a slotted spoon;
drain on an absorbent-paper-lined plate.
6 Divide asparagus spears among serving plates.
Top with crumbled pancetta and poached eggs;
drizzle with butter then top with cheese and freshly
ground black pepper.

preparation time *10 minutes*
cooking time *10 minutes* serves *4*
nutritional count per serving *14.9g total fat (7.3g
saturated fat); 794kJ (190 cal); 1.2g carbohydrate;
12.8g protein; 1g fibre*

herb omelette with sautéed mushrooms

2 tablespoons finely chopped fresh flat-leaf parsley
2 tablespoons finely chopped fresh chervil
2 tablespoons finely chopped fresh chives
2 tablespoons finely chopped fresh tarragon
50g butter
2 tablespoons olive oil
250g swiss brown mushrooms, halved
½ cup (125ml) water
2 teaspoons finely grated lemon rind
1 tablespoon lemon juice
12 eggs

1   Combine herbs in small bowl.
2   Heat 30g of the butter and 1 tablespoon of the oil in large deep frying pan. Cook mushrooms, stirring, 5 minutes. Stir in 2 tablespoons of the water; cook, stirring, until water evaporates and mushrooms are tender. Remove from heat; stir in rind, juice and 2 tablespoons of the herb mixture. Cover to keep warm.
3   Gently whisk eggs and remaining water in a large bowl, whisk in remaining herb mixture.
4   Heat a quarter of the remaining butter and 1 teaspoon of the remaining oil in medium frying pan. When butter mixture bubbles, pour a quarter of the egg mixture into pan; cook over medium heat, tilting pan, until egg is almost set. Tilt pan backwards; fold omelette in half. Cook 30 seconds then slide onto serving plate.
5   Repeat process with remaining butter, oil and egg mixture, wiping out pan between omelettes, to make a total of four omelettes.
6   Serve omelettes topped with sautéed mushrooms.

preparation time *10 minutes*
cooking time *20 minutes* serves *4*
nutritional count per serving *35.3g total fat (12.9g saturated fat); 1714kJ (410 cal); 1g carbohydrate; 22.4g protein; 1.8g fibre*

mushroom, capsicum and cheese omelettes

20g butter
200g mushrooms, sliced thinly
1 small red capsicum (150g), sliced thinly
2 tablespoons finely chopped fresh chives
8 eggs
1 tablespoon milk
4 green onions, sliced thinly
½ cup (60g) coarsely grated cheddar cheese

1   Melt butter in large frying pan; cook mushrooms, capsicum and chives, stirring occasionally, 4 minutes or until vegetables soften. Drain vegetable filling on absorbent-paper-lined plate; cover to keep warm.
2   Whisk eggs in large jug until combined and frothy; whisk in milk and onion.
3   Pour half of the egg mixture into same pan; tilt to cover base with egg mixture. Cook over medium heat about 4 minutes or until omelette is just set. Spoon half of the vegetable filling onto one half of the omelette; sprinkle with half of the cheese. Fold omelette over to cover vegetable filling. Carefully slide onto plate; cover to keep warm. Repeat process with remaining egg mixture, vegetable filling and cheese.
4   Cut each omelette in half to serve.

preparation time *15 minutes*
cooking time *15 minutes* serves *4*
nutritional count per serving *20.3g total fat (9.4g saturated fat); 1141kJ (273 cal); 2.5g carbohydrate; 19.7g protein; 1.9g fibre*

fetta and mint omelettes with crisp bacon

2 tablespoons olive oil
8 slices rindless shortcut bacon (280g)
12 eggs
¼ cup (60ml) water
20g butter
4 green onions, chopped finely
¼ cup fresh mint leaves
120g fetta cheese, crumbled
75g baby spinach leaves

1   Heat 2 teaspoons oil in medium frying pan; cook bacon until crisp. Drain on absorbent paper.
2   Beat eggs and water in large bowl.
3   Heat a quarter of the butter and 1 teaspoon of oil in same pan. When butter is just bubbling, add a quarter of the egg mixture to pan; sprinkle with a quarter of the onion, mint and fetta. Cook on medium heat, tilting pan, until egg is just set. Slide omelette from pan, fold in half. Repeat with remaining butter, oil, egg and filling.
4   Serve omelettes immediately with spinach and bacon.

preparation time *10 minutes*
cooking time *20 minutes* serves *4*
nutritional count per serving *36.8g total fat (14.8g saturated fat); 2036kJ (487 cal); 1.4g carbohydrate; 38.2g protein; 0.7g fibre*

zucchini and mushroom omelette

10g butter
1 clove garlic, crushed
25g button mushrooms, sliced thinly
¼ cup (50g) coarsely grated zucchini
1 green onion, chopped finely
2 eggs
1 tablespoon water
¼ cup (30g) coarsely grated cheddar cheese

1   Heat half of the butter in small non-stick frying pan; cook garlic and mushroom, stirring, over medium heat about 2 minutes or until mushrooms are lightly browned. Add zucchini and onion; cook, stirring, about 1 minute or until zucchini begins to soften. Remove vegetable mixture from pan; cover to keep warm.
2   Beat eggs and the water in small bowl. Add cheese; whisk until combined.
3   Heat remaining butter in same pan; swirl pan so butter covers base. Pour egg mixture into pan; cook, tilting pan, over medium heat until almost set.
4   Place vegetable mixture evenly over half of the omelette; using eggslice, flip other half over vegetable mixture. Slide omelette gently onto serving plate.

preparation time *10 minutes*
cooking time *10 minutes* serves *1*
nutritional count per serving *29.5g total fat (15.3g saturated fat); 1526kJ (365 cal); 2g carbohydrate; 22.5g protein; 2.2g fibre*

smoked salmon omelette

6 eggs
⅔ cup (160ml) cream
⅔ cup (160g) sour cream
2 tablespoons coarsely chopped fresh dill
1 tablespoon lemon juice
1 tablespoon warm water
220g smoked salmon
30g baby rocket leaves

1 Whisk eggs in medium bowl; whisk in cream.
2 Pour a quarter of the egg and cream mixture into heated oiled 22cm non-stick frying pan; cook over medium heat, tilting pan, until omelette is almost set. Run spatula around edge of pan to loosen omelette, turn onto plate; cover to keep warm. Repeat process with remaining egg mixture to make four omelettes.
3 Combine sour cream, dill, juice and the water in small bowl.
4 Fold omelettes into quarters; place on serving plates. Top each with equal amounts of the salmon, sour cream mixture and rocket.

preparation time *10 minutes*
cooking time *15 minutes* serves *4*
nutritional count per serving *43.6g total fat (24.8g saturated fat); 2077kJ (497 cal); 2.8g carbohydrate; 24.6g protein; 0.1g fibre*

denver omelette

10 eggs
⅓ cup (80g) sour cream
2 fresh small red thai chillies, chopped finely
2 teaspoons vegetable oil
3 green onions, sliced thinly
1 medium green capsicum (200g), chopped finely
100g leg ham, chopped finely
2 small tomatoes (260g), seeded, chopped finely
½ cup (60g) coarsely grated cheddar cheese

1 Whisk eggs in large bowl; whisk in sour cream and chilli.
2 Heat oil in large non-stick frying pan; cook onion and capsicum, stirring, until onion softens. Transfer onion mixture to medium bowl with ham, tomato and cheese; toss to combine.
3 Pour ½ cup of the egg mixture into same oiled frying pan; cook, tilting pan, over low heat until almost set. Sprinkle about ⅓ cup of the filling over half of the omelette; using spatula, fold omelette over to completely cover the filling.
4 Pour ¼ cup of the egg mixture into empty half of pan; cook over low heat until almost set. Sprinkle about ⅓ cup of the filling over folded omelette, fold omelette over top of first omelette to cover filling. Repeat two more times, using ¼ cup of the egg mixture each time, to form one large layered omelette. Carefully slide omelette onto plate; cover to keep warm.
5 Repeat steps 3 and 4 to make second omelette, using remaining egg and filling. Cut each denver omelette in half.

preparation time *10 minutes*
cooking time *15 minutes* serves *4*
nutritional count per serving *30.2g total fat (13.4g saturated fat); 1639kJ (392 cal); 3.5g carbohydrate; 26.7g protein; 1.3g fibre*

egg and cheese tartlets with capsicum relish

2 sheets ready-rolled puff pastry
2 teaspoons olive oil
2 shallots (50g), sliced thinly
4 eggs
¼ cup (60ml) cream
½ cup (40g) finely grated parmesan cheese
30g baby rocket leaves

CAPSICUM RELISH

1 tablespoon olive oil
1 small red onion (100g), sliced thinly
2 medium red capsicum (400g), sliced thinly
⅓ cup (80ml) white balsamic vinegar
2 tablespoons brown sugar
½ cup (125ml) water

1 Preheat oven to 220°C/200°C fan-forced.
Oil a six-hole texas (¾ cup/180ml) muffin pan.
2 Cut pastry sheets in half; cut halves into three rectangles. Overlap two rectangles to form cross shapes; push gently into pan holes to cover bases and sides. Prick bases with fork, cover with baking paper; fill with dried beans or uncooked rice.
3 Bake pastry cases 10 minutes. Remove paper and beans carefully from pan holes; bake pastry cases a further 5 minutes or until browned lightly. Cool cases in pan. Reduce oven to 200°C/180°C fan-forced.
4 Meanwhile, make capsicum relish.
5 Heat oil in small frying pan. Cook shallots until soft.
6 Whisk eggs and cream in medium bowl; mix in cheese and shallots. Fill pastry cases with egg mixture. Bake 15 minutes or until set. Serve with relish and rocket.

CAPSICUM RELISH Heat oil in large frying pan; cook onion and capsicum about 10 minutes or until vegetables soften. Add vinegar, sugar and the water; cook, stirring occasionally, about 15 minutes or until thickened slightly.

preparation time *20 minutes (plus cooling time)*
cooking time *30 minutes* serves *6*
nutritional count per serving *27.3g total fat (12.7g saturated fat); 1697kJ (406 cal); 28g carbohydrate; 11.7g protein; 1.7g fibre*

italian egg, prosciutto and cheese roll

4 eggs
4 focaccia rolls (440g), split
120g taleggio or fontina cheese, sliced thinly
4 slices (60g) prosciutto
8 large fresh basil leaves

TOMATO SAUCE

400g can crushed tomatoes
¼ cup (60ml) red wine vinegar
2 tablespoons brown sugar

1 Make tomato sauce.
2 Preheat grill.
3 Fry eggs in heated oiled medium frying pan until cooked as you like.
4 Spread bottom half of each roll with about one tablespoon of the tomato sauce; place on oven tray. Layer cheese and prosciutto on rolls; grill until cheese starts to melt. Top each with two basil leaves, an egg and remaining tomato sauce; top with remaining roll half.

TOMATO SAUCE Place undrained tomatoes with remaining ingredients in medium saucepan; bring to the boil. Reduce heat; simmer 15 minutes.

preparation time *10 minutes*
cooking time *20 minutes* serves *4*
nutritional count per serving *20.3g total fat (9g saturated fat); 2245kJ (537 cal); 58.8g carbohydrate; 27.5g protein; 4.1g fibre*

home-fried potatoes, chipolatas and tomatoes

400g new potatoes, sliced thinly
2 large tomatoes (500g)
½ cup (85g) polenta
⅓ cup (80ml) olive oil
12 chipolatas (360g)
1 large brown onion (200g), chopped coarsely
¼ cup loosely packed fresh oregano leaves
1 tablespoon fresh rosemary leaves

1   Boil, steam or microwave potato until just tender; drain.
2   Meanwhile, cut tomatoes into four slices; coat one side of each slice with polenta. Heat 1 tablespoon of the oil in large frying pan; cook tomato slices, polenta-side up, until just browned. Turn; cook until just browned. Remove from pan; cover to keep warm.
3   Cook chipolatas in same cleaned pan until browned all over and cooked through. Remove from pan; cover to keep warm.
4   Heat remaining oil in same cleaned pan; cook potato, stirring, until browned lightly. Add onion; cook, stirring, until potato is crisp and onion softened. Stir in oregano and rosemary.
5   Divide potato, chipolatas and tomato among serving plates.

preparation time *10 minutes*
cooking time *25 minutes* serves *4*
nutritional count per serving *39.2g total fat (12.4g saturated fat); 2391kJ (572 cal); 35g carbohydrate; 17.3g protein; 6.7g fibre*

breakfast beans on sourdough toast

2 cups (400g) dried cannellini beans
1 tablespoon olive oil
1 large brown onion (200g), chopped coarsely
2 cloves garlic, sliced thinly
2 rindless bacon rashers (130g), chopped coarsely
2 tablespoons brown sugar
¼ cup (60ml) maple syrup
1 tablespoon dijon mustard
400g can chopped tomatoes
1 litre (4 cups) water
6 x 1cm-thick slices sourdough bread, toasted
2 tablespoons coarsely chopped fresh flat-leaf parsley

1   Place beans in large bowl, cover with water; stand overnight, drain. Rinse under cold water, drain.
2   Heat oil in large saucepan; cook onion, garlic and bacon, stirring, until onion softens. Stir in beans, sugar, syrup and mustard. Add undrained tomatoes and the water; bring to the boil. Reduce heat; simmer, covered, about 2 hours or until beans are tender.
3   Uncover; cook, stirring occasionally, 30 minutes or until mixture thickens. Serve on toast; sprinkle with parsley.

preparation time *10 minutes (plus standing time)*
cooking time *2 hours 45 minutes* serves *6*
nutritional count per serving *6.3g total fat (1.1g saturated fat); 1626kJ (389 cal); 53.1g carbohydrate; 22.2g protein; 14.5g fibre*

tuna and asparagus frittata

5 medium potatoes (1kg), sliced thinly
1 medium brown onion (150g), sliced thinly
1 clove garlic, crushed
340g asparagus, chopped coarsely
425g can tuna, drained
8 eggs, beaten lightly
2 tablespoons finely chopped fresh flat-leaf parsley
cooking-oil spray

1 Boil, steam or microwave potatoes until almost tender.
2 Cook onion and garlic in small heated frying pan, stirring, until onion softens.
3 Combine potato and onion mixture in large bowl with asparagus, tuna, eggs and parsley.
4 Preheat grill.
5 Reheat pan; spray lightly with cooking oil. Spoon frittata mixture into pan; press down firmly. Cook, uncovered, over low heat until almost set; remove from heat. Place under grill until frittata sets and top is browned.

preparation time *10 minutes*
cooking time *30 minutes* serves *4*
nutritional count per serving *14.1g total fat (4.2g saturated fat); 1898kJ (454 cal); 35.8g carbohydrate; 42.3g protein; 6.4g fibre*

fruit scrolls with spiced yogurt

40g butter
1½ tablespoons brown sugar
¼ teaspoon ground nutmeg
1 tablespoon ground cinnamon
1 small apple (130g), peeled, cored, grated coarsely
⅓ cup (50g) finely chopped dried apricots
½ cup (125ml) orange juice
1 sheet ready-rolled puff pastry
½ cup (140g) plain yogurt
1 tablespoon honey

1 Preheat oven to 200°C/180°C fan-forced. Grease oven tray.
2 Melt half of the butter in small saucepan; cook sugar, nutmeg and half of the cinnamon, stirring, over low heat, until sugar dissolves. Stir in apple, apricot and half of the juice; bring to the boil. Reduce heat; simmer, uncovered, 2 minutes. Remove pan from heat; stir in remaining juice.
3 Spread fruit mixture over pastry sheet; roll into log. Cut log into quarters; place on tray, 5cm apart, brush with remaining melted butter.
4 Bake scrolls about 20 minutes or until cooked through.
5 Meanwhile, combine yogurt, honey and remaining cinnamon in small bowl.
6 Serve hot scrolls with spiced yogurt and, if you like, dusted with sifted icing sugar.

preparation time *10 minutes*
cooking time *25 minutes* serves *4*
nutritional count per serving *9.5g total fat (6.2g saturated fat); 790kJ (189 cal); 22.6g carbohydrate; 2.5g protein; 1.6g fibre*

DRINKS
& NIBBLES

sugar syrup

1 cup (220g) sugar
1 cup (250ml) water

1 Stir sugar and water in small saucepan over low heat until sugar dissolves. Bring to the boil. Reduce heat and simmer, uncovered, without stirring, 5 minutes; remove from heat, cool.
2 Refrigerate in an airtight container for up to 2 months.

preparation time *5 minutes*
cooking time *10 minutes* makes *about 350ml*
nutritional count per tablespoon *0g total fat (0g saturated fat); 213kJ (51 cal); 12.6g carbohydrate; 0g protein; 0g fibre*

piña colada

30ml white rum
30ml dark rum
80ml pineapple juice
20ml sugar syrup (recipe above)
40ml coconut cream
dash of Angostura bitters
1 cup ice cubes

1 Blend or process ingredients until smooth.
2 Pour into 400ml tulip-shaped glass.

preparation time *5 minutes* serves *1*
nutritional count per serving *8.4g total fat (7.3g saturated fat); 1179J (282 cal); 19.8g carbohydrate; 1g protein; 0.7g fibre*

classic mojito

1 lime, cut into quarters
15ml sugar syrup (recipe above)
6 sprigs fresh mint
45ml light rum
½ cup ice cubes
150ml soda water

1 Using muddler, crush 3 lime wedges, sugar syrup and mint in cocktail shaker. Add rum and ice cubes; shake vigorously.
2 Strain into 320ml highball glass; top with soda water and garnish with remaining lime wedge.

preparation time *5 minutes* serves *1*
nutritional count per serving *0.2g total fat (0g saturated fat); 543kJ (130 cal); 7.8g carbohydrate; 0.6g protein; 1.4g fibre*

sangria

750ml bottle dry red wine
30ml Cointreau
30ml Bacardi
30ml brandy
½ cup (110g) sugar
2 cinnamon sticks
½ medium orange, peeled, chopped coarsely
½ medium lemon, peeled, chopped coarsely
6 medium strawberries, chopped coarsely
1 cup ice cubes

1 Stir ingredients in a large jug until well combined. Pour into glasses.

preparation time *10 minutes* serves *4*
nutritional count per serving *0.1g total fat (0g saturated fat); 1313kJ (314 cal); 33.3g carbohydrate; 0.9g protein; 1g fibre*

sea breeze

120ml cranberry juice
30ml ruby red grapefruit juice
45ml vodka
1 cup ice cubes

1 Place ingredients in 300ml highball glass; stir well.

preparation time *5 minutes* serves *1*
nutritional count per serving *0g total fat (0g saturated fat); 711kJ (170 cal); 18.9g carbohydrate; 0.4g protein; 0g fibre*

bloody mary

60ml vodka
10ml lemon juice
¼ teaspoon Tabasco sauce
½ teaspoon horseradish
dash worcestershire sauce
pinch celery salt
150ml vegetable juice
1 cup crushed ice

1 Place ingredients in 340ml highball glass; stir to combine. Garnish with cracked black pepper and a trimmed celery stalk, if you like.

preparation time *5 minutes* serves *1*
nutritional count per serving *0.2g total fat (0g saturated fat); 656kJ (157 cal); 6.2g carbohydrate; 1.6g protein; 1.2g fibre*

margarita

45ml tequila
30ml fresh lime juice
30ml Cointreau
1 cup ice cubes

1 Place ingredients and in a cocktail shaker; shake vigorously. Strain into a salt-rimmed 150ml margarita glass. Garnish with slice of lemon, if you like.

preparation time *10 minutes* serves *1*
nutritional count per serving *0.2g total fat (0g saturated fat); 953kJ (228 cal); 14.8g carbohydrate; 0.3g protein; 0.1g fibre*

cosmopolitan

45ml vodka
30ml Cointreau
20ml cranberry juice
10ml lime juice
1 cup ice cubes

1 Place ingredients in cocktail shaker; shake vigorously.
2 Strain into chilled 230ml martini glass. Garnish with 2cm strip orange rind, if you like.

preparation time *5 minutes* serves *1*
nutritional count per serving *0.1g total fat (0g saturated fat); 991kJ (237 cal); 17.4g carbohydrate; 0.2g protein; 0g fibre*

strawberry and cranberry spritzer

300g frozen cranberries, thawed
400g strawberries, hulled
8 large fresh mint leaves, shredded
100g strawberries, extra, sliced thinly
3½ cups (875ml) chilled soda water
crushed ice, to serve

1 Push cranberries and strawberries through juice extractor. Stir in mint leaves, sliced strawberries and soda water. Serve over ice.

preparation time *10 minutes* makes *1.5 litres (6 cups)*
nutritional count per cup *0.2g total fat (0g saturated fat); 151kJ (36 cal); 4.2g carbohydrate; 1.6g protein; 2.8g fibre*

caipiroska

1 lime, cut into eight wedges
2 teaspoons caster sugar
45ml vodka
½ cup crushed ice

1 Using muddler, crush lime wedges with sugar in cocktail shaker. Add vodka and ice; shake vigorously.
2 Pour into 260ml old-fashioned glass.

preparation time *5 minutes* serves *1*
nutritional count per serving *0.1g total fat (0g saturated fat); 564J (135 cal); 9.6g carbohydrate; 0.4g protein; 1g fibre*

frozen mango daiquiri

60ml Bacardi
60ml mango liqueur
30ml fresh lime juice
1 medium ripe mango (430g), peeled,
    chopped coarsely
1 cup ice cubes

1   Blend ingredients until just combined.
2   Pour into 300ml highball glass.

preparation time *10 minutes* serves *1*
nutritional count per serving *0.8g total fat (0g
saturated fat); 2069kJ (495 cal); 62.7g carbohydrate;
3.4g protein; 4.6g fibre*

mai tai

1 cup ice cubes
30ml white rum
30ml dark rum
15ml orange curaçao
15ml Amaretto
15ml fresh lemon juice
15ml sugar syrup (see page 46)
15ml fresh orange juice
15ml bottled pineapple juice
10ml grenadine

1   Place ice cubes in glass; pour remaining ingredients,
except grenadine, one at a time over ice, stir gently.
Carefully add grenadine.

preparation time *5 minutes* serves *1*
nutritional count per serving *0.2g total fat (0g
saturated fat); 1083kJ (259 cal); 22.3g carbohydrate;
0.3g protein; 0g fibre*

manhattan

60ml rye whisky
30ml vermouth rosso
1 cup ice cubes

1   Place ingredients in cocktail shaker; shake vigorously.
2   Strain into chilled 150ml margarita glass. Garnish
with maraschino cherry dropped in the glass, if you like.

preparation time *10 minutes* serves *1*
nutritional count per serving *0g total fat (0g
saturated fat); 644kJ (154 cal); 0.8g carbohydrate;
0.1g protein; 0g fibre*

lime and mint spritzer

1 cup (250ml) sugar syrup (see page 46)
1 cup (250ml) lime juice
1.25 litres (5 cups) chilled mineral water
¼ cup coarsely chopped fresh mint

1   Combine ingredients in large jug.
2   Serve immediately, with ice, if you like.

preparation time *5 minutes* serves *8*
nutritional count per serving *0.1g total fat (0g
saturated fat); 268kJ (64 cal); 15.1g carbohydrate;
0.3g protein; 0.2g fibre*

black russian

½ cup ice cubes
30ml vodka
30ml Kahlua
120ml cola (optional)

1   Place ice cubes in 180ml old-fashioned glass; pour
vodka then Kahlua over ice. Top with cola, if using.

preparation time *5 minutes* serves *1*
nutritional count per serving *5g total fat (3.1g
saturated fat); 915kJ (219 cal); 19.7g carbohydrate;
0.9g protein; 0g fibre*

1 FROZEN MANGO DAIQUIRI 2 MAI TAI
3 MANHATTAN 4 LIME AND MINT SPRITZER

2 litres (8 cups) orange and passionfruit juice drink
850ml can unsweetened pineapple juice
250g strawberries, chopped
¼ cup (60ml) passionfruit pulp
2 medium red apples (300g), chopped
2 medium oranges (360g), peeled, chopped
1.25 litres (5 cups) lemon soda squash
1.25 litres (5 cups) creaming soda
3 cups (750ml) ginger beer
fresh mint sprigs

1   Combine orange and passionfruit juice drink,
pineapple juice and fruit in large bowl.
2   Just before serving, stir in remaining ingredients.
Serve cold.

preparation time *15 minutes* makes *6.5 litres (26 cups)*
nutritional count per 250ml *0.2g total fat (0g*
aturated fat); 456kJ (109 cal); 24.9g carbohydrate;
1g protein; 1.2g fibre

tropical punch

425g can sliced mango in natural juice
3 cups (750ml) tropical fruit juice
300g finely chopped pineapple
250g finely chopped strawberries
2 tablespoons finely shredded fresh mint
1 tablespoon caster sugar
3 cups (750ml) dry ginger ale

1   Strain mango over small bowl; reserve juice. Chop
mango slices finely; combine mango and reserved juice
in large bowl with tropical fruit juice. Stir in pineapple,
strawberries, mint, sugar and ginger ale.
2   Refrigerate punch 2 hours before serving.

preparation time *15 minutes (plus refrigeration time)*
makes *2.5 litres (10 cups)*
nutritional count per 250ml *0.1g total fat (0g*
saturated fat); 435kJ (104 cal); 23.6g carbohydrate;
1.1g protein; 1.7g fibre

1 litre (4 cups) water
4 teabags
1 cinnamon stick
2 cardamom pods
4 whole cloves
1 cup (220g) caster sugar
1½ cups (375ml) cold water, extra
½ cup (125ml) fresh lemon juice
2 cups (500ml) fresh orange juice
¼ cup coarsely chopped fresh mint
1 medium lemon (140g), sliced
1 litre (4 cups) mineral water
1 cup ice cubes

1   Bring the water to the boil in large saucepan; add
teabags, spices and sugar. Stir over low heat for about
3 minutes or until sugar is dissolved; discard teabags.
Refrigerate until cold.
2   Discard spices then stir in the extra water, juices, mint
and lemon. Before serving, add mineral water and ice.

preparation time *15 minutes (plus refrigeration time)*
makes *3 litres (12 cups)*
nutritional count per 250ml *0.1g total fat (0g*
saturated fat); 385kJ (92 cal); 22g carbohydrate;
0.4g protein; 0.3g fibre

planter's punch

50ml white rum
25ml fresh lime juice
20ml lime juice cordial
dash Angostura bitters
1 cup ice cubes
30ml chilled soda water

1   Place ingredients excpet soda water in cocktail
shaker; shake vigorously.
2   Pour into 300ml highball glass; top with soda water.

preparation time *5 minutes* serves *1*
nutritional count per serving *0.1g total fat (0g*
saturated fat); 606kJ (145 cal); 10.4g carbohydrate;
0.2g protein; 0g fibre

mixed berry punch

1 teabag
1 cup (250ml) boiling water
120g raspberries
150g blueberries
125g strawberries, halved
¼ cup loosely packed fresh mint leaves
750ml chilled sparkling apple cider
2½ cups (625ml) chilled lemonade

1 Place teabag in heatproof mug, cover with the water; stand 10 minutes. Squeeze teabag over mug, discard teabag; cool tea 10 minutes.
2 Using fork, crush raspberries in punch bowl; add blueberries, strawberries, mint and tea. Stir to combine, cover; refrigerate 1 hour.
3 Just before serving, stir in cider and lemonade; sprinkle with extra mint leaves, if you like.

preparation time *10 minutes (plus refrigeration time)* serves *8*
nutritional count per serving *0.1g total fat (0g saturated fat); 393kJ (94 cal); 21.6g carbohydrate; 0.6g protein; 1.5g fibre*

citron crush

½ medium lime, cut into 4 wedges
½ medium lemon, cut into 4 wedges
2 tablespoons palm sugar
4 large fresh mint leaves, torn
1 cup crushed ice
120ml lemonade

1 Using a mortar and pestle (or muddler), crush lime, lemon, sugar and mint.
2 Place ice in glass; add fruit mixture, top with lemonade.

preparation time *10 minutes* serves *1*
nutritional count per serving *0.1g total fat (0g saturated fat); 694kJ (166 cal); 39.2g carbohydrate; 0.5g protein; 1.6g fibre*

long island iced tea

15ml vodka
15ml white rum
15ml white tequila
15ml gin
10ml Cointreau
15ml lemon juice
15ml sugar syrup (see page 46)
½ cup ice cubes
80ml cola

1 Place ingredients except cola in cocktail shaker; shake vigorously.
2 Pour into 250ml highball glass. Top with cola; garnish with lemon slice, if you like.

preparation time *5 minutes* serves *1*
nutritional count per serving *0.1g total fat (0g saturated fat); 974kJ (233 cal); 20.9g carbohydrate; 0.1g protein; 0g fibre*

lemon iced tea

3 teabags
3 lemon soother or lemon zinger teabags
1.5 litres (6 cups) boiling water
⅓ cup (80g) caster sugar
2 strips of lemon rind
1 cup ice cubes

1 Combine teabags, the water, sugar and rind in large heatproof jug, stir until sugar is dissolved; cool to room temperature, strain mixture.
2 Refrigerate until cold. Serve with ice cubes.

preparation time *10 minutes (plus refrigeration time)* makes *1.5 litres (6 cups)*
nutritional count per 250ml *0.3g total fat (0g saturated fat); 242kJ (58 cal); 13.4g carbohydrate; 0.3g protein; 0g fibre*

flirtini

6 fresh raspberries
1 cup ice cubes
30ml vodka
15ml Cointreau
15ml cranberry juice
15ml fresh lime juice
15ml bottled pineapple juice
60ml brut champagne

1 Crush raspberries in base of chilled glass;
top with half of the ice.
2 Place remaining ice, vodka, Cointreau and
juices in cocktail shaker; shake vigorously.
3 Strain into glass; top with champagne.

preparation time *5 minutes* serves *1*
nutritional count per serving *0.1g total fat (0g
saturated fat); 706kJ (169 cal); 11.4g carbohydrate;
0.5g protein; 0.6g fibre*

dry martini

45ml gin
15ml dry vermouth
1 cup ice cubes

1 Place ingredients in cocktail shaker; shake vigorously.
2 Strain into chilled 90ml martini glass. Garnish with
a caperberry, if you like.

preparation time *5 minutes* serves *1*
nutritional count per serving *0g total fat (0g
saturated fat); 451kJ (108 cal); 0.4g carbohydrate;
0g protein; 0g fibre*

apple martini

45ml vodka
30ml apple schnapps
5ml sugar syrup (see page 46)
1 cup ice cubes

1 Place ingredients in a cocktail shaker; shake vigorously.
2 Strain into chilled glass.

preparation time *5 minutes* serves *1*
nutritional count per serving *0.1g total fat (0g
saturated fat); 815kJ (195 cal); 14.3g carbohydrate;
0g protein; 0g fibre*

campari lady

30ml gin
45ml Campari
120ml fresh grapefruit juice
30ml tonic water
1 cup ice cubes

1 Place ingredients in cocktail shaker; shake vigorously.
2 Strain into 300ml highball glass with some of the ice.

preparation time *10 minutes* serves *1*
nutritional count per serving *0.3g total fat (0g
saturated fat); 1032kJ (247 cal); 28.2g carbohydrate;
0.7g protein; 0g fibre*

raspberry and cranberry crush

1 cup (250ml) raspberry sorbet
2 cups (500ml) cranberry juice
1 cup (150g) frozen raspberries
2 tablespoons lemon juice

1 Blend ingredients until smooth; serve immediately.

preparation time *10 minutes* makes *1 litre (4 cups)*
nutritional count per 250ml *0.2g total fat (0g
saturated fat); 660kJ (158 cal); 36.4g carbohydrate;
1.2g protein; 2.1g fibre*

smoked salmon cones

800g smoked salmon slices
300ml cream
125g packet cream cheese, softened
¼ cup (50g) roasted pistachios, chopped finely
2 tablespoons finely chopped fresh chives
48 baby spinach leaves (100g)

1 Blend or process 100g of the salmon until chopped finely. Add cream and cheese; process until smooth. Transfer mixture to medium bowl; stir in nuts and chives. Refrigerate until firm.
2 Halve remaining salmon slices widthways; place one spinach leaf on each salmon slice, top with 1 teaspoon of the cheese mixture. Roll into small cone to enclose filling; place on serving tray. Cover; refrigerate 2 hours.

preparation time *40 minutes (plus refrigeration time)* makes *48*
nutritional count per cone *4.9g total fat (2.5g saturated fat); 263kJ (63 cal); 0.4g carbohydrate; 4.4g protein; 0.2g fibre*

smoked salmon roulade

If mascarpone softens while making the roulade, place in the refrigerator until firm.

½ cup (75g) plain flour
2 eggs
2 teaspoons vegetable oil
1 cup (250ml) milk
250g mascarpone cheese
2 tablespoons drained capers, rinsed, chopped coarsely
2 tablespoons finely chopped fresh dill
1 tablespoon finely grated lemon rind
1 clove garlic, crushed
500g thinly sliced smoked salmon
40 fresh dill sprigs

1 Place flour in medium bowl. Make well in centre; gradually whisk in combined eggs, oil and milk. Strain into large jug; stand 30 minutes.
2 Pour ¼ cup batter into heated oiled 19-cm non-stick frying pan, tilting pan to coat base. Cook over low heat, loosening around edge with spatula, until browned. Turn crêpe; cook until browned. Remove from pan; repeat with remaining batter to make a total of five crêpes.
3 Combine mascarpone, capers, chopped dill, rind and garlic in medium bowl.
4 Spread one crêpe with 2 tablespoons of the mascarpone mixture; top with 100g of the salmon. Roll crêpe tightly to enclose filling. Repeat with remaining crêpes, mascarpone mixture and salmon. Trim ends; slice each roll into eight pieces. Garnish each piece with dill sprig.

preparation time *30 minutes (plus standing time)*
cooking time *20 minutes* makes *40*
nutritional count per piece *4.3g total fat (2.4g saturated fat); 259kJ (62 cal); 2g carbohydrate; 3.9g protein; 0.1g fibre*

crab and celeriac remoulade cups

40 wonton wrappers (320g)
cooking-oil spray
¼ cup (60g) sour cream
¼ cup (75g) whole-egg mayonnaise
¼ small celeriac (80g), grated coarsely
1 small green apple (130g), grated coarsely
2 tablespoons finely chopped fresh flat-leaf parsley
1 tablespoon wholegrain mustard
1 tablespoon lemon juice
¾ cup (150g) fresh cooked crab meat, shredded finely

1 Preheat oven to 200°C/180°C fan-forced.
Oil 12-hole mini (1 tablespoon/20ml) muffin pan.
2 Using 7.5cm cutter, cut one round from each wonton
wrapper. Push rounds carefully into pan holes; spray
each lightly with oil. Bake, uncovered, about 7 minutes
or until wonton cups are golden brown. Stand in pan
2 minutes; turn onto wire racks to cool. Repeat process
with remaining wonton wrappers.
3 Combine sour cream, mayonnaise, celeriac, apple,
parsley, mustard and juice in medium bowl; fold crab
meat gently through remoulade mixture. Place one
rounded teaspoon of remoulade in each wonton cup.

preparation time *20 minutes*
cooking time *30 minutes* makes *40*
nutritional count per cup *1.7g total fat (0.5g
saturated fat); 180kJ (43 cal); 5.3g carbohydrate;
1.5g protein; 0.2g fibre*

mozzarella and sun-dried tomato risotto balls

2 cups (500ml) chicken stock
½ cup (125ml) water
1 tablespoon olive oil
1 small brown onion (80g), chopped finely
1 clove garlic, crushed
¾ cup (150g) arborio rice
1 tablespoon finely chopped fresh basil
1 tablespoon finely chopped fresh flat-leaf parsley
2 tablespoons finely chopped semi-dried tomatoes
60g mozzarella cheese, diced into 1cm pieces
¼ cup (25g) packaged breadcrumbs
vegetable oil, for deep-frying

1 Place stock and the water in medium saucepan;
bring to the boil. Reduce heat; simmer, covered.
2 Meanwhile, heat olive oil in medium saucepan;
cook onion and garlic, stirring, until onion softens.
Add rice; stir to coat in onion mixture. Stir in ½ cup of
the simmering stock mixture; cook, stirring, over low
heat until liquid is absorbed. Continue adding stock
mixture, in ½-cup batches, stirring, until liquid is
absorbed after each addition. Total cooking time should
be about 35 minutes or until rice is just tender. Stir in
herbs and tomato, cover; cool 30 minutes.
3 Roll heaped teaspoons of the risotto mixture into
balls; press a piece of cheese into centre of each ball,
roll to enclose. Coat risotto balls in breadcrumbs.
4 Heat oil in wok; deep-fry risotto balls, in batches,
until browned and heated through.

preparation time *25 minutes*
cooking time *50 minutes (plus cooling time)* makes *30*
nutritional count per risotto ball *3g total fat (0.6g
saturated fat); 213kJ (51 cal); 4.9g carbohydrate;
1.3g protein; 0.2g fibre*

risotto-filled zucchini flowers

1 cup (250ml) dry white wine
2 cups (500ml) vegetable stock
½ cup (125ml) water
1 tablespoon olive oil
1 small brown onion (80g), chopped finely
1 clove garlic, crushed
1 cup (200g) arborio rice
150g mushrooms, sliced thinly
2 trimmed silver beet leaves (160g), chopped finely
¼ cup (20g) finely grated parmesan cheese
48 tiny zucchini with flowers attached
cooking-oil spray

1   Combine wine, stock and the water in large saucepan; bring to the boil. Reduce heat; simmer, covered, to keep hot.
2   Meanwhile, heat oil in large saucepan; cook onion and garlic, stirring, until onion softens. Add rice; stir to coat in onion mixture. Stir in 1 cup of the hot stock mixture; cook, stirring, over low heat until liquid is absorbed. Continue adding hot stock mixture, in 1-cup batches, stirring, until liquid is absorbed after each addition. Total cooking time should be about 35 minutes or until rice is tender.
3   Add mushrooms and silver beet; cook, stirring, until mushrooms are just tender. Stir in cheese.
4   Remove and discard stamens from centre of flowers; fill flowers with risotto, twist petal tops to enclose filling.
5   Cook zucchini with flowers, in batches, on heated oiled grill plate (or grill or barbecue) until zucchini are just tender and risotto is heated through.

preparation time *50 minutes*
cooking time *50 minutes* makes *48*
nutritional count per flower *0.8g total fat (0.2g saturated fat); 130kJ (31 cal); 3.8g carbohydrate; 1g protein; 0.6g fibre*

ham and artichoke risotto cakes

¾ cup (180ml) dry white wine
1½ cups (375ml) beef stock
2½ cups (625ml) water
20g butter
1 medium brown onion (150g), chopped finely
2 cloves garlic, crushed
2 cups (400g) arborio rice
1 cup (80g) finely grated parmesan cheese
2 cups (200g) packaged breadcrumbs
vegetable oil, for shallow-frying
1½ cups (390g) bottled tomato pasta sauce
1 teaspoon sambal oelek
150g shaved ham
250g bottled marinated artichokes, sliced thinly

1   Heat wine, stock and the water in large saucepan; cover to keep warm.
2   Melt butter in large saucepan; cook onion and garlic until soft. Add rice and 1 cup hot stock mixture; stir, over low heat, until liquid is absorbed. Keep adding hot stock mixture, in batches, stirring until absorbed. It will take about 35 minutes until rice is tender. Stir in cheese.
3   Spread risotto onto tray; cool.
4   Preheat oven to 240°C/220°C fan-forced.
5   Shape tablespoons of risotto into cakes, coat with breadcrumbs. Heat oil in large frying pan; shallow-fry cakes, in batches, until browned both sides. Drain.
6   Place cakes on oiled oven trays; divide combined sauce and sambal among cakes, top with ham and artichoke. Bake about 5 minutes or until browned.

preparation time *20 minutes (plus cooling time)*
cooking time *45 minutes* makes *64*
nutritional count per risotto cake *3.5g total fat (0.8g saturated fat); 305kJ (73 cal); 7.8g carbohydrate; 2g protein; 0.4g fibre*

fish cakes

500g redfish fillets, skinned and boned
2 tablespoons red curry paste
2 fresh kaffir lime leaves, torn
2 green onions, chopped coarsely
1 tablespoon fish sauce
1 tablespoon lime juice
2 tablespoons finely chopped fresh coriander
3 snake beans (30g), chopped finely
2 fresh small red thai chillies, chopped finely
peanut oil, for deep-frying

1   Cut fish into small pieces. Blend or process fish with curry paste, lime leaves, onion, sauce and juice until mixture forms a smooth paste. Combine fish mixture in medium bowl with coriander, beans and chilli.
2   Roll 1 heaped tablespoon of the fish mixture into ball; flatten into cake shape. Repeat with remaining mixture.
3   Heat oil in wok; deep-fry fish cakes, in batches, until browned and cooked through. Drain on absorbent paper. Serve with fresh coriander leaves and lime wedges, if you like.

preparation time *15 minutes*
cooking time *10 minutes* makes *16 fish cakes*
nutritional count per fish cake *3.7g total fat (0.7g saturated fat); 263kJ (63 cal); 0.4g carbohydrate; 6.7g protein; 0.4g fibre*

deep-fried whitebait

1 cup (150g) plain flour
¼ cup coarsely chopped fresh basil
1 teaspoon garlic salt
500g whitebait
vegetable oil, for deep-frying

SPICED MAYONNAISE DIP

1 cup (300g) mayonnaise
2 cloves garlic, crushed
2 tablespoons lemon juice
1 tablespoon drained capers, chopped finely
1 tablespoon coarsely chopped fresh flat-leaf parsley

1   Combine flour, basil and garlic salt in large bowl. Toss whitebait in flour mixture, in batches, until coated.
2   Heat oil in wok; deep-fry whitebait, in batches, until browned and cooked through; drain on absorbent paper.
3   Make spiced mayonnaise dip; serve with whitebait.

SPICED MAYONNAISE DIP Combine ingredients in small serving bowl.

preparation time *10 minutes*
cooking time *15 minutes* serves *4*
nutritional count per serving *46.2g total fat (7.3g saturated fat); 2880kJ (689 cal); 40.9g carbohydrate; 27.2g protein; 2.2g fibre*

saffron prawns

1kg uncooked king prawns
1½ cups (225g) plain flour
½ teaspoon salt
1½ cups (375ml) light beer
pinch saffron threads
vegetable oil, for deep-frying
lemon wedges, for serving

1   Peel and devein prawns, leaving tails intact.
2   Sift flour and salt into large bowl; whisk in beer and saffron until batter is smooth.
3   Pat prawns dry with absorbent paper. Heat oil in wok; dip prawns in batter, in batches, draining excess batter. Deep-fry prawns, in batches, until just cooked. Remove prawns; drain well on absorbent paper. Repeat process with remaining prawns and batter.
4   Serve prawns immediately with lemon wedges.

preparation time *15 minutes*
cooking time *10 minutes* serves *8*
nutritional count per serving *3.9g total fat (0.5g saturated fat); 757kJ (181 cal); 19.4g carbohydrate; 15.7g protein; 1g fibre*

prawns in wonton wrappers

24 uncooked medium king prawns (1kg)
1 teaspoon sesame oil
1 teaspoon peanut oil
2 cloves garlic, crushed
1 fresh long red chilli, chopped finely
2 green onions
12 wonton wrappers
vegetable oil, for deep-frying

CHILLI PLUM DIP

⅓ cup (110g) plum jam
1 fresh small red thai chilli, sliced thinly
¼ cup (60ml) white vinegar

1   Shell and devein prawns, leaving tails intact.
Combine oils, garlic and chilli in medium bowl with
prawns. Cover; refrigerate 1 hour.
2   Meanwhile, cut green section of each onion into
3cm lengths. Slice each 3cm length in half lengthways;
submerge onion strips in hot water until just pliable.
3   Halve wonton wrappers. Top each wrapper half
with an onion strip then a prawn. Brush edges of
wrapper with a little water; fold wrapper over to
enclose prawn and onion.
4   Heat oil in wok; deep-fry prawns, in batches,
until brown. Drain.
5   Meanwhile, make chilli plum dip.
6   Serve prawns with dip.

CHILLI PLUM DIP Stir ingredients in small saucepan over
low heat until jam melts.

preparation time *20 minutes (plus refrigeration time)*
cooking time *15 minutes* makes *24*
nutritional count per prawn *2g total fat (0.3g
saturated fat); 247kJ (59 cal); 5.3g carbohydrate;
4.8g protein; 0.1g fibre*

deep-fried prawn balls

1kg uncooked large king prawns
5 green onions, chopped finely
2 cloves garlic, crushed
4 fresh small red thai chillies, chopped finely
1 teaspoon grated fresh ginger
1 tablespoon cornflour
2 teaspoons fish sauce
¼ cup coarsely chopped fresh coriander
¼ cup (25g) packaged breadcrumbs
½ cup (35g) stale breadcrumbs
vegetable oil, for deep-frying
⅓ cup (80ml) sweet chilli sauce

1   Shell and devein prawns; cut in half. Blend or
process prawn halves, pulsing, until chopped coarsely.
Place in large bowl with onion, garlic, chilli, ginger,
cornflour, sauce and coriander; mix well.
2   Using hands, roll rounded tablespoons of prawn
mixture into balls. Roll balls in combined breadcrumbs;
place, in single layer, on plastic-wrap-lined tray. Cover;
refrigerate 30 minutes.
3   Heat oil in wok; deep-fry prawn balls, in batches,
until browned and cooked through. Serve with sweet
chilli sauce.

preparation time *25 minutes (plus refrigeration time)*
cooking time *10 minutes* serves *4*
nutritional count per serving *10.9g total fat (1.5g
saturated fat); 1195kJ (286 cal); 17.1g carbohydrate;
28.5g protein; 2.2g fibre*

barbecued pork rice paper rolls

400g chinese barbecued pork, sliced thinly
½ small wombok (350g), shredded finely
1 small carrot (70g), grated coarsely
1 small red capsicum (150g), sliced thinly
1 cup (80g) bean sprouts
3 green onions, sliced thinly
½ cup loosely packed fresh mint leaves
1 tablespoon plum sauce
1 tablespoon sweet chilli sauce
1 tablespoon lime juice
12 x 17cm-square rice paper sheets

PLUM DIPPING SAUCE

2 tablespoons plum sauce
2 tablespoons sweet chilli sauce
2 tablespoons water
1 tablespoon lime juice
1 tablespoon light soy sauce

1 Combine pork, wombok, carrot, capsicum, sprouts, onion, mint, sauces and juice in large bowl.
2 To assemble rolls, place one rice paper sheet in medium bowl of warm water until softened. Lift sheet carefully from water; place, with one corner of the sheet facing you, on board covered with a tea towel. Place a little of the pork filling vertically along centre of sheet; fold top and bottom corners over filling then roll sheet from side to side to enclose filling. Repeat with remaining rice paper sheets and pork filling.
3 Make plum dipping sauce; serve with rolls.

PLUM DIPPING SAUCE Combine ingredients in small bowl.

preparation time *30 minutes* makes *12*
nutritional count per roll *5.5g total fat (2.2g saturated fat); 548kJ (131 cal); 10.2g carbohydrate; 8.9g protein; 2.5g fibre*

duck and mushroom spring rolls

½ chinese barbecued duck (500g)
50g fresh shiitake mushrooms, sliced thinly
50g oyster mushrooms, sliced thinly
50g enoki mushrooms, trimmed
4 green onions, sliced thinly
1 clove garlic, crushed
2cm piece fresh ginger (10g), grated
1 tablespoon hoisin sauce
1 tablespoon lime juice
12 x 21.5cm-square spring roll wrappers
vegetable oil, for deep-frying

1 Remove skin and meat from duck; discard bones. Shred meat and skin finely.
2 Combine duck, mushrooms, onion, garlic, ginger, sauce and juice in medium bowl.
3 To assemble rolls, place one wrapper on board, with one corner of the wrapper facing you. Place a little of the duck filling onto corner; roll once toward opposing corner to cover filling, then fold in two remaining corners to enclose filling. Continue rolling; brush seam with a little water to seal spring roll. Repeat process with remaining wrappers and duck filling.
4 Heat oil in wok; deep-fry spring rolls, in batches, until browned. Drain on absorbent paper. Serve with sweet chilli sauce, if you like.

preparation time *30 minutes*
cooking time *20 minutes* makes *12*
nutritional count per roll *9.6g total fat (2.3g saturated fat); 585kJ (140 cal); 6.8g carbohydrate; 6.3g protein; 1.1g fibre*

gorgonzola and fennel tartlets

120g gorgonzola cheese, crumbled
½ cup (120g) sour cream
2 eggs
1 tablespoon olive oil
2 small fennel bulbs (600g), trimmed, halved,
    sliced thinly
4 sheets fillo pastry
cooking-oil spray

1 Blend or process cheese, sour cream and eggs
until smooth; transfer to large jug.
2 Heat oil in small frying pan; cook fennel, stirring,
until soft.
3 Preheat oven to 180°C/160°C fan-forced. Oil two
12-hole mini (1½-tablespoons/30ml) muffin pans.
4 Cut pastry into 7cm squares. Stack two squares of
pastry on board; spray with oil. Place another two
squares diagonally on top to make star shape; spray
with oil. Press into hole of mini muffin pan; repeat with
remaining pastry. Divide cheese mixture among pastry
cases; top with fennel.
5 Bake tartlets about 15 minutes or until filling sets and
pastry is browned. Stand in pans 5 minutes.

preparation time *20 minutes*
cooking time *20 minutes makes 24*
*nutritional count per tartlet 16.4g total fat (8.3g
saturated fat); 832kJ (199 cal); 6 carbohydrate;
6.5g protein; 1.5g fibre*

asian oysters

24 oysters, on the half shell
¼ cup (60ml) lime juice
1 tablespoon fish sauce
2 teaspoons white sugar
2 tablespoons coconut cream
1 baby onion (25g), sliced thinly
1 fresh long red chilli, sliced thinly
2 tablespoons finely chopped fresh coriander
2 tablespoons finely chopped fresh mint

1 Remove oysters from shells; discard shells.
2 Combine oysters in medium bowl with juice,
sauce and sugar. Cover; refrigerate 1 hour. Stir in
coconut cream.
3 Combine onion, chilli and herbs in small bowl.
4 Place each undrained oyster on chinese spoons,
then place on serving tray; top each with herb mixture.

preparation time *30 minutes (plus refrigeration time)*
makes *24*
*nutritional count per spoon 0.6g total fat (0.4g
saturated fat); 59kJ (14 cal); 0.6g carbohydrate;
1.4g protein; 0.1g fibre*

oysters with two dressings

24 oysters, on the half shell
RED WINE VINEGAR DRESSING
1½ teaspoons finely chopped shallots
1 tablespoon red wine vinegar
1 teaspoon extra virgin olive oil
SPICY LIME DRESSING
1½ tablespoons fresh lime juice
½ teaspoon piri piri sauce
1 teaspoon chopped fresh coriander

RED WINE VINEGAR DRESSING Combine ingredients
in small bowl; spoon over 12 oysters.

preparation time *5 minutes makes 12*
*nutritional count per oyster 1g total fat (0.3g
saturated fat); 92kJ (22 cal); 0.2g carbohydrate;
3.1g protein; 0g fibre*

SPICY LIME DRESSING Combine ingredients in small
bowl; spoon over 12 oysters.

preparation time *5 minutes makes 12*
*nutritional count per oyster 0.6g total fat (0.2g
saturated fat); 79kJ (19 cal); 0.3g carbohydrate;
3.1g protein; 0g fibre*

chicken sausage rolls

1kg chicken mince
1 medium brown onion (150g), chopped finely
½ cup (35g) stale breadcrumbs
1 egg
¼ cup finely chopped fresh basil
½ cup (75g) drained semi-dried tomatoes in oil, chopped finely
2 tablespoons tomato paste
5 sheets ready-rolled puff pastry
1 egg, extra

1 Preheat oven to 220°C/200°C fan-forced. Line oven trays with baking paper.
2 Combine mince, onion, breadcrumbs, egg, basil, semi-dried tomato and paste in large bowl.
3 Cut pastry sheets in half lengthways. Place equal amounts of chicken filling mixture lengthways along centre of each pastry piece; roll pastry to enclose filling. Cut each roll into six pieces; place rolls, seam-side down, on trays. Brush with extra egg.
4 Bake rolls 30 minutes. Serve rolls hot, with tomato sauce, if you like.

preparation time *15 minutes*
cooking time *30 minutes* makes *60*
nutritional count per roll *4.8g total fat (2.2g saturated fat); 359kJ (86 cal); 6g carbohydrate; 4.5g protein; 0.5g fibre*

mini chicken and leek pies

1 cup (250ml) chicken stock
170g chicken breast fillet
1 tablespoon olive oil
1 small leek (200g), sliced thinly
½ trimmed celery stick (50g), chopped finely
2 teaspoons plain flour
2 teaspoons fresh thyme leaves
¼ cup (60ml) cream
1 teaspoon wholegrain mustard
2 sheets ready-rolled shortcrust pastry
1 sheet ready-rolled puff pastry
1 egg yolk
2 teaspoons sesame seeds

1 Bring stock to the boil in small saucepan. Add chicken; return to the boil. Reduce heat; simmer, covered, about 10 minutes or until chicken is just cooked through. Remove from heat; stand chicken in poaching liquid 10 minutes. Remove chicken; chop finely. Reserve ¼ cup of the poaching liquid; discard remainder.
2 Heat oil in medium saucepan; cook leek and celery, stirring, until leek softens. Add flour and half of the thyme; cook, stirring, 1 minute. Gradually stir in reserved liquid and cream; cook, stirring, until mixture boils and thickens. Stir in chicken and mustard. Cool 10 minutes.
3 Preheat oven to 220°C/200°C fan-forced. Oil eight holes in each of two 12-hole patty pans.
4 Using 7cm cutter, cut 16 rounds from shortcrust pastry; press one round into each hole. Spoon 1 tablespoon of the chicken mixture into each pastry case. Using 6cm cutter, cut 16 rounds from puff pastry; top chicken pies with puff pastry lids. Brush lids with yolk; sprinkle with remaining thyme and sesame seeds. Using sharp knife, make two small slits in each lid.
5 Bake pies about 20 minutes or until browned.

preparation time *40 minutes*
cooking time *40 minutes* makes *16*
nutritional count per pie *11.5g total fat (5.6g saturated fat); 740kJ (177 cal); 13.5g carbohydrate; 5.1g protein; 1g fibre*

steak with salsa verde on mini toasts

200g piece beef fillet steak
½ cup finely chopped fresh flat-leaf parsley
¼ cup finely chopped fresh basil
1 tablespoon drained baby capers, rinsed
1 clove garlic, crushed
1 tablespoon lemon juice
1 tablespoon olive oil
1 packet mini toasts (80g)
2 tablespoons dijon mustard

1 Cook steak on heated oiled grill plate (or grill or barbecue) until cooked as desired. Cover steak; stand 10 minutes, slice thinly.
2 Meanwhile, combine herbs, capers, garlic, juice and oil in medium bowl with steak; toss gently to combine.
3 Place mini toasts on serving platter; divide mustard and steak among mini toasts.

preparation time *20 minutes*
cooking time *10 minutes* makes *36*
nutritional count per toast *1g total fat (0.2g saturated fat; 92kJ (22 cal); 1.7g carbohydrate; 1.5g protein; 0.2g fibre*

smoked chicken salad on blini

⅓ cup (50g) buckwheat flour
2 tablespoons plain flour
½ teaspoon baking powder
1 egg
½ cup (125ml) buttermilk
20g butter, melted
100g smoked chicken, shredded
1 small green apple (130g), chopped finely
2 green onions, sliced thinly
¼ cup (75g) whole-egg mayonnaise
2 teaspoons wholegrain mustard
1 tablespoon coarsely chopped fresh chives

1 Sift flours and baking powder into small bowl, gradually whisk in combined egg and buttermilk until mixture is smooth; stir in butter.
2 Cook blini, in batches, by dropping 2 teaspoons of batter into heated large non-stick frying pan; cook blini until browned both sides. Cool on wire racks.
3 Meanwhile, combine remaining ingredients in medium bowl.
4 Place blini on serving platter; divide chicken salad among blini then sprinkle with chives.

preparation time *20 minutes*
cooking time *10 minutes* makes *24*
nutritional count per blini *2.2g total fat (0.8g saturated fat); 171kJ (41 cal); 3.6g carbohydrate; 1.6g protein; 0.2g fibre*

1 STEAK WITH SALSA VERDE ON MINI TOASTS
2 SMOKED CHICKEN SALAD ON BLINI 3 DEEP-FRIED FONTINA BITES [P 66]
4 SCALLOPS WITH SAFFRON CREAM [P 66]

1

2

3

4

deep-fried fontina bites

500g piece fontina cheese
½ cup (75g) plain flour
½ cup (75g) cornflour
1 egg
¾ cup (180ml) water
1½ cups (150g) packaged breadcrumbs
1 tablespoon finely chopped fresh flat-leaf parsley
2 tablespoons finely chopped fresh oregano
½ teaspoon cayenne pepper
vegetable oil, for deep-frying

1 Cut cheese into 1.5cm x 4cm pieces.
2 Combine flour and cornflour in medium bowl;
gradually stir in combined egg and water until batter
is smooth. Combine breadcrumbs, herbs and pepper
in another medium bowl.
3 Dip cheese pieces, one at a time, in batter then in
breadcrumb mixture. Repeat process to double-coat
each piece.
4 Heat oil in wok; deep-fry cheese pieces, in batches,
until browned. Drain on absorbent paper.

preparation time *20 minutes*
cooking time *10 minutes* makes *32*
nutritional count per bite *6.8g total fat (3.3g
saturated fat); 456kJ (109 cal); 6.9g carbohydrate;
5.2g protein; 0.3 fibre*

scallops with saffron cream

12 scallops, on the half shell (480g)
1 teaspoon olive oil
1 small brown onion (80g), chopped finely
2 teaspoons finely grated lemon rind
pinch saffron threads
⅔ cup (160ml) cream
1 tablespoon lemon juice
2 teaspoons salmon roe

1 Remove scallops from shells; wash and dry shells.
Place shells, in single layer, on serving platter.
2 Rinse scallops under cold water; discard scallop roe.
Gently pat scallops dry with absorbent paper.
3 Heat oil in small saucepan; cook onion, stirring,
until softened. Add rind, saffron and cream; bring to
the boil. Reduce heat; simmer, uncovered, 5 minutes or
until mixture has reduced to about ½ cup. Remove from
heat; stand 30 minutes. Stir in juice; stand 10 minutes.
Strain cream mixture into small bowl then back into
cleaned pan; stir over low heat until heated through.
4 Meanwhile, cook scallops, in batches, on heated
oiled grill plate (or grill or barbecue) until browned
lightly and cooked as desired.
5 Return scallops to shells; top with cream sauce
and roe.

preparation time *5 minutes (plus standing time)*
cooking time *10 minutes* makes *12*
nutritional count per scallop *6.4g total fat (4g
saturated fat); 288kJ (69 cal); 0.8g carbohydrate;
2.3g protein; 0.1g fibre*

scallops st jacques-style

24 scallops (500g), roe removed
½ cup (125ml) dry white wine
½ cup (125ml) cream
1 tablespoon fresh chervil leaves

1 Rinse scallops under cold water. Dry on absorbent paper.
2 Bring wine to the boil in medium frying pan; reduce heat then simmer until reduced by half. Whisk in cream; bring to the boil. Reduce heat; simmer, uncovered, about 5 minutes or until liquid has reduced by two-thirds. Add scallops; cook 1 minute. Remove from heat.
3 Place each scallop on a chinese spoon, then on serving tray. Spoon sauce on each scallop, top with chervil.

preparation time *5 minutes*
cooking time *15 minutes* makes *24*
nutritional count per scallop *2.4g total fat (1.5g saturated fat); 159kJ (38 cal); 0.3g carbohydrate; 3g protein; 0g fibre*

sesame-crusted tuna with wasabi mayo

300g sashimi tuna steak
1 tablespoon white sesame seeds
1 tablespoon black sesame seeds
1 tablespoon sesame oil
2 tablespoons mayonnaise
1 teaspoon wasabi paste

1 Coat both sides of tuna with combined seeds.
2 Heat oil in medium frying pan; cook tuna, uncovered, until browned both sides and cooked as desired (do not overcook as tuna has a tendency to dry out).
3 Cut tuna into 24 similar-sized pieces (about 2cm).
4 Serve tuna topped with combined mayonnaise and wasabi; skewer with toothpicks.

preparation time *20 minutes*
cooking time *5 minutes* makes *24*
nutritional count per stick *2.5g total fat (0.5g saturated fat); 155kJ (37 cal); 0.3g carbohydrate; 3.4g protein; 0.1g fibre*

beef and fig cigars

20g butter
1 medium brown onion (150g), chopped finely
½ teaspoon ground cinnamon
2 cloves garlic, crushed
250g beef mince
¾ cup (140g) finely chopped dried figs
1 tablespoon finely chopped fresh chives
8 sheets fillo pastry
cooking-oil spray
½ cup (125ml) plum sauce

1 Melt butter in large frying pan; cook onion, cinnamon and garlic, stirring, until onion softens. Add beef; cook, stirring, until beef is browned. Stir in figs and chives; cool 10 minutes.
2 Meanwhile, preheat oven to 200°C/180°C fan-forced. Oil two oven trays.
3 Spray one pastry sheet with oil; cover with a second pastry sheet. Cut lengthways into three even strips, then crossways into four even strips.
4 Place one rounded teaspoon of the beef mixture along the bottom of one narrow edge of a strip, leaving 1cm border. Fold narrow edge over beef mixture then fold in long sides; roll to enclose filling. Place cigar, seam-side down, on tray; repeat process with remaining pastry and beef mixture.
5 Spray cigars with oil. Bake about 10 minutes or until browned. Serve with plum sauce.

preparation time *30 minutes*
cooking time *30 minutes* makes *48*
nutritional count per cigar *0.9g total fat (0.4g saturated fat); 142kJ (34 cal); 4.9g carbohydrate; 1.5g protein; 0.6g fibre*

salt and pepper quail

6 quails (960g)
½ cup (75g) plain flour
1½ tablespoons sea salt flakes
2 teaspoons coarsely ground black pepper
vegetable oil, for deep-frying

LEMON PEPPER DIPPING SAUCE

¼ cup (60ml) vegetable oil
1 teaspoon finely grated lemon rind
⅓ cup (80ml) lemon juice
2 tablespoons grated palm sugar
1 teaspoon ground white pepper

HERB SALAD

½ cup loosely packed vietnamese mint leaves
½ cup loosely packed fresh coriander leaves
1 cup (80g) bean sprouts
1 fresh long red chilli, sliced thinly

1   Rinse quails under cold water; pat dry. Discard
necks from quails. Using kitchen scissors, cut along
sides of each quail's backbone; discard backbones.
Halve each quail along breastbone.
2   Make lemon pepper dipping sauce.
3   Make herb salad.
4   Toss quail in combined flour, salt and pepper;
shake off excess.
5   Heat oil in wok; deep-fry quail, in batches,
about 6 minutes or until cooked. Drain.
6   Divide quail among serving plates; top with herb
salad. Serve with remaining dipping sauce.

LEMON PEPPER DIPPING SAUCE Place ingredients in
screw-top jar; shake well.

HERB SALAD Combine ingredients in medium bowl with
1 tablespoon of the lemon pepper dipping sauce.

preparation time *30 minutes*
cooking time *20 minutes* serves *4*
nutritional count per serving *34.8g total fat (6.2g
saturated fat); 2098kJ (502 cal); 21.4g carbohydrate;
25.5g protein; 2g fibre*

chilli salt squid

1kg small whole squid
vegetable oil, for deep-frying
2 fresh medium red chillies, sliced
1 cup lightly packed fresh coriander leaves
⅓ cup (50g) plain flour
2 fresh medium red chillies, chopped finely, extra
2 teaspoons sea salt
1 teaspoon ground black pepper
lime wedges, for serving

1   Gently separate body and tentacles of squid by
pulling on tentacles. Cut head from tentacles just below
eyes and discard head. Trim long tentacle of each squid.
2   Remove clear quill from inside the body. Peel side
flaps from body, then peel away the dark skin. Wash
squid well and pat dry with absorbent paper.
3   Cut along one side of the body and open out.
Score inside surface in a criss-cross pattern, using
a small sharp knife. Cut body into 3cm pieces.
4   Heat oil in wok; carefully (the oil will spit) deep-fry
chillies until softened. Drain on absorbent paper.
Deep-fry coriander carefully (oil will spit) 10 seconds or
until changed in colour; drain on absorbent paper.
5   Toss squid in combined flour, extra chilli, salt and
pepper; shake off excess.
6   Deep-fry squid, in batches, until just browned and
tender; drain on absorbent paper. Sprinkle squid with
coriander and chilli; serve immediately with lime wedges.

preparation time *20 minutes*
cooking time *10 minutes* serves *4*
nutritional count per serving *8.1g total fat (1.7g
saturated fat); 807kJ (193 cal); 9.6g carbohydrate;
19.7g protein; 1g fibre*

pea pakoras with coriander raita

1½ cups (225g) besan flour
½ teaspoon bicarbonate of soda
¾ cup (180ml) water
2 teaspoons vegetable oil
2 cloves garlic, crushed
½ teaspoon ground turmeric
½ teaspoon cumin seeds
1 teaspoon ground cumin
½ teaspoon dried chilli flakes
1 tablespoon coarsely chopped fresh coriander
1 cup (120g) frozen peas
2 green onions, chopped finely
40g baby spinach leaves, shredded coarsely
vegetable oil, for deep-frying, extra

CORIANDER RAITA

1 cup (280g) greek-style yogurt
1 cup firmly packed coarsely chopped coriander
½ teaspoon ground cumin

1   Sift flour and soda into medium bowl; whisk in the water to form a smooth batter.
2   Heat oil in small saucepan; cook garlic and spices, stirring, until fragrant. Add mixture to batter with coriander, peas, onion and spinach; mix well.
3   Heat extra oil in wok; deep-fry level tablespoons of the mixture, in batches, about 5 minutes or until browned lightly. Drain on absorbent paper.
4   Make coriander raita.
5   Serve pakoras with raita.

CORIANDER RAITA   Blend or process ingredients until smooth.

preparation time *25 minutes*
cooking time *15 minutes* makes *24*
nutritional count per pakora *3.2g total fat (0.8g saturated fat); 293kJ (70 cal); 7g carbohydrate; 3.1g protein; 1.5g fibre*

prawns and tequila mayo on witlof leaves

900g cooked medium king prawns
1 tablespoon tequila
¼ cup (75g) mayonnaise
1 tablespoon finely chopped fresh chives
3 red witlof (375g)

1   Shell and devein prawns. Chop prawn meat coarsely. Combine prawn meat in medium bowl with tequila, mayonnaise and chives.
2   Trim end from each witlof; separate leaves (you will need 24 leaves). Place one level tablespoon of the prawn mixture on each leaf.

preparation time *20 minutes* makes *24*
nutritional count per leaf *1.1g total fat (0.1g saturated fat); 130kJ (31 cal); 0.7g carbohydrate; 4g protein; 0.3g fibre*

blt on mini toasts

4 rindless bacon rashers (260g)
1 packet (80g) mini toasts
6 butter lettuce leaves
¼ cup (75g) whole-egg mayonnaise
200g grape tomatoes, halved

1   Cut each rasher into pieces slightly smaller than mini toasts.
2   Heat large frying pan; cook bacon, stirring, until browned and crisp, drain on absorbent paper.
3   Cut lettuce into pieces slightly larger than mini toasts.
4   Divide mayonnaise among mini toasts; top each with lettuce, bacon and tomato. Serve at room temperature.

preparation time *20 minutes*
cooking time *5 minutes* makes *40*
nutritional count per blt *2.3g total fat (0.6g saturated fat); 134kJ (32 cal); 1.2g carbohydrate; 1.5g protein; 0.2g fibre*

olive and cheese fritters

2 teaspoons (7g) dried yeast
1 cup (250ml) warm water
2 cups (300g) plain flour
½ teaspoon salt
¼ cup (40g) pitted black olives, chopped coarsely
4 drained anchovy fillets, chopped finely
4 drained sun-dried tomatoes, chopped finely
200g bocconcini cheese, chopped finely
1 small white onion (80g), chopped finely
2 cloves garlic, crushed
vegetable oil, for deep-frying

1 Dissolve yeast in the warm water in medium jug. Place flour and salt in large bowl, gradually stir in yeast mixture to form a sticky, wet batter. Cover, stand in warm place about 1 hour or until doubled in size.
2 Stir in olive, anchovy, tomato, cheese, onion and garlic.
3 Heat oil in wok; deep-fry heaped teaspoons of mixture, in batches, about 3 minutes or until browned and cooked through. Drain on absorbent paper; sprinkle with sea salt, if you like. Stand 2 minutes before serving.

preparation time *15 minutes (plus standing time)*
cooking time *15 minutes* makes *40*
nutritional count per fritter *2.1g total fat (0.7g saturated fat); 213kJ (51 cal); 5.9g carbohydrate; 1.9g protein; 0.5g fibre*

pork dumplings

250g pork mince
½ cup (40g) finely chopped wombok
2 green onions, chopped finely
2 tablespoons finely chopped fresh garlic chives
2cm piece fresh ginger (10g), grated
2 teaspoons light soy sauce
2 teaspoons cornflour
40 wonton wrappers

DIPPING SAUCE

¼ cup (60ml) light soy sauce
2 teaspoons white vinegar
2 teaspoons brown sugar

1 Combine pork, wombok, onion, chives, ginger, sauce and cornflour in medium bowl.
2 Place 1 level teaspoon of the pork mixture into centre of each wonton wrapper; brush edges with a little water, pinch edges together to seal.
3 Place dumplings, in batches, in large baking-paper-lined bamboo steamer. Steam, covered, over large saucepan of boiling water about 4 minutes or until cooked through.
4 Meanwhile, make dipping sauce.
5 Serve dumplings with dipping sauce.

DIPPING SAUCE Combine ingredients in small bowl.

preparation time *25 minutes*
cooking time *15 minutes* makes *40*
nutritional count per dumpling *0.2g total fat (0g saturated fat); 63kJ (15 cal); 0.6g carbohydrate; 2.5g protein; 0g fibre*

grilled salmon on lemon grass skewers

10 x 30cm lemon grass stems
2kg salmon fillets
⅔ cup (160g) sour cream
1 tablespoon coarsely chopped fresh dill
1 tablespoon lemon juice

1 Trim lemon grass tops; cut off hard base of stem.
Cut remaining sticks in half lengthways then widthways;
you will have 40 lemon grass skewers.
2 Remove any skin or bones from fish; cut fish into
40 x 3cm pieces. Using tip of small knife, cut slit
through centre of each piece of fish; thread each piece
on a lemon grass skewer. Cook, in batches, on heated
oiled grill plate (or grill or barbecue) until salmon is
browned lightly all over and cooked as desired.
3 Meanwhile, combine remaining ingredients in bowl.
4 Serve skewers hot with sour cream mixture.

preparation time *30 minutes*
cooking time *20 minutes* makes *40*
nutritional count per skewer *3.6g total fat (0.8g
saturated fat); 298kJ (71 cal); 0g carbohydrate;
9.5g protein; 0g fibre*
nutritional count per teaspoon sauce *1.8g total fat
(1.2g saturated fat); 71kJ (17 cal); 0.1g carbohydrate;
0.1g protein; 0g fibre*

smoked trout on crispy wonton wrappers

1 tablespoon prepared horseradish
1 tablespoon lemon juice
½ cup (120g) sour cream
2 tablespoons finely chopped fresh chives
1½ cups (260g) smoked trout
12 wonton wrappers
vegetable oil, for deep-frying
50g snow pea tendrils
1 tablespoon coarsely chopped fresh chives, extra

1 Combine horseradish, juice, sour cream and chives
in small bowl; fold in trout.
2 Cut each wrapper into four squares. Heat oil in wok;
deep-fry wrappers, in batches, until crisp. Drain.
3 Divide tendrils among wrappers; top each with one
heaped teaspoon of the trout mixture and extra chives.

preparation time *30 minutes*
cooking time *10 minutes* makes *48*
nutritional count per wrapper *1.4g total fat (0.8g
saturated fat); 92kJ (22 cal); 0.5g carbohydrate;
1.7g protein; 0.1g fibre*

1 GRILLED SALMON ON LEMON GRASS SKEWERS 2 SMOKED TROUT ON
CRISPY WONTON WRAPPERS 3 SPICY LAMB AND PINE NUT TRIANGLES [P 74]
4 CHEESE BALLS WITH FOUR COATINGS [P 74]

1

2

3

4

spicy lamb and pine nut triangles

10g butter
1 medium brown onion (150g), chopped finely
1 clove garlic, crushed
½ teaspoon ground mixed spice
½ teaspoon freshly ground black pepper
½ cup (80g) pine nuts, roasted
2 teaspoons sambal oelek
500g lamb mince
2 green onions, sliced thinly
24 sheets fillo pastry
cooking-oil spray

1 Melt butter in medium non-stick frying pan; cook brown onion, garlic, spice, pepper, nuts and sambal, stirring, until onion softens. Add lamb; cook, stirring, until lamb is browned and cooked. Stir in green onion.
2 Preheat oven to 200°C/180°C fan-forced. Oil trays.
3 Spray one pastry sheet with oil, cover with second pastry sheet; cut crossways into six even strips, spray with oil. Repeat with remaining pastry sheets.
4 Place 2 teaspoons of lamb filling on the bottom of narrow edge of one strip, leaving a 1cm border. Fold opposite corner of strip diagonally across filling to form triangle; continue folding to end of strip, retaining triangle shape. Place triangle on tray, seam-side down; repeat with remaining strips and filling. Spray with oil.
5 Bake triangles about 10 minutes or until browned.

preparation time *30 minutes*
cooking time *30 minutes* makes *72*
nutritional count per triangle *1.6g total fat (0.4g saturated fat); 142kJ (34 cal); 2.7g carbohydrate; 0.1g protein; 0.2g fibre*

cheese balls with four coatings

Farm cheese is a fresh cheese from which much of the liquid is pressed. Available at delis and cheese shops.

500g neufchâtel cheese
500g farm cheese
2 teaspoons finely grated lemon rind
2 tablespoons lemon juice
¼ teaspoon sea salt

1 Line four oven trays with baking paper.
2 Blend or process ingredients until smooth; refrigerate about 2 hours or until firm enough to roll.
3 Using hands, roll rounded teaspoons of the mixture into balls; place 16 balls on each tray. Refrigerate, covered, until firm.
4 Make all four coatings; roll 16 balls in each coating.

preparation time *40 minutes (plus refrigeration time)*
makes *64*

PEPPER COATING Combine 1½ tablespoons poppy seeds and 2 teaspoons cracked black pepper; coat balls.

nutritional count per ball *4.9g total fat (2.9g saturated fat); 234kJ (56 cal); 0.3g carbohydrate; 2.8g protein; 0.3g fibre*

PARSLEY COATING Coat balls in ¼ cup finely chopped fresh flat-leaf parsley.

nutritional count per ball *4.4g total fat (2.8g saturated fat); 209kJ (50 cal); 0.2g carbohydrate; 2.6g protein; 0g fibre*

SESAME SEED COATING Coat balls in ¼ cup (35g) sesame seeds.

nutritional count per ball *5.6g total fat (2.9g saturated fat); 263kJ (63 cal); 0.2g carbohydrate; 3.1g protein; 0.2g fibre*

ZA'ATAR COATING Combine 1 tablespoon each of sumac and toasted sesame seeds, 1 teaspoon each of dried oregano, dried marjoram and sweet paprika, and 2 teaspoons dried thyme; coat balls.

nutritional count per ball *4.5g total fat (2.8g saturated fat); 213kJ (51 cal); 0.2g carbohydrate; 2.6g protein; 0g fibre*

lamb and pine nut little boats

2 teaspoons olive oil
1 small brown onion (80g), chopped finely
2 cloves garlic, crushed
2 teaspoons ground cumin
400g lamb mince
1 medium tomato (150g), chopped finely
1 tablespoon finely chopped fresh flat-leaf parsley
1 tablespoon lemon juice
2 tablespoons sumac
3 sheets ready-rolled shortcrust pastry
1 egg, beaten lightly
2 tablespoons pine nuts
1 tablespoon finely chopped fresh flat-leaf parsley
½ cup (140g) yogurt

1 Heat oil in small frying pan; cook onion, garlic and cumin, stirring, until onion softens. Place onion mixture in medium bowl with mince, tomato, parsley, juice and half of the sumac; mix until combined.
2 Preheat oven to 200°C/180°C fan-forced. Oil two oven trays.
3 Cut each pastry sheet into nine squares. Brush egg on two opposing sides of a pastry square; place 1 level tablespoon filling along centre of square. Bring egg-brushed sides together then push the two unbrushed sides inward to widen centre opening, making boat shape and showing filling. Sprinkle some pine nuts on exposed filling; place boat on tray. Repeat process with remaining pastry squares, egg, filling and pine nuts, spacing boats 4cm apart on trays.
4 Bake boats about 20 minutes or until browned and cooked through. Sprinkle with parsley.
5 Meanwhile, combine yogurt and remaining sumac in small bowl.
6 Serve little boats with sumac yogurt.

preparation time *35 minutes*
cooking time *25 minutes* makes *27*
nutritional count per boat *8.4g total fat (3.6g saturated fat); 581kJ (139 cal); 10.4g carbohydrate; 5.6g protein; 0.5g fibre*

chorizo and potato fritters

2 teaspoons vegetable oil
1 chorizo sausage (200g), chopped finely
1 small brown onion (80g), chopped finely
2 fresh small red thai chillies, chopped finely
2 medium zucchini (240g), grated coarsely
450g potatoes, peeled, grated coarsely
1 small kumara (250g), peeled, grated coarsely
3 eggs, beaten lightly
1 cup (150g) plain flour
1 teaspoon sweet paprika
vegetable oil, for deep-frying

SWEET CHILLI DIPPING SAUCE

½ cup (120g) sour cream
2 tablespoons sweet chilli sauce

1 Heat oil in medium frying pan; cook chorizo, onion and chilli, stirring, until onion softens. Add zucchini; cook, stirring, 1 minute. Cool 10 minutes.
2 Meanwhile, make sweet chilli dipping sauce.
3 Combine chorizo mixture in large bowl with potato, kumara, eggs, flour and paprika.
4 Heat oil in wok; deep-fry level tablespoons of the potato mixture, in batches, until fritters are browned lightly. Drain on absorbent paper.
5 Serve fritters with dipping sauce.

SWEET CHILLI DIPPING SAUCE Combine ingredients in small bowl.

preparation time *25 minutes*
cooking time *15 minutes* makes *40*
nutritional count per fritter *4g total fat (0.9g saturated fat); 276kJ (66 cal); 5.1g carbohydrate; 2.3g protein; 0.5g fibre*
nutritional count per teaspoon sauce *1.5g total fat (1g saturated fat); 63kJ (15 cal); 0.4g carbohydrate; 0.1g protein; 0.1g fibre*

spicy carrot and zucchini bhaji

1 cup (150g) besan flour
2 teaspoons coarse cooking salt
½ cup (125ml) cold water
¼ teaspoon ground turmeric
1 teaspoon chilli powder
1 teaspoon garam masala
2 cloves garlic, crushed
2 small brown onions (160g), sliced thinly
1 medium carrot (120g), grated coarsely
1 medium zucchini (120g), grated coarsely
½ cup loosely packed fresh coriander leaves
vegetable oil, for deep-frying
1 cup (320g) mango chutney

1   Whisk besan, salt and the water in medium bowl until mixture forms a smooth thick batter. Stir in spices, garlic, onion, carrot, zucchini and coriander.
2   Heat oil in wok; deep-fry tablespoons of mixture, in batches, until vegetables are tender and bhaji are browned. Drain on absorbent paper.
3   Serve bhaji with chutney.

preparation time *15 minutes*
cooking time *15 minutes* makes *20*
nutritional count per bhaji *2.3g total fat (0.3g saturated fat); 330kJ (79 cal); 12.1g carbohydrate; 2g protein; 1.6g fibre*

za'atar-spiced chicken drumettes

2 tablespoons olive oil
24 chicken drumettes (2kg)

ZA'ATAR

1 tablespoon sumac
1 tablespoon toasted sesame seeds
1 teaspoon dried oregano
1 teaspoon dried marjoram
1 teaspoon sweet paprika
2 teaspoons dried thyme

GARLIC DRESSING

2 cloves garlic, peeled
½ teaspoon salt
2 tablespoons lemon juice
⅔ cup (160ml) olive oil

1   Preheat oven to 220°C/200°C fan-forced.
2   Combine za'atar ingredients and oil in large bowl with drumettes.
3   Place drumettes on metal rack in large shallow baking dish. Roast, uncovered, about 40 minutes or until drumettes are cooked through.
4   Meanwhile, make garlic dressing.
5   Serve drumettes with dressing.

GARLIC DRESSING Using mortar and pestle or mini food processor, crush garlic with salt. Stir in juice then whisk in oil in thin, steady stream until dressing thickens slightly.

preparation time *20 minutes*
cooking time *40 minutes* makes *24*
nutritional count per drumette *12.9g total fat (2.6g saturated fat); 615kJ (147 cal); 0.1g carbohydrate; 8.1g protein; 0.1g fibre*

chorizo taquitos with chunky tomato salsa

450g can refried beans
1 tablespoon water
400g chorizo sausage, chopped finely
½ medium red capsicum (100g), chopped finely
3 green onions, chopped finely
10 large flour tortillas, quartered
vegetable oil, for deep-frying

CHUNKY TOMATO SALSA

425g can peeled tomatoes
2 fresh small red thai chillies, quartered
1 clove garlic, quartered
⅓ cup loosely packed fresh coriander leaves
1 small brown onion (80g), quartered

1   Make chunky tomato salsa.
2   Heat beans with the water in small saucepan.
3   Meanwhile, cook chorizo in large frying pan, stirring, until crisp; drain on absorbent paper.
4   Combine bean mixture and chorizo in medium bowl with capsicum and onion. Divide filling among tortilla pieces; roll each taquito into cone shape, secure with toothpick.
5   Heat oil in large saucepan; deep-fry taquitos, in batches, until browned lightly and crisp. Drain on absorbent paper. Remove toothpicks.
6   Serve hot taquitos with salsa.

CHUNKY TOMATO SALSA Blend or process ingredients until just combined.

preparation time *40 minutes*
cooking time *15 minutes* makes *40*
nutritional count per taquito *6g total fat (1.5g saturated fat); 435kJ (104 cal); 8.2g carbohydrate; 3.8g protein; 1.2g fibre*

prosciutto, blue brie and fig finger sandwiches

Remove cheese from refrigerator 30 minutes before making sandwiches.

50g blue brie, softened
8 slices light rye bread
6 slices prosciutto (90g), halved widthways
4 medium figs (240g), sliced thinly

1   Spread cheese over four bread slices; top with prosciutto, fig and remaining bread.
2   Remove and discard crusts; cut sandwiches into three strips.

preparation time *10 minutes* makes *12*
nutritional count per finger *2.5g total fat (1.1g saturated fat); 368kJ (88 cal); 12g carbohydrate; 4.5g protein; 1.9g fibre*

chicken, capers and mayonnaise finger sandwiches

2 cups (320g) coarsely shredded barbecued chicken
2 tablespoons drained capers, chopped coarsely
2 tablespoons finely chopped fresh chives
⅓ cup (100g) whole-egg mayonnaise
8 slices brown bread
1 lebanese cucumber (130g), sliced thinly

1   Combine chicken, capers, chives and ¼ cup of the mayonnaise in medium bowl.
2   Spread chicken mixture over four bread slices; top with cucumber. Spread remaining mayonnaise over remaining bread; place on top of cucumber.
3   Remove and discard crusts; cut sandwiches into three strips.

preparation time *10 minutes* makes *12*
nutritional count per finger *4.3g total fat (0.7g saturated fat); 422kJ (101 cal); 9.9g carbohydrate; 5.7g protein; 1.2g fibre*

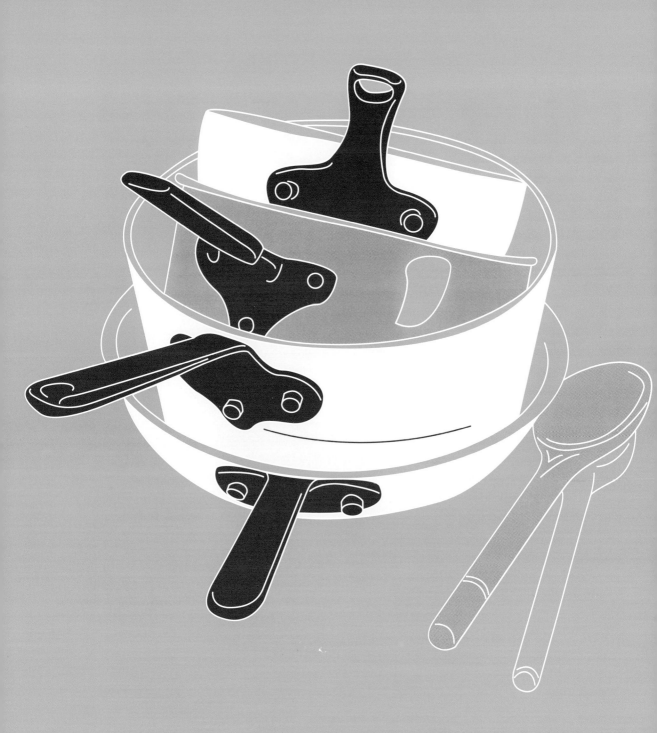

SUPERFAST

cashew and parsley-crumbed chicken with rocket salad

¾ cup (115g) roasted unsalted cashews
¾ cup fresh flat-leaf parsley, chopped finely
1 cup (70g) stale breadcrumbs
2 eggs
4 chicken breast fillets (800g)
⅓ cup (50g) plain flour
2 tablespoons olive oil
250g trimmed rocket
250g yellow grape tomatoes, halved
1 medium red capsicum (200g), sliced thinly

MUSTARD VINAIGRETTE

1½ tablespoons olive oil
1 clove garlic, crushed
1 tablespoon white vinegar
2 teaspoons wholegrain mustard

1 Preheat oven to 180°C/160°C fan-forced.
2 Blend or process nuts until they resemble a coarse meal; combine in medium shallow bowl with parsley and breadcrumbs. Beat eggs lightly in another medium shallow bowl.
3 Halve chicken pieces diagonally; slice through each piece horizontally. Coat pieces in flour; shake away excess. Dip chicken in egg then in breadcrumb mixture.
4 Heat oil in large frying pan; cook chicken, in batches, until browned both sides. Place chicken on tray; bake in oven about 10 minutes or until cooked through.
5 Meanwhile, make mustard vinaigrette.
6 Place rocket, tomato and capsicum in large bowl with vinaigrette; toss gently to combine.
7 Serve chicken with salad.

MUSTARD VINAIGRETTE Place ingredients in screw-top jar; shake well.

preparation time *15 minutes*
cooking time *20 minutes* serves *4*
nutritional count per serving *45.1g total fat (9g saturated fat); 3206kJ (767 cal); 30.1g carbohydrate; 57.7g protein; 6.1g fibre*

grilled citrus chicken with orange and pistachio couscous

3 cloves garlic, crushed
1 tablespoon finely chopped fresh oregano
¼ cup (60ml) lemon juice
½ cup (170g) orange marmalade
2 fresh small red thai chillies, chopped finely
4 chicken breast fillets (800g)
2 cups (500ml) chicken stock
2 cups (400g) couscous
2 medium oranges (480g)
2 green onions, sliced thinly
⅓ cup (45g) roasted unsalted pistachios, chopped coarsely

1 Preheat oven to 200°C/180°C fan-forced. Oil oven tray; line with baking paper.
2 Combine garlic, oregano, juice, marmalade and chilli in medium bowl with chicken.
3 Drain chicken; reserve marmalade mixture. Cook chicken on heated oiled grill plate (or grill or barbecue) until browned both sides. Place chicken on tray, drizzle with reserved marmalade mixture; bake in oven, about 10 minutes or until chicken is cooked through.
4 Meanwhile, bring stock to the boil in medium saucepan. Combine couscous with the stock in large heatproof bowl, cover; stand about 5 minutes or until liquid is absorbed, fluffing with fork occasionally. Segment oranges over couscous; stir in onion and nuts.
5 Serve couscous topped with chicken.

preparation time *10 minutes*
cooking time *15 minutes* serves *4*
nutritional count per serving *18g total fat (4.4g saturated fat); 3620kJ (866 cal); 113g carbohydrate; 60.4g protein; 4.3g fibre*

maple-glazed chicken, shallot and kumara skewers

Soak bamboo skewers in cold water for at least 1 hour to prevent splintering and scorching during cooking.

1 large kumara (500g), cut into 2cm pieces
660g chicken thigh fillets, cut into 3cm pieces
12 shallots (300g), halved
2 tablespoons maple syrup
1 tablespoon cider vinegar
1 teaspoon dijon mustard

1 Boil, steam or microwave kumara until tender; drain. Thread kumara, chicken and shallot, alternately, onto skewers.
2 Combine syrup, vinegar and mustard in small bowl.
3 Cook skewers on heated oiled grill plate (or grill or barbecue), covered with foil, 10 minutes. Uncover, brush all over with syrup mixture. Turn; cook, brushing with syrup mixture, 5 minutes or until chicken is cooked.

preparation time *15 minutes*
cooking time *20 minutes* serves *4*
nutritional count per serving *12.2g total fat (3.6g saturated fat); 1484kJ (355 cal); 26.4g carbohydrate; 33.8g protein; 2.7g fibre*

chicken with roasted cherry tomato and basil sauce

500g cherry tomatoes
5 cloves garlic, unpeeled
2 tablespoons olive oil
4 x 200g chicken breast fillets
¼ cup coarsely chopped fresh basil
¼ cup (60ml) cream

1 Preheat oven to 200°C/180°C fan-forced.
2 Combine tomatoes, garlic and oil in large shallow baking dish. Roast about 20 minutes or until tomatoes soften. When garlic is cool enough to handle, peel.
3 Meanwhile, cook chicken on heated oiled grill plate (or grill or barbecue) until cooked through. Cover; stand 5 minutes.
4 Blend or process garlic and half the tomatoes until smooth. Place in medium saucepan with basil and cream; cook, stirring, over low heat, until heated through.
5 Serve chicken topped with sauce and remaining roasted tomatoes.

preparation time *5 minutes*
cooking time *25 minutes* serves *4*
nutritional count per serving *26.8g total fat (9g saturated fat); 1818kJ (435 cal); 3.6g carbohydrate; 44g protein; 2.7g fibre*

salt and sichuan pepper salmon with wasabi mayonnaise

2 teaspoons sea salt
2 teaspoons sichuan pepper
¼ cup (60ml) vegetable oil
4 x 200g salmon fillets, skin on
½ cup (150g) mayonnaise
2 teaspoons wasabi paste
1 teaspoon finely chopped fresh coriander
1 teaspoon lime juice
watercress, for serving

1 Using mortar and pestle or pepper grinder, grind salt and pepper until fine. Combine pepper mixture, half the oil and fish in large bowl, cover; stand 5 minutes.
2 Meanwhile, combine mayonnaise, wasabi, coriander and juice in small bowl.
3 Heat remaining oil in large frying pan; cook fish, skin-side down, until skin crisps. Turn fish; cook until cooked as desired.
4 Serve fish with wasabi mayonnaise and watercress.

preparation time *10 minutes*
cooking time *15 minutes* serves *4*
nutritional count per serving *40.1g total fat (6.3g saturated fat); 2278kJ (545 cal); 7.5g carbohydrate; 39.4 protein; 0.2g fibre*

prawn and scallop chilli jam stir-fry

1kg uncooked medium king prawns
2 tablespoons peanut oil
300g scallops, roe removed
2 cloves garlic, crushed
2cm piece fresh ginger (10g), grated
200g green beans, cut into 5cm lengths
350g gai lan, trimmed, chopped coarsely
⅔ cup (190g) prepared thai chilli jam
1½ cups (120g) bean sprouts
½ cup firmly packed thai basil leaves

1 Shell and devein prawns, leaving tails intact.
2 Heat half of the oil in wok; stir-fry prawns and scallops, in batches, until cooked as desired. Drain on absorbent paper.
3 Heat remaining oil in wok; stir-fry garlic and ginger until fragrant. Add beans and gai lan; stir-fry until gai lan is wilted. Return prawns and scallops to wok with chilli jam; stir-fry 2 minutes.
4 Stir in sprouts and basil off the heat; serve with steamed jasmine rice, if you like.

preparation time *15 minutes*
cooking time *20 minutes* serves *4*
nutritional count per serving *14.6g total fat (2.9g saturated fat); 1513kJ (362 cal); 16.8g carbohydrate; 38.6g protein; 3.9g fibre*

1 SALT AND SICHUAN PEPPER SALMON WITH WASABI MAYONNAISE
2 PRAWN AND SCALLOP CHILLI JAM STIR-FRY 3 FAST FISH VINDALOO [P 84]
4 CHAR-GRILLED CHILLI SQUID AND RICE NOODLE SALAD [P 84]

1

2

3

4

fast fish vindaloo

We used blue eye fillets in this recipe, but you can use any firm white fish you like.

2 tablespoons olive oil
4 x 200g firm white fish fillets, skin on
1 large brown onion (200g), sliced thinly
2 cloves garlic, crushed
¼ cup (75g) vindaloo curry paste
1 cup (250ml) water
2 medium tomatoes (300g), chopped coarsely
⅓ cup loosely packed fresh coriander leaves

1 Heat half the oil in large frying pan; cook fish, skin-side down, until browned. Turn; cook other side until browned. Remove from pan.
2 Heat remaining oil in same pan; cook onion and garlic, stirring, until onion softens. Add curry paste; cook, stirring, until fragrant. Add the water and tomato; bring to the boil. Reduce heat; simmer, uncovered, 5 minutes.
3 Return fish to pan; simmer, uncovered, about 5 minutes or until fish is cooked through.
4 Serve vindaloo sprinkled with coriander leaves and, if you like, steamed basmati rice, pappadums and raita.

preparation time *10 minutes*
cooking time *20 minutes* serves *4*
nutritional count per serving *16.5g total fat (2.1g saturated fat); 1375kJ (329 cal); 5.7g carbohydrate; 37.5g protein; 3.7g fibre*

char-grilled chilli squid and rice noodle salad

800g cleaned squid hoods
450g fresh wide rice noodles
1 medium red capsicum (200g), sliced thinly
150g snow peas, trimmed, halved
1 lebanese cucumber (130g), seeded, sliced thinly
1 small red onion (100g), sliced thinly
1 cup loosely packed fresh coriander leaves
⅓ cup coarsely chopped fresh mint

SWEET CHILLI DRESSING

⅓ cup (75g) caster sugar
½ cup (125ml) water
1 tablespoon white vinegar
2 fresh small red thai chillies, chopped finely

1 Cut squid down centre to open out; score the inside in a diagonal pattern. Halve squid lengthways; cut squid into 3cm pieces.
2 Make sweet chilli dressing.
3 Cook squid on heated oiled grill plate (or grill or barbecue), in batches, until tender and browned.
4 Place noodles in large heatproof bowl, cover with boiling water; separate with fork, drain.
5 Place noodles and squid in large serving bowl with dressing and remaining ingredients; toss gently to combine.

SWEET CHILLI DRESSING Stir sugar and the water and in small saucepan, over low heat, until sugar dissolves; bring to the boil. Reduce heat; simmer, uncovered, without stirring, about 5 minutes or until syrup thickens slightly. Stir in vinegar and chilli off the heat.

preparation time *15 minutes*
cooking time *15 minutes* serves *4*
nutritional count per serving *3.1g total fat (0.8g saturated fat); 1584kJ (379 cal); 48.3g carbohydrate; 38.1g protein; 2.8g fibre*

steamed salmon with burnt orange sauce

½ cup (110g) caster sugar
⅓ cup (80ml) water
1 teaspoon finely grated orange rind
¼ cup (60ml) orange juice
1 tablespoon olive oil
1 tablespoon rice wine vinegar
4 x 200g salmon fillets
350g watercress, trimmed

1 Stir sugar and the water in small saucepan, without boiling, until sugar dissolves; bring to the boil. Reduce heat; simmer, uncovered, without stirring, until mixture is a light caramel colour.
2 Remove pan from heat; allow bubbles to subside. Carefully stir in rind and juice; return pan to low heat. Stir until any pieces of caramel melt. Remove pan from heat; stir in oil and vinegar.
3 Meanwhile, steam fish in large bamboo steamer over large saucepan of simmering water, covered, 15 minutes.
4 Serve fish with watercress, drizzled with sauce.

preparation time *10 minutes*
cooking time *25 minutes serves 4*
nutritional count per serving *19.1g total fat (3.8g saturated fat); 1940kJ (464 cal); 29.4g carbohydrate; 41.6g protein; 3.4g fibre*

chickpea ratatouille

2 tablespoons olive oil
1 medium red onion (170g), cut into thin wedges
2 cloves garlic, crushed
1 medium eggplant (300g), chopped coarsely
1 medium red capsicum (200g), chopped coarsely
2 medium zucchini (240g), sliced thickly
400g can chickpeas, rinsed, drained
4 small egg tomatoes (240g), chopped coarsely
2 tablespoons tomato paste
½ cup (125ml) water
⅔ cup loosely packed fresh basil leaves

1 Heat half the oil in large frying pan; cook onion and garlic, stirring, about 5 minutes or until onion softens. Remove from pan.
2 Heat remaining oil in same pan; cook eggplant, capsicum and zucchini, stirring, about 5 minutes or until eggplant is browned.
3 Return onion mixture to pan with chickpeas, tomato, paste and the water; simmer, covered, about 10 minutes or until vegetables soften. Remove from heat; stir in basil.

preparation time *10 minutes*
cooking time *25 minutes serves 4*
nutritional count per serving *10.8g total fat (1.4g saturated fat); 857kJ (205 cal); 16.4g carbohydrate; 7.1g protein; 7.7g fibre*

ginger and kaffir lime perch parcels

4 x 180g ocean perch fillets
3 green onions, sliced thinly
5cm piece fresh ginger (25g), sliced thinly
4 fresh kaffir lime leaves, shredded finely
2 teaspoons sesame oil

1 Preheat oven to 180°C/160°C fan-forced.
2 Place each fillet on large square of oiled foil or baking paper; top each with onion, ginger and lime leaves, drizzle with oil. Gather corners together; fold to enclose.
3 Place parcels on oven trays; cook about 15 minutes or until fish is cooked through.
4 Remove fish from parcel, discard topping from fish. Serve with lime wedges and steamed rice, if you like.

preparation time *5 minutes*
cooking time *15 minutes serves 4*
nutritional count per serving *3.4g total fat (0.5g saturated fat); 648kJ (155 cal); 6.3g carbohydrate; 30.4g protein; 0.2g fibre*

ocean trout with lime and lemon grass hollandaise

10cm stick fresh lemon grass (20g), chopped finely
3 fresh kaffir lime leaves, shredded thinly
1 tablespoon finely grated lime rind
⅓ cup (80ml) lime juice
3 egg yolks
200g unsalted butter, melted
3 fresh kaffir lime leaves, chopped finely
4 x 200g ocean trout fillets

1 To make lime and lemon grass hollandaise, combine lemon grass, shredded lime leaves, rind and juice in small saucepan; bring to the boil. Reduce heat; simmer, uncovered, until liquid reduces to 1 tablespoon. Strain through fine sieve into medium heatproof bowl; cool 10 minutes. Discard solids in sieve.
2 Add egg yolks to juice mixture in bowl; set bowl over medium saucepan of simmering water, do not allow water to touch base of bowl. Whisk mixture over heat until thickened.
3 Remove bowl from heat; gradually add melted butter in thin, steady stream, whisking constantly until sauce has thickened. (If sauce is too thick, a tablespoon of hot water can be added.) Stir in finely chopped lime leaves.
4 Meanwhile, cook fish in heated oiled large frying pan until cooked as desired. Serve with hollandaise.

preparation time *20 minutes*
cooking time *10 minutes* serves *4*
nutritional count per serving *52.9g total fat (30.1g saturated fat); 2675kJ (640 cal); 0.7g carbohydrate; 41.6g protein; 0.1g fibre*

fish fillets with chunky tomato, anchovy and caper sauce

We used blue eye fillets in this recipe, but you can use any firm white fish you like.

1 tablespoon olive oil
4 x 200g white fish fillets
1 medium brown onion (150g), chopped finely
2 cloves garlic, crushed
4 medium tomatoes (600g), peeled, seeded, chopped coarsely
4 drained anchovy fillets, chopped finely
1 tablespoon drained capers, rinsed
1 teaspoon white sugar
¼ cup coarsely chopped fresh flat-leaf parsley

1 Heat half the oil in large frying pan; cook fish, uncovered, until cooked as desired.
2 Meanwhile, heat remaining oil in small saucepan; cook onion and garlic, stirring, until onion softens. Add tomato; cook, stirring, 1 minute. Remove from heat; stir in anchovy, capers, sugar and parsley.
3 Serve fish with sauce and, if you like, lemon wedges.

preparation time *15 minutes*
cooking time *15 minutes* serves *4*
nutritional count per serving *7.1g total fat (1.1g saturated fat); 1099kJ (263 cal); 6.4g carbohydrate; 41.8g protein; 2.8g fibre*

honey and five-spice lamb with buk choy

¼ teaspoon five-spice powder
¼ cup (60ml) oyster sauce
2 tablespoons honey
2 tablespoons rice vinegar
2 cloves garlic, crushed
600g lamb fillets, sliced thinly
400g fresh thin rice noodles
1 tablespoon sesame oil
2 fresh long red chillies, sliced thinly
2cm piece fresh ginger (10g), cut into matchsticks
1 medium red onion (150g), sliced thickly
500g baby buk choy, leaves separated
¼ cup firmly packed fresh coriander leaves
1 tablespoon crushed peanuts

1 Combine five-spice, sauce, honey, vinegar and garlic in small bowl.
2 Combine lamb with 1 tablespoon of the five-spice mixture in medium bowl.
3 Place noodles in large heatproof bowl, cover with boiling water; separate noodles with fork, drain.
4 Heat oil in wok; stir-fry lamb, in batches, until browned. Return to wok; add remaining five-spice mixture, chilli, ginger and onion; stir-fry until onion softens. Add noodles and buk choy; stir-fry until hot.
5 Serve stir-fry sprinkled with coriander and nuts.

preparation time *15 minutes*
cooking time *10 minutes* serves *4*
nutritional count per serving *12.2g total fat (3.3g saturated fat); 1781kJ (426 cal); 40.7g carbohydrate; 36.1g protein; 3.3g fibre*

open steak sandwich with roasted capsicum and ricotta

2 medium red capsicums (400g)
¾ cup (180g) ricotta cheese
2 tablespoons coarsely chopped fresh chervil
2 teaspoons lemon juice
4 x 125g beef minute steaks
1 tablespoon cracked black pepper
4 slices rye sourdough bread (180g)
1 tablespoon olive oil
2 cloves garlic, crushed
40g baby rocket leaves

1 Preheat grill.
2 Quarter capsicums; discard seeds and membranes. Roast under grill, skin-side up, until skin blisters and blackens. Cover capsicum pieces in plastic or paper 5 minutes; peel away skin.
3 Meanwhile, combine cheese, chervil and juice in small bowl.
4 Sprinkle steaks both sides with pepper; cook on heated oiled grill plate (or grill or barbecue) until cooked as desired.
5 Brush one side of each bread slice with combined oil and garlic; toast both sides under grill. Spread bread with cheese mixture; top with capsicum, beef then rocket.

preparation time *15 minutes*
cooking time *15 minutes* serves *4*
nutritional count per serving *19.3g total fat (7.6g saturated fat); 1793kJ (429 cal); 25g carbohydrate; 36.8g protein; 3.9g fibre*

1

2

3

4

polenta-crumbed fish with rocket sauce

You can use any firm white fish fillet, such as perch, ling or blue eye, in this recipe.

⅔ cup (200g) mayonnaise
50g baby rocket leaves
1 clove garlic, crushed
600g white fish fillets
1 cup (170g) polenta
2 tablespoons finely chopped fresh flat-leaf parsley
2 teaspoons finely grated lemon rind
2 egg whites
vegetable oil, for shallow-frying

1 Blend or process mayonnaise, rocket and garlic until sauce is smooth.
2 Cut fish into 2cm strips. Combine polenta, parsley and rind in shallow medium bowl. Whisk egg whites lightly in another shallow medium bowl. Dip fish in egg white then coat in polenta mixture.
3 Heat oil in large frying pan; shallow-fry fish, in batches, until cooked through.
4 Serve fish with sauce.

preparation time *15 minutes*
cooking time *15 minutes* serves *4*
nutritional count per serving *28.6g total fat (4g saturated fat); 2370kJ (567 cal); 39.7g carbohydrate; 36.7g protein; 2g fibre*

cheese gnocchi with fresh tomato sauce and pancetta

2 cups (480g) ricotta cheese
1 cup (80g) finely grated parmesan cheese
½ cup (75g) plain flour
2 eggs
1 tablespoon olive oil
4 thin slices pancetta (60g), halved
4 medium tomatoes (600g), chopped coarsely
4 green onions, sliced thinly
2 tablespoons coarsely chopped fresh oregano
2 tablespoons balsamic vinegar

1 Preheat grill.
2 Combine cheeses, flour, eggs and oil in large bowl. Drop rounded tablespoons of mixture into large saucepan of boiling water; cook, without stirring, until gnocchi float to surface. Remove from pan with slotted spoon; drain. Keep warm.
3 Grill pancetta until browned and crisp.
4 Meanwhile, combine tomato, onion, oregano and vinegar in medium bowl.
5 Serve gnocchi topped with fresh tomato sauce and pancetta.

preparation time *15 minutes*
cooking time *20 minutes* serves *4*
nutritional count per serving *29.7g total fat (15g saturated fat); 1952kJ (467 cal); 18.4g carbohydrate; 30.1g protein; 2.7g fibre*

1 POLENTA-CRUMBED FISH WITH ROCKET SAUCE 2 CHEESE GNOCCHI WITH FRESH TOMATO SAUCE AND PANCETTA 3 LAMB AND COUSCOUS TABBOULEH POCKETS [P 90] 4 GRILLED CHICKEN, BRIE AND AVOCADO ON CIABATTA [P 90]

SUPERFAST 89

600g lamb mince
1 tablespoon sumac
6 small pitta pockets
½ cup (140g) yogurt
COUSCOUS TABBOULEH

⅓ cup (65g) couscous
⅓ cup (80ml) boiling water
2 cups coarsely chopped fresh flat-leaf parsley
2 medium tomatoes (300g), seeded,
    chopped finely
1 small red onion (100g), chopped finely
1 tablespoon lemon juice
¼ cup (60ml) olive oil

1   Make couscous tabbouleh.
2   Heat oiled large frying pan; cook lamb and sumac,
stirring, until cooked through.
3   Halve pitta pockets crossways; spread yogurt on
insides. Sandwich lamb mixture and tabbouleh inside
each pocket.

COUSCOUS TABBOULEH Combine couscous with
the water in medium heatproof bowl, cover; stand
about 5 minutes or until water is absorbed, fluffing
with fork occasionally. Stir in parsley, tomato, onion,
juice and oil.

preparation time *10 minutes*
cooking time *15 minutes* serves 6
nutritional count per serving *19.2g total fat (5.4g
saturated fat); 2136kJ (511 cal); 50.9g carbohydrate;
31.1g protein; 4g fibre*

2 chicken breast fillets (400g)
4 thick slices ciabatta (140g)
⅓ cup (80ml) sweet chilli sauce
50g baby rocket leaves
100g brie cheese, cut into 4 slices
1 small avocado (200g), sliced thinly

1   Halve chicken pieces diagonally; slice through each
piece horizontally (you will have eight pieces). Cook
on heated oiled grill plate (or grill or barbecue) until
chicken is browned both sides and cooked through.
2   Toast bread, both sides, on same grill plate.
3   Spread half the sauce over toast slices; top with
rocket, chicken, cheese then avocado. Drizzle with
remaining sauce.

preparation time *5 minutes*
cooking time *15 minutes* serves 4
nutritional count per serving *22.6g total fat (8.3g
saturated fat); 1768kJ (423 cal); 22.9g carbohydrate;
30.6g protein; 2.9g fibre*

grilled chicken with herbed butter, almonds and gruyère

80g butter, softened
1 tablespoon finely chopped fresh flat-leaf parsley
2 teaspoons lemon juice
4 single chicken breast fillets (680g)
3 medium carrots (360g), cut into thin 8cm matchsticks
250g baby green beans
¼ cup (35g) roasted slivered almonds
¼ cup (30g) finely grated gruyère cheese

1 Combine butter, parsley and juice in small bowl, cover; refrigerate.
2 Cook chicken on heated oiled grill plate (or grill or barbecue) until browned both sides and cooked through. Cover loosely to keep warm.
3 Meanwhile, boil, steam or microwave carrot and beans, separately, until tender; drain.
4 Serve chicken on vegetables; divide parsley butter among chicken pieces, sprinkle with nuts and cheese.

preparation time *15 minutes*
cooking time *20 minutes* serves *4*
nutritional count per serving *28.1g total fat (13.6g saturated fat); 2052kJ (491 cal); 6.2g carbohydrate; 51.2g protein; 4.8g fibre*

steamed spinach-wrapped chicken with anchovy and tomato

24 large trimmed spinach leaves (150g)
4 drained anchovy fillets, chopped finely
2 tablespoons drained baby capers, rinsed
1 tablespoon olive oil
¼ cup (35g) drained semi-dried tomatoes, chopped coarsely
½ teaspoon cracked black pepper
2 cloves garlic, crushed
4 x 200g chicken breast fillets

LEMON DRESSING

2 tablespoons olive oil
1 teaspoon finely grated lemon rind
2 tablespoons lemon juice
1 clove garlic, crushed

1 Bring large saucepan of water to the boil; add spinach, one leaf at a time, drain immediately. Place in large bowl of iced water; stand 3 minutes. Drain thoroughly on absorbent paper.
2 Combine anchovy, capers, oil, tomato, pepper and garlic in small bowl.
3 Divide spinach into four portions; spread leaves flat on board. Place one chicken fillet on each spinach portion. Top chicken with anchovy mixture. Wrap spinach around chicken to completely enclose.
4 Place chicken parcels in baking-paper-lined bamboo steamer set over large saucepan of simmering water; steam, covered, about 20 minutes or until chicken is cooked through.
5 Meanwhile, make lemon dressing.
6 Serve chicken with dressing.

LEMON DRESSING Whisk ingredients in small bowl.

preparation time *15 minutes*
cooking time *20 minutes* serves *4*
nutritional count per serving *26.1g total fat (5.6g saturated fat); 1894kJ (453 cal); 4.4g carbohydrate; 49.2g protein; 2.5g fibre*

creamy horseradish chicken with garlic sautéed spinach

1 tablespoon olive oil
4 x 200g chicken breast fillets
1 green onion, sliced thinly
2 tablespoons dry white wine
⅔ cup (160ml) cream
2 tablespoons prepared horseradish
2 teaspoons lemon juice
½ teaspoon dijon mustard
1 teaspoon finely chopped fresh dill
20g butter
2 cloves garlic, crushed
600g trimmed spinach, chopped coarsely

1 Heat half the oil in large frying pan; cook chicken until cooked through. Remove from pan; cover to keep warm.
2 Heat remaining oil in same heated pan. Cook onion, stirring, until soft. Add wine; bring to the boil. Reduce heat; simmer, uncovered, until liquid is reduced by half. Add cream; bring to the boil. Reduce heat; simmer, uncovered, about 2 minutes or until sauce thickens slightly. Add horseradish, juice, mustard and dill; stir over heat until heated through.
3 Meanwhile, melt butter in large saucepan. Add garlic; cook, stirring, 2 minutes. Add spinach; cook over low heat, covered, about 2 minutes or until wilted.
4 Serve chicken and spinach drizzled with sauce.

preparation time *10 minutes*
cooking time *20 minutes* serves *4*
nutritional count per serving *38.6g total fat (18.8g saturated fat); 2366kJ (566 cal); 4g carbohydrate; 47.6g protein; 4.6g fibre*

chicken tandoori pockets with raita

1 tablespoon lime juice
⅓ cup (100g) tandoori paste
¼ cup (70g) yogurt
400g chicken tenderloins
8 large flour tortillas
60g snow pea tendrils

RAITA

1 cup (280g) yogurt
1 lebanese cucumber (130g), halved, seeded, chopped finely
1 tablespoon finely chopped fresh mint

1 Combine juice, paste and yogurt in medium bowl with chicken.
2 Cook chicken, in batches, on heated oiled grill plate (or grill or barbecue) until cooked through. Stand 5 minutes; slice thickly.
3 Meanwhile, heat tortillas according to packet directions.
4 Make raita.
5 Place equal amounts of each of the chicken, tendrils and raita on a quarter section of each tortilla; fold tortilla in half and then in half again to enclose filling and form triangle-shaped pockets.

RAITA Combine ingredients in small bowl.

preparation time *10 minutes*
cooking time *10 minutes* makes *8*
nutritional count per pocket *11.5g total fat (2.7g saturated fat); 1225kJ (293 cal); 27.9g carbohydrate; 17.8g protein; 3.1g fibre*

pork cutlets with fennel apple relish

2 tablespoons cider vinegar
¼ cup (60ml) olive oil
1 tablespoon dijon mustard
2 teaspoons caster sugar
4 x 235g pork cutlets
1 large unpeeled green apple (200g), chopped finely
1 small red onion (100g), chopped finely
1 medium fennel bulb (300g), trimmed, chopped finely

1 Whisk vinegar, oil, mustard and sugar in medium bowl; transfer 2 tablespoons of dressing to large bowl. Place pork in large bowl; turn to coat cutlets in dressing.
2 To make relish, combine apple, onion and fennel in bowl with remaining dressing.
3 Meanwhile, cook drained pork on heated oiled grill plate (or grill or barbecue) until browned both sides and cooked as desired, brushing with dressing occasionally.
4 Serve pork with relish.

preparation time *15 minutes*
cooking time *20 minutes* serves *4*
nutritional count per serving *31.2g total fat (7.9g saturated fat); 1877kJ (449 cal); 9.6g carbohydrate; 32g protein; 2.3g fibre*

lamb chops with capsicum mayonnaise

100g roasted capsicum
½ cup (150g) whole-egg mayonnaise
8 lamb mid-loin chops (800g)

1 Blend or process capsicum and mayonnaise until smooth.
2 Cook lamb, in batches, on heated oiled grill plate (or grill or barbecue) until browned all over and cooked as desired.
3 Top lamb with capsicum mayonnaise; serve with mashed potato with fetta and olives, if you like.

preparation time *5 minutes*
cooking time *20 minutes* serves *4*
nutritional count per serving *32.2g total fat (10.6g saturated fat); 1869kJ (447 cal); 8.2g carbohydrate; 31.5g protein; 0.5g fibre*

marmalade-glazed pork cutlets

½ cup (125ml) dry red wine
⅓ cup (115g) orange marmalade
1 clove garlic, crushed
⅓ cup (80ml) fresh orange juice
1 tablespoon olive oil
4 x 235g pork cutlets

1 Combine wine, marmalade, garlic and juice in small saucepan; bring to the boil. Remove from heat.
2 Heat oil in large frying pan; cook pork until browned both sides and cooked as desired, brushing constantly with marmalade glaze.

preparation time *5 minutes*
cooking time *20 minutes* serves *4*
nutritional count per serving *21.0g total fat (6.3g saturated fat); 1693kJ (405 cal); 20.4g carbohydrate; 28.2g protein; 0.4g fibre*

cashew, lemon and thyme crumbed schnitzel

4 x 150g pork medallions
1 cup (150g) roasted unsalted cashews
½ cup (35g) stale breadcrumbs
2 teaspoons finely grated lemon rind
2 teaspoons finely chopped fresh thyme
1 egg
vegetable oil, for shallow-frying
1 medium lemon (140g), quartered

1 Using meat mallet, gently pound pork, one piece at a time, between sheets of plastic wrap, until about 5mm in thickness.
2 Blend or process nuts until coarsely chopped; combine in shallow medium bowl with breadcrumbs, rind and thyme. Whisk egg in another shallow medium bowl. Dip pork in egg then coat in cashew mixture.
3 Heat oil in large frying pan; cook pork, in batches. Drain on absorbent paper. Serve pork with lemon.

preparation time *20 minutes*
cooking time *15 minutes* serves *4*
nutritional count per serving *38.5g total fat (6.8g saturated); 2391kJ (572 cal); 13g carbohydrate; 42.5g protein; 3.3g fibre*

hokkien noodle and pork stir-fry

600g hokkien noodles
1 tablespoon cornflour
½ cup (125ml) water
¼ cup (60ml) kecap manis
¼ cup (60ml) hoisin sauce
2 tablespoons rice vinegar
2 tablespoons peanut oil
600g pork fillet, sliced thinly
1 medium brown onion (150g), sliced thickly
2 cloves garlic, crushed
1 teaspoon grated fresh ginger
150g sugar snap peas, trimmed
1 medium red capsicum (200g), sliced thinly
1 medium yellow capsicum (200g), sliced thinly
200g baby buk choy, quartered

1 Place noodles in large heatproof bowl, cover with boiling water. Separate noodles with fork; drain.
2 Blend cornflour with the water in small bowl; stir in sauces and vinegar.
3 Heat half of the oil in wok; stir-fry pork, in batches, until browned all over.
4 Heat remaining oil in wok; stir-fry onion, garlic and ginger until onion softens. Add peas, capsicums and buk choy; stir-fry until vegetables are just tender.
5 Return pork to wok with noodles and sauce mixture; stir-fry until sauce thickens slightly.

preparation time *20 minutes*
cooking time *10 minutes* serves *4*
nutritional count per serving *14.3g total fat (3g saturated fat); 2215kJ (530 cal); 52.3g carbohydrate; 43.6g protein; 7.5g fibre*

spiced fried fish

We used bream fillets in this recipe, but you can use any firm white fillets you like.

1 tablespoon plain flour
1½ teaspoons ground cumin
1½ teaspoons ground coriander
1 teaspoon sweet smoked paprika
¼ teaspoon cayenne pepper
8 white fish fillets (800g)
1 tablespoon olive oil

1 Combine flour and spices in medium bowl; add fish, rub spice mixture all over fish.
2 Heat oil in large frying pan; cook fish, in batches, until browned and cooked as desired.
3 Serve fish with couscous with pistachios and lemon wedges, if you like.

preparation time *20 minutes*
cooking time *15 minutes* serves *4*
nutritional count per serving *14.8g total fat (4.2g saturated fat); 1250kJ (299 cal); 2g carbohydrate; 39.5g protein; 0.1g fibre*

chicken with pecan honey sauce

2 tablespoons olive oil
4 x 200g chicken breast fillets
3 shallots (75g), chopped finely
1 clove garlic, crushed
½ cup (125ml) dry white wine
½ cup (125ml) chicken stock
2 tablespoons honey
2 teaspoons dijon mustard
½ cup (60g) roasted pecans, chopped coarsely
100g mesclun
1 tablespoon lemon juice
2 small pears (360g), sliced thinly

1 Heat half the oil in large frying pan; cook chicken, uncovered, until cooked. Remove from pan; keep warm.
2 Cook shallot and garlic in same heated pan, stirring, until onion softens. Add wine; bring to the boil. Reduce heat; simmer, uncovered, until liquid is reduced by half. Add stock, honey and mustard; cook, stirring, about 5 minutes or until liquid is reduced by half. Remove from heat; stir in nuts.
3 Combine mesclun with juice and remaining oil in medium bowl.
4 Cut chicken in half crossways; drizzle with sauce. Serve with mesclun and pear.

preparation time *15 minutes*
cooking time *20 minutes* serves *4*
nutritional count per serving *7.2g total fat (1.3g saturated fat); 560kJ (134 cal); 5.1g carbohydrate; 10.6g protein; 1g fibre*

creamy farfalle with fried zucchini

375g farfalle pasta
2 tablespoons olive oil
3 cloves garlic, crushed
6 small zucchini (540g), grated coarsely
½ cup (40g) finely grated parmesan cheese
3 green onions, sliced thinly
2 teaspoons finely grated lemon rind
1 tablespoon finely chopped fresh flat-leaf parsley
300ml cream

1   Cook pasta in large saucepan of boiling water until just tender.
2   Meanwhile, heat oil in large frying pan; cook garlic, stirring, about 2 minutes or until fragrant. Add zucchini; cook, stirring, 2 minutes.
3   Combine cheese, onion, rind and parsley in bowl.
4   Add cream and drained hot pasta to zucchini mixture; stir gently over low heat until heated through. Serve pasta immediately, topped with cheese mixture.

preparation time *10 minutes*
cooking time *20 minutes* serves *4*
nutritional count per serving *46.3g total fat (25g saturated fat); 3227kJ (772 cal); 68.8g carbohydrate; 17.7g protein; 5.9g fibre*

creamy spinach polenta with roasted vegetables

2 medium zucchini (240g), sliced thickly
6 baby eggplants (360g), sliced thickly
4 medium egg tomatoes (300g), quartered
4 flat mushrooms (320g), quartered
2 tablespoons olive oil
2 cloves garlic, crushed
2⅓ cups (580ml) milk
2 cups (500ml) water
1 cup (170g) polenta
½ cup (40g) finely grated parmesan cheese
250g spinach, trimmed, chopped coarsely

1   Preheat oven to 220°C/200°C fan-forced.
2   Combine zucchini, eggplant, tomato, mushrooms, oil and garlic, in single layer, in large shallow baking dish. Roast, uncovered, about 20 minutes or until vegetables are tender.
3   Meanwhile, combine 2 cups of the milk and the water in large saucepan; bring to the boil. Gradually add polenta to liquid, stirring constantly. Reduce heat; simmer, stirring, about 5 minutes or until polenta thickens. Stir in cheese, spinach and remaining milk.
4   Divide vegetables among serving plates; top with polenta. Sprinkle with extra parmesan, if you like.

preparation time *15 minutes*
cooking time *20 minutes* serves *4*
nutritional count per serving *19.9g total fat (7.2g saturated fat); 1856kJ (443 cal); 43.1g carbohydrate; 19.1g protein; 9.3g fibre*

rigatoni with zucchini, lemon and mint

500g rigatoni pasta
¼ cup (60ml) olive oil
2 cloves garlic, crushed
3 medium zucchini (360g), grated coarsely
¾ cup (180g) ricotta cheese
1 cup coarsely chopped fresh mint
½ cup (70g) roasted slivered almonds
2 tablespoons lemon juice

1 Cook pasta in large saucepan of boiling water until just tender; drain.
2 Meanwhile, heat oil in large frying pan; cook garlic and zucchini, stirring, 2 minutes. Add cheese; cook, stirring, until just heated through.
3 Combine pasta and zucchini mixture in large serving bowl with remaining ingredients.

preparation time *10 minutes*
cooking time *10 minutes* serves *4*
nutritional count per serving *30.3g total fat (6g saturated fat); 3110kJ (744 cal); 88.9g carbohydrate; 23.9g protein; 8.3g fibre*

warm lemon-herbed pasta and fresh salmon salad

Fresh spinach and ricotta agnolotti is found in the refrigerated section in most supermarkets. You can substitute ravioli or tortellini for the agnolotti.

1 cup (120g) frozen peas
170g asparagus, trimmed, chopped coarsely
500g piece salmon fillet
625g spinach and ricotta agnolotti
½ cup fresh flat-leaf parsley leaves
1 tablespoon water
¼ cup (60ml) olive oil
1 teaspoon finely grated lemon rind
¼ cup (60ml) lemon juice

1 Boil, steam or microwave peas and asparagus, separately, until just tender; drain. Rinse under cold water; drain.
2 Cook fish on heated oiled grill plate (or grill or barbecue) until browned and cooked as desired. Place fish in large bowl then, using fork, flake into chunks.
3 Meanwhile, cook pasta in large saucepan of boiling water, uncovered, until just tender; drain. Add to fish.
4 Pour combined parsley, the water, oil, rind and juice over fish, add peas and asparagus; toss to combine.

preparation time *15 minutes*
cooking time *20 minutes* serves *4*
nutritional count per serving *33.7g total fat (10.6g saturated fat); 2428kJ (581 cal); 26.9g carbohydrate; 39.8g protein; 5.5g fibre*

steak with peppercorn and pepita rub

1 clove garlic, quartered
1 tablespoon mixed peppercorns
½ teaspoon sea salt
1 tablespoon olive oil
⅓ cup (65g) toasted pepitas
4 x 200g scotch fillet steaks
25g butter
2 teaspoons red wine vinegar
1 tablespoon redcurrant jelly
420g can white beans, rinsed, drained
250g cherry tomatoes, halved
¼ cup fresh basil leaves
1 small radicchio (150g), trimmed

REDCURRANT DRESSING

¼ cup (60ml) olive oil
2 tablespoons red wine vinegar
1 tablespoon redcurrant jelly

1   Make redcurrant dressing.
2   Using mortar and pestle, crush garlic, peppercorns, salt, oil and 1 tablespoon of the pepitas to form a paste. Rub paste onto beef.
3   Heat butter in large frying pan; cook beef until browned both sides and cooked as desired. Remove from pan; cover to keep warm.
4   Add vinegar and jelly to same pan; stir until combined.
5   Meanwhile, place beans, tomatoes, basil, radicchio, dressing and remaining pepitas in large bowl; toss gently to combine.
6   Serve steak, drizzled with pan juices, with salad.

REDCURRANT DRESSING Place ingredients in screw-top jar; shake well.

preparation time *15 minutes*
cooking time *15 minutes* serves *4*
nutritional count per serving *41.3g total fat (11.3g saturated fat); 2784kJ (666 cal); 20.1g carbohydrate; 50.1g protein; 7.3g fibre*

veal cutlets with green olive salsa

2 tablespoons olive oil
2 cloves garlic, crushed
1 tablespoon finely chopped fresh oregano
2 teaspoons finely grated lemon rind
1 tablespoon lemon juice
4 x 125g veal cutlets

GREEN OLIVE SALSA

1 tablespoon lemon juice
¼ cup coarsely chopped fresh flat-leaf parsley
½ cup (80g) finely chopped large green olives
1 small green capsicum (150g), chopped finely
1 tablespoon olive oil
1 clove garlic, crushed
1 tablespoon finely chopped fresh oregano

1   Make green olive salsa.
2   Combine oil, garlic, oregano, rind and juice in small bowl; brush mixture over veal. Cook veal on heated oiled grill plate (or grill or barbecue) until browned both sides and cooked as desired.
3   Serve veal with salsa and, if you like, barbecued kipfler potatoes.

GREEN OLIVE SALSA Combine ingredients in small bowl.

preparation time *20 minutes*
cooking time *15 minutes* serves *4*
nutritional count per serving *16.3g total fat (2.7g saturated fat); 1112kJ (266 cal); 5.8g carbohydrate; 23.4g protein; 1.2g fibre*

crisp beef with baby buk choy and noodles

2 tablespoons cornflour
½ teaspoon bicarbonate of soda
600g beef rump steak, cut into thin strips
⅔ cup (160ml) peanut oil
2 tablespoons sweet chilli sauce
¼ cup (60ml) kecap manis
1 tablespoon light soy sauce
2 teaspoons sesame oil
1 clove garlic, crushed
2 green onions, chopped finely
400g fresh thin egg noodles
200g shiitake mushrooms, quartered
½ small wombok (400g), shredded coarsely
300g baby buk choy, sliced thinly lengthways

1 Combine cornflour and soda in large bowl with beef; toss to coat all over, shaking off excess.
2 Heat one-third of the peanut oil in wok; stir-fry about one-third of the beef until crisp. Drain on absorbent paper, cover to keep warm. Repeat with remaining peanut oil and beef.
3 Combine sauces, sesame oil, garlic and onion in small bowl.
4 Place noodles in large heatproof bowl, cover with boiling water; separate with fork, drain.
5 Reheat same cleaned wok; stir-fry mushrooms about 2 minutes or until just tender. Add wombok and buk choy; stir-fry 1 minute. Add sauce mixture, noodles and beef; stir-fry until heated through.

preparation time *15 minutes*
cooking time *15 minutes* serves *4*
nutritional count per serving *50.5g total fat (11.7g saturated fat); 3762kJ (900 cal); 60.8g carbohydrate; 48.1g protein; 6.1g fibre*

scotch fillet with pepper thyme sauce

1 tablespoon olive oil
4 x 200g scotch fillet steaks
1 trimmed celery stalk (100g), chopped finely
1 medium brown onion (150g), chopped finely
½ cup (125ml) dry white wine
300ml cream
1 tablespoon mixed peppercorns, crushed
1 tablespoon coarsely chopped fresh thyme

1 Heat half the oil in large frying pan; cook beef until cooked as desired. Remove from pan; cover to keep warm.
2 Heat remaining oil in same pan; cook celery and onion, stirring, until vegetables soften. Add wine; stir until liquid is reduced by half. Add cream and peppercorns; bring to the boil. Reduce heat; simmer, uncovered, stirring occasionally, about 5 minutes or until sauce thickens slightly. Remove from heat; stir in thyme.
3 Serve beef drizzled with sauce, and accompanied with chunky chips, if you like.

preparation time *10 minutes*
cooking time *15 minutes* serves *4*
nutritional count per serving *46.7g total fat (26.3g saturated fat); 2658kJ (636 cal); 5g carbohydrate; 44.2g protein; 1.4g fibre*

chilli and honey barbecued steak

2 tablespoons barbecue sauce
1 tablespoon worcestershire sauce
1 tablespoon honey
1 fresh long red chilli, chopped finely
1 clove garlic, crushed
4 x 200g new-york cut steaks

1 Combine sauces, honey, chilli and garlic in large bowl with beef.
2 Cook beef on heated oiled grill plate (or grill or barbecue) until browned both sides and cooked as desired.
3 Serve steaks with coleslaw or potato salad, if you like.

preparation time *15 minutes*
cooking time *10 minutes* serves *4*
nutritional count per serving *12.1g total fat (5g saturated fat); 1354kJ (324 cal); 11.7g carbohydrate; 42.4g protein; 0.3g fibre*

rump steak in black bean sauce with tangy sprout salad

1 tablespoon black bean sauce
1 tablespoon honey
1 fresh long red chilli, chopped finely
3cm piece fresh ginger (15g), grated
600g piece beef rump steak
¼ cup (60ml) lime juice
1 tablespoon peanut oil
2 teaspoons honey, extra
100g snow pea sprouts, trimmed
1 large red capsicum (350g), sliced thinly
1 lebanese cucumber (130g), seeded, sliced thinly

1 Combine sauce, honey, chilli and one-third of the ginger in large bowl with beef.
2 Cook beef on heated oiled grill plate (or grill or barbecue) until browned both sides and cooked as desired. Cover; stand 5 minutes then slice thickly.
3 Meanwhile, whisk remaining ginger with juice, oil and extra honey in large bowl. Add sprouts, capsicum, cucumber and dressing; toss gently to combine.
4 Serve beef with salad.

preparation time *15 minutes*
cooking time *10 minutes* serves *4*
nutritional count per serving *15.2g total fat (5.4g saturated fat); 1547kJ (370 cal); 19.3g carbohydrate; 37.6g protein; 2.6g fibre*

fennel-flavoured veal chops with garlic mustard butter

2 teaspoons fennel seeds
1 teaspoon sea salt
½ teaspoon cracked black pepper
2 tablespoons olive oil
4 x 200g veal chops
4 flat mushrooms (320g)
80g butter, softened
1 tablespoon coarsely chopped fresh flat-leaf parsley
1 clove garlic, crushed
1 tablespoon wholegrain mustard
80g baby rocket leaves

1 Using mortar and pestle, crush seeds, salt and pepper coarsely; stir in oil. Rub mixture all over veal.
2 Cook veal and mushrooms on heated oiled grill plate (or grill or barbecue) until browned both sides and cooked as desired.
3 Meanwhile, combine butter, parsley, garlic and mustard in small bowl.
4 Divide rocket among serving plates; top each with mushroom, veal then butter.

preparation time *10 minutes*
cooking time *15 minutes* serves *4*
nutritional count per serving *29.7g total fat (13.2g saturated fat); 1831kJ (438 cal); 2.1g carbohydrate; 39.9g protein; 2.7g fibre*

veal with mushrooms and mustard cream sauce

1 tablespoon olive oil
8 veal steaks (640g)
10g butter
1 clove garlic, crushed
150g button mushrooms, sliced thickly
⅓ cup (80ml) dry white wine
1 tablespoon wholegrain mustard
½ cup (125ml) cream
¼ cup (60ml) chicken stock
1 teaspoon fresh thyme leaves

1 Heat oil in large non-stick frying pan; cook veal, in batches, until browned both sides and cooked as desired. Remove from pan; cover to keep warm.
2 Melt butter in same pan; cook garlic and mushrooms, stirring, until mushrooms just soften. Add wine and mustard; cook, stirring, 2 minutes. Add cream and stock; bring to the boil. Reduce heat; simmer, uncovered, about 5 minutes or until sauce thickens slightly. Stir in thyme.
3 Divide veal among serving plates; top with sauce.

preparation time *5 minutes*
cooking time *20 minutes* serves *4*
nutritional count per serving *23.3g total fat (11.8g saturated fat); 1618kJ (387 cal); 1.4g carbohydrate; 39.5g protein; 1.2g fibre*

parmesan-crusted lamb cutlets

⅓ cup (50g) plain flour
12 lamb cutlets (900g)
2 eggs
2 tablespoons milk
1 clove garlic, crushed
½ cup (35g) stale breadcrumbs
½ cup (50g) packaged breadcrumbs
½ cup (40g) finely grated parmesan cheese
1 tablespoon finely chopped fresh oregano
2 tablespoons olive oil

1 Place flour in plastic bag, add cutlets; toss to coat all over, shake off excess flour.
2 Combine eggs, milk and garlic in medium shallow bowl. Combine breadcrumbs, cheese and oregano in another medium shallow bowl. Dip cutlets, one at a time, into egg mixture, then in breadcrumb mixture.
3 Heat oil in large non-stick frying pan; cook cutlets, in batches, until browned both sides and cooked as desired.
4 Serve cutlets sprinkled with fresh whole oregano leaves, if you like.

preparation time *15 minutes*
cooking time *15 minutes* serves *4*
nutritional count per serving *26.7g total fat (9.6g saturated fat); 2036kJ (487 cal); 23.8g carbohydrate; 37.1g protein; 1.5g fibre*

char siu lamb and noodle stir-fry

2 cloves garlic, crushed
2cm piece fresh ginger (10g), grated
1 tablespoon finely grated orange rind
1 teaspoon sesame oil
750g lamb strips
450g hokkien noodles
2 tablespoons peanut oil
200g sugar snap peas
115g baby corn, halved lengthways
2 fresh long red chillies, sliced thinly
⅓ cup (120g) char siu sauce
2 tablespoons water
1 tablespoon rice wine vinegar

1 Combine garlic, ginger, rind, sesame oil in medium bowl with lamb.
2 Place noodles in large heatproof bowl, cover with boiling water; separate with fork, drain.
3 Heat half the peanut oil in wok; stir-fry peas and corn until just tender. Remove from wok.
4 Heat remaining peanut oil in wok; stir-fry lamb, in batches, until browned all over and cooked as desired. Return peas, corn and lamb to wok with noodles, chilli and combined sauce, water and vinegar; stir-fry until heated through.

preparation time *15 minutes*
cooking time *20 minutes* serves *4*
nutritional count per serving *29.2g total fat (9.6g saturated fat); 2725kJ (652 cal); 46.6g carbohydrate; 47.1g protein; 8g fibre*

grilled lamb with paprikash sauce

800g lamb backstraps
1 tablespoon olive oil
1 small brown onion (80g), chopped finely
1 clove garlic, crushed
1 teaspoon smoked paprika
2 teaspoons sweet paprika
pinch cayenne pepper
410g can crushed tomatoes
½ cup (125ml) water

1 Cook lamb on heated oiled grill plate (or grill or barbecue). Cover; stand 5 minutes then slice thickly.
2 Meanwhile, heat oil in medium saucepan; cook onion, stirring, until onion softens. Add garlic and spices; cook, stirring, about 1 minute or until fragrant.
3 Add undrained tomatoes and the water; bring to the boil. Reduce heat; simmer, uncovered, about 5 minutes or until paprikash sauce thickens slightly.
4 Serve lamb with sauce and, if you like, baked potatoes.

preparation time *5 minutes*
cooking time *10 minutes* serves *4*
nutritional count per serving *12g total fat (3.8g saturated fat); 1241kJ (297 cal); 4.4g carbohydrate; 42.1g protein; 1.6g fibre*

lamb, bocconcini and gremolata stacks

4 x 150g lamb leg steaks
1 tablespoon olive oil
1 large red capsicum (350g)
2 tablespoons lemon juice
100g bocconcini cheese, sliced thinly

GREMOLATA

2 tablespoons finely chopped fresh basil
2 cloves garlic, chopped finely
2 teaspoons finely grated lemon rind

1 Preheat grill.
2 Make gremolata.
3 Using meat mallet, gently pound lamb between sheets of plastic wrap until 1cm thick. Heat oil in large frying pan; cook lamb, in batches, until cooked as desired. Place lamb on oven tray.
4 Meanwhile, quarter capsicum, discard seeds and membranes. Roast under grill, skin-side up, until skin blisters and blackens. Cover capsicum pieces in plastic or paper for 5 minutes; peel away skin then slice thickly. Combine capsicum and juice in small bowl.
5 Divide capsicum and bocconcini among lamb steaks; place under grill about 5 minutes or until cheese melts.
6 Serve stacks sprinkled with gremolata and, if you like, a salad of baby rocket leaves.

GREMOLATA Combine ingredients in small bowl.

preparation time *15 minutes*
cooking time *20 minutes* serves *4*
nutritional count per serving *16.7g total fat (6.8g saturated fat); 1346kJ (322 cal); 3.4g carbohydrate; 38.8g protein; 1.2g fibre*

grilled lamb with spicy peach salsa

800g lamb backstraps

SPICY PEACH SALSA

1 small red onion (100g), chopped finely
2 large peaches (440g), chopped finely
2 tablespoons finely chopped fresh flat-leaf parsley
1 fresh long red chilli, chopped finely
1 tablespoon malt vinegar

1   Cook lamb on heated oiled grill plate (or grill or barbecue) until cooked as desired. Stand, covered, 10 minutes then slice thinly.
2   Meanwhile, make spicy peach salsa.
3   Serve lamb with peach salsa and, if you like, barbecued kipfler potatoes.

SPICY PEACH SALSA Combine ingredients in medium bowl.

preparation time *15 minutes*
cooking time *10 minutes* serves *4*
nutritional count per serving *17.7g total fat (8g saturated fat); 1530kJ (366 cal); 7.4g carbohydrate; 43.1g protein; 1.8g fibre*

lamb with white wine and mascarpone sauce

¼ cup (60ml) olive oil
12 fresh sage leaves
100g sliced prosciutto
8 lamb steaks (640g)
1 clove garlic, crushed
¾ cup (180ml) dry white wine
½ cup (120g) mascarpone cheese
¼ cup (60ml) cream

1   Heat oil in medium frying pan; cook sage until crisp. Drain on absorbent paper. Cook prosciutto, stirring, until crisp; drain on absorbent paper.
2   Cook lamb in same pan until browned both sides and cooked as desired. Remove from pan.
3   Cook garlic in same pan, stirring, until fragrant. Add wine; bring to the boil. Reduce heat; simmer, uncovered, until liquid reduces by half. Add mascarpone and cream; cook, stirring, over heat until sauce boils and thickens slightly.
4   Divide lamb among serving plates; top with prosciutto and sage, drizzle with sauce.

preparation time *10 minutes*
cooking time *15 minutes* serves *4*
nutritional count per serving *44.6g total fat (20.6g saturated fat); 2433kJ (582 cal); 1.2g carbohydrate; 38.2g protein; 0.1g fibre*

pear and plum amaretti crumble

825g can plums in syrup, drained,
    halved, stoned
825g can pear halves in natural juice,
    drained, halved
1 teaspoon ground cardamom
125g amaretti (almond macaroons), crushed
⅓ cup (50g) plain flour
⅓ cup (35g) almond meal
½ cup (70g) slivered almonds
100g butter, chopped

1 Preheat oven to 220°C/200°C fan-forced.
Grease deep 6-cup (1.5-litre) ovenproof dish.
2 Combine plums, pears and cardamom in dish.
3 Combine amaretti, flour, almond meal and nuts in
medium bowl. Using fingers, rub butter into amaretti
mixture, sprinkle evenly over plum mixture.
4 Bake crumble about 15 minutes or until golden brown.
Serve with vanilla custard, if you like.

preparation time *10 minutes*
cooking time *15 minutes* serves *4*
nutritional count per serving *43.2g total fat (20.1g
saturated fat); 2801kJ (670 cal); 56.8g carbohydrate;
9.6g protein; 8.8g fibre*

red fruit salad with lemon mascarpone

1kg seedless watermelon
250g strawberries, hulled, quartered
150g raspberries
2 medium plums, sliced thinly
1 tablespoon caster sugar
⅓ cup (80ml) kirsch

LEMON MASCARPONE

250g mascarpone cheese
2 teaspoons finely grated lemon rind
2 teaspoons caster sugar
1 tablespoon lemon juice

1 Using melon baller, scoop watermelon into balls.
Place watermelon in large serving bowl with
strawberries, raspberries, plums, sugar and liqueur;
toss gently to combine. Cover; refrigerate until ready
to serve.
2 Make lemon mascarpone.
3 Serve fruit salad with lemon mascarpone.

LEMON MASCARPONE Combine ingredients in
small bowl.

preparation time *20 minutes* serves *4*
nutritional count per serving *30.3g total fat (20.3g
saturated fat); 2019kJ (483 cal); 33.2g carbohydrate;
5.3g protein; 5.4g fibre*

brandy snap and rhubarb stacks

3¼ cups (400g) coarsely chopped rhubarb
2 tablespoons water
¼ cup (55g) caster sugar
30g butter
2 tablespoons brown sugar
1 tablespoon golden syrup
½ teaspoon ground ginger
2 tablespoons plain flour
¼ cup (70g) yogurt

1 Preheat oven to 180°C/160°C fan-forced.
Grease two oven trays.
2 Place rhubarb, the water and caster sugar in medium saucepan; bring to the boil. Reduce heat; simmer, uncovered, stirring occasionally, about 5 minutes or until rhubarb softens. Drain rhubarb mixture through sieve over medium bowl; reserve liquid. Spread rhubarb mixture onto metal tray; cover with foil, place in freezer.
3 Meanwhile, combine butter, brown sugar, syrup and ginger in same cleaned pan; stir over low heat until butter has melted. Remove from heat, stir in flour.
4 Drop level teaspoons of mixture about 6cm apart onto trays. Bake about 7 minutes or until brandy snaps bubble and become golden brown; cool on trays for 2 minutes then transfer to wire rack to cool completely.
5 Place cooled rhubarb mixture in small bowl; add yogurt, pull skewer backwards and forwards through rhubarb mixture for marbled effect.
6 Sandwich three brandy snaps with a quarter of the rhubarb mixture; repeat with remaining brandy snaps and rhubarb mixture.
7 Place stacks on serving plates; drizzle with reserved rhubarb liquid.

preparation time *10 minutes*
cooking time *15 minutes* serves *4*
nutritional count per serving *7g total fat (4.5g saturated fat); 865kJ (207 cal); 31.7g carbohydrate; 3g protein; 3.4g fibre*

rhubarb galette

20g butter, melted
2½ cups (275g) coarsely chopped rhubarb
⅓ cup (75g) firmly packed brown sugar
1 teaspoon finely grated orange rind
1 sheet ready-rolled puff pastry
2 tablespoons almond meal
10g butter, melted, extra

1 Preheat oven to 240°C/220°C fan-forced.
Line oven tray with baking paper.
2 Combine butter, rhubarb, sugar and rind in medium bowl.
3 Cut 24cm round from pastry, place on tray; sprinkle evenly with almond meal. Spoon rhubarb mixture over pastry, leaving a 4cm border. Fold 2cm of pastry edge up and around filling. Brush edge with extra butter.
4 Bake galette about 20 minutes or until browned.

preparation time *10 minutes*
cooking time *20 minutes* serves *4*
nutritional count per serving *18.2g total fat (4.8g saturated fat); 1354kJ (324 cal); 34.6g carbohydrate; 4g protein; 3.2g fibre*

1

2

3   4

pear, chocolate and almond galette

80g dark cooking chocolate, chopped finely
¼ cup (30g) almond meal
1 sheet ready-rolled puff pastry
1 tablespoon milk
1 medium pear (230g)
1 tablespoon raw sugar

1   Preheat oven to 220°C/200°C fan-forced.
Line oven tray with baking paper.
2   Combine chocolate and 2 tablespoons of the
almond meal in small bowl.
3   Cut pastry sheet into quarters; place quarters
on tray, prick each with a fork, brush with milk.
Divide chocolate mixture onto pastry squares,
leaving 2cm border.
4   Peel and core pear; cut into quarters. Cut each
pear quarter into thin slices then spread one sliced
pear quarter across each pastry square; sprinkle
with sugar then remaining almond meal.
5   Bake galettes about 15 minutes or until pastry is
golden brown.

preparation time *5 minutes*
cooking time *15 minutes* serves *4*
nutritional count per serving *19.9g total fat (11g
saturated fat); 1480kJ (354 cal); 38.4g carbohydrate;
5g protein; 3.5g fibre*

grilled pineapple with coconut ice-cream

1 cup (75g) toasted shredded coconut
2 tablespoons coconut-flavoured liqueur
1 litre vanilla ice-cream, softened
1 tablespoon coconut-flavoured liqueur, extra
2 tablespoons brown sugar
1 large pineapple (2kg), sliced thickly

1   Combine coconut, liqueur and ice-cream in a
medium metal bowl. Freeze for 20 minutes.
2   Combine extra liqueur and sugar in large bowl;
add pineapple, toss to coat in sugar mixture. Brown
pineapple, both sides, on heated oiled grill plate.
3   Serve pineapple with ice-cream.

preparation time *10 minutes (plus freezing time)*
cooking time *5 minutes* serves *4*
nutritional count per serving *26g total fat (19.8g
saturated fat); 2128kJ (509 cal); 49.4g carbohydrate;
7.7g protein; 7.3g fibre*

1 PEAR, CHOCOLATE AND ALMOND GALETTE
2 GRILLED PINEAPPLE WITH COCONUT ICE-CREAM
3 PASSIONFRUIT AND BANANA FOOL [P 114] 4 PAVLOVA TRIFLE [P 114]

SUPERFAST   113

passionfruit and banana fool

6 sponge finger biscuits, chopped coarsely
½ cup (125ml) tropical fruit juice
300ml cream
1 cup (280g) vanilla yogurt
½ cup (125ml) passionfruit pulp
2 small bananas (260g), sliced thinly
2 tablespoons passionfruit pulp, extra

1 Divide biscuits among six 1-cup (250ml) parfait glasses; drizzle with juice equally over biscuits in glasses.
2 Beat cream in small bowl with electric mixer until soft peaks form; fold in yogurt and passionfruit pulp.
3 Spoon half the cream mixture into glasses, top with bananas then remaining cream mixture. Drizzle extra passionfruit pulp over each fool. Refrigerate, covered, for 15 minutes.

preparation time *10 minutes (plus refrigeration time)*
serves *6*
nutritional count per serving *20.4g total fat (13.3g saturated fat); 1271kJ (304 cal); 22.4g carbohydrate; 5.4g protein; 3.7g fibre*

pavlova trifle

¾ cup (180ml) thickened cream
2 tablespoons icing sugar
200g crème fraîche
250g strawberries, quartered
2 medium bananas (400g), sliced thickly
½ cup (125ml) passionfruit pulp
50g meringue, chopped coarsely
3 medium kiwifruit (255g), chopped coarsely

1 Beat cream and icing sugar in small bowl with electric mixer until soft peaks form; stir in crème fraîche.
2 Divide strawberries and banana among four 1½-cup (375ml) glasses. Top with half the passionfruit pulp.
3 Divide crème fraîche mixture among glasses; top with meringue, kiwifruit and remaining passionfruit pulp.

preparation time *25 minutes* serves *4*
nutritional count per serving *36.9g total fat (24.1g saturated fat); 1994kJ (477 cal); 27.1g carbohydrate; 5.7g protein; 8.5g fibre*

citrus salad with lime and mint granita

2 medium oranges (480g)
2 small pink grapefruits (700g)
⅓ cup finely chopped fresh mint
2 tablespoons icing sugar
1 tablespoon lime juice
2 cups ice cubes

1 Segment orange and grapefruit into medium bowl.
2 Blend or process mint, sugar, juice and ice until ice is crushed; serve with fruit.

preparation time *15 minutes* serves *4*
nutritional count per serving *0.4g total fat (0g saturated fat); 385kJ (92 cal); 18.1g carbohydrate; 2.1g protein; 2.7g fibre*

nectarines on brioche

4 nectarines (680g)
40g butter, chopped
¼ cup (55g) firmly packed brown sugar
¼ teaspoon ground nutmeg
200g mascarpone cheese
1 tablespoon icing sugar
1 tablespoon Cointreau
2 teaspoons finely grated orange rind
2 small brioche (200g)
2 teaspoons icing sugar, extra

1 Halve nectarines; cut each half into thirds.
2 Melt butter in medium frying pan; add sugar and nutmeg, stir until sugar dissolves. Add nectarines; cook, stirring, until browned.
3 Meanwhile, combine mascarpone, icing sugar, liqueur and rind in small bowl. Cut each brioche into four slices; toast until browned lightly both sides.
4 Divide brioche slices among serving plates; top with mascarpone mixture and nectarine pieces. Dust with extra sifted icing sugar.

preparation time *15 minutes*
cooking time *5 minutes* serves *4*
nutritional count per serving *38g total fat (24.3g saturated fat); 2567kJ (614 cal); 56.1g carbohydrate; 8.3g protein; 4.6g fibre*

banana caramel sundae

70g dark eating chocolate, chopped finely
⅔ cup (70g) roasted walnuts, chopped coarsely
1 litre vanilla ice-cream
4 medium bananas (800g), chopped coarsely
CARAMEL SAUCE

100g butter
½ cup (125ml) cream
½ cup (110g) firmly packed brown sugar

1 Make caramel sauce.
2 Divide one-third of the sauce among six ¾-cup (180ml) glasses; divide half the chocolate, nuts, ice-cream and banana among glasses. Repeat layering process, ending with a layer of the sauce.

CARAMEL SAUCE Stir ingredients in small saucepan over low heat until sugar dissolves; bring to the boil. Reduce heat; simmer, uncovered, 5 minutes. Cool.

preparation time *10 minutes*
cooking time *10 minutes* serves *6*
nutritional count per serving *41.7g total fat (22.4g saturated fat); 2579kJ (617 cal); 56.1g carbohydrate; 6.9g protein; 2.4g fibre*

banana caramel puddings

90g butter, melted
½ cup (60g) almond meal
3 egg whites
¾ cup (120g) icing sugar
¼ cup (75g) plain flour
50g butter, melted, extra
⅓ cup (75g) firmly packed brown sugar
2 medium bananas (400g), sliced thickly

1 Preheat oven to 200°C/220°C fan-forced. Grease four deep-sided 9.5cm ovenproof dishes; place on oven tray.
2 Place butter, almond meal, egg whites, icing sugar and flour in medium bowl; stir until just mixed together.
3 Divide extra butter among dishes; sprinkle evenly with brown sugar. Divide banana slices then pudding mixture equally among dishes.
4 Bake puddings, uncovered, about 15 minutes or until browned lightly. Stand puddings 2 minutes; turn onto serving plates. Serve with ice-cream, if you like.

preparation time *15 minutes*
cooking time *15 minutes* serves *4*
nutritional count per serving *37.3g total fat (19.5g saturated fat); 2847kJ (681 cal); 75.9g carbohydrate; 9.1g protein; 3.5g fibre*

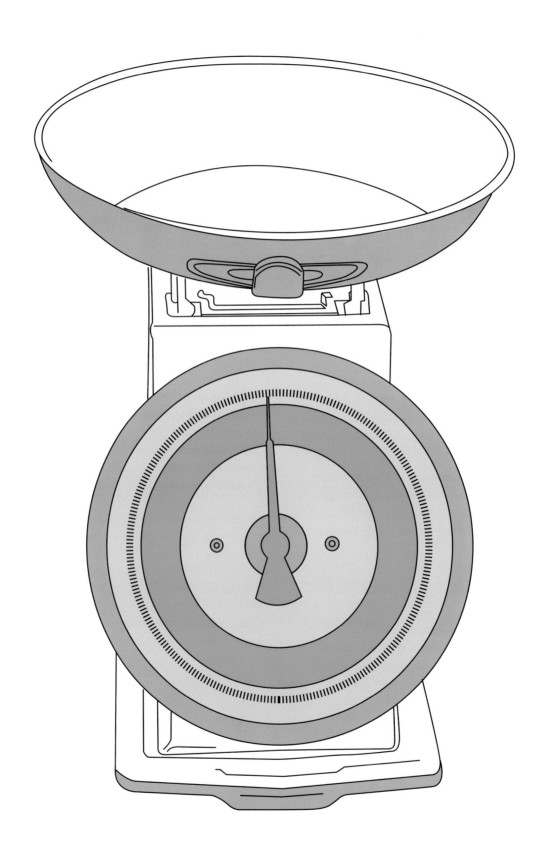

MEGA-HEALTHY

carrot dip

1 medium carrot (120g), grated coarsely
½ cup (125ml) fresh orange juice
2 tablespoons goat milk yogurt
1 tablespoon finely chopped fresh mint
1 tablespoon dried currants
1cm piece fresh ginger (5g), grated

1   Cook carrot and juice in small saucepan,
uncovered, over low heat, about 10 minutes or
until liquid is evaporated. Cool 10 minutes.
2   Blend or process carrot mixture with yogurt;
stir in mint, currants and ginger.

preparation time *10 minutes*
cooking time *10 minutes makes 1 cup*
nutritional count per ¼ cup *0.5g total fat (0.3g
saturated fat); 150kJ (36 cal); 6.2g carbohydrate;
1g protein 1.1g fibre*

white bean and garlic dip

300g can white beans, rinsed, drained
⅓ cup (95g) yogurt
2 tablespoons lemon juice
1 clove garlic, quartered
¼ teaspoon ground cumin

1   Blend or process beans, yogurt, juice and garlic
until smooth. Sprinkle dip with cumin.
2   Serve dip with raw vegetable sticks.

preparation time *5 minutes makes 1 cup*
nutritional count per ¼ cup *0.9g total fat (0.6g
saturated fat); 138kJ (33 cal); 2.6g carbohydrate;
2.4 protein; 1.1g fibre*

watercress and yogurt dip

1 cup loosely packed fresh watercress leaves
1 teaspoon ground cumin
¼ teaspoon cayenne pepper
1 cup (280g) yogurt

1   Blend or process watercress, cumin, cayenne
and 2 tablespoons of the yogurt until smooth;
transfer to small bowl, stir in remaining yogurt.
2   Serve with raw vegetable sticks.

preparation time *10 minutes makes 1 cup*
nutritional count per ¼ cup *2.4g total fat (1.5g
saturated fat); 222kJ (53 cal); 3.4g carbohydrate;
3.6g protein; 0.4g fibre*

thai soy bean salad with grapes and pink grapefruit

½ cup (100g) dried soya beans
2 small pink grapefruit (700g), segmented
100g green grapes, halved
2 small white onion (160g), chopped finely
100g snow pea sprouts, trimmed
½ cup finely chopped fresh coriander
½ cup finely chopped fresh mint
2 fresh kaffir lime leaves, shredded finely
¼ cup (60ml) lime juice

1   Place beans in small bowl, cover with water; stand
overnight, drain. Rinse under cold water; drain.
2   Cook beans in medium saucepan of boiling water,
uncovered, until just tender; drain. Rinse under cold
water; drain.
3   Place beans in medium bowl with remaining
ingredients; toss gently to combine.

preparation time *15 minutes (plus standing time)*
cooking time *20 minutes serves 2*
nutritional count per serving *11.3g total fat (1.6g
saturated fat); 1517kJ (363 cal); 38.3g carbohydrate;
24.6g protein; 16.9g fibre*

tofu and vegie burger

300g firm silken tofu
1 tablespoon olive oil
1 medium brown onion (150g), chopped finely
2 cloves garlic, crushed
¼ teaspoon sweet paprika
1 teaspoon ground turmeric
2 teaspoons ground coriander
1 small zucchini (90g), grated coarsely
2 cups (140g) fresh breadcrumbs
¾ cup (190g) hummus
¼ cup (70g) greek-style yogurt
1 loaf turkish bread (430g)
⅓ cup coarsely chopped fresh mint
½ cup coarsely chopped fresh flat-leaf parsley
1 green onion, sliced thinly
30g snow pea sprouts, trimmed

1 Pat tofu dry with absorbent paper. Place tofu on absorbent-paper-lined tray; cover with more paper, stand 20 minutes.
2 Meanwhile, heat oil in medium frying pan; cook brown onion and garlic, stirring, until onion softens. Add spices; cook, stirring, until fragrant.
3 Place onion mixture in large bowl with tofu, zucchini and breadcrumbs; mash to combine. Shape mixture into four patties. Cover; refrigerate 30 minutes.
4 Meanwhile, combine hummus and yogurt in small bowl.
5 Cut bread into four pieces. Split each piece in half horizontally; toast cut sides in heated oiled grill pan.
6 Cook patties in same oiled grill pan until browned both sides and hot.
7 Spread bread with hummus mixture; sandwich combined mint, parsley and green onion, patties and sprouts between bread pieces.

preparation time *20 minutes (plus standing time)* cooking time *20 minutes (plus refrigeration time)* serves *4*
nutritional count per serving *24.1g total fat (4.6g saturated fat); 2880kJ (689 cal); 81.5g carbohydrate; 30.2g protein; 11.7g fibre*

lavash wrap

2 slices wholemeal lavash
½ small avocado (100g)
2 teaspoons tahini
1 cup (120g) coarsely grated uncooked beetroot
⅔ cup (100g) coarsely grated uncooked pumpkin
½ small red capsicum (80g), sliced thinly
100g mushrooms, sliced thinly
½ small red onion (50g), sliced thinly

1 Spread bread with avocado and tahini.
2 Place remaining ingredients on long side of bread; roll to enclose filling.

preparation time *15 minutes* serves *2*
nutritional count per serving *12.9g total fat (2.5g saturated fat); 1526kJ (365 cal); 44.6g carbohydrate; 12.4g protein; 10.2g fibre*

salad, goats cheese and pecan sandwich

80g goats cheese
2 tablespoons finely chopped pecans
2 tablespoons coarsely chopped fresh flat-leaf parsley
4 slices wholemeal bread (90g)
2 small tomato (180g), sliced thinly
1 lebanese cucumber (130g), sliced thinly lengthways
1 small carrot (70g), sliced thinly lengthways
4 small baby cos lettuce leaves

1 Combine cheese, nuts and parsley in small bowl.
2 Spread cheese mixture on each slice of bread; top two slices with tomato, cucumber, carrot and lettuce. Top with remaining slices.

preparation time *15 minutes* serves *2*
nutritional count per serving *16.5g total fat (5g saturated fat); 1593kJ (381 cal); 40.8g carbohydrate; 17.1g protein; 10.6g fibre*

pepper-crusted beef fillet with vegetable and polenta chips

3 cups (750ml) water
¾ cup (120g) polenta
2 tablespoons wholegrain mustard
2 teaspoons cracked black pepper
600g beef eye fillet
1 large kumara (500g)
2 large parsnips (700g)
2 large carrots (360g)
2 teaspoons olive oil
cooking-oil spray
½ cup coarsely chopped fresh flat-leaf parsley
¼ cup (60ml) balsamic vinegar
¼ cup (60ml) water, extra
1 tablespoon wholegrain mustard, extra
1 tablespoon honey

1 Oil deep 23cm-square cake pan.
2 Bring the water to the boil in medium saucepan. Gradually add polenta to liquid, stirring constantly. Reduce heat; cook, stirring constantly, about 10 minutes or until polenta thickens. Stir in half of the mustard; spread polenta into cake pan. Cover; refrigerate about 1 hour or until firm.
3 Preheat oven to 200°C/180°C fan-forced.
4 Spread combined remaining mustard and pepper all over beef. Cut peeled vegetables into similar-sized baton shapes. Place combined vegetables, in single layer, in large shallow flameproof baking dish; drizzle with oil. Roast, uncovered, 10 minutes. Add beef to dish; roast, uncovered, about 35 minutes or until vegetables are crisp and beef is cooked as desired.
5 Meanwhile, turn polenta onto board; cut into baton shapes similar to vegetables. Coat polenta with cooking-oil spray; place, in single layer, on oven tray. Place polenta in same oven with beef and vegetables for about the last 20 minutes of cooking time or until browned lightly.
6 Remove beef from baking dish. Cover beef; stand 5 minutes before slicing thinly. Place vegetables in large bowl with parsley; toss gently to combine. Cover to keep warm.
7 Place baking dish over high heat; add vinegar, the extra water, extra mustard and honey. Cook, stirring, about 5 minutes or until sauce bubbles and thickens.
8 Serve vegetables, polenta and beef, drizzled with sauce.

preparation time *20 minutes (plus refrigeration time)* cooking time *1 hour 5 minutes* serves *4* nutritional count per serving *11.1g total fat (3.3g saturated fat); 2140kJ (512 cal); 61.1g carbohydrate; 40.7g protein; 9.6g fibre*

roasted tomato and capsicum soup

8 large tomatoes (1.6kg), chopped coarsely
2 large red capsicum (700g), chopped coarsely
1 small brown onion (80g), chopped coarsely
2 cloves garlic, sliced thinly
1 tablespoon finely shredded fresh basil

1   Preheat oven to 180°C/160°C fan-forced.
2   Combine tomato, capsicum, onion and garlic in large baking dish; roast, covered, about 30 minutes or until vegetables soften.
3   Push vegetables through mouli or fine sieve into small saucepan; discard solids.
4   Reheat soup; serve topped with basil.

preparation time *10 minutes*
cooking time *35 minutes* serves *2*
nutritional count per serving *2.4g total fat (1.5g saturated fat); 222kJ (53 cal); 3.4g carbohydrate; 3.6g protein; 0.4g fibre*

caprese salad with figs

Buy the best flavoured tomatoes you can find to make the most of this salad.

4 large tomatoes (480g), sliced thinly
4 large fresh figs (320g), sliced thinly
25 cherry bocconcini cheeses (375g), drained, sliced thinly
½ small red onion (50g), chopped finely
¼ cup firmly packed fresh basil leaves
2 tablespoons olive oil
1 tablespoon balsamic vinegar

1   Overlap slices of tomato, fig and cheese on serving plate; sprinkle with onion and basil.
2   Drizzle with combined oil and vinegar.

preparation time *20 minutes* serves *4*
nutritional count per serving *23.7g total fat (10.7g saturated fat); 1367kJ (327 cal); 8.8g carbohydrate; 18.5g protein; 3.4g fibre*

chicken, pea and asparagus soup with pistou

You need 450g of fresh peas in the pod or 2 cups (240g) frozen peas for this recipe.

3 cups (750ml) chicken stock
3 cups (750ml) water
1 clove garlic, crushed
¼ teaspoon coarsely ground black pepper
400g chicken breast fillets
170g asparagus, trimmed, chopped coarsely
1½ cups (240g) shelled fresh peas
1 tablespoon lemon juice

PISTOU

½ cup coarsely chopped fresh flat-leaf parsley
½ cup coarsely chopped fresh mint
¼ cup coarsely chopped fresh garlic chives
2 teaspoons finely grated lemon rind
1 clove garlic, crushed
2 teaspoons olive oil

1 Bring stock, the water, garlic and pepper to the boil in large saucepan. Add chicken; return to boil. Reduce heat; simmer, covered, about 10 minutes or until chicken is cooked through. Cool in poaching liquid 10 minutes. Remove chicken from pan; slice thinly.
2 Meanwhile, make pistou.
3 Add remaining ingredients to soup; bring to the boil. Return chicken to pan; simmer, uncovered, about 3 minutes or until vegetables are just tender.
4 Divide soup among serving bowls; top with pistou.

PISTOU Pound ingredients using mortar and pestle until smooth.

preparation time *5 minutes*
cooking time *25 minutes* serves *4*
nutritional count per serving *5.7g total fat (1.3g saturated fat); 861kJ (206 cal); 7.3g carbohydrate; 28.9g protein; 4.4g fibre*

grilled chicken with coriander and chilli

8 chicken thigh cutlets (1.6kg)

CORIANDER AND CHILLI PASTE

2 teaspoons coriander seeds
4 fresh small red thai chillies, chopped coarsely
1 teaspoon ground cumin
2 whole cloves
2 cardamom pods, bruised
¼ teaspoon ground turmeric
10cm stick fresh lemon grass (20g), chopped coarsely
2 medium brown onions (300g), chopped coarsely
4 cloves garlic
⅓ cup (80ml) lime juice
2 teaspoons coarse cooking salt
2 tablespoons peanut oil

1 Make coriander and chilli paste.
2 Pierce chicken all over with sharp knife. Combine paste and chicken in large bowl, rubbing paste into cuts. Cover; refrigerate overnight.
3 Cook chicken, covered, on heated oiled grill plate (or grill or barbecue), 5 minutes. Uncover; cook, turning occasionally, about 20 minutes or until cooked.
4 Serve chicken with lime wedges, if you like.

CORIANDER AND CHILLI PASTE Blend or process ingredients until mixture forms a smooth paste.

preparation time *10 minutes (plus refrigeration time)*
cooking time *25 minutes* serves *4*
nutritional count per serving *29.5g total fat (7.8g saturated fat); 2094kJ (501 cal); 5.2g carbohydrate; 53.5g protein; 1.7g fibre*

lentil and vegetable soup

1 litre (4 cups) vegetable stock
½ cup (100g) french green lentils
2 cloves garlic, crushed
1 untrimmed celery stalk (150g)
2 medium carrot (240g), chopped coarsely
100g mushrooms, chopped coarsely
2 tablespoons coarsely chopped fresh flat-leaf parsley

1   Combine stock, lentils, garlic and celery leaves
in medium saucepan; bring to the boil. Reduce heat;
simmer, covered, about 20 minutes or until lentils
just soften. Discard celery leaves.
2   Add coarsely chopped celery stalk, carrot and
mushroom; bring to the boil. Reduce heat; simmer,
covered, about 15 minutes or until vegetables are
tender. Stir in parsley.

preparation time *10 minutes*
cooking time *45 minutes* serves *2*
nutritional count per serving *1.7g total fat (0.2g
saturated fat); 978kJ (234 cal); 37.5g carbohydrate;
18g protein; 17.7g fibre*

white bean and chicken stew

1 cup (200g) dried cannellini beans
1kg chicken thigh fillets, chopped coarsely
¼ cup finely chopped fresh oregano
1 tablespoon olive oil
1 medium fennel bulb (300g)
2 medium brown onions (300g), sliced thinly
2 cloves garlic, crushed
6 medium tomatoes (900g), peeled, seeded,
   chopped coarsely
3 large zucchini (450g), chopped coarsely
½ cup coarsely chopped fresh basil

1   Cover beans with cold water in medium bowl; stand
overnight. Drain beans; rinse under cold water, drain.
Place beans in medium saucepan of boiling water;
return to the boil. Reduce heat; simmer, uncovered, about
30 minutes or until beans are almost tender. Drain.
2   Meanwhile, combine chicken and oregano in
medium bowl. Heat oil in large saucepan; cook
chicken, in batches, until browned.
3   Trim then slice fennel thinly. Coarsely chop enough
fennel fronds to make 2 tablespoons; reserve.
4   Cook onion, garlic and sliced fennel in same dish,
stirring, until vegetables just soften. Return chicken to
dish with tomato, zucchini and beans; cook, covered,
over low heat, about 15 minutes or until chicken is
cooked through. Uncover; simmer 5 minutes.
5   Remove pan from heat; stir in basil and reserved
fronds. Serve stew with french bread, if you like.

preparation time *35 minutes (plus standing time)*
cooking time *35 minutes* serves *4*
nutritional count per serving *23.3g total fat (6.2g
saturated fat); 2119kJ (507 cal); 16.2g carbohydrate;
54.5g protein; 9g fibre*

black bean, corn and papaya salad

1 cup (200g) dried black beans
1 trimmed corn cob (250g)
5 medium egg tomatoes (375g), seeded
4 green onions, sliced thinly
1 cup (170g) diced papaya
⅓ cup coarsely chopped fresh coriander
4 large iceberg lettuce leaves

LIME DRESSING

1 clove garlic, crushed
2 tablespoons lime juice
2 tablespoons olive oil
1 tablespoon white wine vinegar
½ teaspoon white sugar
1 fresh small red thai chilli, chopped finely

1 Cover beans with cold water in medium bowl; stand overnight, drain. Rinse beans under cold water; drain.
2 Cook beans in medium saucepan of boiling water, uncovered, until beans are just tender. Drain.
3 Meanwhile, microwave, steam or grill corn until tender; cut kernels from cobs.
4 Blend or process tomato until just finely chopped.
5 Make lime dressing.
6 Place beans, corn and tomato in large bowl with onion, papaya, coriander and dressing; toss gently to combine. Divide salad among lettuce leaves.

LIME DRESSING Place ingredients in screw-top jar; shake well.

preparation time *30 minutes (plus standing time)*
cooking time *45 minutes* serves *4*
nutritional count per serving *9.9g total fat (1.4g saturated fat); 711kJ (170 cal);13g carbohydrate; 4.4g protein; 5.4g fibre*

cauliflower and green olive salad

1 small cauliflower (1kg), trimmed, cut into florets
1 cup (120g) large green olives, seeded, halved
1 trimmed celery stalk (100g), sliced thinly
1 cup loosely packed celery leaves
½ cup loosely packed fresh flat-leaf parsley leaves
1 small red onion (100g), sliced thinly
2 tablespoons lemon juice
1 tablespoon finely chopped preserved lemon
2 tablespoons olive oil
1 clove garlic, crushed
125g fetta cheese, crumbled

1 Boil, steam or microwave cauliflower until tender; drain.
2 Combine cauliflower in medium bowl with olives, celery, celery leaves, parsley, onion, juice, preserved lemon, oil and garlic.
3 Serve salad sprinkled with cheese.

preparation time *15 minutes*
cooking time *5 minutes* serves *4*
nutritional count per serving *17.2g total fat (6.1g saturated fat); 1087kJ (260 cal); 12.3g carbohydrate; 11.3g protein; 5.5g fibre*

roasted pumpkin, pecan and fetta salad

200g pumpkin, chopped coarsely
cooking-oil spray
100g rocket leaves
⅓ cup (40g) roasted pecans
100g goat fetta cheese, crumbled

CITRUS DRESSING

2 tablespoons fresh orange juice
2 tablespoons fresh lemon juice
1 tablespoon grapeseed oil

1 Preheat oven to 240°C/220°C fan-forced.
2 Place pumpkin on lightly oiled oven tray; spray with oil. Roast, uncovered, about 20 minutes or until tender.
3 Make citrus dressing.
4 Place pumpkin in medium bowl with remaining ingredients and dressing; toss gently to combine.

CITRUS DRESSING Place ingredients in screw-top jar; shake well.

preparation time *15 minutes*
cooking time *20 minutes* serves *2*
nutritional count per serving *27.3g total fat (6.7g saturated fat); 1404kJ (336 cal); 9.9g carbohydrate; 11.8g protein; 3.5g fibre*

cos, snow pea and roasted celeriac salad

200g celeriac, chopped coarsely
4 cloves garlic, unpeeled
cooking-oil spray
100g baby green beans, trimmed, chopped coarsely
¼ cup (60ml) fresh lemon juice
2 tablespoons walnut oil
½ baby cos lettuce (90g), torn
50g snow peas, trimmed, sliced thinly
½ cup (50g) roasted walnuts, chopped coarsely

1 Preheat oven to 240°C/220°C fan-forced.
2 Place celeriac and garlic on shallow oven tray; spray with oil. Roast, uncovered, about 20 minutes or until celeriac is just tender and garlic softens.
3 Meanwhile, boil, steam or microwave beans until tender; drain. Rinse under cold water; drain.
4 When garlic is cool enough to handle, squeeze garlic from skins into screw-top jar. Add juice and oil; shake well.
5 Place celeriac and beans in medium bowl with lettuce, snow peas, nuts and dressing; toss gently to combine.

preparation time *15 minutes*
cooking time *20 minutes* serves *2*
nutritional count per serving *46.9g total fat (13.2g saturated fat); 2215kJ (530 cal); 14g carbohydrate; 13.7g protein; 14.1g fibre*

1

2

3

4

glazed pork and watercress salad

¼ cup (90g) honey
¼ cup (85g) tamarind concentrate
3cm piece fresh ginger (15g), grated
2 cloves garlic, crushed
800g pork fillets
100g watercress, trimmed
1 medium red onion (170g), sliced thinly
2 lebanese cucumbers (260g), seeded, sliced thinly
1 medium yellow capsicum (200g), sliced thinly
½ cup (75g) roasted unsalted cashews

1 Combine honey, tamarind, ginger and garlic in small jug. Combine pork with a third of the honey mixture in medium bowl.
2 Cook pork on heated oiled grill plate (or grill or barbecue) until browned all over and cooked as desired. Cover; stand 10 minutes then slice thickly.
3 Meanwhile, combine remaining ingredients with half the remaining honey mixture in medium bowl.
4 Drizzle pork with remaining honey mixture; serve with salad.

preparation time *15 minutes*
cooking time *15 minutes* serves *4*
nutritional count per serving *14.1g total fat (3.2g saturated fat); 1885kJ (451 cal); 29.9g carbohydrate; 49.6g protein; 4.3g fibre*

lemon chilli pork with italian brown rice salad

2 teaspoons finely grated lemon rind
2 tablespoons lemon juice
½ teaspoon dried chilli flakes
1 tablespoon olive oil
4 x 240g pork cutlets

ITALIAN BROWN RICE SALAD

1 cup (200g) brown long-grain rice
1 medium red capsicum (200g), chopped finely
½ cup (60g) seeded black olives, chopped coarsely
2 tablespoons drained capers, rinsed
½ cup coarsely chopped fresh basil
⅓ cup coarsely chopped fresh flat-leaf parsley
2 tablespoons lemon juice
1 tablespoon olive oil

1 Combine rind, juice, chilli, oil and pork in medium bowl. Cover; refrigerate until required.
2 Make italian brown rice salad.
3 Cook pork, uncovered, in large heated frying pan about 15 minutes or until cooked as desired.
4 Serve pork with rice salad.

ITALIAN BROWN RICE SALAD Cook rice in large saucepan of boiling water, uncovered, until tender; drain. Rinse under cold water; drain. Place rice in large bowl with remaining ingredients; toss gently to combine.

preparation time *35 minutes*
cooking time *50 minutes* serves *4*
nutritional count per serving *14.7g total fat (2.9g saturated fat); 1969kJ (471 cal); 46.4g carbohydrate; 35.7g protein; 3g fibre*

1 GLAZED PORK AND WATERCRESS SALAD 2 LEMON CHILLI PORK WITH ITALIAN BROWN RICE SALAD 3 HOT AND SOUR GREEN PAPAYA AND PORK SALAD [P 130] 4 SEAFOOD PAELLA [P 130]

MEGA HEALTHY 129

hot and sour green papaya and pork salad

½ cup (125ml) water
600g pork fillets
1 small green papaya (650g)
1 large carrot (180g)
2 teaspoons vegetable oil
1 cup firmly packed fresh coriander leaves
⅓ cup (45g) coarsely chopped
   roasted unsalted peanuts

CHILLI AND TAMARIND DRESSING

4 cloves garlic, crushed
4 fresh small red thai chillies, chopped finely
⅔ cup (200g) tamarind concentrate
1 tablespoon finely grated lime rind
½ cup (125ml) lime juice
2 shallots (50g), sliced thinly
⅓ cup (90g) grated palm sugar

1 Make chilli and tamarind dressing.
2 Place the water in large frying pan with ½ cup of the dressing. Add pork; bring to the boil. Reduce heat; simmer, covered, 20 minutes or until pork is cooked through. Remove pork from pan; cover, stand 10 minutes then slice thinly.
3 Peel then halve papaya; remove seeds. Using vegetable peeler, slice papaya and carrot lengthways into thin strips.
4 Stir oil into remaining dressing. Place pork, papaya, carrot, coriander and dressing in medium bowl; toss gently to combine. Serve salad topped with nuts.

CHILLI AND TAMARIND DRESSING Combine ingredients in small jug.

preparation time *20 minutes*
cooking time *25 minutes* serves *4*
nutritional count per serving *11.4g total fat (2.3g saturated fat); 1643kJ (393 cal); 31.7g carbohydrate; 37.9g protein; 6.6g fibre*

seafood paella

8 uncooked large king prawns (560g)
500g small black mussels
600g squid hoods, cleaned
1 uncooked blue swimmer crab (325g)
1 tablespoon olive oil
6 green onions, chopped coarsely
2 cloves garlic, crushed
1 fresh long red chilli, chopped finely
1 medium yellow capsicum (200g), chopped coarsely
2 cups (400g) brown rice
pinch saffron threads
1 cup (250ml) dry white wine
4 medium tomatoes (600g), chopped coarsely
1 tablespoon tomato paste
1 litre (4 cups) chicken stock

1 Shell and devein prawns, leaving tails intact. Scrub mussels; remove beards. Cut squid down centre to open out; score inside in diagonal pattern then cut into thick strips.
2 To prepare crab, lift tail flap then, with a peeling motion, lift off the back shell. Remove and discard whitish gills, liver and brain matter. Rinse crab well under cold water; cut crab body in quarters.
3 Heat oil in large deep frying pan; cook onion, garlic, chilli and capsicum, stirring, until onion softens. Add rice and saffron; stir to coat in onion mixture. Stir in wine, tomato and paste. Cook, stirring, until wine has almost evaporated.
4 Add 1 cup of stock; cook, stirring, until absorbed. Add remaining stock; cook, covered, stirring occasionally, about 1 hour or until rice is tender.
5 Uncover rice; place seafood on top of the rice (do not stir to combine). Cover pan; simmer about 5 minutes or until seafood has changed in colour and mussels have opened (discard any that do not).

preparation time *30 minutes*
cooking time *1 hour 15 minutes* serves *4*
nutritional count per serving *10g total fat (2.1g saturated fat); 2759kJ (660 cal); 85.4g carbohydrate; 43.2g protein; 5.4g fibre*

chipotle, corn, tomato and chickpea salad

1 chipotle chilli
2 tablespoons boiling water
½ cup (130g) bottled tomato pasta sauce
1 tablespoon lime juice
1 teaspoon ground cumin
2 trimmed corn cobs (500g)
420g can chickpeas, drained, rinsed
250g cherry tomatoes, halved
1 small red onion (100g), sliced thinly
1 cup loosely packed fresh coriander leaves

1 Place chilli and the water in small bowl; stand 15 minutes. Discard stalk; blend or process chilli, soaking liquid and sauce until mixture is smooth. Transfer to small bowl; stir in lime juice.
2 Dry-fry cumin in small frying pan, stirring, until fragrant; stir into chilli sauce mixture.
3 Cook corn on heated oiled grill plate (or grill or barbecue) until browned and tender. Cut kernels from cobs.
4 Combine chilli mixture and corn in large bowl with remaining ingredients.

preparation time *20 minutes (plus standing time)* cooking time *15 minutes* serves *4* nutritional count per serving *2.9g total fat (0.3g saturated fat); 853kJ (204 cal); 30.5g carbohydrate; 9.5g protein; 9.4g fibre*

borlotti bean, brown rice and almond salad

½ cup (100g) dried borlotti beans
½ cup (100g) brown long-grain rice
1 small red onion (100g), chopped finely
¼ cup finely chopped fresh flat-leaf parsley
¼ cup finely chopped fresh mint
2 medium tomato (300g), chopped finely
2 tablespoons roasted slivered almonds
2 tablespoons fresh lemon juice
1 tablespoon olive oil

1 Place beans in small bowl, cover with water; stand overnight, drain. Rinse under cold water; drain.
2 Cook beans in medium saucepan of boiling water, uncovered, until just tender; drain. Rinse under cold water; drain.
3 Meanwhile, cook rice in small saucepan of boiling water, uncovered, until rice is tender; drain. Rinse under cold water; drain.
4 Place beans and rice in medium bowl with remaining ingredients; toss gently to combine.

preparation time *10 minutes (plus standing time)* cooking time *20 minutes* serves *2* nutritional count per serving *18.4g total fat (2.1g saturated fat); 2140kJ (512 cal); 63.4g carbohydrate; 21.3g protein; 13.4g fibre*

white bean salad

100g mesclun
1 cup (200g) canned white beans, rinsed, drained
2 tablespoons coarsely chopped fresh tarragon
2 tablespoons coarsely chopped fresh flat-leaf parsley
2 small carrot (140g), cut into matchsticks
1 lebanese cucumber (130g), cut into matchsticks
2 red radishes (70g), trimmed, cut into matchsticks
2 tablespoons fresh apple juice
1 tablespoon cider vinegar
1 tablespoon olive oil
1 tablespoon toasted sunflower seeds
1 tablespoon toasted pepitas

1 Place mesclun, beans, herbs, carrot, cucumber, radish in medium bowl with combined juice, vinegar and oil; toss gently to combine.
2 Serve salad topped with seeds.

preparation time *15 minutes* serves *2* nutritional count per serving *16.5g total fat (2.3g saturated fat); 1170kJ (280 cal); 19g carbohydrate; 10.3g protein; 9.6g fibre*

balsamic-seared steak with kipflers and mushrooms

¼ cup (60ml) balsamic vinegar
2 cloves garlic, crushed
4 beef scotch fillet steaks (800g)
1kg kipfler potatoes, quartered lengthways
1 tablespoon olive oil
500g flat mushrooms, sliced thickly
2 tablespoons dry red wine
1 tablespoon plum jam
1 tablespoon cornflour
¾ cup (180ml) beef stock

1 Combine vinegar and garlic in medium bowl with beef; toss beef to coat in marinade. Cover; refrigerate 3 hours or overnight.
2 Preheat oven to 200°C/180°C fan-forced.
3 Place potato, in single layer, in large shallow baking dish; drizzle with oil. Roast, uncovered, stirring occasionally, about 30 minutes or until browned and crisp.
4 Meanwhile, cook steaks on heated oiled grill plate (or grill or barbecue) until cooked as desired. Remove; cover to keep warm.
5 Cook mushroom on same heated grill plate (or grill or barbecue) until just tender.
6 Place wine in small saucepan; bring to the boil. Add jam and blended cornflour and stock; stir until sauce boils and thickens slightly.
7 Serve steaks with mushrooms, potato and sauce.

preparation time *15 minutes (plus refrigeration time)*
cooking time *15 minutes* serves *4*
nutritional count per serving *13.7g total fat (4.3g saturated fat); 2165kJ (518 cal); 40.8g carbohydrate; 54.2g protein; 8.4g fibre*

grilled vegetables with garlic rosemary dressing

1 medium red capsicum (200g)
1 medium yellow capsicum (200g)
¼ cup (60ml) olive oil
1 clove garlic, crushed
1 teaspoon finely grated lemon rind
2 teaspoons finely chopped fresh rosemary
1 medium red onion (170g), cut into wedges
2 small leeks (400g), trimmed, cut into 2cm pieces
1 medium eggplant (300g), sliced thickly
2 medium zucchini (240g), sliced thickly
4 flat mushrooms (320g), quartered
3 cloves garlic, unpeeled
⅓ cup (100g) mayonnaise
1 tablespoon lemon juice

1 Preheat grill.
2 Quarter capsicums, discard seeds and membranes. Roast under grill or in very hot oven, skin-side up, until skin blisters and blackens. Cover capsicum pieces in plastic or paper for 5 minutes; peel away skin, slice thickly.
3 Combine oil, crushed garlic, rind and half the rosemary in small bowl.
4 Brush onion, leek, eggplant, zucchini, mushrooms and unpeeled garlic with oil mixture; cook vegetables, in batches, on heated oiled grill plate (or grill or barbecue) until tender.
5 Squeeze cooked garlic into small jug; discard skins. Whisk in remaining rosemary, mayonnaise and juice. Serve vegetables with dressing.

preparation time *30 minutes*
cooking time *30 minutes* serves *4*
nutritional count per serving *22.8g total fat (2.9g saturated fat); 1325kJ (317 cal); 16.9g carbohydrate; 7.9g protein; 8.4g fibre*

poached fish with herb salad

3 cups (750ml) water
2 cloves garlic, crushed
5cm piece fresh ginger (25g), sliced thinly
4 white fish fillets (440g)
1 lime, cut into wedges

HERB SALAD

¼ cup loosely packed fresh mint leaves
¼ cup loosely packed fresh coriander leaves
¼ cup loosely packed fresh basil leaves, torn
½ small red onion (50g), sliced thinly
1 lebanese cucumber (130g), seeded, sliced thinly
2 tablespoons fresh lime juice
1 tablespoon olive oil
1cm piece fresh ginger (5g), grated

1 Place the water, garlic and ginger in medium frying
pan; bring to the boil. Add fish, reduce heat; simmer,
uncovered, about 5 minutes or until fish is cooked as
desired. Remove fish with slotted spoon; discard liquid.
2 Combine ingredients for herb salad in medium bowl;
serve with fish and lime wedges.

preparation time *20 minutes*
cooking time *10 minutes* serves *2*
nutritional count per serving *11.7g total fat (2.2g
saturated fat); 1350kJ (323 cal); 4.4g carbohydrate;
48.1g protein; 3.2g fibre*

ocean trout tartare

600g piece sashimi ocean trout
2 teaspoons finely grated lemon rind
1 tablespoon lemon juice
1 tablespoon olive oil
1 clove garlic, crushed
⅓ cup finely chopped fresh flat-leaf parsley
1 medium red onion (170g), chopped finely
4 drained anchovy fillets, rinsed, chopped finely
2 tablespoons drained baby capers, rinsed,
   chopped coarsely
1 small french bread stick (150g), sliced thinly
1 lemon, cut into wedges

1 Chop trout into 5mm pieces; combine in medium
bowl with rind, juice, oil and garlic.
2 Divide tartare mixture among serving plates, shaping
into mound. Mound equal amounts of parsley, onion,
anchovy and capers around tartare mixture on plates;
serve with bread slices and lemon wedges.

preparation time *35 minutes* serves *4*
nutritional count per serving *12.2g total fat (2.3g
saturated fat); 1471kJ (352 cal); 23.4g carbohydrate;
34.4g protein; 3g fibre*

salmon en papillote

1 medium tomato (150g), seeded, chopped finely
1 tablespoon drained baby capers, rinsed
1 small red onion (100g), chopped finely
2 teaspoons finely grated lemon rind
4 x 220g salmon fillets
1 tablespoon lemon juice
1 tablespoon olive oil
80g baby rocket leaves
2 tablespoons finely shredded fresh basil

1 Preheat oven to 200°C/180°C fan-forced.
2 Combine tomato, capers, onion and rind in small bowl.
3 Place each fillet, skin-side down, on large square of
oiled foil. Top each fillet with equal amounts of tomato
mixture. Gather corners of square together above fish;
twist to enclose securely.
4 Place parcels on oven tray; bake about 10 minutes
or until fish is cooked as desired.
5 Combine lemon juice and oil in small jug. Divide
rocket among serving plates.
6 Unwrap parcels just before serving; place fish on
rocket. Top with basil, drizzle with oil mixture.

preparation time *15 minutes*
cooking time *10 minutes* serves *4*
nutritional count per serving *19g total fat (3.8g
saturated fat); 11434kJ (343 cal); 2.6g carbohydrate;
40.1g protein; 1g fibre*

grilled fish with gai lan

We used blue-eye in this recipe, but you can use any firm white fish.

2 x 200g white fish fillets
400g gai lan, chopped coarsely
GINGER AND GARLIC DRESSING
4cm piece fresh ginger (20g), grated
1 clove garlic, crushed
2 tablespoons water
2 tablespoons tamari

1 Cook fish in heated oiled small frying pan until cooked through.
2 Meanwhile, boil, steam or microwave gai lan until tender; drain.
3 Make ginger and garlic dressing.
4 Serve fish with gai lan; drizzle with dressing.

GINGER AND GARLIC DRESSING Place ingredients in screw-top jar; shake well.

preparation time *10 minutes*
cooking time *10 minutes* serves *2*
nutritional count per serving *1.7g total fat (0.2g saturated fat); 3.5g carbohydrate; 828kJ (198 cal); 41.2g protein; 8.2g fibre*

steamed asian fish

We used bream in this recipe, but you can use any firm white fish.

2 whole white fish (440g)
3cm piece fresh ginger (15g), cut into matchsticks
2 green onions, sliced thinly
2 small carrot (140g), cut into matchsticks
2 tablespoons tamari
2 teaspoons sesame oil

1 Preheat oven to 200°C/180°C fan-forced.
2 Oil sheet of foil large enough to enclose fish. Place fish on foil, fill cavity with half of the vegetables. Brush with combined tamari and oil; top with remaining vegetables.
3 Fold edges of foil to enclose fish; place fish parcel on oven tray. Cook about 15 minutes or until fish is cooked as desired. Serve sprinkled with fresh coriander leaves, if you like.

preparation time *10 minutes*
cooking time *15 minutes* serves *2*
nutritional count per serving *11.2g total fat (2.9g saturated fat); 957kJ (229 cal); 5g carbohydrate; 26.8g protein; 2.4g fibre*

ocean trout in baby buk choy parcels

4 dried shiitake mushrooms
2 green onions, chopped finely
3cm piece fresh ginger (15g), grated
5cm stick fresh lemon grass (10g), chopped finely
2 cloves garlic, crushed
1 teaspoon sambal oelek
2 tablespoons soy sauce
4 ocean trout fillets (600g)
4 large baby buk choy (600g)
1½ cups (300g) jasmine rice

GINGER DRESSING

2cm piece fresh ginger (10g), grated
2 tablespoons rice wine vinegar
1 tablespoon vegetable oil
1 teaspoon sesame oil
2 tablespoons mirin
1 tablespoon soy sauce

1 Place mushrooms in small heatproof bowl, cover with boiling water, stand 20 minutes; drain. Discard stems; chop caps finely.
2 Meanwhile, place ginger dressing ingredients in screw-top jar; shake well.
3 Combine mushroom, onion, ginger, lemon grass, garlic, sambal and sauce in small bowl; divide mushroom mixture among flesh side of fish fillets. Carefully insert one fillet, mushroom-side up, inside leaves of each buk choy; wrap leaves around fillet then tie parcels with kitchen string.
4 Place parcels in large steamer fitted over large saucepan of boiling water; steam, covered, about 10 minutes or until fish is cooked as desired.
5 Meanwhile, cook rice in large saucepan of boiling water, uncovered, until rice is just tender; drain. Divide rice among plates; top with parcels, drizzle with dressing.

preparation time *20 minutes (plus standing time)*
cooking time *15 minutes* serves *4*
nutritional count per serving *12.3g total fat (2.2g saturated fat); 2195kJ (525 cal); 64.6g carbohydrate; 37.1g protein; 3.6g fibre*

creamy barley and mixed mushroom pilaf

2 cups (500ml) vegetable stock
3 cups (750ml) water
40g butter
150g button mushrooms, sliced thinly
150g swiss brown mushrooms, sliced thinly
150g oyster mushrooms, sliced thinly
1 teaspoon olive oil
1 medium brown onion (150g), chopped finely
2 cloves garlic, crushed
¾ cup (150g) pearl barley
⅓ cup (80ml) dry white wine
100g enoki mushrooms
½ cup coarsely chopped fresh garlic chives
¼ cup coarsely chopped fresh flat-leaf parsley

1 Combine stock and the water in medium saucepan; bring to the boil, simmer, covered.
2 Heat butter in large deep frying pan; cook button, swiss and oyster mushrooms, stirring, 5 minutes or until tender. Remove from pan.
3 Heat oil in same pan; cook onion and garlic, stirring, until onion softens. Stir in barley. Add wine; cook, stirring, until liquid has almost evaporated. Add ½ cup simmering stock mixture; cook, stirring, over low heat until liquid is absorbed. Continue adding stock mixture, in ½-cup batches, stirring until absorbed after each addition. Total cooking time should be about 40 minutes or until barley is just tender.
4 Remove from heat; stir in mushroom mixture, enoki mushrooms and herbs.

preparation time *25 minutes*
cooking time *55 minutes* serves *4*
nutritional count per serving *11.2g total fat (6g saturated fat); 1195kJ (286 cal); 28.1g carbohydrate; 10.4g protein; 9.5g fibre*

cashew patty salad with spiced yogurt

⅓ cup (55g) burghul
⅔ cup (160ml) boiling water
1½ cups (225g) roasted unsalted cashews
⅓ cup (50g) wholemeal plain flour
1 medium brown onion (150g), quartered
2 cloves garlic, halved
1⅓ cups firmly packed fresh flat-leaf parsley leaves
2 tablespoons vegetable oil
200g baby spinach leaves
1 lebanese cucumber (130g), chopped coarsely
250g cherry tomatoes, halved

SPICED YOGURT

1 cup (280g) yogurt
1 tablespoon lime juice
1 teaspoon ground cumin
2 green onions, chopped finely

1 Place burghul in medium heatproof bowl, add the water; stand 10 minutes.
2 Meanwhile, make spiced yogurt.
3 Blend or process nuts, flour, onion, garlic and ⅓ cup of the parsley until smooth. Combine nut mixture with burghul mixture in medium bowl. Using hands, shape mixture into 24 patties.
4 Heat oil in large frying pan; cook patties, in batches, until browned all over and heated through.
5 Combine remaining parsley in large bowl with remaining ingredients.
6 Serve salad topped with patties; drizzle with yogurt.

SPICED YOGURT Combine ingredients in small bowl.

preparation time *25 minutes*
cooking time *10 minutes* serves *4*
nutritional count per serving *37.1g total fat (7g saturated fat); 2324kJ (556 cal); 32.5g carbohydrate; 17.6g protein; 11.1g fibre*

grilled zucchini with pumpkin and couscous

½ cup (100g) couscous
½ cup (125ml) boiling water
2 tablespoons lemon juice
2 teaspoons olive oil
¼ cup (40g) pine nuts
1 clove garlic, crushed
½ small red onion (50g), chopped finely
1 teaspoon sweet smoked paprika
½ teaspoon ground cumin
½ teaspoon cayenne pepper
½ small red capsicum (75g), chopped finely
200g piece pumpkin, chopped finely
2 tablespoons finely chopped fresh flat-leaf parsley
6 medium zucchini (720g), halved lengthways

PRESERVED LEMON YOGURT

½ cup (140g) greek-style yogurt
2 tablespoons finely chopped preserved lemon
2 tablespoons water

1 Make preserved lemon yogurt.
2 Combine couscous with the water and juice in large heatproof bowl, cover; stand about 5 minutes or until water is absorbed, fluffing with fork occasionally.
3 Heat oil in large saucepan; cook nuts, stirring, until browned lightly. Add garlic, onion and spices; cook, stirring, until onion softens. Add capsicum and pumpkin; cook, stirring, until pumpkin is just tender. Stir in couscous and parsley.
4 Meanwhile, cook zucchini on heated oiled grill plate (or grill or barbecue) until just tender.
5 Serve zucchini topped with couscous and drizzled with yogurt.

PRESERVED LEMON YOGURT Combine ingredients in small bowl.

preparation time *20 minutes*
cooking time *20 minutes* serves *4*
nutritional count per serving *12.7g total fat (2.5g saturated fat); 1200kJ (287 cal); 30.1g carbohydrate; 10.1g protein; 4.9g fibre*

layered grapevine leaves, eggplant and lamb

2 large red capsicums (700g)
1 medium eggplant (300g), cut crossways into 12 slices
1 medium brown onion (150g), chopped finely
1 clove garlic, crushed
500g lamb mince
2 teaspoons baharat
1 tablespoon brandy
1 tablespoon tomato paste
½ cup (125ml) beef stock
1 tablespoon lime juice
1 tablespoon toasted pine nuts
1 cup coarsely chopped fresh flat-leaf parsley
8 fresh grapevine leaves

1 Preheat grill.
2 Quarter capsicums; remove seeds and membrane. Place capsicum, skin-side up, and eggplant on oiled oven tray under grill or in hot oven until skin blisters. Cover capsicum with plastic wrap or paper for 5 minutes; peel away skin, then slice thinly.
3 Meanwhile, cook onion and garlic in heated oiled large frying pan, stirring, until onion just softens. Add mince and spice; cook, stirring, until mince changes colour. Stir in combined brandy, paste and stock; bring to the boil. Reduce heat; simmer, uncovered, stirring, 2 minutes or until liquid reduces by half. Remove from heat; stir in juice, nuts and parsley. Cover to keep warm.
4 Place vine leaves in large saucepan of boiling water, uncovered, for about 30 seconds or just until pliable; drain, in single layer, on absorbent paper.
5 Place one leaf on each plate; layer each leaf with one slice of eggplant, a few capsicum slices, ¼ cup mince mixture and another vine leaf. Repeat layering with remaining eggplant, capsicum and mince.

preparation time *20 minutes*
cooking time *20 minutes* serves *4*
nutritional count per serving *15.5g total fat (5.9g saturated fat); 1321kJ (316 cal); 10.4g carbohydrate; 31.1g protein; 5.6g fibre*

chilli coriander lamb with barley salad

1 tablespoon coriander seeds, crushed lightly
½ teaspoon dried chilli flakes
2 cloves garlic, crushed
4 lamb backstraps (800g)
1 cup (200g) pearl barley
¼ teaspoon ground turmeric
⅓ cup coarsely chopped fresh mint
⅓ cup coarsely chopped fresh coriander
1 small red onion (100g), chopped finely
250g cherry tomatoes, quartered
¼ cup (60ml) lemon juice
2 teaspoons olive oil

1 Combine seeds, chilli and garlic in medium bowl, add lamb; toss lamb to coat in mixture. Cover; refrigerate until required.
2 Meanwhile, cook barley in large saucepan of boiling water, uncovered, about 20 minutes or until just tender; drain. Rinse under cold water; drain.
3 Cook lamb on heated lightly oiled grill plate (or grill or barbecue) until cooked as desired. Cover lamb; stand 5 minutes before slicing thickly.
4 Combine remaining ingredients in large bowl, add barley; toss gently to combine. Serve salad with lamb.

preparation time *20 minutes*
cooking time *30 minutes* serves *4*
nutritional count per serving *10.9g total fat (3.8g saturated fat) 1822kJ (436 cal) 33.8g carbohydrate 49.2g protein 7.8g fibre*

tofu zucchini patties

You need to cook ⅔ cup (130g) of brown rice for this recipe.

300g firm silken tofu, chopped coarsely
1½ cups cooked brown rice
3 medium zucchini (360g), grated coarsely
1 medium brown onion (150g), chopped finely
1 cup (100g) packaged breadcrumbs
2 eggs
2 tablespoons finely chopped fresh flat-leaf parsley
1 clove garlic, crushed
2 tablespoons olive oil
2 lemons, cut into wedges

1   Blend or process tofu until smooth; transfer to large bowl. Add rice, zucchini, onion, breadcrumbs, eggs, parsley and garlic; mix well. Shape mixture into 12 patties.
2   Heat oil in large frying pan; cook patties, in batches, about 3 minutes each side or until browned and heated through. Drain on absorbent paper.
3   Serve patties with lemon wedges and, if desired, watercress and yogurt.

preparation time *15 minutes*
cooking time *15 minutes* serves *4*
nutritional count per serving *18.8g total fat (3.2g saturated fat); 1831kJ (438 cal); 43.2g carbohydrate; 19.8g protein; 6.6g fibre*

dhal with vegetables

1 teaspoon vegetable oil
2cm piece fresh ginger (10g), grated
4cm piece fresh turmeric (20g), grated
1 clove garlic, crushed
1 cup (200g) yellow split peas
2 small carrots (140g), chopped coarsely
1 litre (4 cups) water
2 small zucchini (180g), chopped coarsely

GINGER YOGURT

2 tablespoons finely chopped fresh coriander
2cm piece fresh ginger (10g), grated
2 tablespoons fresh lime juice
¼ cup (70g) sheep milk yogurt

1   Heat oil in medium saucepan; cook ginger, turmeric and garlic, stirring, until fragrant. Add peas, carrot and the water; bring to the boil. Reduce heat; simmer, covered, about 25 minutes or until peas are almost tender. Add zucchini; cook, covered, about 5 minutes or until zucchini is just tender.
2   Meanwhile, make ginger yogurt.
3   Serve dhal with ginger yogurt.

GINGER YOGURT Combine ingredients in small bowl.

preparation time *10 minutes*
cooking time *35 minutes* serves *2*
nutritional count per serving *10g total fat (0.8g saturated fat); 1764kJ (422 cal); 54.8g carbohydrate; 27.3g protein; 14.5g fibre*

beetroot risotto with rocket

2 medium beetroot (350g), peeled, grated coarsely
3 cups (750ml) vegetable stock
3 cups (750ml) water
1 tablespoon olive oil
1 large brown onion (200g), chopped finely
2 cloves garlic, crushed
1½ cups (300g) arborio rice
¼ cup (20g) coarsely grated parmesan cheese
50g baby rocket leaves
1 tablespoon finely chopped fresh flat-leaf parsley

1 Bring beetroot, stock and the water in large saucepan
to the boil. Reduce heat; simmer, uncovered.
2 Meanwhile, heat oil in large saucepan; cook
onion and garlic, stirring, until onion softens. Add rice;
stir rice to coat in onion mixture. Stir in 1 cup simmering
beetroot mixture; cook, stirring, over low heat until
liquid is absorbed. Continue adding beetroot mixture,
in 1-cup batches, stirring, until liquid is absorbed
after each addition. Total cooking time should be
about 35 minutes or until rice is just tender; gently
stir in cheese.
3 Serve risotto topped with combined rocket leaves
and parsley.

preparation time *30 minutes*
cooking time *45 minutes* serves *4*
nutritional count per serving *7.6g total fat (2.1g
saturated fat); 1643kJ (393 cal); 69.4g carbohydrate;
11.5g protein; 4.1g fibre*

brown rice pilaf

2 small kumara (500g), chopped coarsely
cooking-oil spray
3 cups (750ml) vegetable stock
2 teaspoons olive oil
1 small brown onion (80g), chopped finely
1 clove garlic, crushed
2 trimmed celery stalks (200g), chopped finely
150g mushrooms, chopped coarsely
1½ cup (300g) brown medium-grain rice
1 tablespoon finely grated lemon rind
½ cup loosely packed fresh flat-leaf parsley leaves

1 Preheat oven to 180°C/160°C fan-forced.
2 Place kumara on oiled oven tray; spray with oil.
Roast, uncovered, about 25 minutes or until tender.
3 Meanwhile, bring stock to the boil in medium
saucepan. Reduce heat; simmer, uncovered.
4 Heat oil in medium saucepan; cook onion, garlic
and celery, stirring, until onion softens. Add mushroom
and rice; cook, stirring, 2 minutes. Add stock, reduce
heat; simmer, covered, about 50 minutes or until
stock is absorbed and rice is tender. Stir in kumara,
rind and parsley.

preparation time *15 minutes*
cooking time *1 hour* serves *2*
nutritional count per serving *11.1g total fat (1.6g
saturated fat); 3515kJ (841 cal); 161.4g carbohydrate;
22.2g protein; 18g fibre*

grilled lamb cutlets with warm risoni salad

1 clove garlic, crushed
1 tablespoon finely chopped fresh oregano
1 tablespoon finely chopped fresh chives
2 tablespoons lemon juice
¼ cup (60ml) dry white wine
12 french-trimmed lamb cutlets (700g)

WARM RISONI SALAD

500g pumpkin, diced into 3cm pieces
1 clove garlic, crushed
1 tablespoon olive oil
1 cup (220g) risoni
150g baby spinach leaves
2 tablespoons lemon juice
2 tablespoons coarsely chopped fresh chives
2 tablespoons fresh oregano leaves

1   Combine garlic, oregano, chives, juice and wine in large bowl, add lamb; toss lamb to coat in marinade. Cover; refrigerate until required.
2   Meanwhile, make warm risoni salad.
3   Drain lamb; discard marinade. Cook lamb, in batches, on heated oiled grill plate (or grill or barbecue) until cooked as desired. Serve cutlets with salad.

WARM RISONI SALAD Preheat oven to 200°C/180°C fan-forced. Place pumpkin, in single layer, on oven tray; drizzle with combined garlic and half of the oil. Roast, uncovered, about 15 minutes or until pumpkin is browned and tender. Meanwhile, cook pasta in large saucepan of boiling water, uncovered, until just tender; drain. Place pasta and spinach in large bowl with pumpkin, juice, herbs and remaining oil; toss gently to combine.

preparation time *15 minutes*
cooking time *35 minutes* serves *4*
nutritional count per serving *11.5g total fat (3.6g saturated fat); 1735kJ (415 cal); 46.4g carbohydrate; 28g protein; 5.4g fibre*

veal cutlets with onion marmalade

2 teaspoons olive oil
1 clove garlic, crushed
1 teaspoon cracked black pepper
4 veal cutlets (680g)
20g butter
2 large red onions (600g), sliced thinly
⅓ cup (75g) firmly packed brown sugar
¼ cup (60ml) cider vinegar
2 tablespoons orange juice
2 teaspoons finely chopped fresh rosemary
2 cobs corn (800g), trimmed, cut into 3cm pieces
500g asparagus, trimmed

1   Combine oil, garlic and pepper in large bowl with veal. Cover; refrigerate until required.
2   Meanwhile, heat butter in medium frying pan; cook onion, stirring, until soft and browned lightly. Add sugar, vinegar and juice; cook, stirring, about 15 minutes or until onion caramelises. Remove from heat; stir in rosemary.
3   Cook corn and asparagus, in batches, on heated oiled grill plate (or grill or barbecue) until browned and cooked as desired. Remove; cover to keep warm.
4   Cook veal on same grill plate (or grill or barbecue) until cooked as desired.
5   Serve veal, corn and asparagus topped with onion marmalade.

preparation time *15 minutes*
cooking time *40 minutes* serves *4*
nutritional count per serving *11.7g total fat (4.1g saturated fat); 1965kJ (470 cal); 50.8g carbohydrate; 40.1g protein; 10.4g fibre*

pork cutlets with apple and cranberry relish

2 tablespoons cider vinegar
2 tablespoons olive oil
1 tablespoon dijon mustard
2 teaspoons caster sugar
4 x 235g pork cutlets
2 large unpeeled green apples (400g),
    chopped finely
1 small red onion (100g), chopped finely
½ cup (65g) dried cranberries
¼ cup (60ml) water

1 Whisk vinegar, oil, mustard and sugar in medium bowl; transfer 2 tablespoons of dressing to large bowl. Place pork in large bowl; turn to coat cutlets in dressing.
2 Combine apple, onion and cranberries in small saucepan with remaining dressing and the water. Bring to the boil; reduce heat. Simmer, covered, 5 minutes or until soft.
3 Meanwhile, cook drained pork on heated oiled grill plate (or grill or barbecue) until browned both sides and cooked as desired, brushing with dressing occasionally. Serve pork with relish.

preparation time *15 minutes*
cooking time *20 minutes* serves *4*
nutritional count per serving *25.9g total fat (7.0g saturated fat); 1877kJ (449 cal); 23.8g carbohydrate; 29.1g protein; 2.8g fibre*

mulled-wine pork and stone fruits

2 cups (500ml) water
1 cup (250ml) dry white wine
½ cup (110g) sugar
2 cinnamon sticks
5 cloves
¼ cup (60ml) brandy
2 medium peaches (300g), stoned, quartered
4 medium plums (450g), stoned, quartered
2 medium nectarines (340g), stoned, quartered
4 medium apricots (200g), stoned, quartered
800g pork fillets, trimmed
1 fresh long red chilli, sliced thinly
1 long green chilli, sliced thinly

1 Combine the water, wine and sugar in heated large frying pan, stirring constantly, without boiling, until sugar dissolves; bring to the boil. Add cinnamon, cloves, brandy and fruit, reduce heat; simmer, uncovered, about 5 minutes or until fruit is just tender. Using slotted spoon, transfer fruit to large bowl; cover to keep warm.
2 Return poaching liquid to the boil; add pork. Reduce heat; simmer, covered, about 10 minutes or until pork is cooked as desired. Cool pork in liquid 10 minutes then slice thickly. Discard poaching liquid.
3 Combine chillies with fruit; divide fruit and any fruit juices among serving bowls, top with pork.

preparation time *15 minutes*
cooking time *15 minutes* serves *4*
nutritional count per serving *4.9g total fat (1.6g saturated fat); 2094kJ (501 cal); 46.5g carbohydrate; 46.2g protein; 5.5g fibre*

thai pork salad
with kaffir lime dressing

600g pork fillets
2 tablespoons grated palm sugar
1 tablespoon finely grated lime rind
2 teaspoons peanut oil
350g watercress, trimmed
1 cup loosely packed fresh thai basil leaves
½ cup loosely packed fresh coriander leaves
½ cup loosely packed fresh mint leaves
1½ cups (120g) bean sprouts
1 medium green capsicum (200g), sliced thinly

KAFFIR LIME DRESSING

2 cloves garlic, crushed
3 shallots (75g), sliced thinly
1 fresh small red thai chilli, sliced thinly
3 fresh kaffir lime leaves, sliced thinly
¼ cup (60ml) lime juice
⅓ cup (80ml) fish sauce
2 teaspoons grated palm sugar

1   Cut pork fillets in half horizontally. Combine sugar, rind and oil in large bowl, add pork; toss pork to coat in mixture. Cook pork, in batches, in heated lightly oiled large frying pan, over medium heat, about 15 minutes or until cooked as desired. Cover pork; stand 5 minutes, then slice thinly.
2   Meanwhile, make kaffir lime dressing.
3   Place pork in large bowl with remaining ingredients and dressing; toss gently to combine.

KAFFIR LIME DRESSING Place ingredients in screw-top jar; shake well.

preparation time *15 minutes*
cooking time *15 minutes* serves *4*
nutritional count per serving *6.4g total fat (1.6g saturated fat); 1104kJ (264 cal); 12.2g carbohydrate; 38.8g protein; 5.8g fibre*

orange-glazed pork cutlets
with spinach and pecan salad

½ cup (125ml) orange juice
¼ cup (55g) white sugar
2 cloves garlic, crushed
4 pork cutlets (950g), trimmed

SPINACH AND PECAN SALAD

150g baby spinach leaves
¼ cup (35g) roasted pecans, chopped coarsely
150g snow peas, trimmed, halved
4 medium oranges (960g)

CITRUS DRESSING

2 tablespoons orange juice
1 tablespoon lemon juice
½ teaspoon dijon mustard
½ teaspoon white sugar
2 teaspoons olive oil

1   Combine juice, sugar and garlic in small saucepan, bring to the boil. Reduce heat; simmer, without stirring, about 10 minutes or until glaze reduces to about ⅓ cup.
2   Brush cutlets both sides with glaze; cook, uncovered, in heated oiled large frying pan about 10 minutes or until cooked as desired, brushing frequently with remaining glaze. Remove from pan; cover to keep warm.
3   Meanwhile, make spinach and pecan salad.
4   Make citrus dressing ingredients; pour over salad, toss gently to combine.
5   Serve cutlets with salad.

SPINACH AND PECAN SALAD Place spinach, nuts and snow peas in large bowl. Segment peeled oranges over salad to catch juice; add segments to salad.

CITRUS DRESSING Place ingredients in screw-top jar; shake well.

preparation time *20 minutes*
cooking time *20 minutes* serves *4*
nutritional count per serving *17g total fat (3.8g saturated fat); 1935kJ (463 cal); 33.2g carbohydrate; 44.1g protein; 6.4g fibre*

eggplant with salsa fresca

6 baby eggplants (360g), halved lengthways

SALSA FRESCA

1 small green capsicum (150g), chopped finely
1 small yellow capsicum (150g), chopped finely
2 small tomato (180g), seeded, chopped finely
2 tablespoons finely shredded fresh basil
2 tablespoons fresh lemon juice

1 Cook eggplant on heated oiled grill plate (or grill or barbecue) until tender.
2 Combine ingredients for salsa fresca in small bowl.
3 Serve grilled eggplant topped with salsa fresca.

preparation time *15 minutes*
cooking time *15 minutes* serves *2*
nutritional count per serving *0.8g total fat (0g saturated fat); 288kJ (69 cal); 9.6g carbohydrate; 4.6g protein; 5.9g fibre*

stir-fried asian greens with tofu

1 tablespoon peanut oil
4cm piece fresh ginger (20g), cut into slivers
1 clove garlic, crushed
200g gai lan, chopped coarsely
200g broccolini, chopped coarsely
300g baby buk choy, chopped coarsely
200g firm tofu, chopped coarsely
2 tablespoons water
1 tablespoon tamari
1 tablespoon coarsely chopped roasted peanuts

1 Heat oil in wok; stir-fry ginger and garlic until fragrant. Add vegetables, tofu, the water and tamari; stir-fry until greens are just tender.
2 Serve stir-fry sprinkled with nuts.

preparation time *10 minutes*
cooking time *10 minutes* serves *2*
nutritional count per serving *19.6g total fat (3.1g saturated fat); 1221kJ (292 cal); 6.1g carbohydrate; 23g protein; 12.8g fibre*

roasted vegetable stack

2 baby fennel bulbs (260g)
2 medium egg tomatoes (150g), halved lengthways
1 small red capsicum (150g), sliced thickly
1 medium zucchini (120g), sliced thickly lengthways
2 baby eggplants (120g), sliced thickly
cooking-oil spray
2 tablespoons finely chopped fresh flat-leaf parsley
2 tablespoons fresh lemon juice
2 teaspoons olive oil

1 Preheat oven to 200°C/180°C fan-forced.
2 Reserve fennel tips from fennel; slice fennel thinly.
3 Place vegetables on oiled oven tray; spray with oil. Roast, uncovered, about 20 minutes or until vegetables soften. Stir in half of the parsley.
4 Stack vegetables on serving plate; drizzle with combined juice and oil, sprinkle with remaining parsley and coarsely chopped reserved fennel tips.

preparation time *10 minutes*
cooking time *20 minutes* serves *2*
nutritional count per serving *7.2g total fat (0.8g saturated fat); 514kJ (123 cal); 9.7g carbohydrate; 4.1g protein; 6.5g fibre*

chive wontons with choy sum in asian broth

150g firm silken tofu
500g choy sum, trimmed
2 tablespoons finely chopped fresh chives
190g can water chestnuts, rinsed, drained, chopped finely
2 fresh long red chillies, chopped finely
30 wonton wrappers
1 litre (4 cups) vegetable stock
1 litre (4 cups) water
10cm stick fresh lemon grass (20g), chopped coarsely
2cm piece fresh ginger (10g), chopped coarsely
1 clove garlic, quartered
2 fresh kaffir lime leaves
¼ cup (60ml) light soy sauce

1   Dry tofu with absorbent paper then chop coarsely. Stand tofu on several layers of absorbent paper, cover with more paper; stand for 20 minutes. Chop finely.
2   Chop a quarter of the choy sum finely. Combine in medium bowl with tofu, chives, water chestnut and half the chilli.
3   Centre level tablespoons of tofu mixture on a wrapper. Brush wrapper edges with water; gather edges above filling, pinching together to seal. Repeat process with remaining wrappers and filling.
4   Place stock, the water, lemon grass, ginger, garlic, lime leaves, sauce and remaining chilli in large saucepan; bring to the boil. Reduce heat; simmer, uncovered, 5 minutes. Strain into large bowl; discard solids.
5   Return broth to pan; bring to the boil; cook wontons, in two batches, about 4 minutes or until cooked through. Transfer wontons to individual serving bowls.
6   Cook remaining choy sum in broth until just tender. Divide choy sum among bowls then ladle broth over choy sum and wontons.

preparation time *40 minutes (plus standing time)*
cooking time *15 minutes* serves 6
nutritional count per serving *3.2g total fat (0.7g saturated fat); 782kJ (187 cal); 27g carbohydrate; 10.9g protein; 2.2g fibre*

chickpea patties with tomato and cucumber salad

2 medium potatoes (400g)
2 x 300g cans chickpeas, rinsed, drained
1 clove garlic, crushed
2 green onions, sliced thinly
½ cup coarsely chopped fresh coriander
2 tablespoons polenta
1 lebanese cucumber (130g)
2 small egg tomatoes (130g), sliced thickly
2 tablespoons fresh lime juice
2 teaspoons pepitas
2 teaspoons sesame seeds
½ cup (140g) sheep milk yogurt

1   Preheat oven to 180°C/160°C fan-forced.
2   Boil, steam or microwave potato until tender; drain. Mash potato and chickpeas in medium bowl; stir in garlic, onion and coriander. Using hands; shape mixture into four patties. Coat with polenta; refrigerate 1 hour.
3   Cook patties in oiled medium frying pan until browned. Transfer to oven tray; bake 15 minutes or until heated.
4   Meanwhile, slice half of the cucumber thinly; combine with tomato, juice and seeds in medium bowl. Cut remaining cucumber coarsely; combine with yogurt in small bowl.
5   Serve patties with salad and yogurt.

preparation time *20 minutes (plus refrigeration time)*
cooking time *40 minutes* serves 2
nutritional count per serving *21.1g total fat (1.4g saturated fat); 2491kJ (596 cal); 64.6g carbohydrate; 24.5g protein; 18.5g fibre*

1

2

3   4

poached chicken in citrus wakame broth

5g dried wakame
3cm piece fresh ginger (15g), sliced thinly
1 fresh small red thai chilli, sliced thinly
2 cloves garlic, sliced thinly
2 kaffir lime leaves, torn
1 litre (4 cups) chicken stock
2 cups (500ml) water
2 chicken breast fillets (400g)
100g dried soba noodles
½ cup (40g) bean sprouts
2 tablespoons fish sauce
⅓ cup (80ml) lime juice
2 baby buk choy (300g), leaves separated

1 Place wakame in small bowl, cover with cold water; stand about 10 minutes or until softened. Drain then squeeze out excess water. Chop coarsely, removing any hard ribs or stems.
2 Combine ginger, chilli, garlic, lime leaves, stock, the water and chicken in large saucepan; bring to the boil. Reduce heat; simmer, uncovered, about 10 minutes or until cooked through. Cool chicken in broth 10 minutes; remove from pan. Strain broth through muslin-lined sieve over large bowl; discard solids, return broth to pan. Slice chicken thinly.
3 Meanwhile, cook noodles in large saucepan of boiling water, uncovered, until just tender; drain. Divide noodles, wakame and sprouts among serving bowls.
4 Bring broth to the boil; reduce heat and stir in sauce, juice and buk choy. Serve broth topped with chicken, and accompanied with lime wedges, if you like.

preparation time *25 minutes*
cooking time *25 minutes* serves *4*
nutritional count per serving *3.9g total fat (1.2g saturated fat); 1053kJ (252 cal); 20.9g carbohydrate; 30.7g protein; 3.3g fibre*

japanese prawn and soba salad

200g dried soba noodles
10g dried wakame
1 medium carrot (120g)
1 lebanese cucumber (130g)
16 uncooked medium king prawns (720g)
½ sheet toasted nori, shredded finely

MISO DRESSING

1 tablespoon water
2 tablespoons rice vinegar
1 tablespoon yellow miso
1 fresh long red chilli, chopped finely
2cm piece fresh ginger (10g), grated finely
1 clove garlic, crushed
1 tablespoon peanut oil

1 Cook noodles in medium saucepan of boiling water, uncovered, until just tender; drain. Rinse noodles under cold water; drain.
2 Place wakame in small bowl, cover with cold water; stand about 10 minutes or until softened. Drain then squeeze out excess water. Chop coarsely, removing hard ribs or stems.
3 Meanwhile, make miso dressing.
4 Using vegetable peeler, slice carrot and cucumber lengthways into thin ribbons.
5 Shell and devein prawns, leaving tails intact. Cook prawns in medium saucepan of boiling water, uncovered, until changed in colour. Drain on absorbent paper; cool.
6 Place noodles, wakame, carrot, cucumber and prawns in large bowl with dressing; toss gently to combine. Serve salad sprinkled with nori.

MISO DRESSING Place ingredients in screw-top jar;. shake well.

preparation time *35 minutes (plus standing time)*
cooking time *15 minutes* serves *4*
nutritional count per serving *6.1g total fat (1.1g saturated fat); 1329kJ (318 cal); 37.7g carbohydrate; 25.4g protein; 3.9g fibre*

1 POACHED CHICKEN IN CITRUS WAKAME BROTH 2 JAPANESE PRAWN AND SOBA SALAD 3 PEPITA AND SESAME CHICKEN CUTLETS WITH MINT AND PARSLEY SALAD [P 150] 4 ASIAN MILLET AND TOFU SALAD [P 150]

pepita and sesame chicken cutlets with mint and parsley salad

1 tablespoon sesame seeds
⅓ cup (65g) pepitas
2 teaspoons finely grated lime rind
2 tablespoons lime juice
2 cloves garlic, crushed
4 chicken thigh cutlets (800g)
1 egg white, beaten lightly

MINT AND PARSLEY SALAD

1 tablespoon macadamia oil
2 tablespoons lime juice
1 tablespoon cider vinegar
1 cup firmly packed fresh flat-leaf parsley leaves
1 cup firmly packed fresh mint leaves
125g cherry tomatoes, halved
2 green onions, sliced thinly

1 Preheat oven to 200°C/180°C fan-forced.
2 Combine seeds, pepitas, rind, juice and garlic in small bowl.
3 Brush chicken all over with egg white; press seed mixture onto top side only. Refrigerate chicken on oven tray, seeded-side up, 10 minutes.
4 Bake cutlets, covered, 30 minutes. Uncover; cook further 20 minutes.
5 Meanwhile, make mint and parsley salad.
6 Serve chicken with salad.

MINT AND PARSLEY SALAD Whisk oil, juice and vinegar in medium bowl. Add remaining ingredients; toss gently to combine.

preparation time *20 minutes (plus refrigeration time)*
cooking time *50 minutes* serves *4*
nutritional count per serving *21.9g total fat (4g saturated fat); 1542kJ (369 cal); 2g carbohydrate; 28.8g protein; 4.5g fibre*

asian millet and tofu salad

1 cup (200g) millet
2 fresh long red chillies, chopped finely
⅓ cup (45g) roasted unsalted coarsely chopped peanuts
400g firm marinated tofu, cut into batons
100g snow peas, trimmed, sliced lengthways
230g can bamboo shoots, rinsed, drained, sliced thinly
½ small red onion (50g), sliced thinly

MIRIN DRESSING

¼ cup (60ml) mirin
1 tablespoon japanese soy sauce
1 tablespoon rice vinegar
1 clove garlic, crushed

1 Cook millet in medium saucepan of boiling water, uncovered, until just tender; drain. Cool.
2 Meanwhile, make mirin dressing.
3 Combine millet in large bowl with chilli, nuts and half the dressing.
4 Place tofu in medium bowl with remaining ingredients and remaining dressing; toss gently to combine.
5 Serve millet mixture topped with tofu salad.

MIRIN DRESSING Place ingredients in screw-top jar; shake well.

preparation time *20 minutes*
cooking time *15 minutes* serves *4*
nutritional count per serving *14.4g total fat (2.2g saturated fat); 1676kJ (401 cal); 39.3g carbohydrate; 22g protein; 8.8g fibre*

blueberry scones with vanilla fromage frais

2 cups (300g) self-raising flour
2 tablespoons icing sugar
1¼ cups (310ml) buttermilk
150g blueberries
200g vanilla fromage frais

1 Preheat oven to 240°C/220°C fan-forced. Grease shallow 20cm-round sandwich pan.
2 Sift flour and icing sugar into large bowl; pour in enough buttermilk to mix to a sticky dough. Fold in blueberries.
3 Gently knead dough on floured surface until smooth; use hand to flatten out dough to about a 3cm thickness. Cut eight 5.5cm rounds from dough; place rounds, slightly touching, in pan.
4 Bake scones about 20 minutes or until browned; turn onto wire rack. Serve with fromage frais.

preparation time *10 minutes*
cooking time *20 minutes* makes *8*
nutritional count per scone *2.6g total fat (1.5g saturated fat); 832kJ (199 cal); 36.2g carbohydrate; 7.1g protein; 1.8g fibre*

cranberry, apricot and currant rock cakes

2 cups (300g) self-raising flour
¼ teaspoon ground cinnamon
90g cold butter, chopped
⅓ cup (75g) caster sugar
½ cup (75g) dried currants
½ cup (75g) dried apricots, chopped coarsely
½ cup (75g) dried cranberries
1 egg, beaten lightly
½ cup (125ml) milk, approximately
1 tablespoon raw sugar

1 Preheat oven to 200°C/180°C fan-forced. Grease two oven trays.
2 Combine flour and cinnamon in large bowl; rub in butter. Stir in caster sugar, fruit, egg and enough milk to give a moist but still firm consistency.
3 Drop rounded tablespoons of mixture about 5cm apart on trays; sprinkle with raw sugar.
4 Bake rock cakes about 15 minutes or until browned. Loosen cakes; cool on trays.

preparation time *15 minutes*
cooking time *15 minutes* makes *20*
nutritional count per rock cake *4.2g total fat (2.6g saturated fat); 564kJ (135 cal); 22.4g carbohydrate; 2.4g protein; 1.3g fibre*

caramelised figs with spiced yogurt

1 cup (280g) low-fat yogurt
¼ cup (35g) roasted pistachios, chopped coarsely
¼ teaspoon ground nutmeg
1 tablespoon caster sugar
6 large fresh figs (480g)
1 tablespoon honey

1 Combine yogurt, nuts, nutmeg and sugar in small bowl.
2 Halve figs lengthways. Brush cut-side of figs with honey.
3 Cook figs, cut-side down, uncovered, in heated large non-stick frying pan 5 minutes. Turn figs; cook, uncovered, 5 minutes or until browned.
4 Serve figs with spiced yogurt.

preparation time *10 minutes*
cooking time *10 minutes* serves *4*
nutritional count per serving *6g total fat (1.3g saturated fat); 777kJ (186 cal); 26.1g carbohydrate; 6.8g protein; 3.6g fibre*

lime sorbet

2 tablespoons finely grated lime rind
1 cup (220g) caster sugar
2½ cups (625ml) water
¾ cup (180ml) lime juice
1 egg white

1 Stir rind, sugar and water in medium saucepan over high heat until sugar dissolves; bring to the boil. Reduce heat; simmer without stirring, uncovered, 5 minutes. Transfer to large heatproof jug, cool to room temperature; stir in juice.
2 Pour sorbet mixture into loaf pan; cover tightly with foil; freeze 3 hours or overnight.
3 Process mixture with egg white until smooth. Return to loaf pan, cover; freeze until firm. Serve sprinkled with extra lime rind, if you like.

preparation time *20 minutes* cooking time *10 minutes (plus cooling and freezing time)* serves *8* nutritional count per serving *0.1g total fat (0g saturated fat); 472kJ (113 cal); 27.9g carbohydrate; 0.7g protein; 0.2g fibre*

grapefruit sorbet

2 tablespoons finely grated ruby grapefruit rind
1 cup (220g) caster sugar
2½ cups (625ml) water
¾ cup (180ml) ruby red grapefruit juice
1 egg white

1 Stir rind, sugar and water in medium saucepan over high heat until sugar dissolves; bring to the boil. Reduce heat; simmer without stirring, uncovered, 5 minutes. Transfer to large heatproof jug, cool to room temperature; stir in juice.
2 Pour sorbet mixture into loaf pan; cover tightly with foil; freeze 3 hours or overnight.
3 Process mixture with egg white until smooth. Return to loaf pan, cover; freeze until firm. Serve sprinkled with extra grapefruit rind, if you like.

preparation time *20 minutes* cooking time *10 minutes (plus cooling and freezing time)* serves *8* nutritional count per serving *0g total fat (0g saturated fat); 481kJ (115 cal); 29.3g carbohydrate; 0.6g protein; 0.1g fibre*

blood orange sorbet

2 tablespoons finely grated blood orange rind
1 cup (220g) caster sugar
2½ cups (625ml) water
1 cup (250ml) blood orange juice
1 egg white

1 Stir rind, sugar and water in medium saucepan over high heat until sugar dissolves; bring to the boil. Reduce heat; simmer without stirring, uncovered, 5 minutes. Transfer to large heatproof jug, cool to room temperature; stir in juice.
2 Pour sorbet mixture into loaf pan; cover tightly with foil; freeze 3 hours or overnight.
3 Process mixture with egg white until smooth. Return to loaf pan, cover; freeze until firm. Serve sprinkled with extra orange rind, if you like.

preparation time *20 minutes* cooking time *10 minutes (plus cooling and freezing time)* serves *8* nutritional count per serving *0g total fat (0g saturated fat); 497kJ (119 cal); 30.2g carbohydrate; 0.6g protein; 0.1g fibre*

FROM TOP TO BOTTOM: LIME SORBET, GRAPEFRUIT SORBET, BLOOD ORANGE SORBET

plum and apple crumble

4 medium blood plums (450g), cut into thin wedges
2 tablespoons lemon juice
2 tablespoons water
4 medium apples (600g), cut into thin wedges
1 tablespoon honey

CRUMBLE TOPPING

½ cup (45g) rolled oats
½ cup (100g) pepitas
½ cup (75g) sunflower seed kernels
½ cup (70g) coarsely chopped roasted hazelnuts
2 tablespoons honey
1 tablespoon walnut oil

RICOTTA CREAM

⅔ cup (130g) low-fat ricotta cheese
1 teaspoon ground cinnamon
2 tablespoons low-fat milk

1   Preheat oven to 180°C/160°C fan-forced.
Grease six 1¼-cup (310ml) ovenproof dishes.
2   Combine plum, half the juice and half the water
in medium saucepan; cook over low heat, stirring
occasionally, 10 minutes.
3   Combine apple, remaining juice and the remaining
water in another medium saucepan; cook over low
heat, stirring occasionally, 5 minutes. Combine plum
and apple mixtures in medium bowl with honey.
4   Meanwhile, make crumble topping.
5   Divide fruit mixture among dishes; sprinkle with crumble
topping. Bake 30 minutes or until golden brown.
6   Make ricotta cream.
7   Serve plum and apple crumble with ricotta cream.

CRUMBLE TOPPING Combine ingredients in small bowl.

RICOTTA CREAM Beat ingredients in small deep bowl
with electric mixer until smooth.

preparation time *15 minutes*
cooking time *45 minutes* serves *6*
nutritional count per serving *24.8g total fat (2.4g
saturated fat); 1810kJ (433 cal); 31.2g carbohydrate;
8.6g protein; 7.4g fibre*

date and apple muesli slice

2 medium apples (300g), grated coarsely
2 tablespoons lemon juice
¼ cup (60ml) water
50g butter
2 cups (340g) seeded dates
2 cups (220g) natural muesli
1 cup (220g) firmly packed brown sugar
1 cup (150g) plain flour
1 teaspoon ground cinnamon

1   Preheat oven to 180°C/160°C fan-forced.
Grease 25cm x 30cm swiss roll pan.
2   Combine apple, juice, the water, butter and dates
in medium saucepan; bring to the boil. Reduce heat;
simmer, covered, about 5 minutes or until apple is soft.
Uncover; cook, stirring occasionally, about 5 minutes or
until mixture thickens to a paste-like consistency.
3   Meanwhile, place muesli in large frying pan; stir
over low heat about 5 minutes or until browned.
4   Combine muesli in large bowl with sugar, flour and
cinnamon; stir in date mixture. Spread mixture into pan.
5   Bake slice, uncovered, about 20 minutes or until firm.
Cool in pan before cutting.

preparation time *15 minutes*
cooking time *35 minutes* makes *32*
nutritional count per piece *1.6g total fat (1g
saturated fat); 326kJ (79 cal); 15.6g carbohydrate;
1g protein; 1g fibre*

pear, rhubarb and ricotta tarts

1¼ cups (250g) low-fat ricotta cheese
2 egg yolks
2 tablespoons caster sugar
2 teaspoons plain flour
½ cup (55g) finely chopped fresh rhubarb
1 small pear (180g), quartered, sliced thinly
    lengthways
1 tablespoon caster sugar, extra

1 Preheat oven to 200°C/180°C fan-forced. Grease
four 10cm-round deep fluted tins; place on oven tray.
2 Beat cheese, egg yolks, sugar and flour in small
bowl with electric mixer until smooth; stir in rhubarb.
3 Spread mixture into tins; top each with pear, sprinkle
with extra sugar.
4 Bake tarts about 25 minutes or until filling sets. Cool
10 minutes, cover; refrigerate until cold.

preparation time *15 minutes* cooking time *25 minutes*
(plus refrigeration time) makes 4
nutritional count per tart *8.3g total fat (4.4g*
saturated fat); 803kJ (192 cal); 21.2g carbohydrate;
8.5g protein; 1.4g fibre

cranberry, oatmeal and cinnamon scones

1 cup (160g) wholemeal self-raising flour
1 cup (150g) self-raising flour
½ cup (70g) fine oatmeal
1 teaspoon ground cinnamon
½ teaspoon finely grated lemon rind
30g butter
¾ cup (105g) dried cranberries
1 cup (250ml) milk
2 tablespoons honey
1 tablespoon milk, extra
1 tablespoon oatmeal, extra
1 cup (200g) ricotta cheese

1 Preheat oven to 220°C/200°C fan-forced.
Grease and flour deep19cm-square cake pan.
2 Combine flours, oatmeal, cinnamon and rind
in large bowl; rub in butter. Stir in cranberries, milk
and honey.
3 Knead dough on floured surface until smooth. Press
dough to a 2cm-thickness. Cut 12 x 5.5cm rounds
from dough; place in pan. Brush with extra milk then
sprinkle with extra oatmeal.
4 Bake scones about 25 minutes. Serve warm with
cheese, and extra honey, if you like.

preparation time *10 minutes*
cooking time *25 minutes* makes *12*
nutritional count per scone *6.1g total fat (3.5g*
saturated fat); 836kJ (200 cal); 27.6g carbohydrate;
7g protein; 3.5g fibre

frozen passionfruit yogurt

You need approximately six passionfruit for this recipe.

½ cup (110g) caster sugar
¼ cup (60ml) water
1 teaspoon gelatine
2 cups (560g) low-fat yogurt
½ cup (125ml) passionfruit pulp

1 Stir sugar and the water in small saucepan over
low heat until sugar dissolves; transfer to medium jug.
2 Sprinkle gelatine over sugar syrup, stirring until
gelatine dissolves.
3 Combine yogurt and pulp in jug with syrup.
Pour yogurt mixture into loaf pan, cover tightly
with foil; freeze 3 hours or until almost set.
4 Scrape yogurt from bottom and sides of pan
with fork; return to freezer until firm.

preparation time *10 minutes (plus freezing time)*
cooking time *5 minutes* serves *4*
nutritional count per serving *2.5g total fat (1.5g*
saturated fat); 924kJ (221 cal); 39.9g carbohydrate;
8.6g protein; 4.3g fibre

summer berry stack

450g brioche loaf
250g strawberries, sliced thickly
150g raspberries
150g blueberries
1 tablespoon icing sugar

BLACKBERRY COULIS

300g frozen blackberries
¼ cup (40g) icing sugar
¼ cup (60ml) water

1 Make blackberry coulis.
2 Cut 12 x 1cm-thick slices from brioche loaf;
using 7cm cutter, cut one round from each slice.
3 Combine berries in medium bowl.
4 Place one round on each plate; divide a third of
the berries among rounds. Place another round on
top of each stack; divide half of the remaining berries
among stacks. Place remaining rounds on berry stacks;
top with remaining berries.
5 Pour coulis over stacks; dust with sifted icing sugar.

BLACKBERRY COULIS Stir ingredients in medium
saucepan over high heat; bring to the boil. Reduce
heat; simmer, uncovered, 3 minutes. Strain coulis into
medium jug; cool 10 minutes.

preparation time *20 minutes*
cooking time *5 minutes* serves *4*
nutritional count per serving *7.2g total fat (3g
saturated fat); 1313kJ (314 cal); 55.3g carbohydrate;
7.5g protein; 9.7g fibre*

spiced stone-fruit strudel

2 medium peaches (300g), quartered, sliced thinly
2 medium nectarines (340g), quartered, sliced thinly
2 tablespoons brown sugar
½ cup (80g) sultanas
1½ teaspoons ground cinnamon
½ teaspoon ground nutmeg
⅓ cup (25g) fresh breadcrumbs
6 sheets fillo pastry
20g butter, melted
2 tablespoons milk
2 teaspoons icing sugar

1 Combine peach, nectarine, brown sugar, sultanas,
spices and breadcrumbs in medium bowl.
2 Preheat oven to 200°C/180°C fan-forced.
Grease oven tray; line with baking paper.
3 Stack fillo sheets, brushing all sheets with half of
the combined butter and milk. Cut fillo stack in half
widthways; cover one stack with baking paper, then
with a damp tea towel, to prevent drying out.
4 Place half of the fruit mixture along centre of
uncovered fillo stack; roll from one side to enclose
filling, sealing ends of roll with a little of the remaining
butter mixture. Place strudel, seam-side down, on tray;
brush all over with a little of the remaining butter mixture.
Repeat process with remaining fillo stack, fruit mixture
and butter mixture.
5 Bake strudels, uncovered, about 25 minutes or until
browned. Cut each strudel in half widthways; divide
among plates, dust with sifted icing sugar.

preparation time *20 minutes*
cooking time *25 minutes* serves *4*
nutritional count per serving *5.5g total fat (3.1g
saturated fat); 1191kJ (285 cal); 53.1g carbohydrate;
5.9g protein; 4.2g fibre*

1 SUMMER BERRY STACK 2 SPICED STONE-FRUIT STRUDEL
3 BANANA MUFFINS WITH CRUNCHY TOPPING [P 158]
4 PAVLOVA ROLL WITH BANANA, KIWI AND PASSIONFRUIT [P 158]

1

2

3

4

banana muffins with crunchy topping

You need approximately two large (460g) overripe bananas for this recipe.

1¾ cups (280g) wholemeal self-raising flour
¾ cup (165g) firmly packed brown sugar
1 cup mashed banana
1 egg, beaten lightly
1 cup (250ml) buttermilk
¼ cup (60ml) vegetable oil

CRUNCHY OAT TOPPING

1 cup (90g) rolled oats
½ teaspoon ground nutmeg
2 tablespoons honey

1   Preheat oven to 200°C/180°C fan-forced. Grease 12-hole (⅓-cup/80ml) muffin pan.
2   Make crunchy oat topping.
3   Sift flour and sugar into large bowl; stir in banana, egg, buttermilk and oil. Divide mixture among pan holes; sprinkle with topping.
4   Bake muffins about 20 minutes. Stand in pan 5 minutes; turn onto wire rack to cool.

CRUNCHY OAT TOPPING   Blend or process oats until coarsely chopped. Combine oats with nutmeg and honey in small bowl.

preparation time *20 minutes*
cooking time *20 minutes* makes *12*
nutritional count per muffin *6.6g total fat (1.2g saturated fat); 1041kJ (249 cal); 42.5g carbohydrate; 5.6g protein; 3.7g fibre*

pavlova roll with banana, kiwi and passionfruit

You need approximately four passionfruit for this recipe.

4 egg whites
¾ cup (165g) caster sugar
1 teaspoon cornflour
1 teaspoon white vinegar
1 teaspoon vanilla extract
1 tablespoon icing sugar
300ml thickened light cream
1 large banana (230g), halved lengthways, sliced thinly
2 medium kiwifruit (170g), quartered lengthways
⅓ cup (80ml) passionfruit pulp

1   Preheat oven to 160°C/140°C fan-forced. Grease 25cm x 30cm swiss roll pan; line base with baking paper, extending paper 5cm over long sides of pan.
2   Beat egg whites in small bowl with electric mixer until soft peaks form. Gradually add caster sugar, 1 tablespoon at a time, beating until sugar dissolves between additions; fold in cornflour, vinegar and extract. Spread meringue mixture into pan
3   Bake meringue, uncovered, about 20 minutes or until browned. Turn meringue onto sheet of baking paper sprinkled with half of the sifted icing sugar; remove lining paper, trim short ends of meringue.
4   Beat cream and remaining sifted icing sugar in small bowl with electric mixer until soft peaks form.
5   Spread cream mixture over slightly warm meringue; place fruit lengthways along centre of meringue. Roll meringue firmly from long side, using paper as a guide. Refrigerate until ready to serve.

preparation time *25 minutes*
cooking time *20 minutes* serves *10*
nutritional count per serving *8.1g total fat (5.3g saturated fat); 748kJ (179 cal); 24.6g carbohydrate; 3g protein; 1.9g fibre*

pineapple and kiwifruit salad in basil lemon syrup

1½ cups (375ml) water
2 x 5cm strips lemon rind
½ cup (125ml) lemon juice
1 tablespoon caster sugar
¼ cup firmly packed fresh basil leaves
1 small pineapple (900g), quartered, sliced thinly
6 medium kiwifruit (510g), sliced thinly
⅓ cup (80ml) passionfruit pulp
1 tablespoon finely shredded fresh basil

1 Combine the water, rind, juice, sugar and basil leaves in medium frying pan; bring to the boil. Reduce heat; simmer, uncovered, 20 minutes. Strain syrup into medium jug; discard rind and basil. Cool 10 minutes; refrigerate.
2 Just before serving, combine syrup in large bowl with remaining ingredients.

preparation time *20 minutes (plus refrigeration time)* cooking time *20 minutes* serves *4*
nutritional count per serving *0.5g total fat (0g saturated fat); 627kJ (150 cal); 26.6g carbohydrate; 3.6g protein; 9g fibre*

frozen mango parfait

1 medium mango (430g), chopped coarsely
2 cups (440g) low-fat ricotta cheese
¾ cup (165g) caster sugar
300ml light thickened cream

TROPICAL FRUIT SALSA

¼ cup (55g) caster sugar
¼ cup (60ml) water
2 medium kiwifruit (170g), chopped coarsely
1 medium mango (430g), chopped coarsely
2 kaffir lime leaves, sliced thinly

1 Line base of 14cm x 21cm loaf pan with foil, extending 5cm over edges.
2 Blend or process mango until smooth.
3 Beat ricotta and sugar in small bowl with electric mixer until smooth; transfer mixture to large bowl.
4 Beat cream in small bowl with electric mixer until soft peaks form; fold cream into ricotta mixture.
5 Drop alternate spoonfuls of ricotta mixture and mango pulp into pan. Pull skewer backwards and forwards through mixture several times for marbled effect; smooth surface with spatula. Cover with foil; freeze overnight.
6 Make tropical fruit salsa 1 hour before serving. Cover; refrigerate until cold.
7 Serve parfait topped with salsa.

TROPICAL FRUIT SALSA Combine sugar and the water in small saucepan; bring to the boil. Reduce heat; simmer, uncovered, without stirring, 5 minutes; cool. Combine sugar syrup with remaining ingredients in medium bowl.

preparation time *20 minutes (plus freezing time)* serves *12*
nutritional count per serving *12.3g total fat (8g saturated fat); 986kJ (236 cal); 27.4g carbohydrate; 4.7g protein; 1.2g fibre*

TRIED & TRUE

roast loin of pork with balsamic glaze

2 sprigs fresh rosemary
2.5kg boneless loin of pork, rind on
1 tablespoon olive oil
1 tablespoon sea salt flakes
700g spring onions
2 bulbs garlic

BALSAMIC GLAZE

½ cup (125ml) balsamic vinegar
1⅓ cups (330ml) chicken stock
1 teaspoon cornflour
1 tablespoon water
10g butter

1 Preheat oven to 250°C/230°C fan-forced.
2 Tuck the rosemary into the string under the pork. Place pork in large baking dish. Rub the rind with oil then salt. Roast, uncovered, about 40 minutes or until rind blisters. Drain excess fat from dish.
3 Meanwhile, trim onions, leaving 4cm long stems. Cut tops from garlic bulbs.
4 Reduce oven to 180°C/160°C fan-forced. Place onions and garlic in baking dish with pork. Roast about 1 hour or until pork is cooked through.
5 Transfer pork to heated plate; cover with foil, stand while making balsamic glaze. Drain juices from dish into a large heatproof jug; skim fat from top.
6 Make balsamic glaze.
7 Serve pork with vegetables and glaze.

BALSAMIC GLAZE Heat same baking dish on stove; add vinegar, simmer, uncovered, until syrupy and reduced to about 2 tablespoons. Whisk in stock, reserved pan juices with blended cornflour and the water. Stir until mixture boils and thickens slightly. Add butter, stir until melted. Strain glaze through a fine sieve.

preparation time *10 minutes*
cooking time *1 hour 45 minutes serves 9*
nutritional count per serving *23.6g total fat (8.2g saturated fat); 1956kJ (468 cal); 2.7g carbohydrate; 60.3g protein; 2.1g fibre*

chicken, mushroom and asparagus creamy pasta bake

375g rigatoni pasta
60g butter
600g chicken breast fillets, cut into 1cm pieces
100g button mushrooms, sliced thinly
2 tablespoons plain flour
2 cups (500ml) milk
½ cup (40g) coarsely grated romano cheese
1¼ cups (150g) coarsely grated cheddar cheese
170g asparagus, trimmed, chopped coarsely
¼ cup coarsely chopped fresh flat-leaf parsley

1 Preheat oven to 200°C/180°C fan-forced.
2 Cook pasta in large saucepan of boiling water, uncovered, until just tender; drain.
3 Meanwhile, heat one-third of the butter in large frying pan; cook chicken, in batches, until browned and cooked through.
4 Heat remaining butter in same pan; cook mushrooms, stirring, until tender. Add flour; cook, stirring, 1 minute. Gradually stir in milk. Stir over medium heat until mixture boils and thickens. Stir in chicken, ¼ cup of the romano, ¾ cup of the cheddar and the asparagus.
5 Combine chicken mixture and drained pasta in 2.5-litre (10-cup) ovenproof dish; sprinkle with remaining cheeses. Bake, uncovered, about 15 minutes or until top browns. Serve pasta bake sprinkled with parsley, and a mixed green salad, if you like.

preparation time *20 minutes*
cooking time *30 minutes serves 4*
nutritional count per serving *37.3g total fat (22.3g saturated fat); 3775kJ (903 cal); 75.2g carbohydrate; 64g protein; 4.8g fibre*

chicken, chorizo and okra gumbo

1.5kg whole chicken
2 medium carrots (240g), chopped coarsely
2 trimmed celery stalks (200g), chopped coarsely
1 medium brown onion (150g), chopped coarsely
12 black peppercorns
1 bay leaf
3 litres (12 cups) water
60g butter
1 small brown onion (80g), chopped finely, extra
2 cloves garlic, crushed
1 medium red capsicum (200g), chopped finely
2 teaspoons dried oregano
1 teaspoon sweet paprika
¼ teaspoon cayenne pepper
¼ teaspoon ground clove
¼ cup (35g) plain flour
¼ cup (70g) tomato paste
400g can crushed tomatoes
100g fresh okra, halved diagonally
1 cup (200g) calrose rice
1 chorizo sausage (170g), sliced thinly

1 Place chicken, carrot, celery, onion, peppercorns, bay leaf and the water in large saucepan; bring to the boil. Reduce heat; simmer, covered, 1½ hours.
2 Remove chicken from pan. Strain broth through muslin-lined sieve or colander into large heatproof bowl; discard solids. When chicken is cool enough to handle, remove and discard skin and bones; shred meat coarsely.
3 Melt butter in large saucepan; cook extra onion and garlic, stirring, until onion softens. Add capsicum, herbs and spices; cook, stirring, until mixture is fragrant. Add flour and paste; cook, stirring, 1 minute. Gradually stir in reserved broth and undrained tomatoes; bring to the boil, stirring. Stir in okra and rice, reduce heat; simmer, uncovered, 15 minutes, stirring occasionally, or until rice is tender.
4 Meanwhile, heat large oiled frying pan; cook chorizo until browned; drain. Add chorizo and chicken to gumbo; stir over medium heat until hot.

preparation time *30 minutes*
cooking time *2 hours 45 minutes* serves *8*
nutritional count per serving *26.8g total fat (5.7g saturated fat); 2011kJ (481 cal); 30.5g carbohydrate; 27.8g protein; 3.9g fibre*

cheese and herb-stuffed beef sirloin roast

2.5kg boneless beef sirloin roast
2 large kumara (1kg)
1kg potatoes, cut into wedges
2 tablespoons olive oil
2 tablespoons lemon juice
2 teaspoons sweet paprika
1 clove garlic, crushed
2 tablespoons plain flour
⅓ cup (80ml) dry red wine
1½ cups (375ml) beef stock

CHEESE AND HERB STUFFING

50g butter
2 rindless bacon rashers (130g), chopped finely
1 medium brown onion (150g), chopped finely
1 clove garlic, crushed
1½ cups (105g) stale breadcrumbs
½ cup (40g) coarsely grated parmesan cheese
1 egg
1 tablespoon wholegrain mustard
2 tablespoons finely chopped fresh oregano
2 tablespoons finely chopped fresh flat-leaf parsley
2 teaspoons finely grated lemon rind

1 Make cheese and herb stuffing.

2 Preheat oven to 220°C/200°C fan-forced.

3 Cut between fat and meat of beef, making a pocket for stuffing; trim and discard a little of the fat. Spoon stuffing into pocket; lay fat over stuffing to enclose. Tie beef with kitchen string at 2cm intervals; place beef on wire rack over shallow large baking dish.

4 Roast, uncovered, about 1½ hours.

5 Meanwhile, cut kumara into thirds crossways; cut each piece into wedges. Combine kumara with potato, oil, juice, paprika and garlic in shallow large baking dish; roast about 1 hour.

6 Remove beef from dish; cover, stand 10 minutes. Slice beef thinly.

7 Reserve 2 tablespoons of beef juices in baking dish; place over heat. Add flour; cook, stirring, until mixture thickens and bubbles. Gradually add wine and stock, stirring, until gravy boils and thickens slightly.

8 Serve beef with potato and kumara wedges and gravy.

CHEESE AND HERB STUFFING Melt butter in medium frying pan; cook bacon, onion and garlic, stirring, until onion softens. Cool. Combine bacon mixture with remaining ingredients in medium bowl.

preparation time *35 minutes*
cooking time *1 hour 50 minutes* serves *8*
nutritional count per serving *43.5g total fat (19g saturated fat); 3716kJ (889 cal); 41.6g carbohydrate; 78.7g protein; 4.8g fibre*

spinach salad with mushrooms, poached egg and anchovy dressing

40g butter
2 flat mushrooms (200g), sliced thickly
100g swiss brown mushrooms, sliced thickly
100g shiitake mushrooms, sliced thickly
4 eggs
270g char-grilled capsicum in oil, drained, sliced thinly
300g baby spinach leaves

ANCHOVY DRESSING

2 tablespoons coarsely chopped fresh sage
1 tablespoon drained capers, rinsed
6 drained anchovy fillets
2 tablespoons balsamic vinegar
¼ cup (60ml) olive oil
2 tablespoons water

1 Make anchovy dressing.
2 Melt butter in large frying pan; cook mushrooms, stirring, until tender. Place in large bowl; cover.
3 Half-fill a large shallow frying pan with water; bring to the boil. Break eggs into cup, one at a time, then slide into pan. When all eggs are in pan, allow water to return to the boil. Cover pan, turn off heat; stand about 4 minutes or until a light film of egg white sets over yolks. Remove eggs, one at a time, using slotted spoon, and place on absorbent-paper-lined saucer to blot up poaching liquid.
4 Add capsicum and half of the dressing to mushroom mixture in large bowl; toss gently to combine.
5 Divide spinach among serving plates; top with mushroom mixture and egg, drizzle with remaining dressing.

ANCHOVY DRESSING Blend or process ingredients until combined.

preparation time *20 minutes*
cooking time *10 minutes* serves *4*
nutritional count per serving *32.6g total fat (9.4g saturated fat); 1526kJ (365 cal); 2.5g carbohydrate; 14.2g protein; 4.6g fibre*

classic caesar salad

½ loaf ciabatta (220g)
1 clove garlic, crushed
⅓ cup (80ml) olive oil
2 eggs
3 baby cos lettuces, trimmed, leaves separated
1 cup (80g) shaved parmesan cheese

CAESAR DRESSING

1 clove garlic, crushed
1 tablespoon dijon mustard
2 tablespoons lemon juice
2 teaspoons worcestershire sauce
2 tablespoons olive oil

1 Preheat oven to 180°C/160°C fan-forced.
2 Cut bread into 2cm cubes; combine garlic and oil in large bowl with bread. Toast bread on oven tray until croutons are browned.
3 Make caesar dressing.
4 Bring water to the boil in small saucepan, add eggs; cover pan tightly, remove from heat. Remove eggs from water after 2 minutes. When cool enough to handle, break eggs into large bowl; add lettuce, mixing gently so egg coats leaves.
5 Add cheese, croutons and dressing to bowl; toss gently to combine.

CAESAR DRESSING Place ingredients in screw-top jar; shake well.

preparation time *30 minutes*
cooking time *15 minutes* serves *4*
nutritional count per serving *39.1g total fat (9.1g saturated fat); 2366kJ (566 cal); 33.1g carbohydrate; 18.4g protein; 5.6g fibre*

hungarian goulash

2 tablespoons olive oil
40g butter
900g boneless veal shoulder, diced into 2cm pieces
2 medium brown onions (300g), chopped finely
1 tablespoon tomato paste
1 tablespoon plain flour
1 tablespoon sweet paprika
2 teaspoons caraway seeds
½ teaspoon cayenne pepper
2 cloves garlic, crushed
2 cups (500ml) water
1.5 litres (6 cups) beef stock
400g can crushed tomatoes
1 large red capsicum (350g), chopped coarsely
1 medium potato (200g), chopped coarsely

SPATZLE

1 cup (150g) plain flour
2 eggs, beaten lightly
¼ cup (60ml) water
½ teaspoon cracked black pepper

1 Heat half the oil and half the butter in large saucepan; cook veal, in batches, until browned all over.
2 Heat remaining oil and remaining butter in same pan; cook onion, stirring, about 5 minutes or until onion is slightly caramelised.
3 Add paste, flour, paprika, seeds, cayenne and garlic; cook, stirring, 2 minutes. Return veal to pan with the water, stock and undrained tomatoes; bring to the boil. Reduce heat; simmer, uncovered, 1½ hours. Add capsicum and potato; simmer, uncovered, about 10 minutes or until potato is tender.
4 Meanwhile, make spätzle.
5 Serve bowls of soup topped with spätzle.

SPATZLE Place flour in small bowl, make well in centre. Gradually add combined egg and the water, stirring, until batter is smooth; stir in pepper. Pour batter into metal colander set over large saucepan of boiling water; using a wooden spoon, push batter through holes of colander. Bring water back to the boil; boil, uncovered, about 2 minutes or until spätzle float to the surface. Use a slotted spoon to remove spätzle; drain.

preparation time *25 minutes*
cooking time *2 hours* serves *4*
nutritional count per serving *27.3g total fat (9.5g saturated fat); 3022kJ (723 cal); 48g carbohydrate; 68.8g protein; 5.8g fibre*

caramelised onion and prosciutto glazed meatloaf

1 tablespoon olive oil
2 large brown onions (400g), sliced thinly
¼ cup (55g) firmly packed brown sugar
¼ cup (60ml) cider vinegar
12 slices prosciutto (180g)
1kg beef mince
1 egg
1 cup (70g) stale breadcrumbs
2 tablespoons tomato paste
1 clove garlic, crushed
⅓ cup (95g) tomato sauce
⅓ cup (95g) barbecue sauce
2 tablespoons wholegrain mustard
2 tablespoons brown sugar, extra
¼ cup (60ml) water

PARSNIP MASH

3 medium potatoes (600g), chopped coarsely
2 medium parsnips (500g), chopped coarsely
40g butter, chopped coarsely
½ cup (125ml) hot milk

1 Heat oil in large frying pan; cook onion, stirring, about 5 minutes or until soft and browned. Add sugar and vinegar; cook, stirring, about 15 minutes or until onion is caramelised. Cool.

2 Preheat oven to 200°C/180°C fan-forced. Oil 14cm x 21cm loaf pan; line base and long sides of pan with prosciutto slices, allowing 7cm overhang on long sides of pan.

3 Combine mince, egg, breadcrumbs, paste and garlic in large bowl. Press two-thirds of the beef mixture into pan; top with onion mixture, cover with remaining beef mixture. Fold prosciutto slices over to cover beef mixture.

4 Bake loaf, covered, 40 minutes. Remove loaf from oven. Drain excess juices from pan.

5 Turn pan upside-down onto foil-lined oven tray; remove pan. Combine half the sauces, half the mustard and half the extra sugar in small bowl. Brush loaf with sauce mixture; bake, uncovered, basting occasionally with sauce mixture, about 20 minutes or until loaf is cooked through. Stand 10 minutes; slice thickly.

6 Meanwhile, make parsnip mash.

7 To make mustard glaze, combine the water with remaining sauces, mustard and sugar in small saucepan; stir over low heat until sugar dissolves. Bring to the boil; reduce heat. Simmer, uncovered, 2 minutes.

8 Serve meatloaf with parsnip mash and mustard glaze.

PARSNIP MASH Boil, steam or microwave potato and parsnip until tender; drain. Mash vegetables in large bowl with butter and milk until smooth.

preparation time *40 minutes*
cooking time *1 hour 30 minutes* serves *4*
nutritional count per serving *36.5g total fat (15.6g saturated fat); 4000kJ (957 cal); 81.1g carbohydrate; 71.3g protein; 8g fibre*

steaks with red wine shallot sauce

1 tablespoon olive oil
4 boneless sirloin steaks (800g)
20g butter
12 shallots (300g), halved
¼ cup (60ml) red wine
1 teaspoon red wine vinegar
1 cup (250ml) beef stock
1 teaspoon worcestershire sauce

HERB MASH

1kg potatoes, peeled, cut into 3cm pieces
40g butter, softened
1 cup (250ml) hot milk
2 teaspoons finely chopped fresh flat-leaf parsley
2 teaspoons finely chopped fresh chives

1 Make herb mash.
2 Meanwhile, heat oil in large frying pan; cook steaks until cooked as desired. Remove from pan, cover to keep warm.
3 Remove excess oil from pan; add butter and shallots. Cook, stirring, until soft. Stir in wine and vinegar; bring to the boil. Add stock and sauce; cook, stirring, until the mixture boils and thickens.
4 Serve steaks with red wine sauce, herb mash and, if you like, steamed green beans.

HERB MASH Boil, steam or microwave potatoes until tender. Mash with butter and milk. Stir in herbs; cover to keep warm.

preparation time *20 minutes*
cooking time *20 minutes* serves *4*
nutritional count per serving *32.2g total fat (15.8g saturated fat); 2675kJ (640 cal); 33.6g carbohydrate; 49.9g protein; 4.1g fibre*

beer-battered fish with lemon mayonnaise

You can use any firm white fish, such as perch, ling or blue-eye, for this recipe.

⅔ cup (200g) mayonnaise
2 teaspoons finely grated lemon rind
¼ teaspoon cracked black pepper
1 teaspoon lemon juice
¾ cup (110g) self-raising flour
¾ cup (110g) plain flour
1 teaspoon five-spice powder
1 egg
1½ cups (375ml) beer
vegetable oil, for deep-frying
600g white fish fillets

1 Combine mayonnaise, rind, pepper and juice in small bowl.
2 Whisk flours, five-spice, egg and beer in medium bowl until smooth.
3 Heat oil in large saucepan. Dip fish in batter; deep-fry fish, in batches, until cooked through.
4 Serve fish with mayonnaise, and lemon wedges, if you like.

preparation time *10 minutes*
cooking time *20 minutes* serves *4*
nutritional count per serving *29.7g total fat (4.4g saturated fat); 2746kJ (657 cal); 51.2g carbohydrate; 38.7g protein; 2.4g fibre*

osso buco with semi-dried tomatoes and olives

12 pieces veal osso buco (3kg)
¼ cup (35g) plain flour
¼ cup (60ml) olive oil
40g butter
1 medium brown onion (150g), chopped coarsely
2 cloves garlic, chopped finely
3 trimmed celery stalks (300g), chopped coarsely
2 large carrots (360g), chopped coarsely
4 medium tomatoes (600g), chopped coarsely
2 tablespoons tomato paste
1 cup (250ml) dry white wine
1 cup (250ml) beef stock
400g can crushed tomatoes
4 sprigs fresh lemon thyme
½ cup (75g) drained semi-dried tomatoes
¼ cup (60ml) lemon juice
1 tablespoon finely grated lemon rind
½ cup (75g) seeded kalamata olives

GREMOLATA

1 tablespoon finely grated lemon rind
⅓ cup finely chopped fresh flat-leaf parsley
2 cloves garlic, chopped finely

1 Coat veal in flour; shake off excess. Heat oil in large deep saucepan; cook veal, in batches, until browned all over.
2 Melt butter in same pan; cook onion, garlic, celery and carrot, stirring, until vegetables just soften. Stir in fresh tomato, paste, wine, stock, undrained tomatoes and thyme. Return veal to pan, fitting pieces upright and tightly together in single layer; bring to the boil. Reduce heat; simmer, covered, 1¾ hours. Stir in semi-dried tomatoes; simmer, uncovered, about 30 minutes or until veal is tender.
3 Meanwhile, make gremolata.
4 Remove veal from pan; cover to keep warm. Bring sauce to the boil; boil, uncovered, about 10 minutes or until sauce thickens slightly. Stir in juice, rind and olives.
5 Divide veal among serving plates; top with sauce, sprinkle with gremolata. Serve veal with soft polenta, if you like.

GREMOLATA Combine ingredients in small bowl.

preparation time *30 minutes*
cooking time *2 hours 45 minutes* serves 6
nutritional count per serving *21.4g total fat (6.6g saturated fat); 2855kJ (683 cal); 22.3g carbohydrate; 89g protein; 8.1g fibre*

caponata

2 medium red capsicums (400g)
3 trimmed celery stalks (300g)
2 small red onions (200g)
2 medium tomatoes (300g)
2 medium eggplants (600g)
1 tablespoon olive oil
1 clove garlic, chopped finely
cooking-oil spray
½ cup (110g) white sugar
1 cup (250ml) red wine vinegar
½ cup (80g) sultanas
100g seeded black olives
⅓ cup (50g) pine nuts, roasted
1½ tablespoons drained capers, rinsed

1 Cut capsicums, celery, onions, tomatoes and eggplants into 2cm pieces.
2 Heat oil in large frying pan, cook capsicum, celery, onion, tomato and garlic, in batches, until soft; transfer to large bowl.
3 Spray eggplant all over with oil, cook eggplant in batches, until browned. Add to capsicum mixture.
4 Cook sugar in medium frying pan over low heat, without stirring or boiling, until dissolved, swirling pan occasionally. Cook about 5 minutes or until browned lightly. Add vinegar, bring to the boil; reduce heat, simmer, uncovered, until liquid is reduced by a third; cool to room temperature.
5 Add vinegar mixture to vegetables with sultanas, olives, nuts and capers; stir until combined. Stand for 1 hour at room temperature before serving.

preparation time *15 minutes* cooking time *20 minutes (plus cooling and standing time)* serves *6* nutritional count per serving *10g total fat (0.8g saturated fat); 1137kJ (272 cal); 40.6g carbohydrate; 4.9g protein; 6.1g fibre*

garlic and rosemary smoked lamb

Smoking chips and smoke box are available from barbecue specialty shops. When using indirect heat with a gas burner, place the food in a preheated, covered barbecue, then turn the burners directly under the food off, while keeping the side burners on.

1kg boned, rolled lamb loin
4 cloves garlic, halved
8 fresh rosemary sprigs
1 teaspoon dried chilli flakes
1 tablespoon olive oil
250g smoking chips

1 Pierce lamb in eight places with sharp knife; push garlic and rosemary into cuts. Sprinkle lamb with chilli; rub with oil. Cover; refrigerate 3 hours or overnight.
2 Soak smoking chips in large bowl of water 2 hours.
3 Cook lamb, uncovered, on heated oiled barbecue until browned all over. Place drained smoking chips in smoke box on barbecue next to lamb. Cook lamb in covered barbecue, using indirect heat and following manufacturer's instructions, about 40 minutes or until cooked as desired.

preparation time *10 minutes (plus refrigeration and soaking time)* cooking time *50 minutes* serves *6* nutritional count per serving *17.8g total fat (7.1g saturated fat); 1250kJ (299 cal); 0.2g carbohydrate; 35g protein; 0.3g fibre*

1 CAPONATA 2 GARLIC AND ROSEMARY SMOKED LAMB
3 GLAZED PORK AND VEAL APPLE MEATLOAF [P 174]
4 ROAST PORK WITH GARLIC AND ROSEMARY [P 174]

TRIED & TRUE   173

glazed pork and veal apple meatloaf

2 teaspoons olive oil
1 small brown onion (80g), chopped finely
2 cloves garlic, sliced thinly
1 trimmed celery stalk (100g), chopped finely
1 medium green apple (150g), peeled,
    grated coarsely
500g pork and veal mince mixture
1 cup (70g) stale breadcrumbs
1 tablespoon coarsely chopped fresh sage
1 egg, beaten lightly
10 thin streaky bacon rashers
1 small green apple (130g), extra, cored,
    sliced thinly
2 tablespoons apple jelly
    (or redcurrant or quince jelly)

1 Heat oil in large frying pan; add onion, garlic
and celery; cook, stirring, until onion is soft. Add
apple and cook, stirring, until all the liquid has
evaporated; cool.
2 Preheat oven to 180°C/160°C fan-forced.
3 Combine onion mixture with mince, breadcrumbs,
sage and egg in large bowl.
4 Transfer mince mixture to large sheet of plastic wrap;
use wrap to roll mixture into 8cm x 24cm log, discard
wrap. Wrap bacon around log, alternating extra apple
slices with bacon.
5 Place meatloaf onto an oiled oven tray, brush all
over with half the warmed jelly. Roast, uncovered,
about 45 minutes, brushing halfway through cooking
with remaining jelly, or until meatloaf is cooked through
and bacon is browned and crisp. Serve with mustard,
if you like.

preparation time *25 minutes*
cooking time *50 minutes (plus cooling time)* serves *4*
nutritional count per serving *18.4g total fat (5.8g
saturated fat); 1919kJ (459 cal); 20.8g carbohydrate;
50.9g protein; 2.6g fibre*

roast pork with garlic and rosemary

1.5kg pork neck
3 cloves garlic, crushed
1 tablespoon chopped fresh rosemary
1 tablespoon coarse cooking salt
2 tablespoons olive oil
3 bay leaves
⅓ cup (80ml) red wine vinegar
1 cup (250ml) water

1 Preheat oven to 200°C/180°C fan-forced.
2 Tie pork with kitchen string at 3cm intervals.
3 Combine garlic, rosemary, salt and oil in small bowl;
rub mixture over pork.
4 Place pork on rack in baking dish; add bay leaves,
vinegar and the water to dish.
5 Roast pork about 1½ hours or until cooked. Cover
pork; stand 10 minutes before slicing.

preparation time *20 minutes*
cooking time *1 hour 30 minutes* serves *6*
nutritional count per serving *26.1g total fat (7.6g
saturated fat); 1877kJ (449 cal); 0.2g carbohydrate;
53.1g protein; 0.3g fibre*

meat pies

1½ cups (225g) plain flour
90g butter, chopped
1 egg
1 tablespoon iced water, approximately
2 sheets ready-rolled puff pastry
1 egg, beaten lightly, extra

BEEF FILLING

1 tablespoon vegetable oil
1 medium (150g) onion, chopped
700g beef mince
425g can tomatoes
2 tablespoons tomato paste
¼ cup (60ml) worcestershire sauce
1 cup (250ml) beef stock
2 tablespoons cornflour
2 tablespoons water

1 Process flour and butter until crumbly. Add egg and enough water to make ingredients just cling together. Knead dough on floured surface until smooth. Roll into a ball; cover with plastic wrap, refrigerate 30 minutes.
2 Oil six ½-cup (125ml) pie tins. Turn a pie tin upside down on puff pastry, cut around tin. Repeat to make six pastry tops; cover and refrigerate. Wrap pastry scraps in plastic and refrigerate; use for decoration.
3 Divide dough into six portions; roll between sheets of baking paper until large enough to line tins. Lift pastry into tins, ease into sides, trim edges. Lightly prick bases with fork; refrigerate 30 minutes.
4 Preheat oven to 200°C/180°C fan-forced.
5 Place cases on oven trays, line each with baking paper; fill with dried beans. Blind-bake 10 minutes. Remove paper and beans; bake 7 minutes or until cases are browned. Cool.
6 Make beef filling.
7 Spoon filling into pastry cases, brushing edges with a little extra egg; top with puff pastry lids, gently press edges to seal. Decorate with pastry scraps, if you like. Brush pies with a little more egg; bake further 20 minutes or until browned.

BEEF FILLING Heat oil in medium saucepan, cook onion, stirring, until soft. Add mince; cook until browned. Add undrained crushed tomatoes, paste, sauce and stock; simmer, uncovered, 20 minutes. Add blended cornflour and water, stir over heat until mixture boils and thickens; cool.

preparation time *35 minutes (plus refrigeration time)* cooking time *1 hour (plus cooling time)* makes *6* nutritional count per pie *37.4g total fat (13.0g saturated fat); 2989kJ (715 cal); 56.9g carbohydrate; 36.0g protein; 3.7g fibre*

traditional turkey with corn bread and candied sweet potato pie

4kg turkey
1 cup (250ml) water
40g butter, melted
⅓ cup (50g) plain flour
1 cup (250ml) dry white wine
1 litre (4 cups) chicken stock

CORN BREAD

½ cup (75g) self-raising flour
½ cup (85g) cornmeal
¼ cup (30g) coarsely grated cheddar cheese
125g can creamed corn
125g can corn kernels, rinsed, drained
⅓ cup (80ml) buttermilk
1 egg, beaten lightly
30g butter, melted

FORCEMEAT STUFFING

40g butter
1 large brown onion (200g), chopped finely
4 thin slices prosciutto (60g), chopped finely
500g chicken mince
1 cup (70g) stale breadcrumbs
½ cup (60g) coarsely chopped roasted pecans
⅓ cup finely chopped fresh flat-leaf parsley
2 tablespoons finely chopped fresh sage

CANDIED SWEET POTATO PIE

2 large kumara (1kg), chopped coarsely
80g butter
2 eggs, beaten lightly
⅓ cup (50g) plain flour
⅓ cup (75g) firmly packed brown sugar
½ teaspoon ground cinnamon
¼ teaspoon ground ginger
¾ cup (90g) coarsely chopped roasted pecans

1 Preheat oven to 200°C/180°C fan-forced; make corn bread.
2 Make forcemeat stuffing.
3 Reduce oven to 180°C/160°C fan-forced.
4 Fill neck cavity of turkey with some of the stuffing; secure skin with toothpicks or small skewers to enclose stuffing. Fill large cavity with remaining stuffing; secure skin. Tie legs together with kitchen string.
5 Place turkey on oiled wire rack in shallow large baking dish; pour the water into dish. Brush turkey all over with butter. Roast, covered, 2 hours. Uncover turkey; roast about 1 hour, basting occasionally with dish juices, until turkey is cooked through.
6 Meanwhile, make candied sweet potato pie.
7 Remove turkey from dish; reserve ⅓ cup juices from dish. Cover turkey; stand 20 minutes.
8 Heat reserved juices in same dish. Add flour; cook, stirring, until mixture is well browned. Gradually stir in wine and stock; stir until gravy boils and thickens. Strain gravy into heatproof jug.
9 Serve turkey with gravy, corn bread and pie.

CORN BREAD Oil 8cm x 26cm bar cake pan; line base with baking paper, extending paper 5cm over long sides. Sift flour into medium bowl; stir in cornmeal and cheese. Stir in combined remaining ingredients. Spread mixture into pan; bake about 30 minutes. Stand 10 minutes; turn onto wire rack to cool.

FORCEMEAT STUFFING Melt butter in medium frying pan; cook onion and prosciutto, stirring, until onion softens. Combine onion mixture and remaining ingredients in bowl.

CANDIED SWEET POTATO PIE Boil, steam or microwave kumara until tender; drain. Mash kumara in medium bowl with half of the butter until smooth; stir in egg. Spread mixture into oiled 2-litre (8-cup) ovenproof dish. Combine flour, sugar and spices in small bowl; using fingertips, rub in remaining butter. Stir in nuts. Sprinkle nut mixture over kumara; bake in oven, uncovered, about 30 minutes or until browned.

preparation time *1 hour (plus standing time)*
cooking time *3 hours 30 minutes* serves *8*
nutritional count per serving *75.2g total fat (26.7g saturated fat); 5338kJ (1277 cal); 61.8g carbohydrate; 81.2g protein; 6.3g fibre*

butterflied lamb with fresh mint sauce

½ cup (110g) firmly packed brown sugar
½ cup (125ml) water
1½ cups (375ml) cider vinegar
½ cup finely chopped fresh mint
1 teaspoon salt
¼ teaspoon coarsely ground black pepper
¼ cup (90g) honey
1 tablespoon wholegrain mustard
2kg butterflied leg of lamb
¼ cup loosely packed fresh rosemary leaves

1 To make mint sauce, stir sugar and the water in small saucepan over heat, without boiling, until sugar dissolves. Simmer, uncovered, without stirring, about 5 minutes or until syrup thickens slightly. Combine syrup, vinegar, mint, salt and pepper in medium jug.
2 Place a quarter of the mint sauce in large shallow dish with honey and mustard, add lamb; coat well in mint sauce mixture. Cover; refrigerate 2 hours or overnight, turning occasionally.
3 Preheat barbecue to medium heat. Place drained lamb, fat-side down, on oiled barbecue (or grill plate). Cover lamb with foil or large upturned baking dish, cook about 10 minutes or until browned underneath. Turn lamb, sprinkle with rosemary; cook, covered, further 10 minutes or until lamb is cooked as desired (or, cook by indirect heat in covered barbecue following the manufacturer's instructions). Cover; stand lamb 10 minutes.
4 Serve sliced lamb with remaining mint sauce.

preparation time *15 minutes (plus refrigeration time)*
cooking time *25 minutes* serves *10*
nutritional count per serving *8.1g total fat (3.6g saturated fat); 1170kJ (280 cal); 18.3g carbohydrate; 33g protein; 0.3g fibre*

chicken and leek lasagne

You need to purchase a large barbecued chicken weighing approximately 900g for this recipe.

60g butter
1 large leek (500g), sliced thinly
¼ cup (35g) plain flour
2 teaspoons dijon mustard
2 cups (500ml) chicken stock, warmed
3 cups (480g) shredded barbecued chicken
4 fresh lasagne sheets (200g), trimmed to fit dish
⅔ cup (80g) coarsely grated cheddar cheese

1 Preheat oven to 180°C/160°C fan-forced.
2 Melt butter in medium saucepan; cook leek, stirring, until soft. Add flour; cook, stirring, until mixture thickens and bubbles. Gradually stir in mustard and stock; stir over medium heat until mixture boils and thickens. Reserve ⅔ cup of the white sauce; stir chicken into remaining sauce.
3 Oil shallow 2-litre (8-cup) ovenproof dish. Cover base with lasagne sheet; top with about a quarter of the warm chicken mixture. Repeat layering with remaining lasagne sheet and chicken mixture, finishing with lasagne sheet. Spread remaining quarter of the chicken mixture over lasagne; top with reserved white sauce and the cheese.
4 Bake lasagne, covered, 30 minutes; uncover, bake further 20 minutes or until browned lightly. Stand 5 minutes before serving.

preparation time *25 minutes*
cooking time *1 hour 10 minutes* serves *4*
nutritional count per serving *24.8g total fat (8.5g saturated fat); 1685kJ (403 cal); 15.5g carbohydrate; 28.8g protein; 2.4g fibre*

minestrone

2 ham hocks (1kg)
1 medium brown onion (150g), quartered
1 trimmed celery stalk (100g), chopped coarsely
1 teaspoon black peppercorns
1 bay leaf
4 litres (16 cups) water
1 tablespoon olive oil
2 trimmed celery stalks (200g), chopped finely
1 large carrot (180g), chopped finely
3 cloves garlic, crushed
¼ cup (70g) tomato paste
2 large tomatoes (440g), chopped finely
1 small leek (200g), sliced thinly
1 cup (100g) small pasta shells
420g can white beans, rinsed, drained
½ cup coarsely chopped fresh flat-leaf parsley
½ cup coarsely chopped fresh basil
½ cup (40g) shaved parmesan cheese

1 Preheat oven to 220°C/200°C fan-forced.

2 Roast hocks and onion in baking dish, uncovered, 30 minutes. Combine with coarsely chopped celery, peppercorns, bay leaf and the water in large saucepan; bring to the boil. Simmer, uncovered, 2 hours.

3 Remove hocks from soup. Strain broth through muslin-lined sieve or colander into large heatproof bowl; discard solids. Allow broth to cool, cover; refrigerate until cold. When cool, remove ham from bones; shred coarsely. Discard bones.

4 Meanwhile, heat oil in large saucepan; cook finely chopped celery and carrot, stirring, 2 minutes. Add ham, garlic, paste and tomato; cook, stirring, 2 minutes.

5 Discard fat from surface of broth. Place broth in measuring jug; add enough water to make 2 litres. Add broth to pan; bring to the boil. Simmer, covered, 20 minutes.

6 Add leek, pasta and beans; bring to the boil. Simmer, uncovered, until pasta is just tender. Remove from heat; stir in herbs. Serve sprinkled with cheese.

preparation time *40 minutes (plus refrigeration time)* cooking time *3 hours 35 minutes* serves *6* nutritional count per serving *7.2g total fat (2.4g saturated fat); 865kJ (207 cal); 19.6g carbohydrate; 12.7g protein; 6.1g fibre*

blackberry and apple pie

9 medium apples (1.4kg)
2 tablespoons caster sugar
1 tablespoon cornflour
1 tablespoon water
300g frozen blackberries
1 tablespoon cornflour, extra
1 tablespoon demerara sugar

PASTRY

2 cups (300g) plain flour
⅔ cup (110g) icing sugar
185g cold butter, chopped
2 egg yolks
1 tablespoon iced water, approximately

1 Make pastry.
2 Grease 23cm pie dish. Roll two-thirds of the pastry between sheets of baking paper until large enough to line pie dish. Ease pastry into dish; trim edge. Cover; refrigerate 30 minutes. Roll remaining pastry between sheets of baking paper until large enough to cover pie.
3 Meanwhile, peel and core apples; slice thinly. Place in large saucepan with caster sugar; cook, covered, over low heat, about 10 minutes or until apples are just tender. Strain over small saucepan; reserve cooking liquid. Place apples in large bowl. Blend cornflour with the water, stir into reserved cooking liquid over heat until mixture boils and thickens; gently stir into apple mixture.
4 Toss blackberries in extra cornflour; stir gently into apple mixture.
5 Preheat oven to 220°C/200°C fan-forced.
6 Spoon fruit mixture into pastry case; top with rolled pastry. Press edges together, trim with knife; decorate edge. Brush pastry with a little water; sprinkle with demerara sugar. Using knife, make three cuts in top of pastry to allow steam to escape. Place pie on oven tray; bake 20 minutes.
7 Reduce oven to 180°C/160°C fan-forced; bake pie further 30 minutes or until pastry is browned lightly. Stand 10 minutes before serving.

PASTRY Blend or process flour, icing sugar and butter until combined. Add egg yolks and enough of the water to make ingredients just come together. Knead dough on floured surface until smooth. Wrap in plastic; refrigerate 30 minutes.

preparation time *50 minutes (plus refrigeration time)* cooking time *1 hour 5 minutes* serves *8* nutritional count per serving *21.1g total fat (13g saturated fat); 2107kJ (504 cal); 69.4g carbohydrate; 5.9g protein; 6.3g fibre*

pink marshmallows

2 tablespoons (28g) gelatine
½ cup (125ml) cold water
2 cups (440g) caster sugar
1 cup (250ml) hot water
1 teaspoon rosewater
pink food colouring
1 cup (80g) desiccated coconut
¼ cup (20g) shredded coconut

1 Grease 25cm x 30cm swiss roll pan.
2 Sprinkle gelatine over the cold water in small bowl.
3 Stir sugar and the hot water in medium saucepan over heat until sugar dissolves; bring to the boil. Add in gelatine mixture; boil, without stirring, 20 minutes. Cool to lukewarm.
4 Beat sugar mixture, flavouring and colouring in large bowl with electric mixer, on high speed, about 5 minutes or until mixture is thick and holds its shape.
5 Spread marshmallow mixture into pan. Sprinkle marshmallow with a little of the combined coconut to cover top evenly. Set at room temperature for about 2 hours or until firm. Cut marshmallow into squares.

preparation time *30 minutes* cooking time *25 minutes (plus standing time)* makes *105*
nutritional count per marshmallow *0.6g total fat (0.5g saturated fat); 100kJ (24 cal); 4.3g carbohydrate; 0.3g protein; 0.1g fibre*

VARIATIONS

ORANGE Instead of the rosewater and pink food colouring, flavour the mixture with 1 teaspoon orange blossom water and tint with orange food colouring.

MINT Instead of the rosewater and pink food colouring, flavour with ½ teaspoon peppermint essence or a few drops of peppermint oil and tint with green food colouring.

triple chocolate fudge

For success every time, you will need to use an accurate candy thermometer for this recipe.

1½ cups (330g) caster sugar
½ cup (110g) firmly packed brown sugar
100g dark eating chocolate, chopped coarsely
2 tablespoons glucose syrup
½ cup (125ml) cream
¼ cup (60ml) milk
40g butter
200g white eating chocolate, melted
50g milk eating chocolate, melted

1 Grease and line an 8cm x 26cm bar cake pan with baking paper, extending paper 2cm above sides of the pan.
2 Stir sugars, dark chocolate, syrup, cream and milk in small saucepan over heat, without boiling, until sugars dissolve. Bring to the boil; boil without stirring, about 10 minutes or until mixture reaches 116°C on candy thermometer. Remove pan immediately from heat, leaving thermometer in mixture; add butter, do not stir.
3 Cool fudge about 40 minutes or until mixture drops to 40°C. Remove thermometer. Stir fudge with wooden spoon about 10 minutes or until a small amount dropped from spoon holds its shape. Spread fudge into cake pan; smooth surface. Cover with foil; stand at room temperature 2 hours.
4 Spread white chocolate over fudge, drizzle with milk chocolate. Pull a skewer through the chocolate topping for a marbled affect. Refrigerate 3 hours or overnight.
5 Remove fudge from pan, cut in half lengthways before slicing thinly.

preparation time *20 minutes (plus cooling and refrigeration time)* cooking time *15 minutes* makes *50*
nutritional count per piece *4g total fat (2.5g saturated fat); 389kJ (93 cal); 13.8g carbohydrate; 0.6g protein; 0g fibre*

sugar and spice snaps

1½ cups (225g) plain flour
¾ cup (165g) firmly packed dark muscovado sugar
2 teaspoons ground ginger
1 teaspoon mixed spice
¼ teaspoon ground clove
150g butter, chopped coarsely
1 egg yolk
¼ cup (55g) raw sugar

1 Process flour, muscovado sugar, spices and butter until crumbly. Add egg yolk; process until combined. Knead dough on floured surface until smooth. Cover; refrigerate 30 minutes.
2 Divide dough in half; roll each half between sheets of baking paper to 3mm thickness. Refrigerate 30 minutes.
3 Preheat oven to 180°C/160°C fan-forced. Line three oven trays with baking paper.
4 Cut 30 x 7cm rounds from dough. Place rounds on trays; sprinkle with raw sugar.
5 Bake snaps about 10 minutes; cool on trays.

preparation time *25 minutes (plus refrigeration time)* cooking time *10 minutes* makes *30* nutritional count per snap *4.3g total fat (2.7g saturated fat); 393kJ (94 cal); 12.8g carbohydrate; 0.9g protein; 0.3g fibre*

jam wreaths

250g butter, softened
1 teaspoon finely grated lemon rind
⅓ cup (75g) caster sugar
2 cups (300g) plain flour
½ cup (100g) rice flour
½ cup (160g) raspberry jam
1 tablespoon caster sugar, extra

1 Beat butter, rind and sugar in medium bowl with electric mixer until combined. Stir in sifted flours, in two batches. Knead dough on floured surface until smooth. Cover; refrigerate 30 minutes.
2 Preheat oven to 180°C/160°C fan-forced. Line two oven trays with baking paper.
3 Roll three-quarters of the dough between sheets of baking paper to 4mm thickness; cut 20 x 6.5cm rounds from dough. Place rounds 4cm apart on oven trays.
4 Roll remaining dough between sheets of baking paper to 4mm thickness. Using a 4cm holly cutter, cut out leaves from dough.
5 Brush edge of each round of dough lightly with water; arrange leaves, overlapping slightly, around edge. Sprinkle leaves lightly with extra sugar. Spoon jam into the centre of each wreath.
6 Bake wreaths about 20 minutes. Cool on trays.

preparation time *25 minutes (plus refrigeration time)* cooking time *20 minutes* makes *20* nutritional count per wreath *10.5g total fat (6.8g saturated fat); 849kJ (203 cal); 24.8g carbohydrate; 2g protein; 0.8g fibre*

chocolate chip cookies

125g butter, softened
½ teaspoon vanilla extract
⅓ cup (75g) caster sugar
⅓ cup (75g) firmly packed brown sugar
1 egg
1 cup (150g) plain flour
½ teaspoon bicarbonate of soda
150g milk eating chocolate, chopped coarsely
½ cup (50g) walnuts, chopped coarsely

1 Preheat oven to 180°C/160°C fan-forced.
Grease oven trays; line with baking paper.
2 Beat butter, extract, sugars and egg in small bowl
with electric mixer until smooth; do not overbeat.
Transfer mixture to medium bowl; stir in sifted flour
and soda then chocolate and nuts. Drop level
tablespoons of mixture onto trays 5cm apart.
3 Bake cookies about 15 minutes; cool on trays.

preparation time *15 minutes*
baking time *15 minutes* makes *24*
nutritional count per cookie *7.9g total fat (4.7g*
saturated fat); 564kJ (135 cal); 14.3g carbohydrate;
1.5g protein; 0.7g fibre

chocolate fudge brownies

150g butter, chopped
300g dark eating chocolate, chopped
1½ cups (330g) firmly packed brown sugar
3 eggs
1 teaspoon vanilla extract
¾ cup (110g) plain flour
¾ cup (140g) dark Choc Bits
½ cup (120g) sour cream
¾ cup (110g) roasted macadamias,
    chopped coarsely

1 Preheat oven to 180°C/160°C fan-forced. Grease
19cm x 29cm rectangular slice pan; line base with
baking paper, extending paper 5cm over sides.
2 Stir butter and chocolate in medium saucepan over
low heat until smooth. Cool 10 minutes.
3 Stir in sugar, eggs and extract then sifted flour, Choc
Bits, sour cream and nuts. Spread mixture into pan.
4 Bake brownies 40 minutes. Cover pan with foil;
bake further 20 minutes. Cool in pan.
5 Serve brownies dusted with cocoa powder, if you like.

preparation time *20 minutes*
cooking time *1 hour 5 minutes* makes *16*
nutritional count per piece *24.8g total fat (12.7g*
saturated fat); 1722kJ (412 cal); 42.8g carbohydrate;
4.2g protein; 1g fibre

chocolate mousse

200g dark eating chocolate, chopped coarsely
30g unsalted butter
3 eggs, separated
300ml thickened cream, whipped

1 Melt chocolate in medium heatproof bowl over
medium saucepan of simmering water. Remove from
heat; add butter, stir until smooth. Stir in egg yolks.
Transfer mixture to large bowl, cover; cool.
2 Beat egg whites in small bowl with electric mixer
until soft peaks form. Fold egg whites and cream into
chocolate mixture, in two batches.
3 Divide mousse among serving dishes; refrigerate
3 hours or overnight.
4 Serve mousse with extra whipped cream, chocolate
curls and fresh raspberries, if you like.

preparation time *20 minutes (plus cooling and*
refrigeration time) cooking time *5 minutes* serves *6*
nutritional count per serving *34.9g total fat (21.4g*
saturated fat); 1777kJ (425 cal); 22.5g carbohydrate;
6.1g protein; 0.4g fibre

1

2

3

4

traditional shortbread

250g butter, softened
⅓ cup (75g) caster sugar
1 tablespoon water
2 cups (300g) plain flour
½ cup (100g) rice flour
2 tablespoons white sugar

1 Preheat oven to 160°C/140°C fan-forced. Grease oven trays.
2 Beat butter and caster sugar in medium bowl with electric mixer until light and fluffy; stir in the water and sifted flours, in two batches. Knead on floured surface until smooth.
3 Divide mixture in half; shape each, on separate trays, into 20cm rounds. Mark each round into 12 wedges; prick with fork. Pinch edges of rounds with fingers; sprinkle with white sugar.
4 Bake about 40 minutes; stand 5 minutes. Using sharp knife, cut into wedges along marked lines. Cool on trays.

preparation time *20 minutes*
cooking time *40 minutes* makes *24*
nutritional count per piece *8.8g total fat (5.7g saturated fat); 644kJ (154 cal); 7g carbohydrate; 1.7g protein; 0.6g fibre*

college pudding

⅓ cup (110g) raspberry jam
1 egg
½ cup (110g) caster sugar
1 cup (150g) self-raising flour
½ cup (125ml) milk
25g butter, melted
1 tablespoon boiling water
1 teaspoon vanilla extract

1 Grease four 1-cup (250ml) metal moulds; divide jam among moulds.
2 Beat egg and sugar in small bowl with electric mixer until thick and creamy. Fold in sifted flour and milk, in two batches; fold in combined butter, the water and extract.
3 Top jam with pudding mixture. Cover each mould with pleated baking paper and foil (to allow puddings to expand as they cook); secure with kitchen string.
4 Place puddings in large saucepan with enough boiling water to come halfway up sides of moulds. Cover pan with tight-fitting lid; boil 25 minutes, replenishing water as necessary to maintain level. Stand puddings 5 minutes before turning onto plate. Serve with cream, if you like.

preparation time *15 minutes* serves *4*
nutritional count per serving *8.1g total fat (4.7g saturated fat); 1676kJ (401 cal); 73.7g carbohydrate; 6.5g protein; 1.8g fibre*

crêpes suzette

¾ cup (110g) plain flour
3 eggs
2 tablespoons vegetable oil
¾ cup (180ml) milk

ORANGE SAUCE

125g butter
½ cup (110g) caster sugar
1½ cups (375ml) orange juice, strained
2 tablespoons lemon juice
⅓ cup (80ml) orange-flavoured liqueur

1   Sift flour into medium bowl, make well in centre; add eggs and oil, gradually whisk in milk until smooth. Pour batter into large jug, cover; stand 1 hour.
2   Heat greased heavy-based crêpe pan or small frying pan; pour ¼ cup of batter into pan, tilting pan to coat base. Cook over low heat until browned lightly, loosening around edge with spatula. Turn crêpe; brown other side. Remove crêpe from pan; cover to keep warm. Repeat with remaining batter to make a total of eight crêpes.
3   Make orange sauce.
4   Fold crêpes in half then in half again, place in sauce; warm over low heat. Divide crêpes among serving plates; pour hot sauce over crêpes. Serve with orange segments and whipped cream, if you like.

ORANGE SAUCE Melt butter in large frying pan; cook sugar, stirring, until mixture begins to brown. Add juices; bring to the boil. Reduce heat; simmer, uncovered, about 3 minutes or until light golden. Add liqueur; remove from heat, ignite.

preparation time *15 minutes (plus standing time)*
cooking time *25 minutes* serves *4*
nutritional count per serving *41g total fat (20.5g saturated fat); 3039kJ (727 cal); 66.9g carbohydrate; 10.3g protein; 1.3g fibre*

sticky date cake with butterscotch sauce

3¾ cups (635g) dried pitted dates
3 cups (750ml) hot water
2 teaspoons bicarbonate of soda
185g butter, chopped
2¼ cups (500g) firmly packed brown sugar
6 eggs
3 cups (450g) self-raising flour
½ cup (60g) coarsely chopped walnuts
½ cup (60g) coarsely chopped pecans

BUTTERSCOTCH SAUCE

2 cups (440g) firmly packed brown sugar
500ml thickened cream
250g butter, chopped

1   Preheat oven to 180°C/160°C fan-forced. Grease 26cm x 36cm baking dish; double-line base and long sides with baking paper, bringing paper 5cm above edges of dish.
2   Combine dates and the water in medium saucepan; bring to the boil. Remove from heat; stir in soda. Stand 5 minutes. Blend or process date mixture until smooth.
3   Beat butter and sugar in large bowl with electric mixer until light and fluffy. Beat in eggs. Stir in date mixture and flour; spread mixture into dish, sprinkle with nuts.
4   Bake cake about 50 minutes. Stand in dish 10 minutes; turn onto wire rack, turn cake top-side up.
5   Meanwhile, make butterscotch sauce.
6   Brush surface of hot cake with ⅓ cup of the hot butterscotch sauce. Serve with remaining sauce.

BUTTERSCOTCH SAUCE Stir ingredients in medium saucepan over heat, without boiling, until sugar dissolves; bring to the boil. Reduce heat; simmer 3 minutes.

preparation time *20 minutes*
cooking time *55 minutes (plus standing time)* serves *20*
nutritional count per serving *34.8g total fat (19.7g saturated fat); 2822kJ (675 cal); 82.4g carbohydrate; 6.2g protein; 4.2g fibre*

lime chiffon pie

250g plain sweet biscuits
125g butter, melted
4 eggs, separated
⅓ cup (75g) caster sugar
3 teaspoons gelatine
2 teaspoons finely grated lime rind
⅓ cup (80ml) lime juice
⅓ cup (80ml) water
⅓ cup (75g) caster sugar, extra

1 Grease deep 23cm pie dish.
2 Process biscuits until fine; add butter, process until combined. Press mixture firmly over base and side of dish; refrigerate 30 minutes.
3 Combine egg yolks, sugar, gelatine, rind, juice and the water in medium heatproof bowl. Whisk over medium saucepan of simmering water until mixture thickens slightly. Remove from heat; pour into large bowl. Cover; cool.
4 Beat egg whites in small bowl with electric mixer until soft peaks form; gradually add extra sugar, beating until sugar dissolves. Fold meringue into filling mixture, in two batches.
5 Spread filling into crumb crust; refrigerate 3 hours.

preparation time *20 minutes (plus refrigeration time)*
cooking time *15 minutes* serves 6
nutritional count per serving *27.3g total fat (15.6g saturated fat); 2094kJ (501 cal); 54.9g carbohydrate; 8.7g protein; 0.9g fibre*

banoffee pie

395g can sweetened condensed milk
75g butter, chopped
½ cup (110g) firmly packed brown sugar
2 tablespoons golden syrup
2 large bananas (460g), sliced thinly
300ml thickened cream, whipped
PASTRY
1½ cups (225g) plain flour
1 tablespoon icing sugar
140g cold butter, chopped
1 egg yolk
2 tablespoons cold water

1 Make pastry.
2 Grease 24cm-round loose-based fluted flan tin. Roll dough between sheets of baking paper until large enough to line tin. Ease dough into tin; press into base and side. Trim edge; prick base all over with fork. Cover; refrigerate 30 minutes.
3 Preheat oven to 200°C/180°C fan-forced.
4 Place tin on oven tray; cover dough with baking paper, fill with dried beans or rice. Bake 10 minutes; remove paper and beans carefully from pie shell. Bake a further 10 minutes; cool.
5 Meanwhile, combine condensed milk, butter, sugar and syrup in medium saucepan; cook over medium heat, stirring, about 10 minutes or until mixture is caramel-coloured. Stand 5 minutes; pour into pie shell, cool.
6 Top caramel with banana, then whipped cream.

PASTRY Process flour, sugar and butter until crumbly; add egg yolk and water, process until ingredients come together. Knead dough on floured surface until smooth. Wrap in plastic; refrigerate 30 minutes.

preparation time *45 minutes (plus refrigeration time)*
cooking time *35 minutes* serves 8
nutritional count per serving *41.6g total fat (27g saturated fat); 3005kJ (719 cal); 76.3g carbohydrate; 9.2g protein; 1.9g fibre*

3 eggs

½ cup (110g) caster sugar

1 tablespoon cornflour

¾ cup (110g) self-raising flour

1 teaspoon butter

¼ cup (60ml) boiling water

⅓ cup (75g) caster sugar, extra

½ cup (125ml) water

2 cups (300g) frozen blackberries

3⅓ cups (500g) frozen mixed berries

¼ cup (80g) blackberry jam

1 Preheat oven to 180°C/160°C fan-forced. Grease 25cm x 30cm swiss roll pan; line base with baking paper, extending paper 5cm over long sides.

2 Beat eggs in small bowl with electric mixer until thick and creamy. Gradually add sugar, beating until sugar dissolves; transfer mixture to large bowl.

3 Fold triple-sifted flours into egg mixture. Pour combined butter and boiling water down side of bowl; fold into egg mixture. Spread mixture into pan.

4 Bake cake 15 minutes. Cool in pan.

5 Meanwhile, combine extra sugar and the water in medium saucepan; bring to the boil. Stir in berries; return to the boil. Reduce heat; simmer, uncovered, until berries soften. Strain over medium bowl; reserve syrup and berries separately.

6 Turn cake onto board. Line 1.25-litre (5-cup) pudding basin with plastic wrap, extending wrap 10cm over side of basin. Cut circle slightly smaller than top edge of basin from cake using tip of sharp knife; cut second circle exact size of base of basin from cake. Cut remaining cake into 10cm long strips.

7 Place small cake circle in base of basin and use cake strips to line side of basin. Pour ⅔ cup of the reserved syrup into small jug; reserve. Fill basin with berries; cover with remaining syrup, top with large cake circle. Cover pudding with overhanging plastic wrap, weight pudding with saucer; refrigerate 3 hours or overnight.

8 Stir jam and two tablespoons of the reserved syrup in small saucepan until heated through. Turn pudding onto serving plate; brush with remaining reserved syrup then jam mixture. Serve with whipped cream, if you like.

preparation time *30 minutes (plus refrigeration time)* cooking time *25 minutes* serves 6
nutritional count per serving *3.7g total fat (1.3g saturated fat); 1338kJ (320 cal); 60.6g carbohydrate; 7.3g protein; 5.8g fibre*

mini chocolate éclairs

To prevent skin forming on the pastry cream, place a piece of plastic wrap over the entire surface until ready to use.

20g butter
¼ cup (60ml) water
¼ cup (35g) plain flour
1 egg
100g dark eating chocolate, melted

PASTRY CREAM

1 cup (250ml) milk
½ vanilla bean, split
3 egg yolks
⅓ cup (75g) caster sugar
2 tablespoons cornflour

1 Preheat oven to 240°C/220°C fan-forced. Grease two oven trays.
2 Combine butter with the water in small saucepan; bring to the boil. Add flour; beat with wooden spoon over heat until mixture comes away from base and side of saucepan and forms a smooth ball.
3 Transfer mixture to small bowl; beat in egg with electric mixer until mixture becomes glossy.
4 Spoon mixture into piping bag fitted with 1cm plain tube. Pipe 5cm lengths of choux pastry mixture 3cm apart onto trays; bake 7 minutes.
5 Reduce oven to 240°C/220°C fan-forced; bake further 10 minutes or until éclairs are browned lightly and crisp. Carefully cut eclairs in half, remove any soft centre; bake further 5 minutes or until éclairs are dried out. Cool to room temperature.
6 Meanwhile, make pastry cream.
7 Spoon pastry cream into piping bag fitted with 1cm plain tube; pipe cream onto 16 éclair halves; top with remaining halves. Place éclairs on foil-covered tray; spread with melted chocolate.

PASTRY CREAM Bring milk, with vanilla bean added, to the boil in small saucepan. Discard vanilla bean. Meanwhile, beat egg yolks, sugar and cornflour in small bowl with electric mixer until thick. With motor operating, gradually beat in milk mixture. Return custard mixture to saucepan; stir over heat until mixture boils and thickens.

preparation time *20 minutes*
cooking time *30 minutes* makes *16*
nutritional count per éclair *4.8g total fat (2.6g saturated fat); 422kJ (101 cal); 12.1g carbohydrate; 2.1g protein; 0.2g fibre*

baked vanilla cheesecake

250g plain sweet biscuits
125g butter, melted
4 eggs
¾ cup (165g) caster sugar
500g cream cheese
1 tablespoon finely grated lemon rind
½ teaspoon mixed spice

1 Process biscuits until fine. Add butter, process until combined. Press mixture over base and sides of 20cm springform tin. Place on oven tray; refrigerate 30 minutes.
2 Preheat oven to 160°C/140°C fan-forced.
3 Beat eggs and sugar in small bowl with electric mixer until thick and creamy. Beat cheese and rind in medium bowl with electric mixer until smooth. Add egg mixture to cheese mixture; beat until combined.
4 Pour filling into tin; bake about 50 minutes. Cool in oven with door ajar. Refrigerate 3 hours or overnight.
5 Serve cheesecake sprinkled with mixed spice.

preparation time *25 minutes (plus refrigeration time)*
cooking time *50 minutes* serves *10*
nutritional count per serving *32.9g total fat (20g saturated fat); 1973kJ (472 cal); 35.6g carbohydrate; 8.6g protein; 0.5g fibre*

vanilla bean ice-cream

2 vanilla beans
1⅔ cups (410ml) milk
600ml thickened cream
8 egg yolks
¾ cup (165g) caster sugar

1 Split vanilla beans lengthways; scrape out seeds into medium saucepan. Add pods, milk and cream; bring to the boil.
2 Meanwhile, whisk egg yolks and sugar in medium bowl until creamy; gradually whisk into hot milk mixture. Stir over low heat, without boiling, until mixture thickens slightly.
3 Strain mixture into medium heatproof bowl; discard pods. Cover surface of custard with plastic wrap; refrigerate about 1 hour or until cold.
4 Pour custard into ice-cream maker, churn according to manufacturer's instructions (or place custard in shallow container, such as an aluminium slab cake pan, cover with foil; freeze until almost firm). Place ice-cream in large bowl, chop coarsely then beat with electric mixer until smooth. Pour into deep container, cover; freeze until firm. Repeat process two more times.

VARIATIONS

PASSIONFRUIT Omit vanilla beans; reduce milk to 1 cup (250ml). Stir ⅔ cup passionfruit pulp into custard before placing in ice-cream maker.

CHOCOLATE Omit vanilla beans; add 20g coarsely chopped dark eating chocolate to milk and cream when heating.

preparation time *15 minutes (plus refrigeration, churning and freezing time)* cooking time *10 minutes* serves *8*
nutritional count per serving *35.5g total fat (21.4g saturated fat); 1843kJ (441 cal); 24.8g carbohydrate; 6.5g protein; 0g fibre*

chocolate soufflé

⅓ cup (75g) caster sugar
50g butter
1 tablespoon plain flour
200g dark eating chocolate, melted
2 egg yolks
4 egg whites

1   Preheat oven to 180°C/160°C fan-forced. Grease four ¾-cup (180ml) soufflé dishes. Sprinkle inside of dishes with a little of the sugar; shake away excess. Place dishes on oven tray.
2   Melt butter in small saucepan, add flour; cook, stirring, about 2 minutes or until mixture thickens and bubbles. Remove from heat; stir in chocolate and egg yolks. Transfer to large bowl.
3   Beat egg whites in small bowl with electric mixer until soft peaks form. Gradually add remaining sugar, beating until sugar dissolves. Fold egg white mixture into chocolate mixture, in two batches. Divide mixture among dishes.
4   Bake soufflés 15 minutes. Dust with cocoa powder, if you like.

preparation time *15 minutes*
cooking time *20 minutes* serves *4*
nutritional count per serving *27.9g total fat (16.1g saturated fat); 2040kJ (488 cal); 52.3g carbohydrate; 8.1g protein; 0.7g fibre*

marshmallow pavlova

4 egg whites
1 cup (220g) caster sugar
½ teaspoon vanilla extract
¾ teaspoon white vinegar
300ml thickened cream, whipped
250g strawberries, halved

1   Preheat oven to 120°C/100°C fan-forced. Line oven tray with foil; grease foil, dust with cornflour, shake away excess. Mark 18cm-circle on foil.
2   Beat egg whites in small bowl with electric mixer until soft peaks form; gradually add sugar, beating until sugar dissolves. Add extract and vinegar; beat until combined.
3   Spread meringue into circle on foil, building up at the side to 8cm in height.
4   Smooth side and top of pavlova gently. Using spatula blade, mark decorative grooves around side of meringue; smooth top again.
5   Bake pavlova about 1½ hours. Turn off oven; cool pavlova in oven with door ajar. When pavlova is cold, cut around top edge (the crisp meringue top will fall slightly on top of the marshmallow). Serve pavlova topped with whipped cream and strawberries; dust lightly with sifted icing sugar, if you like.

preparation time *25 minutes (plus cooling time)*
cooking time *1 hour 30 minutes* serves *8*
nutritional count per serving *14g total fat (9.2g saturated fat); 1070kJ (256 cal); 29.6g carbohydrate; 3.1g protein; 0.7g fibre*

1 CHOCOLATE SOUFFLE   2 MARSHMALLOW PAVLOVA
3 LAMINGTONS [P 196]   4 PEACH MELBA [P 196]

lamingtons

6 eggs
⅔ cup (150g) caster sugar
⅓ cup (50g) cornflour
½ cup (75g) plain flour
⅓ cup (50g) self-raising flour
2 cups (160g) desiccated coconut

ICING

4 cups (640g) icing sugar
½ cup (50g) cocoa powder
15g butter, melted
1 cup (250ml) milk

1 Preheat oven to 180°C/160°C fan-forced. Grease 20cm x 30cm lamington pan; line with baking paper, extending paper 5cm over long sides.
2 Beat eggs in large bowl with electric mixer about 10 minutes or until thick and creamy; gradually beat in sugar, dissolving between additions. Fold in triple-sifted flours. Spread mixture into pan.
3 Bake cake about 35 minutes. Turn immediately onto a baking-paper-covered wire rack to cool.
4 Meanwhile, make icing.
5 Cut cake into 16 squares; dip each square in icing, drain off excess. Toss in coconut; place on wire rack to set.

ICING Sift icing sugar and cocoa into medium heatproof bowl; stir in butter and milk. Set bowl over medium saucepan of simmering water; stir until icing is of a coating consistency.

preparation time *25 minutes*
cooking time *35 minutes* makes *16*
nutritional count per lamington *10.4g total fat (1.8g saturated fat); 1501kJ (359 cal); 59.6g carbohydrate; 5.1g protein; 1.9g fibre*

peach melba

1 litre (4 cups) water
4 medium peaches (600g)
500ml vanilla ice-cream

RASPBERRY SAUCE

200g fresh or thawed frozen raspberries
1 tablespoon icing sugar, approximately

1 Bring the water to the boil in medium saucepan. Add peaches; simmer, uncovered, 5 minutes. Remove peaches; place in bowl of cold water. When peaches are cold, remove skins.
2 Meanwhile, make raspberry sauce.
3 Serve peach halves topped with ice-cream, sauce and extra raspberries, if you like.

RASPBERRY SAUCE Push raspberries through fine sieve into small bowl; sweeten pulp with sifted sugar to taste.

preparation time *5 minutes (plus cooling time)*
cooking time *5 minutes* serves *4*
nutritional count per serving *7.7g total fat (4.8g saturated fat); 861kJ (206 cal); 27.5g carbohydrate; 4.2g protein; 4.5g fibre*

almond macaroons

2 egg whites
½ cup (110g) caster sugar
1¼ cups (150g) almond meal
½ teaspoon almond essence
2 tablespoons plain flour
¼ cup (40g) blanched almonds

1 Preheat oven to 150°C/130°C fan-forced. Grease oven trays.
2 Beat egg whites in small bowl with electric mixer until soft peaks form; gradually add sugar, beating until dissolved between additions. Gently fold in meal, essence and sifted flour, in two batches.
3 Drop level tablespoons of mixture about 5cm apart on trays; press one nut onto each macaroon.
4 Bake macaroons about 20 minutes or until firm and dry; cool on trays.

preparation time *15 minutes*
cooking time *20 minutes* makes *22*
nutritional count per serving *4.8g total fat (0.3g saturated fat); 326kJ (78 cal); 6.1g carbohydrate; 2.2g protein; 0.8g fibre*

crème caramel

¾ cup (165g) caster sugar
½ cup (125ml) water
300ml cream
1¾ cups (430ml) milk
6 eggs
1 teaspoon vanilla extract
⅓ cup (75g) caster sugar, extra

1 Preheat oven to 160°C/140°C fan-forced.
2 Combine sugar and the water in medium frying pan; stir over heat, without boiling, until sugar dissolves. Bring to the boil; boil, uncovered, without stirring, until mixture is deep caramel in colour. Remove from heat; allow bubbles to subside. Pour toffee into deep 20cm-round cake pan.
3 Combine cream and milk in medium saucepan; bring to the boil. Whisk eggs, extract and extra sugar in large bowl; whisking constantly, pour hot milk mixture into egg mixture. Strain mixture into cake pan.
4 Place pan in medium baking dish; add enough boiling water to come half way up side of pan. Bake, uncovered, about 40 minutes or until firm. Remove custard from baking dish, cover; refrigerate overnight.
5 Gently ease crème caramel from side of pan; invert onto deep-sided serving plate.

preparation time *20 minutes (plus refrigeration time)*
cooking time *40 minutes* serves *6*
nutritional count per serving *29.7g total fat (17.7g saturated fat); 2031kJ (486 cal); 45g carbohydrate; 10.1g protein; 0g fibre*

grilled sabayon peaches

6 medium peaches (900g), sliced thickly
4 egg yolks
2 tablespoons caster sugar
2 tablespoons peach liqueur
2 tablespoons apple juice

1 Arrange peach slices in six shallow 1-cup (125ml) ovenproof serving dishes.
2 Combine egg yolks, sugar, liqueur and juice in large bowl. Place bowl over pan of simmering water, ensuring that water doesn't touch bottom of bowl. Whisk constantly about 8 minutes or until mixture is very thick and creamy.
3 Meanwhile, preheat grill.
4 Spoon warm sabayon evenly over peach slices.
5 Place dishes under grill about 1 minute or until just browned lightly. Serve immediately.

preparation time *10 minutes*
cooking time *12 minutes* serves *6*
nutritional count per serving *3.9g total fat (1.2g saturated fat); 564kJ (135 cal); 17.7g carbohydrate; 3.2g protein; 1.8g fibre*

impossible pie

½ cup (75g) plain flour
1 cup (220g) caster sugar
¾ cup (60g) desiccated coconut
4 eggs
1 teaspoon vanilla extract
125g butter, melted
½ cup (40g) flaked almonds
2 cups (500ml) milk

1 Preheat oven to 180°C/160°C fan-forced. Grease deep 24cm pie dish.
2 Combine sifted flour, sugar, coconut, eggs, extract, butter and half the nuts in large bowl; gradually add milk, stirring, until combined. Pour mixture into dish.
3 Bake pie 35 minutes. Sprinkle with remaining nuts; bake further 10 minutes.
4 Serve pie with cream or fruit, if you like.

preparation time *10 minutes*
cooking time *45 minutes* serves *8*
nutritional count per serving *25.7g total fat (15.4g saturated fat); 1747kJ (418 cal); 38.2g carbohydrate; 8.1g protein; 1.9g fibre*

JUST LIKE
MUM MADE

beef stew with
parsley dumplings

1kg beef chuck steak, cut into 5cm pieces
2 tablespoons plain flour
2 tablespoons olive oil
20g butter
2 medium brown onions (300g), chopped coarsely
2 cloves garlic, crushed
2 medium carrots (240g), chopped coarsely
1 cup (250ml) dry red wine
2 tablespoons tomato paste
2 cups (500ml) beef stock
4 sprigs fresh thyme

PARSLEY DUMPLINGS

1 cup (150g) self-raising flour
50g butter
1 egg, beaten lightly
¼ cup (20g) coarsely grated parmesan cheese
¼ cup finely chopped fresh flat-leaf parsley
⅓ cup (50g) drained sun-dried tomatoes,
    chopped finely
¼ cup (60ml) milk

1 Preheat oven to 180°C/160°C fan-forced.
2 Coat beef in flour; shake off excess. Heat oil in large flameproof casserole dish; cook beef, in batches, over heat until browned all over.
3 Melt butter in same dish; cook onion, garlic and carrot, stirring, until vegetables soften. Add wine; cook, stirring, until liquid reduces to ¼ cup. Return beef to dish with paste, stock and thyme; bring to the boil. Cover; cook in oven 1¾ hours.
4 Meanwhile, make parsley dumpling mixture.
5 Remove dish from oven; uncover. Drop level tablespoons of the dumpling mixture, about 2cm apart, onto top of stew. Cook, uncovered, in oven about 20 minutes or until dumplings are browned lightly and cooked through.
6 Serve stew and dumplings with a mixed green salad dressed with vinaigrette, if you like.

PARSLEY DUMPLINGS Place flour in medium bowl; rub in butter. Stir in egg, cheese, parsley, tomato and enough milk to make a soft, sticky dough.

preparation time *20 minutes*
cooking time *2 hours 30 minutes* serves *4*
nutritional count per serving *39.7g total fat (17.4g saturated fat); 3457kJ (827 cal); 43g carbohydrate; 63.9g protein; 6.7g fibre*

corned beef with parsley sauce

1.5kg whole piece beef corned silverside
2 bay leaves
6 black peppercorns
1 large brown onion (200g), quartered
1 large carrot (180g), chopped coarsely
1 tablespoon brown malt vinegar
¼ cup (50g) firmly packed brown sugar

PARSLEY SAUCE

30g butter
¼ cup (35g) plain flour
2½ cups (625ml) milk
⅓ cup (40g) grated cheddar cheese
⅓ cup finely chopped fresh flat-leaf parsley
1 tablespoon mild mustard

1 Place beef, bay leaves, peppercorns, onion, carrot, vinegar and half of the sugar in large saucepan. Add enough water to just cover beef; simmer, covered, about 2 hours or until beef is tender. Cool beef 1 hour in liquid in pan.
2 Remove beef from pan; discard liquid. Sprinkle sheet of foil with remaining sugar, wrap beef in foil; stand 20 minutes before serving.
3 Meanwhile, make parsley sauce.
4 Serve corned beef with sauce.

PARSLEY SAUCE Melt butter in small saucepan, add flour; cook, stirring, until bubbling. Gradually stir in milk; cook, stirring, until sauce boils and thickens. Remove from heat; stir in cheese, parsley and mustard.

preparation time *20 minutes (plus standing time)*
cooking time *2 hours 15 minutes (plus cooling time)*
serves *4*
nutritional count per serving *35.8g total fat (19.3g saturated fat); 3520kJ (842 cal); 31g carbohydrate; 97g protein; 2.5g fibre*

family beef casserole

2 tablespoons vegetable oil
2kg beef chuck steak, chopped coarsely
2 medium brown onions (300g), sliced thinly
2 medium carrots (240g), sliced thickly
3 cloves garlic, crushed
¼ cup finely chopped fresh parsley
¼ cup (70g) tomato paste
2 teaspoons dijon mustard
1 cup (250ml) dry red wine
½ cup (125ml) beef stock

1 Preheat oven to 160°C/140°C fan-forced.
2 Heat oil in 2.5 litre (10-cup) flameproof casserole dish; cook beef, in batches, until browned. Remove from dish. Add onion, carrot and garlic to dish; cook, stirring, until onion is soft.
3 Return beef to dish; stir in parsley, paste, mustard, wine and stock. Cook, covered, in oven about 1¾ hours or until beef is tender.

preparation time *15 minutes*
cooking time *2 hours 15 minutes serves 6*
nutritional count per serving *21.4g total fat (7.1g saturated fat); 2203kJ (527 cal); 6.1g carbohydrate; 69.2g protein; 2.6g fibre*

chunky beef and vegetable pie

1 tablespoon olive oil
1.5kg gravy beef, cut into 2cm pieces
60g butter
1 medium brown onion (150g), chopped finely
1 clove garlic, crushed
¼ cup (35g) plain flour
1 cup (250ml) dry white wine
3 cups (750ml) hot beef stock
2 tablespoons tomato paste
2 trimmed celery stalks (200g), cut into 2cm pieces
2 medium potatoes (400g), cut into 2cm pieces
1 large carrot (180g), cut into 2cm pieces
1 large zucchini (150g), cut into 2cm pieces
150g mushrooms, quartered
1 cup (120g) frozen peas
½ cup finely chopped fresh flat-leaf parsley
2 sheets ready-rolled puff pastry
1 egg, beaten lightly

1 Heat oil in large saucepan; cook beef, in batches, until browned all over.
2 Melt butter in same pan; cook onion and garlic, stirring, until onion softens. Add flour; cook, stirring, until mixture thickens and bubbles. Gradually stir in wine and stock; stir until mixture boils and thickens slightly.
3 Return beef to pan with paste, celery, potato and carrot; bring to the boil. Reduce heat; simmer, covered, 1 hour.
4 Add zucchini and mushrooms; simmer, uncovered, about 30 minutes or until beef is tender. Add peas; stir until heated through. Remove from heat; stir in parsley.
5 Preheat oven to 220°C/200°C fan-forced.
6 Divide warm beef mixture between two deep 25cm pie dishes; brush outside edge of dishes with a little egg. Top each pie with a pastry sheet; pressing edges to seal. Trim pastry; brush pastry with egg.
7 Bake pie about 20 minutes or until browned.

preparation time *40 minutes*
cooking time *2 hours* serves *8*
nutritional count per serving *27.6g total fat (13.3g saturated fat); 2412kJ (577 cal); 28.6g carbohydrate; 46.4g protein; 4.9g fibre*

beef, barley and mushroom stew

1kg beef chuck steak, cut into 3cm pieces
¼ cup (35g) plain flour
2 tablespoons olive oil
20g butter
2 medium brown onions (300g), chopped finely
3 cloves garlic, crushed
1 medium carrot (120g), chopped finely
1 trimmed celery stalk (100g), chopped finely
4 sprigs fresh thyme
1 sprig fresh rosemary
1 bay leaf
½ cup (100g) pearl barley
2 cups (500ml) beef stock
½ cup (125ml) dry white wine
2 cups (500ml) water
200g swiss brown mushrooms, quartered
200g button mushrooms, quartered

1 Preheat oven to 160°C/140°C fan-forced.
2 Coat beef in flour; shake off excess. Heat oil in large flameproof casserole dish; cook beef, in batches, over heat until browned all over.
3 Melt butter in same dish; cook onion, garlic, carrot, celery and herbs, stirring, until vegetables soften. Add barley, stock, wine and the water; bring to the boil. Return beef to dish, cover; cook in oven 1½ hours.
4 Stir in mushrooms; cook, uncovered, a further 30 minutes or until beef and mushrooms are tender.
5 Serve stew, if you like, with a parsnip mash and sprinkled with fresh thyme.

preparation time *35 minutes*
cooking time *2 hours 20 minutes* serves *4*
nutritional count per serving *21.8g total fat (6.3g saturated fat); 2462kJ (589 cal); 28.7g carbohydrate; 60.3g protein; 8.2g fibre*

crumbed marinated lamb cutlets

12 french-trimmed lamb cutlets (600g)
¼ cup (60ml) soy sauce
2 cloves garlic, crushed
¼ cup (35g) plain flour
2 eggs, beaten lightly
¼ cup (60ml) milk
1 cup (70g) stale breadcrumbs, approximately
1 cup (100g) packaged breadcrumbs, approximately
vegetable oil, for shallow-frying

1 Using meat mallet, pound each cutlet between sheets of plastic wrap until cutlets are flattened slightly.
2 Combine soy sauce and garlic in large dish with cutlets. Cover, refrigerate 30 minutes; turn several times while marinating.
3 Place flour in plastic bag; add cutlets. Toss until cutlets are well coated with flour. Dip cutlets in combined egg and milk, then coat with combined breadcrumbs.
4 Heat oil in large frying pan; cook cutlets until browned both sides and cooked as desired. Drain on absorbent paper.

preparation time *25 minutes (plus marinating time)*
cooking time *30 minutes* serves *4*
nutritional count per serving *20.3g total fat (5.9g saturated fat); 1856kJ (444 cal); 35.6g carbohydrate; 28.4g protein; 2.3g fibre*

beef and barley soup

1 tablespoon olive oil
500g gravy beef, trimmed, cut into 2cm pieces
2 cloves garlic, crushed
2 medium brown onions (300g), chopped finely
¾ cup (150g) pearl barley
3 cups (750ml) beef stock
1.5 litres (6 cups) water
1 bay leaf
1 sprig fresh rosemary
1 sprig fresh thyme
2 medium potatoes (400g), cut into 1cm pieces
2 medium carrots (240g), cut into 1cm pieces
2 medium zucchini (240g), cut into 1cm pieces
2 medium yellow patty-pan squash (60g),
   cut into 1cm pieces
100g swiss brown mushrooms, chopped coarsely
½ cup finely chopped fresh flat-leaf parsley

1 Heat half the oil in large saucepan; cook beef,
in batches, until browned.
2 Heat remaining oil in same pan; cook garlic and
onion, stirring, until onion softens. Return beef to pan
with barley, stock, the water, bay leaf, rosemary and
thyme, bring to the boil. Reduce heat; simmer, covered,
about 1 hour or until beef and barley are tender,
skimming fat occasionally.
3 Add potato, carrot, zucchini, squash and mushrooms
to soup; simmer, covered, about 25 minutes or until
vegetables are softened. Remove and discard bay leaf,
rosemary and thyme.
4 Serve bowls of soup sprinkled with parsley.

preparation time *30 minutes*
cooking time *1 hour 45 minutes* serves *6*
nutritional count per serving *8.8g total fat (2.6g
saturated fat); 1350kJ (323 cal); 30g carbohydrate;
26.9g protein; 7.8g fibre*

cream of chicken soup

2 litres (8 cups) water
1 litre (4 cups) chicken stock
1.8kg whole chicken
1 medium carrot (120g), chopped coarsely
1 trimmed celery stalk (100g), chopped coarsely
1 medium brown onion (150g), chopped coarsely
40g butter
⅓ cup (50g) plain flour
2 tablespoons lemon juice
½ cup (125ml) cream
¼ cup finely chopped fresh flat-leaf parsley

1 Place the water and stock in large saucepan with
chicken, carrot, celery and onion; bring to the boil.
Reduce heat; simmer, covered, 1½ hours. Remove
chicken from pan; simmer broth, covered, 30 minutes.
2 Strain broth through muslin-lined sieve or colander
into large heatproof bowl; discard solids. Remove and
discard chicken skin and bones; shred meat coarsely.
3 Melt butter in large saucepan, add flour; cook,
stirring, until mixture thickens and bubbles. Gradually
stir in broth and juice; bring to the boil, stirring.
Add cream, reduce heat; simmer, uncovered, about
25 minutes, stirring occasionally. Add chicken;
stir soup over medium heat until hot.
4 Serve bowls of soup sprinkled with parsley.

preparation time *35 minutes*
cooking time *2 hours 30 minutes* serves *4*
nutritional count per serving *58.6g total fat (14.9g
saturated fat); 3327kJ (796 cal); 15.5g carbohydrate;
51.9g protein; 2.4g fibre*

pork leg roast with sage potatoes

2.5kg boneless pork leg roast, rind on
2 tablespoons olive oil
1 tablespoon sea salt flakes
6 medium potatoes (1.2kg), quartered
2 tablespoons olive oil, extra
2 tablespoons fresh sage leaves
2 tablespoons fresh rosemary leaves

RASPBERRY GLAZE

1 cup (320g) cranberry sauce
⅔ cup (100g) fresh or frozen raspberries
½ cup (110g) sugar
⅓ cup (80ml) balsamic vinegar

1   Preheat oven to 220°C/200°C fan-forced.
2   Score pork rind with sharp knife; rub with oil, then salt. Place pork in large shallow baking dish. Roast, uncovered, 20 minutes.
3   Reduce oven to 180°C/160°C fan-forced. Roast pork, uncovered, further 2 hours.
4   Meanwhile, combine potato with extra oil, sage and rosemary in large bowl. Place in single layer on oven tray. Roast, uncovered, about 35 minutes.
5   Make raspberry glaze.
6   Stand pork covered loosely with foil 10 minutes before slicing. Serve pork and potatoes with glaze.

RASPBERRY GLAZE   Stir ingredients in medium saucepan over heat until sugar dissolves. Reduce heat; simmer, 15 minutes or until mixture is reduced by about half.

preparation time *20 minutes*
cooking time *2 hours 35 minutes (plus standing time)*
serves *9*
nutritional count per serving *30.2g total fat (8.6g saturated fat); 2851kJ (682 cal); 36.3g carbohydrate; 64g protein; 3.7g fibre*

macaroni cheese

300g macaroni
4 rindless bacon rashers (260g), chopped coarsely
50g butter
⅓ cup (50g) plain flour
1 litre (4 cups) milk
1 cup (125g) grated cheddar cheese
½ cup (40g) grated pecorino cheese
2 tablespoons wholegrain mustard
½ cup (35g) stale breadcrumbs
20g butter, chopped, extra

1   Cook pasta in large saucepan of boiling water, uncovered, until just tender; drain.
2   Preheat oven to 200°C/180°C fan-forced.
3   Cook bacon in medium frying pan, stirring, until crisp; drain.
4   Melt butter in same pan, add flour; cook, stirring, 1 minute. Gradually add milk; cook, stirring, until sauce boils and thickens. Cool 2 minutes then stir in cheeses and mustard.
5   Combine pasta, cheese sauce and bacon in large bowl; transfer mixture to oiled deep 2-litre (8-cup) ovenproof dish. Top with breadcrumbs; dot with extra butter. Bake, uncovered, about 30 minutes or until top is browned lightly.

preparation time *10 minutes*
cooking time *50 minutes* serves *4*
nutritional count per serving *43.9g total fat (26.4g saturated fat); 3616kJ (865 cal); 78.7g carbohydrate; 37.8g protein; 3.5g fibre*

fish mornay pies

2½ cups (625ml) milk
½ small brown onion (40g)
1 bay leaf
6 black peppercorns
4 x 170g firm white fish fillets, skinned
3 large potatoes (900g), chopped coarsely
600g celeriac, chopped coarsely
1 egg yolk
½ cup (40g) finely grated parmesan cheese
¾ cup (180ml) cream
60g butter
¼ cup (35g) plain flour
2 tablespoons coarsely chopped fresh flat-leaf parsley

1 Place milk, onion, bay leaf and peppercorns in large saucepan; bring to the boil. Add fish, reduce heat; simmer, covered, about 5 minutes or until cooked through. Remove fish from pan; divide fish among four 1½-cup (375ml) ovenproof dishes. Strain milk through sieve into medium jug. Discard solids; reserve milk.
2 Boil, steam or microwave potato and celeriac, separately, until tender; drain. Push potato and celeriac through sieve into large bowl; stir in yolk, cheese, ¼ cup of the cream and half of the butter until smooth. Cover to keep warm.
3 Meanwhile, melt remaining butter in medium saucepan; add flour, cook, stirring, about 3 minutes or until mixture bubbles and thickens slightly. Gradually stir in reserved milk and remaining cream; cook, stirring, until mixture boils and thickens. Stir in parsley.
4 Preheat grill.
5 Divide mornay mixture among dishes; cover each with potato mixture. Place pies on oven tray; place under grill until browned lightly.

preparation time *25 minutes*
cooking time *35 minutes* serves *4*
nutritional count per serving *47.6g total fat (28.8g saturated fat); 3507kJ (839 cal); 44.7g carbohydrate; 54.2g protein; 9g fibre*

cottage pie

1 tablespoon olive oil
2 cloves garlic, crushed
1 large brown onion (200g), chopped finely
2 medium carrots (240g), peeled, chopped finely
1kg beef mince
1 tablespoon worcestershire sauce
2 tablespoons tomato paste
2 x 425g cans crushed tomatoes
1 teaspoon dried mixed herbs
200g mushrooms, quartered
1 cup (120g) frozen peas
1kg potatoes, peeled, chopped coarsely
¾ cup (180ml) hot milk
40g butter, softened
½ cup (50g) coarsely grated pizza cheese

1 Heat oil in large saucepan; cook garlic, onion and carrot, stirring, until onion softens. Add beef; cook, stirring, about 10 minutes or until changed in colour.
2 Add sauce, paste, undrained tomatoes and herbs; bring to the boil. Reduce heat; simmer, uncovered, about 30 minutes or until mixture thickens slightly. Stir in mushrooms and peas.
3 Meanwhile, preheat oven to 180°C/160°C fan-forced. Boil, steam or microwave potato until tender; drain. Mash potato in large bowl with milk and butter.
4 Pour beef mixture into deep 3-litre (12-cup) ovenproof dish; top with mashed potato mixture; sprinkle with cheese. Bake, uncovered, about 45 minutes or until pie is heated through and top is browned lightly.

preparation time *20 minutes*
cooking time *1 hour 35 minutes* serves *8*
nutritional count per serving *15.7g total fat (7g saturated fat); 1634kJ (391 cal); 24.6g carbohydrate; 34.8g protein; 6.2g fibre*

fish chowder

40g butter
1 large brown onion (200g), chopped coarsely
1 clove garlic, crushed
2 rindless bacon rashers (130g), chopped coarsely
2 tablespoons plain flour
2 medium potatoes (400g), chopped coarsely
3 cups (750ml) milk
2 cups (500ml) vegetable stock
400g firm white fish fillets, chopped coarsely
2 tablespoons finely chopped fresh chives

1 Melt butter in large saucepan; cook onion, garlic
and bacon, stirring, until onion softens.
2 Add flour; cook, stirring, 1 minute. Add potato,
milk and stock; bring to the boil. Reduce heat; simmer,
covered, about 10 minutes or until potato is just tender.
3 Add fish; simmer, uncovered, about 4 minutes or
until fish is cooked through (do not overcook).
4 Serve bowls of soup sprinkled with chives.

preparation time *15 minutes*
cooking time *30 minutes* serves *4*
nutritional count per serving *19.5g total fat (11.6g
saturated fat); 1810kJ (433 cal); 28.4g carbohydrate;
34.8g protein; 2.4g fibre*

pea and ham soup with risoni

2 teaspoons olive oil
1 medium brown onion (150g), chopped coarsely
2 teaspoons ground cumin
2.5 litres (10 cups) water
2 trimmed celery stalks (200g), chopped coarsely
2 dried bay leaves
1.5kg ham bone
1 cup (220g) risoni pasta
2 cups (240g) frozen peas
2 tablespoons finely chopped fresh mint

1 Heat oil in large saucepan; cook onion, stirring,
until softened. Add cumin; cook, stirring, until fragrant.
Add the water, celery, bay leaves and bone; bring
to the boil. Reduce heat; simmer, covered, 1 hour,
skimming occasionally.
2 Remove bone; when cool enough to handle,
cut ham from bone, discarding any skin and fat.
Shred ham finely.
3 Return soup to the boil; stir in ham, pasta and
peas. Cook, uncovered, about 5 minutes or until
pasta is tender.
4 Serve bowls of soup sprinkled with mint.

preparation time *15 minutes*
cooking time *1 hour 15 minutes* serves *6*
nutritional count per serving *3g total fat (0.6g
saturated fat); 811kJ (194 cal); 30g carbohydrate;
9g protein; 4.6g fibre*

roast chicken with tomato braised beans

2kg chicken
1 medium lemon (140g), quartered
6 sprigs fresh thyme
6 cloves garlic, unpeeled
60g butter, softened
2 tablespoons lemon juice
2 cloves garlic, crushed
2 teaspoons finely chopped fresh thyme
1 cup (250ml) water
1 tablespoon olive oil
1 medium brown onion (150g), chopped coarsely
1kg green beans, trimmed
4 medium tomatoes (600g), chopped coarsely

1 Preheat oven to 200°C/180°C fan-forced.
2 Tuck wing tips under chicken. Fill cavity with lemon, thyme sprigs and garlic, fold skin over to enclose filling; secure with toothpicks. Tie legs together with kitchen string.
3 Combine butter, juice, crushed garlic and chopped thyme in small bowl; rub butter mixture all over chicken.
4 Place chicken on oiled rack in large baking dish; pour the water into dish. Roast about 2 hours, basting occasionally with pan juices.
5 Meanwhile, heat oil in large saucepan; cook onion, stirring, until onion softens. Add beans and tomato; cook, covered, stirring occasionally, about 20 minutes or until vegetables soften slightly.
6 Serve chicken with beans.

preparation time *30 minutes*
cooking time *2 hours 10 minutes* serves *6*
nutritional count per serving *33.5g total fat (12.7g saturated fat); 2123kJ (508 cal); 8.3g carbohydrate; 40.3g protein; 7.3g fibre*

winter vegetable gratin

3 medium potatoes (600g)
1 large swede (450g)
1 large kumara (500g)
2 medium carrots (240g)
¾ cup (60g) finely grated parmesan cheese
½ cup (35g) stale breadcrumbs
WHITE SAUCE
40g butter
¼ cup (35g) plain flour
2 cups (500ml) skim milk
pinch ground nutmeg

1 Preheat oven to 200°C/180°C fan-forced. Oil deep 19cm-square cake pan.
2 Make white sauce.
3 Using sharp knife, mandoline or V-slicer, slice vegetables thinly; pat dry with absorbent paper.
4 Layer potato slices in dish; pour a third of the white sauce over potato slices. Layer carrot, another a third of the white sauce, then swede, remaining white sauce and finally the kumara.
5 Bake gratin, covered, about 1½ hours or until vegetables are tender. Top with combined cheese and breadcrumbs; bake, uncovered, a further 20 minutes or until top is browned. Stand 10 minutes before serving.

WHITE SAUCE Melt butter in medium saucepan, add flour; cook, stirring, 1 minute. Remove from heat, gradually stir in milk; cook, stirring, until sauce boils and thickens. Stir in nutmeg.

preparation time *25 minutes*
cooking time *1 hour 50 minutes* serves *4*
nutritional count per serving *13.9g total fat (8.7g saturated fat); 1810kJ (433 cal); 57.6g carbohydrate; 19.1g protein; 8.8g fibre*

slow-cooked lamb and white bean soup

1 cup (200g) dried cannellini beans
2 medium red capsicums (400g)
1 tablespoon olive oil
1.5kg french-trimmed lamb shanks
1 large brown onion (200g), chopped coarsely
2 cloves garlic, quartered
2 medium carrots (240g), chopped coarsely
2 trimmed celery stalks (200g), chopped coarsely
2 tablespoons tomato paste
1 cup (250ml) dry red wine
3 litres (12 cups) water
80g baby spinach leaves

1 Place beans in medium bowl, cover with water, stand overnight; drain. Rinse under cold water; drain.
2 Preheat grill.
3 Quarter capsicums; discard seeds and membranes. Roast under grill or in very hot oven, skin-side up, until skin blisters and blackens. Cover capsicum pieces with plastic or paper for 5 minutes; peel away skin, dice capsicum finely.
4 Heat oil in large saucepan; cook lamb, in batches, until browned all over.
5 Cook onion and garlic in same pan, stirring, until onion softens. Add carrot and celery; cook, stirring, 2 minutes. Add paste and wine; bring to the boil. Reduce heat; simmer, uncovered, 5 minutes.
6 Return lamb to pan with the water; bring to the boil. Reduce heat; simmer, uncovered, 2 hours, skimming fat from surface occasionally.
7 Meanwhile, place beans in medium saucepan of boiling water; return to the boil. Reduce heat; simmer, uncovered, about 30 minutes or until beans are almost tender. Drain.
8 Remove lamb from pan. Strain broth through muslin-lined sieve or colander into large heatproof bowl; discard solids. When lamb is cool enough to handle, remove meat from shanks; shred coarsely. Discard bones.
9 Return broth to same cleaned pan with capsicum, beans and lamb; bring to the boil. Reduce heat; simmer, uncovered, 5 minutes. Remove from heat; stir in spinach.

preparation time *35 minutes (plus standing time)*
cooking time *3 hours 20 minutes* serves *4*
nutritional count per serving *1.8g total fat (0.7g saturated fat); 171kJ (41 cal); 1.4g carbohydrate; 3.8g protein; 0.7g fibre*

quiche lorraine

1¾ cups (255g) plain flour
150g cold butter, chopped
1 egg yolk
2 teaspoons lemon juice, approximately
⅓ cup (80ml) cold water
1 medium brown onion (150g), chopped finely
3 rindless bacon rashers (195g), chopped
3 eggs
300ml cream
½ cup (125ml) milk
¾ cup (120g) grated cheddar cheese

1 Sift flour into bowl; rub in butter. Add egg yolk, juice
and enough water to make ingredients cling together.
Knead gently on floured surface until smooth, cover;
refrigerate 30 minutes.
2 Roll pastry between baking paper large enough to
line a deep 23cm loose-base flan tin. Lift pastry into
flan tin, gently ease pastry into base and side of tin.
Use rolling pin to neatly trim edges of pastry. Place
on oven tray.
3 Preheat oven to 200°C/180°C fan-forced.
4 Line pastry with baking paper, fill with dried beans
or rice; bake 10 minutes. Remove paper and beans;
bake further 10 minutes or until browned. Cool to
room temperature.
5 Reduce oven to 180°C/160°C fan-forced.
6 Cook onion and bacon in oiled small frying pan
until onion is soft; drain away excess fat, cool before
spreading into pastry case.
7 Using whisk, beat eggs in medium bowl; add
cream, milk and cheese. Whisk until just combined;
pour into pastry case.
8 Bake quiche about 35 minutes or until filling is set
and brown. Stand 5 minutes before removing from tin.

preparation time *30 minutes (plus refrigeration and
standing time)* cooking time *1 hour (plus cooling time)*
serves *6*
nutritional count per serving *58.1g total fat (35.4g
saturated fat); 3127kJ (748 cal); 34.8g carbohydrate;
22g protein; 1.9g fibre*

sausage rolls

4 sheets ready-rolled puff pastry
1 egg, beaten lightly
FILLING
750g sausage mince
1 medium white onion (150g), chopped finely
1 cup (70g) stale breadcrumbs
1 teaspoon dried mixed herbs
1 egg, beaten lightly

1 Preheat oven to 200°C/180°C fan-forced.
Oil two oven trays.
2 Cut each sheet of pastry in half.
3 Combine filling ingredients in large bowl; spoon
filling into piping bag.
4 Pipe filling along one long side of each pastry sheet.
Brush opposite edge of pastry with egg; roll up pastry
from filled edge to enclose filling. Cut into six even
pieces, place on trays. Brush with egg; cut small slits
in top of each roll.
5 Bake sausage rolls 25 minutes or until well browned.

preparation time *25 minutes*
cooking time *25 minutes* makes *48*
nutritional count per sausage roll *7.1g total fat (1.9g
saturated fat); 426kJ (102 cal); 6.6g carbohydrate;
3.1g protein; 0.6g fibre*

potato terrine

2 large potatoes (600g)
1 medium red capsicum (200g)
1 large eggplant (500g)
cooking-oil spray
1 large leek (500g)
⅓ cup (80ml) olive oil
3 cloves garlic, crushed
2 tablespoons finely chopped fresh thyme
1 teaspoon ground black pepper
10 slices prosciutto (150g)
250g mozzarella cheese, sliced
1 cup loosely packed fresh basil leaves

SAFFRON VINAIGRETTE

⅓ cup (80ml) olive oil
2 tablespoons lemon juice
pinch saffron threads

1 Preheat oven to 180°C/160°C fan-forced. Oil 14cm x 21cm loaf pan.
2 Cut potatoes into 2mm slices. Add potato to large saucepan of boiling water; cook about 4 minutes or until potatoes are just beginning to soften; drain.
3 Preheat grill. Quarter capsicum, remove seeds and membranes. Roast under grill, skin-side up, until skin blisters and blackens. Cover capsicum pieces in plastic or paper 5 minutes; peel away skin.
4 Cut eggplant lengthways into 5mm slices; spray slices, both sides, with oil. Cook eggplant, in large frying pan, until browned both sides; drain on absorbent paper.
5 Cut white part of leek into 7cm lengths; cut lengths in half. Boil, steam or microwave leek until tender. Drain, rinse under cold water; drain.
6 Combine oil, garlic, thyme and pepper in small bowl.
7 Cover base and long sides of pan with prosciutto, allowing prosciutto to overhang edges. Place half of the potato, overlapping, over base, brush with herb oil mixture; top with half of the cheese, brush with herb oil mixture. Layer capsicum, eggplant, basil and leek, brushing each layer with herb oil mixture. Top leek layer with remaining cheese then remaining potato, brushing with herb oil mixture between layers; press down firmly. Cover terrine with prosciutto slices.
8 Cover terrine with foil, place on oven tray. Bake 1 hour; uncover, cook further 40 minutes. Remove from oven, pour off any liquid. Cool 5 minutes; cover top of terrine with plastic wrap, weight with two large heavy cans for 1 hour.
9 Make saffron vinaigrette. Serve with sliced terrine.

SAFFRON VINAIGRETTE Place ingredients in screw-top jar; shake well.

preparation time *1 hour*
cooking time *2 hours 15 minutes (plus standing time)*
serves *8*
nutritional count per serving *27.1g total fat (7.4g saturated fat); 1476kJ (353 cal); 12.8g carbohydrate; 15.1g protein; 4.3g fibre*

potato salad

2kg potatoes, peeled
2 tablespoons cider vinegar
8 green onions, sliced thinly
¼ cup finely chopped fresh flat-leaf parsley

MAYONNAISE

2 egg yolks
1 teaspoon dijon mustard
2 teaspoons lemon juice
1 cup (250ml) vegetable oil
2 tablespoons hot water, approximately

1 Cut potatoes into 1.5cm pieces. Place potato in large saucepan, barely cover with cold water; cover saucepan, bring to the boil. Reduce heat; simmer, uncovered, stirring occasionally, until just tender. Drain, spread potato on a tray; sprinkle with vinegar. Cool 10 minutes. Refrigerate, covered, until cold.
2 Meanwhile, make mayonnaise.
3 Place potato in large bowl with mayonnaise, onion and parsley; mix gently to combine.

MAYONNAISE Blend or process egg yolks, mustard and juice until smooth. With motor operating, gradually add oil in a thin, steady stream; process until mixture thickens. Add as much of the hot water as required to thin mayonnaise.

preparation time *20 minutes (plus refrigeration time)*
cooking time *20 minutes*
serves *8 (makes 1 cup mayonnaise)*
nutritional count per serving *30.4g total fat (4.1g saturated fat); 1739kJ (416 cal); 28.4g carbohydrate; 6.1g protein; 3.8g fibre*

salmon and potato patties

1kg potatoes, peeled
440g can red salmon
1 small brown onion (80g), chopped finely
1 tablespoon finely chopped fresh flat-leaf parsley
1 teaspoon finely grated lemon rind
1 tablespoon lemon juice
½ cup (75g) plain flour
1 egg
2 tablespoons milk
½ cup (50g) packaged breadcrumbs
½ cup (35g) stale breadcrumbs
vegetable oil, for deep-frying

1 Boil, steam or microwave potatoes until tender; drain. Mash potato in large bowl.
2 Drain salmon; discard any skin and bones. Add salmon to potato with onion, parsley, rind and juice; mix well. Cover; refrigerate 30 minutes.
3 Using floured hands, shape salmon mixture into eight patties. Toss patties in flour; shake away excess. Dip patties, one at a time, in combined egg and milk, then in combined breadcrumbs.
4 Heat oil in wok or large saucepan; deep-fry patties, in batches, until browned. Drain on absorbent paper.

preparation time *20 minutes (plus refrigeration time)*
cooking time *20 minutes* serves *4*
nutritional count per serving *33.4g total fat (6.3g saturated fat); 2792kJ (668 cal); 57.3g carbohydrate; 31.9g protein; 5.4g fibre*

1 POTATO SALAD 2 SALMON AND POTATO PATTIES
3 CREAMED POTATOES WITH ROSEMARY AND CHEESE [P 218]
4 POTATO CROQUETTES [P 218]

JUST LIKE MUM MADE   217

creamed potatoes with rosemary and cheese

1kg potatoes, peeled
300ml cream
2 cloves garlic, crushed
2 chicken stock cubes, crumbled
¼ teaspoon cracked black pepper
1 tablespoon finely chopped fresh rosemary
½ cup (40g) finely grated parmesan cheese

1   Preheat oven to 180°C/160°C fan-forced.
Oil shallow 2.5-litre (10-cup) ovenproof dish.
2   Using sharp knife, mandoline or V-slicer, cut potatoes into thin slices; pat dry with absorbent paper.
3   Combine cream, garlic, stock cubes, pepper and rosemary in small bowl.
4   Layer a quarter of the potato slices, slightly overlapping, in dish; top with a quarter of the cream mixture. Continue layering remaining potato and cream mixture. Press potato firmly with spatula to completely submerge in cream.
5   Cover dish with foil; bake 1 hour. Remove foil; sprinkle with cheese. Bake, uncovered, further 20 minutes or until potato is tender and cheese browns lightly. Stand 10 minutes before serving.

preparation time *15 minutes*
cooking time *1 hour 20 minutes (plus standing time)*
serves *6*
nutritional count per serving *24.1g total fat (15.7g saturated fat); 1375kJ (329 cal); 20.4g carbohydrate; 7.1g protein; 2.4g fibre*

potato croquettes

1kg potatoes, peeled, chopped coarsely
2 egg yolks
20g butter
½ cup (75g) plain flour
½ cup (60g) finely grated cheddar cheese
⅓ cup (50g) plain flour, extra
2 eggs, beaten lightly
2 tablespoons milk
1 cup (100g) packaged breadcrumbs
vegetable oil, for deep-frying

1   Boil, steam or microwave potato until tender; drain. Mash potato in large bowl with yolks, butter, flour and cheese. Cover, refrigerate 30 minutes.
2   Using floured hands, shape heaped tablespoons of the potato mixture into fairly flat fish-finger shapes, dust with extra flour; shake away excess. Dip croquettes, one at a time, in combined egg and milk, then in breadcrumbs. Refrigerate 30 minutes.
3   Heat oil in wok or large saucepan; deep-fry croquettes, in batches, until browned. Drain on absorbent paper.

preparation time *20 minutes (plus refrigeration time)*
cooking time *25 minutes* makes *24*
nutritional count per croquette *5.6g total fat (1.7g saturated fat); 464kJ (111 cal); 11.2g carbohydrate; 3.5g protein; 0.9g fibre*

VARIATION

PESTO & MOZZARELLA Blend or process ¾ cup firmly packed fresh basil leaves, 1 tablespoon toasted pine nuts, 1 tablespoon finely grated parmesan cheese, 1 quartered garlic clove, 1 tablespoon olive oil and 2 teaspoons lemon juice until almost smooth. Add pesto to croquette mixture. Mould croquettes into balls around 5mm-square pieces of mozzarella.

makes *32*
nutritional count per croquette *5.2g total fat (1.5g saturated fat); 389kJ (93 cal); 8.5g carbohydrate; 2.8g protein; 0.8g fibre*

scalloped potatoes

1.2kg potatoes, peeled
150g leg ham, chopped finely
300ml cream
¾ cup (180ml) milk
¾ cup (90g) coarsely grated cheddar cheese

1 Preheat oven to 180°C/160°C fan-forced.
Oil 1.5-litre (6-cup) baking dish.
2 Using sharp knife, mandoline or V-slicer, cut potatoes into very thin slices; pat dry with absorbent paper. Layer a quarter of the potato in dish; top with a third of the ham. Continue layering remaining potato and ham, finishing with potato.
3 Heat cream and milk in small saucepan until almost boiling; pour over potato mixture.
4 Cover dish with foil; bake 30 minutes. Remove foil; bake further 20 minutes. Top with cheese; bake, uncovered, another 20 minutes or until potato is tender. Stand 10 minutes before serving.

preparation time *20 minutes*
cooking time *1 hour 10 minutes (plus standing time)*
serves *6*
nutritional counts per serving *28.9g total fat (18.6g saturated fat); 1764kJ (422 cal); 25.2g carbohydrate; 14.6g protein; 2.7g fibre*

bacon and cheese baked potatoes

6 large potatoes (1.8kg)
1 medium brown onion (150g), chopped finely
3 bacon rashers (210g), chopped coarsely
⅓ cup (80g) sour cream
½ cup (60g) grated cheddar
1 tablespoon finely chopped fresh chives

1 Boil, steam or microwave potatoes until tender; drain.
2 Cook onion and bacon in heated oiled frying pan until browned.
3 Preheat grill.
4 Cut and discard shallow slice from each potato. Scoop two-thirds of potato from each shell; place shells on baking-paper-lined oven tray. Discard half the potato flesh; combine remainder in bowl with bacon mixture, cream and half of the cheese.
5 Spoon mixture into shells; top with remaining cheese. Grill until cheese browns. Sprinkle with chives.

preparation time *20 minutes*
cooking time *30 minutes* serves *6*
nutritional count per serving *11.2g total fat (6.4g saturated fat); 1275kJ (305 cal); 35g carbohydrate; 12.5g protein; 5.4g fibre*

chunky beef and vegetable soup

For an added vegie kick, toss a coarsely chopped trimmed bunch of spinach into the soup when you add the corn and peas.

2 tablespoons olive oil
600g gravy beef, trimmed, cut into 2cm pieces
1 medium brown onion (150g), chopped coarsely
1 clove garlic, crushed
1.5 litres (6 cups) water
1 cup (250ml) beef stock
400g can diced tomatoes
2 trimmed celery stalks (200g), cut into 1cm pieces
1 medium carrot (120g), cut into 1cm pieces
2 small potatoes (240g), cut into 1cm pieces
310g can corn kernels, rinsed, drained
½ cup (60g) frozen peas

1 Heat half the oil in large saucepan; cook beef, in batches, until browned.
2 Heat remaining oil in same pan; cook onion and garlic, stirring, until onion softens. Return beef to pan with the water, stock and undrained tomatoes; bring to the boil. Reduce heat; simmer, covered, 1½ hours.
3 Add celery, carrot and potato to soup; simmer, uncovered, about 20 minutes or until vegetables are tender.
4 Add corn and peas to soup; stir over heat until peas are tender.

preparation time *20 minutes*
cooking time *2 hours* serves *4*
nutritional count per serving *17g total fat (4.3g saturated fat); 1768kJ (423 cal); 26.7g carbohydrate; 36.9g protein; 7.5g fibre*

beef stroganoff

750g piece rump steak
2 tablespoons plain flour
1 teaspoon paprika
60g butter
1 medium onion (150g), chopped finely
2 cloves garlic, crushed
250g small button mushrooms
1 tablespoon lemon juice
¼ cup (60ml) dry red wine
2 tablespoons tomato paste
1 cup (180g) sour cream
1 tablespoon finely chopped fresh chives

1 Wrap steak in plastic wrap; freeze 30 minutes or until partly frozen. Remove plastic; use sharp knife to cut steak into thin slices. Place steak in plastic bag with flour and paprika; shake until steak is well coated with flour mixture.
2 Melt butter in large saucepan; cook onion and garlic, stirring, over medium heat until onion is soft. Increase heat to high; cook steak, in batches, until browned all over.
3 Return steak to pan; add mushrooms, juice and wine, stir until ingredients are combined. Reduce heat; simmer, covered, about 10 minutes or until steak is tender.
4 Stir in paste and sour cream; stir constantly over heat until mixture is heated through.
5 Serve stroganoff with boiled pasta or rice, if you like, and sprinkle with chives.

preparation time *15 minutes (plus freezing time)*
cooking time *15 minutes* serves *4*
nutritional count per serving *39.2g total fat (23.6g saturated fat); 2291kJ (548 cal); 9.1g carbohydrate; 45.7g protein; 3g fibre*

classic trifle

85g packet raspberry jelly crystals
250g sponge cake, cut into 3cm pieces
¼ cup (60ml) sweet sherry
¼ cup (30g) custard powder
¼ cup (55g) caster sugar
½ teaspoon vanilla extract
1½ cups (375ml) milk
825g can sliced peaches, drained
300ml thickened cream
2 tablespoons flaked almonds, roasted

1   Make jelly according to packet directions; pour into shallow container. Refrigerate 20 minutes or until jelly is almost set.
2   Arrange cake pieces in 3-litre (12-cup) bowl; sprinkle with sherry.
3   Blend custard powder, sugar and extract with a little of the milk in small saucepan; stir in remaining milk. Stir over heat until mixture boils and thickens. Cover surface with plastic wrap; cool.
4   Pour jelly over cake; refrigerate 15 minutes. Top with peaches. Stir a third of the cream into custard; pour over peaches.
5   Whip remaining cream; spread over custard, sprinkle with nuts. Refrigerate 3 hours or overnight.

preparation time *30 minutes (plus refrigeration time)*
cooking time *10 minutes* serves *8*
nutritional count per serving *29.5g total fat (14.5g saturated fat); 2123kJ (508 cal); 57.4g carbohydrate; 8.7g protein; 2g fibre*

strawberry powder puffs

2 eggs
⅓ cup (75g) caster sugar
2 tablespoons cornflour
2 tablespoons plain flour
2 tablespoons self-raising flour
½ cup (125ml) thickened cream
2 tablespoons icing sugar
½ cup (65g) finely chopped strawberries

1   Preheat oven to 180°C/160°C fan-forced. Grease and flour two 12-hole shallow round-based patty pans.
2   Beat eggs and sugar in small bowl with electric mixer about 4 minutes or until thick and creamy.
3   Meanwhile, triple-sift flours; fold into egg mixture.
4   Drop 1 teaspoon of mixture into holes of pans. Bake about 7 minutes; turn immediately onto wire racks to cool. Wash, grease and flour pans again; continue using mixture until all puffs are baked.
5   Beat cream and half the sifted icing sugar in small bowl with electric mixer until firm peaks form; fold in strawberries.
6   Sandwich puffs with strawberry cream just before serving. Dust with remaining sifted icing sugar.

preparation time *30 minutes*
cooking time *7 minutes per batch* makes *36*
nutritional count per puff *1.8g total fat (1.1g saturated fat); 150kJ (36 cal); 4.2g carbohydrate; 0.6g protein; 0.1g fibre*

apple and rhubarb turnovers

2 medium apples (300g)
20g butter
2 cups (220g) coarsely chopped trimmed rhubarb
⅓ cup (75g) firmly packed brown sugar
1 tablespoon lemon juice
½ teaspoon ground cinnamon
2 sheets ready-rolled butter puff pastry
1 egg, beaten lightly
1 tablespoon icing sugar

1 Preheat oven to 200°C/180°C fan-forced.
2 Peel and core apples; cut into thin wedges. Melt butter in medium frying pan; cook apple, rhubarb, sugar and juice, stirring occasionally, until sugar dissolves and apple starts to caramelise. Stir in cinnamon; spread mixture on tray. Cool 10 minutes.
3 Cut two 14cm rounds from each pastry sheet. Place a quarter of the fruit mixture on each pastry round; brush around edges with egg. Fold pastry over to enclose filling; pinch edges together to seal. Place turnovers on greased oven tray; brush with egg.
4 Bake turnovers about 15 minutes or until browned lightly. Dust with sifted icing sugar; serve warm with cream or ice-cream, if you like.

preparation time *15 minutes*
cooking time *25 minutes serves 4*
nutritional count per serving *24.5g total fat (13.3g saturated fat); 2069kJ (495 cal); 59.2g carbohydrate; 7.5g protein; 4g fibre*

featherlight sponge

4 eggs
¾ cup (165g) caster sugar
⅔ cup (100g) wheaten cornflour
¼ cup (30g) custard powder
1 teaspoon cream of tartar
½ teaspoon bicarbonate of soda
⅓ cup (110g) apricot jam
300ml thickened cream, whipped

1 Preheat oven to 180°C/160°C fan-forced. Grease and flour two deep 22cm-round cake pans.
2 Beat eggs and sugar in small bowl with electric mixer until thick, creamy and sugar dissolved. Transfer mixture to large bowl; fold in triple-sifted dry ingredients. Divide mixture between pans.
3 Bake sponges about 20 minutes. Turn, top-side up, onto baking-paper-covered wire rack to cool.
4 Sandwich sponges with jam and cream.

preparation time *20 minutes*
cooking time *20 minutes serves 10*
nutritional count per serving *13.3g total fat (8g saturated fat); 1195kJ (286 cal); 37.2g carbohydrate; 3.8g protein; 0.7g fibre*

butterfly cakes

125g butter, softened
1 teaspoon vanilla extract
⅔ cup (150g) caster sugar
3 eggs
1½ cups (225g) self-raising flour
¼ cup (60ml) milk
½ cup (160g) jam
300ml thickened cream

1 Preheat oven to 200°C/180°C fan-forced. Line two deep 12-hole patty pans with paper cases.
2 Beat butter, extract, sugar, eggs, flour and milk in small bowl of electric mixer on low speed until ingredients are just combined. Increase speed to medium, beat about 3 minutes, or until mixture is smooth and changed to a paler colour. Drop slightly rounded tablespoons of mixture into paper cases.
3 Bake cakes about 20 minutes. Turn, top-side up, onto wire racks to cool.
4 Using sharp pointed vegetable knife, cut circle from top of each cake; cut circle in half to make two "wings". Fill cavities with jam and whipped cream. Place wings in position on top of cakes; top with strawberry pieces and dust with a little sifted icing sugar, if you like.

preparation time *30 minutes*
cooking time *20 minutes* makes *24*
nutritional count per cake *9.8g total fat (6.2g saturated fat); 702kJ (168 cal); 17.8g carbohydrate; 2.2g protein; 0.4g fibre*

cinnamon teacake

60g butter, softened
1 teaspoon vanilla extract
⅔ cup (150g) caster sugar
1 egg
1 cup (150g) self-raising flour
⅓ cup (80ml) milk
10g butter, extra, melted
1 teaspoon ground cinnamon
1 tablespoon caster sugar, extra

1 Preheat oven to 180°C/160°C fan-forced. Grease deep 20cm-round cake pan; line base with baking paper.
2 Beat softened butter, extract, sugar and egg in small bowl with electric mixer about 8 minutes or until light and fluffy. Stir in sifted flour and milk. Spread mixture into pan.
3 Bake cake about 30 minutes. Stand 5 minutes before turning top-side up onto wire rack. Brush top with melted butter, sprinkle with combined cinnamon and extra sugar. Serve warm with butter, if you like.

preparation time *15 minutes*
cooking time *30 minutes* serves *10*
nutritional count per serving *6.8g total fat (4.2g saturated fat); 769kJ (189 cal); 27.8g carbohydrate; 2.5g protein; 0.6g fibre*

lemon meringue pie

½ cup (75g) cornflour
1 cup (220g) caster sugar
½ cup (125ml) lemon juice
1¼ cups (310ml) water
2 teaspoons finely grated lemon rind
60g unsalted butter, chopped
3 eggs, separated
½ cup (110g) caster sugar, extra

PASTRY

1½ cups (225g) plain flour
1 tablespoon icing sugar
140g cold butter, chopped
1 egg yolk
2 tablespoons cold water

1 Make pastry.
2 Grease 24cm-round loose-based fluted flan tin. Roll pastry between sheets of baking paper until large enough to line tin. Ease pastry into tin, press into base and side; trim edge. Cover; refrigerate 30 minutes.
3 Preheat oven to 240°C/220°C fan-forced.
4 Place tin on oven tray. Line pastry case with baking paper; fill with dried beans or rice. Bake 15 minutes. Remove paper and beans carefully from pie shell; bake further 10 minutes; cool pie shell, turn oven off.
5 Meanwhile, combine cornflour and sugar in medium saucepan; gradually stir in juice and the water until smooth. Cook, stirring, over high heat, until mixture boils and thickens. Reduce heat; simmer, stirring, 1 minute. Remove from heat; stir in rind, butter and egg yolks. Cool 10 minutes.
6 Spread filling into pie shell. Cover; refrigerate 2 hours.
7 Preheat oven to 240°C/220°C fan-forced.
8 Beat egg whites in small bowl with electric mixer until soft peaks form; gradually add extra sugar, beating until sugar dissolves.
9 Roughen surface of filling with fork before spreading with meringue mixture. Bake about 2 minutes or until browned lightly.

PASTRY Process flour, icing sugar and butter until crumbly. Add egg yolk and the water; process until ingredients come together. Knead dough on floured surface until smooth. Wrap in plastic wrap; refrigerate 30 minutes.

preparation time *30 minutes (plus refrigeration time)* cooking time *35 minutes* serves *10* nutritional count per serving *18.9g total fat (11.6g saturated fat); 1772kJ (424 cal); 57.7g carbohydrate; 5g protein; 0.9g fibre*

rhubarb and pear sponge pudding

825g can pear slices in natural juice
800g rhubarb, trimmed, cut into 4cm pieces
2 tablespoons caster sugar
2 eggs
⅓ cup (75g) caster sugar, extra
2 tablespoons plain flour
2 tablespoons self-raising flour
2 tablespoons cornflour

1 Preheat oven to 180°C/160°C fan-forced.
2 Drain pears; reserve ¾ cup (180ml) of the juice.
3 Cook rhubarb, sugar and reserved juice in large saucepan, stirring occasionally, about 5 minutes or until rhubarb is just tender. Stir in pears. Pour mixture into deep 1.75-litre (7-cup) ovenproof dish.
4 Meanwhile, beat eggs in small bowl with electric mixer until thick and creamy. Gradually add extra sugar, 1 tablespoon at a time, beating until sugar dissolves between additions. Gently fold in combined sifted flours. Spread sponge mixture over hot rhubarb mixture.
5 Bake pudding about 45 minutes or until browned lightly and cooked through.

preparation time *15 minutes*
cooking time *50 minutes* serves *6*
nutritional count per serving *2.1g total fat (0.6g saturated fat); 823kJ (197 cal); 35.7g carbohydrate; 5.4g protein; 5.9g fibre*

banana cake with passionfruit icing

You need approximately two large overripe bananas (460g) and two large passionfruit for this recipe.

125g butter, softened
¾ cup (165g) firmly packed brown sugar
2 eggs
1½ cups (225g) self-raising flour
½ teaspoon bicarbonate of soda
1 teaspoon mixed spice
1 cup mashed banana
½ cup (120g) sour cream
¼ cup (60ml) milk

PASSIONFRUIT ICING

1½ cups (240g) icing sugar
1 teaspoon soft butter
2 tablespoons passionfruit pulp, approximately

1 Preheat oven to 180°C/160°C fan-forced. Grease 15cm x 25cm loaf pan; line base with baking paper.
2 Beat butter and sugar in small bowl with electric mixer until light and fluffy. Beat in eggs, one at a time. Transfer to large bowl; stir in sifted dry ingredients, banana, sour cream and milk. Spread mixture into pan.
3 Bake cake about 50 minutes. Stand 5 minutes; turn, top-side up, onto wire rack to cool.
4 Meanwhile, make passionfruit icing.
5 Spread cake with icing.

PASSIONFRUIT ICING Combine ingredients in small bowl.

preparation time *35 minutes*
cooking time *50 minutes* serves *10*
nutritional count per serving *17g total fat (10.7g saturated fat); 1768kJ (423 cal); 61.5g carbohydrate; 4.7g protein; 1.9g fibre*

baked apples

4 large granny smith apples (800g)
50g butter, melted
⅓ cup (75g) firmly packed brown sugar
½ cup (80g) sultanas
1 teaspoon ground cinnamon

1 Preheat oven to 160°C/140°C fan-forced.
2 Core unpeeled apples about three-quarters of
the way down from stem end, making hole 4cm
in diameter. Use small sharp knife to score around
centre of each apple.
3 Combine remaining ingredients in small bowl;
pack mixture firmly into apples. Stand apples upright
in small baking dish.
4 Bake apples about 45 minutes.

preparation time *15 minutes*
cooking time *45 minutes* serves *4*
nutritional count per serving *10.5g total fat (6.8g
saturated fat); 1292kJ (309 cal); 50.2g carbohydrate;
1.2g protein; 4g fibre*

roasted whole quinces

1.5kg (7 cups) sugar
1.5 litres (6 cups) water
2.4kg whole quinces
1 strip orange rind
1 cinnamon stick
2 cardamom pods
¾ cup (180ml) lemon juice, approximately

1 Preheat oven to 180°C/160°C fan-forced.
2 Stir sugar and the water in medium saucepan over
medium heat, without boiling, until sugar is dissolved.
3 Wash quince well. Put unpeeled quince, rind and
spices into large ovenproof dish; pour syrup over.
4 Bake quinces, covered, about 4 hours, turning
occasionally, or until quinces are tender and deep
pink. Remove quince, add enough juice to the syrup
to adjust sweetness.
5 When cool enough to handle, peel skin from quince.
6 Serve warm quince with syrup and, if you like, cream.

preparation time *10 minutes*
cooking time *4 hours* serves *6*
nutritional count per serving *0.6g total fat (0g saturated
fat); 4213kJ (1008 cal); 235.4g carbohydrate;
1.6g protein; 20.8g fibre*

celebration christmas cakes

3 cups (500g) sultanas
1¾ cups (300g) raisins
1¾ cups (300g) seeded dried dates
1 cup (150g) dried currants
¼ cup (40g) candied orange
⅔ cup (130g) red glacé cherries
¼ cup (55g) glacé ginger
¼ cup (60g) dried apricots
½ cup (125ml) Grand Marnier
250g butter, softened
1 cup (220g) firmly packed brown sugar
5 eggs
1½ cups (225g) plain flour
⅓ cup (50g) self-raising flour
1 teaspoon mixed spice
2 tablespoons Grand Marnier, extra
1kg ready-made white icing
1 egg white
½ cup (80g) icing sugar
20cm-square cake board
60g jar silver cachous
15m silver ribbon

1 Chop all fruit the same size as sultanas. Combine fruit and liqueur in large bowl; cover with plastic wrap, stand overnight.

2 Preheat oven to 150°C/130°C fan-forced. Line two deep 15cm-square cake pans with three thicknesses of baking paper, extending paper 5cm above sides of pans.

3 Beat butter and brown sugar in small bowl with electric mixer until combined; beat in eggs one at a time. Add butter mixture to fruit mixture; mix well. Mix in sifted flours and spice; divide mixture between pans.

4 Bake cakes about 2 hours. Brush hot cakes with extra liqueur. Cover hot cakes in pan tightly with foil, turn upside down, on bench; cool overnight.

5 Trim top of one cake if necessary to make it flat. Mix a walnut-sized piece of white icing with enough cold boiled water to make a sticky paste. Spread half of this mixture into the centre of a sheet of baking paper about 5cm larger than the cake; position cake flat-side down on paper. Using a metal spatula and small pieces of white icing, patch any holes in the cake.

6 Brush egg white evenly over cake. Knead half of the remaining white icing on surface dusted with sifted icing sugar until smooth; roll to 7mm thickness. Lift icing onto cake with rolling pin, smoothing icing over cake with hands dusted with icing sugar. Cut excess icing away from base of cake.

7 Mix icing scraps with cold boiled water to make a sticky paste. Spread half of paste in centre of cake board; centre cake on board. Cut away excess baking paper around base of cake.

8 Gently push a bell-shaped cutter three-quarters of the way into icing. Using a small sharp knife carefully remove about half of the icing inside the bell shape. Carefully pull cutter out of icing. Push cachous gently into icing to fill bell. Secure half the ribbon around cake using pins. Repeat with second cake.

preparation time *1 hour (plus standing time)*
cooking time *2 hours (plus cooling time)* serves *30*
nutritional count per serving *8g total fat (4.8g saturated fat); 1814kJ (434 cal); 82.4g carbohydrate; 3.7g protein; 2.9g fibre*

mini christmas puddings

You need six 30cm squares of unbleached calico for pudding cloths. If calico has not been used before, soak in cold water overnight; next day, boil it 20 minutes then rinse in cold water. Puddings can be cooked in two boilers or in batches, mixture will keep at room temperature for several hours. This recipe will also make one large pudding. You will need a 60cm square of calico. Boil pudding for 6 hours, following the same cooking directions.

1 cup (170g) raisins, chopped coarsely
1 cup (160g) sultanas
1 cup (150g) finely chopped dried dates
½ cup (95g) finely chopped prunes
½ cup (85g) mixed peel
½ cup (125g) finely chopped glacé apricots
1 teaspoon finely grated lemon rind
2 tablespoons lemon juice
2 tablespoons apricot jam
2 tablespoons brandy
250g butter, softened
2 cups (440g) firmly packed brown sugar
5 eggs
1¼ cups (185g) plain flour
½ teaspoon ground nutmeg
½ teaspoon mixed spice
4 cups (280g) stale breadcrumbs

1 Combine fruit, rind, juice, jam and brandy in large bowl; mix well. Cover tightly with plastic wrap; store in a cool, dark place for one week, stirring every day.
2 Beat butter and sugar in small bowl with electric mixer until combined; beat in eggs one at a time. Add butter mixture to fruit mixture, mix well, then mix in sifted dry ingredients and breadcrumbs.
3 Fill boiler three-quarters full of hot water, cover with a tight lid; bring to the boil. Have ready 1m lengths of kitchen string and an extra 1 cup of plain flour. Wearing thick rubber gloves, dip cloths, one at a time, into boiling water; boil 1 minute then remove, squeeze excess water from cloth. Spread hot cloth on bench, rub 2 tablespoons of the flour into centre of each cloth to cover an area about 18cm in diameter, leaving flour a little thicker in centre of cloth where "skin" on the pudding needs to be thickest.
4 Divide pudding mixture among cloths; placing in centre of each cloth. Gather cloths around mixture, avoiding any deep pleats; pat into round shapes. Tie cloths tightly with string as close to mixture as possible. Tie loops in string.
5 Lower three puddings into the boiling water; tie ends of string to handles of boiler to suspend puddings. Cover, boil 2 hours, replenishing water as necessary.
6 Untie puddings from handles; place wooden spoons through string loops. Do not put puddings on bench; suspend from spoon by placing over rungs of upturned stool or wedging handle in drawer. Twist ends of cloth around string to avoid them touching puddings; hang 10 minutes.
7 Place puddings on board; cut string, carefully peel back cloth. Turn puddings onto a plate then carefully peel cloth away completely; cool. Stand at least 20 minutes or until skin darkens and pudding becomes firm.

preparation time *45 minutes (plus standing time)* cooking time *2 hours (plus standing time)* makes 6 nutritional count per pudding *41.1g total fat (24.3g saturated fat); 5618kJ (1344 cal); 215g carbohydrate; 899g protein; 9.8g fibre*

brandied cumquat puddings

You can make your own brandied cumquats (see recipe at right) for this pudding recipe or buy them ready-made from delicatessens and specialist food stores.

2 cups (500g) drained brandied cumquats
185g butter, softened
1 cup (220g) caster sugar
3 eggs
1 cup (150g) self-raising flour
¾ cup (90g) almond meal
2 teaspoons icing sugar

MARMALADE SYRUP

½ cup (110g) caster sugar
¾ cup (180ml) water
⅓ cup (115g) orange marmalade
2 tablespoons brandied cumquat liquid

1 Preheat oven to 180°C/160°C fan-forced. Grease eight 1 cup (250ml) ovenproof dishes or tea cups. Place on oven trays.
2 Blend drained cumquats until pulpy (you will need 1 cup pulp).
3 Beat butter and sugar in small bowl with electric mixer until light and fluffy; beat in eggs one at a time. Transfer mixture to medium bowl; stir in sifted flour, almond meal and pulp. Spoon mixture into dishes.
4 Bake puddings, uncovered, about 40 minutes.
5 Meanwhile, make marmalade syrup.
6 Pour half of the hot syrup over the hot puddings; dust with sifted icing sugar. Serve topped with cumquat wedges and remaining syrup.

MARMALADE SYRUP Stir sugar and the water in small saucepan over low heat, without boiling, until sugar dissolves. Bring to the boil; add marmalade. Reduce heat, simmer, uncovered, about 5 minutes or until syrup is slightly thickened. Stir in reserved brandy syrup.

preparation time *30 minutes*
cooking time *40 minutes* makes *8*
nutritional count per serving *27.4g total fat (13.5g saturated fat); 2985kJ (714 cal); 107g carbohydrate; 447g protein; 2.3g fibre*

brandied cumquats

750g cumquats
2 cinnamon sticks, halved lengthways
2 vanilla beans, halved lengthways
3 cups (660g) caster sugar
2½ cups (625ml) brandy

1 Place clean jars (and lids) on their sides in a large saucepan; cover jars completely with cold water. Put the lid on the pan, bring to the boil, boil for 20 minutes. Remove the jars carefully from the water; drain upright (to allow the water to evaporate) on the sink until the jars are dry.
2 Meanwhile, wash and dry the cumquats well, then prick each one several times with a fine skewer or a thick needle.
3 Place cumquats, cinnamon and vanilla in the jars; pour over enough of the combined sugar and brandy to cover the cumquats completely. Seal.
4 Stand jars in a cool, dark place for at least 2 months before using. Invert jars every few days to help dissolve the sugar.

preparation time *20 minutes (plus standing time)*
makes *7 cups (1.75 litres)*
nutritional count per 1 cup *0.2g total fat (0g saturated fat); 2462kJ (589 cal); 97.3g carbohydrate; 0.8g protein; 3.2g fibre*

1

2

3

4

basic vanilla biscuits

200g butter, softened
½ teaspoon vanilla extract
1 cup (160g) icing sugar
1 egg
1¾ cups (260g) plain flour
½ teaspoon bicarbonate of soda

1 Preheat oven to 160°C/140°C fan-forced.
Grease oven trays; line with baking paper.
2 Beat butter, extract, sifted icing sugar and egg in
small bowl with electric mixer until light and fluffy.
Transfer mixture to medium bowl; stir in sifted flour
and soda, in two batches.
3 Roll level tablespoons of dough into balls; place
on trays 3cm apart.
4 Bake biscuits about 15 minutes; cool on trays.

preparation time *20 minutes*
baking time *15 minutes* makes *30*
nutritional count per serving *5.7g total fat (3.7g
saturated fat); 431kJ (103 cal); 11.6g carbohydrate;
1.2g protein; 0.3g fibre*

VARIATIONS

CRANBERRY & COCONUT Stir ½ cup (65g) dried
cranberries and ½ cup (40g) shredded coconut into
basic biscuit mixture before flour and soda are added.

PEAR & GINGER Stir ¼ cup (35g) finely chopped dried
pears, ¼ cup (55g) coarsely chopped glacé ginger
and ½ cup (45g) rolled oats into basic biscuit mixture
before flour and soda are added.

BROWN SUGAR & PECAN Substitute 1 cup (220g) firmly
packed brown sugar for the icing sugar in the basic
biscuit mixture. Stir ½ cup (60g) coarsely chopped
pecans into basic biscuit mixture before flour and soda
are added.

CHOC CHIP Stir ½ cup (95g) dark Choc Bits into basic
biscuit mixture before flour and soda are added. Roll
level tablespoons of dough into balls then roll balls in
a mixture of 1 tablespoon caster sugar, 2 teaspoons
ground nutmeg and 2 teaspoons ground cinnamon.

1 CRANBERRY AND COCONUT VANILLA BISCUITS 2 PEAR AND GINGER
VANILLA BISCUITS 3 BROWN SUGAR AND PECAN VANILLA BISCUITS
4 CHOC CHIP VANILLA BISCUITS

JUST LIKE MUM MADE   235

berry and rhubarb pies

You need four large stems of rhubarb to get the required amount of chopped rhubarb.

2 cups (220g) coarsely chopped rhubarb
¼ cup (55g) caster sugar
2 tablespoons water
1 tablespoon cornflour
2 cups (300g) frozen mixed berries
1 egg white
2 teaspoons caster sugar, extra

PASTRY

1⅔ cups (250g) plain flour
⅓ cup (75g) caster sugar
150g cold butter, chopped coarsely
1 egg yolk

1 Make pastry.
2 Place rhubarb, sugar and half the water in medium saucepan; bring to the boil. Reduce heat; simmer, covered, about 3 minutes or until rhubarb is tender. Blend cornflour with the remaining water; stir into rhubarb mixture. Stir over heat until mixture boils and thickens. Remove from heat; stir in berries. Cool.
3 Grease six-hole texas (¾-cup/180ml) muffin pan. Roll two-thirds of the pastry between sheets of baking paper to 4mm thickness; cut out six 12cm rounds. Press rounds into pan holes. Refrigerate 30 minutes.
4 Preheat oven to 200°C/180°C fan-forced.
5 Roll remaining pastry between sheets of baking paper to 4mm thickness; cut out six 9cm rounds.
6 Divide fruit mixture among pastry cases.
7 Brush edge of 9cm rounds with egg white; place over filling. Press edges firmly to seal. Brush tops with egg white; sprinkle with extra sugar.
8 Bake pies about 30 minutes. Stand in pan 10 minutes; using palette knife, loosen pies from edge of pan before lifting out. Serve warm with ice-cream if you like.

PASTRY Process flour, sugar and butter until coarse. Add egg yolk; process until combined (if pastry is too dry, add 2 teaspoons water). Knead on floured surface until smooth. Cover; refrigerate 30 minutes.

preparation time *30 minutes (plus refrigeration time)*
cooking time *35 minutes* makes 6
nutritional count per pie *22.1g total fat (13.9g saturated fat); 1946kJ (464 cal); 57.1g carbohydrate; 7.2g protein; 3.9g fibre*

rice pudding

½ cup (100g) uncooked white medium-grain rice
2½ cups (625ml) milk
¼ cup (55g) caster sugar
¼ cup (40g) sultanas
½ teaspoon vanilla extract
2 teaspoons butter
½ teaspoon ground nutmeg

1 Preheat oven to 160°C/140°C fan-forced. Grease shallow 1-litre (4-cup) baking dish.
2 Wash rice under cold water; drain well. Place rice, milk, sugar, sultanas and extract in dish; whisk lightly with fork. Dot with butter.
3 Bake pudding, uncovered, 1 hour, whisking lightly with fork under skin occasionally. Sprinkle with nutmeg; bake further 20 minutes. Serve warm or cold.

preparation time *10 minutes*
cooking time *1 hour 20 minutes* serves 6
nutritional count per serving *5.5g total fat (3.6g saturated fat); 840kJ (201 cal); 32.4g carbohydrate; 4.8g protein; 0.4g fibre*

bread and butter pudding

6 slices white bread (270g)
40g butter, softened
½ cup (80g) sultanas
¼ teaspoon ground nutmeg

CUSTARD

1½ cups (375ml) milk
2 cups (500ml) cream
⅓ cup (75g) caster sugar
½ teaspoon vanilla extract
4 eggs

1 Preheat oven to 160°C/140°C fan-forced. Grease shallow 2-litre (8-cup) ovenproof dish.
2 Make custard.
3 Trim crusts from bread. Spread each slice with butter; cut into four triangles. Layer bread, overlapping, in dish; sprinkle with sultanas. Pour custard over bread; sprinkle with nutmeg.
4 Place dish in large baking dish; add enough boiling water to come halfway up sides of dish.
5 Bake pudding about 45 minutes or until set. Remove pudding from baking dish; stand 5 minutes before serving.

CUSTARD Combine milk, cream, sugar and extract in medium saucepan; bring to the boil. Whisk eggs in large bowl; whisking constantly, gradually add hot milk mixture to egg mixture.

preparation time *20 minutes*
cooking time *50 minutes* serves *6*
nutritional count per serving *48.6g total fat (30.4g saturated fat); 2859kJ (684 cal); 49.3g carbohydrate; 12.4g protein; 1.8g fibre*

chocolate self-saucing pudding

60g butter
½ cup (125ml) milk
½ teaspoon vanilla extract
¾ cup (165g) caster sugar
1 cup (150g) self-raising flour
1 tablespoon cocoa powder
¾ cup (165g) firmly packed brown sugar
1 tablespoon cocoa powder, extra
2 cups (500ml) boiling water

1 Preheat oven to 180°C/160°C fan-forced. Grease 1.5-litre (6-cup) ovenproof dish.
2 Melt butter with milk in medium saucepan. Remove from heat; stir in extract and caster sugar then sifted flour and cocoa. Spread mixture into dish. Sift brown sugar and extra cocoa over mixture; gently pour boiling water over mixture.
3 Bake pudding about 40 minutes or until centre is firm. Stand 5 minutes before serving.

preparation time *20 minutes*
cooking time *45 minutes* serves *6*
nutritional count per serving *9.7g total fat (6.2g saturated fat); 1676kJ (401 cal); 73.4g carbohydrate; 3.8g protein; 1.1g fibre*

quick-mix patty cakes

125g butter, softened
½ teaspoon vanilla extract
¾ cup (165g) caster sugar
3 eggs
2 cups (300g) self-raising flour
¼ cup (60ml) milk

1 Preheat oven to 180°C/160°C fan-forced.
Line two 12-hole patty pans with paper cases.
2 Beat ingredients in medium bowl with electric mixer
on low speed until ingredients are just combined.
Increase speed to medium; beat about 3 minutes or
until mixture is smooth and paler in colour. Drop
rounded tablespoons of mixture into each case.
3 Bake cakes about 20 minutes. Stand in pans
5 minutes; turn, top-side up, onto wire racks to cool.
4 Top cakes with icing of your choice.

preparation time *2 minutes*
cooking time *20 minutes* makes *24*
nutritional count per serving *5.2g total fat (3.1g
saturated fat); 502kJ (120 cal); 15.9g carbohydrate;
2.2g protein; 0.5g fibre*

VARIATIONS

CHOCOLATE & ORANGE Stir in 1 teaspoon finely
grated orange rind and ½ cup (95g) dark Choc Bits
at the end of step 2.

BANANA & WHITE CHOCOLATE CHIP Stir in ½ cup
overripe mashed banana and ½ cup (95g) white
Choc Bits at the end of step 2.

PASSIONFRUIT & LIME Stir in 1 teaspoon finely grated
lime rind and ¼ cup (60ml) passionfruit pulp at the
end of step 2.

MOCHA Blend 1 tablespoon sifted cocoa powder
with 1 tablespoon strong black coffee; stir in at the
end of step 2.

glacé icing

2 cups (320g) icing sugar
20g butter, melted
2 tablespoons hot water, approximately

1 Place sifted icing sugar in small bowl; stir in butter
and enough of the hot water to make a firm paste.
2 Stir mixture over small saucepan of simmering water
until spreadable.

VARIATIONS

CHOCOLATE Stir in 1 teaspoon sifted cocoa powder.

PASSIONFRUIT Stir in 1 tablespoon passionfruit pulp.

COFFEE Dissolve 1 teaspoon instant coffee granules
in the hot water.

banana and cinnamon muffins

You need two large overripe bananas (460g) for this recipe.

2 cups (300g) self-raising flour
⅓ cup (50g) plain flour
1 teaspoon ground cinnamon
½ teaspoon bicarbonate of soda
½ cup (110g) firmly packed brown sugar
1 cup mashed banana
2 eggs
¾ cup (180ml) buttermilk
⅓ cup (80ml) vegetable oil
½ teaspoon ground cinnamon, extra

CREAM CHEESE TOPPING

125g cream cheese, softened
¼ cup (40g) icing sugar

1   Preheat oven to 200°C/180°C fan-forced. Grease 12-hole (⅓-cup/80ml) muffin pan.
2   Sift flours, cinnamon, soda and sugar into large bowl; stir in banana then combined eggs, buttermilk and oil. Divide mixture among pan holes.
3   Bake muffins about 20 minutes. Stand in pan 5 minutes; turn onto wire rack to cool.
4   Make cream cheese topping. Spread cold muffins with topping; sprinkle with extra cinnamon.

CREAM CHEESE TOPPING Beat ingredients in small bowl with electric mixer until smooth.

preparation time *20 minutes*
cooking time *20 minutes* makes *12*
nutritional count per muffin *10.3g total fat (3.2g saturated fat); 1133kJ (271 cal); 37.9g carbohydrate; 5.8g protein; 1.5g fibre*

cashew ginger squares

125g butter
¼ cup (55g) caster sugar
1 cup (150g) self-raising flour
1 teaspoon ground ginger

TOPPING

½ cup (80g) icing sugar
60g butter
2 tablespoons golden syrup
1 cup (150g) unsalted roasted cashews, chopped coarsely
¼ cup (50g) finely chopped glacé ginger

1   Preheat oven to 180°C/160°C fan-forced. Grease 20cm x 30cm lamington pan; line base and two long sides with baking paper, extending paper 2cm above edge of pan.
2   Beat butter and sugar in small bowl with electric mixer until light and fluffy; stir in sifted flour and ginger. Spread mixture evenly over base of pan.
3   Bake slice about 20 minutes or until lightly browned; cool in pan.
4   Make topping; spread hot topping evenly over cold base. Cool.

TOPPING Stir sifted icing sugar, butter and syrup in small saucepan over heat until butter is melted. Stir in nuts and ginger.

preparation time *25 minutes*
cooking time *20 minutes* makes *about 12*
nutritional count per piece *19.2g total fat (9.4g saturated fat); 1241kJ (297 cal); 27.3g carbohydrate; 3.5g protein; 1.1g fibre*

one-bowl sultana loaf

125g butter, melted
750g sultanas
½ cup (110g) firmly packed brown sugar
2 tablespoons marmalade
2 eggs, lightly beaten
¼ cup (60ml) sweet sherry
¾ cup (110g) plain flour
¼ cup (35g) self-raising flour

1 Preheat oven to 150°C/130°C fan-forced. Grease
a 15cm x 25cm loaf pan; line base with baking paper.
2 Beat ingredients in large bowl using a wooden spoon
until combined. Spread mixture into pan (decorate top
with blanched almonds, if you like).
3 Bake loaf 1½ hours. Cover with foil; cool in pan.

preparation time *15 minutes*
cooking time *1 hour 30 minutes* serves *8*
nutritional count per serving *14.7g total fat (8.9g
saturated fat); 2454kJ (587 cal); 102g carbohydrate;
6.3g protein; 4.9g fibre*

baked custard

6 eggs
1 teaspoon vanilla extract
⅓ cup (75g) caster sugar
1 litre (4 cups) hot milk
¼ teaspoon ground nutmeg

1 Preheat oven to 160°C/140°C fan-forced. Grease
shallow 1.5-litre (6-cup) ovenproof dish.
2 Whisk eggs, extract and sugar in large bowl; gradually
whisk in hot milk. Pour into dish; sprinkle with nutmeg.
3 Place dish in larger baking dish; add enough boiling
water to come halfway up sides of dish. Bake, uncovered,
about 45 minutes. Remove custard from large dish;
stand 5 minutes before serving.

preparation time *5 minutes*
cooking time *45 minutes* serves *6*
nutritional count per serving *11.8g total fat (5.9g
saturated fat); 995kJ (238 cal); 20.7g carbohydrate;
12.3g protein; 0g fibre*

last-minute fruit cake

1½ cups (240g) sultanas
1 cup (170g) raisins, chopped coarsely
1 cup (150g) dried currants
½ cup (85g) mixed peel
⅓ cup (70g) glacé cherries, halved
2 tablespoons coarsely chopped glacé pineapple
2 tablespoons coarsely chopped glacé apricots
185g butter, chopped
¾ cup (165g) firmly packed brown sugar
⅓ cup (80ml) brandy
⅓ cup (80ml) water
2 teaspoons finely grated orange rind
1 teaspoon finely grated lemon rind
1 tablespoon treacle
3 eggs, beaten lightly
1¼ cups (185g) plain flour
¼ cup (35g) self-raising flour
½ teaspoon bicarbonate of soda
½ cup (80g) blanched almonds

1 Line deep 20cm-round cake pan with three
thicknesses of baking paper, extending paper
5cm above side.
2 Stir fruit, butter, sugar, brandy and the water in
medium saucepan over medium heat until butter
is melted and sugar is dissolved; bring to the boil.
Remove pan from heat; transfer mixture to large bowl.
Cool to room temperature.
3 Preheat oven to 150°C/130°C fan-forced.
4 Stir rinds, treacle and eggs into fruit mixture then
sifted dry ingredients. Spread mixture into pan;
decorate with nuts.
5 Bake cake, uncovered, about 2 hours. Cover hot
cake with foil; cool in pan overnight.

preparation time *20 minutes*
cooking time *2 hours (plus cooling time)* serves *16*
nutritional count per serving *13.6g total fat (6.8g
saturated fat); 1584kJ (379 cal); 55.1g carbohydrate;
4.8g protein; 2.9g fibre*

3   4

steamed ginger pudding

60g butter
¼ cup (90g) golden syrup
½ teaspoon bicarbonate of soda
1 cup (150g) self-raising flour
2 teaspoons ground ginger
½ cup (125ml) milk
1 egg

SYRUP

⅓ cup (115g) golden syrup
2 tablespoons water
30g butter

1 Grease 1.25-litre (5-cup) pudding steamer.
2 Stir butter and syrup in small saucepan over low heat
until smooth. Remove from heat, stir in soda; transfer
mixture to medium bowl. Stir in sifted dry ingredients
then combined milk and egg, in two batches.
3 Spread mixture into steamer. Cover with pleated
baking paper and foil; secure with lid.
4 Place pudding steamer in large saucepan with
enough boiling water to come halfway up side of
steamer; cover pan with tight-fitting lid. Boil 1 hour,
replenishing water as necessary to maintain level.
Stand pudding 5 minutes before turning onto plate.
5 Meanwhile, make syrup.
6 Serve pudding topped with syrup and, if you like,
whipped cream.

SYRUP Stir ingredients in small saucepan over heat
until smooth; bring to the boil. Reduce heat; simmer,
uncovered, 2 minutes.

preparation time *15 minutes*
cooking time *1 hour* serves *6*
nutritional count per serving *14.3g total fat (9g
saturated fat); 1367kJ (327 cal); 44.5g carbohydrate;
4.5g protein; 1g fibre*

golden syrup dumplings

1¼ cups (185g) self-raising flour
30g butter
⅓ cup (115g) golden syrup
⅓ cup (80ml) milk

SAUCE

30g butter
¾ cup (165g) firmly packed brown sugar
½ cup (175g) golden syrup
1⅔ cups (410ml) water

1 Sift flour into medium bowl; rub in butter. Gradually
stir in golden syrup and milk.
2 Make sauce.
3 Drop rounded tablespoonfuls of mixture into
simmering sauce; simmer, covered, about 20 minutes.
Serve dumplings with sauce.

SAUCE Stir ingredients in medium saucepan over
heat, without boiling, until sugar dissolves. Bring
to the boil, without stirring. Reduce heat; simmer,
uncovered, 5 minutes.

preparation time *10 minutes*
cooking time *25 minutes* serves *4*
nutritional count per serving *13.6g total fat (8.7g
saturated fat); 2792kJ (668 cal); 128.3g carbohydrate;
5.6g protein; 1.8g fibre*

rock cakes

2 cups (300g) self-raising flour
¼ teaspoon ground cinnamon
⅓ cup (75g) caster sugar
90g butter, chopped
1 cup (160g) sultanas
1 egg, beaten lightly
½ cup (125ml) milk
1 tablespoon caster sugar, extra

1   Preheat oven to 200°C/180°C fan-forced.
Grease oven trays.
2   Sift flour, cinnamon and sugar into medium bowl;
rub in butter. Stir in sultanas, egg and milk. Do not
overmix. Drop rounded tablespoons of mixture about
5cm apart onto trays; sprinkle with extra sugar.
3   Bake about 15 minutes; cool on trays.

preparation time *15 minutes*
cooking time *15 minutes* makes *18*
nutritional count per cake *4.9g total fat (3g
saturated fat); 640kJ (153 cal); 24g carbohydrate;
2.5g protein; 1g fibre*

madeira cake

180g butter, softened
2 teaspoons finely grated lemon rind
⅔ cup (150g) caster sugar
3 eggs
¾ cup (110g) plain flour
¾ cup (110g) self-raising flour
⅓ cup (55g) mixed peel
¼ cup (35g) slivered almonds

1   Preheat oven to 160°C/140°C fan-forced. Grease
deep 20cm-round cake pan; line base with paper.
2   Beat butter, rind and sugar in small bowl with
electric mixer until light and fluffy; beat in eggs, one
at a time. Transfer mixture to large bowl, stir in sifted
flours. Spread mixture into pan.
3   Bake cake 20 minutes. Sprinkle with peel and nuts;
bake further 40 minutes. Stand 5 minutes; turn, top-side
up, onto wire rack to cool.

preparation time *15 minutes*
cooking time *1 hour* serves *12*
nutritional count per serving *15.6g total fat (8.7g
saturated fat); 1141kJ (273 cal); 27.9g carbohydrate;
4.9g protein; 1.7g fibre*

date slice

1½ cups (225g) plain flour
1¼ cups (185g) self-raising flour
150g cold butter, chopped
1 tablespoon honey
1 egg
⅓ cup (80ml) milk, approximately
2 teaspoons milk, extra
1 tablespoon white sugar

DATE FILLING

3½ cups (500g) dried seeded dates, chopped coarsely
¾ cup (180ml) water
2 tablespoons finely grated lemon rind
2 tablespoons lemon juice

1   Grease 20cm x 30cm lamington pan; line base with
baking paper, extending paper 5cm over long sides.
2   Sift flours into large bowl; rub in butter until mixture is
crumbly. Stir in combined honey and egg and enough
milk to make a firm dough. Knead on floured surface
until smooth, cover; refrigerate 30 minutes.
3   Meanwhile, make date filling.
4   Preheat oven to 200°C/180°C fan-forced.
5   Divide dough in half. Roll one half large enough to
cover base of pan; press into pan, spread filling over
dough. Roll remaining dough large enough to cover
filling. Brush with extra milk; sprinkle with sugar.
6   Bake slice about 20 minutes; cool in pan.

DATE FILLING Cook ingredients in medium saucepan,
stirring, about 10 minutes or until thick and smooth.
Cool to room temperature.

preparation time *1 hour (plus refrigeration time)*
cooking time *25 minutes* makes *24*
nutritional count per piece *9.3g total fat (5.8g
saturated fat); 1221kJ (292 cal); 45.5g carbohydrate;
4.3g protein; 4.4g fibre*

basic scones

4 cups (600g) self-raising flour
2 tablespoons icing sugar
60g butter
1½ cups (375ml) milk
¾ cup (180ml) water, approximately

1 Preheat oven to 220°C/200°C fan-forced.
Grease 20cm x 30cm lamington pan.
2 Sift flour and sugar into large bowl; rub in butter
with fingertips. Make a well in centre of flour mixture;
add milk and almost all the water. Use knife to "cut"
the milk and water through the flour mixture, mixing
to a soft, sticky dough.
3 Knead dough on floured surface until smooth. Press
dough out to 2cm thickness. Dip 4.5cm round cutter
in flour; cut as many rounds as you can from piece of
dough. Place scones, side by side, just touching, in pan.
Gently knead scraps of dough together; repeat pressing
and cutting of dough, place in same pan. Brush tops
with a little extra milk.
4 Bake scones about 15 minutes or until just browned
and sound hollow when tapped firmly on the top.

preparation time *20 minutes*
cooking time *25 minutes* makes *20*
nutritional count per scone *3.6g total fat (2.2g
saturated fat); 594kJ (142 cal); 23.2g carbohydrate;
3.6g protein; 1.1g fibre*

pumpkin scones

You will need to cook about 250g pumpkin
for this recipe.

40g butter
¼ cup (55g) caster sugar
1 egg, beaten lightly
¾ cup cooked mashed pumpkin
2½ cups (375g) self-raising flour
½ teaspoon ground nutmeg
⅓ cup milk (125ml), approximately

1 Preheat oven to 240°C/220°C fan-forced.
Grease two 20cm round sandwich pans.
2 Beat butter and sugar in small bowl with electric
mixer until light and fluffy; gradually beat in egg. Transfer
mixture to large bowl; stir in pumpkin, then sifted dry
ingredients and enough milk to make a soft sticky dough.
3 Knead dough on floured surface until smooth.
Press dough out to 2cm thickness. Dip 5cm round
cutter in flour; cut rounds from dough. Place rounds,
just touching, in pans. Gently knead scraps of dough
together; repeat pressing and cutting of dough, place
in same pan. Brush tops with a little milk.
4 Bake scones about 15 minutes or until just browned
and sound hollow when tapped firmly on the top.

preparation time *20 minutes*
cooking time *15 minutes* makes *16*
nutritional count per scone *3g total fat (1.7g
saturated fat); 535kJ (128 cal); 21.1g carbohydrate;
3.3g protein; 1.1g fibre*

zucchini walnut loaf

3 eggs
1½ cups (330g) firmly packed brown sugar
1 cup (250ml) vegetable oil
1½ cups finely grated zucchini
1 cup (110g) coarsely chopped walnuts
1½ cups (225g) self-raising flour
1½ cups (225g) plain flour

1 Preheat oven to 180°C/160°C fan-forced.
Grease 15cm x 25cm loaf pan; line base and
sides with baking paper.
2 Beat eggs, sugar and oil in large bowl with
electric mixer until combined. Stir in zucchini, walnuts
and sifted flours, in batches. Spread mixture into pan.
3 Bake loaf about 1¼ hours. Stand in pan 5 minutes;
turn onto wire rack to cool. Serve with butter, if you like.

preparation time *15 minutes*
cooking time *1 hour 15 minutes* serves *10*
nutritional count per serving *32.8g total fat (4g
saturated fat); 2475kJ (592 cal); 64.7g carbohydrate;
8.4g protein; 2.7g fibre*

lumberjack cake

2 large apples (400g), peeled, cored, chopped finely
1 cup (200g) finely chopped dried dates
1 teaspoon bicarbonate of soda
1 cup (250ml) boiling water
125g butter, softened
1 teaspoon vanilla extract
1 cup (220g) caster sugar
1 egg
1½ cups (225g) plain flour

TOPPING

60g butter
½ cup (100g) firmly packed brown sugar
½ cup (125ml) milk
⅔ cup (50g) shredded coconut

1 Preheat oven to 180°C/160°C fan-forced. Grease deep 23cm-square cake pan; line base and sides with baking paper.
2 Combine apple, dates and soda in large bowl, add the water. Cover; stand 10 minutes.
3 Meanwhile, beat butter, extract, sugar and egg in small bowl with electric mixer until light and fluffy. Add butter mixture to apple mixture; stir in flour, in two batches. Pour mixture into pan.
4 Bake cake about 50 minutes.
5 Make topping. Carefully spread warm topping evenly over cake; bake further 20 minutes or until topping has browned.
6 Stand cake in pan 5 minutes; turn, top-side up, onto wire rack to cool.

TOPPING Stir ingredients in medium saucepan over low heat until butter melts and sugar dissolves.

preparation time *30 minutes*
baking time *1 hour 10 minutes* serves *12*
nutritional count per serving *16.5g total fat (11.2g saturated fat); 1613kJ (386 cal); 54g carbohydrate; 3.7g protein; 3.3g fibre*

hummingbird cake

You need two large overripe (460g) bananas for this recipe.

450g can crushed pineapple in syrup
1 cup (150g) plain flour
½ cup (75g) self-raising flour
½ teaspoon bicarbonate of soda
½ teaspoon ground cinnamon
½ teaspoon ground ginger
1 cup (220g) firmly packed brown sugar
½ cup (45g) desiccated coconut
1 cup mashed banana
2 eggs, beaten lightly
¾ cup (180ml) vegetable oil

CREAM CHEESE FROSTING

30g butter, softened
60g cream cheese, softened
1 teaspoon vanilla extract
1½ cups (240g) icing sugar

1 Preheat oven to 180°C/160°C fan-forced. Grease deep 23cm-square cake pan; line base with baking paper.
2 Drain pineapple over medium bowl, pressing with spoon to extract as much syrup as possible. Reserve ¼ cup (60ml) syrup.
3 Sift flours, soda, spices and sugar into large bowl. Stir in drained pineapple, reserved syrup, coconut, banana, egg and oil; pour into pan.
4 Bake cake about 40 minutes. Stand cake in pan 5 minutes; turn, top-side up, onto wire rack to cool.
5 Make cream cheese frosting.
6 Spread cold cake with cream cheese frosting.

CREAM CHEESE FROSTING Beat butter, cream cheese and extract in small bowl with electric mixer until light and fluffy; gradually beat in icing sugar.

preparation time *35 minutes*
cooking time *40 minutes (plus cooling time)* serves *12*
nutritional count per serving *21.4g total fat (6.6g saturated fat); 1881kJ (450 cal); 59.5g carbohydrate; 4.5g protein; 2.2g fibre*

family chocolate cake

2 cups (500ml) water
3 cups (660g) caster sugar
250g butter, chopped
⅓ cup (35g) cocoa powder
1 teaspoon bicarbonate of soda
3 cups (450g) self-raising flour
4 eggs

FUDGE FROSTING

90g butter
½ cup (110g) caster sugar
⅓ cup (80ml) water
1½ cups (240g) icing sugar
⅓ cup (35g) cocoa powder

1 Preheat oven to 180°C/160°C fan-forced. Grease deep 26.5cm x 33cm (3.5-litre/14-cup) baking dish; line base with baking paper.
2 Stir the water, sugar, butter and sifted cocoa and soda in medium saucepan over heat, without boiling, until sugar dissolves. Bring to the boil. Reduce heat; simmer, uncovered, 5 minutes. Transfer mixture to large bowl; cool to room temperature.
3 Add flour and eggs to chocolate mixture; beat with electric mixer until smooth and pale in colour. Pour mixture into pan.
4 Bake cake about 50 minutes. Stand in pan 10 minutes; turn, top-side up, onto wire rack to cool.
5 Meanwhile, make fudge frosting.
6 Spread cold cake with frosting.

FUDGE FROSTING Stir butter, caster sugar and the water in small saucepan over low heat, without boiling, until sugar dissolves. Sift icing sugar and cocoa into small bowl then gradually stir in hot butter mixture. Cover; refrigerate about 20 minutes or until frosting thickens. Beat with wooden spoon until spreadable.

preparation time *20 minutes*
cooking time *50 minutes (plus cooling time)* serves *20*
nutritional count per serving *15.8g total fat (9.8g saturated fat); 1806kJ (432 cal); 67.3g carbohydrate; 4.3g protein; 1g fibre*

honey spice sponge cake

2 eggs
½ cup (110g) caster sugar
⅓ cup (50g) wheaten cornflour
1½ tablespoons custard powder
1 teaspoon mixed spice
½ teaspoon cream of tartar
¼ teaspoon bicarbonate of soda
300ml thickened cream
2 tablespoons honey
1 tablespoon icing sugar

1 Preheat oven to 180°C/160°C fan-forced. Grease 25cm x 30cm swiss roll pan; line base with baking paper, extending paper 5cm over long sides.
2 Beat eggs and ⅓ cup of the caster sugar in small bowl with electric mixer about 10 minutes or until thick and creamy.
3 Meanwhile, triple-sift cornflour, custard powder, spice, cream of tartar and soda onto baking paper. Sift flour mixture over egg mixture; fold ingredients together. Spread mixture into pan.
4 Bake cake 10 minutes.
5 Meanwhile, place piece of baking paper cut the same size as pan on bench; sprinkle with remaining caster sugar. Turn sponge onto paper; peel lining paper away. Cool.
6 Beat cream and honey in small bowl with electric mixer until firm peaks form.
7 Cut edges from all sides of sponge then cut widthways into three rectangles. Place one piece of sponge on plate; spread with half the cream mixture. Top with second piece of sponge and remaining cream. Finish with remaining piece of sponge and dust with sifted icing sugar.

preparation time *15 minutes*
cooking time *10 minutes* serves 6
nutritional count per serving *20.1g total fat (12.6g saturated fat); 1480kJ (354 cal); 39.9g carbohydrate; 3.7g protein; 0.1g fibre*

lemon delicious puddings

125g butter, melted
2 teaspoons finely grated lemon rind
1½ cups (330g) caster sugar
3 eggs, separated
½ cup (75g) self-raising flour
⅓ cup (80ml) lemon juice
1⅓ cups (330ml) milk

1 Preheat oven to 180°C/160°C fan-forced. Grease
six 1-cup (250ml) ovenproof dishes.
2 Combine butter, rind, sugar and yolks in large bowl.
Stir in sifted flour, then juice. Gradually stir in milk;
mixture should be smooth and runny.
3 Beat egg whites in small bowl with electric mixer until
soft peaks form; fold into lemon mixture, in two batches.
4 Place ovenproof dishes in large baking dish; divide
lemon mixture among dishes. Add enough boiling water
to baking dish to come halfway up sides of ovenproof
dishes. Bake, uncovered, about 45 minutes.

preparation time *20 minutes*
cooking time *45 minutes* serves *6*
nutritional count per serving *22g total fat (13.5g
saturated fat); 2069kJ (495 cal); 67.1g carbohydrate;
6.7g protein; 0.5g fibre*

ginger fluff roll

3 eggs
⅔ cup (150g) caster sugar
⅔ cup (100g) wheaten cornflour
1 teaspoon cream of tartar
½ teaspoon bicarbonate of soda
1 teaspoon cocoa powder
2 teaspoons ground ginger
½ teaspoon ground cinnamon
¾ cup (180ml) thickened cream
2 tablespoons golden syrup
1 teaspoon ground ginger, extra

1 Preheat oven to 180°C/160°C fan-forced. Grease
25cm x 30cm swiss roll pan; line base with baking
paper, extending paper 5cm over long sides.
2 Beat eggs and ½ cup of the sugar in small bowl with
electric mixer until thick, creamy and sugar dissolved.
Fold in triple-sifted dry ingredients. Spread sponge
mixture into pan.
3 Bake cake about 12 minutes.
4 Meanwhile, place piece of baking paper cut the
same size as pan on bench; sprinkle with remaining
caster sugar. Turn sponge onto paper; peel lining paper
away. Cool; trim all sides of sponge.
5 Beat cream, syrup and extra ginger in small bowl
with electric mixer until firm peaks form.
6 Spread sponge with ginger cream. Using paper as
a guide, roll sponge from long side. Cover with plastic
wrap; refrigerate 30 minutes.

preparation time *25 minutes*
cooking time *12 minutes (plus refrigeration time)*
serves *10*
nutritional count per serving *8.3g total fat (4.9g
saturated fat); 828kJ (198 cal); 28.1g carbohydrate;
2.5g protein; 0.1g fibre*

1 LEMON DELICIOUS PUDDINGS 2 GINGER FLUFF ROLL 3 HEDGEHOG
SLICE [P 250] 4 MARMALADE ALMOND COCONUT SQUARES [P 250]

hedgehog slice

¾ cup (180ml) sweetened condensed milk
60g butter
125g dark eating chocolate, chopped coarsely
150g plain sweet biscuits
⅓ cup (45g) roasted unsalted peanuts
⅓ cup (55g) sultanas

1 Grease 8cm x 26cm bar pan; line base with baking paper, extending paper 5cm over long sides.
2 Stir condensed milk and butter in small saucepan over low heat until smooth. Remove from heat; stir in chocolate until smooth.
3 Break biscuits into small pieces; place in large bowl with nuts and sultanas. Stir in chocolate mixture until combined. Spread mixture into pan.
4 Cover pan; refrigerate about 4 hours or until firm. Remove from pan; cut into slices.

preparation time *10 minutes (plus refrigeration time)*
cooking time *5 minutes* makes *12*
nutritional count per piece *12.7 total fat (6.9g saturated fat); 1053kJ (252 cal); 29.9g carbohydrate; 4g protein; 0.9g fibre*

marmalade almond coconut squares

125g butter, chopped
1 teaspoon almond essence
¼ cup (55g) caster sugar
1 cup (150g) plain flour
¼ cup (20g) desiccated coconut
⅓ cup (15g) flaked coconut
¼ cup (85g) marmalade, warmed

TOPPING

90g butter, chopped
2 teaspoons grated orange rind
⅓ cup (75g) caster sugar
2 eggs
1 cup (90g) desiccated coconut
1 cup (125g) almond meal

1 Preheat oven to 180°C/160°C fan-forced. Grease 19cm x 29cm rectangular slice pan.
2 Beat butter, essence and sugar in small bowl with electric mixer until smooth. Stir in flour and desiccated coconut; press into pan. Bake 15 minutes or until brown.
3 Meanwhile, make topping; spread over hot slice, sprinkle with flaked coconut. Bake further 20 minutes or until firm. Brush hot slice with marmalade; cool in pan.

TOPPING Beat butter, rind and sugar in small bowl with electric mixer until smooth; beat in eggs until combined. Stir in coconut and almond meal.

preparation time *30 minutes*
cooking time *35 minutes* makes *about 18*
nutritional count per square *18.8g total fat (10.9g saturated fat); 1066kJ (255 cal); 17.2g carbohydrate; 3.5g protein; 2g fibre*

raspberry coconut slice

90g butter
½ cup (110g) caster sugar
1 egg
¼ cup (35g) self-raising flour
⅔ cup (100g) plain flour
1 tablespoon custard powder
⅔ cup (220g) raspberry jam

COCONUT TOPPING

2 cups (160g) desiccated coconut
¼ cup (55g) caster sugar
2 eggs, beaten lightly

1 Preheat oven to 180°C/160°C fan-forced. Grease 20cm x 30cm lamington pan; line base with baking paper, extending paper 5cm over long sides.
2 Beat butter, sugar and egg in small bowl with electric mixer until light and fluffy. Transfer to medium bowl; stir in sifted flours and custard powder. Spread into pan; spread with jam.
3 Combine ingredients for coconut topping in small bowl; sprinkle over jam. Bake about 40 minutes; cool in pan.

preparation time *25 minutes (plus cooling time)*
cooking time *40 minutes* makes *16*
nutritional count per piece *11.6 total fat (8.9g saturated fat); 932kJ (223 cal); 26.7g carbohydrate; 2g protein; 2g fibre*

sweet coconut slice

1 cup (150g) plain flour
½ cup (75g) self-raising flour
2 tablespoons caster sugar
125g cold butter, chopped
1 egg
1 tablespoon iced water
½ cup (160g) apricot jam
10 red glacé cherries, halved

COCONUT FILLING

1 cup (220g) caster sugar
1 cup (250ml) water
3½ cups (280g) desiccated coconut
3 eggs, beaten lightly
60g butter, melted
¼ cup (60ml) milk
1 teaspoon vanilla extract
1 teaspoon baking powder

1 Blend or process flours, sugar and butter until combined. Add egg and the water, process until mixture forms a ball; cover, refrigerate 30 minutes.
2 Meanwhile, make coconut filling.
3 Preheat oven to 180°C/160°C fan-forced. Line 25cm x 30cm swiss roll pan with baking paper, extending paper 5cm over long sides.
4 Roll pastry between sheets of baking paper until 3mm thick and large enough to cover base of pan. Gently ease into base of pan. Brush jam evenly over pastry base. Spread coconut filling over jam. Place cherry halves evenly over slice top.
5 Bake slice about 35 minutes. Cool in pan; cut into squares before serving.

COCONUT FILLING Stir sugar and the water in small saucepan over heat until sugar is dissolved. Bring to the boil, boil 3 minutes without stirring; cool 5 minutes. Place coconut in large bowl, stir in sugar syrup, egg, butter, milk, extract and baking powder.

preparation time *40 minutes (plus refrigeration time)*
cooking time *40 minutes (plus cooling time)* makes *20*
nutritional count per piece *18g total fat (13.5g saturated fat); 1183kJ (283 cal); 28g carbohydrate; 3.6g protein; 2.6g fibre*

passionfruit custard slice

1 cup (150g) plain flour
125g butter, chopped
2 tablespoons icing sugar
2 teaspoons powdered gelatine
⅓ cup (80ml) lemon juice
395g can sweetened condensed milk
⅓ cup (40g) custard powder
1 cup (220g) caster sugar
2 tablespoons milk
1½ cups (375ml) water
20g butter, extra
2 tablespoons lemon juice, extra
⅓ cup (80ml) passionfruit pulp

1 Preheat oven to 180°C/160°C fan-forced. Grease 20cm x 30cm lamington pan; line base and two long sides with baking paper, extending paper 2cm above edge of pan.
2 Process flour, butter and icing sugar until combined. Press over base of pan; bake about 20 minutes. Cool in pan.
3 Sprinkle gelatine over juice in cup; stand in small pan of simmering water, stir until dissolved. Beat gelatine mixture and condensed milk in small bowl with electric mixer about 10 minutes or until mixture thickens. Pour over base.
4 Blend custard powder and caster sugar with milk and the water in small saucepan; cook, stirring, over heat until mixture boils and thickens. Remove from heat, stir in extra butter; cover, stand 10 minutes. Stir in extra juice and passionfruit pulp. Pour over gelatine layer in pan. Refrigerate until set, before cutting.

preparation time *30 minutes (plus refrigeration time)*
cooking time *20 minutes* makes *8*
nutritional count per piece *20g total fat (13g saturated fat); 2182kJ (522 cal); 76.6g carbohydrate; 7.5g protein; 2.2g fibre*

vanilla kisses

125g butter, softened
½ cup (110g) caster sugar
1 egg
⅓ cup (50g) plain flour
¼ cup (35g) self-raising flour
⅔ cup (100g) cornflour
¼ cup (30g) custard powder

VIENNA CREAM

60g butter, softened
½ teaspoon vanilla extract
¾ cup (120g) icing sugar
2 teaspoons milk

1 Preheat oven to 200°C/180°C fan-forced.
Grease oven trays; line with baking paper.
2 Beat butter, sugar and egg in small bowl with
electric mixer until light and fluffy. Stir in sifted dry
ingredients, in two batches.
3 Spoon mixture into piping bag fitted with 1cm-fluted
tube. Pipe 3cm rosettes about 3cm apart on trays.
4 Bake biscuits about 10 minutes; cool on trays.
5 Meanwhile, make vienna cream.
6 Sandwich biscuits with vienna cream.

VIENNA CREAM Beat butter and extract in small bowl
with electric mixer until as white as possible; gradually
beat in sifted icing sugar and milk, in two batches.

preparation time *15 minutes*
cooking time *10 minutes* makes *20*
nutritional count per kiss *7.9g total fat (5.1g
saturated fat); 648kJ (155 cal); 20g carbohydrate;
0.9g protein; 0.2g fibre*

vanilla slice

2 sheets ready-rolled puff pastry
½ cup (110g) caster sugar
½ cup (75g) cornflour
¼ cup (30g) custard powder
2½ cups (625ml) milk
30g butter
1 egg yolk
1 teaspoon vanilla extract
¾ cup (180ml) thickened cream

PASSIONFRUIT ICING

1½ cups (240g) icing sugar
1 teaspoon soft butter
¼ cup (60ml) passionfruit pulp

1 Preheat oven to 240°C/220°C fan-forced.
Grease deep 23cm-square cake pan; line with foil,
extending foil 10cm over sides of pan.
2 Place each pastry sheet on separate oven trays.
Bake about 15 minutes; cool. Flatten pastry with hand;
place one pastry sheet in pan, trim to fit if necessary.
3 Meanwhile, combine sugar, cornflour and custard
powder in medium saucepan; gradually add milk,
stirring until smooth. Add butter; stir over heat until
mixture boils and thickens. Simmer, stirring, about
3 minutes or until custard is thick and smooth. Remove
from heat; stir in egg yolk and extract. Cover surface of
custard with plastic wrap; cool to room temperature.
4 Make passionfruit icing.
5 Whip cream until firm peaks form. Fold cream into
custard, in two batches. Spread custard mixture over
pastry in pan. Top with remaining pastry, trim to fit if
necessary; press down slightly. Spread pastry with
icing; refrigerate 3 hours or overnight.

PASSIONFRUIT ICING Place sifted icing sugar, butter
and pulp in small heatproof bowl over small saucepan
of simmering water; stir until icing is spreadable.

preparation time *20 minutes (plus cooling and
refrigeration time)* cooking time *35 minutes* makes *16*
nutritional count per piece *12.6g total fat (7.6g
saturated fat); 1158kJ (277 cal); 37.2g carbohydrate;
3.1g protein; 0.8g fibre*

anzac biscuits

1 cup (90g) rolled oats
1 cup (150g) plain flour
1 cup (220g) firmly packed brown sugar
½ cup (40g) desiccated coconut
125g butter
2 tablespoons golden syrup
1 tablespoon water
½ teaspoon bicarbonate of soda

1 Preheat oven to 160°C/140°C fan-forced.
Grease oven trays; line with baking paper.
2 Combine oats, sifted flour, sugar and coconut
in large bowl.
3 Stir butter, syrup and the water in small saucepan
over low heat until smooth; stir in soda.
4 Stir syrup into dry ingredients. Roll level tablespoons
of mixture into balls; place about 5cm apart on trays,
flatten slightly.
5 Bake biscuits about 20 minutes; cool on trays.

preparation time *15 minutes*
cooking time *20 minutes* makes *25*
nutritional count per biscuit *5.5g total fat (2.8g
saturated fat); 518kJ (124 cal); 17g carbohydrate;
1.2g protein; 0.7g fibre*

gingernut biscuits

90g butter
⅓ cup (75g) firmly packed brown sugar
⅓ cup (115g) golden syrup
1⅓ cups (200g) plain flour
¾ teaspoon bicarbonate of soda
1 tablespoon ground ginger
1 teaspoon ground cinnamon
¼ teaspoon ground clove

1 Preheat oven to 180°C/160°C fan-forced.
Grease oven trays.
2 Stir butter, sugar and syrup in medium saucepan
over low heat until smooth. Remove from heat;
stir in sifted dry ingredients. Cool 10 minutes.
3 Roll rounded teaspoons of mixture into balls.
Place about 3cm apart on trays; flatten slightly.
4 Bake biscuits about 10 minutes; cool on trays.

preparation time *15 minutes (plus cooling time)*
cooking time *10 minutes* makes *32*
nutritional count per biscuit *2.4g total fat (1.5g
saturated fat); 263kJ (63 cal); 9.5g carbohydrate;
0.7g protein; 0.2g fibre*

oat and bran biscuits

1 cup (150g) plain flour
1 cup (60g) unprocessed bran
¾ cup (60g) rolled oats
½ teaspoon bicarbonate of soda
60g butter, chopped
½ cup (110g) caster sugar
1 egg
2 tablespoons water, approximately

1 Process flour, bran, oats, soda and butter until
crumbly; add sugar, egg and enough of the water
to make a firm dough. Knead dough on floured
surface until smooth; cover, refrigerate 30 minutes.
2 Preheat oven to 180°C/160°C fan-forced.
Grease oven trays; line with baking paper.
3 Divide dough in half; roll each half between sheets
of baking paper to about 5mm thickness. Cut dough
into 7cm rounds; place on trays 2cm apart.
4 Bake biscuits about 15 minutes. Stand on trays
5 minutes; transfer to wire rack to cool.

preparation time *15 minutes (plus refrigeration time)*
baking time *15 minutes* makes *30*
nutritional count per biscuit *2.1g total fat (1.2g
saturated fat); 259kJ (62 cal); 8.8g carbohydrate;
1.3g protein; 1.2g fibre*

vanilla currant cookies

125g butter, softened
1 teaspoon vanilla extract
¾ cup (165g) caster sugar
1 egg
2 cups (300g) self-raising flour
½ cup (40g) desiccated coconut
¼ cup (40g) dried currants
VANILLA ICING

1½ cups (240g) icing sugar
2 teaspoons vanilla extract
1½ teaspoons butter, softened
1 tablespoon milk, approximately

1   Preheat oven to 200°C/180°C fan-forced.
Grease oven trays.
2   Beat butter, extract, sugar and egg in small bowl
with electric mixer until light and fluffy. Transfer mixture
to large bowl; stir in sifted flour, coconut and currants.
3   Shape rounded teaspoons of mixture into balls;
place onto trays about 5cm apart. Flatten with hand
until about 5mm thick.
4   Bake cookies about 10 minutes or until browned
lightly. Cool on trays.
5   Meanwhile, make vanilla icing. Spread cookies
thinly with icing, place on wire racks to set.

VANILLA ICING Sift icing sugar into medium heatproof
bowl, stir in extract and butter, then enough milk to
give a thick paste. Stir over hot water until spreadable.

preparation time *45 minutes*
cooking time *10 minutes per tray (plus cooling time)*
makes *40*
nutritional count per cookie *3.6g total fat (2.4g
saturated fat); 414kJ (99 cal); 16.2g carbohydrate;
1g protein; 0.5g fibre*

honey jumbles

60g butter
½ cup (110g) firmly packed brown sugar
¾ cup (270g) golden syrup
1 egg, beaten lightly
2½ cups (375g) plain flour
½ cup (75g) self-raising flour
½ teaspoon bicarbonate of soda
1 teaspoon ground cinnamon
½ teaspoon ground clove
2 teaspoons ground ginger
1 teaspoon mixed spice
ICING

1 egg white
1½ cups (240g) icing sugar
2 teaspoons plain flour
1 tablespoon lemon juice, approximately
pink food colouring

1   Stir butter, sugar and syrup in medium saucepan over
low heat until sugar dissolves. Cool 10 minutes. Transfer
to large bowl; stir in egg and sifted dry ingredients, in
two batches. Knead dough on floured surface until
dough loses stickiness. Cover; refrigerate 30 minutes.
2   Preheat oven to 160°C/140°C fan-forced.
Grease oven trays.
3   Divide dough into eight portions. Roll each portion
into 2cm-thick sausage; cut each sausage into five 6cm
lengths. Place about 3cm apart on oven trays; round
ends with lightly floured fingers, flatten slightly.
4   Bake jumbles about 15 minutes; cool on trays.
5   Meanwhile, make icing. Spread pink and white
icing on jumbles.

ICING Beat egg white lightly in small bowl; gradually
stir in sifted icing sugar and flour, then enough juice to
make icing spreadable. Place half the mixture in another
small bowl; tint with colouring. Keep icings covered
with a damp tea towel while in use.

preparation time *10 minutes (plus refrigeration time)*
cooking time *15 minutes* makes *40*
nutritional count per jumble *1.5g total fat (0.9g
saturated fat); 456kJ (109 cal); 21.9g carbohydrate;
1.5g protein; 0.4g fibre*

SPICED UP

red curry paste

20 dried long red chillies
1 teaspoon ground coriander
2 teaspoons ground cumin
1 teaspoon hot paprika
2cm piece fresh ginger (10g), chopped finely
3 cloves garlic, quartered
1 medium red onion (170g), chopped coarsely
2 x 10cm sticks fresh lemon grass (40g), sliced thinly
2 tablespoons coarsely chopped fresh
    coriander root and stem mixture
2 teaspoons shrimp paste
1 tablespoon peanut oil

1 Place chillies in small heatproof jug, cover with
boiling water; stand 15 minutes, drain.
2 Meanwhile, dry-fry ground coriander, cumin and
paprika in small frying pan, stirring until fragrant.
3 Blend or process chillies and spices with ginger,
garlic, onion, lemon grass, coriander mixture and paste
until mixture forms a paste.
4 Add oil to paste; continue to blend until smooth.

preparation time *20 minutes (plus standing time)*
cooking time *5 minutes* makes *1 cup*
nutritional count per tablespoon *1.6g total fat (0.3g
saturated fat); 92kJ (22 cal); 1.2g carbohydrate;
0.4g protein; 0.5g fibre*

green curry paste

2 teaspoons ground coriander
2 teaspoons ground cumin
10 long green chillies, chopped coarsely
10 small green chillies, chopped coarsely
1 teaspoon shrimp paste
1 clove garlic, quartered
4 green onions, chopped coarsely
10cm stick fresh lemon grass (20g), chopped finely
1cm piece fresh galangal (5g), chopped finely
¼ cup coarsely chopped fresh coriander
    root and stem mixture
1 tablespoon peanut oil

1 Dry-fry ground coriander and cumin in small frying
pan over medium heat, stirring until fragrant.
2 Blend or process spices with chillies, paste, garlic,
onion, lemon grass, galangal and coriander mixture
until mixture forms a paste.
3 Add oil to paste; continue to blend until smooth.

preparation time *20 minutes*
cooking time *3 minutes* makes *1 cup*
nutritional count per tablespoon *1.6g total fat (0.3g
saturated fat); 67kJ (16 cal); 0.3g carbohydrate;
0.2g protein; 0.2g fibre*

yellow curry paste

2 dried long red chillies
1 teaspoon ground coriander
1 teaspoon ground cumin
½ teaspoon ground cinnamon
2 fresh yellow banana chillies (250g),
    chopped coarsely
1 teaspoon finely chopped fresh turmeric
2 cloves garlic, quartered
1 small brown onion (80g), chopped finely
10cm stick fresh lemon grass (20g), chopped finely
2 teaspoons finely chopped fresh galangal
1 tablespoon coarsely chopped fresh
    coriander root and stem mixture
1 teaspoon shrimp paste
1 tablespoon peanut oil

1 Place chillies in small heatproof jug, cover with
boiling water; stand 15 minutes, drain.
2 Meanwhile, dry-fry ground coriander, cumin and
cinnamon in small frying pan, stirring until fragrant.
3 Blend or process spices and chillies with remaining
ingredients until mixture is smooth.

preparation time *20 minutes (plus standing time)*
cooking time *3 minutes* makes *1 cup*
nutritional count per tablespoon *1.6g total fat (0.3g
saturated fat); 84kJ (20 cal); 0.9g carbohydrate;
0.4g protein; 0.5g fibre*

panang curry paste

25 dried long red chillies
1 teaspoon ground coriander
2 teaspoons ground cumin
2 large cloves garlic, quartered
8 green onions, chopped coarsely
2 x 10cm sticks fresh lemon grass (40g), sliced thinly
2 teaspoons finely chopped fresh galangal
2 teaspoons shrimp paste
½ cup (75g) roasted unsalted peanuts
2 tablespoons peanut oil

1   Place chillies in small heatproof jug, cover with boiling water; stand 15 minutes, drain.
2   Meanwhile, dry-fry ground coriander and cumin in small frying pan, stirring, until fragrant.
3   Blend or process chillies and spices with remaining ingredients, except for the oil, until mixture forms a paste, pausing to scrape down sides occasionally during blending.
4   Add oil to paste; continue to blend until smooth.

preparation time *20 minutes (plus standing time)*
cooking time *3 minutes* makes *1 cup*
nutritional count per tablespoon *6.1g total fat (0.9g saturated fat); 288kJ (69 cal); 1.3g carbohydrate; 1.9g protein; 0.9g fibre*

massaman curry paste

20 dried long red chillies
1 teaspoon ground coriander
2 teaspoons ground cumin
2 teaspoons ground cinnamon
½ teaspoon ground cardamom
½ teaspoon ground clove
5 cloves garlic, quartered
1 large brown onion (200g), chopped coarsely
2 x 10cm sticks fresh lemon grass (40g), sliced thinly
3 fresh kaffir lime leaves, sliced thinly
4cm piece fresh ginger (20g), chopped coarsely
2 teaspoons shrimp paste
1 tablespoon peanut oil

1   Preheat oven to 180°C/160°C fan-forced.
2   Place chillies in small heatproof jug, cover with boiling water; stand 15 minutes, drain.
3   Meanwhile, dry-fry coriander, cumin, cinnamon, cardamom and clove in small frying pan, stirring until fragrant.
4   Place chillies and spices in small shallow baking dish with remaining ingredients. Roast, uncovered, 15 minutes.
5   Blend or process roasted paste mixture until smooth.

preparation time *15 minutes (plus standing time)*
cooking time *20 minutes* makes *1 cup*
nutritional count per tablespoon *1.7g total fat (0.3g saturated fat); 105kJ (25 cal); 1.5g carbohydrate; 0.5g protein; 0.4g fibre*

duck jungle curry

2kg duck
¼ cup (60ml) peanut oil
1 medium brown onion (150g), chopped coarsely
1 medium carrot (120g), chopped coarsely
2 cloves garlic, halved
4cm piece fresh ginger (20g), sliced thickly
½ teaspoon black peppercorns
2 litres (8 cups) cold water
5 fresh kaffir lime leaves, torn
¼ cup (75g) red curry paste (page 258)
150g thai eggplants, halved
1 medium carrot (120g), sliced thinly
100g snake beans, cut into 4cm lengths
230g can bamboo shoots, rinsed, drained
2 x 5cm stems (10g) pickled green peppercorns
½ cup firmly packed fresh thai basil leaves
4 fresh small red thai chillies, chopped coarsely
2 tablespoons fish sauce

1 Discard neck then wash duck inside and out; pat dry with absorbent paper. Using sharp knife, separate drumstick and thigh sections from body; separate thighs from drumsticks. Remove and discard wings. Separate breast and backbone; cut breast from bone. You will have six pieces. Cut duck carcass into four pieces; discard any fat from carcass.

2 Heat 1 tablespoon of the oil in large saucepan; cook carcass pieces, stirring occasionally, about 5 minutes or until browned. Add onion, chopped carrot, garlic and ginger; cook, stirring, about 2 minutes or until onion softens. Add black peppercorns, the water and four of the lime leaves; simmer, uncovered, 1¼ hours, skimming fat from surface of mixture regularly.

3 Strain mixture through muslin-lined sieve into large heatproof jug. Reserve 3 cups of liquid; discard solids and remaining liquid.

4 Preheat oven to 200°C/180°C fan-forced.

5 Heat remaining oil in same cleaned pan; cook thighs, drumsticks and breasts, in batches, until browned. Remove skin from breasts and legs; slice skin thinly. Place sliced duck skin on oven tray; roast, uncovered, about 10 minutes or until crisp.

6 Discard excess oil from pan; reheat pan, cook curry paste, stirring, about 1 minute or until fragrant. Add eggplant, sliced carrot, beans, bamboo shoots, green peppercorns, half of the basil, remaining lime leaf and reserved liquid; simmer, uncovered, 5 minutes. Add duck pieces; simmer, uncovered, about 10 minutes or until vegetables are tender. Stir in chilli and sauce.

7 Place curry in serving bowls; sprinkle with remaining basil and crisped duck skin.

preparation time *40 minutes*
cooking time *2 hours* serves *4*
nutritional count per serving *121g total fat (34.4g saturated fat); 5334kJ (1276 cal); 8.1g carbohydrate; 41g protein; 5.4g fibre*

duck red curry

¼ cup (75g) red curry paste (page 258)
400ml can coconut milk
½ cup (125ml) chicken stock
2 fresh kaffir lime leaves, torn
1 tablespoon fish sauce
1 tablespoon lime juice
⅓ cup firmly packed fresh thai basil leaves
1 whole barbecued duck (1kg), cut into 12 pieces
565g can lychees, rinsed, drained
225g can bamboo shoots, rinsed, drained
3 fresh long red thai chillies, sliced thinly

1   Place curry paste in large saucepan; stir over heat until fragrant. Add coconut milk, stock, lime leaves, sauce and juice; bring to the boil. Reduce heat; simmer, stirring, 5 minutes.
2   Reserve about eight small whole basil leaves for garnish; add remaining basil leaves with duck, lychees and bamboo shoots to curry mixture. Cook, stirring occasionally, about 5 minutes or until heated through.
3   Place curry in serving bowl; sprinkle with sliced chilli and reserved thai basil leaves.

preparation time *15 minutes*
cooking time *15 minutes* serves *4*
nutritional count per serving *63.9g total fat (30g saturated fat); 3377kJ (808 cal); 24.4g carbohydrate; 32.8g protein; 6g fibre*

spicy roast chickens

4 x 500g small chickens
2 teaspoons sweet paprika
2 cloves garlic, crushed
1 teaspoon cumin seeds
2 teaspoons yellow mustard seeds
2 tablespoons finely chopped fresh coriander
2 green onions, chopped finely
⅓ cup (110g) mango chutney
2 tablespoons olive oil

VINAIGRETTE

⅓ cup (80ml) olive oil
2 tablespoons lemon juice
½ teaspoon sugar

1   Using kitchen scissors, cut along each side of chicken backbone; discard backbones. Cut chickens in half along breastbones.
2   Combine chickens in large bowl with paprika, garlic, seeds, coriander, onion, chutney and oil. Cover; refrigerate 3 hours or overnight.
3   Preheat oven to 240°C/220°C fan-forced.
4   Drain chickens; reserve marinade. Place chickens, skin-side up, on rack in baking dish. Bake, uncovered, about 30 minutes or until cooked through, brushing with marinade several times during cooking.
5   Make vinaigrette.
6   Serve chickens drizzled with vinaigrette.

VINAIGRETTE   Place ingredients in screw-top jar; shake well.

preparation *15 minutes (plus refrigeration time)*
cooking time *30 minutes* serves *4*
nutritional count per serving *66.9g total fat (16.2g saturated fat); 3540kJ (847 cal); 13.1g carbohydrate; 49.4g protein; 1g fibre*

lamu chicken

20g butter
4 large brown onions (800g), sliced thinly
2 tablespoons white wine vinegar
1 tablespoon brown sugar
2 tablespoons peanut oil
12 chicken drumsticks (1.8kg)
2 cups (400g) basmati rice
2 cinnamon sticks
2 cups (500ml) chicken stock
2 cups (500ml) water
2 limes, cut into wedges

SPICE PASTE

2 ancho chillies
3 cloves garlic, quartered
2cm piece fresh ginger (10g), quartered
1 small green thai chilli, sliced thinly
1 teaspoon cumin seeds
1 teaspoon coriander seeds
1 teaspoon sea salt
1 teaspoon cracked black pepper
½ teaspoon cardamom seeds
4 whole cloves

1 Make spice paste.
2 Melt butter in large deep saucepan; cook onion, stirring, until soft. Add vinegar and sugar; cook, stirring, about 10 minutes or until onion is caramelised. Transfer to medium bowl; cover to keep warm.
3 Heat half of the oil in same pan; cook chicken, in batches, until browned all over.
4 Heat remaining oil in same pan; cook spice paste, stirring, until fragrant. Add rice and half of the caramelised onion; stir to coat in spice mixture.
5 Return chicken to pan with cinnamon, stock and the water; bring to the boil. Reduce heat; simmer, covered tightly, about 30 minutes or until rice is tender and chicken is cooked through. Discard cinnamon sticks.
6 Divide chicken and rice among plates; top with warmed remaining caramelised onion and lime. Serve with a mixed green salad, if you like.

SPICE PASTE Place ancho chillies in small bowl; cover with warm water. Stand 20 minutes; drain. Discard stems and liquid. Using mortar and pestle, crush ancho chillies with remaining ingredients until mixture forms a thick paste.

preparation time *30 minutes*
cooking time *1 hour 5 minutes* serves *6*
nutritional count per serving *31.2g total fat (9.7g saturated fat); 2876kJ (688 cal); 60.3g carbohydrate; 41.6g protein; 2.4g fibre*

3

4

chicken green curry

1 tablespoon peanut oil
¼ cup (75g) green curry paste (page 258)
3 long green chillies, chopped finely
1kg chicken thigh fillets, cut into 3cm pieces
2 x 400ml cans coconut milk
2 tablespoons fish sauce
2 tablespoons lime juice
1 tablespoon grated palm sugar
150g pea eggplants
1 large zucchini (150g), sliced thinly
⅓ cup loosely packed fresh thai basil leaves
¼ cup loosely packed fresh coriander leaves
2 green onions, chopped coarsely

1   Heat oil in large saucepan; cook paste and about two-thirds of the chilli, stirring, about 2 minutes or until fragrant. Add chicken; cook, stirring, until browned.
2   Add coconut milk, sauce, juice, sugar and eggplants; simmer, uncovered, about 10 minutes or until eggplants are just tender.
3   Add zucchini, basil and coriander; simmer, uncovered, until zucchini is just tender.
4   Serve curry sprinkled with remaining chilli and green onion.

preparation time *20 minutes*
cooking time *30 minutes* serves *4*
nutritional count per serving *67.3g total fat (43.2g saturated fat); 3716kJ (889 cal); 17g carbohydrate; 52.9g protein; 6g fibre*

fish yellow curry

8 new potatoes (320g), halved
400ml can coconut milk
¼ cup (70g) yellow curry paste (page 258)
¼ cup (60ml) fish stock
2 tablespoons fish sauce
1 tablespoon lime juice
1 tablespoon grated palm sugar
800g firm white fish fillets, cut into 3cm pieces
3 green onions, sliced thinly
⅓ cup coarsely chopped fresh coriander
1 fresh long red chilli, sliced thinly
1 tablespoon finely chopped fresh coriander

1   Boil, steam or microwave potato until just tender; drain.
2   Meanwhile, place half of the coconut milk in large saucepan; bring to the boil. Boil, stirring, until milk reduces by half and the oil separates from the coconut milk. Add curry paste; cook, stirring, about 1 minute or until fragrant. Add remaining coconut milk, stock, sauce, juice and sugar; cook, stirring, until sugar dissolves.
3   Add fish and potato to pan; cook, covered, about 3 minutes or until fish is cooked. Stir in onion and coarsely chopped coriander.
4   Divide curry among serving bowls; sprinkle with chilli and finely chopped coriander.

preparation time *20 minutes*
cooking time *20 minutes* serves *4*
nutritional count per serving *23g total fat (18.5g saturated fat); 1960kJ (469 cal); 18.9g carbohydrate; 44.7g protein; 3.9g fibre*

massaman curry

1kg skirt steak, cut into 3cm pieces
2 cups (500ml) beef stock
5 cardamom pods, bruised
¼ teaspoon ground clove
2 star anise
1 tablespoon grated palm sugar
2 tablespoons fish sauce
2 tablespoons tamarind concentrate
2 x 400ml cans coconut milk
2 tablespoons massaman curry paste (page 259)
8 baby brown onions (200g), halved
1 medium kumara (400g), chopped coarsely
¼ cup (35g) coarsely chopped roasted
    unsalted peanuts
2 green onions, sliced thinly

1   Place beef, 1½ cups of the stock, cardamom,
clove, star anise, sugar, sauce, 1 tablespoon of
the tamarind and half of the coconut milk in large
saucepan; simmer, uncovered, about 1½ hours or
until beef is almost tender.
2   Strain beef over large bowl; reserve braising liquid,
discard solids. Cover beef to keep warm.
3   Cook curry paste in same pan, stirring, until fragrant.
Add remaining coconut milk, tamarind and stock;
bring to the boil. Cook, stirring, about 1 minute or
until mixture is smooth. Return beef to pan with brown
onion, kumara and 1 cup of the reserved braising
liquid; simmer, uncovered, about 30 minutes or until
beef and vegetables are tender.
4   Stir nuts and green onion into curry off the heat.

preparation time *20 minutes*
cooking time *2 hours 10 minutes* serves *4*
nutritional count per serving *52.7g total fat (39.5g
saturated fat); 3645kJ (872 cal); 29.2g carbohydrate;
67.4g protein; 7.2g fibre*

thai red beef curry

1 tablespoon peanut oil
4 x 125g scotch fillet steaks
¼ cup (75g) red curry paste (page 258)
225g can bamboo shoots, drained, rinsed
2 x 400ml cans coconut cream
½ cup (125ml) beef stock
2 tablespoons fish sauce
2 tablespoons lime juice
2 fresh kaffir lime leaves, shredded finely
4 large zucchini (600g), sliced thinly
⅓ cup firmly packed fresh thai basil leaves

1   Heat oil in large flameproof casserole dish; cook
beef, in batches, until well-browned both sides.
2   Cook paste in same dish, stirring, until fragrant.
Return beef to dish with bamboo shoots, coconut
cream, stock, sauce, juice and lime leaves; simmer,
uncovered, 1 hour 20 minutes. Add zucchini, simmer
about 5 minutes or until tender.
3   Serve curry sprinkled with basil.

preparation time *15 minutes*
cooking time *1 hour 40 minutes* serves *4*
nutritional count per serving *55.5g total fat (40.6g
saturated fat); 2897kJ (693 cal); 12.3g carbohydrate;
34.1g protein; 7.2g fibre*

pork cutlets with avocado salsa

2 tablespoons taco seasoning mix
¼ cup (60ml) olive oil
4 x 235g pork cutlets
3 small tomatoes (270g), seeded, chopped finely
1 small avocado (200g), chopped finely
1 lebanese cucumber (130g), seeded, chopped finely
1 tablespoon lime juice

1   Combine seasoning, 2 tablespoons of the oil and pork in large bowl.
2   Cook pork on heated oiled grill plate (or grill or barbecue) until cooked.
3   Meanwhile, combine remaining oil in medium bowl with tomato, avocado, cucumber and juice.
4   Serve pork with salsa.

preparation time *10 minutes*
cooking time *10 minutes* serves *4*
nutritional count per serving *42.2g total fat (10.7g saturated fat); 2241kJ (536 cal); 1.2g carbohydrate; 38g protein; 1.2g fibre*

chicken enchiladas

3 chipotle chillies
1 cup (250ml) boiling water
500g chicken breast fillets
1 tablespoon vegetable oil
1 large red onion (300g), chopped finely
2 cloves garlic, crushed
1 teaspoon ground cumin
1 tablespoon tomato paste
2 x 425g cans crushed tomatoes
1 tablespoon finely chopped fresh oregano
⅔ cup (160g) sour cream
1½ cups (240g) coarsely grated cheddar cheese
10 small flour tortillas

1   Cover chillies with the water in small heatproof bowl; stand 20 minutes. Remove stems from chillies; discard stems. Blend or process chillies with soaking liquid until smooth.
2   Meanwhile, place chicken in medium saucepan of boiling water; return to the boil. Reduce heat; simmer, covered, about 10 minutes or until chicken is cooked through. Remove chicken from poaching liquid; cool 10 minutes. Discard poaching liquid; shred chicken finely.
3   Preheat oven to 180°C/160°C fan-forced. Oil a shallow rectangular 3-litre (12-cup) ovenproof dish.
4   Heat oil in large frying pan; cook onion, stirring, until soft. Reserve half of the onion in small bowl.
5   Add garlic and cumin to remaining onion in pan; cook, stirring, until fragrant. Add chilli mixture, tomato paste, undrained tomatoes and oregano; bring to the boil. Reduce heat; simmer, uncovered, 1 minute. Remove sauce from heat.
6   Meanwhile, combine shredded chicken, reserved onion, half of the sour cream and a third of the cheese in medium bowl.
7   Warm tortillas according to instructions on packet. Dip tortillas, one at a time, in tomato sauce in pan; place on board. Place ¼ cup of the chicken mixture along edge of each tortilla; roll enchiladas to enclose filling.
8   Spread ½ cup tomato sauce into dish. Place enchiladas, seam-side down, in dish (they should fit snugly, without overcrowding). Pour remaining tomato sauce over enchiladas; sprinkle with remaining cheese. Cook, uncovered, about 15 minutes or until cheese melts and enchiladas are heated through. Sprinkle with coriander leaves, if you like. Serve with remaining sour cream.

preparation time *50 minutes*
cooking time *35 minutes* serves *10*
nutritional count per serving *9.4g total fat (9.4g saturated fat); 1593kJ (381 cal); 29.4g carbohydrate; 22g protein; 3.1g fibre*

barbecued chicken with nam jim

12 chicken thigh cutlets (2kg)
⅓ cup (90g) grated palm sugar
2 teaspoons ground cumin
1 teaspoon salt
1 cup loosely packed fresh mint leaves
1 cup loosely packed fresh thai basil leaves

NAM JIM

2 cloves garlic, crushed
3 large green chillies, seeded, chopped coarsely
2 coriander roots
2 tablespoons fish sauce
2 tablespoons grated palm sugar
3 shallots (75g), chopped coarsely
¼ cup (60ml) lime juice

1 Cut two deep slashes through the skin and flesh of each chicken thigh. Rub chicken with combined sugar, cumin and salt. Stand 10 minutes.
2 Meanwhile, make nam jim.
3 Place chicken, skin-side down, on heated oiled grill plate (or barbecue) on low heat about 10 minutes. Turn, cover with foil or cover the barbecue; cook until chicken is cooked through.
4 Serve chicken on a bed of herbs with nam jim.

NAM JIM Blend or process ingredients until smooth.

preparation time *15 minutes*
cooking time *20 minutes* serves *4*
nutritional count per serving *20.9g total fat (6.2g saturated fat); 2195kJ (525 cal); 30.1g carbohydrate; 54.1g protein; 2.1g fibre*

chilli cheese polenta with bean and avocado salsa

1 litre (4 cups) water
1 cup (170g) polenta
¼ teaspoon chilli powder
1 cup (120g) coarsely grated cheddar cheese
1 tablespoon vegetable oil

BEAN AND AVOCADO SALSA

3 medium tomatoes (450g), chopped coarsely
1 small red onion (100g), chopped finely
1 medium avocado (250g), chopped coarsely
420g can four-bean mix, rinsed, drained
2 tablespoons sweet chilli sauce

1 Oil 19cm-square cake pan.
2 Place the water in large saucepan; bring to the boil. Gradually stir polenta into the water; reduce heat. Simmer, stirring, about 10 minutes or until polenta thickens. Stir in chilli and cheese; spread polenta into pan, cool 10 minutes. Cover; refrigerate about 1 hour or until polenta firms.
3 Meanwhile, make bean and avocado salsa.
4 Turn polenta onto board; trim edges. Cut polenta into quarters; cut each quarter into three slices. Heat oil in large frying pan; cook polenta, uncovered, until browned both sides.
5 Serve polenta slices topped with salsa.

BEAN AND AVOCADO SALSA Combine ingredients in medium bowl.

preparation time *10 minutes* cooking time *20 minutes (plus refrigeration time)* serves *4*
nutritional count per serving *26.2g total fat (9.4g saturated fat); 2094kJ (501 cal); 44.9g carbohydrate; 17.9g protein; 8.4g fibre*

creamy chicken korma

¼ cup (35g) unsalted cashews
1 teaspoon sesame seeds
500g yogurt
3 cloves garlic, crushed
2cm piece fresh ginger (10g), grated
1 teaspoon dried chilli flakes
½ teaspoon ground turmeric
1kg chicken thigh fillets, cut into 3cm pieces
2 tablespoons vegetable oil
2 medium brown onions (300g), sliced thinly
2 cardamom pods
2 whole cloves
½ teaspoon black cumin seeds
½ cinnamon stick
2 tablespoons lemon juice
⅓ cup (15g) flaked coconut
⅓ cup (50g) unsalted cashews, extra
2 teaspoons kalonji seeds
¼ cup loosely packed fresh coriander leaves

1 Process nuts and sesame seeds until ground finely. Combine nut mixture with yogurt, garlic, ginger, chilli and turmeric in large bowl; add chicken, toss to coat in marinade. Cover; refrigerate 3 hours or overnight.
2 Heat oil in large saucepan; cook onion, stirring, until soft. Add chicken mixture. Reduce heat; simmer, uncovered, 40 minutes, stirring occasionally.
3 Using mortar and pestle, crush cardamom, cloves and cumin seeds.
4 Add spice mixture, cinnamon and juice to chicken mixture; cook, uncovered, about 10 minutes or until chicken is cooked through.
5 Meanwhile, cook coconut and extra nuts in small frying pan, stirring, until browned lightly. Remove from heat; stir in kalonji seeds.
6 Discard cinnamon from curry; serve curry, sprinkled with coconut mixture and coriander, accompanied by steamed basmati rice, if you like.

preparation time *25 minutes (plus refrigeration time)*
cooking time *1 hour* serves *4*
nutritional count per serving *45.7g total fat (13.6g saturated fat); 2918kJ (698 cal); 13.2g carbohydrate; 58.1g protein; 3.7g fibre*

chicken panang curry

2 x 400ml cans coconut milk
3 tablespoons panang curry paste (page 259)
2 tablespoons grated palm sugar
2 tablespoons fish sauce
2 fresh kaffir lime leaves, torn
2 tablespoons peanut oil
1kg chicken thigh fillets, quartered
100g snake beans, chopped coarsely
½ cup firmly packed fresh thai basil leaves
½ cup (75g) coarsely chopped roasted
    unsalted peanuts
2 fresh long red thai chillies, sliced thinly

1 Place coconut milk, paste, sugar, sauce and lime leaves in wok or large frying pan; bring to the boil. Reduce heat; simmer, stirring, about 15 minutes or until curry sauce mixture reduces by about a third.
2 Meanwhile, heat peanut oil in large frying pan; cook chicken, in batches, until browned lightly. Drain on absorbent paper.
3 Add beans, chicken and half of the basil leaves to curry sauce mixture; cook, uncovered, stirring occasionally, about 5 minutes or until beans are just tender and chicken is cooked through.
4 Place curry in serving bowl; sprinkle with peanuts, chilli and remaining basil.

preparation time *15 minutes*
cooking time *20 minutes* serves *4*
nutritional count per serving *82.9g total fat (45g saturated fat); 4406kJ (1054 cal); 17.9g carbohydrate; 57.8g protein; 7.9g fibre*

crying tiger

50g dried tamarind
1 cup (250ml) boiling water
400g beef eye fillet
2 cloves garlic, crushed
2 teaspoons dried green peppercorns, crushed
1 tablespoon peanut oil
2 tablespoons fish sauce
2 tablespoons soy sauce
10cm stick fresh lemon grass (20g), chopped finely
2 fresh small red thai chillies, chopped finely
1 large carrot (180g)
1 cup (80g) thinly sliced wombok

CRYING TIGER SAUCE

¼ cup (60ml) fish sauce
¼ cup (60ml) lime juice
2 teaspoons grated palm sugar
1 teaspoon finely chopped dried red thai chilli
1 green onion, sliced thinly
2 teaspoons finely chopped fresh coriander
reserved tamarind pulp

1 Soak tamarind in the water for 30 minutes. Pour tamarind into a fine strainer set over a small bowl; push as much tamarind pulp through the strainer as possible, scraping underside of strainer occasionally. Discard any tamarind solids left in strainer; reserve ½ cup of pulp for the crying tiger sauce.
2 Halve beef lengthways. Combine remaining tamarind pulp, garlic, peppercorns, oil, sauces, lemon grass and chilli in large bowl; add beef, stir to coat beef all over in marinade. Cover; refrigerate 3 hours or overnight.
3 Make crying tiger sauce.
4 Cook beef on heated oiled grill plate (or grill or barbecue) about 10 minutes or until browned all over and cooked as desired. Cover beef; stand 10 minutes, slice thinly.
5 Meanwhile, cut carrot into 10cm lengths; slice each length thinly, cut slices into thin matchsticks.
6 Place sliced beef on serving dish with carrot and wombok; serve crying tiger sauce separately.

CRYING TIGER SAUCE Whisk ingredients in small bowl until sugar dissolves.

preparation time *20 minutes (plus refrigeration time)*
cooking time *10 minutes* serves *4*
nutritional count per serving *10.9g total fat (3.3g saturated fat); 978kJ (234 cal); 7.8g carbohydrate; 24.8g protein; 2.7g fibre*

mexican bean and shredded pork soup

2 litres (8 cups) water
2 litres (8 cups) chicken stock
1 large carrot (180g), chopped coarsely
1 trimmed celery stalk (100g), chopped coarsely
5 cloves garlic, unpeeled, bruised
6 black peppercorns
3 sprigs fresh oregano
1 bay leaf
1kg piece pork neck
1 tablespoon olive oil
1 large red onion (300g), chopped coarsely
1 medium red capsicum (200g), chopped coarsely
1 medium yellow capsicum (200g), chopped coarsely
2 fresh long red chillies, sliced thinly
2 cloves garlic, crushed
810g can crushed tomatoes
1 teaspoon ground cumin
2 tablespoons coarsely chopped fresh oregano
420g can kidney beans, rinsed, drained

1 Place the water and stock in large saucepan with carrot, celery, bruised garlic, peppercorns, oregano sprigs, bay leaf and pork; bring to the boil. Reduce heat; simmer, covered, 1 hour. Uncover; simmer 1 hour.
2 Transfer pork to medium bowl; using two forks, shred pork coarsely. Strain broth through muslin-lined sieve or colander into large heatproof bowl; discard solids.
3 Heat oil in same cleaned pan; cook onion, capsicums, chilli and crushed garlic, stirring, until vegetables soften. Return pork and broth to pan with undrained tomatoes, cumin and the chopped oregano; bring to the boil. Reduce heat; simmer, covered, 15 minutes. Add beans; simmer, covered, until soup is hot.

preparation time *25 minutes*
cooking time *2 hours 30 minutes* serves *6*
nutritional count per serving *7.4g total fat (1.6g saturated fat); 1490kJ (356 cal); 20.8g carbohydrate; 46.5g protein; 9.1g fibre*

fajitas with guacamole and salsa cruda

3 cloves garlic, crushed
¼ cup (60ml) lemon juice
2 teaspoons ground cumin
1 tablespoon olive oil
600g piece beef eye fillet, sliced thinly
1 large red capsicum (350g), sliced thinly
1 large green capsicum (350g), sliced thinly
1 medium yellow capsicum (200g), sliced thinly
1 large red onion (300g), sliced thinly
8 large flour tortillas

GUACAMOLE

1 large avocado (320g), mashed roughly
¼ cup finely chopped fresh coriander
1 tablespoon lime juice
1 small white onion (80g), chopped finely

SALSA CRUDA

2 medium tomatoes (300g), seeded, chopped finely
1 fresh long red chilli, chopped finely
½ cup coarsely chopped fresh coriander
1 small white onion (80g), chopped finely
1 tablespoon lime juice

1 Combine garlic, juice, cumin, oil and beef in large bowl, cover; refrigerate.
2 Make guacamole. Make salsa cruda.
3 Cook beef, in batches, in heated oiled large frying pan until cooked as desired. Remove from pan; cover to keep warm.
4 Cook capsicum and onion in same pan until softened. Return beef to pan; stir until heated through.
5 Warm tortillas according to packet directions.
6 Divide beef mixture among serving plates; serve with tortillas, guacamole and salsa.

GUACAMOLE Combine ingredients in small bowl.

SALSA CRUDA Combine ingredients in small bowl.

preparation time *25 minutes*
cooking time *15 minutes* serves *4*
nutritional count per serving *31.5g total fat (7.6g saturated fat); 3089kJ (739 cal); 62.7g carbohydrate; 46.2g protein; 8.9g fibre*

mexican beans with sausages

1 cup (200g) dried kidney beans
800g beef sausages, chopped coarsely
1 tablespoon olive oil
1 large white onion (200g), chopped coarsely
3 cloves garlic, crushed
1 large red capsicum (350g), chopped coarsely
½ teaspoon ground cumin
2 teaspoons sweet smoked paprika
1 teaspoon dried chilli flakes
2 x 400g cans crushed tomatoes
2 tablespoons coarsely chopped fresh oregano

1 Place beans in medium bowl, cover with cold water; stand overnight, drain. Rinse under cold water; drain. Place beans in medium saucepan of boiling water; return to the boil. Reduce heat; simmer, uncovered, about 30 minutes or until beans are almost tender. Drain.
2 Cook sausages, in batches, in large deep saucepan until browned; drain on absorbent paper.
3 Heat oil in same pan; cook onion, garlic and capsicum, stirring, until onion softens. Add cumin, paprika and chilli; cook, stirring, about 2 minutes or until fragrant. Add beans and undrained tomatoes; bring to the boil. Reduce heat; simmer, covered, about 1 hour or until beans are tender.
4 Return sausages to pan; simmer, covered, about 10 minutes or until sausages are cooked through. Remove from heat; stir in oregano. Serve with tortillas, if you like.

preparation time *20 minutes (plus standing time)*
cooking time *2 hours 15 minutes* serves *4*
nutritional count per serving *56.9g total fat (25.2g saturated fat); 3323kJ (795 cal); 33.5g carbohydrate; 38.1g protein; 20.2g fibre*

mexican chicken stew

1 tablespoon vegetable oil
8 chicken drumsticks (1.2kg)
1 large red onion (300g), sliced thickly
2 cloves garlic, crushed
2 fresh long red chillies, chopped finely
1 teaspoon ground cumin
4 medium tomatoes (600g), chopped coarsely
1 cup (250ml) chicken stock
⅓ cup loosely packed fresh oregano leaves
420g can kidney beans, rinsed, drained
1 medium yellow capsicum (200g), sliced thickly
1 medium green capsicum (200g), sliced thickly

1 Heat half the oil in large saucepan; cook chicken, in batches, until browned all over.
2 Heat remaining oil in same pan; cook onion, garlic, chilli and cumin, stirring, until onion softens.
3 Return chicken to pan with tomato, stock and ¼ cup of the oregano; bring to the boil. Reduce heat; simmer, covered, 30 minutes. Add beans and capsicums; simmer, uncovered, 20 minutes.
4 Divide stew among bowls; sprinkle with remaining oregano. Serve with sour cream, if you like.

preparation time *20 minutes*
cooking time *1 hour* serves *4*
nutritional count per serving *26.5g total fat (7.1g saturated fat); 2090kJ (500 cal); 19g carbohydrate; 42.6g protein; 8.4g fibre*

black bean, corn and chipotle stew

1½ cups (300g) dried black beans
2 chipotle chillies
½ cup (125ml) boiling water
1 tablespoon cumin seeds
2 trimmed corn cobs (500g)
2 teaspoons olive oil
1 large brown onion (200g), chopped finely
810g can crushed tomatoes
8 small white corn tortillas

SALSA

1 small red onion (100g), chopped coarsely
1 small tomato (90g), chopped coarsely
½ cup coarsely chopped fresh coriander
1 lebanese cucumber (130g), chopped coarsely
1 tablespoon olive oil
2 tablespoons lemon juice

1 Place beans in medium bowl, cover with water; stand overnight, drain. Rinse under cold water; drain. Place beans in medium saucepan of boiling water; return to the boil. Reduce heat; simmer, uncovered, about 15 minutes or until beans are just tender.
2 Preheat oven to 200°C/180°C fan-forced.
3 Place chillies and the boiling water in small bowl; stand 15 minutes. Discard stalks; blend or process chilli and its soaking liquid until smooth.
4 Meanwhile, dry-fry cumin seeds in small frying pan, stirring, until fragrant.
5 Cook corn on heated oiled grill plate (or grill or barbecue) until browned lightly and just tender. When cool enough to handle, cut kernels from cobs with sharp knife.
6 Heat oil in large flameproof dish; cook onion, stirring, until soft. Add drained beans, chilli mixture, cumin, undrained tomatoes and half of the corn; bring to the boil. Cook, uncovered, in oven about 20 minutes or until sauce thickens.
7 Meanwhile, heat tortillas according to packet directions.
8 Combine remaining corn with salsa ingredients in medium bowl. Serve stew with tortillas and salsa.

preparation time *15 minutes (plus standing time)*
cooking time *1 hour* serves *4*
nutritional count per serving *10.4g total fat (1.3g saturated fat); 1839kJ (440 cal); 61.3g carbohydrate; 26.2g protein; 19.5g fibre*

chilli con carne with quesadillas

1 tablespoon olive oil
300g beef mince
1 medium red onion (170g), chopped finely
2 cloves garlic, crushed
1 tablespoon worcestershire sauce
1 tablespoon Tabasco sauce
2 teaspoons ground cumin
2 teaspoons ground coriander
1 teaspoon dried oregano
400g can crushed tomatoes
½ cup (130g) chunky tomato salsa
400g can kidney beans, rinsed, drained
400g can chickpeas, rinsed, drained

QUESADILLAS
¾ cup (90g) coarsely grated cheddar cheese
4 x 20cm flour tortillas
20g butter

1   Heat half the oil in medium saucepan; cook beef, stirring, until browned, remove from pan.
2   Heat remaining oil in same pan; cook onion and garlic, stirring, until onion softens. Return beef to pan with sauces, cumin, coriander and oregano; cook, stirring, 2 minutes.
3   Add undrained tomatoes to pan then stir in salsa, beans and chickpeas; cook, uncovered, 10 minutes.
4   Meanwhile, make quesadillas.
5   Serve chilli with quesadillas.

QUESADILLAS Divide cheese between two tortillas; top with remaining tortillas, pressing firmly to seal. Heat butter in medium frying pan; cook until browned both sides. Cut each quesadilla into quarters.

preparation time *10 minutes*
cooking time *25 minutes serves 4*
nutritional count per serving *26.8g total fat (11.1g saturated fat); 2562kJ (613 cal); 51.7g carbohydrate; 35.5g protein; 11.6g fibre*

char-grilled scallops with corn salsa

36 scallops (900g), roe removed
2 cloves garlic, crushed
2 tablespoons lime juice
1 tablespoon olive oil
2 corn cobs (800g), trimmed
200g grape tomatoes, halved
1 large avocado (320g), chopped coarsely
1 medium red onion (170g), chopped finely
1 medium green capsicum (200g), chopped finely
2 fresh small red thai chillies, chopped finely
¼ cup coarsely chopped fresh coriander
8 corn tortillas
2 limes, cut into wedges

LIME DRESSING
¼ cup (60ml) lime juice
½ teaspoon ground cumin
2 teaspoons olive oil

1   Combine scallops, garlic, juice and oil in large bowl. Cover; refrigerate 3 hours or overnight.
2   Place ingredients for lime dressing in screw-top jar; shake well.
3   Cook corn on heated oiled grill plate (or grill or barbecue) until browned and just tender. Using sharp knife, cut corn kernels from cobs. Place corn kernels in large bowl with tomato, avocado, onion, capsicum, chilli, coriander and dressing; toss gently to combine.
4   Cook drained scallops, in batches, on same grill plate until browned and cooked as desired. Cover to keep warm.
5   Using tongs, place tortillas, one at a time, briefly, on same grill plate to lightly brown both sides (work quickly as tortillas toughen if overcooked). Wrap tortillas in tea towel to keep warm.
6   Serve scallops with salsa, lime wedges and tortillas.

preparation time *25 minutes (plus refrigeration time)*
cooking time *20 minutes serves 4*
nutritional count per serving *24.1g total fat (4.4g saturated fat); 2416kJ (578 cal); 50.6g carbohydrate; 37.8g protein; 12.2g fibre*

vegie nachos

1 tablespoon olive oil
1 medium brown onion (150g), chopped finely
1 clove garlic, crushed
½ teaspoon dried chilli flakes
400g can chopped tomatoes
420g can mexibeans, drained, rinsed
230g packet corn chips
1 cup (120g) grated cheddar cheese
½ cup (120g) sour cream
1 tablespoon chopped fresh coriander

1 Preheat oven to 200°C/180°C fan-forced.
2 Heat oil in medium frying pan; cook onion, garlic
and chilli, stirring, about 5 minutes or until onion softens.
3 Stir in undrained tomatoes and beans; bring to the
boil. Reduce heat; simmer, uncovered, 15 minutes,
stirring constantly, until mixture thickens slightly.
4 Place corn chips onto large ovenproof plate; pour
bean mixture over chips, then sprinkle with cheese.
Bake, uncovered, about 10 minutes or until cheese is
melted. Serve topped with sour cream and coriander.

preparation time *15 minutes*
cooking time *35 minute* serves *4*
nutritional count per serving *43.4g total fat (21.3g
saturated fat); 2867kJ (686 cal); 49.3g carbohydrate;
20.5g protein; 13.3g fibre*

mexican chilli beef

1 tablespoon olive oil
1 medium brown onion (150g), chopped
2 cloves garlic, crushed
1kg minced beef
1 fresh long red chilli, chopped finely
400g can crushed tomatoes
1 cup (250ml) beef stock
¾ cup (180ml) tomato paste
425g can mexican-style baked beans
2 tablespoons chopped fresh parsley

1 Combine oil, onion and garlic in large microwave-
safe bowl; microwave, uncovered, on HIGH (100%)
4 minutes, stirring once during cooking.
2 Stir in beef; microwave, uncovered, on HIGH (100%)
10 minutes, stirring twice. Add chilli, undrained crushed
tomatoes, stock and paste. Microwave, uncovered,
on HIGH (100%) about 25 minutes or until thick,
stirring twice.
3 Stir in beans; microwave, uncovered, on HIGH
(100%) 2 minutes. Stir in parsley.

preparation time *10 minutes*
cooking time *40 minutes* serves *4*
nutritional count per serving *22.9g total fat (8.1g
saturated fat); 2337kJ (559 cal); 23.8g carbohydrate;
59.8g protein; 9.4g fibre*

corn and bean stew
with tortillas

2 teaspoons olive oil
1 medium green capsicum (200g), sliced thinly
1 medium brown onion (150g), sliced thinly
1 cup (165g) fresh corn kernels
3 medium tomatoes (450g), chopped coarsely
420g can kidney beans, rinsed, drained
1 fresh small red thai chilli, chopped finely
8 corn tortillas, warmed

1 Heat half the oil in large frying pan; cook capsicum,
stirring, until just tender. Remove from pan.
2 Heat remaining oil in same pan; cook onion and
corn, stirring, until onion softens. Add tomato, beans
and chilli; simmer, uncovered, 10 minutes.
3 Stir capsicum into tomato mixture; serve with warm
tortillas and guacamole, if you like.

preparation time *15 minutes*
cooking time *15 minutes* serves *4*
nutritional count per serving *9.9g total fat (1.4g
saturated fat); 1935kJ (463 cal); 70.3g carbohydrate;
16.6g protein; 11.5g fibre*

curried lamb and lentil salad

2 tablespoons mild curry paste
¼ cup (60ml) peanut oil
600g lamb backstrap
1 medium brown onion (150g), chopped finely
1 large carrot (180g), chopped finely
1 trimmed celery stalk (100g), chopped finely
1 clove garlic, crushed
⅓ cup (80ml) chicken stock
400g can brown lentils, rinsed, drained
100g baby spinach leaves
½ cup loosely packed fresh coriander leaves

1   Combine 1 tablespoon of the curry paste and
1 tablespoon of the oil in small bowl. Rub lamb with
curry mixture.
2   Cook lamb in heated oiled grill pan until browned
on both sides and cooked as desired. Transfer to plate,
cover, stand for 5 minutes.
3   Meanwhile, heat remaining oil in medium saucepan;
add onion, carrot and celery, cook, stirring, until
vegetables are soft. Add garlic and remaining curry
paste, cook, stirring, until fragrant. Add stock and lentils,
stir until hot. Remove from heat, add spinach and
coriander; toss until combined.
4   Slice lamb; serve with lentil salad.

preparation time *15 minutes*
cooking time *10 minutes* serves *4*
nutritional count per serving *23.1g total fat (5.3g
saturated fat); 1718kJ (411 cal); 12g carbohydrate;
36.1g protein; 6.3g fibre*

curry and lime lentil soup

2 teaspoons vegetable oil
1 tablespoon hot curry paste
1 medium brown onion (150g), chopped finely
2 cloves garlic, crushed
2cm piece fresh ginger (10g), grated
1 teaspoon cumin seeds
1 cup (200g) red lentils
2 cups (500ml) vegetable stock
2½ cups (625ml) water
400g can diced tomatoes
1 teaspoon finely grated lime rind
¼ cup (60ml) lime juice
⅓ cup finely chopped fresh flat-leaf parsley

1   Heat oil in large saucepan; cook curry paste,
stirring, until fragrant. Add onion, garlic, ginger and
cumin; cook, stirring, until onion softens.
2   Add lentils, stock, the water and undrained tomatoes.
Bring to the boil; reduce heat. Simmer, uncovered,
about 20 minutes or until lentils are softened.
3   Stir in rind and juice; return to the boil. Remove from
heat; stir in parsley.

preparation time *15 minutes*
cooking time *30 minutes* serves *4*
nutritional count per serving *6g total fat (0.9g
saturated fat); 991kJ (237 cal); 25.2g carbohydrate;
15.4g protein; 9.9g fibre*

harira

1 cup (200g) dried chickpeas
20g butter
2 medium brown onions (300g), chopped finely
2 trimmed celery stalks (200g), chopped finely
2 cloves garlic, crushed
4cm piece fresh ginger (20g), grated
1 teaspoon ground cinnamon
½ teaspoon ground black pepper
pinch saffron threads
500g diced lamb
3 large tomatoes (660g), seeded, chopped coarsely
2 litres (8 cups) hot water
½ cup (100g) brown lentils
2 tablespoons plain flour
½ cup (100g) cooked white long-grain rice
½ cup firmly packed fresh coriander leaves
2 tablespoons lemon juice

1 Place chickpeas in medium bowl, cover with water, stand overnight; drain. Rinse under cold water; drain.
2 Melt butter in large saucepan; cook onion, celery and garlic, stirring, until onion softens. Add ginger, cinnamon, pepper and saffron; cook, stirring, until fragrant. Add lamb; cook, stirring, about 5 minutes or until lamb is browned. Add chickpeas and tomato; cook, stirring, about 5 minutes or until tomato softens.
3 Stir the water into soup mixture; bring to the boil. Reduce heat; simmer, covered, 45 minutes. Add lentils; simmer, covered, 1 hour.
4 Blend flour with ½ cup of slightly cooled broth in a small bowl; return to pan with rice. Cook, stirring, until soup comes to the boil and thickens slightly. Remove from heat; stir in coriander and juice.

preparation time *25 minutes (plus standing time)*
cooking time *2 hours 15 minutes* serves *8*
nutritional count per serving *8.6g total fat (4g saturated fat); 1095kJ (262 cal); 23.6g carbohydrate; 20.1g protein; 4.8g fibre*

spiced coriander, lentil and barley soup

Soup mix is a packaged blend of various dried pulses and grains, among them, lentils, split peas and barley. It is available from supermarkets.

1 tablespoon coriander seeds
1 tablespoon cumin seeds
1 tablespoon ghee
6 cloves garlic, crushed
2 fresh small red thai chillies, chopped finely
1¼ cups (250g) soup mix
1 litre (4 cups) chicken stock
3½ cups (875ml) water
1 cup coarsely chopped fresh coriander
⅓ cup (95g) greek-style yogurt
1 tablespoon mango chutney

1 Dry-fry seeds in large saucepan, stirring, until fragrant. Using pestle and mortar, crush seeds.
2 Melt ghee in same pan; cook crushed seeds, garlic and chilli, stirring, 5 minutes.
3 Add soup mix, stock and the water; bring to the boil. Reduce heat; simmer, covered, stirring occasionally, 1 hour. Cool 15 minutes.
4 Blend or process half the soup, in batches, until smooth. Return pureed soup to pan with unprocessed soup; stir over medium heat until hot. Remove from heat; stir in coriander.
5 Serve bowls of soup topped with yogurt and chutney.

preparation time *10 minutes (plus cooling time)*
cooking time *1 hour 20 minutes* serves *4*
nutritional count per serving *7.9g total fat (4.6g saturated fat); 1350kJ (323 cal); 49.7g carbohydrate; 11.4g protein; 3g fibre*

lamb shanks massaman

1 tablespoon vegetable oil
8 french trimmed lamb shanks (2kg)
2 large brown onions (400g), chopped coarsely
½ cup (150g) massaman curry paste (page 259)
400ml can coconut milk
2 tablespoons tamarind concentrate
2 cups (500ml) beef stock
700g piece pumpkin, trimmed, cut into 2cm cubes
¼ cup (35g) roasted unsalted peanuts,
    chopped coarsely
2 green onions, sliced thinly

1 Preheat oven to 180°C/160°C fan-forced.
2 Heat half the oil in large flameproof dish; cook lamb, in batches, until browned.
3 Heat remaining oil in same dish; cook brown onion and curry paste, stirring, 2 minutes. Add coconut milk, tamarind and stock; bring to the boil. Remove from heat, add lamb; cook in oven, covered, 2 hours. Remove lamb from dish; cover.
4 Add pumpkin to dish; bring to the boil. Reduce heat; simmer, uncovered, about 10 minutes or until pumpkin is tender and sauce is thickened.
5 Divide lamb, pumpkin and sauce among serving plates, sprinkle with nuts and green onion.

preparation time *30 minutes*
cooking time *2 hours 30 minutes* serves *4*
nutritional count per serving *57.2g total fat (31.4g saturated fat); 3628kJ (868 cal); 20.7g carbohydrate; 65.7g protein; 6g fibre*

rogan josh

1 tablespoon vegetable oil
1kg lamb shoulder, cut into 3cm pieces
3 medium brown onions (450g), sliced thinly
4cm piece fresh ginger (20g), grated
2 cloves garlic, crushed
⅔ cup (200g) rogan josh paste
1½ cups (375ml) water
425g can diced tomatoes
1 cinnamon stick
5 cardamom pods, bruised
2 tablespoons coarsely chopped fresh coriander

1 Heat half the oil in large saucepan; cook lamb, in batches, until browned.
2 Heat remaining oil in same pan; cook onion, stirring, until soft. Add ginger, garlic and paste; cook, stirring, until fragrant.
3 Return lamb to pan; stir to combine with paste mixture. Add the water, undrained tomatoes, cinnamon and cardamom; simmer, covered, about 1½ hours or until lamb is tender.
4 Serve curry sprinkled with coriander.

preparation time *25 minutes*
cooking time *1 hour 50 minutes* serves *6*
nutritional count per serving *28.6g total fat (8.3g saturated fat); 1835kJ (439 cal); 7.8g carbohydrate; 35.7g protein; 5.5g fibre*

spiced salmon with yogurt

1 clove garlic, crushed
1 tablespoon ground coriander
1 teaspoon ground cumin
1 teaspoon ground ginger
½ teaspoon ground turmeric
2 tablespoons olive oil
4 x 200g salmon fillets
400g can cannellini beans, rinsed, drained
½ cup lightly packed fresh coriander leaves
½ cup (140g) plain yogurt

1 Combine garlic, spices and 1 tablespoon of oil in small bowl. Reserve half spice mixture. Rub flesh-side of the salmon with remaining spice mixture.
2 Heat remaining oil in large frying pan; cook salmon, flesh-side down, until browned lightly. Turn; cook salmon until cooked as desired.
3 Meanwhile, heat half the reserved spice mixture in small frying pan until fragrant; add beans, stir until heated through. Remove from heat; add coriander, toss gently.
4 Combine remaining spice mixture with yogurt in a small bowl. Serve salmon on bean mixture, top with spiced yogurt.

preparation *10 minutes*
cooking *15 minutes* serves *4*
nutritional count per serving *24.8g total fat (5.3g saturated fat); 1906kJ (456 cal); 11.1g carbohydrate; 45.1g protein; 4.4g fibre*

fish in spicy coconut cream

2 teaspoons peanut oil
2 cloves garlic, crushed
1 teaspoon grated fresh ginger
20g piece fresh turmeric, grated finely
2 fresh small red thai chillies, sliced thinly
1½ cups (375ml) fish stock
400ml can coconut cream
4cm piece fresh galangal (20g), halved
10cm stick fresh lemon grass (20g),
    cut into 2cm pieces
4 firm white fish fillets (800g)
2 tablespoons fish sauce
2 green onions, sliced thinly

1 Heat oil in wok; cook garlic, ginger, turmeric and chilli, stirring, until fragrant.
2 Add stock, coconut cream, galangal and lemon grass; bring to the boil. Add fish, reduce heat; simmer, covered, about 8 minutes or until fish is cooked as desired. Remove and discard galangal and lemon grass pieces.
3 Using slotted spoon, remove fish carefully from sauce; place in serving bowl, cover to keep warm.
4 Bring sauce to the boil; boil 5 minutes. Remove from heat; stir in fish sauce and onion. Pour sauce over fish in bowl.

preparation time *15 minutes*
cooking time *20 minutes* serves *4*
nutritional count per serving *27.7g total fat (20.1g saturated fat); 1898kJ (454 cal); 5.6g carbohydrate; 44.9g protein; 2.4g fibre*

spicy sardines with orange and olive salad

24 butterflied sardines (1kg)
1 clove garlic, crushed
1 tablespoon olive oil
2 tablespoons orange juice
1 teaspoon hot paprika
1 teaspoon finely chopped fresh oregano

ORANGE AND OLIVE SALAD

2 medium oranges (480g)
⅓ cup (40g) seeded black olives, chopped coarsely
50g baby rocket leaves
1 fresh long red chilli, sliced thinly
1 tablespoon orange juice
½ teaspoon finely chopped fresh oregano
1 tablespoon olive oil

1   Combine sardines and remaining ingredients in medium bowl; mix gently.
2   Make orange and olive salad.
3   Cook sardines, in batches, on heated oiled grill plate (or grill or barbecue) until browned both sides and cooked through.
4   Divide sardines among plates; serve with salad.

ORANGE AND OLIVE SALAD   Peel then segment oranges over medium bowl to catch juices. Add remaining ingredients; toss gently to combine.

preparation time *20 minutes*
cooking time *15 minutes* serves *4*
nutritional count per serving *36.2g total fat (8.3g saturated fat); 2500kJ (598 cal); 11.5g carbohydrate; 56g protein; 2.2g fibre*

fish ball and eggplant red curry

500g firm white fish fillets, chopped coarsely
1 clove garlic, quartered
1 tablespoon finely chopped coriander
   root and stem mixture
1 tablespoon soy sauce
1 tablespoon cornflour
2 teaspoons peanut oil
2 tablespoons red curry paste (page 258)
400ml can coconut milk
½ cup (60g) pea eggplants
2 teaspoons grated palm sugar
1 tablespoon lime juice
1 tablespoon fish sauce
2 green onions, sliced thinly
½ cup (40g) bean sprouts
2 fresh long red thai chillies, sliced thinly
¼ cup loosely packed fresh coriander leaves

1   Blend or process fish with garlic, coriander mixture, soy sauce and cornflour until mixture forms a smooth paste; roll heaped teaspoons of mixture into balls.
2   Place oil and curry paste in large saucepan; stir over heat until fragrant. Add coconut milk; bring to the boil, stirring, until blended. Add fish balls and eggplants, reduce heat; simmer, uncovered, about 5 minutes or until fish balls are cooked through. Stir in sugar, juice, fish sauce and onion; stir until sugar dissolves.
3   Place curry in serving bowl; sprinkle with sprouts, chilli and coriander leaves.

preparation time *20 minutes*
cooking time *15 minutes* serves *4*
nutritional count per serving *29.5g total fat (19.8g saturated fat); 1789kJ (428 cal); 10g carbohydrate; 24.5g protein; 4g fibre*

pumpkin and eggplant curry

2 tablespoons olive oil
1 medium brown onion (150g), sliced thickly
1 clove garlic, crushed
2cm piece fresh ginger (10g), grated
2 fresh small red thai chillies, chopped finely
1 teaspoon ground cumin
½ teaspoon ground turmeric
¼ teaspoon ground cardamom
¼ teaspoon ground fennel
8 baby eggplants (480g), sliced thickly
1kg butternut pumpkin, cut into 2cm pieces
400g can diced tomatoes
400ml can coconut cream
1 cup (250ml) vegetable stock
1 tablespoon tomato paste
400g can chickpeas, rinsed, drained
½ cup coarsely chopped fresh mint

1   Heat oil in large saucepan; cook onion, garlic, ginger and chilli, stirring, until onion softens. Add spices and eggplant; cook, stirring, 2 minutes.
2   Add pumpkin, undrained tomatoes, coconut cream, stock and paste; bring to the boil. Reduce heat; simmer, uncovered, 20 minutes. Add chickpeas; simmer, uncovered, about 10 minutes or until vegetables are tender.
3   Serve bowls of curry sprinkled with mint.

preparation time *20 minutes*
cooking time *40 minutes* serves *6*
nutritional count per serving *22.3g total fat (13.6g saturated fat); 1467kJ (351 cal); 24.5g carbohydrate; 9.5g protein; 8.6g fibre*

spicy pork chops with pumpkin chips

3 fresh long green chillies, chopped coarsely
3 green onions, chopped coarsely
2 cloves garlic, crushed
1 teaspoon ground allspice
1 teaspoon dried thyme
1 teaspoon white sugar
1 tablespoon light soy sauce
1 tablespoon lime juice
4 x 280g pork loin chops
1kg piece pumpkin, trimmed
2 tablespoons vegetable oil

PIRI PIRI DIPPING SAUCE

⅓ cup (100g) mayonnaise
2 tablespoons piri piri sauce

1   Combine chilli, onion, garlic, allspice, thyme, sugar, sauce, juice and pork in medium bowl.
2   Make piri piri dipping sauce.
3   Cut pumpkin into 7cm chips; boil, steam or microwave until tender. Drain. Combine chips with oil in medium bowl. Cook chips on heated oiled grill plate (or barbecue) until browned.
4   Meanwhile, cook pork on same heated oiled grill plate until browned or cooked as desired.
5   Serve pork with chips and dipping sauce.

PIRI PIRI DIPPING SAUCE Combine ingredients in small bowl.

preparation time *15 minutes*
cooking time *25 minutes* serves *4*
nutritional count per serving *21.4g total fat (3.8g saturated fat); 1965kJ (470 cal); 21.6g carbohydrate; 46g protein; 3.6g fibre*

chickpeas in spicy tomato sauce

2 tablespoons ghee
2 teaspoons cumin seeds
2 medium brown onions (300g), chopped finely
2 cloves garlic, crushed
4cm piece fresh ginger (20g), grated
1 tablespoon ground coriander
1 teaspoon ground turmeric
1 teaspoon cayenne pepper
2 tablespoons tomato paste
2 x 400g cans diced tomatoes
2 cups (500ml) water
2 x 420g cans chickpeas, rinsed, drained
1 large kumara (500g), cut into 1.5cm pieces
300g spinach, trimmed, chopped coarsely

1   Heat ghee in large saucepan; cook seeds, stirring, until fragrant. Add onion, garlic and ginger; cook, stirring, until onion softens. Add spices; cook, stirring, until fragrant. Add tomato paste; cook, stirring, 2 minutes.
2   Add undrained tomatoes, the water, chickpeas and kumara; simmer, covered, stirring occasionally, about 30 minutes or until kumara is tender and mixture thickens slightly.
3   Stir in spinach just before serving.

preparation time *15 minutes*
cooking time *45 minutes* serves *6*
nutritional count per serving *8.1g total fat (4.1g saturated fat); 1037kJ (248 cal); 29.1g carbohydrate; 9.9g protein; 9.4g fibre*

spice-rubbed trout with cauliflower puree

1 teaspoon ground cumin
1 teaspoon fennel seeds
½ teaspoon sweet paprika
1 clove garlic, quartered
1 teaspoon coarsely grated lemon rind
1 tablespoon olive oil
4 x 200g ocean trout fillets, skin on
800g cauliflower, chopped coarsely
30g butter
¼ cup (60ml) cream
30g butter, extra
2 tablespoons lemon juice

1   Dry-fry spices in small frying pan, stirring, until fragrant. Using mortar and pestle, grind spice mixture, garlic and rind until crushed.
2   Combine spice mixture, oil and fish in medium bowl. Cook fish in heated oiled large frying pan until cooked through. Remove from pan; cover to keep warm.
3   Meanwhile, boil, steam or microwave cauliflower until tender; drain. Mash cauliflower with butter and cream in large bowl until smooth. Cover to keep warm.
4   Melt extra butter in small saucepan; stir over low heat about 3 minutes or until browned lightly. Remove from heat; stir in juice.
5   Serve trout with puree and browned butter.

preparation time *15 minutes*
cooking time *30 minutes* serves *4*
nutritional count per serving *31.4g total fat (14.8g saturated fat); 2019kJ (483 cal); 5.1g carbohydrate; 43.7g protein; 3.8g fibre*

spicy seafood soup

1 uncooked medium blue swimmer crab (500g)
150g firm white fish fillets
8 medium black mussels (200g)
150g squid hoods
1.25 litres (5 cups) chicken stock
2 x 10cm sticks fresh lemon grass (40g),
    chopped finely
4cm piece fresh galangal (20g), sliced thinly
4 fresh kaffir lime leaves
6 fresh small green thai chillies, chopped coarsely
4 dried long red thai chillies, chopped finely
8 uncooked large prawns (400g)
1 teaspoon grated palm sugar
2 tablespoons fish sauce
1 tablespoon lime juice
¼ cup fresh thai basil leaves

1 Remove and discard back shell and gills of crab;
rinse under cold water. Chop crab body into quarters,
leaving claws intact. Cut fish into bite-sized portions;
scrub mussels, remove beards. Cut squid into 2cm-thick
slices; score the inside in a diagonal pattern.
2 Combine chicken stock, lemon grass, galangal,
lime leaves and both chillies in large saucepan;
bring to the boil.
3 Add prepared seafood and unshelled prawns to
boiling stock mixture; cook, uncovered, about 5 minutes
or until seafood is just cooked through (discard any
mussels that do not open). Remove from heat; stir in
remaining ingredients. Serve hot.

preparation time *20 minutes*
cooking time *15 minutes* serves *4*
nutritional count per serving *3.4g total fat (1.2g
saturated fat); 807kJ (193 cal); 6.1g carbohydrate;
33.9g protein; 0.9g fibre*

gazpacho

1kg ripe tomatoes, peeled, chopped coarsely
2 lebanese cucumbers (260g), seeded,
    chopped coarsely
2 large red capsicums (700g), chopped coarsely
1 large green capsicum (350g), chopped coarsely
1 large red onion (200g), chopped coarsely
2 cloves garlic, chopped coarsely
415ml can tomato juice
2 tablespoons red wine vinegar
1 tablespoon olive oil
2 teaspoons Tabasco sauce
1 medium avocado (250g), chopped finely
1 small yellow capsicum (150g), chopped finely
¼ cup finely chopped fresh coriander

1 Blend or process tomatoes, cucumber, capsicums,
onion, garlic, juice, vinegar, oil and Tabasco, in
batches, until smooth. Pour into large jug. Cover;
refrigerate 3 hours.
2 Stir soup; pour into serving bowls, top with
remaining ingredients. Serve gazpacho sprinkled with
extra Tabasco, if you like.

preparation time *25 minutes (plus refrigeration time)*
serves *6*
nutritional count per serving *10.4g total fat (1.9g
saturated fat); 786kJ (188 cal); 14.5g carbohydrate;
6.2g protein; 6.3g fibre*

lamb stoba

2 tablespoons vegetable oil
1kg lamb shoulder, trimmed, cut into 3cm pieces
2 medium brown onions (300g), sliced thinly
3cm piece fresh ginger (15g), sliced thinly
2 fresh long red chillies, sliced thinly
1 medium red capsicum (200g), chopped coarsely
2 teaspoons ground cumin
2 teaspoons ground allspice
1 cinnamon stick
2 x 400g cans chopped tomatoes
2 teaspoons finely grated lime rind
2 tablespoons lime juice
¼ cup (55g) firmly packed brown sugar

1 Heat half the oil in large saucepan; cook lamb,
in batches, until browned all over.
2 Heat remaining oil in same pan; cook onion,
ginger, chilli, capsicum and spices, stirring, until
onion softens.
3 Add lamb and remaining ingredients; simmer,
covered, about 1 hour or until lamb is tender.

preparation time *10 minutes*
cooking time *1 hour 30 minutes* serves *4*
nutritional count per serving *31.8g total fat (11.2g
saturated fat); 2567kJ (614 cal); 24.4g carbohydrate;
55.8g protein; 4.1g fibre*

afghani lamb and spinach curry

1½ tablespoons vegetable oil
1kg lamb shoulder, trimmed, cut into 3cm pieces
1 large brown onion (200g), chopped finely
4 cloves garlic, crushed
2 teaspoons ground turmeric
½ teaspoon ground nutmeg
½ teaspoon ground cinnamon
½ teaspoon cayenne pepper
400g can chopped tomatoes
2 cups (500ml) beef stock
350g spinach
1 tablespoon finely grated lemon rind
⅓ cup (45g) roasted slivered almonds

1 Heat half the oil in large saucepan; cook lamb,
in batches, until browned all over.
2 Heat remaining oil in same pan; cook onion,
garlic and spices, stirring, until onion softens.
3 Add lamb, undrained tomatoes and stock; simmer,
covered, about 1 hour. Uncover; simmer 15 minutes or
until sauce thickens and lamb is tender. Add spinach
and rind; stir over heat about 1 minute or until spinach
wilts. Serve curry sprinkled with almonds.

preparation time *20 minutes*
cooking time *1 hour 30 minutes* serves *4*
nutritional count per serving *36g total fat (11.4g
saturated fat); 2516kJ (602 cal); 7.2g carbohydrate;
60g protein; 5.9g fibre*

1 LAMB STOBA 2 AFGHANI LAMB AND SPINACH CURRY
3 MALAYSIAN LAMB CURRY [P 290]
4 KEEMA WITH GREEN CHILLI AND TOMATO [P 290]

malaysian lamb curry

2 tablespoons garam masala
1 tablespoon ground cumin
1 tablespoon black mustard seeds
1 teaspoon ground turmeric
1kg diced lamb shoulder
¼ cup (60ml) vegetable oil
2 medium brown onions (300g), sliced thinly
2 cloves garlic, crushed
3 dried long red chillies, chopped coarsely
2 long green chillies, chopped coarsely
400ml can coconut cream
1 cup (250ml) beef stock
200g sugar snap peas, trimmed
½ cup loosely packed fresh coriander leaves

1   Combine spices in large bowl, add lamb; mix well.
2   Heat two tablespoons of the oil in large saucepan; cook lamb mixture, in batches, until browned.
3   Heat remaining oil in same pan; cook onion, garlic and chillies over low heat, stirring, until onion softens.
4   Return lamb to pan with coconut cream and stock; simmer, covered, 1 hour 20 minutes. Uncover, stir in peas off the heat. Serve curry sprinkled with coriander.

preparation time *20 minutes*
cooking time *1 hour 30 minutes* serves *4*
nutritional count per serving *57.4g total fat (30g saturated fat); 3390kJ (811 cal); 12.3g carbohydrate; 58.4g protein; 8.5g fibre*

keema with green chilli and tomato

2 tablespoons ghee
1 medium brown onion (150g), chopped finely
5cm piece fresh ginger (25g), grated
2 cloves garlic, crushed
3 long green chillies, chopped finely
2 teaspoons cumin seeds
2 teaspoons ground coriander
1 teaspoon ground turmeric
2 teaspoons garam masala
800g lamb mince
400g can diced tomatoes
2 large tomatoes (440g), chopped coarsely
⅓ cup (95g) yogurt
1 tablespoon lemon juice
1 cup (120g) frozen peas
2 tablespoons coarsely chopped fresh coriander

1   Heat ghee in large saucepan; cook onion, ginger, garlic and two-thirds of the chilli, stirring, until onion softens. Add spices; cook, stirring, until fragrant. Add mince; cook, stirring, until mince changes colour.
2   Add undrained tomatoes and fresh tomato; cook, stirring occasionally, about 15 minutes or until mince is cooked through and sauce has thickened.
3   Add remaining chilli, yogurt, juice and peas; cook, uncovered, until peas are just tender. Serve curry sprinkled with coriander.

preparation time *20 minutes*
cooking time *45 minutes* serves *4*
nutritional count per serving *4.6g total fat (2.4g saturated fat); 364kJ (87 cal); 2.2g carbohydrate; 8.8g protein; 1.2g fibre*

curried lamb shanks with naan

8 french-trimmed lamb shanks (1.5kg)
¼ cup (35g) plain flour
2 tablespoons peanut oil
1 medium brown onion (150g), chopped finely
2 cloves garlic, crushed
½ cup (150g) rogan josh curry paste
2 cups (500ml) water
400g can crushed tomatoes
1 teaspoon sugar
2 cups (500ml) beef stock
400g cauliflower, chopped coarsely
400g pumpkin, chopped coarsely
¾ cup (150g) red lentils
¼ cup coarsely chopped fresh coriander
4 pieces naan

1 Toss lamb in flour; shake away excess. Heat oil in large saucepan; cook lamb, in batches, until browned all over.
2 Cook onion and garlic in same pan, stirring, until onion softens. Add paste; cook, stirring, until fragrant. Return lamb to pan with the water, undrained tomatoes, sugar and stock; bring to the boil. Reduce heat; simmer, covered, 1½ hours.
3 Preheat oven to 240°C/220°C fan-forced.
4 Add cauliflower, pumpkin and lentils to curry; bring to the boil. Reduce heat; simmer, covered, 15 minutes or until cooked as desired. Remove from heat; stir in coriander.
5 Meanwhile, wrap naan in foil; heat in oven 10 minutes. Serve naan with lamb.

preparation time *20 minutes*
cooking time *2 hours 5 minutes* serves *4*
nutritional count per serving *46.7g total fat (15.3g saturated fat); 4009kJ (958 cal); 62.4g carbohydrate; 64.9g protein; 15.4g fibre*

cajun-spiced beef and garlicky bean salad

750g piece beef fillet
1 tablespoon cajun spice mix
420g can mixed beans, rinsed, drained
2 lebanese cucumbers (260g), halved lengthways, sliced thinly
4 small tomatoes (360g), cut into wedges
1 medium red onion (170g), sliced thinly
1 medium avocado (250g), sliced thickly
½ cup finely chopped fresh coriander

GARLIC VINAIGRETTE

¼ cup (60ml) lemon juice
¼ cup (60ml) olive oil
2 cloves garlic, crushed

1 Make garlic vinaigrette.
2 Sprinkle beef both sides with spice mix; cook on heated oiled grill plate (or grill or barbecue). Cover; stand 5 minutes then slice thinly.
3 Place remaining ingredients in large bowl with vinaigrette; toss gently to combine.
4 Serve salad topped with beef.

GARLIC VINAIGRETTE Combine ingredients in small bowl.

preparation time *15 minutes*
cooking time *10 minutes* serves *4*
nutritional count per serving *35.3g total fat (8.8g saturated fat); 2445kJ (585 cal); 16.3g carbohydrate; 47.5g protein; 7.5 g fibre*

indian rice pilaf with spiced beef

2 tablespoons peanut oil
1 small brown onion (80g), sliced finely
1 clove garlic, crushed
1 teaspoon cumin seeds
1 teaspoon caraway seeds
⅛ teaspoon ground turmeric
1 cup (200g) basmati rice
2 cups (500ml) chicken stock
2 tablespoons currants
500g beef mince
1½ teaspoons curry powder
⅓ cup (80ml) sweet chilli sauce
¼ cup (60ml) water
4 green onions, sliced thinly
⅔ cup (80g) frozen peas
¼ cup firmly packed coriander leaves

1 Heat 1 tablespoon of the oil in a large frying pan; cook brown onion, garlic, seeds and turmeric; cook, stirring, until onion softens.
2 Add rice, stir over heat until rice is coated with oil. Stir in stock; bring to the boil. Reduce heat to low; cook, covered, 12 minutes. Remove from heat; stand, covered, 5 minutes or until rice is tender. Stir in currants.
3 Meanwhile, heat remaining oil in large frying pan; cook beef, stirring, until browned.
4 Add curry powder; cook until fragrant. Stir in sauce, water, green onions and peas; cook, stirring, until peas are soft and heated through.
5 Serve pilaf topped with spiced mince and coriander.

preparation time *10 minutes*
cooking time *30 minutes* serves *4*
nutritional count per serving *19.1g total fat (9.8g saturated fat); 2926kJ (700 cal); 93.2g carbohydrate; 35.7g protein; 4.1g fibre*

harissa chicken with rocket and cucumber salad

4 x 500g small chickens
1 tablespoon harissa paste
1 teaspoon finely grated lemon rind
¼ cup (60ml) olive oil
2 teaspoons cumin seeds
1 teaspoon ground coriander
200g yogurt
1 clove garlic, crushed
2 lebanese cucumbers (260g)
150g baby rocket leaves
2 tablespoons lemon juice

1 Rinse chickens under cold water; pat dry inside and out with absorbent paper. Using kitchen scissors, cut along each side of each chicken's backbone; discard backbone. Place chickens, skin-side up, on board; using heel of hand, press down on breastbone to flatten chickens.
2 Combine paste, rind and 1 tablespoon of the oil in large bowl, add chicken; rub mixture all over chicken.
3 Cook chickens on heated oiled grill plate (or grill or barbecue) 10 minutes. Cover, cook, over low heat, about 10 minutes or until chickens are cooked through.
4 Meanwhile, dry-fry spices in small frying pan, stirring, until fragrant. Cool 10 minutes. Combine spices with yogurt and garlic in small bowl.
5 Using vegetable peeler, slice cucumber lengthways into ribbons. Combine cucumber in large bowl with rocket, juice and remaining oil.
6 Serve chicken with yogurt and salad.

preparation time *25 minutes*
cooking time *20 minutes* serves *4*
nutritional count per serving *55.2g total fat (15.4g saturated fat); 3043kJ (728 cal); 4.9g carbohydrate; 52.8g protein; 1.5g fibre*

shredded beef with spanish rice and peas

1 large carrot (180g), chopped coarsely

1 trimmed celery stalk (100g), chopped coarsely

5 cloves garlic, quartered

6 black peppercorns

1 bay leaf

2 teaspoons dried oregano

1.5kg beef skirt steak

2 litres (8 cups) water

1 tablespoon olive oil

1 medium red capsicum (200g), sliced thickly

1 medium green capsicum (200g), sliced thickly

2 medium brown onions (300g), sliced thickly

400g can whole tomatoes

1 teaspoon ground cumin

1 cup (150g) pimiento-stuffed green olives, halved

¼ cup (60ml) lemon juice

SOFRITO

1 tablespoon olive oil

2 rindless bacon rashers (130g), chopped finely

3 cloves garlic, crushed

1 small brown onion (80g), chopped finely

½ small green capsicum (75g), chopped finely

1 tablespoon tomato paste

2 tablespoons red wine vinegar

SPANISH RICE AND PEAS

3 cups (750ml) water

¼ cup (60ml) olive oil

2 cups (400g) medium-grain white rice

1 cup (120g) frozen peas

1 Place carrot, celery, garlic, peppercorns, bay leaf, 1 teaspoon of the oregano, steak and the water in large deep saucepan; bring to the boil. Reduce heat; simmer, uncovered, about 2 hours or until beef is tender.

2 Meanwhile, make sofrito.

3 Remove beef from braising liquid. Strain liquid over large bowl; discard solids. Using two forks, shred beef coarsely.

4 Heat oil in same cleaned pan; cook sofrito, capsicums and onion, stirring, until vegetables soften. Return beef and braising liquid to pan with undrained tomatoes, cumin and remaining oregano; bring to the boil. Reduce heat; simmer, uncovered, 20 minutes. Remove from heat; stir in olives and juice.

5 Meanwhile, make spanish rice and peas.

6 Serve shredded beef.

SOFRITO Heat oil in small frying pan; cook bacon, garlic, onion and capsicum, stirring, until onions soften. Add paste and vinegar; cook, stirring, until vinegar evaporates. Cool 10 minutes; blend or process until smooth.

SPANISH RICE AND PEAS Combine the water and oil in medium saucepan; bring to the boil. Stir in rice; cook, uncovered, without stirring, about 10 minutes or until liquid has almost evaporated. Reduce heat; simmer, covered, 5 minutes. Gently stir in peas; simmer, covered, about 5 minutes or until rice and peas are tender.

preparation time *40 minutes*
cooking time *2 hours 50 minutes* serves *6*
nutritional count per serving *25.8g total fat (5.6g saturated fat); 3177kJ (760 cal); 63.4g carbohydrate; 67.5g protein; 7.7g fibre*

sri lankan crab curry

If you use uncooked crabs in this recipe, increase the cooking time by about 15 minutes; cook until they change colour.

1 tablespoon peanut oil
2 large brown onions (400g), chopped finely
4 cloves garlic, crushed
3cm piece fresh ginger (15g), grated
1 fresh small red thai chilli, chopped finely
4 dried curry leaves
½ teaspoon fenugreek seeds
1 teaspoon ground cinnamon
1 teaspoon ground turmeric
2 x 400ml cans coconut cream
1 tablespoon fish sauce
2 tablespoons lime juice
2 whole cooked mud crabs (1.6kg)
½ cup (25g) flaked coconut, toasted

1   Heat oil in wok; stir-fry onion, garlic, ginger and chilli until onion softens. Add curry leaves and spices; stir-fry until fragrant. Add coconut cream, sauce and juice; simmer, uncovered, 30 minutes.
2   Meanwhile, prepare crabs. Lift tail flap of each crab then, with a peeling motion, lift off the back of each shell. Remove and discard the gills, liver and brain matter; rinse crabs well. Cut each body in half; separate claws from bodies. You will have eight pieces.
3   Add half of the crab to wok; simmer, covered, about 10 minutes or until crab is heated through. Transfer crab to large serving bowl; cover to keep warm. Repeat with remaining crab pieces.
4   Spoon curry sauce over crab; sprinkle with coconut.

preparation time *30 minutes*
cooking time *55 minutes* serves *4*
nutritional count per serving *52.5g total fat (37.2g saturated fat); 3118kJ (746 cal); 14.4g carbohydrate; 51.9g protein; 6.4g fibre*

chilli crab laksa

2 uncooked whole mud crabs (1.5kg)
2 tablespoons peanut oil
3 fresh long red chillies, chopped finely
2 cloves garlic, crushed
2cm piece fresh ginger (10g), grated
½ cup (125ml) fish stock
⅔ cup (180g) laksa paste
3¼ cups (800ml) coconut milk
1 litre (4 cups) chicken stock
3 fresh kaffir lime leaves, shredded finely
1 fresh long red chilli, chopped finely, extra
1 tablespoon lime juice
1 tablespoon fish sauce
1 tablespoon grated palm sugar
250g rice stick noodles
3 green onions, sliced thinly
3 cups (240g) bean sprouts
½ cup loosely packed fresh coriander leaves

1   Place crabs in large container filled with ice and water; stand 1 hour. Leaving flesh in claws and legs, prepare crab by lifting tail flap and, with a peeling motion, lift off back shell. Remove and discard whitish gills, liver and brain matter; crack claws with back of knife. Rinse crabs well. Using cleaver or heavy knife, chop each body into quarters; crack large claws lightly with back of knife.
2   Heat oil in wok; stir-fry chilli, garlic and ginger until fragrant. Add crab and fish stock to wok; bring to the boil. Reduce heat; simmer, covered, about 20 minutes or until crab is changed in colour. Discard liquid in wok.
3   Meanwhile, cook paste in large saucepan, stirring, until fragrant. Stir in coconut milk, chicken stock, lime leaf and extra chilli; bring to the boil. Reduce heat; simmer, covered, 20 minutes. Stir in juice, sauce and sugar.
4   Meanwhile, place noodles in large heatproof bowl; cover with boiling water. Stand until tender; drain.
5   Divide noodles and crab among bowls; ladle laksa into bowls, top with onion, sprouts and coriander.

preparation time *40 minutes (plus standing time)*
cooking time *30 minutes* serves *4*
nutritional count per serving *68.2g total fat (40g saturated fat); 4088kJ (978 cal); 31.6g carbohydrate; 55.9g protein; 10.8g fibre*

mussels in spiced coconut broth

1kg medium black mussels
1 cup (250ml) water
3 cups (750ml) fish stock
10cm piece fresh ginger (50g), sliced thinly
2 fresh small red thai chillies, sliced thinly
4 cloves garlic, sliced thinly
3 dried curry leaves
4 shallots (100g), sliced thinly
1 tablespoon fish sauce
1 teaspoon finely grated lemon rind
2 teaspoons lemon juice
½ cup (125ml) coconut milk
1 cup firmly packed fresh coriander leaves

1 Scrub mussels; remove beards.
2 Place the water and stock in large saucepan with ginger, chilli, garlic, curry leaves, shallot, sauce, rind, juice and milk; bring to the boil. Reduce heat; simmer, covered, 20 minutes.
3 Add mussels; simmer, covered, about 5 minutes or until mussels open (discard any that do not).
4 Serve bowls of soup sprinkled with coriander.

preparation time *15 minutes*
cooking time *30 minutes* serves *4*
nutritional count per serving *8g total fat (6.2g saturated fat); 585kJ (140 cal); 6.7g carbohydrate; 9.7g protein; 1.7g fibre*

spanish-style barbecued seafood

500g uncooked medium prawns
½ cup (125ml) extra virgin olive oil
2 cloves garlic, crushed
1 teaspoon paprika
2 teaspoons finely grated lemon rind
salt and freshly ground black pepper
650g whiting fillets
2 large zucchini (300g), sliced lengthways
1 large red capsicum (350g), quartered

GARLIC MAYONNAISE

½ cup (150g) whole egg mayonnaise
1 clove garlic, crushed
1 tablespoon lemon juice

1 Peel and devein prawns, leaving tails intact.
2 Combine ⅓ cup (80ml) oil, half the garlic, paprika, rind, salt and pepper, prawns and fish in medium bowl; toss gently to combine.
3 Make garlic mayonnaise.
4 Cook zucchini and capsicum on a heated oiled grill plate (or barbeuce) until browned and tender.
5 Cook prawns and fish on same heated oiled grill plate (or barbeuce) until browned on both sides and just cooked through.
6 Serve prawns and whiting with vegetables, garlic mayonnaise and, if you like, lemon wedges.

GARLIC MAYONNAISE Combine ingredients in small bowl.

preparation time *20 minutes*
cooking time *15 minutes* serves *4*
nutritional count per serving *42.5g total fat (5.8g saturated fat); 2604kJ (623 cal); 12g carbohydrate; 47.6g protein; 2.7g fibre*

prawn and scallop laksa

12 uncooked medium king prawns (540g)
1 litre (4 cups) chicken stock
3¼ cups (810ml) coconut milk
4 fresh kaffir lime leaves, shredded finely
150g rice stick noodles
300g scallops, roe removed
150g marinated tofu, cut into 2cm pieces
2 tablespoons lime juice
2 cups (160g) bean sprouts
4 green onions, sliced thinly
1 fresh long red chilli, sliced thinly
½ cup loosely packed fresh coriander leaves

LAKSA PASTE

3 medium dried chillies
⅓ cup (80ml) boiling water
2 teaspoons peanut oil
1 small brown onion (80g), chopped coarsely
2 cloves garlic, quartered
2cm piece fresh ginger (10g), grated
10cm stick fresh lemon grass (20g), chopped finely
1 tablespoon halved unroasted unsalted macadamias
1 tablespoon coarsely chopped fresh
   coriander root and stem mixture
½ teaspoon ground turmeric
½ teaspoon ground coriander
¼ cup loosely packed fresh mint leaves

1 Shell and devein prawns, leaving tails intact.

2 Make laksa paste.

3 Cook paste in large saucepan, stirring, about
5 minutes or until fragrant. Stir in stock, coconut milk
and lime leaves; bring to the boil. Reduce heat;
simmer, covered, 20 minutes.

4 Meanwhile, place noodles in large heatproof bowl,
cover with boiling water; stand until tender, drain.

5 Add prawns to laksa mixture; simmer, uncovered,
about 5 minutes or until prawns change colour. Add
scallops and tofu; simmer, uncovered, about 3 minutes
or until scallops change colour. Remove from heat;
stir in juice.

6 Divide noodles among serving bowls; ladle laksa
into bowls, top with sprouts, onion, chilli and coriander.

LAKSA PASTE Cover chillies with the water in small
heatproof bowl, stand 10 minutes; drain. Blend or
process chillies with remaining ingredients until smooth.

preparation time *45 minutes*
cooking time *30 minutes* serves 6
nutritional count per serving *35.4g total fat (25.9g
saturated fat); 2207kJ (528 cal); 25.1g carbohydrate;
25.7g protein; 5g fibre*

texan-style spareribs

3kg american-style pork spareribs
2 tablespoons sweet paprika
1 tablespoon ground cumin
1 teaspoon cayenne pepper
2 x 800ml bottles beer
1 cup (250ml) barbecue sauce
¼ cup (60ml) water
¼ cup (60ml) maple syrup
¼ cup (60ml) cider vinegar

1 Place ribs on large tray. Combine spices in small bowl, rub spice mixture all over ribs. Cover; refrigerate 3 hours or overnight.
2 Preheat oven to 180°C/160°C fan-forced.
3 Bring beer to the boil in medium saucepan. Reduce heat; simmer, uncovered, 20 minutes. Divide beer and ribs between two large shallow baking dishes; cook in oven, covered, 1½ hours. Remove from oven; discard beer.
4 Meanwhile, combine sauce, the water, syrup and vinegar in small saucepan; bring to the boil. Reduce heat; simmer, uncovered, 5 minutes.
5 Cook ribs, in batches, on heated oiled grill plate (or grill or barbecue), turning and brushing with sauce occasionally, until browned all over.

preparation time *20 minutes (plus refrigeration time)*
cooking time *2 hours 5 minutes* serves *8*
nutritional count per serving *17.5g total fat (6.1g saturated fat); 2123kJ (508 cal); 25.4g carbohydrate; 49.8g protein; 0.4g fibre*

piri piri chicken thigh fillets

4 fresh long red chillies, chopped coarsely
1 teaspoon dried chilli flakes
2 cloves garlic, quartered
1 teaspoon sea salt
2 tablespoons olive oil
1 tablespoon apple cider vinegar
2 teaspoons brown sugar
8 x 125g chicken thigh fillets

1 Using mortar and pestle, grind fresh chilli, chilli flakes, garlic and salt to make piri piri paste.
2 Combine paste with oil, vinegar, sugar and chicken in medium bowl.
3 Cook chicken on heated oiled grill plate (or grill or barbecue) until cooked through.
4 Serve chicken with lime wedges, if you like.

preparation time *10 minutes*
cook time *15 minutes* serves *4*
nutritional count per serving *27.2g total fat (6.8g saturated fat); 1822kJ (436 cal); 1.8g carbohydrate; 46.6g protein; 0.3g fibre*

chilli-rubbed hickory-smoked steaks

The hickory smoking chips called for here are available at most barbecue supply stores, as are other varieties of wood chips that can also be used to smoke meat on the barbecue.

1 tablespoon finely grated lemon rind
2 teaspoons chilli powder
2 teaspoons dried thyme
1 teaspoon sweet smoked paprika
2 tablespoons olive oil
2 cloves garlic, crushed
4 x 200g beef rib-eye steaks
100g hickory smoking chips
2 cups (500ml) water

1 Combine rind, chilli, thyme, paprika, oil and garlic in large bowl with steaks. Cover; refrigerate 3 hours or overnight.
2 Soak chips in the water in medium bowl; stand 3 hours or overnight.
3 Place drained chips in smoke box alongside steaks on grill plate. Cook steaks, covered, using indirect heat, about 10 minutes or until cooked.

preparation time *10 minutes (plus refrigeration and standing time)* cooking time *10 minutes* serves *4* nutritional count per serving *27.3g total fat (8.9g saturated fat); 1726kJ (413 cal); 0.4g carbohydrate; 41.1g protein; 0.7g fibre*

cajun prawns with bean and coriander salad

1 tablespoon hot paprika
1 teaspoon chilli powder
1 teaspoon ground ginger
2 teaspoons ground cumin
1 teaspoon ground cardamom
1 teaspoon ground coriander
1 tablespoon vegetable oil
1 medium red onion (150g), chopped coarsely
1 clove garlic, crushed
24 uncooked medium king prawns (1kg)
1 teaspoon vegetable oil, extra
1 tablespoon lime juice
1 lime, cut into wedges

BEAN AND CORIANDER SALAD

400g green beans, halved crossways
1 cup loosely packed fresh coriander leaves
4 small vine-ripened tomatoes (120g), quartered
1 medium red onion (150g), sliced thinly
1 teaspoon coarsely grated lime rind
2 tablespoons lime juice
1 clove garlic, crushed
1 teaspoon sugar

1 Blend or process spices, oil, onion and garlic until a paste. Shell and devein prawns, leaving tails intact.
2 Make bean and coriander salad.
3 Heat extra oil in wok; stir-fry prawns, in batches, until just changed in colour.
4 Cook paste, stirring, in same wok about 2 minutes or until fragrant. Return prawns to wok with juice; stir-fry until prawns are heated through. Serve prawns with salad and lime wedges.

BEAN AND CORIANDER SALAD Boil, steam or microwave beans until just tender; drain. Rinse; drain. Place beans in bowl with coriander, tomato, onion and combined rind, juice, garlic and sugar; toss gently to combine.

preparation time *30 minutes* cooking time *15 minutes* serves *4* nutritional count per serving *6.9g total fat (0.7g saturated fat); 953kJ (228 cal); 9g carbohydrate; 29.8g protein; 5g fibre*

1

2

3

4

assamese sour fish curry

We used blue eye in this recipe, but you can use any firm white fish.

1 tablespoon coriander seeds
2 teaspoons cumin seeds
½ teaspoon ground turmeric
1 teaspoon black peppercorns
2cm piece fresh ginger (10g), chopped coarsely
2 cloves garlic, chopped coarsely
2 long green chillies, chopped coarsely
2 tablespoons vegetable oil
4 firm white fish cutlets (800g)
2 medium brown onions (300g), sliced thinly
1½ teaspoons black mustard seeds
4 fresh curry leaves
¾ cup (180ml) water
⅓ cup (80ml) fish stock
¼ cup (60ml) lime juice
1 tablespoon fish sauce

1 Dry-fry coriander and cumin seeds and turmeric in small frying pan, stirring, until fragrant. Using mortar and pestle, crush spices with peppercorns, ginger, garlic and chilli to form a paste.
2 Heat half of the oil in large frying pan; cook fish, uncovered, until browned both sides. Remove from pan; cover to keep warm.
3 Heat remaining oil in same pan; cook onion, mustard seeds and curry leaves, stirring, about 5 minutes or until onion is browned. Add spice paste; cook, stirring, until fragrant. Add the water, stock, juice and sauce; bring to the boil. Return fish to the pan; simmer, covered, about 5 minutes or until fish is cooked as desired.

preparation time *20 minutes*
cooking time *20 minutes* serves *4*
nutritional count per serving *12.9g total fat (2.3g saturated fat); 1150kJ (275 cal); 3.8g carbohydrate; 34.7g protein; 1.6g fibre*

lemon grass chicken curry

1 tablespoon vegetable oil
24 chicken drumettes (1.7kg)
1 medium brown onion (150g), sliced thinly
3 cloves garlic, crushed
½ teaspoon cracked black pepper
3 x 10cm sticks fresh lemon grass (60g), chopped finely
1 long green chilli, chopped finely
¼ cup (75g) mild curry paste
1 tablespoon grated palm sugar
½ cup (125ml) chicken stock
½ cup (125ml) water
1 medium red capsicum (200g), sliced thinly
1 medium carrot (120g), cut into matchsticks
4 green onions, sliced thinly

1 Heat oil in large flameproof casserole dish; cook chicken, in batches, until browned. Drain and discard cooking juices.
2 Cook brown onion, garlic, pepper, lemon grass and chilli in same pan, stirring, until onion softens. Add paste; cook, stirring, until fragrant. Return chicken to dish; cook, stirring, 5 minutes.
3 Add sugar, stock and the water; cook, covered, 10 minutes. Uncover; simmer about 10 minutes or until chicken is cooked through. Remove chicken from dish; cover to keep warm. Add capsicum and carrot; cook, uncovered, about 5 minutes or until curry sauce thickens and vegetables are just tender. Stir green onion into curry off the heat.
4 Serve chicken topped with curried vegetable mixture.

preparation time *25 minutes*
cooking time *45 minutes* serves *4*
nutritional count per serving *36.3g total fat (9g saturated fat); 2286kJ (547 cal); 9.9g carbohydrate; 43.8g protein; 4.3g fibre*

kofta curry

800g chicken mince
2cm piece fresh ginger (10g), grated
½ teaspoon ground cinnamon
⅓ cup coarsely chopped fresh coriander
4 cloves garlic, crushed
2 tablespoons ghee
1 medium brown onion (150g), chopped finely
2 fresh long red chillies, chopped finely
2 teaspoons ground coriander
1 teaspoon ground cumin
½ teaspoon ground turmeric
1 teaspoon ground fenugreek
1 teaspoon garam masala
4 medium tomatoes (600g), peeled,
   chopped coarsely
2 cups (500ml) chicken stock
½ cup firmly packed fresh coriander leaves

1   Combine mince, ginger, cinnamon, chopped coriander and half the garlic in medium bowl; roll level tablespoons of the mixture into balls. Place balls on tray, cover; refrigerate 30 minutes.
2   Meanwhile, heat 1 tablespoon of the ghee in large saucepan; cook onion, chilli, spices and remaining garlic, stirring, until onion is browned lightly. Add tomato; cook, stirring, about 5 minutes or until tomato softens. Add stock; simmer, uncovered, about 15 minutes or until sauce thickens slightly.
3   Heat remaining ghee in medium frying pan; cook kofta, in batches, until browned. Add kofta to sauce; simmer, uncovered, about 10 minutes or until kofta are cooked through. Stir in coriander leaves off the heat.

preparation time *35 minutes (plus refrigeration time)*
cooking time *1 hour* serves *4*
nutritional count per serving *25.7g total fat (10.8g saturated fat); 1797kJ (430 cal); 6.4g carbohydrate; 42.2g protein; 3.1g fibre*

coconut chicken curry

2 tablespoons vegetable oil
12 chicken drumsticks (1.8kg)
2 tablespoons ground coriander
3 cloves garlic, crushed
5cm piece fresh ginger (25g), grated
10cm stick fresh lemon grass (20g), chopped finely
10 fresh curry leaves, torn
1 large brown onion (200g), sliced thinly
1 cinnamon stick
2 cardamom pods, bruised
1 tablespoon tamarind concentrate
400g can coconut milk
1 cup (250ml) chicken stock
1 large kumara (500g), chopped coarsely
1 clove garlic, chopped finely
2cm piece fresh ginger (10g), chopped finely
1 fresh small red thai chilli, chopped finely
1 long green chilli, chopped finely
¼ cup finely chopped fresh coriander
2 teaspoons finely grated lemon rind

1   Heat oil in large deep flameproof casserole dish; cook chicken, in batches, until browned.
2   Cook ground coriander, crushed garlic, ginger, lemon grass and curry leaves in same pan, stirring, until fragrant.
3   Add onion; cook, stirring, about 5 minutes or until onion softens. Return chicken to pan with cinnamon, cardamom, tamarind, coconut milk and stock; simmer, uncovered, 30 minutes.
4   Add kumara; simmer, uncovered, 30 minutes or until kumara is just tender and chicken is cooked through. Discard cinnamon and cardamom.
5   Meanwhile, combine chopped garlic, chopped ginger, chillies, fresh coriander and rind in small bowl; sprinkle mixture over curry.

preparation time *30 minutes*
cooking time *1 hour 30 minutes* serves *4*
nutritional count per serving *61.4g total fat (28.6g saturated fat); 3645kJ (872 cal); 22.8g carbohydrate; 55.8g protein; 5.2g fibre*

kenyan chicken curry

8cm piece fresh ginger (40g), grated
6 cloves garlic, crushed
2 teaspoons ground turmeric
½ cup (125ml) lemon juice
⅓ cup (80ml) vegetable oil
1 teaspoon ground cumin
3 teaspoons garam masala
1 tablespoon ground coriander
1 teaspoon paprika
1 teaspoon chilli flakes
¼ cup (70g) yogurt
1kg chicken thigh fillets, cut into 3cm pieces
3 large brown onions (600g), chopped coarsely
2 teaspoons chilli powder
2 teaspoons ground fenugreek
2 x 400g cans crushed tomatoes
1 stick cinnamon
2 long green chillies, chopped finely
300ml cream
1 tablespoon honey
¼ cup coarsely chopped fresh coriander

1 Combine half the ginger, half the garlic, half the turmeric, half the juice and half the oil in large bowl with all the cumin, garam masala, ground coriander, paprika, chilli flakes and yogurt, add chicken; turn to coat in marinade. Cover; refrigerate 30 minutes.
2 Preheat oven to 240°C/220°C fan-forced.
3 Cook chicken, in oiled medium shallow flameproof baking dish, uncovered, over heat, 10 minutes.
4 Heat remaining oil in large saucepan; cook onion, chilli powder, fenugreek and remaining ginger, garlic and turmeric, stirring, until onion softens. Add undrained tomatoes, cinnamon, green chilli and remaining juice. Simmer, covered, 10 minutes. Stir in cream and honey; simmer, uncovered, 1 minute.
5 Add chicken; simmer 5 minutes or until chicken is cooked through. Remove from heat, stir in fresh coriander.

preparation time *30 minutes (plus refrigeration time)*
cooking time *30 minutes* serves *6*
nutritional count per serving *58.9g total fat (24g saturated fat); 3035kJ (726 cal); 15.6g carbohydrate; 32.5g protein; 4.9g fibre*

cauliflower and green pea curry

600g cauliflower florets
2 tablespoons ghee
1 medium brown onion (150g), chopped finely
2 cloves garlic, crushed
2cm piece fresh ginger (10g), grated
¼ cup (75g) hot curry paste
¾ cup (180ml) cream
2 large tomatoes (440g), chopped coarsely
1 cup (120g) frozen peas
1 cup (280g) yogurt
3 hard-boiled eggs, sliced thinly
¼ cup finely chopped fresh coriander

1 Boil, steam or microwave cauliflower until just tender; drain.
2 Meanwhile, heat ghee in large saucepan; cook onion, garlic and ginger, stirring, until onion softens. Add paste; cook, stirring, until mixture is fragrant.
3 Add cream; bring to the boil. Reduce heat. Add cauliflower and tomato; simmer, uncovered, 5 minutes, stirring occasionally.
4 Add peas and yogurt; stir over low heat about 5 minutes or until peas are just cooked.
5 Serve curry sprinkled with egg and coriander.

preparation time *20 minutes*
cooking time *30 minutes* serves *4*
nutritional count per serving *40.9g total fat (21.9g saturated fat); 2132kJ (510 cal); 15.5g carbohydrate; 17g protein; 8.6g fibre*

nepalese meatball curry

2 tablespoons vegetable oil
1 small white onion (80g), chopped finely
3 cloves garlic, crushed
5cm piece fresh ginger (25g), grated
750g lamb mince
1 egg
1 egg yolk
1 fresh long red chilli, chopped finely
1 teaspoon ground cumin
½ teaspoon ground turmeric
¼ cup coarsely chopped fresh coriander
2 tablespoons stale breadcrumbs
¼ cup (60ml) lemon juice

CURRY SAUCE

1 tablespoon vegetable oil
1 medium white onion (150g), chopped finely
1 clove garlic, crushed
3cm piece fresh ginger (15g), grated
1 tablespoon coarsely chopped fresh
   coriander root and stem mixture
2 teaspoons ground cumin
1 teaspoon ground fenugreek
1 teaspoon yellow mustard seeds
1 teaspoon ground turmeric
2 x 400g cans crushed tomatoes
1 cup (250ml) beef stock

1 Make curry sauce.
2 Meanwhile, heat half of the oil in large frying pan; cook onion, garlic and ginger, stirring, until onion softens. Cool 10 minutes.
3 Combine mince, whole egg and yolk, chilli, spices, coriander, breadcrumbs and onion mixture in large bowl; roll level tablespoons of the lamb mixture into balls.
4 Heat remaining oil in same pan; cook meatballs, in batches, until browned all over.
5 Add meatballs to curry sauce; cook, uncovered, about 20 minutes or until meatballs are cooked through. Stir juice into curry off the heat.

CURRY SAUCE Heat oil in large saucepan; cook onion, garlic and ginger, stirring, until onion softens. Add coriander mixture and spices; cook, stirring, until fragrant. Add undrained tomatoes and stock; simmer, covered, 1 hour.

preparation time *30 minutes*
cooking time *1 hour 20 minutes* serves *4*
nutritional count per serving *29.9g total fat (8.4g saturated fat); 2086kJ (499 cal); 12.2g carbohydrate; 43.7g protein; 4.1g fibre*

spiced fish with lemon yogurt sauce

We used perch in this recipe, but you can use any firm white fish.

2 cups (400g) long-grain white rice
1 medium lemon, sliced thinly
1 teaspoon ground cumin
1 teaspoon ground cinnamon
2 teaspoons hot paprika
1 tablespoon plain flour
4 skinless white fish fillets (800g)
1 tablespoon olive oil
400g baby carrots
¾ cup (200g) low-fat yogurt
1 tablespoon lemon juice
2 tablespoons coarsely chopped fresh coriander

1   Cook rice in large saucepan of boiling water, uncovered, until tender; drain.
2   Meanwhile, heat large oiled frying pan; cook lemon, uncovered, until lightly browned both sides. Remove from pan.
3   Combine spices and flour in small bowl; sprinkle over fish. Heat oil in same pan; cook fish, uncovered, until browned both sides and cooked as desired.
4   Meanwhile, boil, steam or microwave carrots until just tender; drain.
5   Combine yogurt, juice and coriander in small bowl.
6   Serve fish on rice with lemon, carrots and yogurt mixture.

preparation time *15 minutes*
cooking time *15 minutes* serves *4*
nutritional count per serving *8.6g total fat (1.8g saturated fat); 2579kJ (617 cal); 89g carbohydrate; 41.3g protein; 5.8g fibre*

dry thai prawn curry

5 dried long red chillies
1.5kg uncooked medium prawns
2cm piece fresh galangal (10g), chopped coarsely
10cm stick fresh lemon grass (20g), chopped coarsely
2 tablespoons coarsely chopped fresh coriander root and stem mixture
2 cloves garlic, crushed
1 teaspoon shrimp paste
2 tablespoons vegetable oil
8 fresh kaffir lime leaves, torn
2 tablespoons water
1 tablespoon fish sauce
1 teaspoon caster sugar
1 medium green apple (150g), unpeeled, cut into matchsticks
2 shallots (50g), sliced thinly
½ cup firmly packed fresh coriander leaves
2 fresh long red chillies, sliced thinly

1   Place dried chillies in small heatproof jug, cover with boiling water; stand 15 minutes, drain.
2   Shell and devein prawns, leaving tails intact.
3   Blend or process soaked chillies, galangal, lemon grass, coriander mixture, garlic, paste, half of the oil and half of the lime leaf until mixture forms a paste.
4   Transfer curry paste mixture to large bowl, add prawns; mix well.
5   Heat remaining oil in wok; stir-fry prawn mixture with remaining lime leaf until prawns are changed in colour. Add the water, sauce and sugar; stir-fry 1 minute. Remove from heat; toss apple, shallot, coriander leaves and fresh chilli into curry.

preparation time *10 minutes (plus standing time)*
cooking time *15 minutes* serves *4*
nutritional count per serving *10.6g total fat (1.4g saturated fat); 1183kJ (283 cal); 6.1g carbohydrate; 40g protein; 1.5g fibre*

coconut fish curry

We used ling in this recipe, but you can use any firm white fish.

¼ cup (60ml) vegetable oil
800g firm white fish fillets, cut into 3cm pieces
1 medium brown onion (150g), sliced thinly
2 cloves garlic, crushed
2 long green chillies, sliced thinly
3 teaspoons garam masala
1⅔ cups (410ml) coconut milk
2 tablespoons lemon juice
¼ cup (60ml) tamarind concentrate
1 large tomato (220g), chopped coarsely
1 medium red capsicum (200g), chopped coarsely
⅓ cup firmly packed fresh coriander leaves
1 medium lemon (140g), cut into wedges

1   Heat 2 tablespoons of the oil in large saucepan; cook fish, in batches, until browned all over.
2   Heat remaining oil in same pan; cook onion, garlic and half of the chilli, stirring, until onion softens. Add garam masala; cook, stirring, until fragrant. Add coconut milk, juice, tamarind, tomato and capsicum; bring to the boil. Add fish, reduce heat; simmer, covered, about 5 minutes or until fish is cooked as desired.
3   Divide curry among serving bowls; top with coriander and remaining chilli. Serve with lemon wedges and your choice of warmed naan, chapati or pappadum, if you like.

preparation time *25 minutes*
cooking time *20 minutes* serves *4*
nutritional count per serving *36.5g total fat (20.6g saturated fat); 2257kJ (540 cal); 9.1g carbohydrate; 43.7g protein; 4.6g fibre*

ginger and chilli baked fish

1.6kg whole white fish
cooking-oil spray
2 limes, sliced thinly
2cm piece fresh ginger (10g), sliced thinly
1 tablespoon peanut oil
1 tablespoon fish sauce
8cm piece fresh ginger (40g), grated finely, extra
1 clove garlic, crushed
2 tablespoons grated palm sugar
1 fresh large red chilli, sliced
1 tablespoon fish sauce, extra
1 tablespoon lime juice

1   Preheat oven to 240°C/220°C fan-forced.
2   Make four deep slits diagonally across both sides of fish. Place a large sheet of foil, with sides overlapping, in large, shallow baking dish. Spray foil with oil, place fish on foil. Fill fish cavity with layers of lime and ginger.
3   Combine oil, sauce, extra ginger and garlic in small bowl; rub into cuts in fish and all over surface. Bring foil up around sides of fish to catch cooking juices; do not cover top.
4   Bake fish 20 minutes or until almost cooked through.
5   Meanwhile, combine sugar, chilli, extra sauce and juice in small bowl; spoon over fish. Bake fish further 5 minutes or until browned and just cooked through.

preparation time *10 minutes*
cooking time *25 minutes* serves *4*
nutritional count per serving *11.1g total fat (3.2g saturated fat); 1321kJ (316 cal); 7.7g carbohydrate; 45.3g protein; 1g fibre*

tofu and vegetable curry

300g firm silken tofu
6 cloves garlic, quartered
3 fresh small red thai chillies, chopped coarsely
10cm stick fresh lemon grass (20g), chopped coarsely
1.5cm piece fresh turmeric (20g), chopped coarsely
4cm piece fresh ginger (20g), chopped coarsely
1 medium brown onion (150g), chopped finely
1 tablespoon vegetable oil
400ml can coconut milk
1 cup (250ml) vegetable stock
2 fresh kaffir lime leaves
4 medium zucchini (480g), chopped coarsely
1 small cauliflower (1kg), cut into florets
1 tablespoon soy sauce
1 tablespoon lime juice
⅓ cup firmly packed fresh coriander,
   chopped coarsely
¼ cup loosely packed fresh thai basil leaves

1 Press tofu between two chopping boards with
a weight on top, raise one end; stand 10 minutes.
Cut tofu into 2cm cubes; pat dry between layers of
absorbent paper.
2 Blend or process garlic, chilli, lemon grass, turmeric,
ginger, onion and oil until mixture forms a paste.
3 Cook paste in large saucepan, stirring, 5 minutes.
Add coconut milk, stock and lime leaves; simmer,
uncovered, stirring occasionally, 10 minutes.
4 Add zucchini and cauliflower; simmer, uncovered,
about 5 minutes or until vegetables are tender.
5 Discard lime leaves; stir in tofu, sauce, juice and
coriander. Sprinkle with basil before serving.

preparation time *25 minutes (plus standing time)*
cooking time *25 minutes* serves *4*
nutritional count per serving *31.7g total fat (19.7g
saturated fat); 1843kJ (441 cal); 14.8g carbohydrate;
19.8g protein; 11g fibre*

sri lankan fried pork curry

2 tablespoons vegetable oil
20 fresh curry leaves
½ teaspoon fenugreek seeds
1 large brown onion (200g), chopped finely
4 cloves garlic, crushed
3cm piece fresh ginger (15g), grated
1 tablespoon curry powder
2 teaspoons cayenne pepper
1kg pork belly, chopped coarsely
1 tablespoon white wine vinegar
2 tablespoons tamarind concentrate
1 cinnamon stick
4 cardamom pods, bruised
1½ cups (375ml) water
400ml can coconut milk

1 Heat half the oil in large saucepan; cook curry
leaves and seeds until seeds pop and mixture is
fragrant. Add onion, garlic and ginger; cook, stirring,
until onion softens.
2 Add curry powder and cayenne to pan, then pork;
stir well to combine. Add vinegar, tamarind, cinnamon,
cardamom and the water; simmer, covered, 1 hour.
3 Heat remaining oil in large frying pan. Transfer pork
to pan; cook, stirring, until pork is browned and crisp.
4 Meanwhile, add coconut milk to curry sauce;
simmer, stirring, about 5 minutes or until curry thickens
slightly. Return pork to curry; stir to combine.

preparation time *20 minutes*
cooking time *1 hour 20 minutes* serves *4*
nutritional count per serving *78.2g total fat (35.7g
saturated fat); 3766kJ (901 cal); 8g carbohydrate;
42.1g protein; 3.6g fibre*

pork and vegetable vindaloo

Portuguese for vinegar and garlic, vindaloo is a highly flavoured, but also fiercely hot curry. If you like, you can reduce the amount of chilli in the recipe.

2 teaspoons cumin seeds
2 teaspoons garam masala
1 teaspoon ground cinnamon
2 cloves garlic, quartered
4 fresh small red thai chillies, chopped coarsely
2cm piece fresh ginger (10g), sliced thinly
1 large brown onion (200g) chopped coarsely
2 tablespoons white vinegar
2 tablespoons vegetable oil
1kg boneless pork shoulder, cut into 2cm pieces
2 cups (500ml) beef stock
2 medium potatoes (400g), cut into 2cm pieces
2 medium carrots (240g), cut into 2cm pieces
150g green beans, trimmed, chopped coarsely

1 Dry-fry spices in small frying pan, stirring, until fragrant; cool.
2 Blend or process spices, garlic, chilli, ginger, onion and vinegar until mixture forms a smooth paste.
3 Heat half the oil in large saucepan; cook pork, in batches, until browned.
4 Heat remaining oil in same pan; cook paste, stirring, 5 minutes. Return pork to pan with stock; bring to the boil. Reduce heat; simmer, covered, 30 minutes. Add potato, carrot and beans; simmer, uncovered, about 30 minutes or until pork is tender and sauce thickens slightly.
5 Serve vindaloo with steamed rice and coriander, if you like.

preparation time *30 minutes*
cooking time *1 hour* serves *6*
nutritional count per serving *19.9g total fat (5.4g saturated fat); 1664kJ (398 cal); 13.6g carbohydrate; 39.3g protein; 3.8g fibre*

sour pork curry

1 tablespoon vegetable oil
1kg pork neck
1 teaspoon shrimp paste
¼ cup coarsely chopped fresh coriander root and stem mixture
2cm piece fresh galangal (10g), chopped finely
5 dried long red chillies, chopped finely
3 fresh long red chillies, chopped finely
2 tablespoons fish sauce
¾ cup (235g) tamarind concentrate
2 tablespoons caster sugar
2 cups (500ml) chicken stock
1 litre (4 cups) water
½ cup fresh thai basil leaves, chopped coarsely

1 Heat oil in large flameproof casserole dish; cook pork, uncovered, until browned. Remove from dish.
2 Preheat oven to 160°C/140°C fan-forced.
3 Add paste, coriander mixture, galangal and chillies to same dish; cook, stirring, until fragrant. Add sauce, tamarind, sugar, stock and the water; bring to the boil. Return pork to dish, cover; cook in oven 1 hour. Uncover; cook 1 hour.
4 Remove pork from dish, cover; stand 10 minutes before slicing thickly. Stir basil into curry sauce off the heat.

preparation time *30 minutes*
cooking time *2 hours 15 minutes* serves *4*
nutritional count per serving *9.3g total fat (2.1g saturated fat); 1680kJ (402 cal); 18.3g carbohydrate; 59.7g protein; 1.5g fibre*

pork and pickled garlic green curry

Sweet and subtle pickled garlic, or kratien dong, is the young green bulb, packed whole and unpeeled in vinegar brine. Eaten as a snack in Thailand, it can be served as a condiment or used in cooking.

¼ cup (35g) coarsely chopped fresh ginger
3 cloves garlic, quartered
1 medium brown onion (150g), chopped coarsely
1 teaspoon ground turmeric
2 tablespoons green curry paste (page 258)
10 fresh kaffir lime leaves, torn
750g pork fillet, cut into 2cm cubes
¼ cup (60ml) peanut oil
1 tablespoon tamarind concentrate
1 cup (250ml) boiling water
2 tablespoons fish sauce
2 bulbs pickled garlic (50g), drained, chopped coarsely
2 teaspoons grated palm sugar

1 Blend or process ginger, fresh garlic, onion, turmeric, curry paste and half of the lime leaves until mixture is almost smooth; combine with pork in large bowl. Cover; refrigerate at least 30 minutes.
2 Heat oil in large saucepan; cook pork mixture, stirring, until lightly browned all over.
3 Meanwhile, blend tamarind and the water in small jug; stir in fish sauce. Add tamarind mixture to pan; cook, uncovered, about 10 minutes or until pork is tender.
4 Add pickled garlic and sugar; simmer, stirring occasionally, 5 minutes or until sauce thickens slightly.
5 Place curry in serving bowl; sprinkle with finely shredded remaining kaffir lime leaves.

preparation time *20 minutes (plus refrigeration time)*
cooking time *20 minutes* serves *4*
nutritional count per serving *32.8g total fat (8g saturated fat); 2098kJ (502 cal); 7.4g carbohydrate; 42.7g protein; 4.6g fibre*

chilli corn fritters with roasted tomatoes

¼ cup (35g) plain flour
1 tablespoon rice flour
½ teaspoon baking powder
¼ teaspoon salt
1 teaspoon chilli powder
½ teaspoon smoked paprika
1 egg, beaten lightly
¼ cup (60ml) milk
1½ cups (250g) fresh corn kernels
2 green onions, sliced thinly
2 tablespoons finely chopped fresh coriander

ROASTED TOMATOES

12 cherry tomatoes, halved
2 teaspoons balsamic vinegar
2 teaspoons olive oil

1 Make roasted tomatoes.
2 Meanwhile, sift flours, baking powder, salt and spices into medium bowl; gradually whisk in combined egg and milk until smooth. Stir in corn, onion and coriander.
3 Cook fritters in batches, by dropping 2 teaspoons of batter into a large, heated, oiled frying pan; cook fritters until lightly browned.
4 Serve fritters topped with roasted tomatoes.

ROASTED TOMATOES Preheat oven to 200°C/180°C fan-forced. Place tomatoes on small baking-paper-lined oven tray; drizzle with vinegar and oil, and sprinkle with salt and pepper. Roast tomatoes about 15 minutes or until beginning to collapse.

preparation *15 minutes*
cooking *25 minutes* makes *24*
nutritional count per serving *0.9g total fat (0.2g saturated fat); 117kJ (28 cal); 3.6g carbohydrate; 1.1g protein; 0.7g fibre*

trinidadian beef

2 tablespoons coriander seeds
2 tablespoons cumin seeds
½ teaspoon fennel seeds
½ teaspoon black mustard seeds
½ teaspoon fenugreek seeds
1 teaspoon black peppercorns
1 medium brown onion (150g), chopped finely
2 cloves garlic, quartered
¼ cup coarsely chopped fresh coriander
1 tablespoon fresh thyme leaves
3 fresh small red thai chillies, chopped coarsely
½ teaspoon ground ginger
2 tablespoons coarsely chopped fresh flat-leaf parsley
⅓ cup (80ml) peanut oil
1kg gravy beef, cut into 3cm pieces
3 cloves garlic, crushed
1 tablespoon hot curry powder
3 cups (750ml) beef stock
2 fresh small red thai chillies, sliced thinly

1   Dry-fry seeds and peppercorns in small frying pan, stirring, about 1 minute or until fragrant. Crush mixture using mortar and pestle.
2   Blend or process onion, quartered garlic, coriander, thyme, chopped chilli, ginger, parsley and 1 tablespoon of the oil until mixture forms a paste. Transfer curry paste to large bowl; add beef, turn to coat in paste. Cover; refrigerate 30 minutes.
3   Heat remaining oil in large saucepan; cook crushed garlic and curry powder, stirring, 1 minute. Add beef mixture; cook, stirring, over medium heat 10 minutes. Add stock and crushed spice mixture; simmer, covered, 1 hour. Uncover; simmer about 1 hour, stirring occasionally, or until meat is tender and sauce thickens slightly. Serve curry sprinkled with sliced chilli.

preparation time *25 minutes (plus refrigeration time)*
cooking time *2 hours 15 minutes* serves *4*
nutritional count per serving *30.2g total fat (8.3g saturated fat); 2111kJ (505 cal); 3.7g carbohydrate; 53.9g protein; 1.9g fibre*

xacutti

1 cup (80g) desiccated coconut
½ teaspoon ground cinnamon
4 whole cloves
8 dried long red chillies
1 teaspoon ground turmeric
1 tablespoon poppy seeds
1 tablespoon cumin seeds
1 tablespoon fennel seeds
2 tablespoons coriander seeds
2 teaspoons black peppercorns
2 star anise
6 cloves garlic, quartered
2 tablespoons ghee
1 large brown onion (200g), chopped finely
1kg diced rump
2 cups (500ml) water
2 cups (500ml) beef stock
2 tablespoons lime juice

1   Dry-fry coconut in large frying pan over medium heat, stirring, until browned lightly; remove coconut from pan. Dry-fry cinnamon, cloves, chillies, turmeric, seeds, peppercorns and star anise in same pan, stirring, about 1 minute or until fragrant.
2   Blend or process coconut, spice mixture and garlic until fine.
3   Heat ghee in large saucepan; cook onion, stirring, until onion softens. Add coconut spice mixture; cook, stirring, until fragrant. Add beef; cook, stirring, about 2 minutes or until beef is coated with coconut spice mixture.
4   Add the water and stock; simmer, covered, 30 minutes, stirring occasionally. Uncover; cook 30 minutes or until beef is tender and sauce thickened slightly. Stir juice into curry off the heat; sprinkle with fresh sliced chilli, if you like.

preparation time *25 minutes*
cooking time *1 hour 15 minutes* serves *4*
nutritional count per serving *38.2g total fat (23.8g saturated fat); 2512kJ (600 cal); 5g carbohydrate; 57.5g protein; 5.2g fibre*

1 TRINIDADIAN BEEF 2 XACUTTI 3 AROMATIC VIETNAMESE BEEF CURRY [P 314]
4 MEATBALLS IN SPICY COCONUT MILK [P 314]

aromatic vietnamese beef curry

2 tablespoons peanut oil
800g beef strips
1 medium brown onion (150g), chopped finely
3 cloves garlic, crushed
1 fresh long red chilli, chopped finely
10cm stick) fresh lemon grass (20g, chopped finely
1 star anise
1 cinnamon stick
4 cardamom pods, bruised
350g snake beans, cut in 4cm lengths
2 tablespoons ground bean sauce
2 tablespoons fish sauce
½ cup coarsely chopped fresh coriander
½ cup (40g) toasted almond flakes

1   Heat half of the oil in wok; stir-fry beef, in batches, until browned. Cover to keep warm.
2   Heat remaining oil in wok; stir-fry onion until soft. Add garlic, chilli, lemon grass, star anise, cinnamon, cardamom and beans; stir-fry until beans are tender. Discard star anise, cinnamon and cardamom.
3   Return beef to wok with sauces; stir-fry until heated through. Stir in coriander and nuts off the heat.

preparation time *15 minutes*
cooking time *20 minutes* serves *4*
nutritional count per serving *27.2g total fat (7.1g saturated fat); 2011kJ (481 cal); 7.4g carbohydrate; 49.6g protein; 4.9g fibre*

meatballs in spicy coconut milk

800g beef mince
2 eggs
2 teaspoons cornflour
2 cloves garlic, crushed
1 tablespoon finely chopped fresh coriander
1 fresh long red chilli, chopped finely
2 purple shallots (50g), chopped coarsely
3 cloves garlic, quartered
1 teaspoon chilli flakes
7 fresh long red chillies, chopped coarsely
2 tablespoons peanut oil
2cm piece fresh galangal (10g), sliced thinly
3 large tomatoes (660g), seeded, chopped coarsely
400ml can coconut milk
1 tablespoon kecap asin
1 large tomato (220g), seeded, diced
½ cup (40g) fried shallots
1 fresh small red chilli, sliced thinly

1   Combine mince, eggs, cornflour, crushed garlic, coriander and finely chopped chilli in medium bowl; roll level tablespoons of mixture into balls. Place meatballs, in single layer, in large baking-paper-lined bamboo steamer. Steam, covered, over wok of simmering water 10 minutes.
2   Meanwhile, blend or process purple shallots, quartered garlic, chilli flakes, coarsely chopped chilli and half of the oil until mixture forms a paste.
3   Heat remaining oil in wok; cook shallot paste and galangal, stirring, about 1 minute or until fragrant. Add chopped tomato; cook, stirring, 1 minute. Add coconut milk, kecap asin and meatballs; simmer, uncovered, stirring occasionally, about 5 minutes or until meatballs are cooked through and sauce thickens slightly.
4   Serve curry topped with diced tomato, fried shallots and thinly sliced chilli.

preparation time *25 minutes*
cooking time *20 minutes* serves *4*
nutritional count per serving *47.1g total fat (26.5g saturated fat); 2721kJ (651 cal); 8.3g carbohydrate; 47.7g protein; 3.9g fibre*

lamb meatball korma

½ cup (40g) desiccated coconut
⅓ cup (80ml) hot water
¼ cup (40g) unsalted roasted cashews
500g lamb mince
1 large brown onion (200g), chopped finely
½ cup (35g) stale breadcrumbs
1 egg
2 tablespoons ghee
2 bay leaves
1 cinnamon stick
5 cardamom pods, bruised
5 cloves
1 medium red onion (170g), sliced thinly
2cm piece fresh ginger (10g), grated
2 cloves garlic, crushed
½ teaspoon chilli powder
½ teaspoon ground turmeric
1 teaspoon ground coriander
½ teaspoon ground cumin
2 medium tomatoes (300g), chopped coarsely
1½ cups (375ml) water, extra
¾ cup (180ml) cream

1   Place coconut in small heatproof bowl, cover with the hot water; stand 1 hour, drain. Blend or process coconut and nuts until mixture forms a thick puree.
2   Mix 2 tablespoons of the coconut mixture, lamb, brown onion, breadcrumbs and egg in medium bowl; roll level tablespoons of mixture into balls.
3   Melt half the ghee in large saucepan; cook meatballs, in batches, until browned. Drain on absorbent paper.
4   Heat remaining ghee in same cleaned pan; add leaves, cinnamon, cardamom and cloves. Cook, stirring, until fragrant. Add red onion; cook, stirring, until browned. Add ginger, garlic, chilli, turmeric, coriander and cumin; cook, stirring, 1 minute. Add tomato; cook, stirring, about 5 minutes or until mixture thickens slightly. Add remaining coconut mixture and extra water; simmer, uncovered, 20 minutes.
5   Return meatballs to pan; simmer, covered, about 20 minutes or until cooked through. Stir in cream; simmer, stirring, until hot.

preparation time *45 minutes (plus standing time)*
cooking time *1 hours 10 minutes* serves *4*
nutritional count per serving *50.1g total fat (29.1g saturated fat); 2755kJ (659 cal); 17g carbohydrate; 34g protein; 5.5g fibre*

lamb and macadamia curry

1 cup (140g) roasted unsalted macadamias
2 tablespoons vegetable oil
800g diced lamb shoulder
1 medium brown onion (150g), chopped coarsely
1 clove garlic, crushed
2 fresh small red thai chillies, chopped finely
2cm piece fresh ginger (10g), grated
1 teaspoon ground cumin
1 teaspoon ground turmeric
½ teaspoon ground cinnamon
½ teaspoon ground cardamom
½ teaspoon ground fennel
400g can diced tomatoes
400ml can coconut milk
1 cup (250ml) beef stock
½ cup loosely packed fresh coriander leaves

1   Blend or process half the nuts until finely ground; coarsely chop remaining nuts.
2   Heat half the oil in large saucepan; cook lamb, in batches, until browned.
3   Heat remaining oil in same pan; cook onion, garlic, chilli and ginger, stirring, until onion softens. Add spices; cook, stirring, until fragrant. Return lamb to pan with ground nuts, undrained tomatoes, coconut milk and stock; bring to the boil. Reduce heat; simmer, covered, about 1¼ hours or until lamb is tender. Uncover; simmer about 15 minutes or until sauce thickens slightly.
4   Sprinkle curry with remaining nuts and coriander.

preparation time *20 minutes*
cooking time *2 hours 20 minutes* serves *4*
nutritional count per serving *68.4g total fat (28.4g saturated); 3561kJ (852cal); 11.6g carbohydrate; 47g protein; 5.9g fibre*

pork and lemon grass curry

3 x 10cm sticks fresh lemon grass (60g),
  chopped finely
4 cloves garlic, quartered
4cm piece fresh galangal (20g), sliced thinly
1 teaspoon ground turmeric
2 fresh jalapeño chillies, quartered
½ cup (125ml) water
¼ cup (60ml) peanut oil
½ teaspoon shrimp paste
2 x 400ml cans coconut milk
3 fresh kaffir lime leaves, torn
1kg pork fillet, cut into 1cm slices
2 tablespoons lime juice

1 Blend or process lemon grass, garlic, galangal,
turmeric and chilli with the water until mixture forms
a paste.
2 Heat 1 tablespoon of the oil in large saucepan;
cook lemon grass paste and shrimp paste, stirring,
about 1 minute or until fragrant. Add coconut milk and
lime leaves; simmer, uncovered, about 30 minutes or
until sauce thickens slightly.
3 Meanwhile, heat remaining oil in large frying pan.
Cook pork, in batches, until browned. Add pork and
juice to curry sauce; simmer, uncovered, about 2 minutes
or until pork is cooked.

preparation time *20 minutes*
cooking time *45 minutes* serves *4*
nutritional count per serving *75.2g total fat (45.6g
saturated fat); 3925kJ (939 cal); 8.3g carbohydrate;
57.3g protein; 4.2g fibre*

tamarind and citrus pork curry

70g dried tamarind, chopped coarsely
¾ cup (180ml) boiling water
1 tablespoon peanut oil
1 large red onion (300g), chopped finely
1 fresh long red chilli, sliced thinly
5cm piece fresh ginger (25g), grated
2 cloves garlic, crushed
10 fresh curry leaves
2 teaspoons fenugreek seeds
½ teaspoon ground turmeric
1 teaspoon ground coriander
1 teaspoon finely grated lime rind
1 tablespoon lime juice
400ml can coconut cream
6 baby eggplants (360g), chopped coarsely
1kg pork fillet, cut into 2cm dice

1 Soak tamarind in the boiling water 30 minutes.
Place fine sieve over small bowl; push tamarind through
sieve. Discard solids in sieve; reserve pulp in bowl.
2 Heat oil in large saucepan; cook onion, chilli,
ginger, garlic, curry leaves, seeds and spices, stirring,
until onion softens.
3 Add pulp, rind, juice, coconut cream and eggplant;
simmer, covered, 20 minutes. Add pork; simmer,
uncovered, about 20 minutes or until pork is cooked.

preparation time *20 minutes (plus standing time)*
cooking time *50 minutes* serves *4*
nutritional count per serving *45.8g total fat (25.7g
saturated fat); 3060kJ (732 cal); 19.7g carbohydrate;
57.7g protein; 6.8g fibre*

raan

1.5kg boneless leg of lamb
1 cup (250ml) water

INDIAN SPICE PASTE

2 teaspoons coriander seeds
1 teaspoon cumin seeds
2 cardamom pods, bruised
1 cinnamon stick
1 star anise
1 teaspoon ground turmeric
½ teaspoon chilli powder
1 medium brown onion (150g), chopped coarsely
2 cloves garlic, peeled
4cm piece fresh ginger (20g), grated finely
1 teaspoon salt
2 teaspoons brown sugar
2 tablespoons lemon juice
⅓ cup (80ml) peanut oil

CORIANDER YOGURT

1 cup (280g) yogurt
¼ cup coarsely chopped fresh coriander

1 Make indian spice paste.
2 Using the point of a sharp knife, pierce lamb all over with deep cuts. Place lamb and indian spice paste in a large resealable plastic bag or large shallow dish. Rub lamb with indian spice paste to ensure an even coating; cover, refrigerate 3 hours or overnight.
3 Preheat oven to 180°C/160°C fan-forced.
4 Pour the water into large baking dish; place lamb on rack in dish. Cover with foil; roast 1 hour. Remove foil, roast 30 minutes or until lamb is browned and cooked as desired. Stand, covered, 15 minutes before slicing.
5 Meanwhile, make coriander yogurt. Serve with lamb.

INDIAN SPICE PASTE Dry-fry seeds, cardamom, cinnamon and star anise in heated frying pan, stirring, until fragrant. Add turmeric and chilli, remove from heat. Blend or process spices with onion, garlic, ginger, salt, sugar and juice until smooth. With motor operating, gradually add oil until well combined.

CORIANDER YOGURT Combine yogurt and coriander in small bowl.

preparation time *15 minutes (plus refrigeration time)*
cooking time *1 hour 30 minutes (plus standing time)*
serves *6*
nutritional count per serving *23.8g total fat (7.7g saturated fat); 1710kJ (409 cal); 5.1g carbohydrate; 43.6g protein; 0.6g fibre*

balti beef curry

1 tablespoon vegetable oil
750g beef skirt steak, cut into 2cm dice
1 clove garlic, crushed
1 medium brown onion (150g), chopped coarsely
2cm piece fresh ginger (10g), grated
½ cup (150g) balti curry paste
410g can crushed tomatoes
¾ cup (180ml) water
½ cup (125ml) buttermilk
½ cup coarsely chopped fresh coriander leaves
1 medium tomato (150g), seeded, sliced thinly

1 Heat half the oil in large deep frying pan; cook beef, in batches, until browned all over.
2 Heat remaining oil in pan; cook garlic, onion and ginger, stirring, until onion softens. Add curry paste; cook, stirring, until paste is blended with onion mixture.
3 Return beef to pan with undrained tomatoes and the water; bring to the boil. Reduce heat; simmer, covered, 45 minutes. Uncover; simmer about 10 minutes or until beef is tender, stirring occasionally. Remove from heat; stir in buttermilk.
4 Sprinkle curry with coriander and tomato, and serve with steamed basmati rice, if you like.

preparation time *10 minutes*
cooking time *1 hour 10 minutes* serves *4*
nutritional count per serving *21.8g total fat (4.1g saturated fat); 1839kJ (440 cal); 10.7g carbohydrate; 47.3g protein; 6.2g fibre*

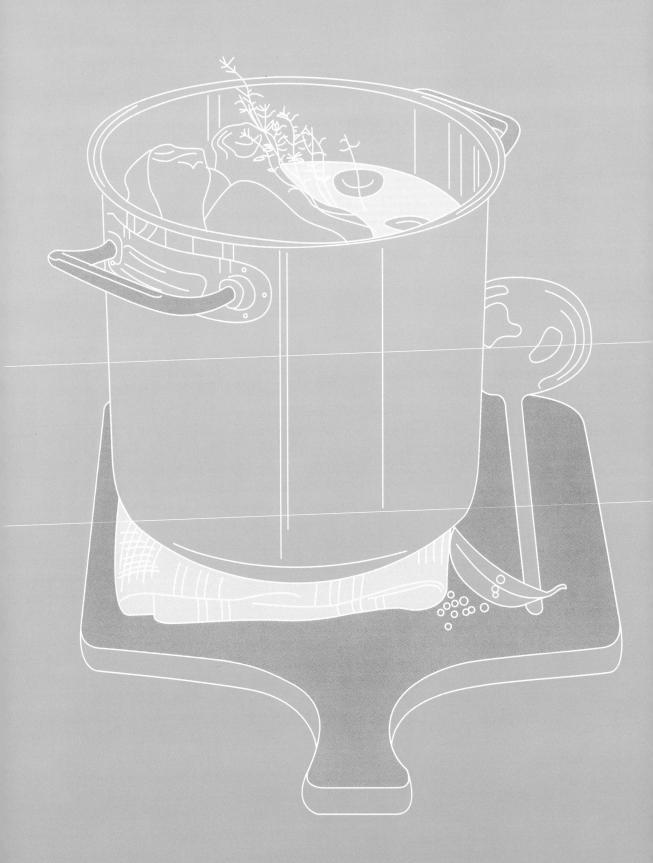

PENNY PINCHING

spanish cheese and tomato tortilla

4 green onions, sliced thickly
1 medium red capsicum (200g), chopped coarsely
2 cloves garlic, crushed
1 fresh long red chilli, chopped finely
2 medium tomatoes (300g), chopped coarsely
200g fetta cheese, crumbled
8 eggs
300ml cream
¼ cup coarsely chopped fresh flat-leaf parsley

1 Heat oiled 26cm frying pan; cook onion, capsicum, garlic and chilli, stirring, until vegetables are just tender. Remove from heat; stir in tomato and cheese.
2 Whisk eggs, cream and parsley in large jug. Pour over capsicum mixture; stir gently.
3 Preheat grill.
4 Return pan to low heat; cook tortilla, uncovered, until just set. Place pan under grill to brown tortilla top (protect handle with foil). Cut into wedges to serve.

preparation time *15 minutes*
cooking time *20 minutes* serves *4*
nutritional count per serving *49.9g total fat (29g saturated fat); 2424kJ (580 cal); 7.6g carbohydrate; 25.6g protein; 2.2g fibre*

potato frittata

600g baby new potatoes
1 tablespoon olive oil
1 medium red capsicum (200g)
1 small brown onion (80g)
¼ cup coarsely chopped fresh basil
¼ cup coarsely chopped fresh flat-leaf parsley
10 eggs
½ cup (40g) grated parmesan cheese

1 Boil, steam or microwave potatoes until just tender; when cool enough to handle, cut potatoes into quarters.
2 Meanwhile, heat oil in large non-stick frying pan; cook capsicum and onion, stirring, until softened.
3 Combine potato, basil, parsley and eggs in large bowl. Pour egg mixture into pan. Cook, over low heat, about 8 minutes or until edges are set.
4 Meanwhile, preheat grill.
5 Sprinkle top with cheese. If necessary, cover pan handle with foil then place pan under hot grill until frittata is just set.

preparation time *10 minutes*
cooking time *15 minutes* serves *4*
nutritional count per serving *22.9g total fat (7.3g saturated fat); 1647kJ (394 cal); 20.1g carbohydrate; 26.8g protein; 3g fibre*

free-form caramelised leek tarts

2 tablespoons olive oil
2 medium brown onions (300g), sliced thinly
2 medium leeks (700g), trimmed, sliced thinly
1 tablespoon fresh thyme leaves
2 cups (400g) ricotta cheese
⅓ cup (25g) coarsely grated parmesan cheese
1 egg, separated
4 sheets ready-rolled shortcrust pastry

1 Heat oil in large frying pan; cook onion and leek, stirring, about 15 minutes or until mixture starts to caramelise. Stir in thyme; cool.
2 Meanwhile, combine ricotta, parmesan and egg yolk in small bowl.
3 Preheat oven to 200°C/180°C fan-forced. Oil two oven trays; line with baking paper.
4 Using 20cm plate as a guide, cut 1 round from each pastry sheet; place two rounds on each tray. Divide ricotta mixture among rounds, leaving 4cm border around edges.
5 Divide leek mixture over rounds. Turn border of each tart up around filling; brush upturned edges with egg white.
6 Bake tarts about 35 minutes or until pastry is browned lightly.

preparation time *30 minutes*
cooking time *50 minutes* serves *4*
nutritional count per serving *70g total fat (34.3g saturated fat); 4531kJ (1084 cal); 83.2g carbohydrate; 28.3g protein; 7.1g fibre*

chicken and vegetable pasties

2 teaspoons vegetable oil
2 cloves garlic, crushed
1 medium brown onion (150g), chopped finely
1½ cups (240g) coarsely chopped leftover cooked chicken
2 cups (240g) frozen pea, corn and carrot mixture
½ cup (120g) sour cream
2 teaspoons dijon mustard
¼ cup (30g) coarsely grated cheddar cheese
4 sheets ready-rolled puff pastry
1 egg, beaten lightly

1 Preheat oven to 220°C/200°C fan-forced. Oil oven tray.
2 Heat oil in large frying pan; cook garlic and onion, stirring, until onion softens.
3 Add chicken, frozen vegetables, sour cream, mustard and cheese; stir until hot.
4 Cut one 22cm round from each pastry sheet. Place a quarter of the filling in centre of each round. Brush edge of pastry with egg; fold over to enclose filling, pinching edge together to seal. Place pasties on tray; brush with remaining egg.
5 Bake pasties about 30 minutes or until browned.

preparation time *15 minutes*
cooking time *30 minutes* serves *4*
nutritional count per serving *62.5g total fat (32.3g saturated fat); 4063kJ (972 cal); 69.1g carbohydrate; 31.4g protein; 5.9g fibre*

vegetarian paella

2 cups (500ml) vegetable stock
3 cups (750ml) water
1 tablespoon olive oil
2 cloves garlic, crushed
1 medium red onion (170g), chopped finely
2 medium tomatoes (300g), seeded, chopped finely
1 medium red capsicum (200g), chopped finely
¼ teaspoon ground turmeric
2 teaspoons smoked sweet paprika
1¾ cups (350g) arborio rice
1 cup (120g) frozen peas
100g frozen baby beans
¼ cup (40g) sliced black olives
⅓ cup finely chopped fresh flat-leaf parsley

1 Combine stock and the water in medium saucepan; bring to the boil. Remove from heat.
2 Heat oil in large frying pan; cook garlic, onion, tomato, capsicum, turmeric and paprika, stirring, until vegetables soften. Add rice; stir to coat in spice mixture. Stir in stock mixture; bring to the boil. Reduce heat; simmer, uncovered, about 20 minutes or until rice is almost tender.
3 Sprinkle peas and beans evenly over surface of paella; simmer, covered, about 5 minutes or until rice is tender. Add olives and parsley; stand, covered, 5 minutes.

preparation time *25 minutes*
cooking time *40 minutes* serves *4*
nutritional count per serving *6g total fat (1g saturated fat); 1823kJ (437 cal); 80.3g carbohydrate; 11.6g protein; 5.7g fibre*

tuna spinach mornay pie with mash

50g butter
1 medium brown onion (150g), sliced thinly
¼ cup (35g) plain flour
2 cups (500ml) milk, warmed
150g baby spinach leaves
425g can tuna in springwater, drained
2 tablespoons lemon juice

POTATO AND CELERIAC MASH

400g potatoes, chopped coarsely
300g celeriac, chopped coarsely
2 tablespoons milk
30g butter
¼ cup (20g) finely grated parmesan cheese

1 Make potato and celeriac mash.
2 Melt butter in medium saucepan; cook onion, stirring, about 5 minutes or until softened. Add flour; cook, stirring, until mixture thickens and bubbles. Gradually add milk; stir until mixture boils and thickens. Remove from heat; stir in spinach, tuna and juice.
3 Preheat grill.
4 Spoon tuna mixture into shallow 1.5-litre (6-cup) flameproof dish; top with mash. Place under grill until browned lightly.

POTATO AND CELERIAC MASH Boil, steam or microwave potato and celeriac, separately, until tender; drain. Mash potato and celeriac in large bowl with milk and butter until smooth. Stir in cheese; cover to keep warm.

preparation time *20 minutes*
cooking time *30 minutes* serves *4*
nutritional count per serving *25.8g total fat (12.1g saturated fat); 2040kJ (488 cal); 29.7g carbohydrate; 31.7g protein; 5.8g fibre*

1 VEGETARIAN PAELLA 2 TUNA SPINACH MORNAY PIE WITH MASH
3 CHINESE BARBECUED SPARERIBS [P 324]
4 PORK AND BLACK-EYED BEANS [P 324]

PENNY PINCHING   323

chinese barbecued spareribs

¾ cup (180ml) barbecue sauce
2 tablespoons dark soy sauce
1 tablespoon honey
¼ cup (60ml) orange juice
2 tablespoons brown sugar
1 clove garlic, crushed
2cm piece fresh ginger (10g), grated
2kg slabs american-style pork spareribs

1   Combine sauces, honey, juice, sugar, garlic and
ginger in large shallow dish; add ribs, turn to coat in
marinade. Cover; refrigerate 3 hours or overnight.
2   Preheat oven to 180°C/160°C fan-forced.
3   Brush ribs both sides with marinade; place, in single
layer, in large shallow baking dish. Roast, covered,
45 minutes. Uncover; roast about 15 minutes or until
ribs are browned. Serve with fried rice, if you like.

preparation time *15 minutes (plus refrigeration time)*
cooking time *1 hour* serves *4*
nutritional count per serving *26.4g total fat (10.2g
saturated fat); 2675kJ (640 cal); 35.2g carbohydrate;
64.7g protein; 0.8g fibre*

pork and black-eyed beans

1 cup (200g) black-eyed beans
1kg pork neck, sliced thickly
⅓ cup (50g) plain flour
2 tablespoons olive oil
1 medium brown onion (150g), chopped coarsely
2 cloves garlic, crushed
½ teaspoon five-spice powder
1 teaspoon sichuan peppercorns, crushed coarsely
½ teaspoon chilli powder
½ cup (125ml) dry white wine
3 cups (750ml) chicken stock
2 teaspoons finely grated orange rind
½ cup coarsely chopped fresh flat-leaf parsley

1   Place beans in medium bowl, cover with cold water;
stand overnight, drain. Rinse under cold water; drain.
2   Coat pork in flour, shake away excess. Heat half
the oil in large flameproof casserole dish; cook pork,
in batches, until browned all over.
3   Heat remaining oil in same dish; cook onion, garlic,
five-spice, peppercorns and chilli, stirring, until spices
are fragrant and onion softens. Add beans, wine and
stock; bring to the boil.
4   Return pork to dish; simmer, covered, 40 minutes.
Uncover; simmer about 30 minutes or until pork is
tender and sauce thickens slightly, stirring occasionally.
Remove from heat; stir in rind and parsley.

preparation time *20 minutes (plus standing time)*
cooking time *1 hour 30 minutes* serves *4*
nutritional count per serving *19.9g total fat (5.1g
saturated fat); 2608kJ (624 cal); 30.3g carbohydrate;
71.4g protein; 8.5g fibre*

spinach and corn pasties

1 tablespoon vegetable oil
2 medium potatoes (400g), cut into 1cm pieces
1 small brown onion (80g), chopped finely
250g frozen spinach, thawed, drained
2 x 310g cans creamed corn
3 sheets ready-rolled shortcrust pastry
2 tablespoons milk

1 Heat half the oil in large frying pan; cook potato, stirring, until browned lightly. Add onion; cook, stirring, until soft. Combine potato, onion, spinach and corn in large bowl.
2 Preheat oven to 200°C/180°C fan-forced. Oil two oven trays.
3 Cut pastry sheets in half diagonally. Divide filling among triangles, placing on one side; fold pastry in half to enclose filling, pressing edges with fork to seal. Place on trays; brush with milk.
4 Bake pasties about 30 minutes or until browned lightly. Serve with sweet chilli sauce, if you like.

preparation time *20 minutes*
cooking time *45 minutes* serves *6*
nutritional count per serving *27.1g total fat (12.6g saturated fat); 2291kJ (548 cal); 62.7g carbohydrate; 9.8g protein; 7.5g fibre*

bacon and potato hash

8 rindless bacon rashers (500g)
3 medium potatoes (600g), cut into 1cm pieces
1 large red capsicum (350g), chopped coarsely
5g butter
3 shallots (75g), chopped coarsely
½ teaspoon smoked paprika

LEMON VINAIGRETTE

1 teaspoon dijon mustard
2 tablespoons lemon juice
1 tablespoon olive oil

1 Cook bacon in heated large frying pan, in batches, until beginning to crisp. Coarsely chop half the bacon; keep warm.
2 Meanwhile, boil, steam or microwave potato and capsicum, separately, until almost tender; drain well.
3 Make lemon vinaigrette.
4 Melt butter in same frying pan; add potato, cook, stirring occasionally, about 10 minutes or until browned lightly. Add shallot, paprika, chopped bacon and capsicum; cook, stirring, until shallot softens. Remove from heat; drizzle with vinaigrette.
5 Serve hash topped with remaining bacon.

LEMON VINAIGRETTE Place ingredients in screw-top jar; shake well.

preparation time *10 minutes*
cooking time *25 minutes* serves *4*
nutritional count per serving *12.8g total fat (3.8g saturated fat); 1454kJ (348 cal); 24.1g carbohydrate; 31.8g protein; 4g fibre*

pork salad with chilli plum dressing

1 medium wombok (1kg), shredded finely
½ cup finely shredded fresh mint
1 small red onion (100g), sliced thinly
400g leftover roast pork, shredded finely
½ cup firmly packed fresh mint leaves

CHILLI PLUM DRESSING

½ cup (150g) mayonnaise
½ cup (125ml) plum sauce
1 teaspoon dried chilli flakes
2 tablespoons water

1 Make chilli plum dressing.
2 Combine half the dressing in large bowl with wombok, shredded mint, onion and half the pork.
3 Divide wombok mixture among serving plates; top with remaining pork and mint leaves, drizzle with remaining dressing.

CHILLI PLUM DRESSING Whisk ingredients in small bowl.

preparation time *20 minutes* serves *4*
nutritional count per serving *16.6g total fat (4g saturated fat); 1889kJ (452 cal); 31.7g carbohydrate; 32.8g protein; 8.9g fibre*

salmon and green bean potato patties

150g green beans
800g potatoes, chopped coarsely
20g butter
⅓ cup (25g) finely grated parmesan cheese
1 egg
415g can red salmon
⅓ cup (35g) packaged breadcrumbs
vegetable oil, for shallow-frying
150g baby spinach leaves
1 medium lemon (140g), cut into wedges

1 Boil, steam or microwave beans until tender; drain. Rinse under cold water; drain. Chop coarsely.
2 Boil, steam or microwave potatoe until tender; drain. Mash potato in large bowl with butter, cheese and egg until smooth.
3 Drain salmon; discard skin and bones. Add salmon and beans to potato mixture; mix well. Shape salmon mixture into 12 patties; coat in breadcrumbs. Place patties on tray, cover; refrigerate 30 minutes.
4 Heat oil in large frying pan; shallow-fry patties, in batches, until browned lightly and heated through. Drain on absorbent paper; serve on baby spinach with lemon wedges.

preparation time *20 minutes (plus refrigeration time)*
cooking time *30 minutes* serves *4*
nutritional count per serving *51.7g total fat (8.7g saturated fat); 2959kJ (708 cal); 29.6g carbohydrate; 29.5g protein; 5.6g fibre*

potato and pea curry

3 medium potatoes (600g), chopped coarsely
1 tablespoon vegetable oil
2 cloves garlic, crushed
2cm piece fresh ginger (10g), grated
¼ cup (75g) tikka masala curry paste
300ml cream
1½ cups (180g) frozen peas
½ cup (140g) yogurt
2 tablespoons lime juice
4 small pappadams
4 hard-boiled eggs, halved

1   Boil, steam or microwave potato until just tender; drain.
2   Meanwhile, heat oil in large saucepan; cook garlic and ginger, stirring, 2 minutes. Add paste; cook, stirring, until fragrant.
3   Add cream, bring to the boil; reduce heat. Add potato; simmer, uncovered, 5 minutes. Add peas and yogurt; stir over low heat about 5 minutes or until peas are heated through. Stir in juice.
4   Cook pappadams, in microwave oven, following packet directions.
5   Top curry with egg; serve with pappadams.

preparation time *15 minutes*
cooking time *25 minutes* serves *4*
nutritional count per serving *51.8g total fat (25.5g saturated fat); 3106kJ (743 cal); 37.8g carbohydrate; 22.7g protein; 24.5g fibre*

potato and tuna bake

3 medium potatoes (600g), cut into 1cm pieces
20g butter
1 tablespoon olive oil
3 shallots (75g), chopped coarsely
425g can tuna in oil, drained
250g frozen spinach, thawed, drained
½ cup (125ml) milk
1½ cups (180g) coarsely grated cheddar cheese
½ cup (75g) drained semi-dried tomatoes, chopped coarsely

1   Preheat oven to 220°C/200°C fan-forced. Oil four 1-cup (250ml) shallow baking dishes.
2   Boil, steam or microwave potato until almost tender; drain.
3   Heat butter and oil in large frying pan; add potato, cook, stirring occasionally, about 10 minutes or until browned lightly. Add shallot; cook, stirring, until shallot softens. Transfer mixture to medium bowl; coarsely crush potato mixture with fork.
4   Stir tuna, spinach, milk, ½ cup of the cheese and tomatoes into potato mixture. Divide mixture among dishes; sprinkle with remaining cheese.
5   Bake tuna bake, uncovered, in oven, about 10 minutes or until browned lightly.

preparation time *15 minutes*
cooking time *25 minutes* serves *4*
nutritional count per serving *38.8g total fat (15.9g saturated fat); 2696kJ (645 cal); 28.6g carbohydrate; 41.5g protein; 8.8g fibre*

chicken fried rice

1 tablespoon vegetable oil
2 eggs, beaten lightly
3 rindless bacon rashers (195g), chopped coarsely
2 cloves garlic, crushed
2cm piece fresh ginger (10g), grated
1½ cups (240g) coarsely chopped leftover
    cooked chicken
4 cups cold cooked rice
1 cup (140g) frozen pea and corn mixture
¼ cup (60ml) light soy sauce
1 cup (80g) bean sprouts
6 green onions, sliced thinly

1   Heat half the oil in wok; cook egg over medium heat, swirling wok to form thin omelette. Remove from wok; cool. Roll omelette tightly; cut into thin strips.
2   Heat remaining oil in wok; stir-fry bacon, garlic and ginger until bacon is crisp.
3   Add chicken; stir-fry 1 minute. Add rice, frozen vegetables and sauce; stir-fry until hot. Add sprouts, onion and omelette; stir-fry 1 minute.

preparation time *10 minutes*
cooking time *15 minutes* serves *4*
nutritional count per serving *21.9g total fat (5.9g saturated fat); 2362kJ (565 cal); 52.6g carbohydrate; 37.2g protein; 3.8g fibre*

curried sausages

800g thick beef sausages
20g butter
1 medium brown onion (150g), chopped coarsely
1 tablespoon curry powder
2 teaspoons plain flour
2 large carrots (360g), chopped coarsely
2 trimmed celery stalks (200g), chopped coarsely
500g baby new potatoes, halved
2 cups (500ml) beef stock
1 cup loosely packed fresh flat-leaf parsley leaves

1   Cook sausages, in batches, in heated deep large frying pan until cooked through. Cut each sausage into thirds.
2   Melt butter in same cleaned pan; cook onion, stirring, until soft. Add curry powder and flour; cook, stirring, 2 minutes.
3   Add vegetables and stock; bring to the boil. Reduce heat; simmer, covered, about 15 minutes or until vegetables are tender. Add sausages; simmer, uncovered, until sauce thickens slightly. Stir in parsley.

preparation time *20 minutes*
cooking time *45 minutes* serves *4*
nutritional count per serving *55.8g total fat (27.3g saturated fat); 3177kJ (760 cal); 29.8g carbohydrate; 30.1g protein; 12.8g fibre*

warm lentil and sausage salad

1 cup (200g) brown lentils
3 medium tomatoes (450g), quartered
1 tablespoon olive oil
1 medium brown onion (150g), chopped finely
1 teaspoon ground cumin
8 thick chicken sausages (960g)
½ cup coarsely chopped fresh flat-leaf parsley

WHITE WINE VINAIGRETTE

⅓ cup (80ml) white wine vinegar
¼ cup (60ml) olive oil
1 clove garlic, crushed

1 Make white wine vinaigrette.
2 Preheat oven to 220°C/200°C fan-forced.
3 Cook lentils, uncovered, in large saucepan of boiling water until just tender; drain. Place lentils in large bowl with half the vinaigrette; toss gently to combine.
4 Place tomato on oven tray; drizzle with half the oil. Roast, uncovered, in oven about 10 minutes or until tender.
5 Meanwhile, heat remaining oil in large frying pan; cook onion and cumin, stirring, until onion softens. Transfer onion mixture to bowl with lentils.
6 Cook sausages in same pan until cooked through. Drain on absorbent paper.
7 Meanwhile, add remaining vinaigrette, sliced sausage, tomato and parsley to bowl with lentil mixture; toss gently to combine.

WHITE WINE VINAIGRETTE Place ingredients in screw-top jar; shake well.

preparation time *15 minutes*
cooking time *45 minutes* serves *4*
nutritional count per serving *73.6g total fat (21g saturated fat); 4034kJ (965 cal); 28.3g carbohydrate; 41.8g protein: 16.4g fibre*

oven-baked tuna risotto

3½ cups (875ml) chicken stock
10g butter
2 teaspoons olive oil
1 medium brown onion (150g), chopped finely
1 clove garlic, crushed
1½ cups (300g) arborio rice
425g can tuna in oil, drained
1 cup (120g) frozen peas
250g cherry tomatoes, halved
2 tablespoons lemon juice

1 Preheat oven to 180°C/160°C fan-forced.
2 Bring stock to the boil in medium saucepan.
3 Meanwhile, melt butter with oil in large saucepan; cook onion and garlic, stirring, until onion softens. Add rice; stir to coat in onion mixture. Stir in hot stock and tuna.
4 Place risotto mixture in a large 2.5 litre (10-cup) shallow baking dish; cover with foil. Bake, in oven, 15 minutes, stirring halfway through cooking time. Uncover; bake 20 minutes. Stir in peas, top with tomato; bake, uncovered, about 15 minutes or until rice is tender. Remove from oven, stir in juice.

preparation time *20 minutes*
cooking time *1 hour* serves *4*
nutritional count per serving *25.8g total fat (5.2g saturated fat); 2583kJ (618 cal); 66.3g carbohydrate; 28g protein; 4g fibre*

baked risotto with spicy sausage and cherry tomatoes

5 thin spicy Italian-style sausages (400g)
3½ cups (875ml) chicken stock
2 teaspoons olive oil
1 large brown onion (200g), chopped finely
1 clove garlic, crushed
1½ cups (300g) arborio rice
250g cherry tomatoes
2 tablespoons fresh marjoram leaves

1 Preheat oven to 180°C/160°C fan-forced.
2 Cook sausages, uncovered, in heated large frying pan until browned all over and cooked through. Drain on absorbent paper; slice thickly.
3 Meanwhile, bring stock to the boil in medium saucepan. Reduce heat; simmer, covered.
4 Heat oil in same frying pan; cook onion and garlic, stirring, until onion softens. Add rice; stir to coat in onion mixture. Stir in stock and sausages.
5 Place risotto mixture in large shallow ovenproof dish; cover with foil. Bake in oven 15 minutes, stirring halfway during cooking time. Uncover; bake 15 minutes. Add tomatoes; bake about 15 minutes or until tomatoes soften and rice is tender. Remove from oven, sprinkle with marjoram.

preparation time *15 minutes*
cooking time *1 hour* serves *4*
nutritional count per serving *29.1g total fat (13g saturated fat); 2587kJ (619 cal); 67.1g carbohydrate; 20.1g protein; 5g fibre*

pork sausages with grilled polenta and tomato sauce

1 litre (4 cups) water
1 cup (170g) polenta
1 cup (120g) coarsely grated cheddar cheese
2 teaspoons olive oil
1 medium red onion (170g), sliced thinly
1 clove garlic, crushed
1 fresh small red thai chilli, chopped finely
4 medium tomatoes (600g), chopped coarsely
8 thick pork sausages (960g)

1 Bring the water to the boil in medium saucepan; gradually stir in polenta. Reduce heat; simmer, stirring, until polenta thickens. Stir in cheese. Spread polenta into oiled deep 19cm-square cake pan, cover; refrigerate about 1 hour or until polenta firms.
2 Meanwhile, heat oil in medium saucepan; cook onion, garlic and chilli, stirring, until onion softens. Add tomato; simmer, covered, until tomato softens.
3 Cut polenta into quarters. Cook polenta and sausages, in batches, on heated oiled grill plate (or grill or barbecue) until polenta is browned both sides and sausages are cooked through.
4 Serve sausages on polenta squares, topped with spicy tomato sauce. Serve sprinkled with fresh thyme leaves, if you like.

preparation time *20 minutes*
cooking time *15 minutes (plus refrigeration time)*
serves *4*
nutritional count per serving *8.9g total fat (3.8g saturated fat); 527kJ (126 cal); 5.6g carbohydrate; 5.6g protein; 0.9g fibre*

citrus chicken
with vermicelli salad

¼ cup (60ml) lemon juice
2 fresh small red thai chillies, sliced thinly
¼ cup (85g) orange marmalade
2 cloves garlic, crushed
4 chicken marylands (1.4kg)
250g rice vermicelli
2 medium oranges (480g)
⅔ cup loosely packed fresh mint leaves
1 medium lebanese cucumber (130g), seeded,
   sliced thinly crossways

CITRUS DRESSING

2 tablespoons lemon juice
2 tablespoons orange marmalade
2 teaspoons vegetable oil

1 Combine juice, chilli, marmalade and garlic in large
bowl. Pierce chicken all over with skewer, add to bowl;
coat in marinade. Cover; refrigerate 3 hours or overnight.
2 Preheat oven to 200°C/180°C fan-forced.
3 Place drained chicken on oiled wire rack in large
shallow baking dish; reserve marinade. Roast,
uncovered, about 45 minutes or until cooked through,
brushing occasionally with reserved marinade.
4 Meanwhile, place vermicelli in large heatproof bowl,
cover with boiling water. Stand until just tender; drain.
Rinse vermicelli under cold water; drain. Using scissors,
cut vermicelli into random lengths.
5 Segment orange over small bowl; reserve 2 teaspoons
of juice. Make citrus dressing.
6 Place vermicelli and orange segments in large bowl
with mint, cucumber and dressing; toss gently to
combine. Serve salad with chicken.

CITRUS DRESSING Place ingredients and reserved
orange juice in screw-top jar; shake well.

preparation time *15 minutes (plus refrigeration time)*
cooking time *45 minutes* serves *4*
nutritional count per serving *36.1g total fat (10.9g
saturated fat); 3520kJ (842 cal); 75g carbohydrate;
51.1g protein; 4.8g fibre*

chicken, leek and
mushroom pies

1 tablespoon vegetable oil
1 medium leek (350g), sliced thinly
2 rindless bacon rashers (130g), sliced thinly
200g mushrooms, halved
1 tablespoon plain flour
1 cup (250ml) chicken stock
⅓ cup (80ml) cream
1 tablespoon dijon mustard
3 cups (480g) coarsely chopped barbecued chicken
1 sheet ready-rolled puff pastry, quartered

1 Preheat oven to 200°C/180°C fan-forced.
2 Heat oil in medium saucepan; cook leek, bacon and
mushrooms, stirring, until leek softens. Stir in flour; cook,
stirring, until mixture thickens and bubbles. Gradually
add stock; cook, stirring, until mixture boils and thickens.
Stir in cream, mustard and chicken.
3 Divide mixture among four 1-cup (250ml) ovenproof
dishes; top each with a pastry quarter. Bake, uncovered,
about 20 minutes or until browned.

preparation time *15 minutes*
cooking time *45 minutes* serves *4*
nutritional count per serving *44.7g total fat (13.1g
saturated fat); 2780kJ (665 cal); 20.4g carbohydrate;
44.5g protein; 3.7g fibre*

caramelised chicken cutlets

2 teaspoons vegetable oil
4 chicken thigh cutlets (800g), skin on
1 medium red onion (170g), sliced thinly
3 cloves garlic, sliced thinly
¼ cup (55g) brown sugar
1 tablespoon dark soy sauce
1 tablespoon fish sauce
⅓ cup coarsely chopped fresh coriander

1 Preheat oven to 200°C/180°C fan-forced.
2 Heat oil in large frying pan; cook chicken, both sides, until browned. Place chicken, in single layer, in baking dish. Roast chicken, uncovered, in oven, about 25 minutes or until cooked through.
3 Meanwhile, heat same frying pan; cook onion and garlic, stirring, until onion softens. Add sugar and sauces; cook, stirring, 3 minutes. Return chicken to pan with coriander; turn chicken to coat in mixture.

preparation time *20 minutes*
cooking time *35 minutes* serves *4*
nutritional count per serving *22.4g total fat (6.9g saturated fat); 1538kJ (368 cal); 16.3g carbohydrate; 24.8g protein; 1g fibre*

chickpea and kumara salad

1 cup (200g) dried chickpeas
1 medium red onion (170g), chopped coarsely
1 medium red capsicum (200g), sliced thickly
1 medium kumara (400g), cut into 1cm pieces
2 cloves garlic, unpeeled
⅓ cup (80ml) olive oil
¼ cup (60ml) lemon juice
1 teaspoon english mustard
150g baby spinach leaves

1 Place chickpeas in medium bowl, cover with cold water; stand overnight, drain. Rinse under cold water; drain.
2 Preheat oven to 220°C/200°C fan-forced.
3 Place chickpeas in medium saucepan of boiling water; return to the boil. Reduce heat; simmer, uncovered, about 1 hour or until chickpeas are tender. Drain.
4 Meanwhile, toss onion, capsicum, kumara, garlic and 1 tablespoon of the oil in shallow baking dish. Bake, uncovered, about 30 minutes or until kumara is tender. Cool 10 minutes; remove garlic from dish.
5 Using back of fork, crush peeled garlic in large bowl; whisk in remaining oil, juice and mustard.
6 Combine chickpeas, roasted vegetables and spinach with garlic vinaigrette in bowl.

preparation time *20 minutes (plus standing time)*
cooking time *30 minutes* serves *4*
nutritional count per serving *21.5g total fat (3g saturated fat); 1685kJ (403 cal); 34.9g carbohydrate; 12.7g protein; 10.3g fibre*

lentil cottage pie

4 medium potatoes (800g), chopped coarsely
½ cup (125ml) milk, warmed
4 green onions, chopped finely
½ cup (100g) french green lentils
1 tablespoon olive oil
1 large brown onion (200g), chopped finely
1 medium red capsicum (200g), chopped coarsely
2 medium zucchini (240g), chopped coarsely
1 medium eggplant (300g), chopped coarsely
2 cloves garlic, crushed
410g can crushed tomatoes

1 Boil, steam or microwave potato until tender; drain. Mash potato in large bowl with milk and green onion until smooth.
2 Meanwhile, cook lentils in small saucepan of boiling water until just tender; drain. Rinse; drain.
3 Preheat oven to 200°C/180°C fan-forced.
4 Heat oil in medium saucepan; cook brown onion, capsicum, zucchini, eggplant and garlic, stirring, until vegetables soften. Add lentils and undrained tomato; bring to the boil. Reduce heat; simmer, about 10 minutes or until mixture has thickened.
5 Spoon mixture into oiled shallow 2.5 litre (10-cup) baking dish; spread with potato.
6 Bake pie, uncovered, about 30 minutes or until top browns lightly.

preparation time *20 minutes*
cooking time *1 hour 15 minutes* serves *4*
nutritional count per serving *7.3g total fat (1.5g saturated fat); 1384kJ (331 cal); 44.8g carbohydrate; 15.4g protein; 11.8g fibre*

clam chowder

1kg baby clams
2 tablespoons coarse cooking salt
40g butter
1 large brown onion (200g), chopped coarsely
2 rindless bacon rashers (130g), chopped coarsely
1 clove garlic, crushed
2 tablespoons plain flour
3 cups (750ml) milk, warmed
2 cups (500ml) vegetable stock, warmed
2 medium potatoes (400g), chopped coarsely
2 tablespoons finely chopped fresh chives

1 Rinse clams under cold water; place in large bowl, sprinkle with salt, cover with water. Stand 1 hour; rinse, drain.
2 Meanwhile, melt butter in large saucepan; cook onion, bacon and garlic, stirring, until onion softens. Add flour to pan; cook, stirring, until mixture thickens and bubbles. Gradually stir in milk and stock; stir until mixture boils and thickens slightly. Add potato, reduce heat; simmer, covered, until potato is tender.
3 Add clams; simmer, covered, about 5 minutes or until clams open (discard any that do not). Remove from heat; stir in chives.
4 Serve chowder with grilled slices of french bread, if you like.

preparation time *15 minutes (plus standing time)*
cooking time *25 minutes* serves *4*
nutritional count per serving *19.4g total fat (8.8g saturated fat); 1672kJ (400 cal); 28.7g carbohydrate; 26.4g protein; 2.5g fibre*

1 LENTIL COTTAGE PIE 2 CLAM CHOWDER
3 PASTA SALAD WITH GREEN BEANS AND TUNA [P 336]
4 CHILLI AND MINT EGGPLANT BURGERS [P 336]

pasta salad with green beans and tuna

375g large pasta spirals
250g green beans, trimmed, halved crossways
425g can tuna in oil
1 medium red capsicum (200g), sliced thinly
¾ cup loosely packed fresh flat-leaf parsley leaves

LEMON DRESSING

2 cloves garlic, crushed
1 tablespoon finely grated lemon rind
1 teaspoon cracked black pepper
1 tablespoon lemon juice

1 Cook pasta in large saucepan of boiling water, uncovered, until tender; drain. Rinse pasta under cold water; drain.
2 Meanwhile, boil, steam or microwave beans until just tender; drain. Rinse under cold water; drain.
3 Drain tuna over small bowl; reserve oil for dressing. Flake tuna in large chunks with fork.
4 Make lemon dressing.
5 Place pasta, beans and tuna in large bowl with dressing and remaining ingredients; toss gently to combine.

LEMON DRESSING Place ingredients with reserved oil in screw-top jar; shake well.

preparation time *10 minutes*
cooking time *10 minutes* serves *4*
nutritional count per serving *26g total fat (3.9g saturated fat); 2750kJ (658 cal); 67.5g carbohydrate; 35g protein; 6.2g fibre*

chilli and mint eggplant burgers

¼ cup (35g) plain flour
2 eggs
½ cup (85g) polenta
1 teaspoon hot paprika
1 medium eggplant (300g)
vegetable oil, for shallow-frying
1 large loaf turkish bread (430g), quartered
8 large butter lettuce leaves
80g cheddar cheese, cut into 4 slices
½ cup loosely packed fresh mint leaves
⅓ cup (80ml) sweet chilli sauce

1 Place flour in small shallow bowl; beat eggs in second small shallow bowl; combine polenta and paprika in third small shallow bowl.
2 Slice eggplant into 8 slices crossways; discard two skin-side pieces. Coat slices, one at a time, in flour, shake away excess, dip in egg then coat in polenta mixture.
3 Heat oil in large frying pan; shallow-fry eggplant, in batches, until browned lightly both sides. Drain on absorbent paper.
4 Meanwhile, preheat grill.
5 Halve each quarter of bread horizontally. Toast cut sides under grill.
6 Sandwich lettuce, eggplant, cheese, mint and sauce between toasted bread quarters.

preparation time *20 minutes*
cooking time *10 minutes* serves *4*
nutritional count per serving *23g total fat (6g saturated fat); 2684kJ (642 cal); 77.9g carbohydrate; 24.3g protein; 12.3g fibre*

pea and salmon pasta bake

375g rigatoni pasta
40g butter
2 tablespoons plain flour
2 cups (500ml) milk
1½ cups (180g) frozen peas
½ cup (40g) coarsely grated parmesan cheese
1¼ cups (150g) coarsely grated cheddar cheese
415g can pink salmon, drained,
    skin and bones removed

1 Preheat oven to 200°C/180°C fan-forced.
2 Cook pasta in large saucepan of boiling water,
uncovered, until tender; drain.
3 Meanwhile, melt butter in medium saucepan. Add
flour; cook, stirring, until mixture thickens and bubbles.
Gradually stir in milk; stir over medium heat until sauce
boils and thickens. Stir in peas, ¼ cup parmesan and
¾ cup cheddar.
4 Combine sauce mixture with pasta and salmon in
shallow 2.5-litre (10-cup) oiled ovenproof dish; sprinkle
with remaining combined cheeses. Bake, uncovered,
in oven, about 20 minutes or until browned lightly.

preparation time *15 minutes*
cooking time *35 minutes* serves *6*
nutritional count per serving *23.8g total fat (13.7g
saturated fat); 2345kJ (561 cal); 51.2g carbohydrate;
33.1g protein; 3.9g fibre*

meatloaf with stir-fried cabbage

700g beef mince
2 cloves garlic, crushed
1 small brown onion (80g), chopped finely
1 small carrot (70g), grated coarsely
⅓ cup (35g) packaged breadcrumbs
1 egg
4cm piece fresh ginger (20g), chopped finely
2 tablespoons light soy sauce
¼ cup (60ml) hoisin sauce
1 tablespoon peanut oil
4 cups (320g) finely sliced cabbage
1 teaspoon sesame oil

1 Preheat oven to 180°C/160°C fan-forced.
2 Combine beef, garlic, onion, carrot, breadcrumbs,
egg, half the ginger, half the soy sauce and 2 tablespoons
of the hoisin sauce in large bowl. Press mixture firmly
into oiled 14cm x 21cm loaf pan; bake, uncovered,
about 45 minutes or until meatloaf shrinks from the sides
of the pan.
3 Meanwhile, heat peanut oil in wok; stir-fry remaining
ginger. Add cabbage; stir-fry until wilted. Remove from
heat; stir in sesame oil.
4 Slice meatloaf; drizzle with combined remaining
sauces. Serve with stir-fried cabbage.

preparation time *15 minutes*
cooking time *45 minutes* serves *4*
nutritional count per serving *20.5g total fat (6.7g
saturated fat); 1777kJ (425 cal); 16.4g carbohydrate;
40.9g protein; 6.1g fibre*

caramelised corned beef with sweet mustard sauce

1.5kg piece corned silverside
2 dried bay leaves
1 medium brown onion (150g), chopped coarsely
½ cup (125ml) red wine vinegar
¾ cup (165g) firmly packed brown sugar
8 baby new potatoes (320g), halved
2 medium carrots (240g), quartered lengthways
80g butter
8 pickling onions (320g), halved
2 medium zucchini (240g), quartered lengthways
2 teaspoons fresh thyme leaves
1 tablespoon plain flour
1 tablespoon wholegrain mustard

1 Cover beef, bay leaves, brown onion, half the vinegar and a third of the brown sugar with cold water in large saucepan; bring to the boil. Reduce heat; simmer, uncovered, about 1½ hours or until beef is tender. Remove from heat; stand, covered, 30 minutes.
2 Meanwhile, boil, steam or microwave potato and carrot, separately, until almost tender. Drain; cover to keep warm.
3 Drain beef over medium bowl; reserve 2 cups cooking liquid, discard remaining liquid and solids.
4 Melt butter in same cleaned pan; cook pickling onion, stirring, until softened. Stir in remaining vinegar and brown sugar. Add potato, carrot, zucchini and thyme; cook, stirring, until vegetables are caramelised. Transfer vegetables to serving dish; cover to keep warm.
5 Return beef to pan; cook, turning, about 5 minutes or until caramelised. Remove beef; stand, covered, 5 minutes then slice thinly.
6 Meanwhile, add flour to same pan; cook, stirring, until mixture thickens and bubbles. Add mustard then reserved cooking liquid; stir until mixture boils and thickens slightly. Serve beef and vegetables drizzled with mustard sauce.

preparation time *20 minutes*
cooking time *2 hours (plus standing time)* serves *4*
nutritional count per serving *28.8g total fat (4.5g saturated fat); 3357kJ (803 cal); 62.3g carbohydrate; 70g protein; 5.9g fibre*

beef and onion casserole

1kg beef chuck steak, cut into 2cm dice
⅓ cup (50g) plain flour
2 tablespoons olive oil
2 small brown onions (200g), chopped coarsely
2 cloves garlic, crushed
150g mushrooms, quartered
1 cup (250ml) dry red wine
400g can crushed tomatoes
2 cups (500ml) beef stock
2 tablespoons tomato paste

1   Coat beef in flour, shake away excess. Heat half the oil in large saucepan; cook beef, in batches, until browned all over.
2   Heat remaining oil in same pan; cook onion, garlic and mushrooms, stirring, until onion softens.
3   Return beef to pan with wine, undrained tomatoes, stock and paste; bring to the boil. Reduce heat; simmer, covered, 40 minutes. Uncover; simmer, stirring occasionally, about 40 minutes or until meat is tender and sauce thickens slightly.

preparation time *20 minutes*
cooking time *1 hour 30 minutes* serves *4*
nutritional count per serving *21.2g total fat (6.2g saturated fat); 2245kJ (537 cal); 17.4g carbohydrate; 56.8g protein; 4g fibre*

lamb fritters with spicy yogurt

2 teaspoons ground cumin
1 cup (280g) greek-style yogurt
1 egg
1¾ cups (260g) self-raising flour
1½ cups (375ml) buttermilk
150g piece pumpkin, grated finely
2 green onions, chopped finely
300g leftover roast lamb, chopped coarsely
vegetable oil, for shallow-frying

1   Dry-fry cumin in large frying pan, stirring, until fragrant.
2   Combine yogurt with half the cumin in small bowl.
3   Combine egg, flour and buttermilk in large bowl with pumpkin, onion, lamb and remaining cumin; mix well.
4   Heat oil in same pan; shallow-fry quarter cups of batter, in batches, until fritters are browned lightly. Drain on absorbent paper; serve with yogurt.

preparation time *10 minutes*
cooking time *20 minutes* serves *4*
nutritional count per serving *49.2g total fat (13.3g saturated fat); 3511kJ (840 cal); 60.3g carbohydrate; 37.6g protein; 3g fibre*

lamb and barley soup

1.5kg french-trimmed lamb shanks
3 litres (12 cups) water
¾ cup (150g) pearl barley
1 medium carrot (120g), sliced thinly
1 medium leek (350g), sliced thinly
2 trimmed celery stalks (200g), sliced thinly
1 tablespoon curry powder
250g trimmed silver beet, chopped coarsely

1 Combine lamb, the water and barley in large saucepan; bring to the boil. Reduce heat; simmer, uncovered, 1 hour, skimming surface and stirring occasionally. Add carrot, leek and celery; simmer, uncovered, 10 minutes.
2 Remove lamb from soup mixture. When cool enough to handle, remove meat; chop coarsely. Discard bones and any fat or skin.
3 Dry-fry curry powder in small saucepan until fragrant. Return meat to soup with curry powder and silver beet; cook, uncovered, until silver beet wilts.

preparation time *15 minutes*
cooking time *1 hour 25 minutes* serves *6*
nutritional count per serving *13.3g total fat (5.7g saturated fat); 1404kJ (336 cal); 18.9g carbohydrate; 31.8g protein; 6.4g fibre*

tomato braised lamb shanks with creamy polenta

2 tablespoons olive oil
16 french-trimmed lamb shanks (4kg)
1 large red onion (300g), sliced thinly
1 clove garlic, crushed
2 tablespoons tomato paste
1 cup (250ml) dry red wine
2 cups (500ml) chicken stock
1 cup (250ml) water
400g can diced tomatoes
2 tablespoons coarsely chopped fresh rosemary

CREAMY POLENTA

3 cups (750ml) water
2 cups (500ml) milk
1 cup (250ml) chicken stock
1½ cups (250g) polenta
½ cup (40g) coarsely grated parmesan cheese
1 cup (250ml) cream

1 Preheat oven to 200°C/180°C fan-forced.
2 Heat half the oil in large baking dish; brown lamb, in batches.
3 Heat remaining oil in same dish; cook onion and garlic, stirring, until onion softens. Add paste; cook, stirring, 2 minutes. Add wine; bring to the boil. Boil, uncovered, until liquid reduces by about half.
4 Return lamb to dish with stock, the water, undrained tomatoes and rosemary; cover, cook in oven, turning lamb occasionally, about 3 hours. Remove lamb from dish; cover to keep warm. Reserve pan juices.
5 Meanwhile, make creamy polenta.
6 Divide polenta among serving plates; top with lamb, drizzle with juices.

CREAMY POLENTA Bring the water, milk and stock to the boil in medium saucepan; gradually stir in polenta. Cook, stirring, about 5 minutes or until polenta thickens slightly. Stir in cheese and cream.

preparation time *30 minutes*
cooking time *3 hours 30 minutes* serves *8*
nutritional count per serving *28g total fat (14.8g saturated fat); 2826kJ (676 cal); 30.3g carbohydrate; 69.1g protein; 2.3g fibre*

thai potato and salmon rösti

4 medium potatoes (800g)
1 teaspoon coarse cooking salt
1 tablespoon fish sauce
1 tablespoon red curry paste
1 tablespoon lime juice
1 tablespoon plain flour
415g can pink salmon, drained
1 tablespoon coarsely chopped fresh coriander
vegetable oil, for shallow-frying
CUCUMBER DIPPING SAUCE

1 lebanese cucumber (130g), seeded, sliced thinly
½ cup (125ml) water
¼ cup (55g) white sugar
¼ cup (60ml) white wine vinegar
1 teaspoon sambal oelek

1   Grate potatoes coarsely into large bowl; stir in salt, squeeze out excess moisture. Stir in sauce, paste, juice, flour, salmon and coriander. Shape mixture into 12 x 8cm-wide patties. Place on tray, cover; refrigerate 30 minutes.
2   Meanwhile, make cucumber dipping sauce.
3   Heat oil in large frying pan; cook rösti, in batches, until browned and heated through.
4   Serve rösti with dipping sauce.

CUCUMBER DIPPING SAUCE Place cucumber in heatproof bowl. Combine the water, sugar and vinegar in small saucepan; stir over heat, without boiling, until sugar is dissolved. Remove from heat; stir in sambal. Pour over cucumber.

preparation time *25 minutes (plus refrigeration time)*
cooking time *1 hour* serves *4*
nutritional count per serving *32.4g total fat (4.9g saturated fat); 2395kJ (573 cal); 43.6g carbohydrate; 24.5g protein; 5.2g fibre*

tuna and chilli pasta

375g angel hair pasta
425g can tuna in oil
4 cloves garlic, sliced thinly
1 teaspoon dried chilli flakes
⅓ cup (80ml) dry white wine
400g can chopped tomatoes
1 tablespoon lemon juice

1   Cook pasta in large saucepan of boiling water until tender; drain, reserving ¼ cup cooking liquid. Rinse pasta under cold water, drain.
2   Meanwhile, drain tuna, reserving 2 tablespoons of the oil.
3   Heat reserved oil in medium frying pan; cook garlic, stirring, until fragrant. Add chilli and wine; cook, uncovered, until wine is almost evaporated. Add undrained tomatoes, tuna and reserved cooking liquid; simmer until liquid has reduced slightly. Remove from heat; stir in juice.
4   Combine pasta and sauce in large bowl.

preparation time *5 minutes*
cooking time *10 minutes* serves *4*
nutritional count per serving *22.3g total fat (3.2g saturated fat); 2617kJ (626 cal); 67.5g carbohydrate; 32.5g protein; 4.8g fibre*

1 THAI POTATO AND SALMON ROSTI 2 TUNA AND CHILLI PASTA
3 BAKED PENNE WITH KUMARA AND SPINACH [P 344]
4 CHICKEN AND PUMPKIN CURRY [P 344]

PENNY PINCHING   343

baked penne with kumara and spinach

2 medium red onions (340g), cut into wedges
2 small kumara (600g), sliced thickly
2 tablespoons olive oil
375g penne pasta
250g frozen spinach, thawed, drained
1½ cups (360g) ricotta cheese
1 clove garlic, crushed
¼ cup (60ml) cream
2 x 400g cans crushed tomatoes
¼ cup (40g) pine nuts
½ cup (40g) finely grated parmesan cheese

1 Preheat oven to 220°C/200°C fan-forced.
2 Combine onion and kumara with oil in large baking dish; roast, uncovered, stirring once, about 40 minutes or until tender.
3 Meanwhile, cook pasta in large saucepan of boiling water until tender; drain.
4 Combine pasta in large bowl with spinach, ricotta, garlic, cream and tomatoes.
5 Spread kumara mixture over base of 3-litre (12-cup) baking dish. Top with pasta mixture; sprinkle with nuts and parmesan. Bake, covered, 10 minutes. Uncover; bake about 5 minutes or until browned lightly.

preparation time *15 minutes*
cooking time *55 minutes* serves *6*
nutritional count per serving *25.3g total fat (9.8g saturated fat); 2450kJ (586 cal); 63.4g carbohydrate; 21.9g protein; 8.4g fibre*

chicken and pumpkin curry

2 teaspoons ground cumin
2 teaspoons ground ginger
1 teaspoon ground coriander
1 teaspoon dried chilli flakes
5 dried curry leaves
1 tablespoon peanut oil
2 cloves garlic, crushed
1 medium red onion (170g), sliced thinly
2 x 400ml cans coconut milk
2 tablespoons kecap asin
1 tablespoon brown sugar
800g butternut pumpkin, chopped coarsely
600g chicken thigh fillets, chopped coarsely
250g snow peas, trimmed
⅓ cup (80ml) lime juice
⅔ cup (90g) coarsely chopped roasted unsalted peanuts

1 Dry-fry spices in wok over medium heat, stirring, about 1 minute or until fragrant.
2 Add curry leaves, oil, garlic and onion; stir-fry until onion softens.
3 Add coconut milk, kecap asin, sugar, pumpkin and chicken; simmer, uncovered, about 20 minutes or until pumpkin softens. Remove from heat, stir in snow peas and juice. Serve sprinkled with nuts.

preparation time *25 minutes*
cooking time *35 minutes* serves *4*
nutritional count per serving *68.5g total fat (42.3g saturated fat); 3900kJ (933 cal); 31.4g carbohydrate; 44.8g protein; 10g fibre*

curried pea soup

10g butter
1 tablespoon olive oil
1 medium brown onion (150g), chopped coarsely
2 tablespoons tikka masala curry paste
1kg frozen peas
3 cups (750ml) chicken stock
1 cup (250ml) water
½ cup (140g) yogurt

1 Melt butter with oil in large saucepan; cook onion, stirring, about 5 minutes or until soft.
2 Add paste to onion mixture; cook, stirring, until fragrant. Add peas, stock and the water; bring to the boil. Reduce heat, simmer, uncovered, 5 minutes. Cool 15 minutes.
3 Blend or process soup, in batches, with yogurt, until smooth. Return soup to pan, stir until heated through.

preparation time *10 minutes (plus cooling time)*
cooking time *15 minutes* serves *4*
nutritional count per serving *13.2g total fat (3.5g saturated fat); 1333kJ (319 cal); 24.7g carbohydrate; 16.9g protein; 17.9g fibre*

spicy rocket pasta

2 tablespoons olive oil
1 teaspoon dried chilli flakes
2 cloves garlic, crushed
½ teaspoon cracked black pepper
¼ cup (60ml) lemon juice
375g angel hair pasta
80g rocket leaves
2 medium tomatoes (300g), seeded, chopped coarsely
⅔ cup firmly packed fresh basil leaves

1 Heat oil in large frying pan; cook chilli and garlic, stirring, until fragrant. Add pepper and juice; stir until hot.
2 Meanwhile, cook pasta in large saucepan of boiling water until tender; drain.
3 Combine chilli mixture and pasta in large bowl with rocket, tomato and basil.

preparation time *15 minutes*
cooking time *10 minutes* serves *4*
nutritional count per serving *10.4g total fat (1.5g saturated fat); 1756kJ (420 cal); 66.4g carbohydrate; 12.1g protein; 4.8g fibre*

mashed potato casserole

500g potatoes, peeled, chopped coarsely
30g butter, softened
2 eggs, beaten lightly
300ml cream
1 cup (120g) coarsely grated cheddar cheese
2 tablespoons coarsely chopped fresh chives

1 Preheat oven to 180°C/160°C fan-forced.
2 Boil, steam or microwave potato until tender; drain. Mash potato in large bowl with butter until smooth; spread over base of oiled shallow 1.5-litre (6-cup) baking dish.
3 Combine remaining ingredients in medium bowl; pour over potato.
4 Bake casserole, uncovered, about 40 minutes or until top sets and is browned.

preparation time *10 minutes*
cooking time *1 hour* serves *4*
nutritional count per serving *51.4g total fat (32.7g saturated fat); 2445kJ (585 cal); 16.3g carbohydrate; 15g protein; 1.7g fibre*

corn chowder

40g butter
1 clove garlic, crushed
1 medium leek (350g), trimmed, sliced thinly
½ cup (125ml) dry white wine
2 trimmed celery stalks (200g), chopped finely
800g desiree potatoes, peeled, chopped coarsely
2 cups (500ml) chicken stock
2 cups (500ml) water
2 cups (320g) frozen corn kernels
½ cup (125ml) cream
1 tablespoon finely chopped fresh flat-leaf parsley

1 Melt butter in large saucepan; cook garlic and leek, stirring, until leek softens. Add wine; cook, stirring, until liquid reduces by half. Add celery, potato, stock and the water; bring to the boil. Reduce heat; simmer, covered, until potato is just tender. Cool 10 minutes.
2 Blend or process 3 cups of the soup, in batches, until smooth. Return blended soup to remaining unprocessed soup; add corn and cream. Bring to the boil. Reduce heat; simmer, stirring, until corn is just tender. Remove from heat; stir in parsley.

preparation time *20 minutes*
cooking time *30 minutes* serves *6*
nutritional count per serving *15.6g total fat (9.8g saturated fat); 1215kJ (305 cal); 28.6g carbohydrate; 6.7g protein; 5.2g fibre*

potato and beef pasties

500g potatoes, peeled, chopped coarsely
1 tablespoon olive oil
1 small brown onion (80g), chopped finely
2 cloves garlic, crushed
1 medium carrot (120g), chopped finely
1 trimmed celery stalk (100g), chopped finely
350g beef mince
⅓ cup (80ml) dry red wine
1 cup (250ml) beef stock
¼ cup (70g) tomato paste
½ cup (60g) frozen peas
8 sheets ready-rolled puff pastry, thawed
1 egg, beaten lightly

1 Boil, steam or microwave potato until tender; drain. Mash in medium bowl.
2 Meanwhile, heat oil in medium saucepan; cook onion and garlic, stirring, until onion softens. Add carrot and celery; cook, stirring, until vegetables are tender. Add beef; cook, stirring, until changed in colour.
3 Stir in wine, stock, paste and peas; cook, uncovered, about 5 minutes or until mixture thickens slightly. Stir potato into beef mixture; cool 10 minutes.
4 Preheat oven to 180°C/160°C fan-forced. Oil two oven trays.
5 Cut two 14cm-rounds from one pastry sheet; place rounds on oven tray. Place about ¹⁄₁₆ of the filling in centre of each round. Brush edge of pastry with egg; fold over to enclose filling, pressing around edge with fork to seal. Repeat process with remaining pastry sheets, one at a time as above, and remaining filling.
6 Bake pasties, uncovered, about 30 minutes or until browned lightly.

preparation time *30 minutes*
cooking time *45 minutes* makes *16*
nutritional count per pasty *22g total fat (11.1g saturated fat); 1626kJ (389 cal); 34.9g carbohydrate; 10.9g protein; 2.3g fibre*

bubble and squeak

450g nadine potatoes, peeled, chopped coarsely
250g cabbage, chopped coarsely
4 rindless bacon rashers (260g), chopped coarsely
1 medium brown onion (150g), chopped coarsely

1 Boil, steam or microwave potato and cabbage,
separately, until just tender; drain. Mash potato in
medium bowl until smooth.
2 Meanwhile, cook bacon in large heated non-stick
frying pan, stirring, until crisp; drain on absorbent paper.
3 Cook onion in same pan, stirring, until softened.
Add potato, cabbage and bacon; stir to combine.
Flatten mixture to form large cake-shape; cook,
uncovered, until bottom of cake is just browned.
Carefully invert onto plate, then slide back into frying
pan; cook, uncovered, until browned on other side.

preparation time *10 minutes*
cooking time *30 minutes* serves *4*
nutritional count per serving *9.5g total fat (3.4g
saturated fat); 1250kJ (299 cal); 16.5g carbohydrate;
17.3g protein; 4.3g fibre*

portuguese potatoes

600g potatoes, peeled, chopped coarsely
2 tablespoons olive oil
2 cloves garlic, crushed
1 large brown onion (200g), chopped coarsely
4 medium tomatoes (760g), chopped coarsely
2 teaspoons sweet paprika
2 teaspoons finely chopped fresh thyme
½ cup (125ml) chicken stock
1 tablespoon piri piri sauce
1 tablespoon coarsely chopped fresh flat-leaf parsley

1 Preheat oven to 240°C/220°C fan-forced.
2 Toss potato and half of the oil in medium shallow
baking dish. Roast, uncovered, about 30 minutes or
until browned lightly.
3 Meanwhile, heat remaining oil in large frying pan;
cook garlic and onion, stirring, until onion softens.
Add tomato, paprika and thyme; cook, stirring, about
1 minute or until tomato just softens. Add stock and
sauce; bring to the boil. Reduce heat; simmer, uncovered,
stirring occasionally, about 10 minutes or until sauce
thickens slightly.
4 Remove potato from oven; reduce oven to
180°C/160°C fan-forced.
5 Pour sauce over potato; bake, uncovered, further
20 minutes or until potato is tender. Serve sprinkled
with parsley.

preparation time *15 minutes*
cooking time *50 minutes* serves *6*
nutritional count per serving *6.5g total fat (0.9g
saturated fat); 602kJ (144 cal); 15.6g carbohydrate;
4g protein; 3.6g fibre*

warm split pea and sausage salad

1½ cups (300g) yellow split peas
2 rindless bacon rashers (130g), chopped coarsely
6 thin sausages (480g), chopped coarsely
1 medium carrot (120g), chopped coarsely
1 trimmed celery stalk (100g), chopped coarsely
1 medium brown onion (150g), chopped coarsely
2 cloves garlic, sliced thinly
250g grape tomatoes, halved
400g can white beans, rinsed, drained
2 teaspoons finely grated orange rind
⅓ cup (80ml) orange juice

1 Place peas in medium bowl, cover with cold water; stand overnight. Drain peas, rinse under cold water; drain.
2 Place peas in medium saucepan, cover with boiling water. Simmer, covered, about 10 minutes or until peas are tender; rinse under cold water, drain.
3 Meanwhile, cook bacon and sausage in large heated saucepan, in batches, until sausage is cooked.
4 Add carrot, celery, onion and garlic to pan; cook, stirring, until carrot softens slightly. Add tomatoes; cook, stirring, 2 minutes. Add beans, peas, bacon and sausage; stir to combine. Remove from heat; stir in rind and juice.

preparation time *15 minutes (plus standing time)*
cooking time *25 minutes* serves *4*
nutritional count per serving *33.9g total fat (15.1g saturated fat); 2985kJ (714 cal); 51.2g carbohydrate; 43g protein; 16.8g fibre*

soup au pistou

1 tablespoon olive oil
1 small brown onion (80g), chopped finely
2 cloves garlic, sliced thinly
1 large carrot (180g), chopped finely
1 trimmed celery stalk (100g), chopped finely
1 medium potato (200g), cut into 1cm cubes
⅓ cup (75g) risoni
3 cups (750ml) chicken stock
1 cup (250ml) water
400g can white beans, rinsed, drained
2 tablespoons lemon juice
⅓ cup (90g) basil pesto

1 Heat oil in large saucepan, add onion, garlic, carrot and celery; cook, stirring, until onion softens. Add potato, risoni, stock and the water; bring to the boil. Reduce heat; cook about 10 minutes or until risoni is tender.
2 Stir in beans; cook, uncovered, 1 minute.
3 Remove from heat; stir in juice. Serve with basil pesto.

preparation time *10 minutes*
cooking time *25 minutes* serves *4*
nutritional count per serving *14.8g total fat (3g saturated fat); 1342kJ (321 cal); 31.4g carbohydrate; 12g protein; 7.5g fibre*

1 WARM SPLIT PEA AND SAUSAGE SALAD 2 SOUP AU PISTOU
3 KUMARA, BACON AND EGG BAKE [P 350]
4 SPINACH AND PUMPKIN FILLO PIE [P 350]

1

2

3

4

kumara, bacon and egg bake

1 large kumara (500g), sliced thinly
1½ teaspoons ground cumin
5 rindless bacon rashers (325g), chopped finely
1 medium brown onion (150g), chopped finely
8 eggs
¼ cup (60ml) cream
1 cup (120g) coarsely grated cheddar cheese

1   Preheat oven to 180°C/160°C fan-forced.
Oil 2.5 litre (10-cup) baking dish.
2   Boil, steam or microwave kumara 5 minutes. Drain;
pat dry with absorbent paper. Place in single layer over
base of dish; sprinkle with ½ teaspoon of the cumin.
3   Meanwhile, cook bacon and onion over heat in
medium frying pan about 5 minutes or until onion
softens. Stir in remaining cumin; spread bacon mixture
over kumara.
4   Whisk eggs, cream and cheese in medium bowl;
pour over kumara mixture. Bake, uncovered, in oven,
30 minutes.

preparation time *15 minutes*
cooking time *45 minutes* serves *4*
nutritional count per serving *31.7g total fat (15.6g*
saturated fat); 2195kJ (525 cal); 18.1g carbohydrate;
41.1g protein; 2.4g fibre

spinach and pumpkin fillo pie

75g butter, melted
1 tablespoon olive oil
1 medium brown onion (150g), chopped finely
2 cloves garlic, crushed
1kg butternut pumpkin, chopped finely
1 tablespoon brown sugar
1 teaspoon ground cumin
½ teaspoon ground nutmeg
2 x 250g frozen spinach, thawed, drained
1 cup (200g) fetta cheese
2 eggs, beaten lightly
6 sheets fillo pastry

1   Brush 24cm ovenproof pie dish with some of
the butter.
2   Heat oil in large frying pan; cook onion and
garlic, stirring, until onion softens. Add pumpkin,
sugar and spices; cook, covered, about 20 minutes
or until pumpkin is tender. Stir in spinach and ¾ cup
of the cheese. Remove from heat; cool 5 minutes.
Stir in egg.
3   Preheat oven to 180°C/160°C fan-forced.
4   Layer two sheets of pastry, brushing each with butter;
fold pastry in half widthways, place in pie dish, edges
overhanging. Brush pastry with butter again. Repeat
with remaining pastry, overlapping the pieces clockwise
around the dish. Fold over edges to make a rim around
the edge of the pie; brush with remaining butter. Spoon
pumpkin mixture into dish.
5   Bake pie about 40 minutes or until browned lightly.
Sprinkle with remaining cheese.

preparation time *25 minutes*
cooking time *55 minutes* serves *6*
nutritional count per serving *24.4g total fat (13.4g*
saturated fat); 1588kJ (380 cal); 23.2g carbohydrate;
15g protein; 5.1g fibre

creamy fish pie

10g butter
2 teaspoons olive oil
1 small brown onion (80g), chopped finely
1 medium carrot (120g), chopped finely
1 trimmed celery stalk (100g), chopped finely
1 tablespoon plain flour
1 cup (250ml) fish stock
500g firm white fish fillets, chopped coarsely
½ cup (125ml) cream
1 tablespoon english mustard
1 cup (120g) frozen peas
½ cup (40g) finely grated parmesan cheese
1 sheet ready-rolled puff pastry
1 egg, beaten lightly

1 Preheat oven to 220°C/200°C fan-forced.
2 Melt butter with oil in large saucepan; cook onion,
carrot and celery, stirring, until carrot softens. Stir in
flour; cook, stirring, 2 minutes. Add stock and fish;
cook, stirring, until fish is cooked through and mixture
boils and thickens. Remove from heat; stir in cream,
mustard, peas and cheese.
3 Spoon mixture into a shallow small 1.5 litre (6-cup)
baking dish; top with pastry, brush top with egg.
4 Bake pie about 20 minutes or until browned.

preparation time *20 minutes*
cooking time *40 minutes* serves *4*
nutritional count per serving *35.1g total fat (19.1g
saturated fat); 2366kJ (566 cal); 23.5g carbohydrate;
37.5g protein; 4.1g fibre*

smoked salmon pie

1kg potatoes, peeled, chopped coarsely
40g butter, softened
¼ cup (60g) sour cream
200g smoked salmon, chopped coarsely
2 eggs, separated
2 green onions, chopped finely

1 Preheat oven to 200°C/180°C fan-forced.
2 Boil, steam or microwave potato until tender;
drain. Mash potato in large bowl with butter and
sour cream. Stir in salmon, one of the egg yolks,
egg whites and onion.
3 Spoon mixture into deep 22cm-round loose-base
flan tin; smooth top with spatula, brush with remaining
egg yolk.
4 Bake pie about 25 minutes or until heated through
and browned lightly.

preparation time *10 minutes*
cooking time *35 minutes* serves *6*
nutritional count per serving *12.9g total fat (7g
saturated fat); 1049kJ (251 cal); 19.1g carbohydrate;
13.6g protein; 2.3g fibre*

gnocchi with tomato and basil sauce

1 litre (4 cups) milk
1 cup (180g) semolina
4 egg yolks
⅔ cup (50g) finely grated parmesan cheese
2 tablespoons semolina, extra
2 tablespoons olive oil
4 cloves garlic, crushed
½ cup coarsely chopped fresh basil
2 cups (520g) bottled tomato pasta sauce
40g butter, melted
½ cup (40g) finely grated parmesan cheese, extra

1 Bring milk to the boil in medium saucepan. Gradually add semolina, stirring constantly. Reduce heat; simmer, stirring, about 5 minutes or until mixture thickens. Remove from heat; stir in egg yolks and cheese. Stand 5 minutes.
2 Sprinkle extra semolina on flat surface; roll semolina mixture into two 5cm-thick sausage shapes. Wrap in plastic; refrigerate 1 hour or until firm.
3 Meanwhile, heat oil in small saucepan; cook garlic and basil, stirring, until fragrant. Add pasta sauce; bring to the boil. Reduce heat; simmer, covered, 2 minutes.
4 Preheat grill.
5 Cut refrigerated semolina into 2cm gnocchi pieces. Place gnocchi, in single layer, on oiled oven trays. Brush gnocchi with melted butter; sprinkle with extra cheese. Grill about 3 minutes or until cheese browns lightly. Serve gnocchi topped with tomato sauce and sprinkled with fresh basil leaves, if you like.

preparation time *15 minutes*
cooking time *15 minutes (plus refrigeration time)*
serves *6*
nutritional count per serving *27.9g total fat (13.2g saturated fat); 2023kJ (484 cal); 38.7g carbohydrate; 18.4g protein; 3.2g fibre*

baked potatoes with salmon and peas

4 large potatoes (1.2kg), unpeeled
½ cup (60g) frozen peas
50g butter, softened
½ cup (120g) sour cream
100g smoked salmon, chopped coarsely
2 tablespoons coarsely chopped fresh dill

1 Preheat oven to 180°C/160°C fan-forced.
2 Pierce skin of potatoes with fork; wrap each potato in foil, place on oven tray. Bake about 1 hour or until tender.
3 Meanwhile, boil, steam or microwave peas until tender; drain.
4 Combine butter and sour cream in medium bowl.
5 Remove potatoes from oven; fold back foil to reveal tops of potatoes. Increase oven to 240°C/220°C fan-forced.
6 Cut 0.5cm from top of each potato; chop coarsely, add to bowl with butter mixture. Carefully scoop out flesh from potatoes, leaving skins intact. Add potato flesh to butter mixture.
7 Mash potato mixture until almost smooth; stir in peas, salmon and dill. Divide mixture among potato shells. Bake about 10 minutes or until browned lightly.

preparation time *20 minutes*
cooking time *1 hour 10 minutes* serves *4*
nutritional count per serving *22.7g total fat (14.8g saturated fat); 1873kJ (448 cal); 41.1g carbohydrate; 14.6g protein; 6.9g fibre*

tuna and cannellini bean salad

2 cups (400g) dried cannellini beans
425g can tuna in springwater, drained
1 small red onion (100g), sliced thinly
2 trimmed celery stalks (200g), sliced thinly

ITALIAN DRESSING

⅓ cup (80ml) olive oil
⅓ cup (80ml) lemon juice
1 tablespoon finely chopped fresh oregano
2 cloves garlic, crushed

1   Place beans in medium bowl, cover with cold water; stand overnight, drain. Rinse under cold water; drain. Place beans in medium saucepan of boiling water; return to the boil. Reduce heat; simmer, uncovered, about 1 hour or until beans are almost tender. Drain.
2   Meanwhile, make italian dressing.
3   Palce beans and dressing in large bowl with tuna, onion and celery; toss gently to combine.

ITALIAN DRESSING   Place ingredients in screw-top jar; shake well.

preparation time *10 minutes (plus standing time)*
cooking time *1 hour*   serves *4*
nutritional count per serving *21.6g total fat (3.8g saturated fat); 1651kJ (395 cal); 17.3g carbohydrate; 28.8g protein; 8.5g fibre*

white bean and chickpea soup with risoni

1 tablespoon olive oil
1 medium brown onion (150g), chopped coarsely
1 large carrot (180g), chopped coarsely
2 cloves garlic, sliced thinly
2 tablespoons tomato paste
2 teaspoons ground cumin
2 x 400g cans crushed tomatoes
1 litre (4 cups) vegetable stock
400g can chickpeas, rinsed, drained
400g can white beans, rinsed, drained
⅓ cup (75g) risoni

1   Heat oil in large saucepan; cook onion and carrot, stirring, until carrot softens. Add garlic, paste and cumin; cook, stirring, until garlic softens.
2   Add undrained tomatoes and stock to pan; bring to the boil. Add chickpeas and beans; return to the boil. Add risoni; boil about 10 minutes or until risoni is tender.

preparation time *15 minutes*
cooking time *30 minutes*   serves *4*
nutritional count per serving *7.8g total fat (1.4g saturated fat); 1359kJ (325 cal); 41.9g carbohydrate; 15.5g protein; 11.6g fibre*

lemon, pea and ricotta pasta

375g angel hair pasta
2 cups (240g) frozen peas
2 tablespoons olive oil
2 cloves garlic, sliced thinly
2 teaspoons finely grated lemon rind
½ cup (125ml) lemon juice
¾ cup (180g) ricotta cheese, crumbled

1 Cook pasta in large saucepan of boiling water until tender; add peas during last minute of pasta cooking time. Drain, reserving ¼ cup cooking liquid. Rinse pasta and peas under cold water; drain.
2 Meanwhile, heat oil in small frying pan; cook garlic, stirring, until fragrant.
3 Combine pasta and peas in large bowl with reserved cooking liquid, garlic mixture, rind and juice; stir in cheese.

preparation time *5 minutes*
cooking time *10 minutes* serves *4*
nutritional count per serving *15.6g total fat (4.7g saturated fat); 2123kJ (508 cal); 69g carbohydrate; 19g protein; 6.9g fibre*

scotch broth

1kg lamb neck chops
¾ cup (150g) pearl barley
2.25 litres (9 cups) water
1 large brown onion (200g), cut into 1cm pieces
2 medium carrots (240g), cut into 1cm pieces
1 medium leek (350g), sliced thinly
2 cups (160g) finely shredded savoy cabbage
½ cup (60g) frozen peas
2 tablespoons coarsely chopped fresh flat-leaf parsley

1 Place lamb, barley and the water in large saucepan; bring to the boil. Reduce heat; simmer, covered, 1 hour, skimming fat from surface occasionally. Add onion, carrot and leek; simmer, covered, about 30 minutes or until carrot is tender.
2 Remove lamb from pan. When cool enough to handle, remove and discard bones; shred lamb coarsely.
3 Return lamb to soup with cabbage and peas; cook, uncovered, about 10 minutes or until cabbage is just tender.
4 Serve bowls of soup sprinkled with parsley.

preparation time *30 minutes*
cooking time *1 hour 45 minutes* serves *4*
nutritional count per serving *24.4g total fat (10.7g saturated fat); 2274kJ (544 cal); 32.8g carbohydrate; 43.2g protein; 10.7g fibre*

antipasto picnic loaf

2 medium red capsicums (400g)
1 medium eggplant (300g), sliced thinly
2 large flat mushrooms (160g), sliced thinly
1 round cob loaf (450g)
⅓ cup (95g) wholegrain mustard
⅓ cup (100g) mayonnaise
200g leftover roast beef, sliced thinly
½ small green coral lettuce, trimmed, leaves separated

1 Preheat oven to 220°C/200°C fan-forced.
2 Quarter capsicums; discard seeds and membranes.
Roast, skin-side up, until skin blisters and blackens. Cover
capsicum pieces with plastic or paper for 5 minutes;
peel away skin.
3 Place eggplant and mushrooms on oiled oven tray.
Roast about 15 minutes or until tender; cool.
4 Cut shallow lid from top of loaf; remove soft bread
inside, leaving 2cm-thick shell.
5 Spread half the combined mustard and mayonnaise
inside bread shell and lid. Place beef inside bread
shell; top with mushroom then capsicum and eggplant,
pressing layers down firmly. Spread with remaining
mayonnaise mixture; top with lettuce. Replace lid;
press down firmly.
6 Wrap loaf tightly with kitchen string and plastic wrap;
refrigerate 2 hours or until required.

preparation time *20 minutes (plus refrigeration time)*
cooking time *25 minutes* serves *4*
nutritional count per serving *24g total fat (3.6g
saturated fat); 2692kJ (644 cal); 67.7g carbohydrate;
34.5g protein; 8.9g fibre*

lamb and burghul burgers

½ cup (80g) burghul
½ cup (125ml) boiling water
250g minced lamb
1 small brown onion (80g), chopped finely
1 small zucchini (90g), grated coarsely
¼ cup finely chopped fresh mint
1 egg
1 tablespoon olive oil
4 turkish bread rolls (660g)
½ baby cos lettuce, torn
1 large tomato (220g), sliced thinly
1 cup (240g) hummus

1 Place burghul in small bowl, cover with the boiling
water; stand 10 minutes or until burghul softens and
water is absorbed.
2 Combine burghul in medium bowl with lamb, onion,
zucchini, mint and egg. Shape mixture into four patties.
3 Heat oil in large frying pan; cook patties, over medium
heat, until browned both sides and cooked through.
4 Meanwhile, preheat grill.
5 Split rolls in half; toast, cut-side up, under grill.
Sandwich lettuce, patties, tomato and hummus between
roll halves.

preparation time *25 minutes*
cooking time *20 minutes* serves *4*
nutritional count per serving *28.3g total fat (6.9g
saturated fat); 3407kJ (815 cal); 94.2g carbohydrate;
38.3g protein; 14.7g fibre*

banana and coconut cream parfait

¾ cup (180ml) thickened cream
2 tablespoons icing sugar
2 tablespoons coconut-flavoured liqueur, optional
4 scoops mango coconut crème ice-cream
4 large bananas (920g), sliced thinly
½ cup (25g) flaked coconut, toasted

1 Beat cream, icing sugar and liqueur in small bowl with electric mixer until soft peaks form.
2 Layer ice-cream, bananas, coconut and cream mixture in four 1½-cup (375ml) serving glasses.

preparation time *15 minutes* serves *4*
nutritional count per serving *28.5g total fat (19.5g saturated fat); 2149kJ (514 cal); 55.4g carbohydrate; 6.7g protein; 4.7g fibre*

warm lemon meringue pots

2 tablespoons cornflour
½ cup (110g) caster sugar
¼ cup (60ml) lemon juice
½ cup (125ml) water
1 teaspoon finely grated lemon rind
2 eggs, separated
30g butter, chopped
2 tablespoons thickened cream
⅓ cup (75g) caster sugar, extra

1 Preheat oven to 200°C/180°C fan-forced.
2 Stir cornflour, sugar, juice and the water in small saucepan until mixture boils and thickens. Reduce heat; simmer, 1 minute. Remove from heat; stir in rind, egg yolks, butter and cream.
3 Divide lemon mixture among four ½-cup (125ml) ovenproof dishes; place dishes on oven tray.
4 Meanwhile, beat egg whites in small bowl with electric mixer until soft peaks form; gradually add extra sugar, 1 tablespoon at a time, beating until sugar dissolves between additions. Spoon meringue evenly over lemon mixture.
5 Bake pots about 5 minutes or until meringue is browned lightly.

preparation time *20 minutes*
cooking time *7 minutes* serves *4*
nutritional count per serving *12.9g total fat (7.4g saturated fat); 1384kJ (331 cal); 51.6g carbohydrate; 4.2g protein; 0.1g fibre*

warm chocolate pavlovas

2 egg whites
1⅓ cups (215g) icing sugar
⅓ cup (80ml) boiling water
1 tablespoon cocoa powder, sifted
500ml chocolate ice-cream

CHOCOLATE CUSTARD SAUCE

1 tablespoon cornflour
1 tablespoon cocoa powder, sifted
1 tablespoon caster sugar
1 cup (125ml) milk
2 egg yolks

1 Preheat oven to 180°C/160°C fan-forced.
Line large oven tray with baking paper.
2 Beat egg whites, icing sugar and the water in
small bowl with electric mixer about 10 minutes or
until firm peaks form.
3 Fold sifted cocoa into meringue. Drop six equal
amounts of mixture onto tray; use the back of a spoon
to create well in centre of mounds.
4 Bake pavlovas about 25 minutes or until firm to touch.
5 Meanwhile, make chocolate custard sauce.
6 Serve pavlovas straight from the oven, topped with
ice-cream and sauce.

CHOCOLATE CUSTARD SAUCE Blend cornflour, cocoa
and sugar with milk in small saucepan. Stir in egg yolks.
Stir over heat until sauce boils and thickens.

preparation time *5 minutes*
cooking time *35 minutes* serves *4*
nutritional count per serving *14.5g total fat (9g*
saturated fat); 2011kJ (481 cal); 79.5g carbohydrate;
7.4g protein; 0.2g fibre

spiced apple and fillo cups

425g can pie apples
½ teaspoon ground cinnamon
¼ teaspoon ground nutmeg
½ cup (35g) stale breadcrumbs
¾ cup (120g) sultanas
1½ tablespoons caster sugar
4 sheets fillo pastry
30g butter, melted
1 tablespoon icing sugar

1 Preheat oven to 200°C/180°C fan-forced. Grease
eight holes of 12-hole (⅓-cup/80ml) muffin pan.
2 Combine apple, cinnamon, nutmeg, breadcrumbs,
sultanas and caster sugar in medium bowl.
3 Place pastry on a board; brush one sheet with a
little of the butter, then top with another sheet. Repeat
brushing and layering with remaining butter and pastry.
Cut pastry stack into quarters vertically, then across the
centre horizontally; you will have eight rectangles. Press
one pastry rectangle into each of the muffin pan holes.
4 Divide apple mixture evenly among pastry cases;
bake about 10 minutes or until pastry is browned lightly.
Using spatula, carefully remove fillo cups from pan;
cool 5 minutes on wire rack. Serve fillo cups dusted
with sifted icing sugar.

preparation time *20 minutes*
cooking time *10 minutes* serves *4*
nutritional count per serving *7g total fat (4.2g*
saturated fat); 1262kJ (302 cal); 57.7g carbohydrate;
3.7g protein; 3.6g fibre

apple and blackberry jellies

85g packet blackcurrant jelly crystals
1 cup (150g) frozen blackberries
1 medium apple (150g), peeled, cored,
   chopped finely
½ cup (125ml) thickened cream
1 tablespoon icing sugar

1   Prepare jelly according to packet directions.
2   Divide blackberries and apple among four ¾-cup
(180ml) glasses then pour jelly over the top. Refrigerate
about 3 hours or until jelly has set.
3   Beat cream and icing sugar in small bowl with
electric mixer until soft peaks form. Serve jellies topped
with whipped cream.

preparation time *10 minutes (plus refrigeration time)*
serves *4*
nutritional count per serving *11.6g total fat (7.6g
saturated fat); 986kJ (239 cal); 30.1g carbohydrate;
2.9g protein; 1.4g fibre*

passionfruit soufflés

1 tablespoon caster sugar
2 egg yolks
⅓ cup (80ml) fresh passionfruit pulp
2 tablespoons Cointreau
½ cup (80g) icing sugar
4 egg whites
2 teaspoons icing sugar, extra

1   Preheat oven to 180°C/160°C fan-forced. Grease
four 1-cup (250ml) ovenproof dishes. Sprinkle insides
of dishes evenly with caster sugar; shake away excess.
Place dishes on oven tray.
2   Whisk egg yolks, passionfruit pulp, liqueur and
2 tablespoons of the icing sugar in large bowl until
mixture is combined.
3   Beat egg whites in small bowl with electric mixer
until soft peaks form. Gradually add remaining icing
sugar; beat until firm peaks form.
4   Gently fold egg white mixture, in two batches, into
passionfruit mixture; divide mixture among dishes.
5   Bake soufflés, uncovered, about 12 minutes or until
puffed and browned lightly. Dust tops with extra sifted
icing sugar.

preparation time *10 minutes*
cooking time *15 minutes*   serves *4*
nutritional count per serving *2.9g total fat (0.9g
saturated fat); 815kJ (195 cal); 31.1g carbohydrate;
5.8g protein; 2.7g fibre*

1 APPLE AND BLACKBERRY JELLIES 2 PASSIONFRUIT SOUFFLES
3 FLOATING ISLANDS IN CARDAMOM CREAM [P 362]
4 WHITE CHOCOLATE AND BLACK CHERRY CREAMED RICE [P 362]

floating islands
in cardamom cream

2 egg whites
⅓ cup (75g) caster sugar
⅔ cup (160ml) cream
2 teaspoons honey
½ teaspoon ground cardamom
⅓ cup (60g) coarsely chopped pistachios

1   Preheat oven to 160°C/140°C fan-forced. Grease
four ¾-cup (180ml) ovenproof dishes.
2   Beat egg whites in small bowl with electric mixer until
soft peaks form; gradually add sugar, 1 tablespoon at a
time, beating until sugar dissolves between additions.
3   Divide egg white mixture among dishes; using
spatula, smooth tops. Place dishes in baking dish;
pour enough boiling water into large deep baking dish
to come halfway up sides of dishes.
4   Bake, uncovered, about 12 minutes or until floating
islands have risen by about a third. Stand in baking
dish 2 minutes.
5   Meanwhile, combine cream, honey and cardamom
in small jug.
6   Divide cardamom cream among serving plates;
turn floating islands onto cream, sprinkle with nuts.

preparation time *15 minutes*
cooking time *15 minutes* serves *4*
nutritional count per serving *24.9g total fat (12.3g
saturated fat); 1768kJ (423 cal); 43.9g carbohydrate;
5.5g protein; 1.4g fibre*

white chocolate and
black cherry creamed rice

1.5 litres (6 cups) milk
⅔ cup (130g) arborio rice
2 tablespoons caster sugar
90g white chocolate, chopped finely
425g can seedless black cherries, drained

1   Place milk, rice, sugar and half the chocolate in
medium saucepan; bring to the boil. Reduce heat;
simmer over very low heat, stirring often, about
40 minutes or until rice is tender.
2   Serve rice warm, topped with cherries and remaining
chocolate. Serve sprinkled with nutmeg, if you like.

preparation time *5 minutes*
cooking time *50 minutes* serves *6*
nutritional count per serving *22.3g total fat (14.4g
saturated fat); 2261kJ (541 cal); 67.9g carbohydrate;
22.3g protein; 1.1g fibre*

apple and marmalade streusel puddings

20g butter
4 medium apples (600g), peeled, cored, sliced thinly
2 tablespoons water
1 tablespoon caster sugar
½ cup (170g) orange marmalade

STREUSEL

½ cup (75g) plain flour
¼ cup (35g) self-raising flour
⅓ cup (75g) firmly packed brown sugar
½ teaspoon ground cinnamon
100g butter, chopped

1 Make streusel.
2 Preheat oven to 200°C/180°C fan-forced. Grease four ¾-cup (180ml) ovenproof dishes.
3 Melt butter in medium frying pan; cook apple, the water and sugar, stirring, about 10 minutes or until apple is tender. Stir in marmalade. Divide apple mixture among dishes.
4 Coarsely grate streusel onto baking paper; sprinkle over apple mixture.
5 Bake puddings in oven about 20 minutes or until browned lightly.

STREUSEL Blend or process ingredients until combined. Roll into a ball; wrap in plastic. Freeze streusel about 1 hour or until firm.

preparation time *15 minutes (plus freezing time)*
cooking time *30 minutes* serves *4*
nutritional count per serving *25.1g total fat (16.3g saturated fat); 2458kJ (588 cal); 8.2g carbohydrate; 3.4g protein; 3.6g fibre*

watermelon and mint granita

1 cup (220g) white sugar
2 cups (500ml) water
1.6kg coarsely chopped watermelon
2 cups firmly packed fresh mint leaves

1 Stir sugar and the water in medium saucepan over low heat, without boiling, until sugar dissolves; bring to the boil. Reduce heat; simmer, uncovered, without stirring, about 5 minutes or until syrup thickens slightly but does not colour.
2 Blend or process watermelon and mint, in batches, until almost smooth; push batches through sieve into large bowl. Stir in sugar syrup.
3 Pour mixture into two 20cm x 30cm lamington pans, cover with foil; freeze about 3 hours or until almost set.
4 Using fork, scrape granita from bottom and sides of pans, mixing frozen with unfrozen mixture. Cover, return to freezer. Repeat process every hour for about 4 hours or until large ice crystals form and granita has a dry, shard-like appearance. Scrape again with fork before serving.

preparation time *10 minutes (plus freezing time)*
cooking time *10 minutes* serves *8*
nutritional count per serving *0.5g total fat (0g saturated fat); 698kJ (167 cal); 38.1g carbohydrate; 1g protein; 2.1g fibre*

CAFE FAVOURITES

white bean dip

2 x 400g cans white beans, rinsed, drained
2 cloves garlic, crushed
2 tablespoons lemon juice
⅓ cup (80ml) olive oil
1 tablespoon fresh basil leaves

1   Blend or process beans, garlic, juice and oil until almost smooth.
2   Sprinkle dip with basil. Serve with toasted turkish bread, if you like.

preparation time *5 minutes* makes *2 cups*
nutritional count per tablespoon *3.1g total fat (0.4g saturated fat); 138kJ (33 cal); 0.6g carbohydrate; 0.5g protein; 0.9g fibre*

artichoke spinach dip

340g jar marinated artichokes, rinsed, drained
250g frozen chopped spinach, thawed
½ cup (120g) sour cream
¼ cup (75g) mayonnaise
¾ cup (60g) coarsely grated parmesan cheese
1 clove garlic, crushed

1   Preheat oven to 200°C/180°C fan-forced.
2   Chop artichokes coarsely; combine with remaining ingredients in medium bowl. Transfer mixture to 2-cup (500ml) ovenproof dish; cook, covered, in oven 20 minutes.
3   Serve dip with toasted turkish bread, if you like.

preparation time *10 minutes*
cooking time *20 minutes* makes *2 cups*
nutritional count per tablespoon *2.7g total fat (1.3g saturated fat); 130kJ (31 cal); 0.7g carbohydrate; 1.1g protein; 0.4g fibre*

black olive tapenade

2 cups (240g) seeded black olives
1 drained anchovy fillet, rinsed
1 tablespoon drained capers, rinsed
2 teaspoons dijon mustard
2 tablespoons olive oil

1   Rinse and drain olives on absorbent paper. Blend or process olives with anchovy, capers and mustard until smooth.
2   With motor operating, add oil in a thin steady stream, processing until tapenade is smooth.
3   Serve tapenade with toasted turkish bread, if you like.

preparation time *5 minutes* makes *1 cup*
nutritional count per tablespoon *3.3g total fat (0.5g saturated fat); 213kJ (51 cal); 4.6g carbohydrate; 0.6g protein; 0.3g fibre*

bruschetta

2 medium tomatoes (300g), seeded, chopped finely
½ small red onion (50g), chopped finely
1 clove garlic, crushed
1 tablespoon red wine vinegar
2 tablespoons olive oil
1 small french bread stick (150g), cut into 2.5cm slices
cooking-oil spray
2 tablespoons finely shredded fresh basil

1   Preheat oven to 220°C/200°C fan-forced.
2   Combine tomato, onion, garlic, vinegar and oil in small bowl. Stand 20 minutes.
3   Meanwhile, place bread on oiled oven tray; spray with cooking oil. Toast, in oven (or under grill), until browned both sides.
4   Stir basil into tomato mixture, spoon over toast.

preparation time *10 minutes (plus standing time)*
cooking time *5 minutes* makes *12*
nutritional count per bruschetta *4.3g total fat (0.5g saturated fat); 318kJ (76 cal); 7.4g carbohydrate; 1.5g protein; 0.9g fibre*

bean nachos

2 x 420g cans kidney beans, rinsed, drained
⅓ cup (85g) chunky tomato salsa
⅓ cup finely chopped fresh coriander
230g bag corn chips
1½ cups (180g) coarsely grated cheddar cheese
2 cups (120g) finely shredded iceberg lettuce
1 small tomato (90g), chopped coarsely
½ small avocado (100g), chopped coarsely
2 tablespoons lime juice

1   Preheat oven to 220°C/200°C fan-forced.
2   Combine half the beans with salsa; mash until chunky.
Stir in remaining beans and coriander.
3   Spread half the chips in medium shallow baking dish;
top with half the cheese and half the bean mixture. Top
with remaining chips, remaining cheese then remaining
bean mixture. Cook 10 minutes.
4   Toss lettuce, tomato and avocado in medium bowl
with juice. Serve nachos topped with salad.

preparation time *10 minutes*
cooking time *10 minutes* serves *6*
nutritional count per serving *24.5g total fat (11.6g
saturated fat); 1856kJ (444 cal); 33.7g carbohydrate;
17.3g protein; 10.8g fibre*

corn and goats cheese quesadillas

2 corn cobs (500g) trimmed
240g soft goats cheese
8 large (20cm) flour tortillas
½ cup (100g) char-grilled capsicum, sliced thinly
40g jalapeño chilli slices, drained
⅓ cup coarsely chopped fresh coriander
20g butter
40g baby spinach leaves
1 lime, cut into wedges

1   Cook cobs on heated oiled grill plate (or grill or
barbecue) until kernels are tender and browned lightly;
when cool enough to handle, cut kernels from cobs.
2   Spread cheese gently over tortillas. Top 4 of the
tortillas with corn, capsicum, chilli and coriander;
top with remaining tortillas. Press around edges firmly
to seal quesadillas.
3   Heat butter in medium frying pan; cook quesadillas,
one at a time, until browned both sides and heated
through. Serve with spinach and lime wedges.

preparation time *10 minutes*
cooking time *20 minutes* serves *4*
nutritional count per serving *21.7g total fat (10g
saturated fat); 2169kJ (519 cal); 57g carbohydrate;
19.8g protein; 8.6g fibre*

warm pork and mandarin salad with honey dressing

600g pork fillets
2 medium mandarins (400g), peeled
2 tablespoons olive oil
1 tablespoon honey
1 fresh long red chilli, chopped finely
2 medium radicchio (400g), trimmed
1 cup (50g) snow pea sprouts
¾ cup (115g) roasted unsalted cashews

1   Cook pork, uncovered, in heated oiled large frying
pan until cooked as desired. Cover; stand 5 minutes
then slice thickly.
2   Meanwhile, segment mandarins into large bowl.
Add oil, honey and chilli; stir gently to combine. Add
pork, radicchio, sprouts and nuts; toss gently to combine.
Serve salad warm.

preparation time *10 minutes*
cooking time *10 minutes* serves *4*
nutritional count per serving *27.2g total fat (5g
saturated fat); 2098kJ (502 cal); 20.7g carbohydrate;
41g protein; 5.9g fibre*

gruyère, leek and bacon tart

50g butter
2 medium leeks (700g), sliced thinly
2 rindless bacon rashers (130g), chopped finely
2 sheets ready-rolled puff pastry
2 eggs
½ cup (125ml) cream
1 teaspoon fresh thyme leaves
½ cup (60g) finely grated gruyère cheese

1 Preheat oven to 220°C/200°C fan-forced. Oil 24cm-round loose-based flan tin; place tin on oven tray.
2 Melt butter in medium frying pan; cook leek, stirring occasionally, about 15 minutes or until soft. Remove from pan. Cook bacon in same pan, stirring, until crisp; drain on absorbent paper.
3 Meanwhile, place one pastry sheet in flan tin; overlap with second sheet to form cross shape, trim away overlapping pastry. Prick pastry base with fork. Line pastry with baking paper; fill with dried beans or uncooked rice. Bake 20 minutes. Remove paper and beans; cool pastry case.
4 Reduce oven to 200°C/180°C fan-forced.
5 Whisk eggs, cream and thyme in small bowl.
6 Spread leek into pastry case; top with bacon. Pour in egg mixture; sprinkle with cheese. Bake, about 20 minutes or until filling sets. Cool 10 minutes before serving. Serve with a baby rocket and parmesan salad, if you like.

preparation time *25 minutes*
cooking time *45 minutes* serves 6
nutritional count per serving *34.8g total fat (20.2g saturated fat); 1948kJ (466 cal); 24.5g carbohydrate; 14.4g protein; 2.8g fibre*

fetta and spinach fillo bundles

350g spinach, trimmed
1 tablespoon olive oil
1 medium brown onion (150g), chopped finely
2 cloves garlic, crushed
½ teaspoon ground nutmeg
150g fetta cheese, crumbled
3 eggs
2 teaspoons finely grated lemon rind
¼ cup coarsely chopped fresh mint
2 tablespoons finely chopped fresh dill
80g butter, melted
6 sheets fillo pastry

1 Boil, steam or microwave spinach until wilted; drain. Refresh in cold water; drain. Squeeze out excess moisture. Chop spinach coarsely; spread out on absorbent paper.
2 Heat oil in small frying pan; cook onion and garlic, stirring, until onion softens. Add nutmeg; cook, stirring, until fragrant. Cool.
3 Combine onion mixture and spinach in medium bowl with cheese, eggs, rind and herbs.
4 Preheat oven to 200°C/180°C fan-forced. Brush 6-hole texas (¾-cup/180ml) muffin pan with a little of the butter.
5 Brush each sheet of fillo with melted butter; fold in half to enclose buttered side. Gently press one sheet into each pan hole.
6 Divide spinach mixture among pastry cases; fold fillo over filling to enclose. Brush with butter.
7 Bake bundles about 15 minutes. Turn bundles out, top-side up, onto baking-paper-lined oven tray; bake further 5 minutes or until browned lightly. Stand 5 minutes before serving, top-side up.

preparation time *20 minutes*
cooking time *25 minutes* makes 6
nutritional count per bundle *22.9g total fat (12.3g saturated fat); 1200kJ (287 cal); 9.6g carbohydrate; 10.4g protein; 1.8g fibre*

grilled pork medallions with capsicum cream sauce

1 medium red capsicum (200g)
1 medium tomato (150g), halved, seeded
2 teaspoons olive oil
1 clove garlic, crushed
1 small brown onion (80g), chopped finely
½ trimmed celery stalk (50g), chopped finely
2 tablespoons water
1 teaspoon finely chopped fresh rosemary
4 x 150g pork medallions
½ cup (125ml) cream

1 Preheat grill.
2 Quarter capsicum; discard seeds and membranes. Roast capsicum and tomato under grill or in very hot oven, skin-side up, until capsicum skin blisters and blackens. Cover capsicum and tomato pieces with plastic or paper for 5 minutes; peel away skins then slice capsicum thickly.
3 Heat oil in large frying pan; cook garlic, onion and celery until softened. Add capsicum, tomato and the water; cook, uncovered, 5 minutes. Remove from heat; stir in rosemary.
4 Meanwhile, cook pork on heated oiled grill plate (or grill or barbecue) until cooked as desired. Cover to keep warm.
5 Blend or process capsicum mixture until smooth. Return to same pan, add cream; bring to the boil. Reduce heat; simmer, uncovered, 5 minutes.
6 Serve pork with sauce.

preparation time *15 minutes*
cooking time *15 minutes* serves *4*
nutritional count per serving *19.4g total fat (10.5g saturated fat); 1404kJ (336 cal); 4.7g carbohydrate; 35g protein; 1.8g fibre*

lentil and garlic soup with minted yogurt

1 tablespoon olive oil
10 cloves garlic, sliced thinly
2 sprigs fresh thyme
2 cups (400g) french green lentils
2 cups (500ml) vegetable stock
2 litres (8 cups) water
175g watercress, trimmed, chopped coarsely

MINTED YOGURT

1 cup (280g) yogurt
1 tablespoon lemon juice
¼ cup coarsely chopped fresh mint

1 Heat oil in large saucepan; cook garlic and thyme, stirring, until garlic softens. Stir in lentils then stock and the water; bring to the boil. Reduce heat; simmer, covered, about 35 minutes or until lentils soften.
2 Meanwhile, make minted yogurt.
3 Blend or process soup, in batches, until pureed; return to pan. Add watercress to soup; cook, stirring, until wilted.
4 Serve bowls of soup with minted yogurt.

MINTED YOGURT Combine ingredients in medium bowl.

preparation time *10 minutes*
cooking time *45 minutes serves 6*
nutritional count per serving *6.5g total fat (1.9g saturated fat); 1158kJ (277 cal); 28.9g carbohydrate; 20.1g protein; 16.7g fibre*

seafood chowder

1 tablespoon olive oil
3 rindless bacon rashers (195g), sliced thinly
1 medium brown onion (150g), chopped finely
1 small fennel bulb (200g), sliced thinly
3 cloves garlic, sliced thinly
2 medium tomatoes (300g), seeded, chopped coarsely
2 tablespoons tomato paste
1 teaspoon hot paprika
½ cup (125ml) dry white wine
2 x 400g cans whole tomatoes
3 cups (750ml) fish stock
1 litre (4 cups) water
500g kipfler potatoes, cut into 3cm pieces
1.2kg marinara mix
½ cup coarsely chopped fresh flat-leaf parsley

1 Heat oil in large saucepan, add bacon; cook until
crisp. Drain on absorbent paper.
2 Add onion, fennel and garlic to pan; cook until
vegetables soften. Add fresh tomato; cook until soft.
Add tomato paste and paprika; cook, stirring, 2 minutes.
Return bacon to pan with wine; cook, stirring, 2 minutes.
3 Slice canned tomatoes thickly. Add slices with juice
from can, stock, the water and potato to pan; bring
to the boil. Reduce heat; simmer, covered, about
20 minutes or until potato is soft.
4 Add marinara mix; cook, covered, about 3 minutes.
Stir in parsley.

preparation time *20 minutes*
cooking time *30 minutes* serves *6*
nutritional count per serving *8.8g total fat (2.2g
saturated fat); 1781kJ (426 cal); 24.5g carbohydrate;
50.5g protein; 5.7g fibre*

black-eyed bean and ham soup

1 cup (200g) black-eyed beans
1 tablespoon olive oil
1 trimmed celery stalk (100g), chopped coarsely
1 small brown onion (80g), chopped coarsely
1 medium carrot (120g), chopped coarsely
1 bay leaf
2 cloves garlic
1.2kg ham hock
1 litre (4 cups) chicken stock
2 litres (8 cups) water
½ bunch trimmed silver beet (125g), shredded finely
2 tablespoons cider vinegar

1 Place beans in medium bowl, cover with water;
stand overnight, rinse, drain.
2 Heat oil in large saucepan, add celery, onion and
carrot; cook until vegetables are soft. Add bay leaf,
garlic, ham hock, stock and the water; bring to the boil.
Reduce heat; simmer, uncovered, 1 hour.
3 Add beans to soup; simmer, uncovered, about 1 hour
or until beans are tender.
4 Remove hock from soup. When cool enough to
handle, remove meat from hock. Discard bone; shred
meat coarsely, return to soup.
5 Add silver beet to soup; cook, stirring, until wilted.
Remove from heat; stir in vinegar.

preparation time *25 minutes (plus standing time)*
cooking time *2 hours 30 minutes* serves *6*
nutritional count per serving *7.2g total fat (1.8g
saturated fat); 945kJ (226 cal); 16.1g carbohydrate;
21.2g protein; 6.3g fibre*

salade niçoise

200g baby green beans, trimmed
2 tablespoons olive oil
1 tablespoon lemon juice
2 tablespoons white wine vinegar
4 medium tomatoes (600g), cut into wedges
4 hard-boiled eggs, quartered
425g can tuna in springwater, drained, flaked
½ cup (80g) drained caperberries, rinsed
½ cup (60g) seeded small black olives
¼ cup firmly packed fresh flat-leaf parsley leaves
440g can drained whole baby new potatoes,
     rinsed, halved

1   Boil, steam or microwave beans until tender; drain.
Rinse under cold water; drain.
2   Whisk oil, juice and vinegar in large bowl, add
beans and remaining ingredients; toss gently to combine.

preparation time *15 minutes*
cooking time *5 minutes* serves *4*
nutritional count per serving *16.9g total fat (3.7g*
saturated fat); 1522kJ (364 cal); 19.5g carbohydrate;
30.9g protein; 5.2g fibre

greek salad with grilled lamb

¼ cup (70g) yogurt
⅓ cup (80ml) lemon juice
¼ cup (60ml) olive oil
2 cloves garlic, crushed
600g lamb fillets
3 medium tomatoes (450g), cut into thin wedges
1 small red onion (100g), sliced thinly
2 medium red capsicums (400g), chopped coarsely
2 lebanese cucumbers (260g), chopped coarsely
½ cup (75g) seeded kalamata olives
400g can chickpeas, rinsed, drained
1 cup firmly packed fresh flat-leaf parsley leaves
100g fetta cheese, crumbled

1   Combine yogurt, 1 tablespoon of the juice,
1 tablespoon of the oil and half the garlic in medium
bowl with lamb. Cover; refrigerate until needed.
2   Meanwhile, place remaining juice, oil and garlic
in screw-top jar; shake well.
3   Drain lamb; cook on heated oiled grill plate
(or grill or barbecue) until cooked as desired.
Cover; stand 5 minutes then slice thickly.
4   Combine remaining ingredients in large bowl with
lemon dressing. Serve salad topped with lamb.

preparation time *20 minutes*
cooking time *5 minutes (plus standing time)* serves *4*
nutritional count per serving *27.5g total fat (8.8g*
saturated fat); 2215kJ (530 cal); 23.1g carbohydrate;
44g protein; 7.8g fibre

salade composé

1 small french bread stick (150g), cut into 1cm slices
2 cloves garlic, crushed
¼ cup (60ml) olive oil
6 rindless bacon rashers (390g), sliced thickly
150g mesclun
6 medium egg tomatoes (450g), sliced thinly
4 hard-boiled eggs, halved lengthways

RED WINE VINAIGRETTE

¼ cup (60ml) red wine vinegar
3 teaspoons dijon mustard
⅓ cup (80ml) extra virgin olive oil

1   Preheat grill. Brush both sides bread slices with
combined garlic and oil; toast under grill.
2   Cook bacon in large frying pan until crisp; drain.
3   Meanwhile, make red wine vinaigrette.
4   Layer bread and bacon in large bowl with mesclun
and tomato, top with egg; drizzle with vinaigrette.

RED WINE VINAIGRETTE Place ingredients in screw-top
jar; shake well.

preparation time *15 minutes*
cooking time *20 minutes* serves *4*
nutritional count per serving *48.3g total fat (9.9g*
saturated fat); 2575kJ (616 cal); 19.7g carbohydrate;
25.2g protein; 3.5g fibre

beetroot, pumpkin and spinach salad with fetta polenta

2 cups (500ml) water
2 cups (500ml) vegetable stock
1 cup (170g) polenta
200g fetta cheese, crumbled
10 small beetroots (600g)
2 tablespoons olive oil
700g peeled pumpkin, diced into 4cm pieces
150g baby spinach leaves
¾ cup (75g) roasted walnuts, chopped coarsely

WALNUT VINAIGRETTE

2 tablespoons walnut oil
¼ cup (60ml) olive oil
¼ cup (60ml) lemon juice

1 Preheat oven to 200°C/180°C fan-forced. Oil 20cm x 30cm lamington pan; line with baking paper.
2 Bring the water and stock in large saucepan to the boil. Gradually add polenta, stirring constantly. Reduce heat; cook, stirring, about 10 minutes or until polenta thickens. Stir in cheese then spread polenta into pan. Cool 10 minutes then cover; refrigerate about 1 hour or until polenta is firm.
3 Meanwhile, discard beetroot stems and leaves; quarter unpeeled beetroots then place in large shallow baking dish; drizzle with half of the oil. Roast, uncovered, 15 minutes. Add pumpkin; drizzle with remaining oil. Roast, uncovered, about 30 minutes or until vegetables are tender.
4 Make walnut vinaigrette.
5 When cool enough to handle, peel beetroot. Place in large bowl with dressing; toss gently to combine.
6 Turn polenta onto board; trim edges. Cut polenta into 12 pieces; cook, in batches, on heated oiled grill plate (or grill or barbecue) until browned both sides and heated through.
7 Add pumpkin, spinach and nuts to beetroot mixture; toss gently to combine. Divide polenta pieces among serving plates; top with salad.

WALNUT VINAIGRETTE Place ingredients in screw-top jar; shake well.

preparation time *20 minutes (plus refrigeration time)*
cooking time *1 hour 15 minutes* serves *4*
nutritional count per serving *58.8g total fat (13.3g saturated fat); 3515kJ (841 cal); 51.8g carbohydrate; 23g protein; 9.3g fibre*

lamb and fetta salad with warm walnut dressing

1 tablespoon vegetable oil
600g lamb fillets
200g fetta cheese, crumbled
250g witlof, trimmed, leaves separated
150g baby spinach leaves, trimmed

WARM WALNUT DRESSING

2 cloves garlic, crushed
1 teaspoon finely grated lemon rind
¼ cup (60ml) olive oil
2 tablespoons cider vinegar
½ cup (55g) coarsely chopped roasted walnuts

1 Heat oil in large frying pan; cook lamb, uncovered, about 10 minutes. Remove from pan; cover, stand 5 minutes then slice thickly.
2 Make warm walnut dressing.
3 Combine lamb in medium bowl with cheese, witlof and spinach. Serve salad drizzled with dressing.

WARM WALNUT DRESSING Stir garlic, rind, oil and vinegar in small saucepan until hot. Remove from heat; stir in nuts.

preparation time *15 minutes*
cooking time *10 minutes* serves *4*
nutritional count per serving *52.8g total fat (16.8g saturated fat); 2742kJ (656 cal); 1.2g carbohydrate; 43.8g protein; 3.2g fibre*

caesar salad with salt and pepper squid

1 tablespoon sichuan peppercorns
2 tablespoons sea salt
1 cup (200g) rice flour
600g cleaned squid hoods with tentacles
vegetable oil, for deep-frying
1 tablespoon sea salt, extra
2 baby cos lettuces (360g)

CAESAR DRESSING

1 cup (300g) mayonnaise
1 clove garlic, crushed
2 tablespoons lime juice
1 tablespoon milk
1 teaspoon worcestershire sauce

1   Dry-fry peppercorns in small frying pan until fragrant; using mortar and pestle, crush peppercorns coarsely. Combine crushed pepper, salt and flour in medium bowl.
2   Cut squid hoods down centre to open out; score inside in diagonal pattern then cut into thick strips. Toss squid pieces in flour mixture; shake off excess.
3   Make caesar dressing.
4   Heat oil in wok; deep-fry squid, in batches, until browned lightly. Drain on absorbent paper; sprinkle with extra salt.
5   Divide leaves among serving plates; top with squid, drizzle with dressing.

CAESAR DRESSING Whisk ingredients in small bowl.

preparation time *15 minutes*
cooking time *5 minutes* serves *4*
nutritional count per serving *34.7g total fat (4.5g saturated fat); 2688kJ (643 cal); 51g carbohydrate; 30g protein; 3.7g fibre*

goats cheese, fig and prosciutto salad

Freeze soft goats cheese for 10 minutes to make crumbling easier.

6 slices prosciutto (90g)
120g baby rocket leaves, trimmed
4 large fresh figs (320g), quartered
150g soft goats cheese, crumbled

HONEY CIDER DRESSING

¼ cup (60ml) cider vinegar
2 tablespoons olive oil
1 tablespoon wholegrain mustard
1 tablespoon honey

1   Preheat grill.
2   Make honey cider dressing.
3   Place prosciutto under grill until crisp; drain on absorbent paper, chop coarsely.
4   Serve rocket topped with fig, cheese and prosciutto; drizzle with dressing.

HONEY CIDER DRESSING Place ingredients in screw-top jar; shake well.

preparation time *10 minutes*
cooking time *5 minutes* serves *4*
nutritional count per serving *16.9g total fat (5.7g saturated fat); 1062kJ (254 cal); 13.7g carbohydrate; 11.1g protein; 2.6g fibre*

1 CAESAR SALAD WITH SALT AND PEPPER SQUID 2 GOATS CHEESE, FIG AND PROSCIUTTO SALAD 3 CRAB CAKES WITH AVOCADO SALSA [P 376] 4 PRAWN, CRAB AND AVOCADO SALAD [P 376]

crab cakes with avocado salsa

600g cooked crab meat
1 cup (70g) stale white breadcrumbs
1 egg
1 clove garlic, crushed
2 tablespoons mayonnaise
¼ cup finely chopped fresh coriander
½ teaspoon cayenne pepper
15g butter
1 tablespoon olive oil

AVOCADO SALSA

2 small avocados (400g), chopped coarsely
1 medium tomato (150g), chopped coarsely
¾ cup loosely packed fresh coriander leaves
2 teaspoons Tabasco sauce
1 tablespoon lime juice
1 tablespoon olive oil

1   Combine crab meat, breadcrumbs, egg, garlic, mayonnaise, coriander and pepper in medium bowl. Shape mixture into eight patties; place on tray. Cover; refrigerate 1 hour.
2   Meanwhile, make avocado salsa.
3   Heat butter and oil in large frying pan; cook crab cakes, in batches, until browned both sides and heated through. Serve crab cakes topped with salsa.

AVOCADO SALSA Combine ingredients in medium bowl.

preparation time *20 minutes (plus refrigeration time)* cooking time *10 minutes* serves *4*
nutritional count per serving *34.1g total fat (7.8g saturated fat); 2011kJ (481 cal); 17.6g carbohydrate; 25.3g protein; 2.8g fibre*

prawn, crab and avocado salad

16 cooked medium king prawns (800g)
4 large butter lettuce leaves
250g crab meat, shredded coarsely
1 large avocado (320g), sliced thinly

THOUSAND ISLAND DRESSING

½ cup (150g) mayonnaise
1 tablespoon tomato sauce
½ small red capsicum (75g), chopped finely
½ small white onion (40g), grated finely
8 pimiento-stuffed green olives, chopped finely
1 teaspoon lemon juice

1   Make thousand island dressing.
2   Shell and devein prawns, leaving tails intact.
3   Divide lettuce leaves among serving plates; divide prawns, crab and avocado among lettuce leaves. Drizzle with dressing.

THOUSAND ISLAND DRESSING Combine ingredients in small bowl.

preparation time *25 minutes* serves *4*
nutritional count per serving *26.5g total fat (4.4g saturated fat); 1718kJ (411 cal); 11.5g carbohydrate; 30.7g protein; 2.8g fibre*

crab, fennel and herb quiches

3 sheets ready-rolled shortcrust pastry
1 tablespoon olive oil
1 medium fennel bulb (300g), sliced thinly
250g crab meat
2 tablespoons finely chopped fennel fronds
2 tablespoons finely chopped fresh flat-leaf parsley
½ cup (60g) coarsely grated cheddar cheese

FILLING

300ml cream
¼ cup (60ml) milk
3 eggs

1 Preheat oven to 200°C/180°C fan-forced.
Oil 12-hole (⅓-cup/80ml) muffin pan.
2 Cut 12 x 9cm rounds from pastry; press rounds into pan holes.
3 Heat oil in large frying pan; cook fennel, stirring, about 5 minutes or until fennel softens and browns slightly. Divide fennel among pastry cases; top with combined crab, fronds, parsley and cheese.
4 Whisk ingredients for filling in large jug; pour into pastry cases.
5 Bake quiches about 25 minutes. Stand in pan 5 minutes before serving with lime wedges, if you like.

preparation time *20 minutes*
cooking time *30 minutes* makes *12*
nutritional count per quiche *27.1g total fat (15g saturated fat); 1509kJ (361 cal); 20.3g carbohydrate; 9g protein; 1.3g fibre*

goats cheese and zucchini flower quiches

3 sheets ready-rolled shortcrust pastry
12 baby zucchini with flowers (240g)
100g firm goats cheese, chopped finely
⅓ cup (25g) finely grated parmesan cheese
2 tablespoons finely chopped garlic chives

FILLING

300ml cream
¼ cup (60ml) milk
3 eggs

1 Preheat oven to 200°C/180°C fan-forced.
Oil 12-hole (⅓-cup/80ml) muffin pan.
2 Cut 12 x 9cm rounds from pastry; press rounds into pan holes.
3 Remove flowers from zucchini; remove and discard stamens from flowers. Slice zucchini thinly. Divide combined sliced zucchini, cheeses and chives into pastry cases.
4 Whisk ingredients for filling in large jug; pour into pastry cases. Top each quiche with a zucchini flower.
5 Bake quiches about 25 minutes. Stand in pan 5 minutes before serving.

preparation time *25 minutes*
cooking time *25 minutes* makes *12*
nutritional count per quiche *25.8g total fat (15g saturated fat); 1421kJ (340 cal); 19.9g carbohydrate; 7.1g protein; 1.1g fibre*

crumbed chicken schnitzel with mixed bean salad

300g green beans
200g yellow beans
4 medium tomatoes (600g), seeded, sliced thickly
2 tablespoons olive oil
1 tablespoon red wine vinegar
2 teaspoons wholegrain mustard
2 tablespoons coarsely chopped fresh tarragon
2 tablespoons coarsely chopped fresh chervil
2 teaspoons drained green peppercorns, crushed
4 chicken breast fillets (800g)
¼ cup (35g) plain flour
2 eggs, beaten lightly
1 tablespoon milk
2 teaspoons finely grated lemon rind
½ cup (85g) polenta
½ cup (50g) packaged breadcrumbs
vegetable oil, for shallow-frying

1 Boil, steam or microwave beans until tender. Rinse under cold water; drain. Place beans in large bowl with tomato, olive oil, vinegar, mustard, herbs and peppercorns; toss gently to combine. Cover; refrigerate until required.
2 Using meat mallet, gently pound chicken, one piece at a time, between sheets of plastic wrap until 1cm thick.
3 Whisk flour, egg, milk and rind together in shallow bowl; combine polenta and breadcrumbs in a second shallow bowl. Coat chicken pieces, first in egg mixture then in breadcrumb mixture.
4 Heat vegetable oil in large frying pan; shallow-fry chicken, in batches, until browned and cooked through. Drain on absorbent paper.
5 Serve schnitzel, sliced, with bean salad.

preparation time *25 minutes*
cooking time *20 minutes* serves *4*
nutritional count per serving *35.4g total fat (5.8g saturated fat); 2897kJ (693 cal); 33.5g carbohydrate; 57.1g protein; 5.8g fibre*

pappardelle with chicken and creamy mushroom sauce

2 tablespoons olive oil
1 clove garlic, crushed
1 small onion (80g), chopped finely
250g swiss brown mushrooms, sliced thinly
1 cup (250ml) cream
2 teaspoons finely chopped fresh rosemary
50g butter, chopped
500g pappardelle pasta
200g cooked chicken, shredded thinly
½ cup (50g) walnut pieces, roasted
¾ cup (60g) finely grated parmesan cheese
¼ cup chopped fresh flat-leaf parsley

1 Heat oil in large frying pan; cook garlic and onion, stirring, until onion softens. Add mushroom; cook, stirring, until tender.
2 Add cream and rosemary to pan; bring to the boil. Reduce heat; simmer, uncovered, about 3 minutes or until sauce thickens. Stir in butter.
3 Meanwhile, cook pasta in large saucepan of boiling water, uncovered, until just tender. Drain; return to pan.
4 Add hot cream sauce to hot pasta with chicken, nuts, half of the cheese, and parsley; toss gently to combine. Serve immediately, topped with remaining cheese.

preparation time *15 minutes*
cooking time *12 minutes* serves *6*
nutritional count per serving *43.5g total fat (20.6g saturated fat); 3085kJ (738 cal); 59.4g carbohydrate; 25g protein; 5.5g fibre*

gnocchi with classic pesto

1kg russet burbank potatoes, unpeeled
2 eggs, beaten lightly
30g butter, melted
¼ cup (20g) finely grated parmesan cheese
2 cups (300g) plain flour, approximately

CLASSIC PESTO

2 cloves garlic, quartered
¼ cup (40g) roasted pine nuts
¼ cup (20g) finely grated parmesan cheese
1 cup firmly packed fresh basil leaves
⅓ cup (80ml) olive oil
½ cup (125ml) cream

1 Boil or steam whole potatoes until tender; drain.
Peel when cool enough to handle. Mash, using ricer,
food mill (mouli), or sieve and wooden spoon, into
large bowl; stir in eggs, butter, parmesan and enough
of the flour to make a firm dough.
2 Divide dough into eight equal portions; roll each
portion on floured surface into 2cm-thick sausage-shape.
Cut each sausage-shape into 2cm pieces; roll into balls.
3 Roll each ball along the inside tines of a fork,
pressing lightly on top of ball with index finger to form
classic gnocchi shape, grooved on one side and
dimpled on the other. Place gnocchi, in single layer,
on floured tray, cover; refrigerate 1 hour.
4 Meanwhile, make classic pesto.
5 Cook gnocchi, uncovered, in large saucepan of
boiling salted water about 3 minutes or until gnocchi
float to the surface. Remove from pan with slotted
spoon; drain. Return to pan; add pesto. Toss gently.

CLASSIC PESTO Blend or process garlic, pine nuts,
cheese and basil until finely chopped. With motor
operating, gradually add oil until pesto is thick. Transfer
pesto to small saucepan, add cream; stir, uncovered,
over low heat until heated through.

preparation time *35 minutes (plus refrigeration time)*
cooking time *25 minutes* serves *8*
nutritional count per serving *25.8g total fat (9.5g
saturated fat); 1944kJ (465 cal); 44.2g carbohydrate;
11.7g protein; 4.4g fibre*

penne puttanesca

500g penne pasta
⅓ cup (80ml) extra virgin olive oil
3 cloves garlic, crushed
1 teaspoon chilli flakes
5 medium tomatoes (950g), chopped coarsely
200g seeded kalamata olives
8 drained anchovy fillets, chopped coarsely
⅓ cup (65g) rinsed drained capers
⅓ cup coarsely chopped fresh flat-leaf parsley
2 tablespoons finely shredded fresh basil

1 Cook pasta in large saucepan of boiling water,
uncovered, until just tender; drain.
2 Meanwhile, heat oil in large frying pan; cook
garlic, stirring, until fragrant. Add chilli and tomato;
cook, stirring, 5 minutes. Add remaining ingredients;
cook, stirring occasionally, about 5 minutes or until
sauce thickens slightly.
3 Add pasta to sauce; toss gently to combine.

preparation time *10 minutes*
cooking time *20 minutes* serves *4*
nutritional count per serving *21.1g total fat (3.1g
saturated fat); 2884kJ (690 cal); 10.2g carbohydrate;
18.6g protein; 7.9g fibre*

roasted capsicum and goats cheese terrine

3 large red capsicums (1kg)
1½ cups (360g) ricotta cheese, chopped coarsely
250g firm goats cheese, chopped coarsely
¼ cup finely chopped fresh chives
2 tablespoons lemon juice
1 clove garlic, crushed

SPINACH AND WALNUT PESTO

¼ cup (20g) finely grated parmesan cheese
100g baby spinach leaves
¼ cup (25g) roasted walnuts
1 clove garlic, quartered
¼ cup (60ml) olive oil
2 tablespoons lemon juice
1 tablespoon water

1 Preheat oven to 240°C/220°C fan-forced. Oil six holes of eight-hole (½-cup/125ml) petite loaf pan. Line base and two long sides of each hole with a strip of baking paper, extending 5cm over sides.
2 Halve capsicums; discard seeds and membranes. Place on oven tray; roast, skin-side up, about 15 minutes or until skin blisters and blackens. Cover with plastic wrap for 5 minutes then peel away skin. Cut capsicum into strips; line base and two long sides of pan holes with capsicum strips, extending 2cm over edges.
3 Combine remaining ingredients in medium bowl; spoon cheese mixture into pan holes, pressing down firmly. Fold capsicum strips over to enclose filling. Cover; refrigerate 1 hour.
4 Meanwhile, make spinach and walnut pesto.
5 Carefully remove terrines from pan holes; serve with spinach and walnut pesto. Sprinkle with chopped fresh chives.

SPINACH AND WALNUT PESTO Process cheese, spinach, nuts and garlic until chopped finely. With motor operating, gradually add combined oil, juice and the water in a thin, steady stream; process until pesto is smooth.

preparation time *30 minutes (plus refrigeration time)*
cooking time *15 minutes* makes 6
nutritional count per terrine *26.8g total fat (10.8g saturated fat); 1417kJ (339 cal); 7.5g carbohydrate; 16.5g protein; 2.6g fibre*

sun-dried tomato puttanesca pasta with meatballs

500g pork and veal mince
½ cup (35g) stale breadcrumbs
1 egg
¼ cup (20g) finely grated parmesan cheese
1 tablespoon olive oil
1 medium brown onion (150g), chopped coarsely
2 cloves garlic, quartered
1 fresh small red thai chilli
6 anchovy fillets
1 cup (150g) drained sun-dried tomatoes
¼ cup (70g) tomato paste
1 cup (250ml) chicken stock
12 pimiento-stuffed olives, sliced thinly
375g spaghetti
⅓ cup coarsely chopped fresh flat-leaf parsley

1   Combine mince, breadcrumbs, egg and cheese in medium bowl; roll level tablespoons of mixture into balls.
2   Heat oil in medium frying pan; cook meatballs, uncovered, until browned.
3   Blend or process onion, garlic, chilli, anchovy, tomatoes and paste until smooth. Combine tomato mixture with stock in medium saucepan; bring to the boil. Add meatballs and olives; simmer, uncovered, 15 minutes.
4   Meanwhile, cook spaghetti in large saucepan of boiling water until tender; drain.
5   Serve spaghetti topped with meatballs and sauce; sprinkle with parsley.

preparation time *25 minutes*
cooking time *25 minutes serves 4*
nutritional count per serving *20.6g total fat (6.3g saturated fat); 2964kJ (709 cal); 78.8g carbohydrate; 47.5g protein; 7.9g fibre*

mixed mushroom fettuccine boscaiola

10g dried porcini mushrooms
¼ cup (60ml) boiling water
375g fettuccine
1 tablespoon olive oil
200g pancetta, chopped coarsely
100g button mushrooms, sliced thinly
100g swiss brown mushrooms, sliced thinly
1 flat mushroom (80g), sliced thinly
2 cloves garlic, crushed
¼ cup (60ml) dry white wine
300ml cream
1 tablespoon lemon juice
½ cup (40g) finely grated parmesan cheese
2 tablespoons coarsely chopped fresh chives
2 tablespoons finely grated parmesan cheese, extra

1   Combine porcini mushrooms and the water in small heatproof bowl; cover, stand 15 minutes or until mushrooms are tender. Drain; reserve soaking liquid, chop mushrooms coarsely.
2   Cook pasta in large saucepan of boiling water until tender; drain.
3   Meanwhile, heat oil in large frying pan; cook pancetta until crisp. Add all mushrooms and garlic; cook, stirring, until mushrooms are browned lightly. Add wine; bring to the boil. Boil, uncovered, until liquid has almost evaporated. Add cream, juice and reserved soaking liquid; simmer, uncovered, until sauce reduces by half and thickens slightly. Stir in cheese and chives.
4   Combine pasta and sauce in large bowl. Serve bowls of pasta sprinkled with extra parmesan cheese.

preparation time *20 minutes (plus standing time)*
cooking time *20 minutes serves 4*
nutritional count per serving *45.5g total fat (26.1g saturated fat); 3390kJ (811 cal); 66.9g carbohydrate; 28.9g protein; 5.3g fibre*

pasta with capers and anchovies

A teaspoon of dried chilli flakes cooked with the garlic makes a deliciously hot alternative. If you have some, stir in ¼ cup coarsely chopped fresh flat-leaf parsley or a handful of baby rocket leaves before serving.

375g spaghetti
2 tablespoons olive oil
3 cloves garlic, sliced thinly
¼ cup (50g) drained baby capers, rinsed
10 drained anchovy fillets, chopped finely
1 tablespoon finely grated lemon rind
1 tablespoon lemon juice

1 Cook pasta in large saucepan of boiling water until tender; drain.
2 Meanwhile, heat oil in medium frying pan; cook garlic, stirring, until fragrant. Add capers and anchovies; stir gently until hot.
3 Pour garlic mixture over pasta; stir in rind and juice.

preparation time *10 minutes*
cooking time *10 minutes* serves *4*
nutritional count per serving *11.1g total fat (1.7g saturated fat); 1781kJ (426 cal); 65.6g carbohydrate; 13.3g protein; 3.8g fibre*

chilli and garlic spaghettini with breadcrumbs

375g spaghettini
⅓ cup (80ml) olive oil
50g butter
4 cloves garlic, crushed
4 fresh small red thai chillies, chopped finely
2 cups (140g) stale breadcrumbs
½ cup coarsely chopped fresh flat-leaf parsley
2 teaspoons finely grated lemon rind

1 Cook pasta in large saucepan of boiling water, uncovered, until just tender.
2 Meanwhile, heat half of the oil in large frying pan with butter. After butter melts, add garlic, chilli and breadcrumbs; cook, stirring, until breadcrumbs are browned lightly.
3 Combine drained hot pasta and breadcrumb mixture in large bowl with parsley, rind and remaining oil.

preparation time *10 minutes*
cooking time *10 minutes* serves *4*
nutritional count per serving *30.9g total fat (9.8g saturated fat); 2959kJ (708 cal); 88.4g carbohydrate; 15.9g protein; 4.6g fibre*

pork, rocket and sopressa pasta

100g baby rocket leaves
¼ cup (60ml) olive oil
2 tablespoons lemon juice
375g fettuccine
600g pork fillets
1 medium brown onion (150g), chopped finely
1 clove garlic, crushed
100g hot sopressa, sliced thinly

1 Blend or process rocket, oil and juice until rocket is finely chopped.
2 Cook pasta in large saucepan of boiling water, uncovered, until tender.
3 Meanwhile, cook pork, uncovered, in heated oiled large frying pan, until cooked as desired. Remove from pan; cover to keep warm.
4 Cook onion, garlic and salami in same pan, stirring, until onion softens.
5 Combine drained pasta in large bowl with thinly sliced pork, and rocket and salami mixtures.

preparation time *15 minutes*
cooking time *20 minutes* serves *4*
nutritional count per serving *27.8g total fat (6.4g saturated fat); 3047kJ (729 cal); 67.2g carbohydrate; 50.1g protein; 4.1g fibre*

grilled beef and vegetable burgers

600g beef mince
2 teaspoons ground cumin
2 cloves garlic, crushed
¼ cup finely chopped fresh coriander
8 large slices sourdough bread
4 baby eggplants (240g), sliced thickly
3 medium egg tomatoes (225g), sliced thickly
1 medium brown onion (150g), sliced thinly
½ cup (130g) hummus
2 teaspoons lemon juice
1 teaspoon olive oil
100g rocket leaves, trimmed

1 Combine mince, cumin, garlic and coriander in medium bowl. Using your hands, shape mixture into four patties to fit the size of the bread slices.
2 Grill bread on heated oiled grill plate (or grill or barbecue) until browned on both sides. Transfer to a plate.
3 Cook patties, eggplant, tomatoes and onion on same heated oiled grill plate (or barbecue) until patties and vegetables are browned and just cooked through.
4 Meanwhile, combine hummus, juice and oil in small bowl.
5 Layer four toasted bread slices with rocket, eggplant, patties, tomatoes, hummus and onion. Top with remaining bread slices before serving.

preparation *15 minutes*
cooking *10 minutes* serves *4*
nutritional count per serving *4.2g total fat (1.2g saturated fat); 577kJ (138 cal); 14.2g carbohydrate; 9.5g protein; 2.5g fibre*

cheeseburgers with caramelised onion

500g beef mince
4 thin slices (40g) cheddar cheese
4 hamburger buns, split
1 small tomato (90g), sliced thinly
8 large butter lettuce leaves
4 large dill pickles (240g), sliced thinly
1 tablespoon american-style mustard
⅓ cup (95g) tomato sauce

CARAMELISED ONION

2 tablespoons olive oil
2 medium white onions (300g), sliced thinly
1 tablespoon brown sugar
2 tablespoons balsamic vinegar
2 tablespoons water

1 Make caramelised onion.
2 Shape beef into four patties; cook on heated oiled grill plate (or grill or barbecue) until cooked through. Top each patty with cheese slices during last minute of cooking time.
3 Meanwhile, toast buns, cut-sides down, on same grill plate (or grill or barbecue).
4 Place cheeseburgers, onion, tomato, lettuce and pickle between buns; serve with mustard and sauce.

CARAMELISED ONION Heat oil in large frying pan; cook onion, stirring, until soft. Add sugar, vinegar and the water; cook, stirring, until onion is caramelised.

preparation time *15 minutes*
cooking time *40 minutes* serves *4*
nutritional count per serving *23.6g total fat (7.4g saturated fat); 2378kJ (569 cal); 51.6g carbohydrate; 34.9g protein; 5g fibre*

coppa and ricotta panini

We used coppa in this sandwich, but you can use parma ham or prosciutto, if you prefer. Coppa is a salted and dried sausage made from the neck or shoulder of pork. It is deep red in colour and can be found in both mild and spicy versions; it is more marbled with fat so it's less expensive.

⅓ cup (80g) black olive tapenade
¼ cup (60ml) balsamic vinegar
4 focaccia rolls (440g), halved
240g ricotta cheese
½ teaspoon finely grated lemon rind
1 teaspoon lemon juice
16 slices coppa (240g)
40g baby rocket leaves

1   Combine tapenade with 2 tablespoons of the vinegar in small bowl; spread over bottom half of each roll.
2   Combine cheese with rind and juice in small bowl; spread over tapenade.
3   Top ricotta with coppa and rocket; drizzle with remaining vinegar then top with roll halves.
4   Cook panini in preheated sandwich press until browned lightly and heated through.

preparation time *10 minutes*
cooking time *20 minutes* serves *4*
nutritional count per serving *18.2g total fat (6.7g saturated fat); 2036kJ (487 cal); 51.3g carbohydrate; 27.6g protein; 3g fibre*

turkish chicken club sandwich

⅓ cup (80ml) lime juice
2 tablespoons olive oil
2 teaspoons sumac
2 chicken thigh fillets (400g)
1 large turkish bread (430g)
1 lebanese cucumber (130g), sliced thinly
1 medium tomato (150g), sliced thinly
24 small butter lettuce leaves

CORIANDER AIOLI

½ cup (150g) mayonnaise
1 tablespoon lime juice
1 clove garlic, crushed
2 tablespoons finely chopped fresh coriander

1   Combine juice, oil, sumac and chicken in medium bowl, cover; refrigerate 30 minutes.
2   Meanwhile, make coriander aïoli.
3   Drain chicken; reserve marinade. Cook chicken on heated oiled grill plate (or grill or barbecue) until cooked through, brushing with reserved marinade after turning. Cover; stand 5 minutes then slice thinly.
4   Halve bread horizontally; cut each piece into six slices. Toast slices lightly.
5   Spread each toast slice with aïoli. Layer four toast slices with half the chicken, cucumber, tomato and lettuce, then top with toasts; layer with remaining chicken, cucumber, tomato and lettuce then top with remaining toast. Cut in half to serve, if you like.

CORIANDER AIOLI Combine ingredients in small bowl.

preparation time *15 minutes (plus refrigeration time)*
cooking time *15 minutes* makes *4*
nutritional count per sandwich *32.1g total fat (5.4g saturated fat); 2700kJ (646 cal); 57.5g carbohydrate; 29.6g protein; 4.6g fibre*

1

2

3

4

steak sandwich with tarragon and tomato salsa

Use ciabatta, focaccia or even individual turkish bread for the bread in this recipe if you like.

4 x 125g scotch fillet steaks
2 cloves garlic, crushed
1 tablespoon dijon mustard
1 tablespoon olive oil
8 thick slices bread (320g)
⅓ cup (100g) mayonnaise
40g trimmed watercress

TARRAGON AND TOMATO SALSA

2 cloves garlic, crushed
3 large egg tomatoes (270g), quartered, sliced thinly
½ small red onion (50g), sliced thinly
1 tablespoon finely chopped fresh tarragon

1 Combine beef, garlic, mustard and half the oil in medium bowl.
2 Make tarragon and tomato salsa.
3 Cook beef on heated grill plate (or grill or barbecue) until cooked as desired. Remove from heat, cover; stand 5 minutes.
4 Meanwhile, brush both sides of bread with remaining oil; toast on same grill plate (or grill or barbecue). Spread one side of each slice with mayonnaise; sandwich watercress, beef and salsa between slices.

TARRAGON AND TOMATO SALSA Combine ingredients in medium bowl.

preparation time *15 minutes*
cooking time *15 minutes* serves *4*
nutritional count per serving *21.6g total fat (4.6g saturated fat); 2161kJ (517 cal); 43.3g carbohydrate; 35g protein; 4.2g fibre*

steak sandwich with beetroot relish

While this recipe makes 2 cups of relish, you'll only need about half of it for this recipe. Refrigerate the remaining relish in an airtight glass container for up to 2 weeks.

¼ cup (60ml) light soy sauce
2 cloves garlic, crushed
400g beef rump steak
1 long french bread stick (300g)
175g watercress, trimmed

BEETROOT RELISH

1 tablespoon olive oil
10g butter
1 medium red onion (170g), sliced thinly
2 large beetroots (400g), peeled, grated coarsely
½ cup (125ml) red wine vinegar
1 cup (250ml) water
¾ cup (165g) caster sugar
1 cup (130g) dried cranberries
1½ tablespoons prepared horseradish

1 Combine sauce and garlic in medium bowl with beef. Cover; refrigerate 1 hour.
2 Meanwhile, make beetroot relish.
3 Drain beef; cook on heated oiled grill plate (or grill or barbecue) until cooked as desired. Cover; stand 5 minutes then slice thinly.
4 Cut bread into quarters; slice each quarter in half horizontally. Divide beef among bread bases; top each with ¼ cup of the beetroot relish, a quarter of the watercress and remaining bread pieces.

BEETROOT RELISH Heat oil and butter in large deep saucepan; cook onion, stirring, until soft. Add beetroot; cook, stirring, 5 minutes. Add remaining ingredients; bring to the boil. Reduce heat; simmer, uncovered, about 35 minutes or until relish is thickened.

preparation time *15 minutes (plus refrigeration time)*
cooking time *50 minutes* serves *4*
nutritional count per serving *13.2g total fat (4g saturated fat); 2730kJ (653 cal); 93.9g carbohydrate; 34.3g protein; 7.9g fibre*

1 STEAK SANDWICH WITH TARRAGON AND TOMATO SALSA 2 STEAK SANDWICH WITH BEETROOT RELISH 3 VEGETARIAN LASAGNE [P 388] 4 SPINACH AND RICOTTA-STUFFED CHICKEN PARMIGIANA [P 388]

vegetarian lasagne

3 medium red capsicums (600g)
1 medium eggplant (300g), sliced thinly
1 tablespoon coarse cooking salt
3 medium zucchini (360g), sliced thinly
1 medium kumara (400g), sliced thinly
cooking-oil spray
2 cups (500g) bottled tomato pasta sauce
250g instant lasagne sheets
2½ cups (250g) coarsely grated mozzarella cheese
⅓ cup (25g) coarsely grated parmesan cheese
WHITE SAUCE

40g butter
2 tablespoons plain flour
1¼ cups (310ml) milk
¼ cup (20g) coarsely grated parmesan cheese

1 Preheat grill. Quarter capsicums; discard seeds and membranes. Roast under grill, skin-side up, until skin blisters and blackens. Cover capsicum pieces in plastic or paper for 5 minutes; peel away skin.
2 Place eggplant in colander, sprinkle all over with salt; stand 20 minutes. Rinse eggplant under cold water; drain on absorbent paper.
3 Preheat oven to 200°C/180°C fan-forced.
4 Meanwhile, make white sauce.
5 Place eggplant, zucchini and kumara, in single layer, on oven trays; spray with oil. Roast, uncovered, in oven about 20 minutes or until browned and tender.
6 Oil deep rectangular 2-litre (8-cup) ovenproof dish. Spread ⅔-cup of the pasta sauce into dish; top with a quarter of the lasagne sheets, ⅓-cup of the pasta sauce, eggplant and a third of the mozzarella. Layer cheese with another quarter of the lasagne sheets, ⅓-cup of the pasta sauce, capsicum, and another third of the mozzarella. Layer mozzarella with another quarter of the lasagne sheets, ⅓-cup of the pasta sauce, zucchini, kumara, remaining mozzarella, remaining lasagne sheets and remaining pasta sauce. Top with white sauce, sprinkle with parmesan.
7 Bake lasagne, uncovered, about 30 minutes or until browned lightly. Stand 10 minutes before serving.

WHITE SAUCE Heat butter in small saucepan; add flour, cook stirring, until mixture thickens and bubbles. Gradually stir in milk; stir until mixture boils and thickens. Remove from heat; stir in cheese.

preparation time *40 minutes*
cooking time *1 hour 30 minutes* serves *4*
nutritional count per serving *32.5g total fat (19g saturated fat); 3189kJ (763 cal); 82g carbohydrate; 37.5g protein; 9.9g fibre*

spinach and ricotta-stuffed chicken parmigiana

8 x 100g chicken schnitzels
40g baby spinach leaves
1⅓ cups (320g) ricotta cheese
¼ cup (35g) plain flour
2 eggs
2 tablespoons milk
1½ cups (105g) stale breadcrumbs
vegetable oil, for shallow-frying
1 cup (260g) bottled tomato pasta sauce
1 cup (100g) coarsely grated mozzarella cheese

1 Preheat oven to 200°C/180°C fan-forced.
2 Top each schnitzel with spinach and cheese, leaving 1cm border around edges. Fold in half to secure filling; press down firmly.
3 Coat schnitzels in flour; shake off excess. Dip in combined egg and milk, then in breadcrumbs.
4 Heat oil in large frying pan; cook schnitzels, in batches, until browned and cooked through. Drain on absorbent paper.
5 Place schnitzels in oiled shallow large baking dish; top with sauce and cheese. Roast, uncovered, about 10 minutes or until cheese melts.

preparation time *15 minutes*
cooking time *20 minutes* serves *4*
nutritional count per serving *40.2g total fat (15.3g saturated fat); 3194kJ (764 cal); 31.9g carbohydrate; 67.2g protein; 2.9g fibre*

mushroom risotto

3 cups (750ml) chicken stock
1 litre (4 cups) water
2 tablespoons olive oil
1 small brown onion (80g), chopped finely
10g butter
2 cloves garlic, sliced thinly
100g shiitake mushrooms, sliced thinly
100g button mushrooms, sliced thinly
100g oyster mushrooms, sliced thinly
2 cups (400g) arborio rice
½ cup (125ml) dry white wine
75g baby spinach leaves
⅓ cup (25g) coarsely grated parmesan cheese
⅓ cup (50g) roasted pine nuts
¼ cup finely chopped fresh chives

1 Place stock and the water in large saucepan; bring to the boil. Reduce heat; simmer, covered.
2 Heat oil in large saucepan; cook onion, stirring, until soft. Add butter, garlic and mushrooms; cook, stirring, until vegetables soften. Add rice; stir to coat in mixture. Add wine; cook, stirring until liquid is almost evaporated.
3 Stir 1 cup simmering stock mixture into rice mixture; cook, stirring, over low heat until liquid is absorbed. Continue adding stock mixture in 1-cup batches, stirring, until absorbed after each addition. Total cooking time should be about 35 minutes or until rice is tender.
4 Stir spinach and cheese into risotto. Remove from heat; stir in nuts and half the chives. Serve sprinkled with remaining chives.

preparation time *20 minutes*
cooking time *45 minutes* serves *6*
nutritional count per serving *15.7g total fat (3.3g saturated fat); 1781kJ (426 cal); 55.2g carbohydrate; 16.8g protein; 3.3g fibre*

seafood risotto

1.5 litres (6 cups) chicken stock
2 cups (500ml) water
2 tablespoons olive oil
1 medium leek (350g), sliced thinly
1 fresh small red thai chilli, chopped finely
3 cups (600g) arborio rice
pinch saffron threads
1 cup (250ml) dry white wine
2 tablespoons tomato paste
1.5kg marinara mix
1 cup (120g) frozen peas
2 teaspoons finely grated lemon rind
1 cup loosely packed fresh flat-leaf parsley leaves

1 Combine stock and the water in medium saucepan; bring to the boil. Simmer, covered.
2 Heat oil in large saucepan; cook leek and chilli, stirring, until leek softens. Add rice and saffron; stir to coat in leek mixture. Add wine and paste; cook, stirring, until wine has almost evaporated.
3 Add ½ cup simmering stock to the rice mixture. Cook, stirring, over low heat, until liquid is absorbed. Continue adding stock mixture, in ½ cup batches, stirring until liquid is absorbed after each addition. Total cooking time should be about 30 minutes.
4 Add marinara mix and peas; mix gently. Simmer, covered, 5 minutes. Uncover; simmer until all stock has been absorbed and seafood is tender.
5 Stir in rind and parsley.

preparation time *35 minutes*
cooking time *40 minutes* serves *8*
nutritional count per serving *5.9g total fat (1.1g saturated fat); 1547kJ (370 cal); 63.2g carbohydrate; 8.9g protein; 2.9g fibre*

old-fashioned cherry pie

2¼ cups (335g) plain flour
⅔ cup (110g) icing sugar
185g butter, chopped
1 egg
2 teaspoons iced water, approximately
600g frozen pitted cherries
2 tablespoons cornflour
1 tablespoon lemon juice
⅓ cup (75g) white sugar
½ teaspoon ground cinnamon
20g butter, cut into 1cm cubes, extra
1 egg, beaten lightly, extra

1 Process flour, icing sugar and butter until mixture resembles breadcrumbs. Add egg and enough water to process until ingredients just come together. Knead dough on floured surface until smooth. Cover; refrigerate 30 minutes.
2 Meanwhile, place thawed cherries in a colander over a bowl 30 minutes to drain well.
3 Grease 23cm pie dish. Roll two-thirds of the pastry between sheets of baking paper until large enough to line dish. Lift pastry into dish, smooth over base and side; trim edge. Cover; freeze 10 minutes.
4 Preheat oven to 180°C/160°C fan-forced. Place dish on oven tray. Line pastry case with baking paper, fill with dried beans or rice. Bake 15 minutes; remove paper and beans. Bake 20 minutes or until base is browned and cooked through. Cool.
5 Combine drained cherries, cornflour, juice, ¼ cup of the sugar and cinnamon in medium bowl. Spoon filling into pastry case. Dot with extra butter.
6 Roll out remaining pastry until large enough to cover pie. Brush edges with a little extra egg, place pastry over filling. Press edges together, trim with a knife; crimp edge gently if you like. Brush lightly with egg, sprinkle with remaining sugar.
7 Bake pie about 40 minutes or until browned.

preparation time *30 minutes (plus refrigeration and cooling time)* cooking time *1 hour 15 minutes* serves *8* nutritional count per serving *23g total fat (14.3g saturated fat); 2073kJ (496 cal); 63.6g carbohydrate; 7.1g protein; 2.9g fibre*

pecan pie

1¼ cups (185g) plain flour
⅓ cup (55g) icing sugar
125g cold butter, chopped
1 egg yolk
1 teaspoon water
1 cup (120g) pecans, chopped coarsely
2 tablespoons cornflour
1 cup (220g) firmly packed brown sugar
60g butter, melted
2 tablespoons cream
1 teaspoon vanilla extract
3 eggs
⅓ cup (40g) pecans, extra
2 tablespoons apricot jam, warmed, sieved

1 Process flour, icing sugar and butter until crumbly. Add egg yolk and the water; process until ingredients just come together. Knead dough on floured surface until smooth. Cover; refrigerate 30 minutes.
2 Grease 24cm-round loose-based flan tin. Roll pastry between sheets of baking paper until large enough to line tin. Ease pastry into tin, press into base and side; trim edge. Cover; refrigerate 30 minutes.
3 Preheat oven to 180°C/160°C fan-forced.
4 Place tin on oven tray. Line pastry case with baking paper, fill with dried beans or rice. Bake 10 minutes; remove paper and beans from pie shell. Bake about 5 minutes; cool.
5 Reduce oven to 160°C/140°C fan-forced.
6 Combine chopped nuts and cornflour in medium bowl. Add brown sugar, butter, cream, extract and eggs; stir until combined. Pour mixture into shell, sprinkle with extra nuts.
7 Bake about 45 minutes. Cool; brush pie with jam.

preparation time *25 minutes (plus refrigeration time)* cooking time *1 hour* serves *10* nutritional count per serving *30.8g total fat (12.5g saturated fat); 2048kJ (490 cal); 46.5g carbohydrate; 6.1g protein; 2.1g fibre*

ginger sticky date pudding

1 cup (140g) seeded dried dates
¼ cup (55g) glacé ginger
1 teaspoon bicarbonate of soda
1 cup (250ml) boiling water
50g butter, chopped
½ cup (110g) firmly packed brown sugar
2 eggs
1 cup (150g) self-raising flour
1 teaspoon ground ginger

BUTTERSCOTCH SAUCE

300ml cream
¾ cup (165g) firmly packed brown sugar
75g butter, chopped

1 Preheat oven to 200°C/180°C fan-forced.
Grease deep 20cm-round cake pan; line base with
baking paper.
2 Place dates, ginger, soda and the water in food
processor; stand 5 minutes then add butter and sugar.
Process until mixture is almost smooth. Add eggs,
flour and ginger; process until combined. Pour mixture
into pan.
3 Bake pudding about 45 minutes. Stand in pan
10 minutes; turn onto serving plate.
4 Meanwhile, make butterscotch sauce.
5 Serve pudding warm with sauce.

BUTTERSCOTCH SAUCE Stir ingredients in medium
saucepan over low heat until sauce is smooth.

preparation time *10 minutes*
cooking time *45 minutes* serves *8*
nutritional count per serving *30.1g total fat (19.6g
saturated fat); 2337kJ (559 cal); 65.1g carbohydrate;
4.7g protein; 2.4g fibre*

dark chocolate mud cake

675g dark eating chocolate, chopped
400g unsalted butter, chopped
1½ tablespoons instant coffee granules
1¼ cups (310ml) water
1¼ cups (275g) firmly packed brown sugar
1¾ cups (260g) plain flour
½ cup (75g) self-raising flour
4 eggs
⅓ cup (80ml) coffee-flavoured liqueur

DARK CHOCOLATE GANACHE

½ cup (125ml) cream
400g dark eating chocolate, chopped

1 Preheat oven to 160°C/140°C fan-forced.
Grease deep 19cm-square cake pan; line with
baking paper.
2 Combine chocolate, butter, coffee, the water
and sugar in large saucepan; stir over low heat
until smooth. Cool 15 minutes.
3 Whisk in sifted flours, eggs and liqueur into
chocolate mixture. Pour mixture into pan.
4 Bake cake about 2½ hours. Cool in pan.
5 Meanwhile, make dark chocolate ganache.
6 Turn cake, top-side up, onto plate; spread with
ganache. Top with raspberries, if you like.

DARK CHOCOLATE GANACHE Bring cream to the boil
in small saucepan; remove from heat, add chocolate,
stir until smooth. Refrigerate, stirring occasionally, about
30 minutes or until spreadable.

preparation time *20 minutes (plus cooling time)*
cooking time *2 hours 40 minutes* serves *16*
nutritional count per serving *45.7g total fat (28.3g
saturated fat); 3135kJ (750 cal); 75.3g carbohydrate;
7.8g protein; 1.7g fibre*

gourmet chocolate tart

1½ cups (225g) plain flour
½ cup (110g) caster sugar
140g cold butter, chopped
1 egg, beaten lightly

FILLING

2 eggs
2 egg yolks
¼ cup (55g) caster sugar
250g dark eating chocolate, melted
200g butter, melted

1 Blend or process flour, sugar and butter until crumbly; add egg, process until ingredients just come together. Knead dough on floured surface until smooth. Enclose in plastic wrap; refrigerate 30 minutes.
2 Grease 24cm-round loose-base flan tin. Roll dough between sheets of baking paper until large enough to line tin. Lift dough onto tin; press into side, trim edge, prick base all over with fork. Cover; refrigerate 30 minutes.
3 Preheat oven to 200°C/180°C fan-forced. Place tin on oven tray. Line pastry with baking paper, fill with dried beans or rice. Bake 10 minutes. Remove paper and beans from tin; bake about 5 minutes or until tart shell browns lightly. Cool to room temperature.
4 Reduce oven to 180°C/160°C fan-forced.
5 Make filling; pour into shell.
6 Bake tart about 10 minutes or until filling is set; cool 10 minutes. Refrigerate 1 hour. Serve dusted with cocoa powder, if you like.

FILLING Whisk eggs, egg yolks and sugar in medium heatproof bowl over medium saucepan of simmering water about 15 minutes or until light and fluffy. Gently whisk chocolate and butter into egg mixture.

preparation time *40 minutes (plus refrigeration time)* cooking time *30 minutes (plus refrigeration time)* serves *8* nutritional count per serving *48.1g total fat (32.7g saturated fat); 2959kJ (708 cal); 60.4g carbohydrate; 8g protein; 2.6g fibre*

chocolate caramel slice

½ cup (75g) self-raising flour
½ cup (75g) plain flour
1 cup (80g) desiccated coconut
1 cup (220g) firmly packed brown sugar
125g butter, melted
395g can sweetened condensed milk
30g butter, extra
2 tablespoons golden syrup
200g dark eating chocolate, chopped coarsely
2 teaspoons vegetable oil

1 Preheat oven to 180°C/160°C fan-forced. Grease 20cm x 30cm lamington pan; line with baking paper, extending paper 5cm over long sides.
2 Combine sifted flours, coconut, sugar and butter in medium bowl; press mixture evenly over base of pan. Bake about 15 minutes or until browned lightly.
3 Meanwhile, make caramel filling by combining condensed milk, extra butter and syrup in small saucepan. Stir over medium heat about 15 minutes or until caramel mixture is golden brown; pour over base. Bake 10 minutes; cool.
4 Make topping by combining chocolate and oil in small saucepan; stir over low heat until smooth. Pour warm topping over caramel. Refrigerate 3 hours or overnight.

preparation time *20 minutes (plus cooling and refrigeration time)* cooking time *25 minutes* makes *16* nutritional count per piece *17.7g total fat (11.8g saturated fat); 1492kJ (357 cal); 44.6g carbohydrate; 4.1g protein; 1.2g fibre*

dark chocolate and almond torte

160g dark eating chocolate, chopped coarsely
160g unsalted butter
5 eggs, separated
¾ cup (165g) caster sugar
1 cup (125g) almond meal
⅔ cup (50g) roasted flaked almonds,
    chopped coarsely
⅓ cup (35g) coarsely grated dark eating chocolate
1 cup (140g) vienna almonds

DARK CHOCOLATE GANACHE

125g dark eating chocolate, chopped coarsely
⅓ cup (80ml) thickened cream

1 Preheat oven to 180°C/160°C fan-forced. Grease deep 22cm round cake pan; line base and side with two layers of baking paper.
2 Stir chopped chocolate and butter in small saucepan over low heat until smooth; cool to room temperature.
3 Beat egg yolks and sugar in small bowl with electric mixer until thick and creamy. Transfer to large bowl; fold in chocolate mixture, almond meal, flaked almonds and grated chocolate.
4 Beat egg whites in small bowl with electric mixer until soft peaks form; fold into chocolate mixture, in two batches. Pour mixture into pan.
5 Bake cake about 45 minutes. Stand in pan 15 minutes; turn cake, top-side up, onto wire rack to cool.
6 Meanwhile, make dark chocolate ganache.
7 Spread ganache over cake, decorate cake with vienna almonds; stand 30 minutes before serving.

DARK CHOCOLATE GANACHE Stir ingredients in small saucepan over low heat until smooth.

preparation time *20 minutes (plus standing time)*
cooking time *55 minutes* serves *14*
nutritional count per serving *30.2g total fat (12.7g saturated fat); 1781kJ (426 cal); 30.6g carbohydrate; 7.5g protein; 1.9g fibre*

flourless chocolate dessert cake

100g dark eating chocolate, chopped
100g butter, chopped
2 tablespoons marsala
½ cup (110g) caster sugar
⅔ cup (80g) almond meal
1 tablespoon instant coffee powder
1 tablespoon hot water
3 eggs, separated
2 tablespoons icing sugar

STRAWBERRY COULIS

250g strawberries, hulled
¼ cup (40g) icing sugar

1 Preheat oven to 180°C/160°C fan-forced. Grease deep 20cm-round cake pan; line base and side with baking paper.
2 Stir chocolate and butter in small saucepan over low heat until both are melted.
3 Combine chocolate mixture with marsala, sugar, almond meal and combined coffee and the water in large bowl; beat in egg yolks, one at a time.
4 Beat egg whites in small bowl with electric mixer until soft peaks form; gently fold into chocolate mixture, in two batches. Pour mixture into pan.
5 Bake about 45 minutes; cover with foil during baking if overbrowning. Cool cake in pan. Cover; refrigerate several hours or overnight.
6 Make strawberry coulis.
7 Carefully turn cake onto board; cut into slices with a hot knife. Dust cake with sifted icing sugar; serve with strawberry coulis and whipped cream, if you like.

STRAWBERRY COULIS Blend or process ingredients until mixture is smooth.

preparation time *20 minutes*
cooking time *50 minutes (plus refrigeration time)*
serves *10*
nutritional count per serving *17.1g total fat (7.9g saturated fat); 1179kJ (282 cal); 25.2g carbohydrate; 4.8g protein; 1.6g fibre*

chocolate ganache and raspberry cake

⅓ cup (35g) cocoa powder
⅓ cup (80ml) water
150g dark eating chocolate, melted
150g butter, melted
1⅓ cups (300g) firmly packed brown sugar
1 cup (125g) almond meal
4 eggs, separated
200g dark eating chocolate, chopped coarsely
⅔ cup (160ml) thickened cream
300g raspberries

1 Preheat oven to 160°C/140°C fan-forced. Grease deep 22cm-round cake pan; line base and side with baking paper.
2 Blend sifted cocoa with the water in large bowl until smooth. Stir in melted chocolate, butter, sugar, almond meal and egg yolks.
3 Beat egg whites in small bowl with electric mixer until soft peaks form. Fold egg whites into chocolate mixture, in two batches. Pour mixture into pan.
4 Bake cake about 1¼ hours. Stand in pan 15 minutes; turn, top-side up, onto wire rack to cool.
5 Stir chopped chocolate and cream in small saucepan over low heat until smooth.
6 Place raspberries on top of cake; drizzle chocolate mixture over raspberries. Stand cake at room temperature until chocolate sets.

preparation time *25 minutes*
cooking time *1 hour 25 minutes (plus standing time)*
serves *12*
nutritional count per serving *31.5g total fat (16.1g saturated fat); 2082kJ (498 cal); 45.7g carbohydrate; 7.1g protein; 2.7g fibre*

ice-cream sundae with berry sauce and almond wafers

⅓ cup (75g) firmly packed brown sugar
25g butter
½ cup (125ml) thickened cream
1 cup (150g) frozen mixed berries
500ml vanilla ice-cream
500ml strawberry ice-cream

ALMOND WAFERS

1 egg white
2 tablespoons caster sugar
2 tablespoons plain flour
20g butter, melted
2 tablespoons flaked almonds

1 Make almond wafers.
2 Place sugar, butter and cream in small saucepan; bring to the boil. Reduce heat; simmer, uncovered, stirring, about 5 minutes or until slightly thickened. Remove from heat; stir in berries.
3 Divide both ice-creams among four 1½-cup (375ml) serving glasses; drizzle with berry sauce. Serve with almond wafers.

ALMOND WAFERS Preheat oven 180°C/160°C fan-forced. Grease two oven trays. Beat egg white in small bowl with electric mixer until soft peaks form. Gradually add sugar, beating until dissolved after each addition; fold in flour and butter. Drop rounded teaspoons of mixture 10cm apart on oven trays (about four per tray); sprinkle with nuts. Bake, about 5 minutes or until wafers are browned lightly; cool on trays.

preparation time *20 minutes*
cooking time *10 minutes* serves *4*
nutritional count per serving *31.2g total fat (22.6g saturated fat); 2479kJ (593 cal); 58.7g carbohydrate; 8g protein; 1.4g fibre*

polenta and almond orange cake

2 medium oranges (480g)
⅔ cup (110g) roasted blanched almonds
¾ cup (165g) caster sugar
1 teaspoon baking powder
6 eggs
1 cup (120g) almond meal
1 cup (170g) polenta
50g butter, melted

1 Cover unpeeled whole oranges in medium saucepan with cold water, bring to the boil. Boil, uncovered, 30 minutes; drain. Repeat process with fresh water, boil about 1 hour or until oranges are tender; drain. Cool oranges.
2 Preheat oven to 200°C/180°C fan-forced. Grease deep 22cm-round cake pan; line base and side with baking paper.
3 Blend or process nuts with 1 tablespoon of the sugar until coarse.
4 Trim ends from oranges then cut in half; discard seeds. Blend or process oranges, including rind, with baking powder until mixture is pulpy.
5 Beat eggs with remaining sugar in small bowl with electric mixer until light and fluffy. Transfer to large bowl; fold in nut mixture, almond meal, polenta, butter and orange pulp. Spread mixture into pan.
6 Bake cake about 50 minutes. Cool in pan 5 minutes; turn, top-side up, onto serving plate; serve dusted with sifted icing sugar, if you like.

preparation time *30 minutes (plus cooling time)*
cooking time *2 hours 45 minutes* serves *12*
nutritional count per serving *17g total fat (3.8g saturated fat); 1271kJ (304 cal); 27.8g carbohydrate; 8.8g protein; 2.9g fibre*

orange syrup cake

1 large orange (300g)
2 cups (500ml) water
2 cups (440g) caster sugar
⅔ cup (160ml) brandy
250g unsalted butter, softened
1 cup (220g) caster sugar, extra
4 eggs
1½ cups (225g) self-raising flour
2 tablespoons cornflour

1 Preheat oven to 160°C/140°C fan-forced. Grease deep 22cm round cake pan; line base and side with baking paper.
2 Peel orange. Chop both the peel and the flesh of orange finely; discard seeds.
3 Stir flesh and peel in medium saucepan with the water, sugar and brandy over medium heat until sugar dissolves; bring to the boil. Reduce heat; simmer, uncovered, about 15 minutes or until orange skin is tender. Strain syrup into jug; reserve orange solids separately.
4 Beat butter and extra sugar in small bowl with electric mixer until light and fluffy. Add eggs, one at a time, beating until just combined between additions. Transfer mixture to large bowl; stir in combined sifted flour and cornflour, and reserved orange solids. Pour mixture into pan.
5 Bake cake about 50 minutes.
6 Meanwhile, simmer reserved syrup over heat in small saucepan until thickened slightly.
7 Stand cake in pan 5 minutes; turn, top-side up, onto wire rack set over tray. Pour hot syrup over hot cake; serve warm.

preparation time *25 minutes*
cooking time *1 hour 10 minutes* serves *12*
nutritional count per serving *19.3g total fat (12g saturated fat); 2128kJ (509 cal); 71.5g carbohydrate; 4.4g protein; 1.1g fibre*

rhubarb and almond cakes

½ cup (125ml) milk
¼ cup (40g) blanched almonds, roasted
80g butter, softened
1 teaspoon vanilla extract
½ cup (110g) caster sugar
2 eggs
1 cup (150g) self-raising flour

POACHED RHUBARB

250g trimmed rhubarb, chopped coarsely
¼ cup (60ml) water
½ cup (110g) white sugar

1 Preheat oven to 180°C/160°C fan-forced.
Grease a 6-hole texas (¾-cup/180ml) muffin pan.
2 Make poached rhubarb.
3 Meanwhile, blend or process milk and nuts
until smooth.
4 Beat butter, extract and sugar in small bowl
with electric mixer until light and fluffy. Beat in eggs;
transfer to large bowl. Stir in sifted flour and almond
mixture. Spoon mixture equally among pan holes.
5 Bake cakes 10 minutes. Carefully remove muffin
pan from oven; divide drained rhubarb over ckaes,
bake further 15 minutes.
6 Stand cakes in pan 5 minutes; turn, top-side up,
onto wire rack to cool. Serve warm or cold with
rhubarb syrup.

POACHED RHUBARB Bring ingredients to the boil in
medium saucepan. Reduce heat; simmer, uncovered,
about 10 minutes or until rhubarb is just tender. Drain
rhubarb over medium bowl; reserve rhubarb and
syrup separately.

preparation time *20 minutes*
cooking time *40 minutes* serves *6*
nutritional count per serving *17.6g total fat (8.5g
saturated fat); 1735kJ (415 cal); 55.2g carbohydrate;
7.3g protein; 2.8g fibre*

lime and poppy seed syrup cake

¼ cup (40g) poppy seeds
½ cup (125ml) milk
250g butter, softened
1 tablespoon finely grated lime rind
1¼ cups (275g) caster sugar
4 eggs
2¼ cups (335g) self-raising flour
¾ cup (110g) plain flour
1 cup (240g) sour cream

LIME SYRUP

½ cup (125ml) lime juice
1 cup (250ml) water
1 cup (220g) caster sugar

1 Preheat oven to 180°C/160°C fan-forced.
Grease base and sides of deep 23cm-square
cake pan.
2 Combine poppy seeds and milk in small jug;
soak 10 minutes.
3 Beat butter, rind and sugar in small bowl with
electric mixer until light and fluffy. Add eggs, one
at a time, beating until combined between additions;
transfer mixture to large bowl. Stir in sifted flours,
cream and poppy seed mixture, in two batches.
Spread mixture into pan.
4 Bake cake about 1 hour.
5 Meanwhile, make lime syrup.
6 Stand cake 5 minutes; turn, top-side up, onto wire
rack over tray. Pour hot lime syrup over hot cake.

LIME SYRUP Stir ingredients in small saucepan over heat,
without boiling, until sugar dissolves. Simmer, uncovered,
without stirring, 5 minutes.

preparation time *20 minutes*
cooking time *1 hour* serves *16*
nutritional count per serving *21.9g total fat (13.1g
saturated fat); 1797kJ (430 cal); 51.8g carbohydrate;
5.7g protein; 1.6g fibre*

upside-down toffee date and banana cake

1½ cups (330g) caster sugar
1½ cups (375ml) water
3 star anise
2 medium bananas (400g), sliced thinly
1 cup (140g) dried seeded dates
¾ cup (180ml) water, extra
½ cup (125ml) dark rum
1 teaspoon bicarbonate of soda
60g butter, chopped
½ cup (110g) firmly packed brown sugar
2 eggs
2 teaspoons mixed spice
1 cup (150g) self-raising flour
½ cup mashed banana
300ml thickened cream

1 Preheat oven to 180°C/160°C fan-forced. Grease deep 22cm-round cake pan; line base with baking paper.
2 Stir caster sugar, the water and star anise in medium saucepan over low heat, without boiling, until sugar dissolves. Bring to the boil; boil syrup, uncovered, without stirring, about 5 minutes or until thickened slightly. Strain ½ cup of the syrup into small heatproof jug; reserve to flavour cream. Discard star-anise.
3 To make toffee, continue boiling remaining syrup, uncovered, without stirring, about 10 minutes or until toffee is golden brown. Pour hot toffee into cake pan; top with sliced banana.
4 Combine dates, the extra water and rum in small saucepan; bring to the boil then remove from heat. Stir in soda; stand 5 minutes. Blend or process date mixture with butter and brown sugar until almost smooth. Add eggs, spice and flour; blend or process until just combined. Stir in mashed banana. Pour into pan.
5 Bake cake about 40 minutes. Turn onto serving plate; stand 2 minutes. Remove pan then baking paper.
6 For star anise cream, beat cream in small bowl with electric mixer until firm peaks form. Stir in reserved syrup.
7 Serve cake warm or at room temperature with star anise cream.

preparation time *20 minutes*
cooking time *1 hour 10 minutes* serves *12*
nutritional count per serving *14.5g total fat (9.1g saturated fat); 1726kJ (413 cal); 60.3g carbohydrate; 3.7g protein; 2.3g fibre*

plum and hazelnut upside-down cake

50g butter, chopped
½ cup (110g) firmly packed brown sugar
6 medium plums (680g), halved, stones removed
185g butter, softened, extra
1 cup (220g) firmly packed brown sugar, extra
3 eggs
½ cup (50g) hazelnut meal
½ cup (75g) self-raising flour
½ cup (75g) plain flour

1 Preheat oven to 180°C/160°C fan-forced. Grease deep 22cm-round cake pan; line base with baking paper.
2 Stir butter and sugar in small saucepan over low heat until smooth; pour over cake pan base. Place plums, cut-side down, over pan base.
3 Beat extra butter and extra sugar in small bowl with electric mixer until creamy. Add eggs, one at a time, beating until combined between additions. Transfer mixture to large bowl; stir in hazelnut meal and sifted flours. Spread mixture into pan.
4 Bake cake about 1 hour. Stand in pan 5 minutes; turn onto serving plate.

preparation time *15 minutes*
cooking time *1 hour* serves *8*
nutritional count per serving *30.2g total fat (16.7g saturated fat); 2232kJ (534 cal); 58.4g carbohydrate; 6g protein; 2.8g fibre*

pistachio shortbread mounds

⅔ cup (70g) shelled pistachios, roasted
250g butter, softened
1 cup (160g) icing sugar
1½ cups (225g) plain flour
2 tablespoons rice flour
2 tablespoons cornflour
¾ cup (90g) almond meal
⅓ cup (55g) icing sugar, extra

1 Preheat oven to 160°C/140°C fan-forced.
Grease oven trays; line with baking paper.
2 Coarsely chop half the nuts.
3 Beat butter and sifted icing sugar in small bowl
with electric mixer until light and fluffy. Transfer mixture
to large bowl; stir in sifted flours, almond meal and
chopped nuts.
4 Shape level tablespoons of mixture into mounds;
place about 3cm apart on oven trays. Press one
whole nut on each mound.
5 Bake mounds about 25 minutes. Stand on trays
5 minutes; place on wire racks to cool. Serve dusted
with extra sifted icing sugar.

preparation time *30 minutes*
cooking time *25 minutes* makes *40*
nutritional count per mound *7.3g total fat (3.6g
saturated fat); 485kJ (116 cal); 10.8g carbohydrate;
1.5g protein; 6.6g fibre*

white chocolate macadamia cookies

1½ cups (225g) plain flour
½ teaspoon bicarbonate of soda
¼ cup (55g) caster sugar
⅓ cup (75g) firmly packed brown sugar
125g butter, melted
½ teaspoon vanilla extract
1 egg
180g white eating chocolate, chopped coarsely
¾ cup (105g) roasted macadamias, chopped coarsely

1 Preheat oven to 200°C/180°C fan-forced.
Grease two oven trays; line with baking paper.
2 Sift flour, soda and sugars into large bowl. Stir
in butter, extract and egg then chocolate and nuts.
3 Drop rounded tablespoons of mixture, 5cm apart
on trays. Bake about 10 minutes. Cool on trays.

preparation time *10 minutes*
cooking time *10 minutes* makes *24*
nutritional count per cookie *10.4g total fat (4.9g
saturated fat); 706kJ (169 cal); 16.4g carbohydrate;
2.2g protein; 0.6g fibre*

peanut butter choc-chunk cookies

75g butter, softened
1 teaspoon vanilla extract
¼ cup (55g) caster sugar
¼ cup (55g) firmly packed brown sugar
⅔ cup (190g) smooth peanut butter
1 egg
1 cup (150g) plain flour
½ teaspoon bicarbonate of soda
150g milk eating chocolate, chopped coarsely

1 Preheat oven to 180°C/160°C fan-forced.
Grease two oven trays; line with baking paper.
2 Beat butter, extract and sugars in small bowl
with electric mixer until smooth. Add peanut butter;
beat until combined. Add egg; beat until combined.
Stir in sifted flour and soda, then chocolate.
3 Drop level tablespoons of mixture, about 5cm apart,
onto trays; press down slightly to flatten.
4 Bake cookies about 10 minutes or until beginning
to brown; cool on trays.

preparation time *15 minutes*
cooking time *10 minutes* makes *28*
nutritional count per cookie *7.3g total fat (3g
saturated fat); 531kJ (127 cal); 11.7g carbohydrate;
3.1g protein; 1g fibre*

chocolate melting moments

125g butter, softened
2 tablespoons icing sugar
¾ cup (110g) plain flour
2 tablespoons cornflour
1 tablespoon cocoa powder
¼ cup (85g) chocolate hazelnut spread

1 Preheat oven to 180°C/160°C fan-forced. Grease oven trays; line with baking paper.
2 Beat butter and sifted sugar in small bowl with electric mixer until light and fluffy. Stir in sifted dry ingredients.
3 Spoon mixture into piping bag fitted with 1cm-fluted tube. Pipe stars about 3cm apart on trays.
4 Bake biscuits about 10 minutes; cool on trays. Sandwich biscuits with hazelnut spread.

preparation time *15 minutes*
cooking time *10 minutes* makes *20*
nutritional count per biscuit *6.7g total fat (3.8g saturated fat); 410kJ (98 cal); 8.5g carbohydrate; 1g protein; 0.3g fibre*

mini florentines

¾ cup (120g) sultanas
2 cups (80g) corn flakes
¾ cup (60g) roasted flaked almonds
½ cup (100g) red glacé cherries
⅔ cup (160ml) sweetened condensed milk
60g white eating chocolate, melted
60g dark eating chocolate, melted

1 Preheat oven to 180°C/160°C fan-forced. Grease oven trays; line with baking paper.
2 Combine sultanas, corn flakes, nuts, cherries and condensed milk in medium bowl.
3 Drop level tablespoons of mixture about 5cm apart on trays. Bake 5 minutes; cool on trays.
4 Spread half the florentine bases with white chocolate; spread remaining half with dark chocolate. Run fork through chocolate to make waves; allow to set at room temperature.

preparation time *10 minutes (plus standing time)*
cooking time *5 minutes* makes *25*
nutritional count per biscuit *3.7g total fat (1.5g saturated fat); 451kJ (108 cal); 16.4g carbohydrate; 1.8g protein; 0.6g fibre*

pistachio and cranberry biscotti

60g unsalted butter, softened
1 teaspoon vanilla extract
1 cup (220g) caster sugar
2 eggs
1¾ cups (260g) plain flour
½ teaspoon bicarbonate of soda
1 cup (130g) dried cranberries
¾ cup (110g) coarsely chopped roasted pistachios
1 egg, extra
1 tablespoon water
2 tablespoons caster sugar, extra

1 Beat butter, extract and sugar in medium bowl until combined. Beat in eggs, one at a time. Stir in sifted flours and soda then cranberries and nuts. Cover; refrigerate 1 hour.
2 Preheat oven to 180°C/160°C fan-forced. Grease oven tray.
3 Knead dough on floured surface until smooth but still sticky. Halve dough; shape each half into 30cm log. Place logs on oven tray.
4 Combine extra egg with the water in small bowl. Brush egg mixture over logs; sprinkle with extra sugar. Bake 20 minutes or until firm; cool 3 hours or overnight.
5 Preheat oven to 160°C/140°C fan-forced.
6 Using serrated knife, cut logs diagonally into 1cm slices. Place slices on ungreased oven trays. Bake about 15 minutes or until dry and crisp, turning halfway through baking time; cool on wire racks.

preparation time *20 minutes (plus refrigeration and cooling time)* cooking time *40 minutes* makes *60*
nutritional count per biscotti *2.1g total fat (0.7g saturated fat); 259kJ (62 cal); 9.2g carbohydrate; 1.2g protein; 0.4g fibre*

very berry cupcakes

125g butter, softened
½ teaspoon vanilla extract
⅔ cup (150g) caster sugar
2 eggs
1 cup (150g) dried mixed berries
½ cup (70g) slivered almonds
⅔ cup (100g) plain flour
⅓ cup (50g) self-raising flour
¼ cup (60ml) milk

SUGARED FRUIT

150g fresh blueberries
120g fresh raspberries
1 egg white, beaten lightly
2 tablespoons vanilla sugar

CREAM CHEESE FROSTING

30g butter, softened
80g cream cheese, softened
1½ cups (240g) icing sugar

1 Prepare sugared fruit.
2 Preheat oven to 160°C/140°C fan-forced. Line 12-hole (⅓-cup/80ml) muffin pan with paper cases.
3 Beat butter, extract, sugar and eggs in small bowl with electric mixer until light and fluffy.
4 Stir in fruit and nuts, then sifted flours and milk. Divide mixture among cases; smooth surface.
5 Bake about 35 minutes. Turn onto wire rack to cool.
6 Make cream cheese frosting.
7 Spread cakes with frosting; top with sugared fruit.

SUGARED FRUIT Brush each berry lightly with egg white; roll in sugar. Place fruit on baking-paper-lined tray. Leave about 1 hour or until sugar is dry.

CREAM CHEESE FROSTING Beat butter and cheese in small bowl with electric mixer until light and fluffy; gradually beat in sifted icing sugar.

preparation time *25 minutes*
cooking time *35 minutes* makes *12*
nutritional count per cupcake *17.4g total fat (9.1g saturated fat); 1689kJ (404 cal); 55.3g carbohydrate; 5.1g protein; 2.5g fibre*

turkish delight cupcakes

60g white eating chocolate, chopped roughly
2 tablespoons rosewater
½ cup (125ml) water
⅓ cup (45g) pistachios
90g butter, softened
1 cup (220g) firmly packed brown sugar
2 eggs
⅔ cup (100g) self-raising flour
2 tablespoons plain flour

DECORATIONS

⅔ cup (90g) coarsely chopped pistachio nuts
300g white eating chocolate, melted
900g turkish delight, chopped

1 Preheat oven to 180°C/160°C fan-forced. Line 12-hole (⅓-cup/80ml) muffin pan with paper cases.
2 Stir chocolate, rosewater and the water in small saucepan over low heat until smooth.
3 Blend or process nuts until fine.
4 Beat butter, sugar and eggs in small bowl with electric mixer until combined. Fold in sifted flours, ground pistachios and warm chocolate mixture. Divide mixture among cases.
5 Bake about 25 minutes. Turn onto wire rack to cool.
6 Cut a 3cm deep hole in the centre of each cake; fill with a few chopped nuts. Drizzle with a little chocolate; replace lids.
7 Decorate cakes with pieces of turkish delight and chopped nuts dipped in chocolate.

preparation time *25 minutes*
cooking time *30 minutes* makes *12*
nutritional count per cupcake *22.8g total fat (11.3g saturated fat); 2629kJ (629 cal); 97.6g carbohydrate; 7g protein; 1.4g fibre*

1 VERY BERRY CUPCAKES 2 TURKISH DELIGHT CUPCAKES
3 LEMON MERINGUE CUPCAKES [P 404]
4 CARROT CUPCAKES WITH MAPLE FROSTING [P 404]

1

2

3

4

lemon meringue cupcakes

125g butter, softened
2 teaspoons finely grated lemon rind
⅔ cup (150g) caster sugar
2 eggs
⅓ cup (80ml) milk
¾ cup (60g) desiccated coconut
1¼ cups (185g) self-raising flour

LEMON CURD

4 egg yolks
⅓ cup (75g) caster sugar
2 teaspoons finely grated lemon rind
¼ cup (60ml) lemon juice
40g butter

COCONUT MERINGUE

4 egg whites
1 cup (220g) caster sugar
1⅓ cups (95g) shredded coconut, chopped finely

1   Make lemon curd.
2   Preheat oven to 180°C/160°C fan-forced. Line
12-hole (⅓-cup/80ml) muffin pan with paper cases.
3   Beat butter, rind, sugar and eggs in small bowl
with electric mixer until light and fluffy. Stir in milk and
coconut, then sifted flour. Divide mixture among cases;
smooth surface.
4   Bake about 20 minutes. Turn onto wire rack to cool.
5   Increase oven to 220°C/200°C fan-forced.
6   Cut a 2cm deep hole in the centre of each cake,
fill with curd; discard cake tops.
7   Make coconut meringue; spoon into a piping bag
fitted with a 1cm plain tube. Pipe meringue on top of
each cake; place cakes on oven tray. Bake 5 minutes
or until meringue is browned lightly.

LEMON CURD Place ingredients in small heatproof bowl
over small saucepan of simmering water, stirring constantly,
until mixture thickens slightly and coats back of a spoon.
Remove from heat. Cover tightly; refrigerate until cold.

COCONUT MERINGUE Beat egg whites in small bowl
with electric mixer until soft peaks form; gradually add
sugar, beating until sugar dissolves. Fold in coconut.

preparation time *30 minutes*
cooking time *25 minutes* makes *12*
nutritional count per cupcake *22.9g total fat (15.9g
saturated fat); 1810kJ (433 cal); 49.5g carbohydrate;
6g protein; 2.5g fibre*

carrot cupcakes with maple frosting

½ cup (125ml) vegetable oil
3 eggs
1½ cups (225g) self-raising flour
1 cup (220g) firmly packed brown sugar
2 teaspoons mixed spice
2 cups (480g) firmly packed coarsely grated carrot
¾ cup (90g) coarsely chopped roasted pecans
6 roasted pecans, halved

MAPLE FROSTING

30g butter, softened
80g cream cheese, softened
2 tablespoons maple syrup
1¼ cups (200g) icing sugar

1   Preheat oven to 180°C/160°C fan-forced. Line
12-hole (⅓-cup/80ml) muffin pan with paper cases.
2   Stir oil, eggs, sifted flour, sugar and spice in medium
bowl until combined. Stir in carrot and chopped nuts.
Divide mixture among paper cases.
3   Bake about 30 minutes. Stand 5 minutes; turn,
top-side up, onto wire rack to cool.
4   Meanwhile, make maple frosting.
5   Spread frosting over cupcakes; top each with a nut.

MAPLE FROSTING Beat butter, cream cheese and
syrup in small bowl with electric mixer until light and
fluffy; gradually beat in sifted icing sugar until frosting
is spreadable.

preparation time *30 minutes*
cooking time *30 minutes* makes *12*
nutritional count per cupcake *22.4g total fat (4.8g
saturated fat); 1848kJ (442 cal); 53.4g carbohydrate;
5.4g protein; 2.9g fibre*

apple and pecan streusel muffins

4 medium apples (600g)
20g butter
⅓ cup (75g) firmly packed brown sugar
2 cups (300g) self-raising flour
¾ cup (165g) caster sugar
1 cup (120g) coarsely chopped roasted pecans
¾ cup (180ml) buttermilk
90g butter, melted
1 egg, beaten lightly

STREUSEL TOPPING

⅓ cup (50g) plain flour
2 tablespoons self-raising flour
¼ cup (55g) firmly packed brown sugar
½ teaspoon mixed spice
80g butter, chopped coarsely

1 Make streusel topping.
2 Preheat oven to 180°C/160°C fan-forced.
Grease two 6-hole texas (¾-cup/180ml) muffin pans.
3 Peel, core and quarter apples; slice thinly. Melt butter
in large frying pan; cook apple, stirring, about 5 minutes
or until browned lightly. Add brown sugar; cook, stirring,
about 5 minutes or until mixture thickens slightly.
4 Sift flour into large bowl; stir in remaining ingredients
(do not overmix, the batter should be lumpy).
5 Spoon mixture into pan holes; top with apple
mixture. Coarsely grate streusel topping over muffins.
6 Bake about 35 minutes. Stand in pan 5 minutes;
turn, top-side up, onto wire rack to cool.

STREUSEL TOPPING Process ingredients until they come
together. Enclose in plastic wrap; freeze about 1 hour
or until firm.

preparation time *20 minutes (plus freezing time)*
cooking time *45 minutes* makes *12*
nutritional count per muffin *21.3g total fat (9.4g
saturated fat); 1793kJ (429 cal); 52.5g carbohydrate;
5.5g protein; 2.7g fibre*

citrus poppy seed muffins

125g softened butter, chopped
2 teaspoons finely grated lemon rind
2 teaspoons finely grated lime rind
2 teaspoons finely grated orange rind
⅔ cup (150g) caster sugar
2 eggs, beaten lightly
2 cups (300g) self-raising flour
½ cup (125ml) milk
2 tablespoons poppy seeds
1 medium orange (240g)
icing sugar, for dusting

1 Preheat oven to 180°C/160°C fan-forced.
Grease 12-hole (⅓-cup/80ml) muffin pan.
2 Beat butter, rinds, caster sugar, egg, sifted flour
and milk in medium bowl with electric mixer until
just combined. Increase speed to medium; beat until
mixture is just changed in colour; stir in poppy seeds.
Divide mixture among pan holes.
3 Bake muffins about 20 minutes. Stand in pan for a
few minutes; turn onto wire rack.
4 Peel rind thinly from orange, avoiding any white pith.
Cut rind into thin strips. To serve, dust muffins with icing
sugar; top with orange strips.

preparation time *15 minutes*
cooking time *20 minutes* makes *12*
nutritional count per muffin *11g total fat (6.3g
saturated fat); 1037kJ (248 cal); 32g carbohydrate;
4.5g protein; 1.7g fibre*

roasted stone fruit with caramel

60g butter
½ cup (110g) firmly packed brown sugar
1 vanilla bean, halved lengthways
2 medium peaches (300g)
2 medium nectarines (340g)
2 medium apricots (100g)
2 medium plums (220g)

1 Preheat oven to 200°C/180°C fan-forced.
2 Combine butter, sugar and vanilla bean in large shallow ovenproof dish; place in oven until butter is melted.
3 Meanwhile, halve peaches, nectarines and apricots; remove stones, leave plums whole. Place fruit in dish, cut-side up; bake about 1 hour, turning fruit frequently and basting occasionally with caramel mixture, or until fruit is browned and tender.
4 Serve fruit drizzled with remaining caramel mixture.

preparation time *15 minutes*
cooking time *1 hour* serves *4*
nutritional count per serving *12.5g total fat (8.1g saturated fat); 1225kJ (293 cal); 41g carbohydrate; 2g protein; 4.1g fibre*

runny chocolate fruit puddings

½ cup (160g) bottled fruit mince
50g dark eating chocolate (70% cocoa solids), chopped coarsely
150g butter, chopped coarsely
3 eggs
⅓ cup (75g) firmly packed brown sugar
½ cup (75g) plain flour
¼ cup (35g) self-raising flour
1 tablespoon cocoa powder

CHOCOLATE RUM SAUCE

150g dark eating chocolate (70% cocoa solids), chopped coarsely
⅓ cup (80ml) cream
2 tablespoons dark rum

1 Spoon fruit mince into 6 holes of 1 tablespoon (20ml) ice-cube tray; freeze for 3 hours.
2 Preheat oven to 200°C/180°C fan-forced. Grease six 1-cup (250ml) pudding moulds.
3 Stir chocolate and butter in small saucepan over low heat until smooth. Cool 10 minutes.
4 Beat eggs and sugar in small bowl with electric mixer until thick and creamy. Transfer mixture to medium bowl; fold in sifted flours and cocoa, then chocolate mixture.
5 Spoon pudding mixture into moulds. Remove frozen fruit mince cubes from tray; press one cube into centre of each pudding.
6 Bake puddings 12 minutes.
7 Meanwhile, make chocolate rum sauce.
8 Serve puddings drizzled with sauce.

CHOCOLATE RUM SAUCE Stir ingredients in small saucepan over low heat until smooth.

preparation time *20 minutes (plus freezing time)*
cooking time *15 minutes* serves *6*
nutritional count per serving *39.6g total fat (24.2g saturated fat); 2704kJ (647 cal); 60.8g carbohydrate; 8g protein; 2g fibre*

fruity almond pistachio slice

¾ cup (180ml) sweetened condensed milk
125g butter, chopped
2 teaspoons grated lemon rind
1½ cups (150g) plain sweet biscuit crumbs
½ cup (125g) coarsely chopped red glacé cherries
½ cup (150g) coarsely chopped glacé figs
½ cup (125g) coarsely chopped glacé peaches
⅓ cup (55g) coarsely chopped almond kernels, roasted
⅓ cup (50g) coarsely chopped pistachios, roasted
¾ cup (65g) desiccated coconut
100g dark eating chocolate, melted
60g butter, melted, extra
1 tablespoon coarsely chopped almond kernels, extra
1 tablespoon coarsely chopped pistachios, extra

1 Grease 19cm x 29cm rectangular slice pan; line base and two opposite sides with baking paper.
2 Stir condensed milk, butter and rind in medium saucepan over heat until butter is melted. Stir in biscuit crumbs, fruit, nuts and coconut. Press mixture evenly over base of pan.
3 Spread with combined chocolate and extra butter, sprinkle with extra nuts; refrigerate until set.

preparation time *20 minutes (plus refrigeration time)*
cooking time *5 minutes* makes *24*
nutritional count per piece *14.2g total fat (7.7g saturated fat); 995kJ (238 cal); 24.2g carbohydrate; 2.9g protein; 1.2g fibre*

banana bread

90g unsalted butter, softened
1 teaspoon vanilla extract
1 cup (220g) firmly packed brown sugar
2 eggs
1 cup mashed banana
1 cup (150g) plain flour
1 cup (150g) self-raising flour

1 Preheat oven to 180°C/160°C fan-forced. Grease 14cm x 21cm loaf pan; line base and long sides with baking paper, extending paper 5cm above long sides.
2 Beat butter, extract and sugar in small bowl with electric mixer until light and fluffy. Beat in eggs, one at a time. Transfer to large bowl; stir in banana then sifted flours, in two batches. Spread into pan.
3 Cover pan with pleated foil; bake 40 minutes. Uncover, bake 30 minutes. Stand 5 minutes; cool on wire rack.

preparation time *10 minutes*
cooking time *1 hour 10 minutes* makes *12 slices*
nutritional count per slice *9.5g total fat (5.6g saturated fat); 1296kJ (309 cal); 49.7g carbohydrate; 5.1g protein; 1.7g fibre*

crème brûlée

1 vanilla bean
3 cups (750ml) thickened cream
6 egg yolks
¼ cup (55g) caster sugar
¼ cup (40g) pure icing sugar

1 Preheat oven to 180°C/160°C fan-forced. Grease six ½-cup (125ml) ovenproof dishes.
2 Split vanilla bean in half lengthways; scrape seeds into medium heatproof bowl. Heat pod with cream in small saucepan, without boiling.
3 Add egg yolks and caster sugar to seeds in bowl; gradually whisk in hot cream mixture. Set bowl over medium saucepan of simmering water; stir over heat about 10 minutes or until custard mixture thickens slightly and coats the back of a spoon; discard pod.
4 Place dishes in large baking dish; divide custard among dishes. Add enough boiling water to baking dish to come halfway up sides of ovenproof dishes. Bake, uncovered, in oven about 20 minutes or until custard sets. Remove custards from dish; cool. Cover; refrigerate overnight.
5 Preheat grill.
6 Place custards in shallow flameproof dish filled with ice cubes; sprinkle custards evenly with sifted icing sugar. Using finger, spread sugar over the surface of each custard, pressing in gently; grill until tops of crème brûlée caramelise.

preparation time *15 minutes (plus refrigeration time)*
cooking time *40 minutes* serves *6*
nutritional count per serving *52.1g total fat (32.3g saturated fat); 2358kJ (564 cal); 19.8g carbohydrate; 5.8g protein; 8g fibre*

new york cheesecake

250g plain sweet biscuits
125g butter, melted

FILLING

750g cream cheese, softened
2 teaspoons finely grated orange rind
1 teaspoon finely grated lemon rind
1 cup (220g) caster sugar
3 eggs
¾ cup (180g) sour cream
¼ cup (60ml) lemon juice

SOUR CREAM TOPPING

1 cup (240g) sour cream
2 tablespoons caster sugar
2 teaspoons lemon juice

1 Process biscuits until fine. Add butter, process until combined. Press mixture over base and side of 24cm springform tin. Place tin on oven tray; refrigerate 30 minutes.
2 Preheat oven to 180°C/160°C fan-forced.
3 Make filling by beating cheese, rinds and sugar in medium bowl with electric mixer until smooth. Beat in eggs, one at a time, then cream and juice. Pour filling into tin.
4 Bake cheesecake 1¼ hours. Remove from oven; cool 15 minutes.
5 Make sour cream topping by combining ingredients in small bowl; spread over cheesecake.
6 Bake cheesecake further 20 minutes; cool in oven with door ajar.
7 Refrigerate cheesecake 3 hours or overnight.

preparation time *20 minutes*
cooking time *1 hour 35 minutes (plus cooling and refrigeration time)* serves *12*
nutritional count per serving *47.8g total fat (30.1g saturated fat); 2587kJ (619 cal); 39g carbohydrate; 9.2g protein; 0.4g fibre*

macadamia and maple tarts

1¼ cups (185g) plain flour
¼ cup (55g) caster sugar
125g cold butter, chopped coarsely
1 egg
½ cup (110g) firmly packed brown sugar
1 tablespoon cornflour
2 tablespoons maple syrup
25g butter, melted
2 eggs
2 tablespoons cream
1 teaspoon finely grated orange rind
1 cup (140g) unsalted macadamias
2 teaspoons of icing sugar

1   Process flour, sugar and butter until crumbly. Add egg; process until combined. Knead on floured surface until smooth. Cover; refrigerate 30 minutes.
2   Divide pastry into six portions. Roll portions, one at a time, between sheets of baking paper into rounds large enough to line six deep 10cm-round loose-based flan tins. Lift rounds into tins; press into sides, trim edges. Prick bases all over with fork. Refrigerate 30 minutes.
3   Preheat oven to 200°C/180°C fan-forced.
4   Place tins on oven tray; line each with baking paper then fill with dried beans or uncooked rice. Bake about 10 minutes. Remove paper and beans from tins; bake further 5 minutes. Cool pastry cases.
5   Reduce oven to 160°C/140°C fan-forced.
6   Combine brown sugar and flour in medium bowl; whisk in syrup, butter, eggs, cream and rind. Divide nuts among pastry cases; pour over maple mixture.
7   Bake tarts about 25 minutes; cool. Refrigerate for 30 minutes. Serve tarts dusted with sifted icing sugar.

preparation time *30 minutes (plus refrigeration time)* cooking time *40 minutes* makes *6*
nutritional count per serving *53g total fat (22.4g saturated fat); 3365kJ (805 cal); 70.8g carbohydrate; 10.5g protein; 3.1g fibre*

lemon tart

1¼ cups (185g) plain flour
⅓ cup (55g) icing sugar
¼ cup (30g) almond meal
125g cold butter, chopped
1 egg yolk

LEMON FILLING

1 tablespoon finely grated lemon rind
½ cup (125ml) lemon juice
5 eggs
¾ cup (165g) caster sugar
1 cup (250ml) thickened cream

1   Process flour, icing sugar, almond meal and butter until combined. Add egg yolk, process until ingredients just come together. Knead on floured surface until smooth. Cover; refrigerate 30 minutes.
2   Roll pastry between sheets of baking paper until large enough to line 24cm-round loose-based flan tin. Lift pastry into tin; press into side, trim edge. Cover; refrigerate 30 minutes.
3   Preheat oven to 200°C/180°C fan-forced.
4   Place flan tin on oven tray. Line pastry case with baking paper, fill with dried beans or rice. Bake 15 minutes. Remove paper and beans; bake about 10 minutes or until browned lightly.
5   Meanwhile, whisk ingredients for lemon filling in medium bowl; stand 5 minutes.
6   Reduce oven to 180°C/160°C fan-forced.
7   Pour lemon filling into pastry case; bake about 30 minutes or until filling has set slightly. Cool.
8   Refrigerate tart until cold. Serve dusted with sifted icing sugar, if you like.

preparation time *30 minutes (plus refrigeration time)* cooking time *55 minutes* serves *8*
nutritional count per serving *30.7g total fat (17.4g saturated fat); 2040kJ (488 cal); 45.9g carbohydrate; 8.6g protein; 1.3g fibre*

lime curd tart

1¼ cups (185g) plain flour
½ cup (80g) icing sugar
¼ cup (20g) desiccated coconut
125g cold unsalted butter
¼ cup (60ml) iced water, approximately
1 cup (50g) flaked coconut

LIME CURD

3 eggs
4 egg yolks
2 teaspoons finely grated lime rind
½ cup (125ml) lime juice
1 cup (220g) caster sugar
200g unsalted butter, chopped

1 Process flour, sugar, coconut and butter until crumbly; add enough of the water to make ingredients come together. Knead dough gently on floured surface until smooth. Wrap in plastic; refrigerate 30 minutes.
2 Grease 24cm-round loose-based flan tin. Roll pastry between sheets of baking paper until large enough to line tin. Ease pastry into tin, press into base and side; trim, prick base with fork. Cover; refrigerate 30 minutes.
3 Preheat oven to 200°C/180°C fan-forced.
4 Place tin on oven tray. Line pastry with baking paper; fill with dried beans or uncooked rice. Bake 15 minutes. Remove paper and beans from pastry case; bake about 10 minutes; cool.
5 Meanwhile, make lime curd.
6 Pour lime curd into pastry case. Refrigerate 2 hours before serving sprinkled with coconut.

LIME CURD Stir eggs, yolks, rind, juice, sugar and butter in medium saucepan over medium heat, without boiling, about 15 minutes or until mixture coats the back of a spoon. Strain lime curd through sieve into medium bowl; stand 10 minutes.

preparation time *20 minutes (plus refrigeration time)* cooking time *25 minutes* serves *10*
nutritional count per serving *35.4g total fat (22.9g saturated fat); 2178kJ (521 cal); 44.2g carbohydrate; 6g protein; 1.8g fibre*

chocolate raspberry tart

1¼ cups (185g) plain flour
½ cup (80g) icing sugar
125g cold unsalted butter, chopped coarsely
¼ cup (60ml) iced water, approximately
¾ cup (240g) raspberry jam
120g raspberries

CHOCOLATE FILLING

200g dark eating chocolate, chopped finely
25g unsalted butter, melted
⅔ cup (160ml) cream, warmed

1 Process flour, icing sugar and butter until crumbly; add enough of the water to make ingredients come together. Knead dough gently on floured surface until smooth. Wrap in plastic; refrigerate 30 minutes.
2 Grease 12.5cm x 35cm (or 24cm-round) loose-based flan tin. Roll pastry between sheets of baking paper until large enough to line tin. Ease pastry into tin, press into base and side; trim edge, prick base with fork. Cover; refrigerate 30 minutes.
3 Preheat oven to 200°C/180°C fan-forced.
4 Place tin on oven tray. Line pastry with baking paper; fill with dried beans or uncooked rice. Bake 15 minutes. Remove paper and beans from pastry case; bake about 10 minutes. Spread jam over pastry base; return to oven 2 minutes. Cool.
5 Make chocolate filling; pour into pastry case. Refrigerate 2 hours.
6 Just before serving, top tart with raspberries.

CHOCOLATE FILLING Whisk ingredients in medium bowl until smooth.

preparation time *20 minutes (plus refrigeration time)* cooking time *25 minutes* serves *12*
nutritional count per serving *21g total fat (13.4g saturated fat); 1559kJ (373 cal); 42.4g carbohydrate; 3g protein; 1.6g fibre*

jaffa rocky road

3 slices (60g) glacé orange, chopped finely
200g white marshmallows, chopped coarsely
½ cup (70g) unsalted pistachios, chopped coarsely
250g milk eating chocolate, chopped coarsely
100g dark eating chocolate, chopped coarsely
60g butter

1 Grease deep 19cm-square cake pan; line base
and two opposite sides with baking paper, extending
paper 5cm above sides.
2 Combine orange, marshmallow and nuts in large bowl.
3 Stir chocolates and butter in medium heatproof
bowl, over medium saucepan of simmering water until
smooth. Pour chocolate mixture over orange mixture;
stir until combined.
4 Spoon rocky road mixture into pan; refrigerate
until set. Remove rocky road from pan before cutting
into squares.

preparation time *15 minutes (plus refrigeration time)*
cooking time *5 minutes* makes *16*
nutritional count per piece *11.4g total fat (6g
saturated fat); 932kJ (223 cal); 26.8g carbohydrate;
3g protein; 0.6g fibre*

hazelnut brownies

125g butter
200g dark eating chocolate
½ cup (110g) caster sugar
2 eggs, beaten lightly
1¼ cups (185g) plain flour
½ cup (70g) roasted hazelnuts, chopped coarsely
1 cup (190g) white Choc Bits

1 Preheat oven to 180°C/160°C fan-forced.
Grease deep 19cm-square cake pan; line base
and two opposite sides with baking paper, extending
paper 5cm above sides.
2 Melt butter and chocolate in medium saucepan
over low heat. Stir in sugar; cook, stirring, 5 minutes.
Cool 10 minutes.
3 Stir in egg and sifted flour then nuts and Choc Bits.
Spread mixture into pan.
4 Bake brownies about 30 minutes. Cool in pan
before cutting into squares. Serve dusted with icing
sugar, if you like.

preparation time *15 minutes*
cooking time *25 minutes* makes *9*
nutritional count per brownie *30g total fat (15.5g
saturated fat); 2174kJ (520 cal); 54.7g carbohydrate;
7.2g protein; 2.1g fibre*

1 JAFFA ROCKY ROAD 2 HAZELNUT BROWNIES
3 BANANA SPLIT [P 414] 4 BERRY YOGURT MUFFINS [P 414]

banana split

4 medium bananas (800g), halved lengthways
2 tablespoons brown sugar
100g dark eating chocolate
300ml thickened cream
1 tablespoon dark rum
4 scoops (240ml) vanilla ice-cream
4 scoops (240ml) chocolate ice-cream
⅔ cup (80g) coarsely chopped roasted pecans
⅓ cup (25g) toasted shredded coconut

1 Preheat grill.
2 Place bananas, cut-sides up, on oven tray; sprinkle with sugar. Grill about 3 minutes or until sugar melts.
3 Meanwhile, melt chocolate with 2 tablespoons of the cream in small bowl set over small saucepan of simmering water.
4 Beat remaining cream with rum in small bowl with electric mixer until soft peaks form.
5 Place 2 banana halves in each of four dishes; top each with a scoop of the vanilla and chocolate ice-cream. Top each with cream; drizzle with chocolate then sprinkle with nuts and coconut.

preparation time *20 minutes*
cooking time *10 minutes* serves *4*
nutritional count per serving *60.1g total fat (31.7g saturated fat); 3618kJ (865 cal); 65.7g carbohydrate; 9.9g protein; 5.8g fibre*

berry yogurt muffins

1½ cups (225g) self-raising flour
⅓ cup (30g) rolled oats
3 eggs
¾ cup (165g) firmly packed brown sugar
¾ cup (200g) yogurt
⅓ cup (80ml) vegetable oil
180g fresh or frozen berries

1 Preheat oven to 200°C/180°C fan-forced. Grease 6-hole texas (¾-cup/180ml) muffin pan.
2 Combine sifted flour with oats in medium bowl. Stir in eggs, sugar, yogurt and oil; add berries, stir gently into muffin mixture. Spoon mixture into pan holes.
3 Bake muffins 20 minutes. Stand in pan 5 minutes; turn, top-side up, onto wire rack to cool.

preparation time *10 minutes*
cooking time *20 minutes* makes *6*
nutritional count per muffin *16.9g total fat (3.2g saturated fat); 1806kJ (432 cal); 58.8g carbohydrate; 9.7g protein; 2.5g fibre*

pear and almond friands

6 egg whites
185g butter, melted
1 cup (120g) almond meal
1½ cups (240g) icing sugar
¾ cup (110g) plain flour
1 small pear (180g), peeled, cored, chopped finely
¼ cup (20g) flaked almonds

1 Preheat oven to 200°C/180°C fan-forced. Grease 12-hole (⅓-cup/80ml) muffin pan.
2 Whisk egg whites in medium bowl until frothy. Add butter, meal, sifted icing sugar and flour, then pear; stir until combined. Place ¼-cups of mixture into pan holes; sprinkle with nuts.
3 Bake friands 20 minutes. Stand in pan 5 minutes; turn, top-side up, onto wire rack to cool.

preparation time *15 minutes*
cooking time *25 minutes* makes *12*
nutritional count per friand *19.2g total fat (8.8g saturated fat); 1300kJ (311 cal); 28.8g carbohydrate; 5.3g protein; 1.6g fibre*

coffee and walnut friands

1¼ cups (125g) roasted walnuts
2 teaspoons instant coffee granules
2 teaspoons boiling water
6 egg whites
185g butter, melted
1½ cups (240g) icing sugar
½ cup (75g) plain flour
24 whole coffee beans

1   Preheat oven to 200°C/180°C fan-forced.
Grease 12-hole (½-cup/125ml) oval friand pan.
2   Process nuts until ground finely.
3   Stir coffee and the water in small jug until dissolved.
4   Whisk egg whites in medium bowl with fork until
combined. Add butter, sifted icing sugar and flour,
ground walnuts and coffee mixture; stir until combined.
Divide mixture among pans; top each friand with two
coffee beans.
5   Bake friands 20 minutes. Stand in pan 5 minutes;
turn, top-side up, onto wire rack to cool.

preparation time *15 minutes*
cooking time *20 minutes* makes *12*
nutritional count per friand *19.9g total fat (8.8g*
saturated fat); 1237kJ (296 cal); 24.9g carbohydrate;
4.1g protein; 0.9g fibre

VARIATION

HAZELNUT AND COFFEE FRIANDS Omit the walnuts
and replace with 125g hazelnut meal.

lemon and coconut friands

6 egg whites
185g butter, melted
1 cup (100g) hazelnut meal
1½ cups (240g) icing sugar
½ cup (75g) plain flour
2 teaspoons finely grated lemon rind
1 tablespoon lemon juice
¼ cup (20g) desiccated coconut
⅓ cup (15g) flaked coconut

1   Preheat oven to 200°C/180°C fan-forced.
Grease 12-hole (⅓-cup/80ml) muffin pan.
2   Whisk egg whites in medium bowl until frothy.
Add butter, hazelnut meal, sifted icing sugar and flour,
rind, juice and desiccated coconut; stir until combined.
Place ¼-cups of mixture into pan holes; sprinkle with
flaked coconut.
3   Bake friands 20 minutes. Stand in pan 5 minutes;
turn, top-side up, onto wire rack to cool.

preparation time *15 minutes*
cooking time *20 minutes* makes *12*
nutritional count per friand *19.7g total fat (10.2g*
saturated fat); 1237kJ (296 cal); 25.3g carbohydrate;
4g protein; 1.6g fibre

pistachio and lime friands

1 cup (140g) unsalted roasted pistachios
6 egg whites
185g butter, melted
1½ cups (240g) icing sugar
½ cup (75g) plain flour
2 teaspoons finely grated lime rind
1 tablespoon lime juice

1   Preheat oven to 200°C/180°C fan-forced. Line
12-hole (½-cup/125ml) oval friand pan.
2   Process nuts until ground finely.
3   Whisk egg whites in medium bowl with fork until
combined. Add butter, sifted icing sugar and flour, rind,
juice and ground pistachios; stir until combined. Divide
mixture among pan holes.
4   Bake friands 25 minutes. Stand in pan 5 minutes;
tun, top-side up, onto wire rack to cool. Serve dusted
with a little sifted icing sugar, if you like.

preparation time *15 minutes*
cooking time *25 minutes* makes *12*
nutritional count per friand *18.6g total fat (9g*
saturated fat); 1229kJ (294 cal); 26.4g carbohydrate;
4.9g protein; 1.3g fibre

CLASSIC COMBOS

spaghetti napoletana

⅓ cup (80ml) olive oil
1 medium brown onion (150g), chopped finely
3 cloves garlic, crushed
¼ cup loosely packed fresh basil leaves
1 teaspoon sea salt
2 tablespoons tomato paste
1.5kg ripe tomatoes, chopped coarsely
500g spaghetti

1 Heat half of the oil in large saucepan; cook onion, garlic, basil and salt, stirring, until onion softens. Add paste; cook, stirring, 1 minute.
2 Add tomato; bring to the boil. Reduce heat; simmer, uncovered, stirring occasionally, about 45 minutes or until sauce thickens. Stir in remaining oil; simmer, uncovered, 5 minutes.
3 Meanwhile, cook pasta in large saucepan of boiling water until tender; drain.
4 Add pasta to sauce; toss to combine. Serve with shaved parmesan, if you like.

preparation time *15 minutes*
cooking time *1 hour* serves *4*
nutritional count per serving *20.1g total fat (2.8g saturated fat); 2771kJ (663 cal); 95.8g carbohydrate; 18.9g protein; 10g fibre*

shepherd's pie

30g butter
1 medium brown onion (150g), chopped finely
1 medium carrot (120g), chopped finely
½ teaspoon dried mixed herbs
4 cups (750g) chopped cooked lamb
¼ cup (70g) tomato paste
¼ cup (60ml) tomato sauce
2 tablespoons worcestershire sauce
2 cups (500ml) beef stock
2 tablespoons plain flour
⅓ cup (80ml) water

POTATO TOPPING

5 medium potatoes (1kg), chopped
60g butter, chopped
¼ cup (60ml) milk

1 Preheat oven to 200°C/180°C fan-forced. Oil shallow 2.5-litre (10 cup) ovenproof dish.
2 Heat butter in large saucepan; cook onion and carrot, stirring, until tender. Add mixed herbs and lamb; cook, stirring, 2 minutes. Stir in paste, sauces and stock, then blended flour and water; stir over heat until mixture boils and thickens. Pour mixture into dish.
3 Place heaped tablespoons of potato topping on lamb mixture.
4 Bake shepherd's pie about 20 minutes or until browned lightly and heated through.

POTATO TOPPING Boil, steam or microwave potatoes until tender; drain. Mash potatoes with butter and milk until smooth.

preparation time *20 minutes*
cooking time *45 minutes* serves *4*
nutritional count per serving *36.2g total fat (20.2g saturated fat); 2976kJ (712 cal); 44.7g carbohydrate; 48.8g protein; 6g fibre*

bangers and mash with caramelised onion

60g butter
1 clove garlic, crushed
4 medium red onions (680g), sliced thinly
2 tablespoons sugar
2 tablespoons red wine vinegar
1kg potatoes, chopped coarsely
½ cup (120g) sour cream
¼ cup (60ml) milk
8 beef sausages (800g)
2 tablespoons finely chopped fresh flat-leaf parsley

1 Heat butter in large frying pan; cook garlic and onion, stirring, until onion softens and browns lightly. Add sugar and vinegar; cook, stirring, about 15 minutes or until mixture caramelises.
2 Meanwhile, boil, steam or microwave potato until tender; drain. Mash potato in large bowl with sour cream and milk until smooth.
3 Cook sausages on heated oiled grill plate (or grill or barbecue) until browned all over and cooked through.
4 Serve sausages and mash topped with caramelised onion and sprinkled with parsley.

preparation time *15 minutes*
cooking time *30 minutes* serves *4*
nutritional count per serving *76g total fat (40.7g saturated fat); 4347kJ (1040 cal); 53g carbohydrate; 32.5g protein; 11.4g fibre*

potato wedges with sloppy joe topping

4 medium potatoes (800g)
2 tablespoons olive oil
1 clove garlic, crushed
1 large brown onion (200g), chopped finely
1 small green capsicum (150g), chopped finely
1 trimmed celery stalk (100g), chopped finely
750g beef mince
2 tablespoons mild american mustard
2 tablespoons cider vinegar
1 cup (250ml) tomato sauce
½ cup (60g) coarsely grated cheddar cheese
2 green onions, sliced thinly

1 Preheat oven to 220°C/200°C fan-forced.
2 Cut each potato into eight wedges; place in large shallow baking dish, drizzle with half of the oil. Roast about 30 minutes or until wedges are tender.
3 Meanwhile, heat remaining oil in large frying pan; cook garlic, brown onion, capsicum and celery, stirring, until vegetables soften. Add mince; cook, stirring, until changed in colour. Stir in mustard, vinegar and sauce; bring to the boil. Reduce heat; cook, stirring, until sloppy joe is cooked through and slightly thickened.
4 Serve wedges topped with sloppy joe mixture; sprinkle with cheese and green onion.

preparation time *10 minutes*
cooking time *30 minutes* serves *4*
nutritional count per serving *26.8g total fat (9.3g saturated fat); 2562kJ (613 cal); 42.1g carbohydrate; 48g protein; 5.7g fibre*

spaghetti with pesto

2 cloves garlic, chopped coarsely
⅓ cup (50g) roasted pine nuts
½ cup (40g) finely grated parmesan cheese
2 cups firmly packed fresh basil leaves
½ cup (125ml) olive oil
500g spaghetti
½ cup (40g) shaved parmesan cheese

1 Blend or process garlic, nuts, grated cheese and basil until almost smooth. Gradually add oil in a thin, steady stream, processing until thick.
2 Cook pasta in large saucepan of boiling water, until just tender; drain, reserve ¼ cup of the cooking liquid.
3 Combine pasta, pesto and reserved cooking liquid in large bowl. Serve with shaved cheese.

preparation time *10 minutes*
cooking time *15 minutes* serves *4*
nutritional count per serving *45.2g total fat (8.9g saturated fat); 3578kJ (859 cal); 86.2g carbohydrate; 23.6g protein; 5.6g fibre*

pear and roquefort salad

1 small french bread stick (150g), sliced thinly
100g roquefort cheese, softened
2 small pears (360g), sliced thinly
1 cup (110g) coarsely chopped roasted walnuts
1 butter lettuce, leaves separated
100g baby spinach leaves

BUTTERMILK DRESSING

¼ cup (60ml) buttermilk
1 tablespoon lemon juice
1 tablespoon olive oil
½ teaspoon caster sugar
1 clove garlic, crushed

1 Preheat oven to 200°C/180°C fan-forced.
2 Place bread on oven tray; toast, in oven, until browned both sides.
3 Meanwhile, make buttermilk dressing.
4 Spread toast with cheese.
5 Place pears, walnuts, lettuce and spinach in large serving bowl with dressing; toss gently to combine. Serve salad with cheese toast.

BUTTERMILK DRESSING Whisk ingredients in medium bowl.

preparation time *15 minutes*
cooking time *5 minutes* serves *4*
nutritional count per serving *33.7g total fat (7.4g saturated fat); 2082kJ (498 cal); 31.2g carbohydrate; 14.6g protein; 7.7g fibre*

1 SPAGHETTI WITH PESTO 2 PEAR AND ROQUEFORT SALAD
3 HONEY, SOY AND SESAME CHICKEN WINGS [P 422]
4 CHICKEN AND CHIPS [P 422]

CLASSIC COMBOS   421

honey, soy and sesame chicken wings

1kg chicken wings
¼ cup (60ml) japanese soy sauce
2 tablespoons honey
1 clove garlic, crushed
2cm piece fresh ginger (10g), grated
2 teaspoons sesame seeds
1 teaspoon sesame oil
2 green onions, sliced thinly

1   Cut chicken wings into three pieces at joints; discard tips. Combine sauce, honey, garlic, ginger, seeds and oil in large bowl with chicken. Cover; refrigerate 3 hours or overnight.
2   Preheat oven to 220°C/200°C fan-forced.
3   Place chicken, in single layer, on oiled wire rack over shallow large baking dish; brush remaining marinade over chicken. Roast about 30 minutes or until chicken is cooked.
4   Serve chicken wings sprinkled with onion.

preparation time *15 minutes (plus refrigeration time)*
cooking time *30 minutes* serves *4*
nutritional count per serving *10.3g total fat (3g saturated fat); 1233kJ (295 cal); 12.6g carbohydrate; 37.4g protein; 0.4g fibre*

chicken and chips

The 12 boxes called for here, chinese takeaway food containers, come in various sizes and colours and are available from some homeware shops, craft stores and party outlets.

1kg kipfler potatoes
1 tablespoon olive oil
12 chicken drumettes (1kg)
¼ cup (35g) plain flour
2 eggs, beaten lightly
2 teaspoons sweet paprika
1 teaspoon ground cumin
½ teaspoon cayenne pepper
2 teaspoons dried oregano
½ cup (50g) packaged breadcrumbs

1   Preheat oven to 240°C/220°C fan-forced.
2   Quarter unpeeled potatoes lengthways. Toss potato and oil in large shallow baking dish. Roast 50 minutes or until browned lightly, turning occasionally.
3   Meanwhile, coat drumettes in flour, shaking away excess; dip drumettes into egg then into combined spices, oregano and breadcrumbs. Place in large oiled shallow baking dish.
4   Roast drumettes alongside potato in oven, about 30 minutes or until cooked through. Serve drumettes and chips in chinese takeaway food containers.

preparation time *30 minutes*
cooking time *50 minutes* serves *12*
nutritional count per serving *6.7g total fat (1.8g saturated fat); 698kJ (167 cal); 14.4g carbohydrate; 11.9g protein; 1.4g fibre*

gorgonzola fritters

Gorgonzola is a creamy, Italian blue cheese. If unavailable, use blue castello or a similar soft blue cheese.

1 cup (200g) ricotta cheese
1 cup (185g) coarsely chopped gorgonzola cheese
2 eggs, beaten lightly
½ cup (75g) plain flour
vegetable oil, for deep-frying
1 cup (80g) finely grated parmesan cheese

1 Combine ricotta, gorgonzola and egg in medium bowl. Whisk in flour; stand 1 hour.
2 Heat oil in large saucepan; deep-fry heaped teaspoons of cheese mixture, turning occasionally, until fritters are browned lightly all over and cooked through. (Do not have oil too hot or fritters will over-brown before cooking through.)
3 Place parmesan in medium bowl; toss hot fritters, in batches, to coat as they are cooked.

preparation time *15 minutes (plus standing time)*
cooking time *15 minutes* makes *36*
nutritional count per fritter *3.9g total fat (2.1g saturated fat); 226kJ (54 cal); 1.6g carbohydrate; 3.1g protein; 0.1g fibre*

duck, pear and blue cheese salad

4 duck breast fillets (600g)
1 small red oak lettuce, trimmed
2 witlof (250g), trimmed
1 medium pear (230g), halved, cored, sliced thinly
1 cup (100g) roasted walnuts
150g soft blue cheese, crumbled

RED WINE VINAIGRETTE
¼ cup (60ml) olive oil
¼ cup (60ml) red wine vinegar
2 teaspoons wholegrain mustard

1 Cook duck, skin-side down, in heated large frying pan about 5 minutes or until skin is browned and crisp. Turn duck; cook about 5 minutes or until cooked as desired. Drain on absorbent paper; slice thinly.
2 Meanwhile, make red wine vinaigrette.
3 Place duck in large bowl with lettuce, witlof, pear and nuts; toss gently to combine. Drizzle with vinaigrette, sprinkle with cheese.

RED WINE VINAIGRETTE Place ingredients in screw-top jar; shake well.

preparation time *10 minutes*
cooking time *15 minutes* serves *4*
nutritional count per serving *99g total fat (27.5g saturated fat); 4431kJ (1060 cal); 8.8g carbohydrate; 33.1g protein; 6.5g fibre*

baked three cheese pasta

375g macaroni pasta
300ml cream
⅓ cup (80ml) vegetable stock
1¼ cups (125g) grated fontina cheese
⅓ cup (75g) crumbled gorgonzola cheese
1¼ cups (100g) coarsely grated parmesan cheese
1 teaspoon dijon mustard
2 tablespoons finely chopped fresh flat-leaf parsley
1 tablespoon finely chopped fresh chives

1   Preheat oven to 180°C/160°C fan-forced.
2   Cook pasta in large saucepan of boiling water, uncovered, until just tender; drain.
3   Meanwhile, heat cream and stock in medium saucepan until hot. Remove from heat, add fontina, gorgonzola and half the parmesan; stir until melted. Add mustard and herbs.
4   Combine cream mixture with drained pasta. Pour pasta mixture into 2.5 litre (10-cup) ovenproof dish; sprinkle with remaining parmesan.
5   Bake pasta about 20 minutes or until browned.

preparation time *10 minutes*
cooking time *30 minutes* serves *4*
nutritional count per serving *58.9g total fat (37.8g saturated fat); 3929kJ (940 cal); 66.4g carbohydrate; 35.4g protein; 3.3g fibre*

leek and fetta triangles

100g butter
2 cloves garlic, crushed
2 medium leeks (700g), sliced thinly
1 tablespoon caraway seeds
150g fetta cheese, chopped coarsely
⅓ cup (40g) coarsely grated cheddar cheese
4 sheets fillo pastry
2 teaspoons sesame seeds

1   Heat half of the butter in large frying pan; cook garlic and leek, stirring occasionally, until leek softens. Stir in caraway seeds; cook, stirring, 2 minutes.
2   Combine leek mixture in medium bowl with fetta and cheddar.
3   Preheat oven to 200°C/180°C fan-forced. Oil oven tray.
4   Melt remaining butter in small saucepan. Brush one sheet of the fillo with a little butter; fold in half lengthways. Place a quarter of the leek mixture at bottom of one narrow edge of fillo, leaving a 1cm border. Fold opposite corner of fillo diagonally across the filling to form a triangle; continue folding to end of fillo, retaining triangular shape. Place on tray, seam-side down; repeat with remaining butter, fillo and filling to make four triangles in total.
5   Brush triangles with butter; sprinkle with sesame seeds. Bake about 10 minutes or until browned lightly.

preparation time *15 minutes*
cooking time *15 minutes* serves *4*
nutritional count per serving *34.2g total fat (21.6g saturated fat); 1772kJ (424 cal); 14.5g carbohydrate; 13.6g protein; 3.9g fibre*

pork cutlets with charcuterie sauce

1 tablespoon olive oil
4 pork cutlets (950g)
1 small brown onion (80g), chopped finely
2 rindless bacon rashers (130g), sliced thinly
⅔ cup (160ml) dry white wine
⅔ cup (160ml) chicken stock
⅓ cup (60g) cornichons, sliced thinly lengthways
⅓ cup (40g) seeded green olives, sliced thinly
2 teaspoons dijon mustard
2 tablespoons finely chopped fresh flat-leaf parsley

1 Heat oil in large frying pan; cook pork, in batches, until browned both sides and cooked as desired. Remove from pan; cover to keep warm.
2 Cook onion and bacon in same pan, stirring, until onion softens.
3 Deglaze pan with wine, stirring until mixture reduces by half.
4 Stir in remaining ingredients; bring to the boil. Boil, uncovered, about 1 minute or until sauce thickens slightly. Serve sauce over cutlets.

preparation time *10 minutes*
cooking time *25 minutes serves 4*
nutritional count per serving *24.1g total fat (7.4g saturated fat); 1697kJ (406 cal); 7.7g carbohydrate; 33g protein; 0.9g fibre*

pork ribs with hoisin and peanut sauce

2kg american-style pork spareribs
2 tablespoons peanut oil
2 tablespoons caster sugar
¼ cup (60ml) rice vinegar
¾ cup (180ml) water
¾ cup (180ml) hoisin sauce
2 tablespoons crushed unsalted peanuts, roasted

1 Preheat oven to 180°C/160°C fan-forced.
2 Place ribs in large oiled baking dish; brush all over with oil. Roast, covered, 1 hour.
3 Meanwhile, stir sugar, vinegar and the water in small saucepan over heat until sugar dissolves. Add sauce; bring to the boil. Reduce heat; simmer, uncovered, about 5 minutes or until thickened slightly.
4 Brush ribs all over with half of the sauce; roast, uncovered, further 30 minutes or until browned and cooked through.
5 Stir nuts into remaining sauce; serve with ribs.

preparation time *5 minutes*
cooking time *1 hour 30 minutes serves 4*
nutritional count per serving *32.3g total fat (8.4g saturated fat); 2554kJ (611 cal); 27.8g carbohydrate; 50g protein; 5.5g fibre*

roasted pork fillet with pear and apricot relish

410g can sliced pears in natural juice
410g can apricot halves in natural juice
600g pork fillets
1 tablespoon olive oil
½ cup (125ml) water
2 tablespoons white vinegar
1 fresh long red chilli, chopped finely
¼ cup (40g) sultanas
2 tablespoons white sugar

1 Preheat oven to 240°C/220°C fan-forced.
2 Drain pears over small bowl. Reserve juice; chop pears coarsely. Drain apricots, discarding juice. Chop apricots coarsely.
3 Place pork in oiled baking dish; drizzle with oil. Roast about 20 minutes or until cooked as desired. Cover; stand 5 minutes, then slice thickly.
4 Meanwhile, combine pear, apricot, reserved juice and remaining ingredients in medium saucepan; bring to the boil. Reduce heat; simmer, uncovered, about 20 minutes or until relish thickens slightly.
5 Serve pork with relish and steamed snow peas, if you like.

preparation time *10 minutes*
cooking time *20 minutes* serves *4*
nutritional count per serving *8g total fat (1.8g saturated fat); 1400kJ (335 cal); 29.2g carbohydrate; 34.2g protein; 3.3g fibre*

sage roasted pork loin

10 fresh sage leaves
1kg boneless loin of pork, rind off
2 tablespoons sea salt flakes
2 tablespoons crushed dried green peppercorns
2 tablespoons coarsely chopped fresh sage
1 tablespoon olive oil

1 Preheat barbecue.
2 Lay sage leaves in the middle of pork loin; roll pork to enclose leaves. Tie pork at 10cm intervals with kitchen string.
3 Combine salt, peppercorns and chopped sage in small bowl.
4 Brush pork with oil; rub with salt mixture.
5 Place pork in disposable aluminium baking dish. Cook pork in covered barbecue, using indirect heat, about 1 hour or until cooked through.
6 Cover pork loosely with foil; stand for 10 minutes before slicing.

preparation time *15 minutes (plus standing time)*
cooking time *1 hour* serves *6*
nutritional count per serving *5.7g total fat (1.3g saturated fat); 861kJ (206 cal); 0.7g carbohydrate; 37.7g protein; 0g fibre*

sirloin steak with herbed butter

3 large potatoes (900g)
1½ tablespoons cracked black pepper
2 teaspoons salt
4 x 250g beef sirloin steaks
peanut oil, for deep-frying
1 tablespoon olive oil

HERBED BUTTER

1 clove garlic
60g butter, softened
2 tablespoons finely chopped fresh basil
2 tablespoons finely chopped fresh flat-leaf parsley

1   Cut peeled potatoes into 5mm slices; cut each slice into 5mm strips. Place potato in large bowl, cover with water; stand 1 hour. Drain; pat dry with absorbent paper.
2   Meanwhile, make herbed butter.
3   Combine pepper and salt on oven tray; press both sides of beef into pepper and salt mixture. Rest beef on oven tray while making frites.
4   Heat peanut oil in wok or large saucepan; cook potato, in batches, about 3 minutes or until just tender, but not browned. Drain on absorbent paper.
5   Meanwhile, heat olive oil in large frying pan; cook beef until browned both sides and cooked as desired. Cover; stand 5 minutes.
6   Reheat oil in wok; cook potato, in batches, until browned lightly and crisp. Drain frites on absorbent paper.
7   Divide beef among serving plates; top with herbed butter, serve with pommes frites.

HERBED BUTTER Beat ingredients in small bowl until combined. Place on piece of plastic wrap, wrap tightly, shape into rectangle; refrigerate until just firm.

preparation time *20 minutes (plus standing time)*
cooking time *30 minutes* serves *4*
nutritional count per serving *49.4g total fat (20.7g saturated fat); 3269kJ (782 cal); 26g carbohydrate; 57.1g protein; 4g fibre*

grilled steak with béarnaise

2 tablespoons white vinegar
2 tablespoons water
1 shallot (25g), chopped finely
2 teaspoons coarsely chopped fresh tarragon
½ teaspoon black peppercorns
4 x 220g scotch fillet steaks
3 egg yolks
200g unsalted butter, melted
1 tablespoon finely chopped fresh tarragon

1   Combine vinegar, the water, shallot, coarsely chopped tarragon and peppercorns in small saucepan; bring to the boil. Reduce heat; simmer, uncovered, about 2 minutes or until liquid reduces by half. Strain over medium heatproof bowl; discard solids. Cool 10 minutes.
2   Meanwhile, cook steaks in heated oiled grill pan (or grill or barbecue) until cooked as desired.
3   Whisk egg yolks into vinegar mixture until combined. Set bowl over medium saucepan of simmering water; do not allow water to touch base of bowl. Whisk mixture over heat until thickened. Remove bowl from heat; gradually whisk in melted butter in thin, steady stream until béarnaise thickens slightly. Stir finely chopped tarragon into sauce.
4   Serve steak with sauce and chips, if you like.

preparation time *20 minutes*
cooking time *20 minutes* serves *4*
nutritional count per serving *58.4g total fat (33.9g saturated fat); 2997kJ (717 cal); 0.5g carbohydrate; 48.8g protein; 0.1g fibre*

potato and leek soup

2 medium potatoes (400g), chopped coarsely
2 medium carrots (240g), chopped coarsely
1 large brown onion (200g), chopped coarsely
1 medium tomato (150g), chopped coarsely
1 trimmed celery stalk (100g), chopped coarsely
1.5 litres (6 cups) water
1 tablespoon olive oil
50g butter
4 medium potatoes (800g), chopped coarsely, extra
1 large leek (500g), sliced thickly
300ml cream
2 tablespoons finely chopped fresh chives
1 tablespoon finely chopped fresh basil
1 tablespoon finely chopped fresh dill

1 Place potato, carrot, onion, tomato, celery and the water in large saucepan; bring to the boil. Reduce heat; simmer, uncovered, 20 minutes. Strain broth through muslin-lined sieve or colander into large heatproof bowl; discard solids.
2 Heat oil and butter in same cleaned pan; cook extra potato and leek, covered, 15 minutes, stirring occasionally. Add broth; bring to the boil. Reduce heat; simmer, covered, 15 minutes. Cool 15 minutes.
3 Blend or process soup, in batches, until smooth. Return soup to same cleaned pan, add cream; stir over medium heat until hot.
4 Serve bowls of soup sprinkled with combined herbs and, if you like, topped with croûtons.

preparation time *30 minutes (plus cooling time)*
cooking time *55 minutes* serves *4*
nutritional count per serving *47.9g total fat (28.8g saturated fat); 2822kJ (675 cal); 46.3g carbohydrate; 11g protein; 9.8g fibre*

cauliflower cheese

1 small cauliflower (1kg), cut into florets
50g butter
¼ cup (35g) plain flour
2 cups (500ml) milk
¾ cup (90g) coarsely grated cheddar cheese

1 Boil, steam or microwave cauliflower until tender; drain.
2 Melt butter in medium saucepan, add flour; cook, stirring, until mixture bubbles and thickens. Gradually add milk; cook, stirring, until mixture boils and thickens. Stir in half of the cheese.
3 Preheat grill.
4 Place cauliflower in 1.5-litre (6-cup) shallow flameproof dish; pour cheese sauce over cauliflower, sprinkle with remaining cheese. Place under grill about 10 minutes or until browned lightly.

preparation time *10 minutes*
cooking time *30 minutes* serves *6*
nutritional count per serving *15.5g total fat (9.9g saturated fat); 970kJ (232 cal); 11.4g carbohydrate; 10.5g protein; 2.9g fibre*

grilled pork loin chops with apple and onion plum sauce

2 medium apples (300g)
1 tablespoon olive oil
1 medium red onion (170g), cut into thin wedges
4 x 280g pork loin chops
½ cup (125ml) plum sauce
¼ cup (60ml) lemon juice
⅓ cup (80ml) chicken stock

1 Preheat barbecue.
2 Cut each unpeeled, uncored apple horizontally into four slices. Heat oil in grill pan; cook apple and onion, turning, until softened.
3 Meanwhile, cook pork on heated oiled grill plate.
4 Stir sauce, juice and stock into apple mixture; simmer 1 minute.
5 Serve pork with sauce.

preparation time *10 minutes*
cooking time *20 minutes* serves *4*
nutritional count per serving *8.7g total fat (1.9g saturated fat); 1718kJ (411 cal); 31.8g carbohydrate; 49.7g protein; 1.8g fibre*

braised oxtails with orange gremolata

1.5kg oxtails, cut into 5cm pieces
2 tablespoons plain flour
2 tablespoons olive oil
1 medium brown onion (150g), chopped coarsely
2 cloves garlic, crushed
½ cup (125ml) sweet sherry
400g can crushed tomatoes
1 cup (250ml) beef stock
1 cup (250ml) water
4 sprigs fresh thyme
2 bay leaves
10cm strip orange rind
4 medium tomatoes (600g), chopped coarsely

ORANGE GREMOLATA

¼ cup finely chopped fresh flat-leaf parsley
1 tablespoon finely grated orange rind
1 clove garlic, crushed

1 Preheat oven to 160°C/140°C fan-forced.
2 Coat oxtail in flour; shake off excess. Heat half of the oil in large flameproof casserole dish; cook oxtail pieces, in batches, until browned all over.
3 Heat remaining oil in same dish; cook onion and garlic, stirring, until onion softens.
4 Return oxtails to dish with sherry, undrained tomatoes, stock, the water, herbs and rind; cook, covered, in oven about 3 hours or until oxtail is tender. Stir in chopped tomato.
5 Meanwhile, make orange gremolata.
6 Serve oxtail sprinkled with gremolata on mashed potato, if you like.

ORANGE GREMOLATA Combine ingredients in small bowl.

preparation time *20 minutes*
cooking time *3 hours 15 minutes* serves *4*
nutritional count per serving *110.2g total fat (40g saturated fat); 5656kJ (1353 cal); 15.8g carbohydrate; 69.5g protein; 4.1g fibre*

braised lamb shanks with white bean puree

1 tablespoon olive oil
8 french-trimmed lamb shanks (2kg)
1 large red onion (300g), chopped coarsely
2 cloves garlic, crushed
1 cup (250ml) chicken stock
2 cups (500ml) water
400g can diced tomatoes
1 tablespoon fresh rosemary leaves
4 drained anchovy fillets, chopped coarsely
2 large red capsicums (700g)
2 large green capsicums (700g)

WHITE BEAN PUREE

20g butter
1 small brown onion (80g), chopped finely
1 clove garlic, crushed
¼ cup (60ml) dry white wine
¾ cup (180ml) chicken stock
2 x 400g cans white beans, rinsed, drained
2 tablespoons cream

1 Heat oil in large deep saucepan; cook lamb, in batches, until browned all over.
2 Cook onion and garlic in same pan, stirring, until onion softens. Add stock, the water, undrained tomatoes, rosemary and anchovy; bring to the boil.
3 Return lamb to pan, reduce heat; simmer, covered, 1 hour, stirring occasionally. Uncover; simmer about 45 minutes or until lamb is tender.
4 Meanwhile, quarter capsicums; discard seeds and membranes. Roast under hot grill or in very hot oven, skin-side up, until skin blisters and blackens. Cover capsicum pieces with plastic wrap or paper 5 minutes; peel away skin, slice thickly.
5 Meanwhile, make white bean puree.
6 Add capsicum to lamb; cook, uncovered, 5 minutes. Serve lamb on white bean puree.

WHITE BEAN PUREE Melt butter in medium frying pan; cook onion and garlic, stirring, until onions softens. Add wine; cook, stirring, until liquid is reduced by half. Add stock and beans; bring to the boil. Reduce heat; simmer, uncovered, about 10 minutes or until liquid is almost evaporated. Blend or process bean mixture with cream until smooth.

preparation time *40 minutes*
cooking time *2 hours 30 minutes* serves *4*
nutritional count per serving *18.8g total fat (8.4g saturated fat); 2312kJ (553 cal); 21g carbohydrate; 72.1g protein; 8.6g fibre*

pappardelle marinara

1 tablespoon olive oil
1 small brown onion (80g), chopped finely
2 tablespoons tomato paste
½ cup (125ml) dry white wine
800g marinara mix
pinch saffron threads
500g pappardelle
NAPOLETANA SAUCE

⅓ cup (80ml) olive oil
1 medium brown onion (150g), chopped finely
3 cloves garlic, crushed
¼ cup loosely packed fresh basil leaves
1 teaspoon sea salt
2 tablespoons tomato paste
1.5kg ripe tomatoes, chopped coarsely

1 Make napoletana sauce.
2 Heat oil in large saucepan; cook onion, stirring, until soft. Add paste; cook, stirring, 1 minute. Add wine; bring to the boil. Reduce heat; simmer, uncovered, 3 minutes.
3 Add napoletana sauce, marinara mix and saffron; bring to the boil. Reduce heat; simmer, uncovered, about 5 minutes or until seafood is cooked through.
4 Meanwhile, cook pasta in large saucepan of boiling water until tender; drain.
5 Add pasta to sauce; toss to combine. Serve with shaved parmesan cheese, if you like.

NAPOLETANA SAUCE Heat half of the oil in large saucepan; cook onion, garlic, basil and salt, stirring, until onion softens. Add paste; cook, stirring, 1 minute. Add tomato; bring to the boil. Reduce heat; simmer, uncovered, stirring occasionally, 45 minutes or until thickened. Stir in remaining oil; simmer, uncovered, 5 minutes.

preparation time *35 minutes*
cooking time *1 hour 10 minutes* serves *6*
nutritional count per serving *20.1g total fat (3.3g saturated fat); 2479kJ (593 cal); 52.3g carbohydrate; 43.4g protein; 6.5g fibre*

surf and turf

4 x 220g new york-cut steaks
30g butter
2 tablespoons plain flour
1¼ cups (310ml) hot milk
1 cup (250ml) dry white wine
¾ cup (180ml) cream
250g marinara mix, drained
2 tablespoons finely chopped fresh dill
1 tablespoon lemon juice

1 Heat oil in large frying pan; cook beef, uncovered, until cooked as desired.
2 Meanwhile, melt butter in medium saucepan, add flour; cook, stirring, until mixture bubbles and thickens. Gradually add milk, stirring, until mixture boils and thickens.
3 Bring wine to the boil in medium frying pan then reduce heat. Simmer, uncovered, until reduced by half.
4 Add white sauce, cream and marinara mix to medium frying pan; bring to the boil. Reduce heat; simmer, uncovered, about 5 minutes or until seafood is cooked through. Stir in dill and juice.
5 Serve steak topped with seafood sauce.

preparation time *10 minutes*
cooking time *20 minutes* serves *4*
nutritional count per serving *43.7g total fat (24.9g saturated fat); 3081kJ (737 cal); 10.1g carbohydrate; 66.1g protein; 0.2g fibre*

1 PAPPARDELLE MARINARA 2 SURF AND TURF
3 SALMON AND BEURRE BLANC [P 436]
4 FISH WITH CREAMY WHITE WINE SAUCE [P 436]

salmon and beurre blanc

6 x 200g salmon fillets
¼ cup (60ml) dry white wine
1 tablespoon lemon juice
¼ cup (60ml) cream
125g cold butter, chopped

1   Cook salmon in heated oiled large frying pan until cooked as desired.
2   Meanwhile, combine wine and juice in small saucepan; bring to the boil. Boil, without stirring, until reduced by two-thirds. Add cream; return to the boil then reduce heat. Whisk in cold butter, piece by piece, whisking between additions, until sauce is smooth and thickened slightly.
3   Serve salmon topped with sauce.

preparation time *15 minutes*
cooking time *10 minutes* serves *4*
nutritional count per serving *53.4g total fat (26g saturated fat); 3031kJ (725 cal); 0.8g carbohydrate; 59g protein; 0g fibre*

fish with creamy white wine sauce

4 x 200g firm white fish fillets
20g butter
2 shallots (50g), chopped finely
1 teaspoon mustard powder
¾ cup (180ml) dry white wine
¾ cup (180ml) fish stock
300ml cream

1   Cook fish in heated oiled large frying pan until cooked as desired.
2   Meanwhile, melt butter in medium frying pan; cook shallot and mustard powder, stirring, about 3 minutes or until shallot softens. Add wine; cook, uncovered, until wine reduces by two-thirds. Add stock; bring to the boil. Boil, uncovered, about 7 minutes or until reduced by half.
3   Add cream to pan; bring to the boil. Reduce heat; simmer, uncovered, about 15 minutes or until sauce thickens slightly.
4   Serve fish drizzled with sauce.

preparation time *10 minutes*
cooking time *20 minutes* serves *4*
nutritional count per serving *41.5g total fat (25.6g saturated fat); 2445kJ (585 cal); 3.1g carbohydrate; 43.4g protein; 0.1g fibre*

smoky octopus stew with red wine and olives

1kg cleaned baby octopus
2 bay leaves
2 tablespoons olive oil
2 cloves garlic, crushed
1 large brown onion (200g), sliced thinly
1½ teaspoons bittersweet smoked paprika
5 medium tomatoes (750g), peeled, chopped coarsely
2 tablespoons tomato paste
¾ cup (180ml) dry red wine
⅓ cup (50g) drained sun-dried tomatoes, chopped coarsely
¼ cup (60ml) water
1¼ cups (200g) seeded kalamata olives
2 tablespoons coarsely chopped fresh flat-leaf parsley

1   Cut heads from octopus; cut tentacles into two pieces.
2   Place octopus and bay leaves in large saucepan of water; bring to the boil. Reduce heat; simmer, covered, about 30 minutes or until octopus is just tender, drain. Discard bay leaves.
3   Heat oil in same cleaned pan; cook garlic and onion, stirring, until onions softens. Add paprika, fresh tomato, tomato paste, wine, sun-dried tomato, the water and octopus; bring to the boil. Reduce heat; simmer, covered, 30 minutes. Stir in olives.
4   Sprinkle stew with parsley; serve with warmed sourdough bread, if you like.

preparation time *20 minutes*
cooking time *1 hour 10 minutes* serves *4*
nutritional count per serving *15.1g total fat (2.4g saturated fat); 2169kJ (519 cal); 23.8g carbohydrate; 63.6g protein; 5.7g fibre*

mussels with beer

1kg large black mussels
1 tablespoon olive oil
2 cloves garlic, crushed
1 large red onion (300g), sliced thinly
2 fresh long red chillies, seeded, sliced thinly
1½ cups (375ml) beer
2 tablespoons sweet chilli sauce
1 cup coarsely chopped fresh flat-leaf parsley

GARLIC BREAD

1 loaf turkish bread (430g)
50g butter, melted
2 cloves garlic, crushed
2 tablespoons finely chopped fresh flat-leaf parsley

1   Scrub mussels; remove beards.
2   Make garlic bread.
3   Meanwhile, heat oil on heated flat plate; cook garlic, onion and chilli, stirring, until onion softens. Add mussels and combined beer and chilli sauce; cook, covered, about 5 minutes or until mussels open (discard any that do not). Remove from heat; stir in parsley.
4   Serve mussels with garlic bread.

GARLIC BREAD Halve bread horizontally; cut each half into four pieces, brush with combined butter, garlic and parsley. Cook bread on heated oiled grill plate (or grill) until browned both sides.

preparation time *20 minutes*
cooking time *15 minutes* serves *4*
nutritional count per serving *19.7g total fat (8.3g saturated fat); 2174kJ (520 cal); 58.3g carbohydrate; 17.6g protein; 5.6g fibre*

roasted chicken with 40 cloves of garlic

3 bulbs garlic
60g butter, softened
1.5kg chicken
2 teaspoons salt
2 teaspoons cracked black pepper
1 cup (250ml) water

ROASTED POTATOES

1kg baby new potatoes
cooking-oil spray

1 Preheat oven to 200°C/180°C fan-forced.
2 Separate cloves from garlic bulb, leaving peel intact. Rub butter over outside of chicken and inside cavity; press combined salt and pepper onto skin and inside cavity. Place half of the garlic inside cavity; tie legs together with kitchen string.
3 Place remaining garlic cloves, in single layer, in medium baking dish; place chicken on garlic. Pour the water carefully into dish; roast chicken, uncovered, in moderately hot oven, brushing occasionally with pan juices, about 1 hour 20 minutes or until browned and cooked through.
4 Meanwhile, make roasted potatoes.
5 Stand chicken on serving platter, covered with foil, 15 minutes; serve with roasted garlic and potatoes.

ROASTED POTATOES Boil steam or microwave potatoes 5 minutes; drain. Pat dry with absorbent paper; cool 10 minutes. Place potatoes, in single layer, in large oiled baking dish; spray with cooking-oil spray. Roast, uncovered, for the last 30 minutes of chicken cooking time or until potatoes are tender.

preparation time *20 minutes*
cooking time *1 hour 20 minutes (plus standing time)*
serves *4*
nutritional count per serving *45g total fat (17.9g saturated fat); 3219kJ (770 cal); 38.4g carbohydrate; 46.8g protein; 14.1g fibre*

croque madame

8 slices wholemeal bread (360g)
8 slices leg ham (240g)
40g butter
4 eggs

CHEESE BECHAMEL

20g butter
1 tablespoon plain flour
¾ cup (180ml) milk
½ cup (60g) finely grated cheddar cheese
1 tablespoon finely chopped fresh flat-leaf parsley

1 Make cheese béchamel.
2 Spread béchamel onto bread slices. Top four slices with ham then remaining bread.
3 Melt butter in large frying pan. Fry sandwiches, in batches, until browned both sides.
4 Fry eggs in same pan until cooked. Top each sandwich with an egg.

CHEESE BECHAMEL Melt butter in small saucepan, add flour; cook, stirring, until mixture bubbles and thickens. Gradually add milk; cook, stirring, until sauce boils and thickens. Remove from heat; stir in cheese and parsley.

preparation time *15 minutes*
cooking time *20 minutes serves 4*
nutritional count per serving *29.2g total fat (15.2g saturated fat); 2328kJ (557 cal); 38.6g carbohydrate; 32.3g protein; 5.8g fibre*

1 ROASTED CHICKEN WITH 40 CLOVES OF GARLIC
2 CROQUE MADAME 3 CASHEW FISH FINGERS WITH MUSHY MINTED PEAS [P 440] 4 STEAK DIANE [P 440]

1

2

3

4

cashew fish fingers with mushy minted peas

1kg firm white fish fillets, chopped coarsely
2 tablespoons coarsely chopped fresh flat-leaf parsley
2 teaspoons finely grated lemon rind
1 tablespoon lemon juice
1 clove garlic, quartered
½ cup (75g) plain flour
2 eggs, beaten lightly
⅔ cup (70g) packaged breadcrumbs
⅔ cup (90g) finely chopped roasted unsalted cashews
vegetable oil, for shallow-frying
2 cups (250g) frozen peas
20g butter
2 tablespoons finely chopped fresh mint

1 Grease 19cm x 29cm slice pan.
2 Process fish, parsley, rind, juice and garlic until smooth. Using spatula, press mixture evenly into pan; turn onto baking-paper-lined tray. Cut into eight 19cm slices; cut each slice in half crossways to make 16 fingers. Cover; refrigerate 30 minutes.
3 Pat fish fingers with flour; shake off excess. Dip in egg, then in combined breadcrumbs and nuts.
4 Heat oil in large frying pan; shallow-fry fingers, in batches, until browned lightly and cooked through. Drain on absorbent paper.
5 Meanwhile, boil, steam or microwave peas until tender; drain. Coarsely crush peas with butter in medium bowl; stir in mint.
6 Serve fish fingers with mushy minted peas, and mayonnaise and lemon wedges, if you like.

preparation time *30 minutes (plus refrigeration time)*
cooking time *15 minutes* serves *4*
nutritional count per serving *37.1g total fat (9g saturated fat); 3127kJ (748 cal); 33.5g carbohydrate; 66.7g protein; 6.9g fibre*

steak diane

1 tablespoon olive oil
4 x 220g new york-cut steaks
⅓ cup (80ml) brandy
1 clove garlic, crushed
¼ cup (60ml) worcestershire sauce
2 teaspoons dijon mustard
300ml cream

1 Heat oil in large frying pan; cook steaks, uncovered, until cooked as desired. Remove from pan; cover to keep warm.
2 Deglaze pan with brandy, stirring until mixture bubbles and starts to thicken.
3 Add remaining ingredients; bring to the boil then reduce heat. Simmer, uncovered, about 5 minutes or until sauce thickens slightly.

preparation time *5 minutes*
cooking time *15 minutes* serves *4*
nutritional count per serving *50.1g total fat (27.6g saturated fat); 2926kJ (700 cal); 5.6g carbohydrate; 48.4g protein; 0.3g fibre*

singapore chilli crab

2 uncooked whole mud crabs (1.5kg)
1 tablespoon peanut oil
1 small brown onion (80g), chopped finely
½ teaspoon cayenne pepper
400g can crushed tomatoes
1 tablespoon soy sauce
2 tablespoons brown sugar
2 cloves garlic, crushed
3cm piece fresh ginger (15g), grated
1 fresh small red thai chilli, sliced thinly
1 teaspoon cornflour
½ cup (125ml) water

1 Place crabs in large container filled with ice water; stand about 1 hour.
2 Prepare crabs, leaving flesh in claws and legs. Using a cleaver or heavy knife, chop each body into sixths.
3 Heat oil in wok; stir-fry onion until softened. Add pepper, undrained tomatoes, sauce, sugar, garlic, ginger and chilli; bring to the boil, then reduce heat. Add crab; simmer, covered, 15 minutes.
4 Add blended cornflour and the water to wok; stir until tomato mixture boils and thickens.

preparation time *25 minutes (plus standing time)*
cooking time *20 minutes* serves *4*
nutritional count per serving *6.2g total fat (1.1g saturated fat); 1012kJ (242 cal); 14g carbohydrate; 31.1g protein; 1.8g fibre*

veal marsala

1 tablespoon olive oil
4 x 150g veal escalopes
20g butter
2 shallots (50g), chopped finely
2 teaspoons plain flour
½ cup (125ml) marsala
½ cup (125ml) beef stock

1 Heat oil in large frying pan; cook escalopes, uncovered, until cooked as desired. Remove from pan; cover to keep warm.
2 Melt butter in same pan; cook shallot, stirring, until soft. Add flour; cook, stirring, 2 minutes.
3 Stir in marsala; bring to the boil. Reduce heat; simmer, uncovered, 2 minutes. Add stock; bring to the boil. Reduce heat; simmer, uncovered, about 4 minutes or until sauce has reduced by half.
4 Serve veal topped with sauce.

preparation time *10 minutes*
cooking time *15 minutes* serves *4*
nutritional count per serving *11g total fat (4g saturated fat); 1225kJ (293 cal); 5.4g carbohydrate; 34.2g protein; 0.2g fibre*

gnocchi with burnt butter and tomato

3 large potatoes (900g), peeled, chopped coarsely
1 clove garlic, crushed
2 tablespoons milk
2 egg yolks
⅓ cup (25g) finely grated parmesan cheese
1 cup (150g) plain flour, approximately
100g butter, chopped coarsely
⅓ cup baby basil leaves
3 medium egg tomatoes (225g), chopped coarsely

1 Boil or steam potato until tender; drain. Cool potato slightly, mash with a masher, ricer or mouli until smooth; stir in garlic and milk. Stir in egg yolks, cheese and enough of the sifted flour to form a firm dough.
2 Roll a quarter of the dough on floured surface into 2cm thick log. Cut log into 1.5cm lengths and shape each into an oval. Press and roll dough with a floured fork to mark one side of gnocchi. Place on floured tray in single layer. Repeat with remaining dough. Cover; refrigerate 1 hour.
3 Cook gnocchi, in batches, in large saucepan of boiling water about 3 minutes or until they float to the surface. Remove with a slotted spoon; drain well.
4 Meanwhile, melt butter in medium frying pan, add basil leaves; cook until crisp. Remove basil from pan with a slotted spoon; drain on absorbent paper. Add tomato; cook, stirring, until tomato softens.
5 Place drained gnocchi and tomato mixture in large bowl; toss gently. Divide among serving dishes, sprinkle with basil. Serve with extra grated parmesan, if you like.

preparation time *40 minutes (plus refrigeration time)*
cooking time *25 minutes* serves *4*
nutritional count per serving *26.5g total fat (16g saturated fat); 2174kJ (520 cal); 51.1g carbohydrate; 13.7g protein; 5.5g fibre*

standing rib roast with horseradish cream

1.2kg standing rib roast
¼ cup (60ml) olive oil
2 green onions, chopped finely
¼ cup (60ml) dry white wine
¼ cup (70g) prepared horseradish
300g sour cream
2 tablespoons lemon juice
1 teaspoon dijon mustard
2 teaspoons finely chopped fresh dill
2 tablespoons hot water

1 Preheat oven to 200°C/180°C fan-forced.
2 Brush roast with 1 tablespoon of the oil. Heat 1 tablespoon of the oil in large flameproof baking dish; cook roast, uncovered, over high heat until browned all over. Place dish in oven; roast about 50 minutes or until cooked as desired.
3 Meanwhile, heat remaining oil in medium frying pan; cook onion, stirring, until soft. Add wine; bring to the boil. Reduce heat; simmer, uncovered, until liquid has almost evaporated.
4 Add horseradish, sour cream, juice and mustard; cook, stirring, until sauce is heated through. Stir in dill and the hot water off the heat.
5 Stand roast 10 minutes before serving with horseradish cream.

preparation time *15 minutes*
cooking time *1 hour* serves *4*
nutritional count per serving *56.5g total fat (27.3g saturated fat); 2943kJ (704 cal); 5.3g carbohydrate; 42.4g protein; 0.5g fibre*

apple pie

1 cup (150g) plain flour
½ cup (75g) self-raising flour
¼ cup (35g) cornflour
¼ cup (30g) custard powder
1 tablespoon caster sugar
100g cold butter, chopped
1 egg, separated
¼ cup (60ml) cold water
1 tablespoon caster sugar, extra

FILLING

10 medium granny smith apples (1.5kg),
   peeled, cored, sliced thickly
½ cup (125ml) water
¼ cup (55g) caster sugar
1 teaspoon finely grated lemon rind
¼ teaspoon ground cinnamon

1   Process flours, custard powder, sugar and butter until crumbly. Add egg yolk and the water; process until ingredients just come together. Knead on floured surface until smooth. Cover; refrigerate 30 minutes.
2   Meanwhile, make filling.
3   Preheat oven to 220°C/200°C fan-forced. Grease deep 25cm pie dish.
4   Divide pastry in half. Roll one half between sheets of baking paper until large enough to line dish. Spoon filling into pastry case; brush pastry edge with egg white.
5   Roll remaining pastry large enough to cover filling. Press edges together. Brush pastry with egg white; sprinkle with extra sugar. Bake 20 minutes.
6   Reduce oven to 180°C/160°C fan-forced; bake pie further 25 minutes.

FILLING Bring apple and the water to the boil in large saucepan. Reduce heat; simmer, covered, about 10 minutes or until apples soften. Drain; stir in sugar, rind and cinnamon. Cool.

preparation time *45 minutes (plus refrigeration time)*
cooking time *1 hour 10 minutes* serves *8*
nutritional count per serving *11.4g total fat (7g saturated fat); 1446kJ (346 cal); 54.2g carbohydrate; 4.3g protein; 3.7g fibre*

apple crumble

5 large apples (1kg)
¼ cup (55g) caster sugar
¼ cup (60ml) water

CRUMBLE

½ cup (75g) self-raising flour
¼ cup (35g) plain flour
½ cup (110g) firmly packed brown sugar
100g cold butter, chopped
1 teaspoon ground cinnamon

1   Preheat oven to 180°C/160°C fan-forced. Grease deep 1.5-litre (6-cup) baking dish.
2   Peel, core and quarter apples. Cook apple, sugar and the water in large saucepan over low heat, covered, about 10 minutes. Drain; discard liquid.
3   Meanwhile, make crumble.
4   Spoon apple mixture into dish; sprinkle with crumble. Bake about 25 minutes.

CRUMBLE Blend or process ingredients until combined.

preparation time *15 minutes*
cooking time *35 minutes* serves *4*
nutritional count per serving *21g total fat (13.6g saturated fat); 2245kJ (537 cal); 80.7g carbohydrate; 3.6g protein; 4.5g fibre*

VARIATIONS

NUT CRUMBLE Stir in ⅓ cup roasted slivered almonds and ⅓ cup coarsely chopped roasted hazelnuts to crumble mixture.

MUESLI CRUMBLE Prepare half the amount of basic crumble mixture; stir in 1 cup toasted muesli.

fudge sauce

This recipe makes enough sauce for four servings of ice-cream.

200g dark eating chocolate
20g butter
¼ teaspoon vanilla extract
½ cup (125ml) cream

1 Place chocolate and butter in small heatproof bowl set over small saucepan of simmering water; do not allow water to touch base of bowl. Stir until chocolate is melted.
2 Stir in extract and cream until combined.
3 Serve sauce warm with ice-cream.

preparation time *5 minutes*
cooking time *10 minutes* makes *1 cup*
nutritional count per tablespoon *10.6g total fat (6.7g saturated fat); 585kJ (140 cal); 10.7g carbohydrate; 1.1g protein; 0.2g fibre*

strawberries and cream

500g strawberries, halved
1½ tablespoons orange-flavoured liqueur
2 teaspoons icing sugar
2 tablespoons icing sugar, extra
½ cup (125ml) thickened cream

1 Combine strawberries, liqueur and icing sugar in large bowl; refrigerate 30 minutes.
2 Drain strawberries over small bowl; reserve liquid. Divide three-quarters of the strawberries among serving dishes.
3 Blend or process remaining strawberries, extra icing sugar and reserved liquid until smooth.
4 Beat cream in small bowl with electric mixer until soft peaks form; fold in strawberry mixture.
5 Top strawberries with strawberry cream.

preparation time *10 minutes (plus refrigeration time)*
serves *4*
nutritional count per serving *11.8g total fat (7.6g saturated fat); 790kJ (189 cal); 14.2g carbohydrate; 2.8g protein; 2.8g fibre*

pears with red wine and cinnamon

4 medium pears (600g), peeled
1½ cups (330g) caster sugar
1 tablespoon lemon juice
2 tablespoons water
½ cup (125ml) dry red wine
1 star anise
¼ teaspoon ground cinnamon

1 Place pears and half of the sugar in large saucepan of water; bring to the boil. Reduce heat; simmer, covered, 30 minutes or until pears are tender.
2 Meanwhile, stir remaining sugar, juice and the water in small saucepan over low heat, without boiling, until sugar dissolves. Bring to the boil. Boil, uncovered, without stirring, about 10 minutes or until mixture turns a caramel colour.
3 Remove sauce from heat; stir in wine, star anise and cinnamon (the caramel will splutter and harden at this stage). Return sauce to low heat, stirring, to dissolve any hardened caramel. Cool 10 minutes; strain into small jug.
4 Serve pears drizzled with sauce.

preparation time *15 minutes*
cooking time *30 minutes* serves *4*
nutritional count per serving *0.2g total fat (0g saturated fat); 3152kJ (754 cal); 179.5g carbohydrate; 0.5g protein; 2.4g fibre*

waffles and ice-cream à la suzette

125g butter
½ cup (110g) caster sugar
2 teaspoons finely grated orange rind
1 tablespoon orange juice
¼ cup (60ml) Cointreau
8 belgian-style waffles
200ml vanilla ice-cream

1 Melt butter in small heavy-base saucepan, add sugar, rind, juice and liqueur; stir over low heat, without boiling, until sugar dissolves. Bring to the boil. Reduce heat; simmer, uncovered, without stirring, about 1 minute or until sauce thickens slightly.
2 Warm waffles according to packet directions.
3 Divide half of the waffles among serving plates; top with ice-cream, remaining waffles and suzette sauce.

preparation time *10 minutes*
cooking time *10 minutes* serves *4*
nutritional count per serving *42.8g total fat (24.6g saturated fat); 3148kJ (753 cal); 73.3g carbohydrate; 9.1g protein; 1.7g fibre*

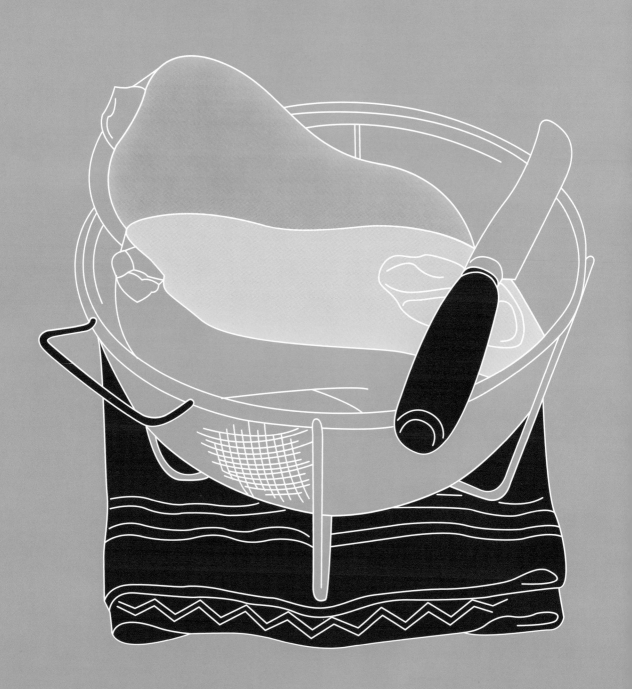

OFFSHORE

baba ghanoush

2 large eggplants (1kg)
¼ cup (70g) tahini
¼ cup (60ml) lemon juice
3 cloves garlic, quartered
1 teaspoon salt
1 tablespoon finely chopped fresh flat-leaf parsley

1 Preheat oven to 220°C/200°C fan-forced.
2 Pierce eggplants all over with fork or skewer; place whole eggplants on oiled oven tray. Bake about 1 hour or until soft. Stand 15 minutes.
3 Peel eggplants, discard skins; chop flesh coarsely.
4 Blend or process eggplant with tahini, juice, garlic and salt, until combined. Spoon into serving bowl; sprinkle with parsley.

preparation time *15 minutes (plus standing time)* cooking time *1 hour* makes *3 cups (700g)* nutritional count per tablespoon *1.3g total fat (0.1g saturated fat); 79kJ (19 cal); 0.8g carbohydrate; 0.7g protein; 1g fibre*

guacamole

1 medium white onion (150g)
2 small tomatoes (260g), seeded
2 medium avocados (500g)
2 tablespoons lime juice
2 tablespoons finely chopped fresh coriander

1 Chop onion and tomatoes finely.
2 Using a fork, mash avocados in medium bowl until almost smooth. Add onion, tomato, juice and coriander; mix well.

preparation time *20 minutes* makes *2½ cups (600g)* nutritional count per tablespoon *2.7g total fat (0.6g saturated fat); 117kJ (28 cal); 0.5g carbohydrate; 0.4g protein; 0.4g fibre*

hummus

¾ cup (150g) dried chickpeas
1 teaspoon salt
1 clove garlic, quartered
⅓ cup (90g) tahini
¼ cup (60ml) lemon juice
pinch cayenne pepper
1 tablespoon finely chopped fresh flat-leaf parsley
2 teaspoons extra virgin olive oil

1 Place chickpeas in medium bowl, cover with cold water; stand overnight.
2 Drain chickpeas, place in medium saucepan, cover with fresh water. Bring to the boil; simmer, covered, about 50 minutes or until chickpeas are tender. Drain chickpeas over large heatproof bowl. Reserve ⅓ cup (80ml) chickpea liquid; discard remaining liquid.
3 Blend or process chickpeas with salt, garlic, tahini, juice and reserved liquid until almost smooth.
4 Spoon into serving bowl; sprinkle with pepper and parsley. Drizzle with olive oil.

preparation time *10 minutes (plus standing time)* cooking time *50 minutes* makes *2 cups (470g)* nutritional count per tablespoon *3g total fat (0.4g saturated fat); 196kJ (47 cal); 2.4g carbohydrate; 1.9g protein; 1.3g fibre*

potato and cheese kofta with tomato tamarind sauce

2 medium potatoes (400g)
2 tablespoons finely chopped fresh coriander
½ cup (75g) roasted unsalted cashews, chopped finely
½ cup (60g) frozen peas, thawed
vegetable oil, for deep-frying
4 hard-boiled eggs, halved

CHEESE

1 litre (4 cups) milk
2 tablespoons lemon juice

TOMATO TAMARIND SAUCE

1 tablespoon olive oil
1 clove garlic, crushed
3cm piece fresh ginger (15g), grated
½ teaspoon dried chilli flakes
1 teaspoon ground cumin
1 teaspoon ground coriander
½ teaspoon mustard seeds
¼ cup (60ml) tamarind concentrate
2 x 400g cans crushed tomatoes

1 Make cheese. Make tomato tamarind sauce.
2 Meanwhile, boil, steam or microwave potato until tender; drain.
3 Mash potato in large bowl; stir in cheese, coriander, nuts and peas.
4 Heat oil in wok; deep-fry level tablespoons of the potato mixture, in batches, until cooked through. Drain on absorbent paper.
5 Add koftas to tomato tamarind sauce; simmer, uncovered, 5 minutes. Divide koftas and sauce among serving plates; top with egg.

CHEESE Bring milk to the boil in medium saucepan. Remove from heat; stir in juice. Cool 10 minutes. Pour through muslin-lined sieve into medium bowl; stand cheese mixture in sieve over bowl for 40 minutes. Discard liquid in bowl.

TOMATO TAMARIND SAUCE Heat oil in large saucepan; cook garlic and ginger, stirring, until fragrant. Add chilli, spices and seeds; cook, stirring, 1 minute. Add tamarind and undrained tomatoes; bring to the boil. Reduce heat; simmer, uncovered, 5 minutes.

preparation time *30 minutes (plus standing time)*
cooking time *35 minutes* serves *4*
nutritional count per serving *29.7g total fat (6.7g saturated fat); 2144kJ (513 cal); 37g carbohydrate; 25.3g protein; 6.2g fibre*

tabbouleh

¼ cup (40g) burghul
3 medium tomatoes (450g)
3 cups coarsely chopped fresh flat-leaf parsley
3 green onions, chopped finely
½ cup coarsely chopped fresh mint
1 clove garlic, crushed
¼ cup (60ml) lemon juice
¼ cup (60ml) olive oil

1 Place burghul in shallow medium bowl. Halve tomatoes, scoop pulp from tomato over burghul. Chop tomato flesh finely; spread over burghul. Cover; refrigerate 1 hour.
2 Place burghul mixture in large bowl with remaining ingredients; toss gently to combine.

preparation time *30 minutes (plus refrigeration time)*
serves *4*
nutritional count per serving *14.2g total fat (2g saturated fat); 790kJ (189 cal); 9.4g carbohydrate; 3.6g protein; 5.9g fibre*

felafel

2 cups (400g) dried chickpeas
1 medium brown onion (150g), chopped coarsely
2 cloves garlic, quartered
½ cup coarsely chopped fresh flat-leaf parsley
2 teaspoons ground coriander
1 teaspoon ground cumin
1 teaspoon bicarbonate of soda
2 tablespoons plain flour
1 teaspoon salt
vegetable oil, for deep frying

1 Place chickpeas in large bowl, cover with cold water; stand overnight, drain.
2 Combine chickpeas, onion, garlic, parsley and spices in large bowl.
3 Blend or process chickpea mixture, in two batches, until almost smooth; return mixture to large bowl. Add soda, flour and salt to chickpea mixture; knead on floured surface for 2 minutes. Stand 30 minutes.
4 Roll level tablespoons of mixture into balls; stand 10 minutes.
5 Heat oil in wok; deep-fry balls, in batches, until golden brown. Serve with separate bowls of dukkah and yogurt for dipping, if you like.

preparation time *45 minutes (plus standing time)*
cooking time *20 minutes* makes *50*
nutritional count per felafel *0.9g total fat (0.1g saturated fat); 79kJ (19 cal); 1.8g carbohydrate; 0.7g protein; 0.6g fibre*

herbed baked ricotta

1kg ricotta cheese
2 tablespoons finely chopped fresh thyme
2 cloves garlic, crushed
2 eggs, beaten lightly
1 tablespoon finely chopped garlic chives
1 tablespoon finely grated lemon rind

1 Preheat oven to 180°C/160°C fan-forced.
Grease deep 20cm-round cake pan; line base with
baking paper.
2 Combine cheese, thyme, garlic, egg, chives and
rind in large bowl. Spoon cheese mixture into pan.
3 Bake cheese mixture about 1 hour or until browned
lightly and firm to touch; cool in pan.

preparation time *15 minutes*
cooking time *1 hour (plus cooling time)* serves *8*
nutritional count per serving *15.5g total fat (9.4g*
saturated fat); 853kJ (204 cal); 1.7g carbohydrate;
14.9g protein; 0.2g fibre

panzanella

½ long loaf ciabatta (250g)
1 clove garlic, crushed
¼ cup (60ml) olive oil
500g cherry tomatoes, halved
1 lebanese cucumber (130g), seeded, sliced thinly
1 medium avocado (250g), chopped coarsely
¼ cup (50g) drained capers, rinsed
1 large yellow capsicum (350g), chopped coarsely
2 x 400g cans white beans, rinsed, drained
½ cup coarsely chopped fresh basil
TOMATO VINAIGRETTE

½ cup (125ml) tomato juice
¼ cup (60ml) red wine vinegar
⅓ cup (80ml) olive oil

1 Preheat oven to 200°C/180°C fan-forced.
2 Cut bread into 2cm cubes. Place bread in large
bowl with combined garlic and oil; toss to coat bread
in oil mixture. Place bread, in single layer, on oven tray;
bake about 10 minutes or until browned lightly.
3 Meanwhile, make tomato vinaigrette.
4 Place bread in same large bowl with remaining
ingredients and vinaigrette; toss gently to combine.

TOMATO VINAIGRETTE Place ingredients in screw-top
jar; shake well.

preparation time 15 minutes
cooking time 10 minutes serves 4
nutritional count per serving *44.7g total fat (7g*
saturated fat); 2951kJ (706 cal); 54.7g carbohydrate;
15.9g protein; 13g fibre

carpaccio with fennel salad

400g beef eye fillet
2 medium fennel bulbs (600g)
2 trimmed celery stalks (200g)
2 tablespoons finely chopped fresh flat-leaf parsley
2 tablespoons lemon juice
1 clove garlic, crushed
¼ teaspoon white sugar
½ teaspoon dijon mustard
⅓ cup (80ml) olive oil

1 Remove any excess fat from fillet, wrap tightly in
plastic wrap; freeze about 1 hour or until partially
frozen. Using sharp knife, slice fillet as thinly as possible.
2 Meanwhile, slice fennel and celery thinly. Place
in medium bowl with remaining ingredients; toss gently
to combine.
3 Arrange beef slices in single layer on serving plates;
top with fennel salad. Serve accompanied with sliced
Italian bread, if you like.

preparation time *10 minutes (plus freezing time)*
serves *4*
nutritional count per serving *24.4g total fat (5.1g*
saturated fat); 1371kJ (328 cal); 3.8g carbohydrate;
22.3g protein; 3.3g fibre

stracciatella

Stracciatella, when translated from Italian to English, means strings or torn rags. This satisfying soup is thus aptly named, since this is what the parmesan-and-egg mixture resembles once it meets the hot stock.

5 eggs
½ cup (40g) finely grated parmesan cheese
1.5 litres (6 cups) chicken stock
2 tablespoons finely chopped fresh flat-leaf parsley
pinch nutmeg

1 Whisk eggs and cheese in medium jug until combined.
2 Bring stock to the boil in large saucepan. Remove from heat; gradually pour in egg mixture, whisking constantly.
3 Return mixture to heat; simmer, stirring constantly, about 5 minutes or until egg mixture forms fine shreds. Stir in parsley and nutmeg.

preparation time *5 minutes*
cooking time *10 minutes* serves *6*
nutritional count per serving *4.1g total fat (2.2g saturated fat); 288kJ (69 cal); 1.8g carbohydrate; 6.5g protein; 0.1g fibre*

lamb kofta platter

650g lamb mince
1 medium brown onion (150g), chopped finely
1 clove garlic, crushed
1 teaspoon ground cumin
1 teaspoon ground coriander
1 cup (70g) stale breadcrumbs
1 egg, beaten lightly
4 pocket pitta
1 tablespoon olive oil
250g tabbouleh
1 medium tomato (150g), chopped finely
200g hummus
1 teaspoon extra virgin olive oil, extra
¼ teaspoon ground paprika
200g beetroot dip

1 Combine lamb mince, onion, garlic, spices, breadcrumbs and egg in medium bowl.
2 Shape the mixture into 12 ovals and thread onto skewers. Cook skewers on heated oiled grill plate (or grill or barbecue) until browned and cooked through.
3 Brush bread with oil, cook in heated oiled grill pan (or grill or barbecue) until browned.
4 Combine tabbouleh and tomato in bowl. Drizzle hummus with extra oil, sprinkle with paprika.
5 Arrange kofta skewers, bread, tabbouleh, hummus, beetroot dip and lemon wedges, if you like, on serving platter.

preparation time *20 minutes*
cooking time *15 minutes* serves *4*
nutritional count per serving *38.3g total fat (9.7g saturated fat); 3612kJ (864 cal); 70g carbohydrate; 53.5g protein; 12.5g fibre*

kashmiri lamb with spicy dhal

1 cup (200g) dried chickpeas
1 cup (200g) yellow split peas
1 teaspoon hot paprika
2 teaspoons ground coriander
2 teaspoons ground cumin
¼ cup (60ml) vegetable oil
600g lamb backstraps
1 medium brown onion (150g), chopped finely
2 cloves garlic, crushed
2cm piece fresh ginger (10g), grated
½ teaspoon ground turmeric
1 teaspoon garam masala
1 teaspoon ground chilli
2 medium tomatoes (300g), chopped coarsely
3 cups (750ml) water
½ cup coarsely chopped fresh coriander leaves

1 Place chickpeas and split peas in large bowl; cover with cold water in large bowl. Soak overnight; rinse, drain.

2 Combine paprika, half the ground coriander, half the cumin, 1 tablespoon of the oil and lamb in large bowl. Cover; refrigerate 3 hours or overnight.

3 Heat 1 tablespoon of the remaining oil in large saucepan; cook onion, garlic and ginger, stirring, until onion softens. Stir in remaining ground coriander and cumin, turmeric, garam masala and chilli; cook, stirring, until fragrant.

4 Add chickpeas, split peas, tomato and the water; bring to the boil. Reduce heat; simmer, covered, stirring occasionally, about 1 hour or until dhal is tender. Remove from heat; stir in fresh coriander.

5 Meanwhile, heat remaining oil in large frying pan; cook lamb, uncovered, until browned and cooked as desired. Cover; stand 10 minutes then slice thickly. Serve with dhal, and yogurt, if you like.

preparation time *30 minutes (plus standing and refrigeration time)* cooking time *1 hour 15 minutes* serves *4*
nutritional count per serving *23.2g total fat (4.7g saturated fat); 2625kJ (628 cal); 44.5g carbohydrate; 54.2g protein; 12.9g fibre*

persian lamb and rhubarb stew

40g butter
1kg diced lamb
1 medium brown onion (150g), sliced thinly
¼ teaspoon saffron threads
½ teaspoon ground cinnamon
¼ teaspoon ground turmeric
1 cup (250ml) water
2 cups (500ml) chicken stock
2 tablespoons tomato paste
2¾ cups (300g) coarsely chopped rhubarb
¼ cup finely chopped fresh mint

1 Melt half of the butter in large deep saucepan; cook lamb, in batches, until browned all over.
2 Melt remaining butter in same pan; cook onion, stirring, until soft. Add spices; cook, stirring, until fragrant. Add the water, stock and paste; bring to the boil. Return lamb to pan, reduce heat; simmer, covered, 1 hour 20 minutes, stirring occasionally.
3 Uncover; simmer about 20 minutes or until lamb is tender. Add rhubarb to lamb mixture; simmer, uncovered, about 10 minutes or until rhubarb has softened.
4 Stir mint into stew off the heat; serve stew over couscous, if you like.

preparation time *20 minutes*
cooking time *2 hours 10 minutes* serves *4*
nutritional count per serving *31g total fat (15.7g saturated fat); 2211kJ (529 cal); 5.6g carbohydrate; 55.8g protein; 3.6g fibre*

dukkah-crusted cutlets with roasted garlic yogurt

6 cloves garlic, unpeeled
1 teaspoon vegetable oil
1 cup (280g) yogurt
2 tablespoons roasted hazelnuts
2 tablespoons roasted pistachios
2 tablespoons sesame seeds
2 tablespoons ground coriander
1 tablespoon ground cumin
12 french-trimmed lamb cutlets (600g)

1 Preheat oven to 180°C/160°C fan-forced.
2 Place garlic on oven tray; drizzle with oil. Roast 10 minutes. Peel garlic then crush in small bowl with yogurt. Cover; refrigerate.
3 To make dukkah, blend or process nuts until chopped finely. Dry-fry seeds and spices in small frying pan until fragrant; combine with nuts in medium bowl.
4 Add cutlets to dukkah mixture, turn to coat. Cook cutlets, both sides, in heated oiled grill pan (or grill or barbecue) until cooked. Serve lamb with garlic yogurt.

preparation time *10 minutes*
cooking time *20 minutes* serves *4*
nutritional count per serving *27.8g total fat (8.7g saturated fat); 1547kJ (370 cal); 5.7g carbohydrate; 22.9g protein; 2.9g fibre*

lemon and garlic kebabs with greek salad

8 x 15cm stalks fresh rosemary
800g lamb fillets, cut into 3cm pieces
3 cloves garlic, crushed
2 tablespoons olive oil
2 teaspoons finely grated lemon rind
1 tablespoon lemon juice

GREEK SALAD

5 medium egg tomatoes (375g), cut into wedges
2 lebanese cucumbers (260g), halved lengthways,
    sliced thinly
1 medium red capsicum (200g), cut into 2cm pieces
1 medium green capsicum (200g), cut into 2cm pieces
1 medium red onion (170g), sliced thinly
¼ cup (40g) seeded kalamata olives
200g fetta cheese, cut into 2cm pieces
2 teaspoons fresh oregano leaves
¼ cup (60ml) olive oil
2 tablespoons cider vinegar

1   Remove leaves from bottom two-thirds of each
rosemary stalk; sharpen trimmed ends to a point.
2   Thread lamb onto rosemary skewers. Brush kebabs
with combined garlic, oil, rind and juice. Cover;
refrigerate until required.
3   Make greek salad.
4   Cook kebabs on heated oiled grill plate (or grill or
barbecue), brushing frequently with remaining garlic
mixture, until cooked. Serve kebabs with greek salad.

GREEK SALAD Place ingredients in large bowl; toss
gently to combine.

preparation time *25 minutes*
cooking time *5 minutes* serves *4*
nutritional count per serving *52.5g total fat (18.9g
saturated fat); 3085kJ (738 cal); 11.2g carbohydrate;
54.1g protein; 4.1g fibre*

duxelles-filled leg of lamb with roasted vegetables

40g butter
150g swiss brown mushrooms, chopped finely
1 clove garlic, crushed
3 shallots (75g), chopped finely
½ cup (125ml) balsamic vinegar
1.2kg easy carve lamb leg
1 teaspoon sea salt
2 large parsnips (700g)
2 large carrots (360g)
1 large kumara (500g)
2 large potatoes (600g)
2 tablespoons olive oil
½ cup (125ml) beef stock

1   Melt butter in large frying pan; cook mushrooms,
garlic and shallot, stirring, until onion softens. Add half
of the vinegar; bring to the boil. Reduce heat; simmer
duxelles, uncovered, about 5 minutes or until liquid
has evaporated.
2   Fill lamb cavity with duxelles; rub lamb all over
with salt.
3   Preheat oven to 180°C/160°C fan-forced.
4   Halve parsnips, carrots and kumara first crossways,
then lengthways; cut pieces into thick slices. Cut
potatoes into wedges. Place vegetables, in single layer,
in large shallow flameproof baking dish; drizzle with
oil. Place lamb on wire rack over vegetables; roast
about 1½ hours or until lamb is cooked as desired and
vegetables are tender. Remove lamb and vegetables
from dish, cover lamb; stand 10 minutes.
5   Meanwhile, place dish containing juices over heat;
stir in stock and remaining vinegar, bring to the boil.
Strain sauce into small jug. Serve vegetables with sliced
lamb, drizzled with sauce.

preparation time *30 minutes*
cooking time *1 hour 45 minutes* serves *4*
nutritional count per serving *34.3g total fat (13.9g
saturated fat); 3432kJ (821 cal); 50.5g carbohydrate;
76.5g protein; 11g fibre*

roasted root vegetable ratatouille

800g celeriac, trimmed, chopped coarsely
2 large carrots (360g), chopped coarsely
2 medium parsnips (500g), chopped coarsely
2 medium kumara (800g), chopped coarsely
⅓ cup (80ml) olive oil
1 large brown onion (200g), chopped finely
3 cloves garlic, crushed
¼ cup loosely packed fresh oregano leaves
1 tablespoon tomato paste
2 x 425g cans crushed tomatoes
½ cup (125ml) dry red wine
1 cup (250ml) water
½ cup (40g) coarsely grated parmesan cheese
2½ cups (250g) coarsely grated mozzarella cheese
1 cup (70g) fresh breadcrumbs
2 teaspoons finely grated lemon rind
½ cup coarsely chopped fresh flat-leaf parsley
2 tablespoons coarsely chopped fresh oregano

1   Preheat oven to 220°C/200°C fan-forced.
2   Combine celeriac, carrot, parsnip, kumara and half of the oil in large deep baking dish. Roast about 50 minutes or until vegetables are tender and browned lightly, stirring halfway through cooking time.
3   Meanwhile, heat remaining oil in large saucepan; cook onion, garlic and oregano leaves, stirring, until onion softens. Add paste; cook, stirring, 1 minute. Add undrained tomatoes, wine and the water; bring to the boil. Boil, uncovered, 10 minutes.
4   Add tomato mixture to vegetables in dish; toss gently to combine. Sprinkle with combined cheeses, breadcrumbs, rind, parsley and chopped oregano. Bake, uncovered, about 20 minutes or until top browns lightly. Serve with a lemon vinaigrette-dressed green leafy salad, if you like.

preparation time *40 minutes*
cooking time *1 hour 30 minutes* serves *6*
nutritional count per serving *24.7g total fat (9.1g saturated fat); 2090kJ (500 cal); 43.9g carbohydrate; 22.1g protein; 12.7g fibre*

greek lamb and lima bean soup

1 cup (200g) dried lima beans
2 tablespoons olive oil
3 lamb shanks (750g)
2 medium brown onions (300g), chopped finely
1 clove garlic, crushed
2 medium carrots (240g), chopped finely
2 trimmed celery stalks (200g), chopped finely
2 cups (500ml) chicken stock
1 litre (4 cups) water
400g can chopped tomatoes
¼ cup coarsely chopped fresh dill
2 tablespoons lemon juice

1   Place beans in medium bowl, cover with water; stand overnight, drain.
2   Heat oil in large saucepan, cook lamb, in batches, until browned all over. Add onion, garlic, carrot and celery to same pan; cook, stirring, until softened.
3   Return lamb to pan with beans, stock and the water; bring to the boil. Simmer, covered, 1 hour, skimming surface occasionally.
4   Remove lamb shanks from pan. When cool enough to handle, remove meat from bones, discard bones; shred meat. Return meat to pan with undrained tomatoes, simmer, covered, 1 hour. Stir in dill and juice.

preparation time *15 minutes (plus standing time)*
cooking time *2 hours 10 minutes* serves *8*
nutritional count per serving *8.3g total fat (2.1g saturated fat); 928kJ (222 cal); 15.3g carbohydrate; 18.2g protein; 6.8g fibre*

tuscan bean soup

2 tablespoons olive oil
3 medium brown onions (450g), chopped coarsely
2 cloves garlic, crushed
200g piece speck, bacon or pancetta,
    chopped coarsely
2 medium carrots (240g), chopped coarsely
2 trimmed celery stalks (200g), chopped coarsely
2 x 400g cans tomatoes
¼ medium savoy cabbage (375g), shredded coarsely
1 medium zucchini (120g), chopped coarsely
2 sprigs fresh thyme
2 cups (500ml) beef stock
2 litres (8 cups) water
400g can borlotti beans, rinsed, drained
6 thick slices ciabatta

1 Heat oil in large saucepan. Cook onion, garlic and speck, stirring, about 5 minutes or until onion is soft.
2 Add carrot, celery, undrained crushed tomatoes, cabbage, zucchini, thyme, stock and the water. Bring to the boil. Reduce heat; simmer, uncovered, 2 hours.
3 Add beans; simmer, uncovered, 20 minutes.
4 Meanwhile, toast or grill bread. Place a slice of bread in the base of six serving bowls, top with soup. Drizzle with extra olive oil, if you like.

preparation time *15 minutes*
cooking time *2 hours 30 minutes* serves *6*
nutritional count per serving *12.1g total fat (2.9g saturated fat); 1154kJ (276 cal); 22.8g carbohydrate; 15.2g protein; 8.3g fibre*

cuban black bean soup

2½ cups (500g) dried black beans
1kg ham bone
¼ cup (60ml) olive oil
2 medium brown onions (300g), chopped finely
1 medium red capsicum (200g), chopped finely
4 cloves garlic, crushed
1 tablespoon ground cumin
1 teaspoon dried chilli flakes
400g can chopped tomatoes
2.5 litres (10 cups) water
1 tablespoon dried oregano
2 teaspoons ground black pepper
¼ cup (60ml) lime juice
2 medium tomatoes (300g), chopped finely
¼ cup coarsely chopped fresh coriander
2 limes, quartered

1 Place beans in medium bowl, cover with water, stand overnight; drain. Rinse under cold water; drain.
2 Preheat oven to 220°C/200°C fan-forced.
3 Roast ham bone on oven tray, uncovered, 30 minutes.
4 Meanwhile, heat oil in large saucepan; cook onion, capsicum and garlic, stirring, until vegetables soften. Add cumin and chilli; cook, stirring, 1 minute. Add beans and ham bone to pan with undrained canned tomatoes, the water, oregano and pepper; bring to the boil. Reduce heat; simmer, uncovered, 1½ hours.
5 Remove ham bone from soup. When cool enough to handle, remove ham from bone, shred coarsely. Discard bone.
6 Return ham to soup; bring to the boil. Reduce heat, simmer, uncovered, until soup is hot. Remove from heat; stir in juice, fresh tomato and coriander.
7 Serve bowls of soup with lime wedges.

preparation time *30 minutes (plus standing time)*
cooking time *2 hours 15 minutes* serves *8*
nutritional count per serving *9.4g total fat (1.6g saturated fat); 1279kJ (306 cal); 29.2g carbohydrate; 20.4g protein; 10.9g fibre*

chicken kofta with date chutney and spiced eggplant

¼ cup (50g) brown rice
1 tablespoon olive oil
1 small brown onion (80g), chopped finely
1 clove garlic, crushed
1 long green chilli, chopped finely
500g chicken mince
½ cup firmly packed fresh coriander leaves
1 egg

SPICED EGGPLANT

1 tablespoon olive oil
2 teaspoons cumin seeds
2 teaspoons yellow mustard seeds
6 baby eggplants (360g), sliced thickly
1 medium brown onion (150g), sliced thinly
1 clove garlic, crushed
½ cup (125ml) water
420g can chickpeas, rinsed, drained
¼ cup firmly packed fresh coriander leaves

DATE CHUTNEY

½ cup (70g) seeded dried dates, chopped finely
¼ cup (60ml) orange juice
¼ cup (60ml) water

1 Cook rice in large saucepan of boiling water, uncovered, until just tender; drain. Rinse under cold water; drain.
2 Heat oil in small frying pan; cook onion, garlic and chilli, stirring, until onion softens. Process onion mixture, chicken mince, rice, coriander and egg until smooth.
3 Shape chicken mixture into 12 patties. Place patties on tray, cover; refrigerate until required.
4 Make spiced eggplant. Make date chutney.
5 Cook kofta patties on heated oiled grill plate (or grill or barbecue) until browned both sides and cooked through. Serve kofta with eggplant; top with date chutney.

SPICED EGGPLANT Heat oil in medium saucepan; fry seeds over low heat until fragrant. Add eggplant, onion and garlic; cook, stirring, about 5 minutes or until just softened. Add the water and chickpeas; bring to the boil. Reduce heat; simmer, uncovered, about 15 minutes or until mixture thickens. Remove from heat; cool 10 minutes then stir in coriander.

DATE CHUTNEY Bring ingredients to the boil in small saucepan. Reduce heat; simmer, uncovered, 5 minutes. Cool 5 minutes; blend or process until smooth.

preparation time *30 minutes (plus refrigeration time)*
cooking time *45 minutes* serves *4*
nutritional count per serving *17.8g total fat (3.5g saturated fat); 1935kJ (463 cal); 37.1g carbohydrate; 35.4g protein; 8.6g fibre*

saltimbocca with risotto milanese

Saltimbocca is a classic Italian veal dish that literally means "jump in the mouth" – just the sensation the wonderful flavours will produce with your first bite. Tinged with the taste and colour of saffron, a milanese is the classic risotto generally served with saltimbocca.

8 veal steaks (680g)
4 slices prosciutto (60g), halved crossways
8 fresh sage leaves
½ cup (50g) finely grated pecorino cheese
40g butter
1 cup (250ml) dry white wine
1 tablespoon coarsely chopped fresh sage

RISOTTO MILANESE

1½ cups (375ml) water
2 cups (500ml) chicken stock
½ cup (125ml) dry white wine
¼ teaspoon saffron threads
20g butter
1 large brown onion (200g), chopped finely
2 cups (400g) arborio rice
¼ cup (20g) finely grated parmesan cheese

1 Place steaks on board. Place one piece prosciutto, one sage leaf and ⅛ of the cheese on each steak; fold in half to secure filling, secure with a toothpick or small skewer.

2 Make risotto milanese.

3 Melt half of the butter in medium non-stick frying pan; cook saltimbocca, in batches, about 5 minutes or until browned both sides and cooked through. Cover to keep warm.

4 Pour wine into same frying pan; bring to the boil. Boil, uncovered, until wine reduces by half. Stir in remaining butter then chopped sage.

5 Divide risotto milanese and saltimbocca among serving plates; drizzle saltimbocca with sauce and accompany with steamed green beans, if you like.

RISOTTO MILANESE Place the water, stock, wine and saffron in medium saucepan; bring to the boil. Reduce heat; simmer, covered. Heat butter in another medium saucepan; cook onion, stirring, until softened. Add rice; stir to coat rice in onion mixture. Stir in ½ cup of the simmering stock mixture; cook, stirring, over low heat, until liquid is absorbed. Continue adding stock mixture, in ½-cup batches, stirring until absorbed after each addition. Total cooking time should be about 35 minutes or until rice is just tender. Stir cheese gently into risotto.

preparation time *10 minutes*
cooking time *25 minutes* serves *4*
nutritional count per serving *23.3g total fat (13.2g saturated fat); 3444kJ (824 cal); 83.1g carbohydrate; 53.7g protein; 1.5g fibre*

chicken and prosciutto cannelloni

Pancetta or double-smoked ham can be substituted for the prosciutto.

50g butter
¼ cup (35g) plain flour
⅔ cup (160ml) milk
1½ cups (375ml) chicken stock
½ cup (40g) finely grated parmesan cheese
400g fontina cheese, grated coarsely
1 tablespoon olive oil
2 medium brown onions (300g), chopped finely
3 cloves garlic, crushed
1kg chicken mince
2 tablespoons finely chopped fresh sage
850g canned tomatoes
½ cup (125ml) dry white wine
¼ cup (70g) tomato paste
3 teaspoons white sugar
12 fresh lasagne sheets
24 slices prosciutto (360g)

1 Heat butter in medium saucepan; cook flour, stirring, until mixture bubbles and thickens. Gradually stir in milk and stock; cook, stirring, until sauce boils and thickens. Remove from heat; stir in parmesan and a quarter of the fontina.
2 Heat oil in large saucepan; cook onion and garlic, stirring, until onion softens. Add chicken; cook, stirring, until browned. Stir in sage. Combine chicken and cheese sauce in large bowl; cool.
3 Cook undrained crushed tomatoes, wine, paste and sugar in same large pan, stirring, 10 minutes. Cool 10 minutes; blend or process, in batches, until smooth.
4 Preheat oven to 180°C/160°C fan-forced.
5 Cut pasta sheets and prosciutto slices in half crossways. Place two pieces of prosciutto on each piece of pasta. Top each piece of pasta with ¼ cup chicken mixture; roll to enclose filling.
6 Oil two 3-litre (12-cup) ovenproof dishes. Pour a quarter of the tomato sauce into base of each dish; place half of the pasta rolls, seam-side down, in each dish. Pour remaining tomato sauce over rolls; sprinkle each dish with remaining fontina.
7 Bake cannelloni, covered, 30 minutes. Uncover, bake further 15 minutes or until cheese melts and browns. Serve with a green salad, if you like.

preparation time *30 minutes*
cooking time *1 hour 10 minutes* serves *8*
nutritional count per serving *36g total fat (18.5g saturated fat); 2746kJ (657 cal); 25.3g carbohydrate; 54.1g protein; 3.2g fibre*

chicken, pea, sage and prosciutto risotto

3 cups (750ml) chicken stock
3 cups (750ml) water
10g butter
2 tablespoons olive oil
1 small brown onion (80g), chopped finely
2 cups (400g) arborio rice
½ cup (125ml) dry white wine
350g chicken breast fillets, chopped coarsely
2 cloves garlic, crushed
1½ cups (180g) frozen peas
6 slices prosciutto (90g)
2 tablespoons finely shredded fresh sage

1 Place stock and the water in large saucepan; bring to the boil. Reduce heat; simmer, covered.
2 Heat butter and half of the oil in large saucepan; cook onion, stirring, until soft. Add rice; stir rice to coat in mixture. Add wine; cook, stirring, until liquid is almost evaporated.
3 Stir in 1 cup simmering stock mixture; cook, stirring, over low heat until liquid is absorbed. Continue adding stock mixture, in 1-cup batches, stirring, until absorbed after each addition. Total cooking time should be about 35 minutes or until rice is tender.
4 Meanwhile, heat remaining oil in medium frying pan; cook chicken, stirring, until cooked through. Add garlic; stir until fragrant. Stir chicken mixture and peas into risotto. .
5 Cook prosciutto in same frying pan until crisp; drain on absorbent paper then break into coarse pieces. Stir sage and half of the prosciutto into risotto; sprinkle remaining prosciutto over individual risotto servings.

preparation time *20 minutes*
cooking time *45 minutes* serves *4*
nutritional count per serving *18.8g total fat (5.1g saturated fat); 2784kJ (666 cal); 84.1g carbohydrate; 24.5g protein; 3.9g fibre*

prawn and asparagus risotto

500g uncooked medium king prawns
3 cups (750ml) chicken stock
3 cups (750ml) water
10g butter
1 tablespoon olive oil
1 small brown onion (80g), chopped finely
2 cups (400g) arborio rice
½ cup (125ml) dry sherry
10g butter, extra
2 teaspoons olive oil, extra
2 cloves garlic, crushed
500g asparagus, chopped coarsely
⅓ cup (25g) coarsely grated parmesan cheese
⅓ cup coarsely chopped fresh basil

1 Shell and devein prawns; chop prawn meat coarsely.
2 Place stock and the water in large saucepan; bring to the boil. Reduce heat; simmer, covered.
3 Meanwhile, heat butter and oil in large saucepan; cook onion, stirring, until soft. Add rice; stir rice to coat in onion mixture. Add sherry; cook, stirring, until liquid is almost evaporated.
4 Stir in 1 cup simmering stock mixture; cook, stirring, over low heat until liquid is absorbed. Continue adding stock mixture, in 1-cup batches, stirring, until absorbed after each addition. Total cooking time should be about 35 minutes or until rice is tender.
5 Heat extra butter and extra oil in medium frying pan; cook prawn meat and garlic, stirring, until prawn just changes colour.
6 Boil, steam or microwave asparagus until just tender; drain. Add asparagus, prawn mixture and cheese to risotto; cook, stirring, until cheese melts. Stir in basil.

preparation time *25 minutes*
cooking time *45 minutes* serves *4*
nutritional count per serving *14.7g total fat (5.5g saturated fat); 2516kJ (602 cal); 82.8g carbohydrate; 26.3g protein; 2.6g fibre*

stuffed squid saganaki

8 small whole squid (600g)
¼ cup (40g) seeded kalamata olives, chopped coarsely
1 teaspoon finely grated lemon rind
¼ teaspoon dried chilli flakes
200g fetta cheese, crumbled
2 teaspoons fresh thyme leaves
1 tablespoon olive oil
1 small red onion (100g), chopped finely
1 clove garlic, crushed
½ cup (125ml) dry white wine
1 cinnamon stick
2 x 400g cans diced tomatoes
3 sprigs fresh thyme
2 teaspoons white sugar

1 Gently separate bodies and tentacles of squid by pulling on tentacles. Cut head from tentacles just below eyes; discard head. Trim long tentacle of each squid; remove the clear quill from inside body. Peel inside flaps from bodies with salted fingers, then peel away dark skin. Wash squid well and pat dry with absorbent paper.

2 Combine olives, rind, chilli, three-quarters of the cheese and half of the thyme leaves in small bowl; stuff cheese mixture into squid bodies. Place tentacles inside opening; secure tentacles to squid with toothpicks. Cover; refrigerate until required.

3 Heat oil in large deep frying pan; cook onion and garlic, stirring, until onion softens. Add wine; bring to the boil. Reduce heat; simmer, uncovered, until liquid is reduced by half.

4 Add cinnamon, undrained tomatoes, thyme sprigs and sugar; bring to the boil. Reduce heat; simmer, uncovered, about 10 minutes or until sauce thickens slightly. Add stuffed squid to pan; simmer, covered, about 15 minutes or until squid are cooked through, turning once halfway through cooking time. Add remaining cheese and remaining thyme leaves; stir until cheese melts slightly. Remove toothpicks; serve with greek-style bread, if you like.

preparation time *50 minutes*
cooking time *45 minutes* serves *4*
nutritional count per serving *18.6g total fat (8.9g saturated fat); 1580kJ (378 cal); 11.7g carbohydrate; 36.1g protein; 3g fibre*

vine-leaf-wrapped swordfish with tomato-olive salsa

16 large fresh grapevine leaves
4 x 200g swordfish steaks

TOMATO-OLIVE SALSA

3 cloves garlic, crushed
1 cup loosely packed fresh flat-leaf parsley leaves
¼ cup coarsely chopped fresh chives
3 small tomatoes (390g), chopped coarsely
½ cup (75g) seeded kalamata olives,
    quartered lengthways
2 tablespoons drained capers, rinsed
2 tablespoons lemon juice
2 teaspoons olive oil

1 Trim vine leaves; using metal tongs, dip, one at a time, in medium saucepan of boiling salted water. Rinse immediately under cold water; drain on absorbent paper.
2 Overlap four vine leaves slightly to form a rectangle large enough to wrap each piece of fish; fold leaves around fish to enclose completely. Place fish parcels in large steamer fitted over large saucepan of boiling water; steam, covered, about 15 minutes or until cooked as desired.
3 Meanwhile, make tomato-olive salsa.
4 Place fish parcels on serving bowls; pull back vine leaves to uncover fish, top with salsa.

TOMATO-OLIVE SALSA Combine ingredients in medium bowl.

preparation time *20 minutes*
cooking time *20 minutes* serves *4*
nutritional count per serving *7.1g total fat (1.8g saturated fat); 1124kJ (269 cal); 6.8g carbohydrate; 42.6g protein; 2.9g fibre*

veal with eggplant, olives and capers

1.5kg diced veal
plain flour
2 tablespoons olive oil
10 spring onions, trimmed, halved
4 cloves garlic, crushed
1 tablespoon drained capers, chopped finely
1 large eggplant (500g), chopped coarsely
10 medium tomatoes (1.3kg), chopped coarsely
¼ cup (60ml) tomato paste
1 cup (250ml) dry white wine
2 teaspoons finely chopped fresh thyme
2 bay leaves
¼ cup (40g) seeded black olives
2 tablespoons roasted pine nuts
2 tablespoons finely chopped fresh mint leaves

1 Preheat oven to 180°C/160°C fan-forced.
2 Toss veal in flour; shake away excess flour. Heat oil in 3 litre (12-cup) flameproof casserole dish; cook veal, in batches, over heat until browned. Remove from dish.
3 Cook onion, garlic, capers and eggplant in same dish, stirring, over heat 5 minutes. Add veal, then stir in tomato, paste, wine, thyme and bay leaves.
4 Cook, covered, in oven about 2 hours or until veal is tender. Discard bay leaves. Serve topped with olives, nuts and mint.

preparation time *20 minutes*
cooking time *2 hours 30 minutes* serves *6*
nutritional count per serving *16.5g total fat (2.8g saturated fat); 2416kJ (578 cal); 22.7g carbohydrate; 66.6g protein; 22.2g fibre*

1

2

3

4

turkish pilaf with chicken, onion and almonds

60g butter
500g chicken strips
1 large brown onion (200g), sliced thinly
4 cloves garlic, crushed
⅓ cup (45g) slivered almonds
1 teaspoon ground allspice
½ teaspoon ground cinnamon
3 drained anchovies, chopped coarsely
2 tablespoons dried currants
1½ cups (300g) basmati rice
2 cups (500ml) chicken stock
1 cup (250ml) water
1 fresh long red chilli, chopped finely

1 Melt a third of the butter in large saucepan; cook chicken, in batches, until just cooked through.
2 Melt remaining butter in same pan; cook onion, garlic and nuts, stirring, until onion softens. Add spices, anchovies and currants; cook, stirring, 2 minutes. Add rice; cook, stirring, 2 minutes. Add stock and the water; bring to the boil. Reduce heat; simmer, covered tightly, 20 minutes or until rice is just tender.
3 Stir chicken into pilaf mixture; cook, covered, until heated through. Serve pilaf sprinkled with chilli, and parsley, if you like.

preparation time *15 minutes*
cooking time *40 minutes* serves *4*
nutritional count per serving *25.1g total fat (10.4g saturated fat); 2696kJ (645 cal); 67g carbohydrate; 36.5g protein; 3.3g fibre*

burghul-stuffed vine leaves with yogurt dip

1 cup (160g) burghul
1 cup (250ml) boiling water
1 tablespoon olive oil
1 green onion, chopped finely
¼ cup (35g) roasted slivered almonds
2 tablespoons finely chopped raisins
2 tablespoons finely chopped fresh mint
1 tablespoon finely chopped fresh coriander
1 tablespoon finely chopped fresh flat-leaf parsley
2 teaspoons ground cinnamon
2 teaspoons finely grated lemon rind
1 tablespoon lemon juice
40 grapevine leaves in brine (200g), rinsed, drained

YOGURT DIP

¾ cup (200g) low-fat yogurt
1 tablespoon finely chopped fresh mint
1 tablespoon finely chopped fresh coriander
1 teaspoon lemon juice
5cm piece fresh ginger (25g), grated

1 Combine burghul and the boiling water in medium heatproof bowl. Cover; stand 5 minutes. Stir in oil, onion, nuts, raisins, herbs, cinnamon, rind and juice.
2 Line base of large bamboo steamer with about 10 vine leaves.
3 Place one of the remaining leaves, vein-side up, on board; place 1 tablespoon of the burghul mixture in centre of leaf. Fold in two opposing sides; roll to enclose filling. Repeat with remaining leaves and burghul mixture.
4 Place rolls, in single layer, on leaves in steamer. Steam, covered, over wok of simmering water about 15 minutes or until rolls are heated through.
5 Meanwhile, make yogurt dip. Serve dip with rolls.

YOGURT DIP Combine ingredients in small bowl.

preparation time *25 minutes (plus standing time)*
cooking time *15 minutes* serves *6*
nutritional count per serving *8g total fat (1.5g saturated fat); 836kJ (200 cal); 21.3g carbohydrate; 7.1g protein; 7g fibre*

1 TURKISH PILAF WITH CHICKEN, ONION AND ALMONDS
2 BURGHUL-STUFFED VINE LEAVES WITH YOGURT DIP 3 BEETROOT WITH
SKORDALIA [P 472] 4 VEAL SCALOPPINE WITH SALSA VERDE [P 472]

beetroot with skordalia

6 medium beetroot (1kg), trimmed

SKORDALIA

1 medium potato (200g), sliced thickly
4 cloves garlic, chopped coarsely
½ teaspoon salt
2 tablespoons cold water
1½ tablespoons lemon juice
⅓ cup (80ml) olive oil

1   Boil or steam unpeeled beetroot until tender; drain.
Peel while still warm. Cut beetroot into wedges;
sprinkle with salt.
2   Make skordalia.
3   Serve beetroot with skordalia.

SKORDALIA   Boil or steam potato until tender; drain.
Mash potato until smooth; cool. Blend or process garlic,
salt, water and juice until smooth. With motor operating,
add oil in a thin stream; blend until thick. Stir in potato.

preparation time *15 minutes*
cooking time *30 minutes (plus cooling time)* serves *8*
nutritional count per serving *9.3g total fat (1.3g
saturated fat); 631kJ (151 cal); 12.3g carbohydrate;
2.7g protein; 4g fibre*

veal scaloppine with salsa verde

2 tablespoons olive oil
8 veal schnitzels (800g)

SALSA VERDE

1 cup coarsely chopped fresh flat-leaf parley
½ cup finely chopped fresh dill
½ cup finely chopped fresh chives
2 tablespoons wholegrain mustard
⅓ cup (80ml) olive oil
¼ cup (60ml) lemon juice
¼ cup (50g) drained baby capers, rinsed
2 cloves garlic, crushed

1   Make salsa verde.
2   Heat oil in large frying pan; cook veal, in batches,
until browned both sides and cooked as desired.
3   Serve veal topped with salsa verde. Serve with
steamed baby new potatoes, if you like.

SALSA VERDE   Combine ingredients in medium bowl.

preparation time *15 minutes*
cooking time *5 minutes* serves *4*
nutritional count per serving *32.4g total fat (5.3g
saturated fat); 2002kJ (479 cal); 2.2g carbohydrate;
44g protein; 1.6g fibre*

veal and tomato dolmades

200g packet grapevine leaves in brine
1 tablespoon olive oil
1 large red onion (300g), chopped finely
4 cloves garlic, crushed
500g veal mince
400g can crushed tomatoes
¼ cup (30g) seeded green olives, chopped finely
¼ cup (35g) drained sun-dried tomatoes,
    chopped finely
1 tablespoon tomato paste

1   Place leaves in large heatproof bowl, cover with
boiling water; stand 10 minutes, drain. Rinse under
cold water; drain. Pat 36 similar-size, well-shaped
leaves dry with absorbent paper; reserve remaining
leaves for another use.
2   Heat oil in large frying pan; cook onion and garlic,
stirring, until onion softens. Add mince; cook, stirring,
until just changed in colour.
3   Add remaining ingredients; bring to the boil.
Reduce heat; simmer, uncovered, about 5 minutes or
until liquid is almost evaporated; cool 15 minutes.
4   Place leaves, vein-side up, on board. Spoon
1 tablespoon of the filling near stem in centre of one
leaf; roll once toward tip of leaf to cover filling then
fold in two sides. Continue rolling toward tip of leaf;
place, seam-side down, in baking-paper-lined steamer.
Repeat process with remaining leaves and filling
mixture, placing rolls about 1cm apart in steamer.
5   Place steamer over large saucepan of boiling water.
Steam, covered, about 15 minutes or until dolmades
are heated through. Serve hot or cold, drizzled with
lemon juice, if you like.

preparation time *40 minutes (plus cooling time)*
cooking time *35 minutes* makes *36*
nutritional count per dolmades *1.6g total fat (0.5g
saturated fat); 146kJ (35 cal); 1.4g carbohydrate;
3.6g protein; 0.7g* fibre

veal shin on mushroom ragoût

40g butter
4 pieces veal osso buco (1kg)
2 cloves garlic, crushed
1 tablespoon fresh rosemary leaves
½ cup (125ml) port
1 cup (250ml) beef stock

MUSHROOM RAGOUT

40g butter
2 cloves garlic, crushed
1 large flat mushroom (100g), sliced thickly
200g swiss brown mushrooms, trimmed
200g shiitake mushrooms, sliced thickly
1 medium red capsicum (200g), sliced thickly
1 medium green capsicum (200g), sliced thickly
½ cup (125ml) beef stock
2 tablespoons port

1   Preheat oven to 200°C/180°C fan-forced.
2   Melt butter in medium flameproof casserole dish;
cook veal, uncovered, over heat until browned both
sides. Add garlic, rosemary, port and stock; cook,
covered, in oven 2¼ hours.
3   Meanwhile, make mushroom ragoût.
4   Divide veal and ragoût among serving dishes.
Serve with soft polenta, if you like.

MUSHROOM RAGOUT Heat butter in large frying pan;
cook garlic, mushrooms and capsicums, stirring, until
vegetables are browned lightly and tender. Stir in stock
and port; cook, covered, 30 minutes.

preparation time *15 minutes*
cooking time *2 hours 15 minutes* serves *4*
nutritional count per serving *17.9g total fat (11.1g
saturated fat); 1743kJ (417 cal); 9.4g carbohydrate;
42.3g protein; 4.5g fibre*

quince and chicken tagine

2 medium quinces (700g), peeled, cored,
    cut into wedges
40g butter
⅓ cup (115g) honey
3 cups (750ml) water
2 teaspoons orange flower water
2 teaspoons olive oil
4 chicken drumsticks (600g)
4 chicken thigh cutlets (800g), skin removed
1 large brown onion (200g), chopped coarsely
3 cloves garlic, crushed
1 teaspoon ground cumin
1 teaspoon ground ginger
pinch saffron threads
2 cups (500ml) chicken stock
2 large zucchini (300g), chopped coarsely
¼ cup coarsely chopped fresh coriander

CORIANDER COUSCOUS

1½ cups (300g) couscous
1½ cups (375ml) boiling water
50g baby spinach leaves, chopped finely
2 tablespoons finely chopped fresh coriander
2 green onions, sliced thinly

1 Place quinces, butter, honey, the water and orange
flower water in medium saucepan; bring to the boil.
Reduce heat; simmer, covered, 1 hour, stirring occasionally.
Uncover, cook, stirring occasionally, about 45 minutes
or until quinces are red in colour.
2 Meanwhile, heat oil in large frying pan; cook
chicken, in batches, until browned.
3 Cook onion, garlic and spices in same frying pan,
stirring, until onion softens. Add stock and chicken; bring
to the boil. Reduce heat; simmer, covered, 20 minutes.
Uncover; simmer, about 20 minutes or until chicken is
cooked though. Add zucchini; cook, uncovered, about
10 minutes or until zucchini is tender. Stir in quinces
and ½ cup of the quince syrup.
4 Meanwhile, make coriander couscous.
5 Divide tagine and couscous among serving plates;
sprinkle with coriander.

CORIANDER COUSCOUS Combine couscous with the
water in large heatproof bowl; cover, stand about
5 minutes or until water is absorbed, fluffing with fork
occasionally. Stir in spinach, coriander and onion.

preparation time *25 minutes*
cooking time *1 hour 50 minutes* serves *4*
nutritional count per serving *32.6g total fat (12.3g
saturated fat); 3913kJ (936 cal); 99g carbohydrate;
56.7g protein; 12.5g fibre*

chicken with capers, anchovies and rosemary

¼ cup (50g) drained capers, rinsed, chopped finely
4 cloves garlic, crushed
6 anchovies, chopped finely
2 teaspoons fresh rosemary leaves
8 chicken thighs (1.6kg)

1 Combine capers, garlic, anchovies and rosemary
in a small bowl.
2 Preheat grill to hot.
3 Cut two deep slashes in each chicken thigh. Place
a teaspoon of caper mixture into each slash.
4 Cook chicken, skin-side down, under grill for about
15 minutes; turn chicken, cook for a further 15 minutes
or until browned and cooked through. Serve with salad
leaves and steamed baby new potatoes, if you like.

preparation time *15 minutes*
cooking time *30 minutes* serves *4*
nutritional count per serving *32.8g total fat (10.8g
saturated fat); 1906kJ (456 cal); 1.3g carbohydrate;
39g protein; 0.7g fibre*

beef and prune tagine

1kg beef blade steak, cut into 4cm pieces
2 large red onions (600g), chopped finely
2 tablespoons olive oil
1 teaspoon cracked black pepper
pinch saffron threads
1 teaspoon ground cinnamon
¼ teaspoon ground ginger
50g butter, chopped
425g can diced tomatoes
1 cup (250ml) water
2 tablespoons white sugar
¾ cup (100g) roasted slivered almonds
1½ cups (250g) seeded prunes
1 teaspoon finely grated lemon rind
¼ teaspoon ground cinnamon, extra

1 Combine beef, onion, oil, pepper, saffron, cinnamon and ginger in large bowl.
2 Place beef mixture in large deep saucepan with butter, undrained tomatoes, the water, half of the sugar and ½ cup of the nuts; bring to the boil. Reduce heat; simmer, covered, 1½ hours. Remove 1 cup cooking liquid; reserve. Simmer tagine, uncovered, 30 minutes.
3 Meanwhile, place prunes in small bowl, cover with boiling water; stand 20 minutes, drain. Place prunes in small saucepan with rind, extra cinnamon, remaining sugar and reserved cooking liquid; bring to the boil. Reduce heat; simmer, uncovered, about 15 minutes or until prunes soften. Stir into tagine.
4 Serve tagine sprinkled with remaining nuts and with couscous, if you like.

preparation time *20 minutes*
cooking time *2 hours 30 minutes* serves *4*
nutritional count per serving *50g total fat (15.9g saturated fat); 3687kJ (882 cal); 41.4g carbohydrate; 62g protein; 10.4g fibre*

kingfish and tomato tagine

2 tablespoons olive oil
2 large brown onions (400g), chopped coarsely
6 cloves garlic, chopped finely
1 fresh small red thai chilli, chopped finely
4 drained anchovy fillets, chopped finely
¾ cup coarsely chopped fresh flat-leaf parsley
1 cup coarsely chopped fresh coriander
¾ cup coarsely chopped fresh mint
200g mushrooms, quartered
2 trimmed celery stalks (200g), sliced thickly
2 teaspoons ground cumin
2 x 425g cans diced tomatoes
4 kingfish cutlets (1kg)
1 medium lemon (140g), cut into wedges
2 tablespoons fresh flat-leaf parsley leaves

1 Preheat oven to 200°C/100°C fan-forced.
2 Heat oil in large deep flameproof baking dish; cook onion, garlic and chilli, stirring, until onion softens. Add anchovy, chopped herbs, mushrooms, celery and cumin; cook, stirring, 5 minutes.
3 Add undrained tomatoes; bring to the boil. Add fish, submerging it in the tomato mixture; return to the boil. Cook, uncovered, in oven about 20 minutes or until liquid has almost evaporated and fish is cooked as desired.
4 Divide fish and lemon wedge among serving plates; sprinkle with parsley. Serve with steamed long-grain white rice, if you like.

preparation time *20 minutes*
cooking time *40 minutes* serves *4*
nutritional count per serving *14.7g total fat (2.8g saturated fat); 1680kJ (402 cal); 14.3g carbohydrate; 48.3g protein; 8.9g fibre*

vegetable pithiviers with roasted tomato sauce

10 large egg tomatoes (900g), quartered
2 teaspoons brown sugar
⅓ cup (80ml) olive oil
2 tablespoons red wine vinegar
2 large red capsicums (700g), halved
30g butter
2 large green zucchini (300g), sliced thinly
7 flat mushrooms (560g), sliced thinly
1 clove garlic, crushed
1 tablespoon port
5 sheets ready-rolled puff pastry
1 egg yolk
1 tablespoon milk
50g baby spinach leaves

1 Preheat oven to 180°C/160°C fan-forced.
2 Combine tomato, sugar, half of the oil and half of the vinegar in large bowl. Place tomato pieces, skin-side down, on oven tray. Roast, uncovered, 1 hour 40 minutes. Remove from oven; return to same bowl; crush with potato masher. Cover to keep warm; reserve tomato sauce.
3 Meanwhile, place capsicum, skin-side up, on oven tray. Roast, uncovered, about 40 minutes or until softened. Place capsicum in plastic bag; close tightly, cool. Discard skin, membrane and seeds; slice thinly.
4 Meanwhile, melt butter in large frying pan; cook zucchini, stirring, about 5 minutes or until softened. Place zucchini in small bowl; cover to keep warm.
5 Cook mushrooms and garlic in same pan, stirring, about 5 minutes or until mushrooms soften. Add port; cook, stirring, until liquid evaporates.
6 Cut four of the pastry sheets into 16cm squares; cut remaining sheet into quarters. Place one of the small squares on oiled oven tray; centre 9cm cutter on pastry. Layer a quarter of the mushroom mixture, a quarter of the zucchini and a quarter of the capsicum on pastry; remove cutter. Brush border with combined egg yolk and milk; top with one of the large squares, press edges together to seal.
7 Using sharp knife, cut around pithiviers, leaving 5mm border; mark pastry with swirl design from centre to side, taking care not to cut through pastry. Brush lightly with egg mixture. Repeat process with remaining pastry, vegetables and egg mixture.
8 Bake pithiviers about 25 minutes or until pastry is browned lightly.
9 Meanwhile, combine spinach, remaining oil and remaining vinegar in medium bowl; toss gently to combine. Divide salad among serving plates; serve with pithivier and roasted tomato sauce.

preparation time *45 minutes*
cooking time *2 hours 5 minutes* serves *4*
nutritional count per serving *74.3g total fat (32.6g saturated fat); 4786kJ (1145 cal); 89.9g carbohydrate; 23.3g protein; 12.5g fibre*

chicken and merguez cassoulet

1½ cups (290g) lima beans
1 tablespoon vegetable oil
8 chicken thigh cutlets (1.3kg), halved
6 merguez sausages (480g)
1 large brown onion (200g), chopped coarsely
2 medium carrots (240g), cut into 1cm pieces
2 cloves garlic, chopped finely
4 sprigs fresh thyme
2 tablespoons tomato paste
1 teaspoon finely grated lemon rind
425g can diced tomatoes
1 cup (250ml) chicken stock
1 cup (250ml) water
2 cups (140g) fresh breadcrumbs

1   Place beans in medium bowl, cover with cold water; stand overnight, drain. Rinse under cold water; drain. Cook beans in large saucepan of boiling water, uncovered, 10 minutes; drain.
2   Heat oil in large flameproof casserole dish; cook chicken, in batches, until browned all over. Cook sausages, in batches, in same dish until browned all over. Drain on absorbent paper; halve sausages. Reserve 1 tablespoon of fat from dish; discard remainder.
3   Preheat oven to 200°C/180°C fan-forced.
4   Heat fat in same dish; cook onion, carrot, garlic and thyme, stirring, until onion softens. Add paste; cook, stirring, 2 minutes. Return chicken to dish with drained beans, rind, undrained tomatoes, stock and the water; bring to the boil. Cover; cook in oven 40 minutes.
5   Uncover; cook further 1¼ hours or until liquid is almost absorbed and beans are tender.
6   Preheat grill.
7   Sprinkle cassoulet with breadcrumbs; place under grill until breadcrumbs are browned lightly. Serve with couscous, if you like.

preparation time *25 minutes (plus standing time)* cooking time *2 hours 45 minutes* serves *6* nutritional count per serving *37g total fat (12.4g saturated fat); 3206kJ (767 cal); 43g carbohydrate; 59.5g protein; 12.8g fibre*

chicken cacciatore

1 cup (200g) green split peas
2 tablespoons olive oil
1.5kg chicken pieces, skin on
1 medium brown onion (150g), chopped finely
½ cup (125ml) dry white wine
2 tablespoons white wine vinegar
½ cup (125ml) chicken stock
410g can crushed tomatoes
¼ cup (70g) tomato paste
½ cup (60g) seeded black olives, chopped coarsely
2 tablespoons drained capers, rinsed, chopped coarsely
2 cloves garlic, crushed
½ cup coarsely chopped fresh flat-leaf parsley
½ cup coarsely chopped fresh basil

1   Place peas in medium bowl, cover with cold water; stand overnight, drain. Rinse under cold water; drain.
2   Heat half of the oil in large deep saucepan; cook chicken, in batches, until browned all over.
3   Cook onion in same pan, stirring, until onion softens. Stir in wine, vinegar, stock, undrained tomatoes and paste.
4   Return chicken to pan, fitting pieces upright and tightly together in single layer; bring to the boil. Reduce heat; simmer, covered, 1 hour. Uncover; simmer about 45 minutes or until chicken is tender. Skim fat from surface; stir in olives.
5   Meanwhile, place peas in large saucepan of boiling water; return to the boil. Reduce heat; simmer, uncovered, about 40 minutes or until tender. Drain.
6   Place peas, capers, garlic, herbs and remaining oil in large bowl; toss gently to combine. Serve chicken cacciatore with split pea salad.

preparation time *20 minutes (plus standing time)* cooking time *2 hours 10 minutes* serves *4* nutritional count per serving *37.2g total fat (9.7g saturated fat); 2830kJ (677 cal); 34.1g carbohydrate; 47g protein; 8.5g fibre*

spanish chicken casserole

1 tablespoon olive oil
4 chicken drumsticks (600g)
4 chicken thigh cutlets (800g)
1 large brown onion (200g), chopped finely
4 medium potatoes (800g), quartered
½ cup (80g) roasted pine nuts
½ cup (80g) roasted blanched almonds
3 cups (750ml) chicken stock
1 cup (250ml) dry white wine
⅓ cup (80ml) lemon juice
4 cloves garlic, crushed
2 tablespoons fresh thyme leaves
½ cup coarsely chopped fresh flat-leaf parsley
500g baby green beans, trimmed

1   Preheat oven to 180°C/160°C fan-forced.
2   Heat oil in large flameproof casserole dish;
cook chicken, in batches, over heat until browned.
3   Cook onion in same dish, stirring, over heat until
soft. Return chicken to dish with potato, nuts, stock,
wine, juice, garlic, thyme and half of the parsley;
bring to the boil. Cover; cook in oven about
1 hour or until chicken is cooked through.
4   Meanwhile, boil, steam or microwave
beans until tender; drain.
5   Serve chicken with beans; sprinkle with
remaining parsley.

preparation time *10 minutes*
cooking time *1 hour 25 minutes* serves *4*
nutritional count per serving *61.4g total fat (12.4g
saturated fat); 4050kJ (969 cal); 35g carbohydrate;
57g protein; 10.4g fibre*

avgolemono

Arborio rice, otherwise known as white short-grain rice,
is an excellent choice for this recipe due to its high
starch level, making for a deliciously creamy soup.

2 teaspoons olive oil
1 small brown onion (80g), chopped finely
1 litre (4 cups) chicken stock
400g chicken breast fillets, chopped coarsely
⅓ cup (65g) white short-grain rice
2 eggs
⅓ cup (80ml) lemon juice
2 tablespoons finely chopped fresh flat-leaf parsley

1   Heat oil in large saucepan; cook onion, stirring,
until soft. Add stock, chicken and rice; bring to the boil.
Reduce heat; simmer, covered, about 20 minutes or
until rice is tender.
2   Whisk eggs and juice in small bowl until smooth.
Gradually whisk ½ cup hot soup into egg mixture
then stir warmed egg mixture into soup.
3   Serve bowls of soup sprinkled with parsley.

preparation time *10 minutes*
cooking time *35 minutes* serves *4*
nutritional count per serving *8.4g total fat (2.3g
saturated fat); 1099kJ (263 cal); 16.3g carbohydrate;
30.3g protein; 0.5g fibre*

moroccan couscous salad with preserved lemon dressing

1½ cups (300g) couscous
1½ cups (375ml) boiling water
20g butter
420g can chickpeas, rinsed, drained
⅓ cup (55g) sultanas
⅓ cup (50g) roasted pine nuts
100g baby rocket leaves, chopped coarsely
¾ cup finely chopped fresh flat-leaf parsley
1 cup (120g) seeded green olives

PRESERVED LEMON DRESSING

1 tablespoon finely grated lemon rind
¼ cup (60ml) lemon juice
¼ cup (60ml) olive oil
2 tablespoons rinsed and drained finely chopped
    preserved lemon

1   Combine couscous with the water in large
heatproof bowl, cover; stand about 5 minutes or
until water is absorbed, fluffing with fork occasionally.
Stir in butter. Stand 10 minutes.
2   Make preserved lemon dressing.
3   Place couscous in large bowl with remaining
ingredients and dressing; toss gently to combine.

PRESERVED LEMON DRESSING   Place ingredients in
screw-top jar; shake well.

preparation time *20 minutes* serves *4*
nutritional count per serving *29g total fat (5.5g
saturated fat); 268kJ (686 cal); 85.6g carbohydrate;
17.2g protein; 6.5g fibre*

moroccan chicken with pistachio couscous

1 teaspoon ground cumin
1 teaspoon ground coriander
½ teaspoon sweet smoked paprika
¼ teaspoon ground turmeric
¼ teaspoon cayenne pepper
2 teaspoons finely grated lemon rind
600g chicken thigh fillets
1 medium red capsicum (200g), sliced thinly
1½ cups (300g) couscous
1⅓ cups (330ml) boiling water
⅓ cup (80ml) lemon juice
2 tablespoons olive oil
½ cup (70g) roasted pistachios, chopped coarsely
½ cup firmly packed fresh coriander leaves

1   Combine spices, rind and chicken in large bowl,
rubbing spice mixture firmly into chicken.
2   Cook chicken mixture, uncovered, in heated oiled
large frying pan until cooked through. Remove chicken
from pan; slice thickly.
3   Cook capsicum in same cleaned heated pan,
stirring, 1 minute.
4   Meanwhile, combine couscous and the water in
large heatproof bowl. Cover, stand about 5 minutes or
until liquid is absorbed, fluffing with fork occasionally;
stir in juice and oil.
5   Stir nuts and coriander into couscous; toss gently
to combine. Serve couscous topped with chicken
and capsicum.

preparation time *20 minutes*
cooking time *15 minutes* serves *4*
nutritional count per serving *29.3g total fat (5.7g
saturated fat); 2876kJ (688 cal); 62.4g carbohydrate;
41.9g protein; 3.2g fibre*

chicken and olive empanadas

2 cups (500ml) chicken stock
1 bay leaf
3 chicken thigh fillets (330g)
1 tablespoon olive oil
1 small brown onion (80g), chopped finely
2 cloves garlic, crushed
2 teaspoons ground cumin
½ cup (80g) sultanas
⅓ cup (40g) seeded green olives, chopped coarsely
5 sheets ready-rolled shortcrust pastry
1 egg, beaten lightly

1 Bring stock and bay leaf to the boil in medium frying pan. Add chicken, reduce heat; poach chicken, covered, about 10 minutes or until cooked through. Cool chicken in liquid 10 minutes; shred chicken finely. Reserve 1 cup of the poaching liquid; discard remainder (or keep for another use).
2 Meanwhile, heat oil in large frying pan; cook onion, stirring, until softened. Add garlic and cumin; cook, stirring, until fragrant. Add sultanas and reserved poaching liquid; bring to the boil. Reduce heat; simmer, uncovered, about 15 minutes or until liquid is almost evaporated. Stir in chicken and olives.
3 Preheat oven to 200°C/180°C fan-forced. Oil two oven trays.
4 Using 9cm cutter, cut 24 rounds from pastry sheets. Place 1 level tablespoon of the filling in centre of each round; fold round in half to enclose filling, pinching edges to seal. Using tines of fork, press around edges of empanadas to make pattern. Place on oven trays; brush tops with egg.
5 Bake empanadas about 25 minutes or until browned lightly. Serve with yogurt, if you like.

preparation time *25 minutes*
cook time *40 minutes* makes *24*
nutritional count per empanada *11.1g total fat (5.3g saturated fat); 794kJ (190 cal); 17.4g carbohydrate; 5.4g protein; 0.9g fibre*

braised chicken with fennel and ouzo

¼ cup (60ml) olive oil
4 x 500g small chickens
1 medium lemon (140g), quartered
2 large fennel bulbs (1kg), halved, sliced thinly
1 large brown onion (200g), sliced thinly
2 cloves garlic, sliced thinly
¼ cup (60ml) ouzo
2 cups (500ml) chicken stock
3 large zucchini (450g), sliced thinly
2 tablespoons lemon juice
½ cup (125ml) cream
2 tablespoons coarsely chopped fennel fronds

1 Preheat oven to 200°C/180°C fan-forced.
2 Heat 1 tablespoon of the oil in large deep flameproof baking dish; cook chickens, one at a time, over heat until browned all over. Place one lemon quarter in cavity of each chicken.
3 Heat remaining oil in same dish; cook fennel, onion and garlic, stirring, until onion softens. Add ouzo; cook, stirring, until ouzo evaporates. Add stock; bring to the boil. Place chickens on fennel mixture; cook, uncovered, in oven about 35 minutes or until chickens are just cooked through.
4 Add zucchini to dish, submerging into fennel mixture; cook, uncovered, further 5 minutes or until zucchini is tender. Transfer chickens to large plate; cover to keep warm.
5 Bring fennel mixture to the boil. Add juice and cream; return to the boil. Reduce heat; simmer, uncovered, 5 minutes. Stir in half of the fennel fronds.
6 Using slotted spoon, divide fennel mixture among plates; top with chicken. Drizzle with pan juices; sprinkle with remaining fennel fronds, serve with risoni, if you like.

preparation time *30 minutes*
cooking time *1 hour 10 minutes* serves *4*
nutritional count per serving *61.4g total fat (20.8g saturated fat); 3407kJ (815 cal); 10g carbohydrate; 49.1g protein; 6.4g fibre*

baked pumpkin and spinach risotto

500g butternut pumpkin, chopped coarsely
2 tablespoons olive oil
1½ cups (375ml) chicken stock
1.25 litres (5 cups) water
1 large brown onion (200g), chopped coarsely
2 cloves garlic, crushed
2 cups (400g) arborio rice
½ cup (125ml) dry white wine
500g spinach, trimmed, chopped coarsely
½ cup (80g) roasted pine nuts
½ cup (40g) coarsely grated parmesan cheese
½ cup (125ml) cream

1 Preheat oven to 220°C/200°C fan-forced.
2 Combine pumpkin with half of the oil in baking dish. Bake, uncovered, about 20 minutes or until tender.
3 Meanwhile, combine stock and the water in large saucepan; bring to the boil. Reduce heat; simmer.
4 Heat remaining oil in large saucepan; cook onion and garlic, stirring, until onion is soft. Add rice; stir to coat in mixture. Add wine; stir until almost evaporated.
5 Stir in 1 cup (250ml) of the hot stock mixture; cook, stirring, over low heat until liquid is absorbed. Continue adding stock mixture, in 1-cup batches, stirring, until liquid is absorbed after each addition. Total cooking time should be about 30 minutes or until rice is just tender.
6 Add spinach, pine nuts, cheese and cream; cook, stirring, until spinach wilts. Gently stir in baked pumpkin.

preparation time *15 minutes*
cooking time *35 minutes* serves *4*
nutritional count per serving *41.6g total fat (13.8g saturated fat); 3490kJ (835 cal); 91.5g carbohydrate; 19.3g protein; 5.7g fibre*

jambalaya

1 tablespoon olive oil
4 smoked chorizo sausages (680g)
400g chicken breast fillets
1 medium red onion (170g), chopped finely
1 medium red capsicum (200g), chopped finely
2 cloves garlic, crushed
2 tablespoons finely chopped bottled jalapeño chillies
1 teaspoon dried oregano
¼ teaspoon cayenne pepper
1 bay leaf
2 tablespoons tomato paste
1½ cups (300g) white long-grain rice
400g can crushed tomatoes
2 cups (500ml) chicken stock

1 Heat oil in large saucepan; cook sausages, turning occasionally, until browned. Remove from pan; slice thickly.
2 Cook chicken in same pan, turning occasionally, until browned. Remove from pan; slice thickly.
3 Cook onion, capsicum and garlic in same pan, stirring, until capsicum softens. Add chilli; cook, stirring, 1 minute. Add spices, bay leaf and paste; cook, stirring, 2 minutes. Add rice; stir to coat in mixture.
4 Add undrained tomatoes and stock, bring to a simmer; return sausage and chicken to pan. Cook, covered, about 45 minutes or until rice is tender and liquid absorbed.

preparation time *20 minutes*
cooking time *1 hour 10 minutes* serves *4*
nutritional count per serving *62.3g total fat (21.2g saturated fat); 4648kJ (1112 cal); 73g carbohydrate; 63.3g protein; 4.5g fibre*

1 BAKED PUMPKIN AND SPINACH RISOTTO 2 JAMBALAYA
3 PASTITSIO [P 484] 4 COQ A LA BIERE [P 484]

pastitsio

250g macaroni
2 eggs, beaten lightly
¾ cup (60g) coarsely grated parmesan cheese
2 tablespoons stale breadcrumbs

MEAT SAUCE

1 tablespoon olive oil
2 medium brown onions (300g), chopped finely
750g beef mince
400g can chopped tomatoes
⅓ cup (95g) tomato paste
½ cup (125ml) beef stock
¼ cup (60ml) dry white wine
½ teaspoon ground cinnamon
1 egg, beaten lightly

TOPPING

90g butter
½ cup (75g) plain flour
3½ cups (875ml) milk
1 cup (80g) coarsely grated parmesan cheese
2 egg yolks

1 Preheat oven to 180°C/160°C fan-forced.
Oil shallow 2.5-litre (10-cup) ovenproof dish.
2 Cook pasta in large saucepan of boiling water until
just tender; drain. Combine warm pasta, egg and
cheese in bowl. Press pasta mixture over base of dish.
3 Meanwhile, make meat sauce. Make topping.
4 Top pasta evenly with meat sauce, pour over
topping; smooth surface then sprinkle with breadcrumbs.
Bake, uncovered, about 1 hour or until browned lightly.
Stand 10 minutes before serving.

MEAT SAUCE Heat oil in large saucepan; cook onion,
stirring, until onion is soft. Add beef; cook, stirring,
until beef is well browned. Stir in undrained tomatoes,
paste, stock, wine and cinnamon; simmer, uncovered,
until thick. Cool 10 minutes; stir in egg.

TOPPING Melt butter in medium saucepan, add flour, stir
over heat until bubbling. Remove from heat, gradually
stir in milk. Stir over heat until sauce boils and thickens;
stir in cheese. Cool 5 minutes; stir in egg yolks.

preparation time *30 minutes*
cooking time *1 hour 45 minutes* serves *6*
nutritional count per serving *41.7g total fat (21.8g
saturated fat); 3398kJ (813 cal); 54.4g carbohydrate;
54g protein; 3.8g fibre*

coq à la bière

1.4kg chicken
¼ cup (35g) plain flour
20g butter
2 large carrots (360g)
1 tablespoon olive oil
6 shallots (150g), peeled
2 tablespoons brandy
1½ cups (375ml) pale ale
1 cup (250ml) chicken stock
1 bay leaf
2 sprigs fresh thyme
2 sprigs fresh flat-leaf parsley
20g butter, extra
200g mushrooms
½ cup (125ml) cream

1 Halve chicken lengthways; cut halves crossways
through the centre. Separate breasts from wings;
separate thighs from legs. Coat chicken pieces in flour;
shake off excess. Melt butter in large saucepan; cook
chicken, in batches, until browned all over.
2 Meanwhile, cut carrots into 5cm lengths; cut lengths
in half lengthways then cut halves thickly into strips.
3 Heat oil in same cleaned pan; cook shallots, stirring
occasionally, about 5 minutes or until browned lightly.
Add carrot; cook, stirring, 5 minutes. Add brandy;
cook, stirring, until liquid evaporates. Add chicken, ale,
stock and herbs; bring to the boil. Reduce heat; simmer,
uncovered, 1¼ hours.
4 Melt extra butter in medium frying pan; cook
mushrooms, stirring, until just tender. Add mushrooms
and cream to chicken; cook, covered, 15 minutes.

preparation time *30 minutes*
cooking time *1 hour 50 minutes* serves *4*
nutritional count per serving *55g total fat (23.9g
saturated fat); 3168kJ (758 cal); 13.5g carbohydrate;
40.1g protein; 3.9g fibre*

potato, garlic and oregano pizza

2 teaspoons dry yeast
½ teaspoon caster sugar
¾ cup (180ml) warm water
2 cups (300g) plain flour
1 teaspoon salt
2 tablespoons olive oil
2 tablespoons polenta
⅓ cup loosely packed fresh oregano leaves
6 small potatoes (720g), sliced thinly
3 cloves garlic, crushed
2 tablespoons olive oil, extra
½ teaspoon sea salt flakes
1 tablespoon fresh oregano leaves, extra

1 Combine yeast, sugar and the water in small bowl, cover; stand in warm place about 10 minutes or until mixture is frothy.
2 Sift flour and salt into large bowl; stir in yeast mixture and oil. Mix to a soft dough. Bring dough together with hands, adding extra water if necessary.
3 Knead dough on floured surface about 10 minutes or until smooth and elastic. Place in oiled bowl, cover; stand in warm place about 1 hour or until doubled in size.
4 Preheat oven to 240°C/220°C fan-forced. Oil two oven trays.
5 Punch dough down with fist; knead on floured surface until smooth. Divide dough in half; roll halves to 20cm x 30cm rectangle; place on trays. Sprinkle dough with polenta; prick with fork.
6 Divide oregano leaves between bases then layer with potato, overlapping slightly. Brush combined garlic and extra oil over potato.
7 Bake pizzas about 20 minutes or until potato is tender and bases are crisp. Sprinkle with sea salt and extra oregano before serving.

preparation time *25 minutes (plus standing time)*
cooking time *20 minutes* serves *4*
nutritional count per serving *19.5g total fat (2.8g saturated fat); 2328kJ (557 cal); 79.1g carbohydrate; 12.8g protein; 6.1g fibre*

cheesy pesto polenta

2⅓ cups (580ml) water
2⅓ cups (580ml) milk
1 cup (170g) polenta
½ cup (40g) finely grated parmesan cheese
30g butter, chopped

PESTO

2 tablespoons finely grated parmesan cheese
2 tablespoons roasted pine nuts
2 tablespoons olive oil
1 clove garlic, crushed
1 cup firmly packed fresh basil leaves

1 Combine the water and milk in large saucepan; bring to the boil. Gradually sprinkle polenta over milk mixture; cook, stirring, until polenta thickens slightly.
2 Reduce heat; simmer, uncovered, about 20 minutes or until polenta is thickened, stirring occasionally.
3 Meanwhile, make pesto.
4 Stir cheese, butter and pesto into polenta.

PESTO Blend or process ingredients until mixture forms a paste.

preparation time *10 minutes*
cooking time *25 minutes* serves *4*
nutritional count per serving *31.3g total fat (12.3g saturated fat); 2061kJ (493 cal); 37.1g carbohydrate; 14.9g protein; 2.6g fibre*

napoletana pizza

Purchased pizza bases can be used in place of the basic pizza dough. Tomato pizza sauce can be made up to two days ahead; store in the refrigerator.

2 teaspoons (7g) instant yeast
½ teaspoon salt
2½ cups (375g) plain flour
1 cup (250ml) warm water
1 tablespoon olive oil
300g mozzarella cheese, sliced thinly
¼ cup coarsely torn fresh basil

BASIC TOMATO PIZZA SAUCE

1 tablespoon olive oil
1 small white onion (80g), chopped finely
2 cloves garlic, crushed
425g canned tomatoes
¼ cup (70g) tomato paste
1 teaspoon white sugar
1 tablespoon fresh oregano

1 Combine yeast, salt and sifted flour in large bowl; mix well. Gradually stir in combined water and oil. Knead on well-floured surface for about 10 minutes or until smooth and elastic. Place dough in large oiled bowl; cover, stand in warm place about 30 minutes or until dough doubles in size.
2 Meanwhile, make basic tomato pizza sauce.
3 Preheat oven to 200°C/180°C fan-forced. Oil two pizza trays.
4 Punch down dough with fist; knead on floured surface until smooth. Divide in half; roll each half to form 30cm round. Place dough on trays. Spread each with half of the pizza sauce; top with cheese.
5 Bake pizzas about 15 minutes or until crust is golden and cheese is bubbling. Sprinkle with basil just before serving.

BASIC TOMATO PIZZA SAUCE Heat oil in medium frying pan; cook onion, stirring over low heat, until soft. Stir in garlic and undrained, crushed tomatoes, paste, sugar and oregano. Simmer, uncovered, about 15 minutes or until mixture thickens.

preparation time *20 minutes (plus standing time)*
cooking time *30 minutes* serves 6
nutritional count per serving *18.1g total fat (8g saturated fat); 1919kJ (459 cal); 50.2g carbohydrate; 21.4g protein; 4.4g fibre*

sicilian stuffed pizza

¾ cup (180ml) warm water
1½ teaspoons (7g) dried yeast
½ teaspoon sugar
2 cups (300g) plain flour
1 teaspoon salt
⅓ cup (80ml) olive oil
1 cup (70g) stale breadcrumbs
2 cloves garlic, crushed
1 teaspoon ground fennel
1 small red onion (100g), chopped finely
250g beef mince
100g italian salami, chopped finely
425g can crushed tomatoes
¼ cup (40g) roasted pine nuts
¼ cup coarsely chopped fresh flat-leaf parsley
½ cup (50g) finely grated fontina cheese

1 Combine the water, yeast and sugar in small bowl, cover; stand in warm place about 10 minutes or until frothy. Combine flour and salt in large bowl, stir in yeast mixture and half of the oil; mix to a soft dough. Knead on floured surface, about 5 minutes or until smooth and elastic. Place dough in large oiled bowl, cover; stand in warm place about 30 minutes or until dough doubles in size.

2 Meanwhile, heat remaining oil in large frying pan; cook breadcrumbs and half of the garlic, stirring, until crumbs are browned lightly. Remove from pan.

3 Reheat same pan; cook fennel, onion and remaining garlic, stirring, until onion softens. Add mince; cook, stirring, until mince changes colour. Stir in salami and undrained tomatoes. Bring to the boil then reduce heat; simmer, uncovered, stirring occasionally, about 15 minutes or until liquid reduces by half. Remove from heat; stir in nuts and parsley. Cool.

4 Preheat oven to 220°C/200°C fan-forced.

5 Punch down dough with fist; knead on lightly floured surface until smooth; divide in half. Roll each half to form 30cm round. Place one round on oiled pizza or oven tray; top with breadcrumb mixture, mince mixture, cheese then remaining round. Pinch edges together.

6 Bake pizza about 15 minutes or until browned lightly. Stand pizza 10 minutes before cutting into wedges. Serve with a rocket and parmesan salad, if you like.

preparation time *30 minutes (plus standing time)*
cooking time *35 minutes (plus standing time)* serves *4*
nutritional count per serving *46.8g total fat (11.4g saturated fat); 3612kJ (864 cal); 72.4g carbohydrate; 35.3g protein; 6.5g fibre*

janssen's temptation

5 medium potatoes (1kg), sliced thinly
1 large brown onion (200g), sliced thinly
9 drained anchovy fillets, halved lengthways
¼ cup (60ml) lemon juice
¾ cup (180ml) cream
2 tablespoons stale breadcrumbs
2 tablespoons finely chopped fresh flat-leaf parsley
30g butter

1 Preheat oven to 220°C/200°C fan-forced.
Oil medium-deep 22cm-square baking dish.
2 Layer a third of the potato over base of dish; sprinkle
over a third of the onion and a third of the anchovy.
Sprinkle with 1 tablespoon of the juice. Repeat layering
with remaining potato, onion, anchovy and juice.
Pour over cream; sprinkle breadcrumbs and parsley
over top then dot with butter.
3 Bake, covered, about 1 hour or until potato is tender.
Uncover; bake about 15 minutes or until browned lightly.

preparation time *15 minutes*
cooking time *1 hour 15 minutes* serves *4*
nutritional count per serving *26.5g total fat (17.1g
saturated fat); 1868kJ (447 cal); 39.2g carbohydrate;
10.5g protein; 6g fibre*

onion and anchovy tartlets

1 tablespoon olive oil
60g butter
3 medium brown onions (450g), halved, sliced thinly
2 cloves garlic, crushed
1 bay leaf
3 sprigs fresh thyme
⅓ cup coarsely chopped fresh flat-leaf parsley
8 drained anchovy fillets chopped finely
2 tablespoons coarsely chopped kalamata olives
¾ cup (110g) self-raising flour
¾ cup (110g) plain flour
¾ cup (180ml) buttermilk

1 Heat oil and half of the butter in large frying pan;
cook onion, garlic, bay leaf and thyme, stirring
occasionally, about 20 minutes or until onion
caramelises. Discard bay leaf and thyme; stir in
parsley, anchovy and olives.
2 Meanwhile, blend or process flours and remaining
butter until mixture resembles fine breadcrumbs. Add
buttermilk; process until ingredients just come together.
Knead dough on floured surface until smooth.
3 Preheat oven to 220°C/200°C fan-forced.
Oil two oven trays.
4 Divide dough into six pieces; roll each piece of
dough on floured surface into 14cm square. Fold
edges over to form 1cm border.
5 Place squares on trays; place rounded tablespoons
of the onion mixture on each square. Bake, uncovered,
about 15 minutes or until pastry browns lightly.

preparation time *45 minutes*
cooking time *35 minutes* serves *6*
nutritional count per serving *12.9g total fat (6.4g
saturated fat); 1170kJ (280 cal); 31.8g carbohydrate;
7.7g protein; 2.7g fibre*

italian chickpea stew

1 cup (200g) dried chickpeas
1 tablespoon olive oil
1 medium red onion (170g), chopped coarsely
2 cloves garlic, crushed
425g can chopped tomatoes
2 cups (500ml) vegetable stock
1 medium eggplant (300g), chopped coarsely
2 large zucchini (300g), chopped coarsely
2 tablespoons tomato paste
⅓ cup coarsely chopped fresh flat-leaf parsley

1   Place chickpeas in medium bowl, cover with cold water; stand overnight, drain. Rinse under cold water; drain. Place chickpeas in medium saucepan of boiling water; return to the boil. Reduce heat; simmer, uncovered, about 1 hour or until chickpeas are tender. Drain.
2   Heat oil in large saucepan; cook onion and garlic until onion softens. Add chickpeas, undrained tomatoes, stock, eggplant, zucchini and paste; bring to the boil. Reduce heat; simmer, covered, 30 minutes. Uncover; simmer, about 30 minutes or until mixture thickens slightly.
3   Serve stew sprinkled with parsley, and topped with grated parmesan cheese, if you like.

preparation time *15 minutes (plus standing time)*
cooking time *2 hours 10 minutes* serves *4*
nutritional count per serving *8.7g total fat (1.3g saturated fat); 1145kJ (274 cal); 29g carbohydrate; 13.8g protein; 12.2g fibre*

tuscan beef stew

1 tablespoon olive oil
400g spring onions, trimmed
1kg chuck steak, cut into 3cm cubes
30g butter
2 tablespoons plain flour
2 cups (500ml) dry red wine
1 cup (250ml) beef stock
1 cup (250ml) water
2 cloves garlic, crushed
6 sprigs thyme
2 bay leaves
1 trimmed celery stalk (100g), chopped coarsely
400g baby carrots, trimmed, halved
2 cups (250g) frozen peas
⅓ cup coarsely chopped fresh flat-leaf parsley

1   Heat oil in large heavy-based saucepan; cook onions, stirring occasionally, about 10 minutes or until browned lightly, remove from pan.
2   Cook steak in same pan, in batches, over high heat, until browned all over.
3   Melt butter in same pan, add flour; cook, stirring, until mixture bubbles and thickens. Gradually stir in wine, stock and the water; stir until mixture boils and thickens. Return steak to pan with garlic, thyme and bay leaves; bring to the boil. Reduce heat; simmer, covered, 1½ hours.
4   Add onion to pan with celery and carrot; simmer, covered, 30 minutes. Add peas; simmer, uncovered, until peas are just tender. Stir in parsley just before serving. Serve with penne or farfalle, if you like.

preparation time *15 minutes*
cooking time *2 hours 40 minutes* serves *4*
nutritional count per serving *22.6g total fat (9.5g saturated fat); 2504kJ (599 cal); 16.4g carbohydrate; 57.4g protein; 9g fibre*

onion focaccia

2½ cups (375g) plain flour
2 teaspoons (7g) dried yeast
¼ cup (20g) grated parmesan cheese
2 tablespoons coarsely chopped fresh sage
3 teaspoons sea salt flakes
1 cup (250ml) warm water
¼ cup (60ml) olive oil
1 small white onion (80g), sliced thinly

1 Sift flour in large bowl; stir in yeast, cheese, sage
and 1 teaspoon of the salt. Gradually stir in the water
and 2 tablespoons of the oil. Knead on well-floured
surface about 10 minutes or until smooth and elastic.
2 Place dough on oiled oven tray; press into a
24cm-round. Cover with oiled plastic wrap; stand
in warm place until dough doubles in size.
3 Preheat oven to 220°C/200°C fan-forced.
4 Meanwhile, combine onion, remaining salt and
remaining oil in small bowl. Remove plastic wrap from
dough; sprinkle dough with onion mixture.
5 Bake focaccia about 25 minutes or until cooked
when tested; cool on wire rack.

preparation time *20 minutes (plus standing time)*
cooking time *25 minutes (plus cooling time)* serves *8*
nutritional count per serving *8.3g total fat (1.6g
saturated fat); 1016kJ (243 cal); 34.4g carbohydrate;
6.5g protein; 2.1g fibre*

french onion soup with gruyère croûtons

50g butter
4 large brown onions (800g), halved, sliced thinly
¾ cup (180ml) dry white wine
3 cups (750ml) water
1 litre (4 cups) beef stock
1 bay leaf
1 tablespoon plain flour
1 teaspoon fresh thyme leaves

GRUYERE CROUTONS

1 small french bread stick (150g), cut into 1.5cm slices
60g gruyère cheese, grated

1 Melt butter in large saucepan; cook onion, stirring,
about 30 minutes or until caramelised.
2 Meanwhile, bring wine to the boil in large saucepan;
boil 1 minute. Stir in the water, stock and bay leaf;
return to the boil. Remove from heat.
3 Stir flour into onion mixture; cook, stirring, 2 minutes.
Gradually add hot broth mixture, stirring, until mixture
boils and thickens slightly. Reduce heat; simmer,
uncovered, stirring occasionally, 20 minutes. Discard
bay leaf; stir in thyme.
4 Meanwhile, make gruyère croûtons.
5 Serve bowls of soup topped with croûtons.

GRUYERE CROUTONS Preheat grill. Toast bread slices
one side then turn and sprinkle equal amounts of cheese
over untoasted sides; grill until cheese browns lightly.

preparation time *30 minutes*
cooking time *50 minutes* serves *4*
nutritional count per serving *16.7g total fat (10g
saturated fat); 1522kJ (364 cal); 31.1g carbohydrate;
13.4g protein; 3.9g fibre*

pork belly and spicy sausage with braised lettuce

4 merguez sausages (320g)
200g pork mince
1 teaspoon finely chopped fresh thyme
500g boned pork belly, rind removed
1 cup (220g) sugar
½ cup (125ml) apple juice
1¼ cup (310ml) chicken stock
20g butter
2 large butter lettuces (1kg), trimmed,
   shredded finely

1 Using sharp knife, slit sausage skins; discard skins. Combine sausage meat in medium bowl with pork mince and thyme. Roll mixture into sausage shape measuring about 5cm in diameter and 20cm in length. Wrap sausage tightly in baking paper then foil, twisting ends tightly to seal. Wrap sausage once again, this time in plastic wrap, twisting ends tightly; refrigerate 1 hour.

2 Meanwhile, cut pork belly, across grain, into 1cm slices; cut each slice in half. Cook pork in large non-stick frying pan about 10 minutes, pressing down with back of spoon until browned and crisp. Drain on absorbent paper.

3 Cook sausage in large saucepan of boiling water, covered, 30 minutes.

4 Meanwhile, combine sugar and apple juice in large heavy-based saucepan. Stir over heat, without boiling, until sugar dissolves; bring to the boil. Reduce heat; simmer, uncovered, without stirring, about 10 minutes or until mixture is browned lightly. Gradually add 1 cup of the stock, stirring until apple sauce is smooth.

5 Melt butter in large saucepan; cook lettuce, stirring, 5 minutes. Add remaining stock; cook, uncovered, until stock evaporates.

6 Reheat apple sauce until almost boiling; add pork, stir about 2 minutes or until pork is heated through.

7 Remove sausage from wrapping; cut into 12 slices. Divide lettuce mixture, sausage and pork among serving plates; drizzle with apple sauce.

preparation time *40 minutes (plus refrigeration time)*
cooking time *40 minutes* serves *6*
nutritional count per serving *35.9g total fat (13.9g saturated fat); 2002kJ (479 cal); 8.1g carbohydrate; 30.3g protein; 3.5g fibre*

pork souvlaki with garlic and oregano

1kg pork fillet, cut into 2cm cubes
⅓ cup (80ml) extra virgin olive oil
2 tablespoons lemon juice
¼ cup fresh oregano leaves, chopped coarsely
4 cloves garlic, crushed
48 fresh bay leaves
2 lemons, cut into wedges

1 Combine pork, oil, lemon juice, oregano and garlic in large bowl. Cover, refrigerate for 3 hours or overnight, stirring occasionally.
2 Thread pork and bay leaves onto skewers.
3 Cook souvlaki, in batches, on heated, oiled grill plate (or grill or barbecue) until browned all over and just cooked through. Serve with lemon wedges.

preparation time *15 minutes (plus refrigeration time)*
cooking time *25 minutes* serves *8*
nutritional count per serving *12.1g total fat (2.3g saturated fat); 936kJ (224 cal); 0.7g carbohydrate; 27.7g protein; 0.9g fibre*

pork cabbage rolls

18 large cabbage leaves
½ cup (100g) uncooked white long-grain rice
250g pork mince
1 medium brown onion (150g), chopped finely
¼ cup finely chopped fresh dill
1 clove garlic, crushed
1 tablespoon tomato paste
2 teaspoons ground cumin
1 teaspoon ground coriander
1 teaspoon ground allspice
4 cloves garlic, quartered
2 medium tomatoes (300g), chopped coarsely
2 x 400g cans crushed tomatoes
¼ cup (60ml) lemon juice

1 Discard thick stems from 15 cabbage leaves; reserve remaining leaves. Boil, steam or microwave trimmed leaves until just pliable; drain. Rinse under cold water; drain. Pat dry with absorbent paper.
2 Using hand, combine rice, pork, onion, dill, crushed garlic, paste and spices in medium bowl.
3 Place one trimmed leaf, vein-side up, on board; cut leaf in half lengthways. Place 1 rounded teaspoon of the pork mixture at stem end of each half; roll each half firmly to enclose filling. Repeat with remaining trimmed leaves.
4 Place reserved leaves in base of large saucepan. Place only enough rolls, seam-side down, in single layer, to completely cover leaves in base of saucepan. Top with quartered garlic, chopped fresh tomato then remaining rolls.
5 Pour undrained tomatoes and juice over cabbage rolls; bring to the boil. Reduce heat; simmer, covered, 1 hour. Uncover; simmer about 30 minutes or until cabbage rolls are cooked through.
6 Serve with thick greek-style yogurt flavoured with a little finely choppped preserved lemon, if you like.

preparation time *1 hour*
cooking time *1 hour 40 minutes* serves *6*
nutritional count per serving *3.6g total fat (1.1g saturated fat); 803kJ (192 cal); 24.7g carbohydrate; 14.3g protein; 9.7g fibre*

italian braised pork

Ask your butcher to roll and tie the pork shoulder for you.

2 tablespoons olive oil
1.5kg pork shoulder, rolled and tied
2 cloves garlic, crushed
1 medium brown onion (150g), chopped coarsely
½ small fennel bulb (100g), chopped coarsely
8 slices hot pancetta (120g), chopped coarsely
1 tablespoon tomato paste
½ cup (125ml) dry white wine
400g can whole tomatoes
1 cup (250ml) chicken stock
1 cup (250ml) water
2 sprigs fresh rosemary
2 large fennel bulbs (1kg), halved, sliced thickly

SPICE RUB

1 teaspoon fennel seeds
2 teaspoons dried oregano
½ teaspoon cayenne pepper
1 tablespoon cracked black pepper
1 tablespoon sea salt
2 teaspoons olive oil

1 Preheat oven to 180°C/160°C fan-forced.
2 Heat oil in large flameproof casserole dish; cook pork, uncovered, over heat, until browned all over.
3 Meanwhile, combine ingredients for spice rub in small bowl.
4 Remove pork from dish; discard all but 1 tablespoon of the oil in dish. Cook garlic, onion, chopped fennel and pancetta in same dish, stirring, until onion softens. Add paste; cook, stirring, 2 minutes.
5 Meanwhile, rub pork with spice rub.
6 Return pork to dish with wine, undrained tomatoes, stock, the water and rosemary; bring to the boil. Cover; cook in oven 1 hour.
7 Add sliced fennel; cook, covered, in oven 1 hour. Remove pork from dish; discard rind. Cover to keep warm.
8 Meanwhile, cook braising liquid in dish over medium heat, uncovered, until thickened slightly. Return sliced pork to dish; serve pork and sauce with warm italian bread, if you like.

preparation time *25 minutes*
cooking time *2 hours 50 minutes* serves 6
nutritional count per serving *32.8g total fat (10.7g saturated fat); 2525kJ (604 cal); 7.5g carbohydrate; 66.5g protein; 4.6g fibre*

greek roast lamb with skordalia and lemon-scented potatoes

Skordalia is a classic Greek accompaniment to meat, made from either potato or bread pureed with a large amount of garlic plus olive oil, lemon juice or vinegar, herbs and, occasionally, ground nuts.

2kg lamb leg
2 cloves garlic, crushed
½ cup (125ml) lemon juice
2 tablespoons olive oil
1 tablespoon fresh oregano leaves
1 teaspoon fresh lemon thyme leaves
5 large potatoes (1.5kg), cut into 3cm pieces
2 tablespoons olive oil, extra
1 tablespoon finely grated lemon rind
2 tablespoons lemon juice
1 teaspoon fresh lemon thyme leaves

SKORDALIA

1 medium potato (200g), quartered
3 cloves garlic, quartered
1 tablespoon lemon juice
1 tablespoon white wine vinegar
2 tablespoons water
⅓ cup (80ml) olive oil
1 tablespoon warm water

1 Combine lamb with garlic, juice, oil, oregano and thyme in large bowl. Cover; refrigerate 3 hours or overnight.

2 Preheat oven to 160°C/140°C fan-forced.

3 Place lamb in large baking dish; roast, uncovered, in oven 4 hours.

4 Meanwhile, make skordalia.

5 Toss potato in large bowl with combined remaining ingredients; place, in single layer, on oven tray. Roast, uncovered, for last 30 minutes of lamb cooking time.

6 Remove lamb from oven; cover to keep warm.

7 Increase oven to 220°C/200°C fan-forced; roast potatoes, uncovered, about 20 minutes or until crisp and tender. Serve potatoes and lamb with skordalia; sprinkle with extra fresh lemon thyme leaves, if you like.

SKORDALIA Boil, steam or microwave potato until tender; drain. Push potato through food mill or fine sieve into large bowl; cool 10 minutes. Place garlic, juice, vinegar and the water in bowl with potato; stir until well combined. Place potato mixture in blender; with motor operating, gradually add oil in a thin, steady stream, blending only until skordalia thickens (do not overmix). Stir in the water.

preparation time *40 minutes (plus refrigeration time)* cooking time *4 hours 20 minutes* serves *4* nutritional count per serving *57g total fat (14g saturated fat); 4556kJ (1090 cal); 51.5g carbohydrate; 91.2g protein; 6.7g fibre*

seared calves liver with persillade and parsnip mash

1kg parsnips, chopped coarsely
1 large potato (300g), chopped coarsely
3 cloves garlic
½ cup (125ml) cream
100g butter
250g asparagus, trimmed
400g piece calves liver, sliced thinly
1 shallot (25g), chopped finely
½ cup (125ml) chicken stock
1 tablespoon lemon juice
⅓ cup finely chopped fresh flat-leaf parsley

1 Boil, steam or microwave parsnip and potato, separately, until tender; drain. Crush 2 cloves of the garlic; mash in large bowl with parsnip, potato, cream and half of the butter. Cover to keep warm.
2 Boil, steam or microwave asparagus until just tender; drain. Cover to keep warm.
3 Pat liver dry with absorbent paper. Melt about 1 tablespoon of the remaining butter in large frying pan; cook liver quickly, in batches, over high heat until browned both sides and cooked as desired (do not overcook). Cover to keep warm.
4 To make persillade, heat remaining butter in same pan. Finely chop remaining clove of garlic; cook garlic and shallot, stirring, until shallot softens. Add stock and juice; bring to the boil, stirring. Remove from heat; stir in parsley.
5 Serve sliced liver with parsnip mash and asparagus; top liver with persillade.

preparation time *15 minutes*
cooking time *30 minutes* serves *4*
nutritional count per serving *40.3g total fat (24.3g saturated fat); 2604kJ (623 cal); 35.8g carbohydrate; 26.4g protein; 7.8g fibre*

terrine de campagne

350g chicken thigh fillets, chopped coarsely
400g boned pork belly, rind removed,
    chopped coarsely
300g piece calves liver, trimmed, chopped coarsely
3 rindless bacon rashers (195g), chopped coarsely
3 cloves garlic, crushed
2 teaspoons finely chopped fresh thyme
10 juniper berries, crushed
2 tablespoons port
¼ cup (60ml) dry white wine
1 egg
¼ cup (35g) roasted, shelled pistachios

1 Preheat oven to 150°C/130°C fan-forced. Oil 1.5-litre (6-cup) ovenproof terrine dish.
2 Blend or process meats, separately, until coarsely minced; combine in large bowl with remaining ingredients.
3 Press meat mixture into dish; cover with foil. Place terrine dish in baking dish; pour enough boiling water into baking dish to come halfway up side of terrine dish. Cook in oven 1 hour. Uncover; cook further 1 hour or until cooked through.
4 Remove terrine dish from baking dish; cover terrine with baking paper. Weight with another dish filled with heavy cans; cool 10 minutes then refrigerate overnight.
5 Turn terrine onto serving plate; serve sliced terrine, at room temperature, with french bread and cornichons, if you like.

preparation time *20 minutes*
cooking time *2 hours (plus refrigeration time)* serves *6*
nutritional count per serving *30.1g total fat (9.6g saturated fat); 2019kJ (483 cal); 3.6g carbohydrate; 46.2g protein; 0.8g fibre*

veal sweetbreads with duxelles and herb salad

500g veal sweetbreads
¼ cup (35g) plain flour
1 teaspoon salt
½ teaspoon freshly ground black pepper
¼ cup (60ml) olive oil
1 cup loosely packed fresh flat-leaf parsley leaves
1 cup loosely packed fresh basil leaves
1 cup loosely packed fresh chervil leaves
¾ cup coarsely chopped fresh chives
2 tablespoons olive oil, extra
2 tablespoons red wine vinegar

DUXELLES

40g butter
8 shallots (200g), chopped finely
400g swiss brown mushrooms, chopped finely
¼ cup (60ml) port
⅓ cup (80ml) beef stock
2 tablespoons finely chopped fresh flat-leaf parsley

1 Cover sweetbreads with cold water in bowl; refrigerate 4 hours, changing water every hour, until sweetbreads whiten and water is clear. Cook sweetbreads, uncovered, in pan of boiling water 5 minutes; drain. Cool 10 minutes. Remove outer membranes; slice sweetbreads thickly.
2 Meanwhile, make duxelles.
3 Coat sweetbreads in combined flour, salt and pepper; shake away excess. Heat oil in large frying pan; cook sweetbreads, in batches, 5 minutes or until browned and cooked as desired.
4 Meanwhile, combine herbs in large bowl with extra oil and vinegar; toss gently to combine.
5 Serve sweetbreads with duxelles and herb salad.

DUXELLES Heat butter in large frying pan; cook shallot and mushrooms until shallot softens. Add port and stock; bring to the boil. Reduce heat; simmer, 15 minutes or until liquid is evaporated. Stir in parsley off the heat.

preparation time *45 minutes (plus refrigeration time)*
cooking time *20 minutes (plus cooling time)* serves 4
nutritional count per serving *53.1g total fat (18.4g saturated fat); 2893kJ (692 cal); 10.5g carbohydrate; 38.3g protein; 4.7g fibre*

beef bourguignon pies

12 pickling onions (480g)
6 rindless bacon rashers (390g), sliced thinly
2 tablespoons olive oil
400g mushrooms
1kg gravy beef, trimmed, cut into 2cm pieces
¼ cup (35g) plain flour
1 tablespoon tomato paste
2 teaspoons fresh thyme leaves
1 cup (250ml) dry red wine
2 cups (500ml) beef stock
2 sheets ready-rolled butter puff pastry
cooking-oil spray
½ cup finely chopped fresh flat-leaf parsley

1 Peel onions, leaving roots intact; halve lengthways.
2 Cook bacon in heated large heavy-based saucepan, stirring, until crisp; drain on absorbent paper. Cook onion in same heated pan, stirring, until browned all over. Remove from pan.
3 Heat 2 teaspoons of the oil in same pan; cook mushrooms, stirring, until just browned. Remove from pan.
4 Coat beef in flour; shake off excess. Heat remaining oil in same pan; cook beef, in batches, until browned all over. Add bacon and onion with tomato paste and thyme; cook, stirring, 2 minutes. Add wine and stock; bring to the boil. Reduce heat; simmer, covered, 1 hour. Add mushrooms; simmer, uncovered, about 40 minutes or until beef is tender, stirring occasionally.
5 Preheat oven to 220°C/200°C fan-forced.
6 Place pastry sheets on board; using 1¼-cup (310ml) ovenproof dish, cut six lids for pies by tracing around rim of dish with tip of sharp knife. Place lids on oiled oven tray, spray with cooking-oil spray; bake 5 minutes.
7 Meanwhile, stir parsley into beef bourguignon then divide among six 1¼-cup (310ml) ovenproof dishes; top each with pastry lid. Serve with hot chips, if you like.

preparation time *30 minutes*
cooking time *2 hours* serves 6
nutritional count per serving *34.2g total fat (13.4g saturated fat); 2796kJ (669 cal); 29.8g carbohydrate; 51.7g protein; 4g fibre*

1 VEAL SWEETBREADS WITH DUXELLES AND HERB SALAD
2 BEEF BOURGUIGNON PIES 3 TOMATO TARTE TATINS WITH
CREME FRAICHE SAUCE [P 500] 4 CIOPPINO [P 500]

OFFSHORE 499

tomato tarte tatins with crème fraîche sauce

9 small firm tomatoes (800g), peeled, quartered
30g butter
1 clove garlic, crushed
1 tablespoon brown sugar
2 tablespoons balsamic vinegar
1½ sheets ready-rolled butter puff pastry
1 egg, beaten lightly
vegetable oil, for deep-frying
6 sprigs fresh baby basil
CREME FRAICHE SAUCE
20g butter
2 shallots (50g), chopped finely
1 cup (240g) crème fraîche
⅓ cup (80ml) water

1 Preheat oven to 220°C/200°C fan-forced.
2 Discard pulp and seeds from tomato quarters; gently flatten flesh.
3 Melt butter in large frying pan; cook garlic, stirring, over low heat, until fragrant. Add sugar and vinegar; cook, stirring, until sugar dissolves. Place tomato in pan, in single layer; cook, covered, turning once, about 5 minutes or until tomato softens.
4 Oil six 1-cup (250ml) metal pie dishes; cut six 11cm rounds from pastry sheets. Divide tomato among dishes; top each with one pastry round, pressing down gently. Brush pastry with egg; bake about 15 minutes or until pastry is browned lightly and puffed.
5 Meanwhile, heat oil in small saucepan; using metal tongs, place thoroughly dry basil sprigs, one at a time, in pan. Deep-fry about 3 seconds or until basil is crisp. Drain on absorbent paper.
6 Make crème fraîche sauce.
7 Divide sauce among serving plates; turn tarts onto sauce, top with basil.

CREME FRAICHE SAUCE Melt butter in small saucepan; cook shallot, stirring, about 3 minutes or until softened. Add crème fraîche; cook, stirring, over low heat, until heated through. Stir in the water.

preparation time *40 minutes*
cooking time *30 minutes* serves *6*
nutritional count per serving *33.8g total fat (20.4g saturated fat); 1735kJ (415 cal); 21.3g carbohydrate; 6.1g protein; 2.7g fibre*

cioppino

2 teaspoons olive oil
1 medium brown onion (150g), chopped coarsely
1 baby fennel bulb (130g), trimmed, chopped coarsely
3 cloves garlic, crushed
6 medium tomatoes (1kg), chopped coarsely
425g can crushed tomatoes
½ cup (125ml) dry white wine
1½ cups (375ml) fish stock
2 cooked blue swimmer crabs (700g)
500g uncooked large king prawns
450g swordfish steaks
400g clams, rinsed
150g scallops
¼ cup coarsely chopped fresh basil
½ cup coarsely chopped fresh flat-leaf parsley

1 Heat oil in large saucepan; cook onion, fennel and garlic, stirring, until onion softens. Add fresh tomato; cook, stirring, about 5 minutes or until pulpy. Stir in undrained crushed tomatoes, wine and stock; reduce heat, simmer, covered, 20 minutes.
2 Meanwhile, remove back shell from crabs; discard grey gills. Rinse crab; using sharp knife, chop each crab into four pieces. Shell and devein prawns, leaving tails intact. Chop fish into 2cm pieces.
3 Add clams to pan; simmer, covered, about 5 minutes or until clams open (discard any that do not). Add remaining seafood; cook, stirring occasionally, about 5 minutes or until seafood has changed in colour and is cooked as desired. Remove from heat; stir in herbs.

preparation time *30 minutes*
cooking time *40 minutes* serves *4*
nutritional count per serving *6.5g total fat (1.4g saturated fat); 1505kJ (360 cal); 12.3g carbohydrate; 54.4g protein; 5.9g fibre*

salmon and green peppercorn rillettes

1 long french bread stick
3 cups (750ml) water
½ cup (125ml) dry white wine
1 small brown onion (80g), chopped coarsely
1 bay leaf
1 teaspoon black peppercorns
300g salmon fillets
100g smoked salmon, sliced thinly
60g butter, softened
2 teaspoons finely grated lemon rind
1 tablespoon green peppercorns in brine, rinsed,
    drained, chopped coarsely

1 Preheat oven to 160°C/140°C fan-forced.
2 Cut bread into 1cm slices; toast, uncovered, in single layer on oven tray in moderately slow oven about 15 minutes or until bread is dry.
3 Meanwhile, combine the water, wine, onion, bay leaf and black peppercorns in medium saucepan; bring to the boil. Add salmon fillets, reduce heat; simmer, uncovered, about 5 minutes or until almost cooked through. Remove from heat, cool salmon fillets in liquid 5 minutes then drain; discard cooking liquid.
4 Discard any skin and bones from salmon fillets; place in medium bowl, flake with fork. Add smoked salmon, butter, rind and green peppercorns; stir to combine rillettes. Divide rillettes among four ½-cup (125ml) dishes; cool to room temperature. Serve with bread slices.

preparation time *20 minutes*
cooking time *20 minutes (plus cooling time)* serves *4*
nutritional count per serving *21.6g total fat (9.9g saturated fat); 2057kJ (492 cal); 40.5g carbohydrate; 27.4g protein; 3g fibre*

whole fish in a salt crust with gremolata

2 x 1kg whole snapper, cleaned, scales left on
3kg coarse cooking salt, approximately
GREMOLATA
½ cup finely chopped fresh flat-leaf parsley
2 cloves garlic, crushed
1 tablespoon finely grated lemon rind
2 tablespoons extra virgin olive oil

1 Preheat oven to 240°C/220°C fan-forced.
2 Make gremolata.
3 Wash fish, pat dry inside and out. Fill cavities of fish with half the gremolata.
4 Divide half the salt between two ovenproof trays large enough to hold fish (ovenproof metal oval platters are ideal). Place fish on salt.
5 Place remaining salt in large sieve or colander and run quickly under cold water until salt is damp. Press salt firmly over fish to completely cover fish.
6 Bake fish 35 minutes. Remove fish from oven; stand 5 minutes.
7 Using a hammer or meat mallet and old knife, break open the crust then lift away with the scales and skin. Serve fish with remaining gremolata.

GREMOLATA Combine ingredients in small bowl.

preparation time *10 minutes*
cooking time *35 minutes* serves *8*
nutritional count per serving *6.1g total fat (1.2g saturated fat); 560kJ (134 cal); 0.1g carbohydrate; 19.4g protein; 0.4g fibre*

châteaubriand

1kg medium potatoes
40g unsalted butter
¼ cup (60ml) olive oil
2 tablespoons finely chopped fresh garlic chives
750g piece beef eye fillet
400g baby vine-ripened truss tomatoes
400g baby carrots, trimmed
350g broccolini
250g yellow patty-pan squash

BEARNAISE SAUCE

⅓ cup (80ml) white wine vinegar
½ teaspoon black peppercorns
2 green onions, chopped finely
3 egg yolks
150g unsalted butter, melted
2 teaspoons finely chopped fresh tarragon

MUSHROOM SAUCE

1 medium brown onion (150g), chopped finely
150g button mushrooms, quartered
150g oyster mushrooms, sliced thickly
½ cup (125ml) beef stock
¼ cup (60ml) dry red wine
¼ cup (60ml) cream

1 Preheat oven to 220°C/200°C fan-forced.
2 Make béarnaise sauce.
3 Cut potatoes into 1cm slices. Heat butter and half of the oil in large non-stick frying pan; cook potato, uncovered, turning occasionally, until browned. Reduce heat; cook potato, covered, turning occasionally, about 15 minutes or until tender. Stir in chives.
4 Meanwhile, heat remaining oil in medium flameproof casserole dish; cook beef, uncovered, until browned all over. Place dish in oven; roast beef, uncovered, 10 minutes. Add tomatoes to dish; roast, uncovered, about 10 minutes or until beef is cooked as desired and tomatoes are soft. Remove beef and tomatoes from dish; cover to keep warm.
5 Make mushroom sauce, using dish with beef juices.
6 Boil, steam or microwave carrots, broccolini and squash, separately, until just tender; drain.
7 Serve beef with potato and vegetables on large serving platter accompanied with both sauces.

BEARNAISE SAUCE Bring vinegar, peppercorns and onion to the boil in small saucepan. Reduce heat; simmer, uncovered, about 5 minutes or until liquid has reduced by half. Strain over medium heatproof bowl; discard peppercorns and onion. Whisk yolks into liquid in bowl until combined. Set bowl over medium saucepan of simmering water; gradually whisk in melted butter in thin, steady stream until mixture thickens slightly. Remove from heat; stir in tarragon. Cover to keep warm.

MUSHROOM SAUCE Place same flameproof casserole dish with beef juices over medium heat, add onion and mushrooms; cook, stirring, until onion softens. Add stock, wine and cream; bring to the boil. Reduce heat; simmer, uncovered, stirring, about 10 minutes or until sauce thickens slightly and mushrooms are tender. Cover to keep warm.

preparation time *45 minutes*
cooking time *50 minutes* serves *6*
nutritional count per serving *46.5g total fat (23.6g saturated fat); 2943kJ (704 cal); 26.8g carbohydrate; 38.9g protein; 16.4g fibre*

vongole and chorizo linguine

750g vongole (clams)
375g linguine pasta
1 tablespoon extra virgin olive oil
1 chorizo sausage (170g), sliced thinly
2 cloves garlic, crushed
2 long red chillies, sliced thinly
250g cherry tomatoes, halved
¾ cup loosely packed small fresh basil leaves
¼ cup (60ml) extra virgin olive oil, extra

1 Rinse vongole. Place in bowl of cold water 1 hour, then drain.
2 Cook pasta in large saucepan boiling until just tender; drain. Return to pan.
3 Meanwhile, heat oil in large frying pan; cook chorizo until crisp. Remove from pan using a slotted spoon. Cook vongole, covered, in same heated pan about 3 minutes or until vongole open (discard any that do not). Push vongole to one side of the pan.
4 Add garlic, chilli and tomatoes to pan; cook, uncovered, for about 2 minutes or until fragrant and softened.
5 Add chorizo and vongole mixture to hot pasta with basil and extra oil; toss gently to combine.

preparation 15 minutes (plus standing time)
cooking 15 minutes serves 4
nutritional count per serving 32.2g total fat (7.4g saturated fat); 2805kJ (671 cal); 67.1g carbohydrate; 25.8g protein; 4.6g fibre

fettuccine alfredo

500g fettuccine pasta
80g butter
300ml cream
½ cup (40g) finely grated parmesan cheese

1 Cook pasta in large saucepan of boiling water until tender; drain. Retun to pan.
2 Melt butter in medium frying pan. Add cream; bring to the boil. Reduce heat; simmer, uncovered, about 5 minutes or until sauce reduces by half.
3 Add cheese; stir over low heat about 2 minutes or until cheese melts. Add sauce to pasta; toss gently to combine.

preparation time 10 minutes
cooking time 10 minutes serves 4
nutritional count per serving 53.4g total fat (34.5g saturated fat); 3821kJ (914 cal); 87.5g carbohydrate; 19.4g protein; 4.1g fibre

spaghetti bolognese

2 teaspoons olive oil
200g pancetta, chopped finely
1 medium brown onion (150g), chopped finely
1 small carrot (70g), chopped finely
2 trimmed celery stalks (200g), chopped finely
600g beef mince
½ cup (125ml) dry red wine
1 cup (250ml) beef stock
½ cup (140g) tomato paste
2 x 400g cans crushed tomatoes
½ cup coarsely chopped fresh flat-leaf parsley
2 tablespoons coarsely chopped fresh oregano
500g spaghetti

1   Heat oil in large heavy-based pan; cook pancetta, stirring, until crisp. Add onion, carrot and celery; cook, stirring, until vegetables soften. Add beef; cook, stirring occasionally, until beef just changes colour.
2   Add wine; bring to the boil then reduce heat. Simmer 5 minutes. Add stock, paste and undrained tomatoes; bring to the boil. Reduce heat; simmer, covered, 1 hour. Uncover; simmer about 30 minutes or until bolognese thickens. Stir in herbs off the heat.
3   Meanwhile, cook pasta in large saucepan of boiling water until tender; drain. Add spaghetti to bolognese; toss to combine.

preparation time *25 minutes*
cooking time *1 hour 45 minutes* serves *6*
nutritional count per serving *18.3g total fat (6.9g saturated fat); 2567kJ (614 cal); 66.1g carbohydrate; 38.7g protein; 6.8g fibre*

spinach gnocchi

500g spinach
1¼ cups (250g) ricotta cheese
1 cup (80g) finely grated parmesan cheese
1 egg, beaten lightly
¼ teaspoon ground nutmeg
plain flour
45g butter, melted

1   Steam or microwave spinach until wilted. Rinse under cold running water; drain well. Squeeze as much liquid as possible from spinach; chop finely.
2   Combine spinach, ricotta, half of the parmesan, egg and nutmeg in medium bowl.
3   Preheat grill.
4   Using tablespoon and palm of hand, roll mixture into egg shapes. Roll gnocchi in flour.
5   Cook gnocchi, in batches, in large saucepan of boiling water, uncovered, about 3 minutes or until gnocchi float to the surface. Remove from pan with slotted spoon; drain.
6   Arrange gnocchi in ovenproof dish. Pour butter over gnocchi; sprinkle with remaining parmesan. Cook under grill until cheese turns golden brown.

preparation time *30 minutes*
cooking time *20 minutes* serves *4*
nutritional count per serving *24.5g total fat (15.1g saturated fat); 1321kJ (316 cal); 3.7g carbohydrate; 19.2g protein; 3.5g fibre*

lasagne with four cheeses

2 teaspoons olive oil
1 medium brown onion (150g), chopped finely
2 cloves garlic, crushed
500g lean beef mince
2 x 425g cans crushed tomatoes
½ cup (140g) tomato paste
½ teaspoon sugar
½ cup finely chopped fresh basil
¼ cup finely chopped fresh oregano
500g ricotta cheese
1 cup (80g) finely grated parmesan cheese
1 cup (100g) coarsely grated mozzarella cheese
¼ teaspoon ground nutmeg
4 eggs
200g large curly instant lasagne sheets
1 cup (100g) pizza cheese

1 Heat oil in large saucepan; cook onion and garlic, stirring, until onion softens. Add mince; cook, stirring, until mince changes colour. Add undrained tomatoes, paste and sugar; cook, stirring, until sauce thickens. Remove from heat; stir in basil and oregano.
2 Preheat oven to 180°C/160°C fan-forced.
3 Beat ricotta, parmesan, mozzarella and nutmeg in medium bowl with electric mixer until well combined. Add eggs, one at a time, beating until just combined between additions.
4 Place a third of the lasagne sheets in shallow 2.5-litre (10-cup) baking dish; top with half of the meat sauce and half of the cheese mixture. Top with another third of the lasagne sheets, remaining meat sauce, remaining lasagne sheets then remaining cheese mixture. Top with pizza cheese.
5 Bake lasagne about 45 minutes or until top browns lightly. Stand lasagne 5 minutes before serving.

preparation time *25 minutes*
cooking time *55 minutes* serves *6*
nutritional count per serving *32.7g total fat (17.2g saturated fat); 2671kJ (639 cal); 33.2g carbohydrate; 50.9g protein; 4.1g fibre*

spanakopita

1.5kg silver beet, trimmed
1 tablespoon olive oil
1 medium brown onion (150g), chopped finely
2 cloves garlic, crushed
1 teaspoon ground nutmeg
200g fetta cheese, crumbled
1 tablespoon finely grated lemon rind
¼ cup chopped fresh mint
¼ cup chopped fresh flat-leaf parsley
¼ cup chopped fresh dill
4 green onions, chopped finely
16 sheets fillo pastry
125g butter, melted
2 teaspoons sesame seeds

1 Boil, steam or microwave silver beet until just wilted; drain. Squeeze out excess moisture; drain on absorbent paper. Chop coarsely; spread out on absorbent paper.
2 Heat oil in small frying pan; cook brown onion and garlic, stirring, until onion is soft. Add nutmeg; cook, stirring, until fragrant.
3 Combine onion mixture and silver beet in large bowl with fetta, rind, herbs and green onion.
4 Preheat oven to 180°C/160°C fan-forced
5 Brush one sheet of fillo with butter; fold lengthways into thirds, brushing with butter between each fold. Place rounded tablespoon of silver beet mixture at the bottom of one narrow edge of folded fillo sheet, leaving a border. Fold opposite corner of fillo diagonally across the filling to form large triangle; continue folding to end of fillo sheet, retaining triangular shape. Place on oiled oven tray, seam-side down; repeat with remaining ingredients.
6 Brush spanakopita with remaining butter; sprinkle with sesame seeds. Bake, uncovered, about 15 minutes or until browned lightly.

preparation time *40 minutes*
cooking time *30 minutes* makes *16*
nutritional count per triangle *11.1g total fat (6.4g saturated fat); 690kJ (165 cal); 11g carbohydrate; 4.7g protein; 1.5g fibre*

moussaka

2 large eggplants (1kg), sliced thinly
1 tablespoon coarse cooking salt
¼ cup (60ml) olive oil
1 large brown onion (200g), chopped finely
2 cloves garlic, crushed
1kg lamb mince
425g can crushed tomatoes
½ cup (125ml) dry white wine
1 teaspoon ground cinnamon
¼ cup (20g) finely grated parmesan cheese

WHITE SAUCE

80g butter
⅓ cup (50g) plain flour
2 cups (500ml) milk

1   Place eggplant in colander, sprinkle all over with salt; stand 30 minutes. Rinse under cold water; drain. Pat dry with absorbent paper.
2   Heat oil in large frying pan; cook eggplant, in batches, until browned both sides; drain on absorbent paper.
3   Cook onion and garlic in same pan, stirring, until onion softens. Add lamb mince; cook, stirring, until mince changes colour. Stir in undrained tomatoes, wine and cinnamon; bring to the boil. Reduce heat; simmer, uncovered, about 30 minutes or until liquid has evaporated.
4   Meanwhile, preheat oven to 180°C/160°C fan-forced. Oil shallow 2-litre (8-cup) rectangular baking dish.
5   Make white sauce.
6   Place a third of the eggplant in dish, overlapping slices slightly; spread half of the meat sauce over eggplant. Repeat layering with another third of the eggplant, remaining meat sauce and remaining eggplant. Spread white sauce over eggplant; sprinkle with cheese.
7   Bake moussaka about 40 minutes or until top browns lightly. Cover; stand 10 minutes before serving.

WHITE SAUCE Melt butter in medium saucepan. Add flour; cook, stirring, until mixture thickens and bubbles. Gradually add milk; stir until mixture boils and thickens.

preparation time *40 minutes (plus standing time)*
cooking time *1 hour 30 minutes* serves 6
nutritional count per serving *36.6g total fat (16.5g saturated fat); 2420kJ (579 cal); 18g carbohydrate; 41.8g protein; 5.3g fibre*

osso buco milanese

12 pieces veal osso buco (3.5kg)
¼ cup (35g) plain flour
¼ cup (60ml) olive oil
1 medium brown onion (150g), sliced thinly
2 cloves garlic, crushed
4 slices pancetta (60g), chopped coarsely
1 cup (250ml) dry white wine
2½ cups (625ml) chicken stock
¼ cup coarsely chopped fresh sage
1 bay leaf
pinch saffron threads
8 marinated artichoke hearts (100g), quartered
2 teaspoons finely grated lemon rind
2 tablespoons lemon juice

1   Coat veal in flour; shake off excess.
2   Heat 2 tablespoons of the oil in large saucepan; cook veal, in batches, until browned all over.
3   Heat remaining oil in same pan; cook onion, garlic and pancetta, stirring, until onion softens. Stir in wine, stock, sage, bay leaf and saffron.
4   Return veal to pan, fitting pieces upright and tightly together in a single layer; bring to the boil. Reduce heat; simmer, covered, 1½ hours. Stir in artichokes; simmer, uncovered, 30 minutes.
5   Remove veal from pan; cover to keep warm. Bring sauce to the boil; boil, uncovered, about 10 minutes or until sauce thickens slightly. Stir in rind and juice.
6   Divide veal among serving plates; top with sauce. Sprinkle with extra grated lemon rind and fresh sage leaves, if you like.

preparation time *30 minutes*
cooking time *2 hours 30 minutes* serves 6
nutritional count per serving *12.1g total fat (2.2g saturated fat); 2136kJ (511 cal); 7.1g carbohydrate; 85.6g protein; 0.8g fibre*

danish pastries

1 cup (250ml) warm milk
¼ cup (55g) sugar
1 tablespoon (14g) dried yeast
20g butter, melted
1 egg, beaten lightly
2¼ cups (335g) plain flour
1 teaspoon salt
200g butter
825g can whole dark plums, drained, halved, seeded
1 egg, beaten lightly, extra
2 tablespoons milk
⅓ cup (110g) apricot jam
2 tablespoons water

CREME PATISSIERE

2 egg yolks
¼ cup (55g) sugar
2 tablespoons cornflour
¾ cup (180ml) milk
½ cup (125ml) cream
1 vanilla bean
30g butter

1 Whisk warm milk, sugar and yeast in medium jug until yeast dissolves, cover; stand in warm place about 15 minutes or until mixture is frothy. Stir in melted butter and egg.

2 Sift flour and salt into large bowl; stir in yeast mixture, mix to a soft dough. Knead dough on floured surface about 10 minutes or until smooth (dough should be sticky). Place dough in oiled large bowl, turning dough once to coat in oil. Cover with plastic wrap; stand at room temperature 1 hour. Refrigerate overnight.

3 Knead dough on floured surface about 5 minutes or until smooth and elastic. Roll dough into 25cm x 40cm rectangle, keeping corners square. Cut butter into small pieces; scatter half of the butter over two-thirds of the dough. Fold unbuttered section of dough over half of the buttered dough; fold remaining buttered section over it. With seam facing right, roll dough to form 25cm x 40cm rectangle again; fold one third of the dough onto centre third, fold remaining third on top. Enclose with plastic wrap; refrigerate 30 minutes.

4 Unwrap dough; with seam facing right, repeat step 3 with remaining butter.

5 Meanwhile, make crème pâtissière.

6 Unwrap dough; with seam facing right, repeat step 3 with no added butter.

7 Preheat oven to 220°C/200°C fan-forced. Divide dough in half; roll each half into 30cm x 40cm rectangle. Cut each rectangle into 10cm squares; you will have 24 squares.

8 Centre 1 heaped teaspoon of the cold crème pâtissière on each square; top each with one plum half. Brush dough around plum with combined extra egg and milk; bring opposite corners together, pinch gently. Place pastries 5cm apart on ungreased oven trays; brush dough again with egg mixture. Bake, uncovered, about 12 minutes or until browned lightly.

9 Meanwhile, stir jam and the water in small saucepan over low heat until smooth; push mixture through sieve into small bowl. Brush pastries straight from the oven with jam mixture; transfer to wire rack to cool.

CREME PATISSIERE Whisk egg yolks, sugar and cornflour in medium bowl until light and fluffy. Combine milk and cream in medium saucepan. Split vanilla bean in half lengthways; scrape seeds into pan, then add pod. Bring mixture almost to the boil; discard pod. Whisking constantly, gradually pour milk mixture into egg mixture; return custard mixture to same saucepan. Cook over low heat, stirring constantly, until mixture boils and thickens; remove from heat. Return to same cleaned medium bowl with butter; stir until butter melts. Cover surface of crème pâtissière completely with plastic wrap to avoid skin forming; cool to room temperature.

preparation time *1 hour 30 minutes (plus standing and refrigeration time)* cooking time *25 minutes* makes *24* nutritional count per pastry *12.7g total fat (7.9g saturated fat); 918kJ (219 cal); 22.3g carbohydrate; 3.5g protein; 0.9g fibre*

crème catalana

8 egg yolks
1 cup (220g) caster sugar
1.125 litres (4½ cups) milk
2 teaspoons finely grated lemon rind
1 cinnamon stick
½ cup (75g) cornflour
⅓ cup (75g) caster sugar, extra

1 Beat yolks and sugar in large bowl with balloon whisk until creamy.
2 Place 1 litre (4 cups) of the milk, rind and cinnamon in large saucepan; stir over medium heat until mixture just comes to the boil. Remove immediately from heat.
3 Strain milk into large heatproof jug; pour milk into egg mixture, whisking constantly. Stir remaining milk and cornflour in small jug until smooth; add to egg mixture. Return mixture to pan; stir constantly over heat until mixture boils and thickens.
4 Pour mixture into 26cm heatproof pie dish; cover, refrigerate 4 hours or overnight.
5 Just before serving, preheat grill. Sprinkle crème catalana with extra sugar; place under grill until sugar is caramelised.

preparation time *15 minutes*
cooking time *10 minutes (plus refrigeration time)*
serves *8*
nutritional count per serving *11.2g total fat (5.4g saturated fat); 1438kJ (344 cal); 52.3g carbohydrate; 7.9g protein; 0g fibre*

zabaglione

2 eggs
4 egg yolks
½ cup (110g) caster sugar
⅓ cup (80ml) marsala
12 sponge finger biscuits

1 Place eggs, egg yolks and sugar in large heatproof bowl over pan of simmering water, ensuring that water does not touch bottom of bowl.
2 Using an electric mixer or whisk, beat egg mixture constantly until light and fluffy. Gradually add marsala while continuing to whisk for about 10 minutes or until mixture is thick and creamy.
3 Spoon zabaglione into small serving glasses; serve with sponge finger biscuits.

preparation time *10 minutes*
cooking time *10 minutes* serves *6*
nutritional count per serving *6.8g total fat (2.1g saturated fat); 970kJ (232 cal); 34g carbohydrate; 6.5g protein; 0.3g fibre*

apple tarte tatin

6 large apples (1.2kg)
100g unsalted butter, chopped
1 cup (220g) firmly packed brown sugar
2 tablespoons lemon juice
1 cup (150g) plain flour
2 tablespoons caster sugar
80g cold unsalted butter, chopped
2 tablespoons sour cream

1 Peel, core and quarter apples. Melt butter in large heavy-based frying pan; add apple, sprinkle evenly with sugar and juice. Cook, uncovered, over low heat, 1 hour, turning apple as it caramelises.
2 Place apple, rounded-sides down, in 23cm pie dish; drizzle with 1 tablespoon of the caramel in pan. Reserve remaining caramel. Pack apple tightly to avoid any gaps, cover; refrigerate until required.
3 Process flour, sugar, butter and sour cream until ingredients just come together. Knead dough on floured surface until smooth. Cover; refrigerate 30 minutes.
4 Preheat oven to 200°C/180°C fan-forced.
5 Roll dough between sheets of baking paper until large enough to cover apple. Peel away one sheet of baking paper; invert pastry over apple. Remove remaining paper; tuck pastry around apple.
6 Bake tarte tatin about 30 minutes or until browned. Carefully turn onto serving plate.
7 Reheat reserved caramel over low heat; drizzle over apple before serving.

preparation time *40 minutes (plus refrigeration time)*
cooking time *1 hour 45 minutes* serves *8*
nutritional count per serving *20.8g total fat (13.5g saturated fat); 1848kJ (442 cal); 59.5g carbohydrate; 2.7g protein; 2.9g fibre*

palmiers with honey cream

2 tablespoons raw sugar
1 sheet ready-rolled puff pastry
1 teaspoon ground nutmeg
300ml thickened cream
2 teaspoons honey

1 Preheat oven to 180°C/160°C fan-forced. Grease two oven trays; line with baking paper.
2 Sprinkle board with a little of the sugar. Roll pastry on sugared board into 20cm x 40cm rectangle; trim edges. Sprinkle pastry with nutmeg and remaining sugar.
3 Starting from long side, loosely roll one side at a time into the middle of the rectangle, so the two long sides meet.
4 Cut pastry into 5mm-thick pieces. Place, cut-side up, about 5cm apart, on trays. Spread pastry open slightly at folded ends to make a V-shape.
5 Bake palmiers about 15 minutes or until golden brown; transfer to wire rack to cool.
6 Beat cream and honey in small bowl with electric mixer until firm peaks form.
7 Serve palmiers with honey cream.

preparation time *25 minutes*
cooking time *15 minutes* makes *30*
nutritional count per palmier *5g total fat (3.1g saturated fat); 259kJ (62 cal); 3.8g carbohydrate; 0.5g protein; 0.1g fibre*

chocolate marquise

¾ cup (180ml) thickened cream
100g dark eating chocolate, chopped coarsely
4 egg yolks
2 eggs
½ cup (110g) caster sugar
300ml thickened cream, extra
¼ cup (60ml) orange-flavoured liqueur
¾ cup (75g) coarsely grated dark eating chocolate
2 teaspoons finely grated orange rind

CHOCOLATE SPONGE

4 eggs
⅔ cup (150g) caster sugar
⅓ cup (50g) plain flour
1 tablespoon cocoa powder

1 Make chocolate sponge.
2 Line base and long sides of 14cm x 21cm loaf pan with baking paper. Cut two rectangles from cooled sponge, one measuring 13cm x 21cm, the other 11cm x 19cm; discard remaining sponge.
3 Combine cream and chopped chocolate in small saucepan; stir over low heat until smooth. Beat egg yolks, eggs and sugar in medium bowl with electric mixer until thick and creamy; with motor operating, gradually beat hot chocolate mixture into egg mixture. Cover; refrigerate about 30 minutes or until mixture thickens slightly.
4 Meanwhile, beat extra cream in small bowl with electric mixer until soft peaks form; fold cream, liqueur, grated chocolate and rind into cooled chocolate mixture.
5 Place smaller rectangle of sponge in loaf pan; pour in chocolate mixture, top with remaining sponge rectangle. Cover with foil; freeze until firm.
6 Turn marquise out onto board; stand at room temperature about 5 minutes or until softened slightly. Slice thickly, serve with fresh berries macerated in the same orange-flavoured liqueur, if you like.

CHOCOLATE SPONGE Preheat oven to 180°C/160°C fan-forced. Grease 25cm x 30cm swiss roll pan; line base with baking paper. Beat eggs and sugar in small bowl with electric mixer until thick and creamy; transfer to large bowl. Fold in triple-sifted combined flour and cocoa; spread mixture into pan. Bake about 10 minutes. Cool in pan 10 minutes.

preparation time *30 minutes* cooking time *15 minutes (plus refrigeration and freezing time)* serves *10* nutritional count per serving *28.4g total fat (16.4g saturated fat); 1986kJ (475 cal); 44.8g carbohydrate; 7.8g protein; 0.5g fibre*

sacher torte

150g dark eating chocolate, chopped
1 tablespoon water
150g butter
½ cup (110g) caster sugar
3 eggs, separated
1 cup (150g) plain flour
2 tablespoons caster sugar, extra
1 cup (320g) apricot jam

CHOCOLATE ICING

125g dark eating chocolate, chopped
125g butter

1 Preheat oven to 180°C/160°C fan-forced. Grease deep 23cm-round cake pan, line base with baking paper; grease paper.
2 Make chocolate icing.
3 Melt chocolate in small heatproof bowl over small saucepan simmering water. Stir in the water; cool to room temperature.
4 Beat butter and sugar in small bowl with electric mixer until light and fluffy. Beat in egg yolks, one at a time. Transfer mixture to large bowl; stir in chocolate mixture, then sifted flour.
5 Beat egg whites in small bowl until soft peaks form; gradually add extra sugar, beating until dissolved between additions. Fold egg white mixture into chocolate mixture; spread into pan.
6 Bake cake about 30 minutes. Stand in pan 5 minutes; turn onto wire rack to cool. Leave cake upside-down.
7 Split cold cake in half; place one half, cut-side up, on serving plate. Heat and strain jam; brush half of the jam over cake half. Top with remaining cake half, brush cake all over with remaining jam. Stand about 1 hour at room temperature to allow jam to set. Spread top and side of cake with icing, set at room temperature.

CHOCOLATE ICING Stir chocolate and butter in small heatproof bowl over small saucepan of simmering water until smooth. Cool at room temperature until spreadable, stirring occasionally (this can take up to 2 hours). This icing is also suitable for piping.

preparation time *30 minutes (plus standing time)* cooking time *40 minutes (plus cooling time)* serves *10* nutritional count per serving *32.1g total fat (20g saturated fat); 2374kJ (568 cal); 63.9g carbohydrate; 5.3g protein; 1.3g fibre*

plum clafoutis

10 small plums (750g), halved, seeded
1 cinnamon stick, halved
¼ cup (60ml) water
¼ cup (55g) brown sugar
⅔ cup (160ml) milk
⅔ cup (160ml) cream
1 teaspoon vanilla extract
4 eggs
½ cup (110g) caster sugar
¼ cup (35g) plain flour

1 Preheat oven to 200°C/180°C fan-forced. Grease shallow 2.5-litre (10-cup) ovenproof dish.
2 Place plums in medium baking dish with cinnamon and the water; sprinkle with sugar. Cook, in oven, about 15 minutes or until plums soften.
3 Remove cinnamon from dish and add to medium saucepan with milk, cream and extract; bring to the boil. Cool; remove cinnamon stick.
4 Whisk eggs and sugar in medium bowl until light and frothy; whisk in flour then whisk mixture into cream mixture.
5 Place drained plums in shallow ovenproof dish; pour cream mixture over plums. Bake about 30 minutes or until browned lightly. Serve dusted with icing sugar, if you like.

preparation time *20 minutes (plus cooling time)* cooking time *50 minutes* serves *6* nutritional count per serving *16.1g total fat (9.3g saturated fat); 1417kJ (339 cal); 46.2g carbohydrate; 7.1g protein; 2.4g fibre*

cassata

2 eggs, separated
½ cup (110g) icing sugar
½ cup (125ml) cream
few drops almond essence

SECOND LAYER

2 eggs, separated
½ cup (110g) icing sugar
½ cup (125ml) cream
60g dark eating chocolate, melted
2 tablespoons cocoa powder
1½ tablespoons water

THIRD LAYER

1 cup (250ml) cream
1 teaspoon vanilla extract
1 egg white, beaten lightly
⅓ cup (55g) icing sugar
2 tablespoons red glacé cherries, chopped finely
2 glacé apricots, chopped finely
2 glacé pineapple rings, chopped finely
1 tablespoon green glacé cherries, chopped finely
30g flaked almonds, roasted

1 Beat egg whites in small bowl with electric mixer until firm peaks form; gradually beat in icing sugar. Fold in lightly beaten egg yolks.
2 Beat cream and almond essence in small bowl with electric mixer until soft peaks form; fold into egg mixture. Pour mixture into deep 20cm-round cake pan; level surface. Freeze until firm.
3 Make second layer; spread over almond layer. Freeze until firm.
4 Make third layer; spread over second layer. Freeze until firm.
5 Run small spatula around edge of cassata; wipe hot cloth over base and side of pan. Turn cassata out onto serving plate.

SECOND LAYER Beat egg whites in small bowl with electric mixer until firm peaks form; gradually beat in sifted icing sugar. Beat cream in small bowl until soft peaks form; fold in egg white mixture. Place chocolate in small bowl; stir in egg yolks. Stir blended cocoa and water into chocolate mixture; stir chocolate mixture through cream mixture.

THIRD LAYER Beat cream and extract in small bowl with electric mixer until firm peaks form. Beat egg white in small bowl with electric mixer until soft peaks form; gradually add icing sugar to egg white, beating well after each addition. Stir egg white mixture into cream; stir in fruit and almonds.

preparation time *1 hour (plus freezing time)*
serves *8*
nutritional count per serving *34.1g total fat (20.2g saturated fat); 2358kJ (564 cal); 57.8g carbohydrate; 6.7g protein; 0.7g fibre*

chocolate hazelnut gelato

1 cup (125g) hazelnuts
1⅔ cups (400ml) milk
2½ cups (600ml) cream
6 egg yolks
⅓ cup (75g) caster sugar
¾ cup (215g) chocolate hazelnut spread

1   Preheat oven to 180°C/160°C fan-forced.
2   Roast hazelnuts in shallow baking dish about 8 minutes or until skins begin to split and nuts are roasted. Place nuts in clean tea towel; rub vigorously to remove skins. Chop nuts coarsely.
3   Bring milk, cream and hazelnuts to the boil in medium saucepan; cover, remove from heat. Stand 10 minutes; strain, discard hazelnuts.
4   Whisk egg yolks and sugar in medium bowl until creamy. Gradually whisk hot milk mixture into egg mixture. Return to pan, stir over low heat, without boiling, until mixture thickens slightly and coats back of spoon. Whisk in chocolate hazelnut spread until combined.
5   Transfer custard to large bowl, cover surface completely with plastic wrap to avoid skin forming; cool slightly. Refrigerate 2 hours or until cold.
6   Transfer custard to shallow container, cover with foil; freeze until almost firm. Chop gelato coarsely; blend or process until smooth. Pour gelato mixture into deep dish or container; cover, freeze until firm. Serve gelato scooped in cones, if you like.

preparation time *20 minutes (plus cooling and freezing time)* cooking time *20 minutes* serves *8* nutritional count per serving *57.1g total fat (27.2g saturated fat); 2796kJ (669 cal); 30.2g carbohydrate; 9.5g protein; 1.9g fibre*

greek honey puffs

2 teaspoons (7g) dry yeast
1 cup (250ml) warm milk
2 tablespoons caster sugar
1 egg, beaten lightly
60g butter, melted
2 cups (300g) plain flour
vegetable oil, for deep-frying
⅔ cup (230g) honey, warmed
¼ teaspoon ground cinnamon
¼ cup coarsely chopped roasted walnuts

1   Combine yeast, milk, sugar, egg and butter in large bowl; mix well. Gradually stir in sifted flour; beat until smooth. Cover; leave to stand in warm place for about 1½ hours or until batter doubles in size and bubbles appear on the surface.
2   Beat batter with a wooden spoon until smooth.
3   Deep-fry rounded teaspoons of batter, in batches, in hot oil, dipping spoon in hot oil before spooning mixture out of bowl. Turn puffs to brown evenly during frying. Drain puffs on absorbent paper.
4   Divide puffs among serving plates, drizzle with honey, sprinkle with cinnamon and walnuts.

preparation time *15 minutes (plus standing time)* cooking time *15 minutes* serves *8* nutritional count per serving *15.6g total fat (5.9g saturated fat); 1680kJ (402 cal); 56.9g carbohydrate; 7g protein; 1.9g fibre*

1

2

3

4

rosewater baklava

1 cup (160g) blanched almonds
1 cup (140g) shelled pistachios
2 teaspoons ground cinnamon
1 teaspoon ground clove
1 teaspoon ground nutmeg
18 sheets fillo pastry
80g butter, melted

ROSEWATER SYRUP

1 cup (250ml) water
1 cup (220g) caster sugar
¼ cup (90g) honey
1 teaspoon rosewater

1 Preheat oven to 180°C/160°C fan-forced.
Grease deep 23cm-square cake pan.
2 Process nuts and spices until chopped finely;
spread nut mixture onto oven tray. Roast, uncovered,
about 10 minutes or until browned lightly.
3 Increase oven to 200°C/180°C fan-forced.
4 Cut pastry sheets to fit base of pan. Layer three
pastry squares, brushing each with butter; place in pan,
sprinkle with ⅓ cup of the nut mixture. Repeat layering
with remaining pastry, butter and nut mixture, ending
with pastry. Using sharp knife, cut baklava into quarters;
cut each quarter in half on the diagonal, then cut each
triangle in half. Bake baklava 25 minutes.
5 Reduce oven to 150°C/130°C fan-forced; bake
baklava further 10 minutes.
6 Meanwhile, make rosewater syrup.
7 Pour hot syrup over hot baklava; cool in pan.

ROSEWATER SYRUP Stir ingredients in small saucepan
over heat, without boiling, until sugar dissolves; bring
to the boil. Reduce heat; simmer, uncovered, without
stirring, about 5 minutes or until thickened slightly.

preparation time *15 minutes*
cooking time *35 minutes* makes *16*
nutritional count per piece *14.8g total fat (3.6g
saturated fat); 1124kJ (469 cal); 28.7g carbohydrate;
5.4g protein; 1.9g fibre*

italian ricotta cheesecake

90g butter, softened
¼ cup (55g) caster sugar
1 egg
1¼ cups (185g) plain flour
¼ cup (35g) self-raising flour

FILLING

1kg ricotta cheese
1 tablespoon finely grated lemon rind
¼ cup (60ml) lemon juice
1 cup (220g) caster sugar
5 eggs
¼ cup (40g) sultanas
¼ cup (80g) finely chopped glacé fruit salad

1 Grease 28cm springform tin.
2 Beat butter, sugar and egg in small bowl with
electric mixer until combined. Stir in half the sifted flours;
then work in remaining flour with hand. Knead pastry
on floured surface until smooth. Wrap in plastic;
refrigerate 30 minutes.
3 Press pastry over base of tin; prick with fork. Place
on oven tray; refrigerate 30 minutes.
4 Preheat oven to 200°C/180°C fan-forced.
5 Line pastry with baking paper, fill with dried beans
or rice; bake 10 minutes. Remove paper and beans;
bake further 15 minutes or until browned lightly. Cool.
6 Reduce oven to 160°C/140°C fan-forced.
7 Make filling by processing cheese, rind, juice, sugar
and eggs until smooth; stir in fruit. Pour filling into tin.
8 Bake cheesecake about 50 minutes; cool in oven
with door ajar. Refrigerate 3 hours or overnight. Serve
dusted with icing sugar, if you like.

preparation time *25 minutes (plus refrigeration time)*
cooking time *1 hour 15 minutes (plus cooling and
refrigeration time)* serves *16*
nutritional count per serving *13.8g total fat (8.2g
saturated fat); 1262kJ (302 cal); 33.2g carbohydrate;
10.7g protein; 0.7g fibre*

prune and custard tart

1¼ cups (175g) plain flour
⅓ cup (55g) icing sugar
¼ cup (30g) almond meal
125g cold butter, chopped
1 egg yolk
1 tablespoon water
1½ cups (250g) seeded prunes
2 tablespoons brandy
300ml cream
3 whole eggs
⅔ cup (150g) caster sugar
1 teaspoon vanilla extract

1   Process flour, sugar, almond meal and butter until mixture is crumbly. Add egg yolk and the water; process until ingredients just come together. Wrap in plastic wrap; refrigerate 30 minutes.
2   Grease 26cm-round loose-base flan tin. Roll pastry between sheets of baking paper until large enough to line tin. Lift pastry into tin; press into side, trim edge, prick base all over with fork. Cover; refrigerate 20 minutes.
3   Preheat oven to 200°C/180°C fan-forced.
4   Place tin on oven tray; line pastry with baking paper, fill with dried beans or rice. Bake 10 minutes. Remove paper and beans from tin; bake further 5 minutes or until tart shell browns lightly. Cool to room temperature.
5   Reduce oven to 150°C/130°C fan-forced.
6   Blend or process prunes and brandy until mixture forms a paste; spread into tart shell.
7   Bring cream to the boil in small saucepan; remove from heat. Whisk whole eggs, sugar and extract in small bowl until combined; gradually add hot cream, whisking continuously until combined. Pour into tart shell.
8   Bake tart about 20 minutes or until custard just sets. Stand 10 minutes; serve warm or cold dusted with icing sugar, if you like.

preparation time 20 minutes (plus refrigeration time)
cooking time 35 minutes (plus cooling and standing time) serves 8
nutritional count per serving 31.9g total fat (18.6g saturated fat); 2278kJ (545 cal); 53g carbohydrate; 7.6g protein; 3.6g fibre

portuguese custard tarts

3 egg yolks
½ cup (110g) caster sugar
2 tablespoons cornflour
¾ cup (180ml) cream
½ cup (125ml) water
strip of lemon rind
2 teaspoons vanilla extract
1 sheet ready-rolled butter puff pastry

1   Preheat oven to 220°C/200°C fan-forced. Grease 12-hole (⅓-cup/80ml) muffin pan.
2   Whisk egg yolks, sugar and cornflour in medium saucepan until combined. Gradually whisk in cream and the water until smooth.
3   Add rind; stir over medium heat until mixture just comes to the boil. Remove from heat immediately; remove rind and stir in extract.
4   Cut pastry sheet in half. Remove plastic and stack the two halves on top of each other. Stand about 5 minutes or until thawed. Roll the pastry up tightly from the short side then cut the log into 12 x 1cm rounds.
5   Place pastry rounds on floured board; roll each round to about 10cm. Press rounds into pan holes. Spoon custard into pastry cases.
6   Bake tarts about 20 minutes or until well browned. Transfer to wire rack to cool.

preparation time 25 minutes
cooking time 30 minutes (plus cooling time) makes 12
nutritional count per tart 14.1g total fat (8.2g saturated fat); 836kJ (200 cal); 16.3g carbohydrate; 2.2g protein; 0.2g fibre

mille-feuille with almonds and raspberries

Mille-feuille, pronounced meal-fwee, translates as "thousand leaves", and refers to puff pastry used in multi-layered sweet or savoury dishes.

1⅓ cups (330ml) milk
4 egg yolks
½ cup (110g) caster sugar
2 tablespoons plain flour
1 tablespoon cornflour
1 teaspoon vanilla extract
50g butter
1 tablespoon honey
2 sheets fillo pastry
⅓ cup (55g) roasted blanched almonds,
  chopped finely
¾ cup (180ml) thickened cream
300g raspberries

1 Bring milk to the boil in medium saucepan. Combine egg yolks, sugar, flours and extract in medium bowl; gradually whisk in hot milk. Return custard mixture to same pan; stir, over heat, until mixture boils and thickens. Return custard to same bowl, cover; refrigerate about 1 hour or until cold.

2 Meanwhile, combine butter and honey in same cleaned pan; stir, over low heat, until smooth.

3 Preheat oven to 200°C/180°C fan-forced. Grease two oven trays.

4 Brush one fillo sheet with half of the honey mixture; sprinkle with nuts. Top with remaining fillo sheet; brush with remaining honey mixture. Cut fillo stack into 7cm-squares; place squares on trays.

5 Bake pastry squares about 5 minutes or until browned lightly. Cool 10 minutes.

6 Meanwhile, beat cream in small bowl with electric mixer until soft peaks form; fold into cold custard mixture.

7 Place one pastry square on each serving plate; top each with one heaped tablespoon of the custard mixture and a few raspberries. Place second pastry square on each; repeat with another layer of custard and raspberries then top each with third pastry square. Serve mille-feuilles with remaining raspberries; dust with icing sugar, if you like.

preparation time *25 minutes*
cooking time *15 minutes (plus refrigeration and cooling time)* serves *8*
nutritional count per serving *22g total fat (11.1g saturated fat); 1409kJ (337 cal); 27.6g carbohydrate; 6.1g protein; 2.9g fibre*

semolina fritters with almond liqueur syrup

75g butter, chopped
1 cup (250ml) water
½ cup (75g) plain flour
½ cup (90g) ground semolina
1 tablespoon caster sugar
4 eggs, beaten lightly
½ teaspoon almond essence
vegetable oil, for deep-frying
¼ cup (30g) almond meal

ALMOND LIQUEUR SYRUP

2 cups (440g) caster sugar
1¼ cups (310ml) water
1 tablespoon almond-flavoured liqueur

1   Make almond liqueur syrup.
2   Combine butter and the water in medium saucepan; bring to the boil, stirring, until butter is melted. Stir in sifted flour and semolina; stir vigorously over heat until mixture leaves side of pan and forms a smooth ball.
3   Transfer mixture to small bowl of electric mixer; gradually beat in sugar and eggs. Stir in essence.
4   Heat oil in wok or medium saucepan; deep-fry heaped teaspoons of mixture, in batches, until puffed and golden brown. Drain on absorbent paper. Dip fritters in syrup; serve sprinkled with roasted flaked almonds, if you like.

ALMOND LIQUEUR SYRUP Stir sugar and the water in medium saucepan over heat, without boiling, until sugar dissolves; bring to the boil. Reduce heat; simmer, uncovered, without stirring, 8 minutes. Remove from heat, stir in liqueur.

preparation time *25 minutes*
cooking time *25 minutes* serves *8*
nutritional count per serving *16.9g total fat (6.6g saturated fat); 1977kJ (473 cal); 71.7g carbohydrate; 6.1g protein; 1g fibre*

panna cotta with roasted nectarines

300ml thickened cream
1 cup (250ml) milk
1 vanilla bean, split
¼ cup (55g) caster sugar
1½ teaspoons gelatine
1 strip lemon rind

ROASTED NECTARINES

4 medium nectarines (680g), halved, seeded
⅓ cup (75g) caster sugar
½ cup (125ml) dessert wine

1   Stir cream, milk, vanilla bean, sugar, gelatine and rind in pan over low heat until warm. Stand until cool.
2   Strain cream mixture through fine strainer into medium jug; discard vanilla pod. Pour mixture into four ½-cup (125ml) moulds. Cover; refrigerate 6 hours or overnight.
3   Make roasted nectarines.
4   Turn panna cotta from moulds onto serving plates; serve with nectarines and pan juices.

ROASTED NECTARINES Preheat oven to 220°C/200°C fan-forced. Place nectarines, cut-side up, in small ovenproof dish; sprinkle with sugar and drizzle with wine. Roast 15 minutes or until browned lightly and softened. Cool.

preparation time *25 minutes (plus refrigeration time)*
cooking time *20 minutes* serves *4*
nutritional count per serving *36.5g total fat (20g saturated fat); 2316kJ (554 cal); 52.3g carbohydrate; 6.5g protein; 3.6g fibre*

ASIAN NEIGHBOURS

pork, peanut and kaffir lime spring rolls

4 dried shiitake mushrooms
½ cup (75g) roasted unsalted peanuts, chopped finely
2 green onions, chopped finely
1 medium red capsicum (200g), chopped finely
3 fresh kaffir lime leaves, shredded finely
2cm piece fresh ginger (10g), grated
500g pork mince
1 tablespoon soy sauce
2 tablespoons oyster sauce
1 tablespoon chinese cooking wine
20 x 21.5cm square spring roll wrappers (300g)
peanut oil, for deep frying

1   Cover mushrooms with boiling water in small heatproof bowl, cover; stand 20 minutes, drain. Discard stems; chop caps finely.
2   Combine mushrooms in medium bowl with nuts, onion, capsicum, lime leaves, ginger, pork, sauces and wine.
3   Spoon rounded tablespoons of the pork filling onto a corner of one wrapper; roll once toward opposing corner to cover filling then fold in two remaining corners to enclose filling. Continue rolling; brush seam with a little water to seal spring roll. Repeat process with remaining wrappers and filling.
4   Heat oil in wok; deep-fry spring rolls, in batches, until golden brown and cooked through. Drain on absorbent paper.

preparation time *50 minutes (plus standing time)*
cooking time *20 minutes* makes *20*
nutritional count per roll *6.9g total fat (1.5g saturated fat); 506kJ (121 cal); 7.1g carbohydrate; 7.3g protein; 0.8g fibre*

mixed satay sticks

250g chicken breast fillets
250g beef eye fillet
250g pork fillet
2 cloves garlic, crushed
2 teaspoons brown sugar
¼ teaspoon sambal oelek
1 teaspoon ground turmeric
¼ teaspoon curry powder
½ teaspoon ground cumin
½ teaspoon ground coriander
2 tablespoons peanut oil

SATAY SAUCE

½ cup (80g) roasted unsalted peanuts
2 tablespoons red curry paste
¾ cup (180ml) coconut milk
¼ cup (60ml) chicken stock
1 tablespoon kaffir lime juice
1 tablespoon brown sugar

1   Cut chicken, beef and pork into long 1.5cm-thick strips; thread strips onto skewers. Place skewers, in single layer, on tray or in shallow baking dish; brush with combined garlic, sugar, sambal, spices and oil. Cover; refrigerate 3 hours or overnight.
2   Make satay sauce.
3   Cook skewers on heated oiled grill plate (or grill or barbecue) until browned and cooked as desired.
4   Serve skewers immediately with sauce.

SATAY SAUCE Blend or process nuts until chopped finely; add paste, process until just combined. Bring coconut milk to the boil in small saucepan; add peanut mixture, whisking until smooth. Reduce heat, add stock; cook, stirring, about 3 minutes or until sauce thickens slightly. Add juice and sugar, stirring, until sugar dissolves.

preparation time *20 minutes (plus refrigeration time)*
cooking time *15 minutes*
makes *12 skewers and 1¼ cups sauce*
nutritional count per skewer (incl sauce) *13.1g total fat (4.7g saturated fat); 823kJ (197 cal); 3.5g carbohydrate; 15.9g protein; 1.2g fibre*

curry puffs

2 teaspoons peanut oil
2 teaspoons finely chopped coriander root
2 green onions, chopped finely
1 clove garlic, crushed
100g beef mince
½ teaspoon ground turmeric
½ teaspoon ground cumin
¼ teaspoon ground coriander
2 teaspoons fish sauce
1 tablespoon water
½ cup (110g) mashed potato
2 sheets ready-rolled puff pastry
1 egg, beaten lightly
vegetable oil, for deep-frying

SWEET CHILLI DIPPING SAUCE

12 fresh small red thai chillies, chopped coarsely
8 cloves garlic, quartered
2 cups (500ml) white vinegar
1 cup (220g) caster sugar
2 teaspoons salt
2 teaspoons tamarind paste

1 Make dipping sauce (freeze excess for future use).
2 Heat oil in wok; stir-fry coriander root, onion, garlic and mince until mince is changed in colour. Add turmeric, cumin and ground coriander; stir-fry until fragrant. Add fish sauce and the water; simmer, uncovered, until mixture thickens. Stir in potato; cool.
3 Using 9cm cutter, cut four rounds from each pastry sheet. Place 1 level tablespoon of the filling in centre of each round; brush around edge lightly with egg. Fold pastry over to enclose filling, pressing edges together to seal.
4 Just before serving, heat oil in wok; deep-fry curry puffs, in batches, until crisp and browned lightly. Drain on absorbent paper; serve with dipping sauce.

SWEET CHILLI DIPPING SAUCE Stir ingredients in medium saucepan over heat without boiling until sugar dissolves; bring to the boil. Reduce heat; simmer, uncovered, about 20 minutes or until thickened slightly. Cool 5 minutes; blend or process until smooth.

preparation time *30 minutes* cooking time *35 minutes*
makes *8 puffs and 1½ cups dipping sauce*
nutritional count per curry puff *16.5g total fat (2g saturated fat); 1012kJ (242 cal); 16.8g carbohydrate; 6.3g protein; 0.9g fibre*
nutritional count per tablespoon dipping sauce *0g total fat (0g saturated fat); 217kJ (52 cal); 12.9g carbohydrate; 0.1g protein; 0.3g fibre*

seafood and vegetable tempura

540g uncooked medium king prawns
1 medium brown onion (150g)
peanut oil, for deep-frying
450g ocean trout fillets, cut into 3cm pieces
1 large red capsicum (350g), cut into 3cm pieces
1 small kumara (250g), sliced thinly
8 baby zucchini with flowers attached (160g),
   stamens removed
1 cup (150g) plain flour
1 lemon, cut into wedges

TEMPURA BATTER

1 egg white
2 cups (500ml) cold soda water
1¼ cups (185g) plain flour
1¼ cups (185g) cornflour

LEMON DIPPING SAUCE

½ cup (125ml) rice vinegar
¼ cup (55g) caster sugar
1 teaspoon light soy sauce
¼ teaspoon finely grated lemon rind
1 green onion (green part only), sliced thinly

1 Shell and devein prawns, leaving tails intact.
Make three small cuts on the underside of each prawn,
halfway through flesh, to prevent curling when cooked.
2 Halve onion from root end. Push four toothpicks,
at regular intervals, through each onion half to hold
rings together; cut in between toothpicks.
3 Make tempura batter.
4 Make lemon dipping sauce.
5 Heat oil in wok. Dust prawns, onion, fish, capsicum,
kumara and zucchini in flour; shake off excess. Dip,
piece by piece, in batter; deep-fry until crisp. Drain
on absorbent paper.
6 Serve tempura with dipping sauce and lemon
wedges, if you like.

TEMPURA BATTER Whisk egg white in large bowl until
soft peaks form; whisk in soda water to combine. Add
sifted flours, whisk to combine (batter should be lumpy).

LEMON DIPPING SAUCE Heat vinegar, sugar and sauce
in small saucepan, stirring, until sugar dissolves. Remove
from heat, add rind; stand 10 minutes. Strain sauce into
serving dish; discard rind. Sprinkle sauce with onion.

preparation time *35 minutes*
cooking time *25 minutes* serves *6*
nutritional count per serving *16.6g total fat (3.1g
saturated fat); 1831kJ (438 cal); 40.2g carbohydrate;
16.6g protein; 3.5g fibre*

money bags

1 tablespoon peanut oil
1 small brown onion (80g), chopped finely
1 clove garlic, crushed
1 tablespoon grated fresh ginger
100g chicken mince
1 tablespoon finely grated palm sugar
1 tablespoon finely chopped roasted
   unsalted peanuts
2 teaspoons finely chopped fresh coriander
3 green onions
24 x 8cm-square wonton wrappers
vegetable oil, for deep-frying

PEANUT DIPPING SAUCE

1 tablespoon peanut oil
2 cloves garlic, crushed
1 small brown onion (80g), chopped finely
2 fresh small red chillies, chopped coarsely
10cm stick fresh lemon grass (20g), chopped finely
¾ cup (180ml) coconut milk
2 tablespoons fish sauce
¼ cup (55g) dark brown sugar
½ cup (140g) crunchy peanut butter
½ teaspoon curry powder
1 tablespoon lime juice

1   Heat oil in wok; stir-fry onion, garlic and ginger until onion softens. Add chicken mince; stir-fry until mince is changed in colour. Add sugar; stir-fry about 3 minutes or until sugar dissolves. Stir nuts and coriander into filling mixture.

2   Cut upper green half of each onion into four long slices; discard remaining onion half. Submerge onion strips in hot water for a few seconds to make pliable.

3   Place 12 wrappers on board; cover each wrapper with another, placed on the diagonal to form star shape. Place rounded teaspoons of the filling mixture in centre of each star; gather corners to form pouch shape. Tie green onion slice around neck of each pouch to hold closed, secure with toothpick.

4   Make dipping sauce (freeze excess for a future use).

5   Just before serving, heat oil in wok; deep-fry money bags, in batches, until crisp and browned lightly. Drain on absorbent paper; serve with peanut dipping sauce.

PEANUT DIPPING SAUCE   Heat oil in small saucepan; cook garlic and onion until softened. Stir in remaining ingredients; bring to the boil. Reduce heat; simmer, stirring, about 2 minutes or until sauce thickens.

preparation time *30 minutes* cooking time *20 minutes*
makes *12 money bags and 1½ cups dipping sauce*
nutritional count per money bag (incl sauce)
15.7g total fat (4.8g saturated fat); 1007kJ (241 cal); 16.5g carbohydrate; 8.8g protein; 2.4g fibre

tuna sashimi

The fish to use for sashimi and sushi should be fish that are in season and labelled "sashimi quality" as a guarantee of correct health and handling standards. This fish should have a firm texture, a pleasant sea-smell (but not "fishy"), bright red gills and bright, clear eyes (although this last is not an indication on its own because the eyes can sometimes be clouded).

¾ cup (200g) finely shredded daikon
400g block-size piece sashimi tuna
2 teaspoons wasabi paste
2 tablespoons pink pickled ginger

PONZU SAUCE

¼ cup (60ml) lemon juice
¼ cup (60ml) japanese soy sauce
¼ cup (60ml) water or dashi stock
½ cup (120g) grated daikon

1 Soak daikon in medium bowl of iced water for 15 minutes; drain well.
2 Meanwhile, make ponzu sauce.
3 Place tuna on chopping board; using very sharp knife, cut 6mm slices at right angles to the grain of the fish, holding the piece of skinned fish with your fingers and slicing with knife almost horizontal to the board.
4 Divide tuna slices among serving plates; mound equal amounts of daikon next to tuna.
5 Garnish plates with equal amounts of mounded wasabi and ginger; serve with separate bowl of ponzu sauce.

PONZU SAUCE Combine juice, sauce and the water in medium bowl. Squeeze excess liquid from daikon; shape into a small mound. Place in small dish.

preparation time *10 minutes (plus standing time)*
serves *4*
nutritional count per serving *6.3g total fat (2.5g saturated fat); 757kJ (181 cal); 3.6g carbohydrate; 26.7g protein; 1.3g fibre*

yakitori

500g chicken breast fillets
½ cup (125ml) mirin
¼ cup (60ml) kecap manis
1 tablespoon soy sauce
1 teaspoon toasted sesame seeds
1 green onion, sliced thinly

1 Slice chicken into thin diagonal strips; thread strips loosely onto skewers. Place skewers, in single layer, in large shallow dish.
2 Combine mirin, kecap manis and sauce in small jug. Pour half of the marinade over skewers; reserve remaining marinade. Cover; refrigerate 3 hours or overnight.
3 Simmer reserved marinade in small saucepan over low heat until reduced by half.
4 Meanwhile, cook drained skewers on heated oiled grill plate (or grill or barbecue) until chicken is cooked through.
5 Serve skewers drizzled with hot marinade and sprinkled with sesame seeds and onion.

preparation time *20 minutes (plus refrigeration time)*
cooking time *10 minutes* makes *24*
nutritional count per skewer *0.6g total fat (0.1g saturated fat); 121kJ (29 cal); 0.3g carbohydrate; 4.9g protein; 0g fibre*

prawn toasts

16 uncooked large prawns (800g)
2 eggs, beaten lightly
¼ cup (35g) cornflour
8 thick slices white bread
1 green onion, chopped finely
vegetable oil, for deep-frying
SWEET CHILLI DIPPING SAUCE
¼ cup (60ml) sweet chilli sauce
¼ cup (60ml) chicken stock
2 teaspoons soy sauce

1   Shell and devein prawns, leaving tails intact. Cut lengthways along backs of prawns, without separating halves. Toss flattened prawns in medium bowl with combined egg and cornflour; mix well.
2   Remove and discard crusts from bread; cut each slice in half. Place one prawn, cut-side down, on each piece of bread; gently flatten prawn onto bread. Sprinkle prawns with onion; press on firmly.
3   Heat oil in wok; carefully lower prawn toasts, in batches, into hot oil. Deep-fry until browned lightly and cooked through; drain on absorbent paper.
4   Meanwhile, make sweet chilli dipping sauce.
5   Serve toasts with dipping sauce.

SWEET CHILLI DIPPING SAUCE   Combine ingredients in small bowl.

preparation time *30 minutes*
cooking time *15 minutes* makes *16*
nutritional count per toast *4.2g total fat (0.7g saturated fat); 489kJ (117 cal); 1.6g carbohydrate; 7.8g protein; 0.8g fibre*

honey prawns

1.5kg uncooked large prawns
1 cup (150g) self-raising flour
1¼ cups (310ml) water
1 egg, beaten lightly
cornflour
vegetable oil, for deep-frying
2 teaspoons peanut oil
¼ cup (60ml) honey
100g snow pea sprouts
2 tablespoons white sesame seeds, toasted

1   Shell and devein prawns, leaving tails intact.
2   Place self-raising flour in medium bowl; gradually whisk in the water and egg until batter is smooth.
3   Just before serving, coat prawns in cornflour; shake off excess. Dip prawns in batter, one at a time; drain off excess.
4   Heat vegetable oil in wok; deep-fry prawns, in batches, until browned lightly. Drain on absorbent paper.
5   Heat peanut oil in cleaned wok; heat honey, uncovered, until bubbling. Add prawns; stir to coat in honey mixture.
6   Serve prawns on sprouts; sprinkle with seeds.

preparation time *30 minutes*
cooking time *15 minutes* serves *4*
nutritional count per serving *17.9g total fat (2.7g saturated fat); 2353kJ (563 cal); 50.6g carbohydrate; 47.7g protein; 3.1g fibre*

chow mein

1 tablespoon vegetable oil
500g lean beef mince
1 medium brown onion (150g), chopped finely
2 cloves garlic, crushed
1 tablespoon curry powder
1 large carrot (180g), chopped finely
2 trimmed celery stalks (200g), sliced thinly
150g mushrooms, sliced thinly
1 cup (250ml) chicken stock
⅓ cup (80ml) oyster sauce
2 tablespoons soy sauce
450g fresh thin egg noodles
½ cup (60g) frozen peas
½ cup (55g) frozen sliced green beans
½ small wombok (400g), shredded coarsely

1 Heat oil in wok; stir-fry mince, onion and garlic until mince is changed in colour. Add curry powder; stir-fry until fragrant. Add carrot, celery and mushrooms; stir-fry until vegetables soften.
2 Add stock, sauces and noodles, stir-fry gently until combined; bring to the boil. Add peas, beans and wombok, reduce heat; simmer, uncovered, tossing occasionally for about 5 minutes or until vegetables are just soft.

preparation time *30 minutes*
cooking time *25 minutes* serves *4*
nutritional count per serving *14.3g total fat (4.1g saturated fat); 2567kJ (614 cal); 71.9g carbohydrate; 44.1g protein; 8.8g fibre*

pot stickers

300g minced pork
2 tablespoons japanese soy sauce
pinch white pepper
1 teaspoon sugar
1 tablespoon sake
1 egg, beaten lightly
2 teaspoons sesame oil
350g cabbage, chopped finely
4 green onions, chopped finely
30 gow gee wrappers
1 tablespoon vegetable oil

1 Combine pork in medium bowl with sauce, pepper, sugar, sake, egg, sesame oil, cabbage and onion. Refrigerate mixture 1 hour.
2 Wet edge of one side of each wrapper. Place about 2 teaspoons of the pork mixture in centre of each wrapper; pleat damp side of wrapper only. Pinch both sides together to seal.
3 Cover base of large frying pan with water; bring to the boil. Place pouches in pan; reduce heat. Simmer, covered, 3 minutes. Using slotted spoon, remove pouches from pan; drain. Dry pan.
4 Heat vegetable oil in pan; cook pouches, one side and base only, until browned lightly.

preparation time *20 minutes (plus refrigeration time)*
cooking time *10 minutes* makes *30*
nutritional count per pot sticker *1.9g total fat (0.5g saturated fat); 184kJ (44 cal); 3.5g carbohydrate; 3g protein; 0.3g fibre*

1

2

3

4

stir-fried pork, buk choy and water chestnuts

¼ cup (60ml) light soy sauce
2 tablespoons oyster sauce
1 tablespoon honey
1 tablespoon chinese cooking wine
1 teaspoon five-spice powder
½ teaspoon sesame oil
1 clove garlic, crushed
600g pork fillets, sliced thinly
2 tablespoons peanut oil
600g baby buk choy, chopped coarsely
227g can water chestnuts, rinsed, drained, sliced thickly
½ cup (75g) unsalted roasted cashews
2 long green chillies, sliced thinly
1 tablespoon water

1   Combine 2 tablespoons of the soy sauce, 1 tablespoon of the oyster sauce, the honey, wine, five-spice, sesame oil, garlic and pork in large bowl. Cover; refrigerate 3 hours or overnight.
2   Stir-fry pork mixture in heated oiled wok, in batches, until browned.
3   Heat peanut oil in same wok; stir-fry buk choy, water chestnuts, nuts and chilli until tender.
4   Return pork to wok with remaining soy and oyster sauces and the water; stir-fry until hot.

preparation time *15 minutes (plus refrigeration time)* cooking time *15 minutes* serves *4* nutritional count per serving *23g total fat (4.5g saturated fat); 1827kJ (437 cal); 15.8g carbohydrate; 39.1g protein; 4.1g fibre*

shantung chicken

1 clove garlic, crushed
2cm piece fresh ginger (10g), grated
1 tablespoon dark soy sauce
1 tablespoon dry sherry
2 teaspoons sichuan peppercorns, crushed
2 teaspoons peanut oil
1.6kg whole chicken

SHANTUNG SAUCE

⅓ cup (75g) caster sugar
½ cup (125ml) water
2 tablespoons white wine vinegar
1 fresh small red thai chilli, chopped finely

1   Combine garlic, ginger, soy sauce, sherry, pepper and oil in large bowl with chicken. Cover; refrigerate overnight.
2   Preheat oven to 220°C/200°C fan-forced.
3   Half-fill large baking dish with water; place chicken on oiled wire rack set over dish. Roast, uncovered, about 1 hour 20 minutes or until cooked through.
4   Meanwhile, make shantung sauce.
5   Remove chicken from oven; when cool enough to handle, remove bones. Chop meat coarsely; serve drizzled with sauce.

SHANTUNG SAUCE Stir sugar and the water in small saucepan over low heat until sugar dissolves. Bring to the boil; boil, uncovered, without stirring, about 5 minutes or until sauce thickens slightly. Remove from heat; stir in vinegar and chilli.

preparation time *10 minutes (plus refrigeration time)* cooking time *1 hour 20 minutes* serves *4* nutritional count per serving *28.3g total fat (8.6g saturated); 2107kJ (504 cal); 19.2g carbohydrate; 42.1g protein; 0.2g fibre*

1 STIR-FRIED PORK, BUK CHOY AND WATER CHESTNUTS
2 SHANTUNG CHICKEN 3 TONKATSU-DON [P 534]
4 THAI BASIL CHICKEN AND SNAKE BEAN STIR-FRY [P 534]

ASIAN NEIGHBOURS   533

tonkatsu-don

3 cups (750ml) water
1½ cups (300g) koshihikari rice
4 pork steaks (600g)
¼ cup (35g) plain flour
2 eggs
2 teaspoons water, extra
2 cups (100g) japanese breadcrumbs
1 tablespoon peanut oil
2 cloves garlic, sliced thinly
½ small wombok (350g), shredded finely
1 fresh small red thai chilli, chopped finely
1 tablespoon mirin
1 tablespoon light soy sauce
vegetable oil, for deep-frying
2 green onions, sliced thinly

TONKATSU SAUCE

⅓ cup (80ml) tomato sauce
2 tablespoons japanese worcestershire sauce
2 tablespoons cooking sake
1 teaspoon japanese soy sauce
1 teaspoon japanese mustard

1 Make tonkatsu sauce.
2 Combine the water and rice in medium saucepan; bring to the boil. Reduce heat; cook, covered tightly, over very low heat, about 15 minutes or until water is absorbed. Remove from heat; stand, covered, 10 minutes.
3 Meanwhile, pound pork gently with meat mallet; coat in flour, shake off excess. Dip pork in combined egg and extra water then coat in breadcrumbs.
4 Heat peanut oil in wok; cook garlic, stirring, until fragrant. Add wombok and chilli; cook, stirring, 1 minute. Transfer wombok mixture to large bowl with mirin and sauce; toss to combine. Cover to keep warm.
5 Heat vegetable oil in cleaned wok; deep-fry pork, in batches, turning occasionally, about 5 minutes or until golden brown. Drain on absorbent paper. Cut pork diagonally into 2cm slices.
6 Divide rice among serving bowls; top with pork, wombok mixture and onion. Drizzle with sauce.

TONKATSU SAUCE Combine ingredients in small saucepan; bring to the boil. Remove from heat; cool.

preparation time *25 minutes*
cooking time *30 minutes* serves *4*
nutritional count per serving *31.6g total fat (8g saturated fat); 3595kJ (860 cal); 91g carbohydrate; 46.7g protein; 4g fibre*

thai basil chicken and snake bean stir-fry

800g chicken thigh fillets, sliced thinly
¼ cup (60ml) fish sauce
1 tablespoon grated palm sugar
¼ teaspoon ground white pepper
1 tablespoon peanut oil
3 cloves garlic, sliced thinly
2cm piece fresh ginger (10g), sliced thinly
½ teaspoon dried chilli flakes
250g snake beans, cut into 5cm lengths
2 medium yellow capsicums (400g), sliced thinly
⅓ cup (80ml) chinese cooking wine
⅓ cup (80ml) lemon juice
1 tablespoon dark soy sauce
½ cup loosely packed thai basil leaves

1 Combine chicken, fish sauce, sugar and pepper in large bowl. Cover; refrigerate 1 hour.
2 Heat oil in wok; stir-fry chicken mixture about 10 minutes or until almost cooked. Add garlic, ginger, chilli, beans and capsicum; stir-fry until beans are tender.
3 Add wine, juice and soy sauce; bring to the boil. Reduce heat; simmer, uncovered, 2 minutes. Remove from heat; stir in basil. Serve with steamed fresh wide rice noodles, if you like.

preparation time *20 minutes (plus refrigeration time)*
cooking time *20 minutes* serves *4*
nutritional count per serving *19.4g total fat (5.2g saturated fat); 1622kJ (388 cal); 8.6g carbohydrate; 42.4g protein; 3.3g fibre*

age-dashi tofu

Age-dashi (pronounced ah-gah dah-she), a simple dish of deep-fried tofu in a flavourful dressing, is a popular entrée in both Japanese restaurants and homes.

300g firm tofu
1 teaspoon instant dashi
1 cup (250ml) hot water
1 tablespoon sake
1 tablespoon mirin
1½ tablespoons light soy sauce
2 tablespoons cornflour
1 tablespoon toasted sesame seeds
vegetable oil, for deep-frying
2 tablespoons coarsely grated daikon
1cm piece fresh ginger (5g), grated
2 green onions, chopped finely
2 teaspoons dried bonito flakes

1 Press tofu between two chopping boards with weight on top, raise one end; stand 25 minutes.
2 Meanwhile, combine dashi and the water in small saucepan. Add sake, mirin and sauce; bring to the boil. Remove from heat.
3 Cut tofu into eight even-sized pieces; pat dry between layers of absorbent paper then toss in combined cornflour and sesame seeds.
4 Heat oil in wok; deep-fry tofu, in batches, until browned lightly. Drain on absorbent paper.
5 Place two pieces of tofu in each serving bowl. Divide daikon, ginger and onion among bowls; pour dashi dressing over tofu then sprinkle with bonito flakes.

preparation time *15 minutes (plus standing time)*
cooking time *30 minutes* serves *4*
nutritional count per serving *10.5g total fat (1.4g saturated fat); 715kJ (171 cal); 6.4g carbohydrate; 10.2g protein; 1.8g fibre*

oyako donburi

4 dried shiitake mushrooms
2 teaspoons dashi powder
1 cup (250ml) boiling water
1 tablespoon peanut oil
3 large brown onions (600g), sliced thinly
1cm piece fresh ginger (5g), grated
1½ cups (300g) koshihikari rice
3 cups (750ml) cold water
¼ cup (60ml) japanese soy sauce
¼ cup (60ml) mirin
1 teaspoon white sugar
500g chicken breast fillets, sliced thinly
6 eggs, beaten lightly
2 green onions, sliced thinly

1 Soak mushrooms in small heatproof bowl of boiling water 20 minutes; drain. Discard stems; coarsely chop caps. Combine dashi and the boiling water in small jug.
2 Meanwhile, heat oil in large frying pan; cook brown onion and ginger, stirring, over medium heat, 10 minutes or until onion is slightly caramelised. Add half the dashi mixture, reduce heat; simmer, about 5 minutes or until liquid evaporates. Transfer to medium bowl.
3 Bring rice and the cold water to the boil in large saucepan, uncovered, stirring occasionally. Reduce heat to as low as possible; cover with a tight-fitting lid, cook 12 minutes (do not remove lid or stir rice during cooking time). Remove from heat; stand, covered, 10 minutes.
4 Meanwhile, combine sauce, mirin, sugar and remaining dashi mixture to same frying pan; bring to the boil. Add chicken and mushrooms; cook, covered, 5 minutes or until chicken is cooked through.
5 Combine egg with brown onion mixture in medium bowl; add onion mixture to chicken mixture. Cook, covered, over low heat, 5 minutes or until egg just sets.
6 Divide rice among bowls; top with chicken mixture and green onion.

preparation time *30 minutes (plus standing time)*
cooking time *45 minutes* serves *4*
nutritional count per serving *15.8g total fat (4.1g saturated fat); 2567kJ (614 cal); 67.6g carbohydrate; 46.2g protein; 2.7g fibre*

miso soup with pork and beans

1 litre (4 cups) dashi stock
100g pork fillet, sliced thinly
8 green beans, cut into 2cm lengths
¼ cup (75g) red miso paste (karakuchi)
2 teaspoons ginger juice
2 green onions, sliced thinly

1   Bring stock to the boil in medium saucepan.
Add pork and beans; return to the boil. Reduce heat;
simmer, uncovered, 2 minutes.
2   Place miso in small bowl; gradually add 1 cup
(250ml) of the hot stock, stirring until miso dissolves.
Add to saucepan; stir to combine. Bring to the boil;
remove from heat immediately.
3   Divide soup among serving bowls; stir ½ teaspoon
of the juice into each bowl. Just before serving, sprinkle
with onion.

preparation time *15 minutes*
cooking time *10 minutes* serves *4*
nutritional count per serving *3.2g total fat (0.8g
saturated fat); 351kJ (84 cal); 5g carbohydrate;
7.9g protein; 1.6g fibre*

grilled tuna with soba noodles

4 x 200g tuna steaks
½ cup (125ml) mirin
2 teaspoons wasabi paste
½ cup (125ml) japanese soy sauce
1 sheet toasted seaweed (yaki-nori)
300g soba noodles
6 green onions, sliced thinly
2 fresh long red chillies, chopped finely

1   Combine tuna with 2 tablespoons of the mirin, half
of the wasabi and half of the soy sauce in large bowl.
Cover; refrigerate 10 minutes.
2   Meanwhile, using scissors, cut seaweed into four
strips; cut each strip crossways into thin pieces.
3   Cook noodles in large saucepan of boiling water,
uncovered, until just tender; drain. Rinse under cold
water; drain.
4   Meanwhile, cook tuna on heated oiled grill plate
(or grill or barbecue) until browned both sides and
cooked as desired.
5   Combine noodles, onion and chilli in medium bowl
with combined remaining mirin, wasabi and sauce.
Serve noodles with tuna and seaweed.

preparation time *15 minutes*
cooking time *10 minutes* serves *4*
nutritional count per serving *12.3g total fat (4.8g
saturated fat); 2495kJ (597 cal); 53.6g carbohydrate;
60.8g protein; 3.2g fibre*

soba noodles in broth

200g dried soba noodles
3 cups (750ml) dashi stock
¼ cup (60ml) japanese soy sauce
2 tablespoons mirin
1 teaspoon sugar
1 tablespoon vegetable oil
400g chicken breast fillet, sliced thinly
2 medium leeks (700g), sliced thinly
¼ teaspoon seven-spice mix (shichimi togarashi)

1 Cook noodles in large saucepan of boiling water, uncovered, until just tender. Drain; cover to keep warm.
2 Combine stock, 2 tablespoons of the sauce, half of the mirin and half of the sugar in medium saucepan; bring to the boil. Remove from heat; cover to keep hot.
3 Heat oil in medium frying pan; cook chicken and leek, stirring, until chicken is just cooked. Stir in remaining sauce, mirin and sugar; bring to the boil.
4 Divide noodles evenly among serving bowls; top with chicken mixture. Cover with broth; sprinkle with seven-spice mix.

preparation time *10 minutes*
cooking time *15 minutes* serves *4*
nutritional count per serving *11.8g total fat (2.8g saturated fat); 1739kJ (416 cal); 41.3g carbohydrate; 32.1g protein; 4.7g fibre*

tofu and spinach miso

1.5 litres (6 cups) water
¼ cup (75g) yellow miso
1 tablespoon japanese soy sauce
3cm piece fresh ginger (15g), grated
100g dried soba noodles
200g marinated tofu, cut into 2cm pieces
4 green onions, sliced thinly
100g baby spinach leaves
1 fresh long red chilli, sliced thinly

1 Place the water in large saucepan with miso, sauce and ginger; bring to the boil. Add noodles, return to the boil; cook, uncovered, about 3 minutes or until noodles are just tender.
2 Remove pan from heat, add tofu, onion and spinach to broth; stir gently until spinach just wilts.
3 Serve bowls of soup sprinkled with chilli.

preparation time *10 minutes*
cooking time *10 minutes* serves *4*
nutritional count per serving *4.9g total fat (0.7g saturated fat); 803kJ (192 cal); 22.9g carbohydrate; 12.1g protein; 3.8g fibre*

beef samosas with peach and raisin chutney

2 teaspoons vegetable oil
1 small brown onion (80g), chopped finely
2 cloves garlic, crushed
2cm piece fresh ginger (10g), grated
1 tablespoon ground cumin
1 tablespoon ground coriander
1 fresh small red thai chilli, chopped finely
250g beef mince
1 small kumara (250g), chopped finely
⅓ cup (80ml) water
4 sheets ready-rolled shortcrust pastry
1 egg, beaten lightly

PEACH AND RAISIN CHUTNEY

3 medium peaches (450g)
⅓ cup (110g) raisins, chopped finely
½ cup (125ml) cider vinegar
2 tablespoons lemon juice
1 small brown onion (80g), chopped finely
¼ teaspoon ground cinnamon
½ teaspoon ground allspice
1 cup (220g) white sugar

1 Make peach and raisin chutney.
2 Heat oil in large frying pan; cook onion, garlic, ginger and spices, stirring, until onion softens. Add chilli and mince; cook, stirring, until mince browns. Add kumara and the water; bring to the boil. Reduce heat; simmer, uncovered, stirring occasionally, until kumara softens. Stir in ⅓ cup of the chutney. Cool filling 10 minutes, then refrigerate until cold.
3 Preheat oven to 200°C/180°C fan-forced. Oil three oven trays.
4 Using 7.5cm cutter, cut nine rounds from each pastry sheet. Place rounded teaspoons of the filling in centre of each round; brush edge of round with egg, press edges together to enclose filling. Repeat process with remaining rounds and filling.
5 Place samosas on trays; brush tops with any remaining egg. Bake about 20 minutes or until browned lightly. Serve with remaining chutney.

PEACH AND RAISIN CHUTNEY Cover peaches with boiling water in medium heatproof bowl 30 seconds. Peel, seed, then chop peaches finely. Place in medium saucepan with remaining ingredients; bring to the boil. Reduce heat; simmer, uncovered, stirring occasionally, about 45 minutes or until chutney thickens (add a small amount of water to chutney, if necessary).

preparation time *50 minutes*
cooking time *1 hour 25 minutes (plus refrigeration time)*
make *36*
nutritional count per samosa *5.7g total fat (2.8g saturated fat); 560kJ (134 cal); 17.8g carbohydrate; 3.1g protein; 0.8g fibre*

coconut, chicken and kaffir lime soup

1 tablespoon peanut oil
600g chicken thigh fillets, cut into 1cm strips
¼ cup (75g) green curry paste
1 litre (4 cups) chicken stock
3¼ cups (800ml) coconut milk
1 long green chilli, chopped finely
8 fresh kaffir lime leaves, shredded
125g rice vermicelli noodles
2 tablespoons grated palm sugar
2 tablespoons lime juice
2 tablespoons fish sauce
1 cup (80g) bean sprouts
½ cup loosely packed vietnamese mint leaves
1 long green chilli, sliced thinly
2 limes, cut into thin wedges

1   Heat oil in large saucepan; cook chicken, in batches, until browned lightly.
2   Cook paste in same pan, stirring, until fragrant.
3   Return chicken to pan with stock, coconut milk, chopped chilli and lime leaf; bring to the boil. Reduce heat; simmer, uncovered, 30 minutes, skimming fat from surface occasionally. Add noodles; cook, uncovered, until noodles are just tender. Stir in sugar, juice and sauce.
4   Serve bowls of soup sprinkled with sprouts, mint, sliced chilli and lime.

preparation time *15 minutes*
cooking time *45 minutes* serves *4*
nutritional count per serving *63.9g total fat (41.6g saturated fat); 3478kJ (832 cal); 25g carbohydrate; 38g protein; 6.8g fibre*

cantonese chicken dumplings

10 dried shiitake mushrooms
2 teaspoons peanut oil
2 cloves garlic, crushed
2cm piece fresh ginger (10g), grated
1 litre (4 cups) water
1 litre (4 cups) chicken stock
2 tablespoons dark soy sauce
200g baby corn, halved lengthways
150g bean sprouts
3 green onions, sliced thinly

CHICKEN DUMPLINGS

1 tablespoon peanut oil
1 green onion, sliced thinly
2cm piece fresh ginger (10g), grated
1 fresh long red chilli, chopped finely
200g chicken mince
1 teaspoon dark soy sauce
20 wonton wrappers

1   Cover mushrooms with ½ cup cold water in small bowl; stand 15 minutes. Drain over small bowl; reserve soaking liquid. Slice mushrooms thinly.
2   Meanwhile, make chicken dumplings.
3   Heat oil in large saucepan; cook garlic and ginger, stirring, 2 minutes. Stir in the water, stock, sauce and reserved soaking liquid; bring to the boil. Reduce heat; simmer, uncovered, 15 minutes.
4   Add mushrooms, dumplings and corn to soup; bring to the boil. Reduce heat; simmer, about 10 minutes or until dumplings are cooked through.
5   Serve bowls of soup sprinkled with sprouts and onion.

CHICKEN DUMPLINGS Heat oil in medium frying pan; cook onions, ginger and chilli, stirring, until onion softens. Add mince; cook, stirring, until browned. Stir in sauce; cool. Place rounded teaspoon of mixture in centre of each wrapper; brush edges with a little water. Gather edges around filling, pinch together to seal.

preparation time *30 minutes (plus standing time)*
cooking time *30 minutes* serves *4*
nutritional count per serving *13.3g total fat (3.2g saturated fat); 1354kJ (324 cal); 28.2g carbohydrate; 20g protein; 5.6g fibre*

tom ka gai

3 cups (750ml) chicken stock
4cm piece fresh galangal (20g), sliced thickly
2 x 10cm sticks fresh lemon grass (40g),
   cut into 5cm pieces
4 fresh kaffir lime leaves
2 teaspoons coarsely chopped coriander
   root and stem mixture
500g chicken thigh fillets, sliced thinly
200g drained canned straw mushrooms, rinsed
1 cup (250ml) coconut milk
1 tablespoon lime juice
1 tablespoon fish sauce
1 teaspoon grated palm sugar
¼ cup loosely packed fresh coriander leaves
2 fresh small red thai chillies, seeded, sliced thinly
2 fresh kaffir lime leaves, shredded
10cm stick fresh lemon grass (20g), extra, sliced thinly

1   Combine stock, galangal, lemon grass pieces, whole lime leaves and coriander mixture in large saucepan; bring to the boil. Reduce heat; simmer, covered, 5 minutes. Remove pan from heat; stand 10 minutes. Strain stock through muslin into large heatproof bowl; discard solids.
2   Return stock to same cleaned pan. Add chicken and mushrooms; bring to the boil. Reduce heat; simmer, uncovered, about 5 minutes or until chicken is cooked through.
3   Stir in coconut milk, juice, sauce and sugar; cook, stirring, until just heated through (do not allow to boil). Remove from heat; stir in coriander leaves, chilli, shredded lime leaves and lemon grass slices. Serve hot.

preparation time *15 minutes (plus standing time)*
cooking time *35 minutes* serves *4*
nutritional count per serving *22.9g total fat (14.5g saturated fat); 1430kJ (342 cal); 5.2g carbohydrate; 28.3g protein; 2.6g fibre*

tom yum goong

900g uncooked large king prawns
1 tablespoon peanut oil
1.5 litres (6 cups) water
2 tablespoons red curry paste
1 tablespoon tamarind concentrate
2 tablespoons finely chopped fresh lemon grass
1 teaspoon ground turmeric
2 fresh small red thai chillies, chopped coarsely
1 tablespoon grated fresh ginger
6 fresh kaffir lime leaves, shredded finely
1 teaspoon grated palm sugar
100g shiitake mushrooms, halved
2 tablespoons fish sauce
2 tablespoons lime juice
¼ cup loosely packed fresh vietnamese mint leaves
¼ cup loosely packed fresh coriander leaves

1   Shell and devein prawns, leaving tails intact.
2   Heat oil in large saucepan; cook prawn shells and heads, stirring, about 5 minutes or until shells and heads are deep orange in colour.
3   Add 1 cup of the water and curry paste to pan; bring to the boil, stirring. Add remaining water; return to the boil. Reduce heat; simmer, uncovered, 20 minutes. Strain stock through muslin into large heatproof bowl; discard solids.
4   Return stock to same cleaned pan. Add tamarind, lemon grass, turmeric, chilli, ginger, lime leaves and sugar; bring to the boil. Boil, stirring, 2 minutes. Reduce heat; add mushrooms; cook, stirring, 3 minutes.
5   Add prawns; cook, stirring, until prawns are changed in colour. Remove from heat; stir in sauce and juice. Serve soup hot, topped with mint and coriander.

preparation time *20 minutes*
cooking time *40 minutes* serves *4*
nutritional count per serving *9g total fat (1.3g saturated fat); 836kJ (200 cal); 3.6g carbohydrate; 25.2g protein; 2.3g fibre*

asian broth with crisp pork belly

½ cup (100g) dried soy beans
1kg boned pork belly, rind-on
1½ teaspoons cooking salt
1 teaspoon five-spice powder
2 cups (500ml) water
1 litre (4 cups) chicken stock
1 fresh small red thai chilli, chopped finely
2 star anise
5cm piece fresh ginger (25g), slivered
⅓ cup (80ml) hoisin sauce
500g choy sum, sliced thinly
3 green onions, sliced thinly

1 Place beans in small bowl, cover with cold water; stand overnight.
2 Place pork on board, rind-side up; using sharp knife, score pork by making shallow cuts diagonally in both directions at 1cm intervals. Rub combined salt and half the five-spice into cuts; slice pork into 10 pieces. Place pork, rind-side up, on tray, cover loosely; refrigerate overnight.
3 Preheat oven to 240°C/220°C fan-forced.
4 Rinse beans under cold water; drain. Place beans in medium saucepan of boiling water; return to the boil. Reduce heat; simmer, uncovered, until tender. Drain.
5 Meanwhile, place pork on metal rack set over shallow baking dish; roast, uncovered, 30 minutes.
6 Reduce oven to 160°C/140°C fan-forced; roast pork, uncovered, further 45 minutes or until crackling is browned and crisp. Cut pork pieces in half.
7 Place beans in large saucepan with the water, stock, chilli, star anise, ginger, sauce and remaining five-spice; bring to the boil. Reduce heat; simmer, covered, 30 minutes. Stir in choy sum and onion.
8 Serve bowls of soup topped with pork.

preparation time *20 minutes (plus standing and refrigeration time)* cooking time *2 hours* serves *4*
nutritional counter serving *59.6g total fat (20.2g saturated fat); 3687kJ (882 cal); 12.4g carbohydrate; 72.2g protein; 6.2g fibre*

wonton soup

2 teaspoons peanut oil
2 cloves garlic, crushed
2 litres (8 cups) chicken stock
1 tablespoon soy sauce
1 litre (4 cups) water
4 green onions, sliced thinly

WONTONS

1 tablespoon peanut oil
4 green onions, sliced thinly
2 cloves garlic, crushed
1 tablespoon grated fresh ginger
400g pork mince
2 tablespoons soy sauce
36 wonton wrappers
1 egg, beaten lightly

1 Make wontons.
2 Heat oil in large saucepan; cook garlic, stirring, 2 minutes. Stir in stock, sauce and the water; bring to the boil. Reduce heat; simmer, uncovered, 15 minutes.
3 Just before serving, divide wontons among serving bowls. Pour over hot soup; sprinkle with onion.

WONTONS Heat oil in large frying pan; cook onion, garlic and ginger, stirring, until onion is soft. Add pork mince; cook, stirring, until mince is just browned. Stir in sauce. Place rounded teaspoons of cooled pork mixture in centre of each wrapper. Brush edges with egg; pinch edges together to seal.

preparation time *30 minutes*
cooking time *40 minutes* serves *6*
nutritional count per serving *12.3g total fat (3.7g saturated fat); 1225kJ (293 cal); 22.4g carbohydrate; 22.5g protein; 1.6g fibre*

japanese seafood hotpot

We used monkfish in this recipe, but you can use any firm white fish such as perch or blue-eye.

12 medium black mussels (300g)
12 uncooked medium king prawns (540g)
2 teaspoons cooking sake
1 tablespoon japanese soy sauce
2 teaspoons mirin
12 scallops without roe (300g)
400g firm white fish fillets, cut into 4cm pieces
1 tablespoon vegetable oil
2 cloves garlic, crushed
5cm piece fresh ginger (25g), chopped finely
3 cups (750ml) fish stock
1 cup (250ml) water
¼ cup (60ml) cooking sake, extra
¼ cup (60ml) japanese soy sauce, extra
1 teaspoon powdered dashi
1 small kumara (250g), halved lengthways, sliced thinly
250g spinach, chopped coarsely
2 green onions, chopped coarsely
270g dried udon noodles

1 Scrub mussels; remove beards. Shell and devein prawns, leaving tails intact.
2 Combine sake, soy and mirin in large bowl with mussels, prawns, scallops and fish.
3 Heat oil in large saucepan; cook garlic and ginger, stirring, until fragrant. Add stock, the water, extra sake, extra soy and dashi; bring to the boil. Add kumara; cook, uncovered, 2 minutes. Add undrained seafood; cook, covered, about 5 minutes or until mussels open (discard any that do not). Add spinach and onion; cook, uncovered, until spinach just wilts.
4 Meanwhile, cook noodles in large saucepan of boiling water, uncovered, until just tender; drain.
5 Divide noodles among bowls; top with seafood.

preparation time *20 minutes*
cooking time *20 minutes* serves *4*
nutritional count per serving *7.8g total fat (1.3g saturated fat); 2307kJ (552 cal); 57.3g carbohydrate; 56.8g protein; 4.5g fibre*

combination long soup

1 litre (4 cups) water
500g chicken breast fillets
2 litres (8 cups) chicken stock
1 tablespoon japanese soy sauce
2cm piece fresh ginger (10g), grated
225g fresh thin wheat noodles
100g shelled cooked small prawns
200g chinese barbecued pork, sliced thinly
4 green onions, sliced thinly
1 small red capsicum (150g), sliced thinly
100g mushrooms, sliced thinly
1¼ cups (100g) bean sprouts

1 Bring the water to the boil in large saucepan; add chicken, return to the boil. Reduce heat; simmer, covered, about 10 minutes or until chicken is cooked. Cool chicken in poaching liquid 10 minutes. Remove chicken from pan; discard poaching liquid. When cool enough to handle, slice chicken thinly.
2 Bring stock, sauce and ginger to the boil in same cleaned pan; add noodles, separating with a fork. Add chicken and remaining ingredients; reduce heat, simmer, uncovered, about 5 minutes or until soup is hot.

preparation time *10 minutes*
cooking time *30 minutes* serves *4*
nutritional count per serving *26.6g total fat (11.2g saturated fat); 2633kJ (630 cal); 37.9g carbohydrate; 56g protein; 7.8g fibre*

mongolian garlic lamb

3 cloves garlic, crushed
1 tablespoon cornflour
¼ cup (60ml) dark soy sauce
⅓ cup (80ml) sweet sherry
800g lamb backstraps, sliced thinly
2 tablespoons peanut oil
1 tablespoon brown sugar
1 teaspoon sesame oil
8 green onions, sliced thinly

1   Combine garlic, cornflour, half the sauce and
half the sherry in large bowl with lamb.
2   Heat peanut oil in wok; stir-fry lamb mixture,
in batches, until browned.
3   Return lamb to wok with sugar, sesame oil and
remaining sauce and sherry; stir-fry until sauce thickens
slightly. Serve sprinkled with onion.

preparation time *10 minutes*
cooking time *10 minutes* serves *4*
nutritional count per serving *28g total fat (9.8g
saturated fat); 2057kJ (492 cal); 12.4g carbohydrate;
43.1g protein; 0.8g fibre*

sake chicken

800g chicken breast fillets
½ cup (125ml) cooking sake
1 clove garlic, crushed
1 fresh long red chilli, chopped finely
2 tablespoons rice vinegar
2 tablespoons japanese soy sauce
1 tablespoon lemon juice
2 teaspoons sesame oil
1 teaspoon caster sugar
2 green onions, sliced thinly
2 tablespoons pickled ginger, shredded finely

1   Combine chicken, sake, garlic, chilli, vinegar, sauce,
juice, oil and sugar in large frying pan; bring to the boil.
Reduce heat; simmer, covered, about 10 minutes or
until chicken is cooked through. Remove from heat;
stand chicken in poaching liquid 10 minutes before
slicing thickly. Cover to keep warm.
2   Bring poaching liquid to the boil; boil, uncovered,
about 5 minutes or until sauce thickens.
3   Serve chicken drizzled with sauce, topped with
onion and ginger.

preparation time *10 minutes*
cooking time *15 minutes* serves *4*
nutritional count per serving *13.4g total fat (3.7g
saturated); 1413kJ (338cal); 2.9g carbohydrate;
43.6g protein; 0.4g fibre*

vietnamese beef pho

2 litres (8 cups) water
1 litre (4 cups) beef stock
1kg chuck steak
2 star anise
8cm piece fresh ginger (40g), grated
⅓ cup (80ml) japanese soy sauce
200g bean thread noodles
1½ cups (120g) bean sprouts
¼ cup loosely packed fresh coriander leaves
⅓ cup loosely packed fresh mint leaves
4 green onions, sliced thinly
2 fresh long red chillies, sliced thinly
¼ cup (60ml) fish sauce
1 medium lemon (140g), cut into 6 wedges

1 Place the water and stock in large saucepan with beef, star anise, ginger and soy sauce; bring to the boil. Reduce heat; simmer, covered, 30 minutes. Uncover, simmer about 30 minutes or until beef is tender.
2 Meanwhile, place noodles in medium heatproof bowl, cover with boiling water; stand until just tender, drain.
3 Combine sprouts, coriander, mint, onion and chilli in medium bowl.
4 Remove beef from pan. Strain broth through muslin-lined sieve or colander into large heatproof bowl; discard solids. When beef is cool enough to handle, remove and discard fat and sinew. Slice beef thinly, return to same cleaned pan with broth; bring to the boil. Stir in fish sauce.
5 Divide noodles among soup bowls; ladle hot beef broth into bowls, sprinkle with sprout mixture, serve with lemon.

preparation time *20 minutes*
cooking time *1 hour 20 minutes* serves *6*
nutritional count per serving *8g total fat (3.3g saturated fat); 1166kJ (279 cal); 11.8g carbohydrate; 38.3g protein; 2.4g fibre*

vietnamese prawn soup

500g uncooked king prawns
2cm piece fresh ginger (10g), sliced thinly
1 teaspoon black peppercorns
2 cloves garlic, crushed
2 fresh large red chillies, sliced thinly
10cm stick fresh lemon grass (20g), sliced coarsely
3 litres (12 cups) water
400g fresh rice noodles
¼ cup (60ml) lemon juice
⅓ cup (80ml) fish sauce, approximately
2 green onions, sliced thinly
⅓ cup firmly packed fresh coriander leaves
¼ cup firmly packed fresh mint leaves

1 Peel and devein prawns, discard heads. Place prawn shells, ginger, peppercorns, garlic, half of the chilli, lemon grass and the water in large saucepan; bring to the boil. Reduce heat; simmer, uncovered, 20 minutes. Strain stock; return liquid to clean saucepan.
2 Add prawns to stock; simmer, covered, about 3 minutes or until prawns are changed in colour.
3 Meanwhile, pour boiling water over rice noodles in bowl; drain.
4 Add lemon juice to stock, gradually add fish sauce to taste. Divide prawns and noodles evenly among serving bowls, top with stock, green onion, herbs and remaining chilli.

preparation time *30 minutes*
cooking time *25 minutes* serves *6*
nutritional count per serving *0.7g total fat (0.1g saturated fat); 493kJ (118 cal); 15.8g carbohydrate; 11.3g protein; 1g fibre*

vietnamese chicken salad

500g chicken breast fillets
1 large carrot (180g)
½ cup (125ml) rice wine vinegar
2 teaspoons salt
2 tablespoons caster sugar
1 medium white onion (150g), sliced thinly
1½ cups (120g) bean sprouts
2 cups (160g) finely shredded savoy cabbage
¼ cup firmly packed fresh vietnamese mint leaves
½ cup firmly packed fresh coriander leaves
1 tablespoon crushed roasted peanuts
2 tablespoons fried shallots

VIETNAMESE DRESSING

2 tablespoons fish sauce
¼ cup (60ml) water
2 tablespoons caster sugar
2 tablespoons lime juice
1 clove garlic, crushed

1   Place chicken in medium saucepan of boiling water; return to the boil. Reduce heat; simmer, uncovered, about 10 minutes or until cooked through. Cool chicken in poaching liquid 10 minutes; discard liquid (or reserve for another use). Shred chicken coarsely.
2   Meanwhile, cut carrot into matchstick-sized pieces. Combine carrot in large bowl with vinegar, salt and sugar, cover; stand 5 minutes. Add onion, cover; stand 5 minutes. Add sprouts, cover; stand 3 minutes. Drain pickled vegetables; discard liquid.
3   Meanwhile, make vietnamese dressing.
4   Place pickled vegetables in large bowl with chicken, cabbage, mint, coriander and dressing; toss gently to combine. Sprinkle with nuts and shallots.

VIETNAMESE DRESSING   Place ingredients in screw-top jar; shake well.

preparation time *20 minutes*
cooking time *15 minutes* serves *4*
nutritional count per serving *8.9g total fat (2.3g saturated fat); 1271kJ (304 cal); 24.3g carbohydrate; 31g protein; 5.1g fibre*

ginger beef stir-fry

6cm piece fresh ginger (30g)
2 tablespoons peanut oil
600g beef rump steak, sliced thinly
2 cloves garlic, crushed
120g snake beans, cut into 5cm lengths
8 green onions, sliced thinly
2 teaspoons grated palm sugar
2 teaspoons oyster sauce
1 tablespoon fish sauce
1 tablespoon soy sauce
½ cup loosely packed fresh thai basil leaves

1   Slice peeled ginger thinly; stack slices, then slice again into thin slivers.
2   Heat half of the oil in wok; stir-fry beef, in batches, until browned all over.
3   Heat remaining oil in wok; stir-fry ginger and garlic until fragrant. Add beans; stir-fry until just tender.
4   Return beef to wok with onion, sugar and sauces; stir-fry until sugar dissolves and beef is cooked as desired. Remove from heat, toss basil through stir-fry.

preparation time *20 minutes*
cooking time *10 minutes* serves *4*
nutritional count per serving *19.4g total fat (6.2g saturated fat); 1421kJ (340 cal); 4.6g carbohydrate; 35.9g protein; 1.9g fibre*

duck and green onion gyoza

1kg chinese barbecued duck
4 green onions, sliced thinly
1 tablespoon japanese soy sauce
2 tablespoons cooking sake
2cm piece fresh ginger (10g), grated
1 fresh long red chilli, chopped finely
30 gyoza wrappers
2 tablespoons vegetable oil

SAKE DIPPING SAUCE

¼ cup (60ml) cooking sake
2 tablespoons japanese soy sauce
1 tablespoon lime juice
1 teaspoon caster sugar

1   Remove and discard skin and bones from duck;
chop meat finely. Combine duck, onion, sauce, sake,
ginger and chilli in medium bowl.
2   Place one heaped teaspoon of duck mixture in centre
of one wrapper; wet edge around one half of wrapper.
Pleat to seal. Repeat with remaining duck mixture and
wrappers.
3   Cover base of large frying pan with water; bring
to the boil, then add gyoza, in batches. Reduce heat;
simmer, covered, 3 minutes.
4   Meanwhile, make sake dipping sauce.
5   Heat oil in same cleaned pan; cook gyoza on
one side only, uncovered, in batches, until browned
and slightly crisp. Drain on absorbent paper. Serve
immediately with dipping sauce.

SAKE DIPPING SAUCE   Place ingredients in screw-top jar;
shake well.

preparation time *40 minutes*
cooking time *20 minutes* makes *30*
nutritional count per gyoza *6.3g total fat (1.7g
saturated); 393kJ (94 cal); 4.9g carbohydrate;
3.9g protein; 0g fibre*

white-cut chicken

1.6kg whole chicken
2 litres (8 cups) water
¼ cup (60ml) light soy sauce
½ cup (125ml) dark soy sauce
1 cup (250ml) chinese cooking wine
½ cup (135g) coarsely chopped palm sugar
20cm piece fresh ginger (100g), sliced thinly
4 star anise
4 cloves garlic, sliced thinly
1 tablespoon sichuan peppercorns

SOY AND GREEN ONION DRESSING

¼ cup (60ml) dark soy sauce
¼ cup (60ml) rice vinegar
4 green onions, sliced thinly
2 teaspoons peanut oil
½ teaspoon sesame oil

1   Make soy and green onion dressing.
2   Place chicken, breast-side down with remaining
ingredients in large saucepan; bring to the boil. Reduce
heat; simmer, uncovered, 25 minutes. Turn chicken
breast-side up; simmer, uncovered, 5 minutes. Remove
pan from heat; turn chicken breast-side down, stand in
poaching liquid 3 hours.
3   Remove chicken from pan; discard poaching liquid.
Using cleaver, cut chicken in half through the centre of
the breastbone and along one side of backbone; cut
each half into eight pieces.
4   Serve chicken drizzled with dressing. If you like,
serve with steamed jasmine rice and asian greens.

SOY AND GREEN ONION DRESSING   Whisk ingredients
in small bowl.

preparation time *20 minutes (plus standing time)*
cooking time *45 minutes* serves *4*
nutritional count per serving *26.2g total fat (8.7g
saturated fat); 2621kJ (627 cal); 41.3g carbohydrate;
46.3g protein; 1.2g fibre*

1 DUCK AND GREEN ONION GYOZA 2 WHITE-CUT CHICKEN
3 TWICE-FRIED SICHUAN BEEF WITH BUK CHOY [P 550]
4 PAD THAI [P 550]

1

2

3

4

twice-fried sichuan beef with buk choy

½ cup (75g) cornflour
1 tablespoon sichuan peppercorns, crushed coarsely
600g piece beef eye fillet, sliced thinly
vegetable oil, for deep-frying
2 teaspoons sesame oil
1 clove garlic, crushed
2 fresh small red thai chillies, chopped finely
1 medium brown onion (150g), sliced thinly
1 medium carrot (120g), halved, sliced thinly
1 medium red capsicum (200g), sliced thinly
150g sugar snap peas, trimmed
300g baby buk choy, leaves separated
2 tablespoons oyster sauce
¼ cup (60ml) japanese soy sauce
¼ cup (60ml) beef stock
2 tablespoons dry sherry
1 tablespoon brown sugar

1 Combine cornflour and half the pepper in medium bowl with beef.
2 Heat vegetable oil in wok; deep-fry beef, in batches, until crisp. Drain on absorbent paper.
3 Heat sesame oil in cleaned wok; stir-fry garlic, chilli and onion until onion softens. Add carrot and capsicum; stir-fry until vegetables soften.
4 Return beef to wok with remaining ingredients; stir-fry until buk choy is wilted.

preparation time *20 minutes*
cooking time *25 minutes serves 4*
nutritional count per serving *19.5g total fat (5.1g saturated); 1914kJ (458cal); 29.6g carbohydrate; 36.4g protein; 3.8g fibre*

pad thai

540g uncooked medium king prawns
¼ cup (85g) tamarind concentrate
⅓ cup (80ml) sweet chilli sauce
2 tablespoons fish sauce
⅓ cup firmly packed fresh coriander leaves
¼ cup (35g) roasted unsalted peanuts
¼ cup (20g) fried shallots
2 cups (160g) bean sprouts
4 green onions, sliced thinly
375g dried rice stick noodles
1 tablespoon peanut oil
2 cloves garlic, crushed
4cm piece fresh ginger (20g), grated
3 fresh small red thai chillies, chopped finely
250g pork mince
2 eggs, beaten lightly
1 lime, quartered

1 Shell and devein prawns, leaving tails intact.
2 Combine tamarind and sauces in small jug.
3 Combine coriander, nuts, shallots, half the sprouts and half the onion in medium bowl.
4 Place noodles in large heatproof bowl, cover with boiling water; stand until just tender, drain.
5 Meanwhile, heat oil in wok; stir-fry garlic, ginger and chilli until fragrant. Add pork; stir-fry until cooked. Add prawns; stir-fry 1 minute. Add egg; stir-fry until set. Add tamarind mixture, remaining sprouts and onion, and noodles; stir-fry until combined.
6 Divide mixture among serving bowls; sprinkle with coriander mixture, serve with lime quarters.

preparation time *25 minutes*
cooking time *10 minutes serves 4*
nutritional count per serving *17.5g total fat (3.9g saturated fat); 1827kJ (437 cal); 30.3g carbohydrate; 36.8g protein; 4.9g fibre*

vegetarian pad thai

200g rice stick noodles
2 cloves garlic, quartered
2 tablespoons finely chopped preserved turnip
2 fresh small red thai chillies, chopped coarsely
¼ cup (60ml) peanut oil
2 eggs, beaten lightly
1 cup (90g) fried onion
125g fried tofu, cut into small pieces
¼ cup (35g) coarsely chopped roasted
    unsalted peanuts
3 cups (240g) bean sprouts
6 green onions, sliced thinly
2 tablespoons soy sauce
1 tablespoon lime juice
2 tablespoons coarsely chopped fresh coriander

1 Place noodles in large heatproof bowl; cover with boiling water, stand until noodles just soften, drain.
2 Meanwhile, using mortar and pestle, crush garlic, turnip and chilli until mixture forms a paste.
3 Heat 2 teaspoons of the oil in wok; pour in egg, swirl wok to make thin omelette. Cook, uncovered, until egg is just set. Remove from wok; roll omelette, cut into thin strips.
4 Heat remaining oil in wok; stir-fry garlic paste and fried onion until fragrant. Add tofu; stir-fry 1 minute. Add half of the nuts, half of the sprouts and half of the green onion; stir-fry until sprouts are just wilted. Add noodles, sauce and juice; stir-fry, tossing gently until combined.
5 Remove from heat; toss remaining nuts, sprouts and green onion with omelette strips and coriander through pad thai. Serve with lime wedges, if you like.

preparation time *20 minutes (plus standing time)*
cooking time *10 minutes* serves *4*
nutritional count per serving *23.9g total fat (4.2g saturated fat); 1375kJ (329 cal); 14.9g carbohydrate; 12.2g protein; 3.8g fibre*

beef kway teow

¼ cup (60ml) oyster sauce
2 tablespoons kecap manis
2 tablespoons chinese cooking wine
1 teaspoon sambal oelek
3 cloves garlic, crushed
2cm piece fresh ginger (10g), grated
2 tablespoons peanut oil
500g beef strips
450g fresh wide rice noodles
6 green onions, cut into 2cm lengths
1 small red capsicum (150g), sliced thinly
1 small green capsicum (150g), sliced thinly
¼ cup coarsely chopped garlic chives
2 cups (160g) bean sprouts

1 Combine sauces, wine, sambal, garlic and ginger in small jug.
2 Heat half the oil in wok; stir-fry beef, in batches, until browned lightly.
3 Place noodles in large heatproof bowl, cover with boiling water; separate with fork, drain.
4 Heat remaining oil in wok; stir-fry onion and capsicums until tender.
5 Return beef to wok with sauce mixture, noodles, chives and sprouts; stir-fry until hot.

preparation time *10 minutes*
cooking time *10 minutes* serves *4*
nutritional count per serving *17.7g total fat (4.8g saturated fat); 2195kJ (525 cal); 53g carbohydrate; 34.4g protein; 3.8g fibre*

braised sweet ginger duck

2kg duck
3 cups (750ml) water
½ cup (125ml) chinese cooking wine
⅓ cup (80ml) soy sauce
¼ cup (55g) firmly packed brown sugar
1 whole star anise
3 green onions, halved
3 cloves garlic, quartered
10cm piece fresh ginger (50g), unpeeled,
    chopped coarsely
2 teaspoons sea salt
1 teaspoon five-spice powder
800g baby buk choy, halved

1 Preheat oven to 180°C/160°C fan-forced.
2 Discard neck from duck, wash duck; pat dry with
absorbent paper. Score duck in thickest parts of skin; cut
duck in half through breastbone and along both sides of
backbone, discard backbone. Tuck wings under duck.
3 Place duck, skin-side down, in medium shallow
baking dish; add combined water, wine, soy, sugar,
star anise, onion, garlic and ginger. Cover; cook in
oven about 1 hour or until duck is cooked as desired.
4 Increase oven to 220°C/200°C fan-forced. Remove
duck from braising liquid; strain liquid through muslin-
lined sieve into large saucepan. Place duck, skin-side
up, on wire rack in same dish. Rub combined salt and
five-spice all over duck; roast duck, uncovered, in oven
about 30 minutes or until skin is crisp.
5 Skim fat from surface of braising liquid; bring to
the boil. Reduce heat; simmer, uncovered, 10 minutes.
Add buk choy; simmer, covered, about 5 minutes or
until buk choy is just tender.
6 Cut duck halves into two pieces; divide buk choy,
braising liquid and duck among plates. Serve with
steamed jasmine rice, if you like.

preparation time *20minutes*
cooking time *1 hour 50 minutes* serves *4*
nutritional count per serving *105.7g total fat (31.7g
saturated fat); 4974kJ (1190 cal); 17.9g carbohydrate;
40.8g protein; 3.5g fibre*

chengdu-style duck

1 tablespoon finely chopped fresh lemon grass
1 tablespoon coarsely chopped fresh mint
2 cloves garlic, crushed
2 teaspoons sichuan peppercorns
2 teaspoons finely grated lemon rind
½ teaspoon hot paprika
600g duck breast fillets, sliced thinly
1 tablespoon peanut oil
2 tablespoons cornflour
400g baby buk choy, sliced thickly
120g bean sprouts, tips trimmed
¼ cup (60ml) sweet chilli sauce

1 Using blender or mortar and pestle, make a paste
with lemon grass, mint, garlic, peppercorns, rind
and paprika.
2 Combine duck in large bowl with spice paste, oil
and cornflour. Cover; refrigerate 3 hours or until required.
3 Stir-fry duck mixture in heated wok, in batches, until
browned and cooked through.
4 Drain all but 1 tablespoon of fat from wok. Stir-fry
buk choy and sprouts until just wilted.
5 Return duck mixture to wok with sauce; stir-fry,
tossing to combine ingredients.

preparation time *25 minutes (plus refrigeration time)*
cooking time *15 minutes* serves *4*
nutritional count per serving *60.6g total fat (17.6g
saturated fat); 2792kJ (668 cal); 9.2g carbohydrate;
21.8g protein; 3.3g fibre*

peking duck

2kg duck
¼ cup (60ml) honey, warmed
1 lebanese cucumber (130g)
8 green onions

PANCAKES

1½ cups (225g) plain flour
1½ teaspoons sugar
¾ cup (180ml) boiling water

SAUCE

⅓ cup (80ml) hoisin sauce
2 tablespoons chicken stock
1 tablespoon plum sauce

1 Wash duck; drain well. Tie string around neck of duck. Lower duck into large saucepan of boiling water for 20 seconds; remove from pan. Drain well; pat dry with absorbent paper. Tie string to refrigerator shelf and suspend duck, uncovered, over drip tray overnight. Remove duck from refrigerator; suspend duck in front of cold air from an electric fan about 2 hours or until skin is dry to touch.

2 Preheat oven to 180°C/160°C fan-forced.

3 Tuck wings under duck. Place duck, breast-side up, on wire rack in large baking dish; brush entire duck evenly with honey. Bake 30 minutes; turn duck. Reduce oven to 150°C/130°C fan-forced; bake further 1 hour or until tender.

4 Meanwhile, make pancakes. Make sauce.

5 Preheat grill. Place duck on chopping board; remove skin. Place skin in single layer on wire rack over oven tray; cook skin under grill until crisp and browned.

6 Slice skin; slice duck meat. Using teaspoon, remove seeds from cucumber. Cut cucumber and onions into thin 8cm strips. To serve, top warm pancakes with duck meat, crisp skin, cucumber, onion and sauce; roll. Eat with fingers.

PANCAKES Sift flour and sugar in large bowl; add the water. Stir quickly using wooden spoon until ingredients cling together. Knead on floured surface 10 minutes or until smooth. Wrap in plastic; stand 30 minutes at room temperature. Divide dough into 16 pieces; roll one piece into a 16cm round. Heat small heavy-based frying pan; dry-fry pancake about 10 seconds on each side or until browned lightly. Repeat with remaining dough. Wrap pancakes in foil after each is cooked to prevent drying out. (If necessary, pancakes can be reheated in bamboo steamer or microwave oven. Line steamer with cloth; place pancakes in single layer on cloth. Steam over simmering water about 2 minutes or until pancakes are heated through.)

SAUCE Combine ingredients in small bowl.

preparation time *2 hours 30 minutes (plus standing time)* cooking time *1 hour 10 minutes* serves *4*
nutritional count per serving *107.2g total fat (31.9g saturated fat); 5973kJ (1429 cal); 71.9g carbohydrate; 44.2g protein; 5.2g fibre*

thai crab and mango salad

500g fresh crab meat
1 firm medium mango (430g)
100g mizuna
1 cup loosely packed fresh mint leaves

LIME AND CHILLI DRESSING

⅓ cup (80ml) lime juice
2 fresh long red chillies, sliced thinly
5cm piece fresh ginger (25g), cut into matchsticks
2 shallots (50g), sliced thinly
1 tablespoon fish sauce
2 tablespoons grated palm sugar
2 teaspoons peanut oil

1   Make lime and chilli dressing.
2   Combine crab in medium bowl with half the dressing.
3   Using vegetable peeler, slice mango into thin strips. Combine mango, mizuna and mint in large bowl with remaining dressing.
4   Divide salad among serving plates; top with crab.

LIME AND CHILLI DRESSING Place ingredients in screw-top jar; shake well.

preparation time *20 minutes* serves *4*
nutritional count per serving *3.5g total fat (0.6g saturated fat); 790kJ (189 cal); 19.4g carbohydrate; 18g protein; 3g fibre*

thai chicken noodle broth

1 litre (4 cups) chicken stock
2 cups (500ml) water
3cm piece fresh ginger (15g), grated
1 fresh small red thai chilli, chopped finely
400g chicken breast fillets, sliced thinly
400g fresh rice noodles
1 tablespoon fish sauce
1 tablespoon grated palm sugar
1 tablespoon lime juice
2 baby buk choy (300g), quartered
⅓ cup loosely packed fresh thai basil leaves

1   Combine stock, the water, ginger and chilli in large saucepan; cover, bring to the boil. Reduce heat; simmer 5 minutes. Add chicken, noodles, sauce, sugar and juice; simmer, about 5 minutes or until chicken is cooked through and noodles are tender.
2   Divide buk choy among serving bowls; ladle chicken broth into bowls. Sprinkle with basil.

preparation time *15 minutes*
cooking time *15 minutes* serves *4*
nutritional count per serving *7.1g total fat (2.2g saturated fat); 1208kJ (289 cal); 27.5g carbohydrate; 27.6g protein; 1.7g fibre*

tamarind duck stir-fry

25g tamarind pulp
½ cup (125ml) boiling water
6cm piece fresh ginger (30g)
1 tablespoon peanut oil
2 cloves garlic, crushed
2 fresh long red thai chillies, chopped finely
1 large whole barbecued duck (1kg),
    cut into 12 pieces
1 medium red capsicum (200g), sliced thinly
¼ cup (60ml) chicken stock
2 tablespoons oyster sauce
1 tablespoon fish sauce
2 tablespoons grated palm sugar
200g baby buk choy, chopped coarsely
100g snow peas, sliced thinly
8 green onions, cut into 5cm lengths
⅓ cup firmly packed fresh coriander leaves

1   Soak tamarind pulp in the water for 30 minutes. Pour tamarind into a fine strainer over a small bowl; push as much pulp through the strainer as possible, scraping underside of strainer occasionally. Discard any tamarind solids left in strainer; reserve pulp liquid in bowl.
2   Slice peeled ginger thinly; stack slices, then slice again into thin slivers.
3   Heat oil in wok; stir-fry ginger, garlic and chilli until fragrant. Add duck and capsicum; stir-fry until capsicum is tender and duck is heated through.
4   Add stock, sauces, sugar and reserved pulp liquid, bring to the boil; boil, 1 minute. Add buk choy; stir-fry until just wilted. Add snow peas and onion; stir-fry until both are just tender. Remove from heat; toss coriander leaves through stir-fry.

preparation time *20 minutes (plus standing time)*
cooking time *10 minutes* serves *4*
nutritional count per serving *28.4g total fat (7.9g saturated fat); 1689kJ (404 cal); 14.7g carbohydrate; 21.3g protein; 2.9g fibre*

prawn stir-fry with tamarind

1kg uncooked king prawns, shelled
2 tablespoons vegetable oil
1 clove garlic, crushed
2 teaspoons grated fresh ginger
10cm stick fresh lemon grass (20g), chopped finely
4 green onions, chopped finely
1 medium red capsicum (200g), sliced thinly
2 tablespoons thick tamarind concentrate
½ cup (125ml) chicken stock
2 teaspoons cornflour
1 tablespoon water

1   Cut almost through backs of prawns; remove dark veins. Gently press prawns open along cut side with knife.
2   Heat oil in wok; stir-fry garlic, ginger, lemon grass and onion until onion is soft. Add capsicum and prawns; stir-fry about 2 minutes or until prawns just change colour.
3   Stir in combined tamarind and stock; stir-fry over high heat 1 minute. Blend cornflour with the water; stir into wok. Stir over high heat until sauce boils and thickens slightly. Serve over hot noodles, if you like.

preparation time *20 minutes*
cooking time *15 minutes* serves *4*
nutritional count per serving *10.3g total fat (1.4g saturated fat); 932kJ (223 cal); 5.1g carbohydrate; 27g protein; 1.2g fibre*

spiced coconut prawn stir-fry

1.25kg uncooked medium king prawns
500g cauliflower, cut into florets
200g broccoli, cut into florets
1 medium brown onion (150g), sliced thinly
2 cloves garlic, sliced thinly
2 fresh long red chillies, sliced thinly
1 teaspoon ground turmeric
2 teaspoons yellow mustard seeds
¼ teaspoon ground cardamom
½ teaspoon ground cumin
140ml can coconut milk
2 tablespoons mango chutney

1 Shell and devein prawns, leaving tails intact.
2 Combine prawns and remaining ingredients in large bowl.
3 Stir-fry prawn and vegetable mixture in heated oiled wok until vegetables are just tender.

preparation time *10 minutes*
cooking time *10 minutes* serves *4*
nutritional count per serving *8.7g total fat (6.5g saturated fat); 1225kJ (293 cal); 11.9g carbohydrate; 38.5g protein; 6g fibre*

garlic and chilli seafood stir-fry

720g uncooked medium king prawns
2 cleaned squid hoods (300g)
540g octopus, quartered
¼ cup (60ml) peanut oil
6 cloves garlic, sliced thinly
2cm piece fresh ginger (10g), sliced thinly
2 fresh long red chillies, sliced thinly
2 tablespoons chinese cooking wine
1 teaspoon caster sugar
4 green onions, cut in 4cm pieces

CHILLI FRIED SHALLOTS

1 tablespoon fried shallots
1 teaspoon sea salt flakes
½ teaspoon dried chilli flakes

1 Shell and devein prawns, leaving tails intact. Cut squid down centre to open out; score inside in diagonal pattern then cut into thick strips. Quarter octopus lengthways.
2 Make chilli fried shallots.
3 Heat 1 tablespoon of the oil in wok; stir-fry prawns until changed in colour, remove from wok.
4 Heat another tablespoon of the oil in wok; stir-fry squid until cooked through, remove from wok.
5 Heat remaining oil in wok; stir-fry octopus until tender, remove from wok.
6 Stir-fry garlic, ginger and chilli in wok until fragrant. Return seafood to wok with remaining ingredients; stir-fry until hot. Serve stir-fry sprinkled with shallots.

CHILLI FRIED SHALLOTS Combine ingredients in small bowl.

preparation time *25 minutes*
cooking time *20 minutes* serves *4*
nutritional count per serving *4.7g total fat (0.8g saturated fat); 460kJ (110 cal); 0.8g carbohydrate; 15.5g protein; 0.3g fibre*

hokkien mee

450g hokkien noodles
1 tablespoon peanut oil
600g piece beef eye fillet, sliced thinly
1 medium brown onion (150g), sliced thinly
2 cloves garlic, crushed
1 medium red capsicum (200g), sliced thinly
115g baby corn, halved lengthways
150g snow peas, trimmed, halved diagonally
2 baby buk choy (300g), chopped coarsely
¼ cup (60ml) char siu sauce
1 tablespoon dark soy sauce
¼ cup (60ml) chicken stock

1   Place noodles in medium heatproof bowl, cover with boiling water; separate with fork, drain.
2   Heat half the oil in wok; stir-fry beef, in batches, until browned.
3   Heat remaining oil in wok; stir-fry onion, garlic and capsicum until tender.
4   Return beef to wok with noodles, corn, snow peas, buk choy, sauces and stock; stir-fry until vegetables are tender and beef is cooked as desired.

preparation time *15 minutes*
cooking time *15 minutes* serves *4*
nutritional count per serving *32.3g total fat (13.8g saturated fat); 3382kJ (809 cal); 75.5g carbohydrate; 47.1g protein; 13.3g fibre*

singapore noodles

250g dried thin egg noodles
2 tablespoons peanut oil
4 eggs, beaten lightly
3 cloves garlic, crushed
1 tablespoon grated fresh ginger
1 medium white onion (150g), sliced thinly
2 tablespoons mild curry paste
230g can water chestnuts, drained, chopped coarsely
3 green onions, chopped diagonally
200g chinese barbecued pork, sliced
500g uncooked medium prawns, shelled, deveined
2 tablespoons light soy sauce
2 tablespoons oyster sauce

1   Cook noodles in large saucepan of boiling water, uncovered, until just tender; drain.
2   Meanwhile, heat half of the oil in wok; add half of the egg, swirl wok to make a thin omelette. Remove omelette from wok; roll omelette, cut into thin strips. Repeat with remaining egg.
3   Heat remaining oil in wok; stir-fry garlic and ginger 1 minute. Add white onion and paste; stir-fry until fragrant.
4   Add water chestnuts, green onion and pork; stir-fry about 2 minutes or until chestnuts are browned lightly.
5   Add prawns; stir-fry until prawns are just changed in colour. Add noodles, combined sauces and omelette; stir-fry, tossing, until sauce thickens and noodles are heated through.

preparation time *30 minutes*
cooking time *15 minutes* serves *4*
nutritional count per serving *27.4g total fat (7.1g saturated fat); 2696kJ (645 cal); 54.6g carbohydrate; 40.7g protein; 6.2g fibre*

beef rendang

2 medium red onions (340g), chopped finely
4 cloves garlic, peeled
4 fresh small red thai chillies
1 tablespoon grated fresh ginger
½ x 10cm stick fresh lemon grass (20g),
    chopped finely
1 teaspoon ground turmeric
2 teaspoons ground coriander
1⅔ cups (410ml) coconut milk
1kg beef blade steak, cut into 3cm cubes
1 cinnamon stick
1 tablespoon thick tamarind concentrate
8 curry leaves
1 teaspoon sugar

1 Blend or process onion, garlic, chillies, ginger,
lemon grass, turmeric, coriander and ⅓ cup (80ml) of
the coconut milk until smooth.
2 Combine beef, coconut mixture, remaining coconut
milk, cinnamon stick, tamarind concentrate and curry
leaves in large saucepan; simmer, uncovered, about
1½ hours, stirring occasionally, or until beef is tender.
3 Add sugar; cook, stirring, about 15 minutes or until
beef is dark and most of the sauce has evaporated.

preparation time *20 minutes*
cooking time *1 hour 45 minutes* serves *4*
nutritional count per serving *16.4g total fat (7g
saturated fat); 1643kJ (393 cal); 6.3g carbohydrate;
53.9g protein; 1.8g fibre*

asian prawn and noodle soup

3 cups (750ml) water
3 cups (750ml) fish stock
10cm stick fresh lemon grass (20g), chopped coarsely
4 fresh kaffir lime leaves, torn
8cm piece fresh ginger (40g), sliced thinly
2 fresh small red thai chillies, chopped coarsely
1 tablespoon fish sauce
1kg uncooked medium king prawns
100g rice stick noodles
230g can bamboo shoots, rinsed, drained
100g fresh shiitake mushrooms, sliced thickly
3 green onions, sliced thinly

1 Place the water and stock in large saucepan with
lemon grass, lime leaf, ginger, chilli and sauce; bring to
the boil. Reduce heat; simmer, uncovered, 10 minutes.
2 Meanwhile, shell and devein prawns.
3 Strain broth through muslin-lined sieve or colander
into large heatproof bowl; discard solids.
4 Return broth to same cleaned pan with noodles,
bamboo and mushrooms. Simmer, uncovered, about
5 minutes or until noodles are just tender. Add prawns;
simmer, uncovered, about 5 minutes or until prawns
are cooked.
5 Serve bowls of soup sprinkled with onion.

preparation time *10 minutes*
cooking time *20 minutes* serves *4*
nutritional count per serving *1.3g total fat (0.3g
saturated fat); 757kJ (181 cal); 9.6g carbohydrate;
30.4g protein; 2.3g fibre*

green papaya salad

10cm stick fresh lemon grass (20g)
1 small green papaya (650g)
2 cups (160g) bean sprouts
1 cup (100g) coarsely grated fresh coconut
¾ cup loosely packed fresh coriander leaves
¾ cup loosely packed fresh mint leaves
2 purple shallots (50g), sliced thinly
½ cup (70g) roasted unsalted peanuts,
    chopped coarsely

CHILLI CITRUS DRESSING

¼ cup (60ml) lime juice
¼ cup (60ml) lemon juice
1 tablespoon grated palm sugar
2 teaspoons fish sauce
1 fresh small red thai chilli, chopped finely

1 Soak lemon grass in medium heatproof bowl of
boiling water about 4 minutes or until tender. Drain;
slice lemon grass thinly.
2 Meanwhile, make chilli citrus dressing.
3 Peel papaya, quarter lengthways, discard seeds;
grate papaya coarsely.
4 Place lemon grass, dressing, papaya, sprouts,
coconut, coriander, mint and shallot in large bowl;
toss gently to combine. Divide salad among serving
bowls; sprinkle with nuts.

CHILLI CITRUS DRESSING Place ingredients in screw-top
jar; shake well.

preparation time *20 minutes* serves *4*
nutritional count per serving *15.5g total fat (7.3g
saturated fat); 1049kJ (251 cal); 16.3g carbohydrate;
7.9g protein; 8.4g fibre*

pork and lychee salad

1 tablespoon peanut oil
300g pork fillet
565g can lychees, rinsed, drained, halved
1 medium red capsicum (200g), sliced thinly
10cm stick fresh lemon grass (20g), sliced thinly
2 fresh kaffir lime leaves, shredded finely
100g watercress
2 tablespoons coarsely chopped fresh vietnamese mint
2 tablespoons drained thinly sliced pickled ginger
2 tablespoons fried shallots

PICKLED GARLIC DRESSING

1 tablespoon drained finely chopped pickled garlic
2 fresh small red thai chillies, seeded, sliced thinly
1 tablespoon rice vinegar
1 tablespoon lime juice
1 tablespoon fish sauce
1 tablespoon palm sugar

1 Heat oil in wok; cook pork, turning, until browned all
over and cooked as desired. Cover; stand 10 minutes,
slice thinly.
2 Meanwhile, make pickled garlic dressing.
3 Combine pork and dressing in medium bowl.
Stand 10 minutes.
4 Meanwhile, combine lychees, capsicum, lemon
grass, lime leaves, watercress and mint in large bowl.
5 Add pork mixture to lychee mixture; toss gently to
combine. Serve salad sprinkled with pickled ginger
and fried shallot.

PICKLED GARLIC DRESSING Place ingredients in screw-top
jar; shake well.

preparation time *20 minutes (plus standing time)*
cooking time *10 minutes* serves *4*
nutritional count per serving *6.9g total fat (1.5g
saturated fat); 911kJ (218 cal); 18.1g carbohydrate;
19.1g protein; 3.3g fibre*

thai beef salad

¼ cup (60ml) fish sauce
¼ cup (60ml) lime juice
500g beef rump steak
3 lebanese cucumbers (390g), seeded, sliced thinly
4 fresh small red thai chillies, sliced thinly
4 green onions, sliced thinly
250g cherry tomatoes, halved
¼ cup firmly packed fresh vietnamese mint leaves
½ cup firmly packed fresh coriander leaves
½ cup firmly packed fresh thai basil leaves
1 tablespoon grated palm sugar
2 teaspoons soy sauce
1 clove garlic, crushed

1   Combine 2 tablespoons of the fish sauce and
1 tablespoon of the juice in medium bowl, add beef;
toss beef to coat in marinade. Cover; refrigerate
3 hours or overnight.
2   Drain beef; discard marinade. Cook beef on heated
oiled grill plate (or grill or barbecue) until cooked as
desired. Cover, beef, stand 5 minutes; slice beef thinly.
3   Meanwhile, combine cucumber, chilli, onion, tomato
and herbs in large bowl.
4   Place sugar, soy sauce, garlic, remaining fish sauce
and remaining juice in screw-top jar; shake well. Add
beef and dressing to salad; toss gently to combine.

preparation time *25 minutes (plus refrigeration time)*
cooking time *10 minutes* serves *4*
nutritional count per serving *8.7g total fat (3.8g
saturated fat); 986kJ (236 cal); 8.2g carbohydrate;
30.6g protein; 3.4g fibre*

larb gai

2 tablespoons long-grain white rice
1 tablespoon peanut oil
½ x 10cm stick fresh lemon grass (20g), chopped finely
2 fresh small red thai chillies, chopped finely
2 cloves garlic, crushed
1cm piece fresh galangal (5g), chopped finely
750g chicken mince
1 lebanese cucumber (130g), seeded, sliced thinly
1 small red onion (100g), sliced thinly
100g bean sprouts
½ cup loosely packed fresh thai basil leaves
1 cup loosely packed fresh coriander leaves
8 large butter lettuce leaves
DRESSING
⅓ cup (80ml) lime juice
2 tablespoons fish sauce
2 tablespoons kecap manis
2 tablespoons peanut oil
2 teaspoons grated palm sugar
½ teaspoon sambal oelek

1   Heat dry wok; stir-fry rice until lightly browned.
Blend or process (or crush using mortar and pestle)
rice until it resembles fine breadcrumbs.
2   Meanwhile, make dressing.
3   Heat oil in same wok; stir-fry lemon grass, chilli,
garlic and galangal until fragrant. Remove from wok.
4   Stir-fry chicken, in batches, until changed in colour
and cooked through.
5   Return chicken and lemon grass mixture to wok with
about one-third of the dressing; stir-fry about 5 minutes
or until mixture thickens slightly.
6   Place remaining dressing in large bowl with chicken,
cucumber, onion, sprouts and herbs; toss gently to
combine. Place lettuce leaves on serving plates; divide
larb salad among leaves, sprinkle with ground rice.

DRESSING Place ingredients in screw-top jar; shake well.

preparation time *25 minutes*
cooking time *20 minutes* serves *4*
nutritional count per serving *21.8g total fat (4.7g
saturated fat); 1772kJ (424 cal); 12.3g carbohydrate;
43g protein; 3.1g fibre*

pork larb with broccolini

1 tablespoon peanut oil
2 cloves garlic, crushed
600g pork mince
⅓ cup (90g) grated palm sugar
2 tablespoons fish sauce
4 kaffir lime leaves, sliced finely
½ cup (40g) fried shallots
⅓ cup (45g) roasted unsalted peanuts
350g broccolini, trimmed, halved lengthways
1 tablespoon lime juice
1 cup loosely packed fresh coriander leaves
1 fresh long red chilli, sliced thinly
2 tablespoons coarsely chopped roasted
    unsalted peanuts

1   Heat oil in wok; stir-fry garlic and pork mince
until mince is browned. Remove from wok.
2   Add sugar, sauce, lime leaves, shallots and nuts
to wok; bring to the boil. Reduce heat; simmer,
uncovered, 1 minute. Return mince to wok; cook,
uncovered, about 2 minutes or until larb mixture is
slightly dry and sticky.
3   Meanwhile, boil, steam or microwave broccolini;
drain.
4   Stir juice and three-quarters of the coriander into
larb off the heat. Spoon larb over broccolini and
sprinkle with remaining coriander, chilli and coarsely
chopped nuts.

preparation time *15 minutes*
cooking time *10 minutes* serves *4*
nutritional count per serving *16g total fat (3g
saturated fat); 1806kJ (432 cal); 25g carbohydrate;
44.1g protein; 5.5g fibre*

chicken larb with thai pickle

¼ cup (60ml) chicken stock
2 tablespoons lime juice
1 tablespoon fish sauce
1 tablespoon grated palm sugar
500g chicken mince
1 clove garlic, crushed
2 shallots (50g), sliced thinly
2 tablespoons finely chopped fresh coriander
1 tablespoon finely chopped fresh mint
1 fresh long red chilli, sliced thinly
1 medium iceberg lettuce, shredded coarsely

THAI PICKLE

½ cup (110g) white sugar
½ cup (125ml) white vinegar
1 tablespoon coarse cooking salt
½ cup (125ml) water
1 small red capsicum (150g), sliced thinly
½ cup (40g) bean sprouts
1 lebanese cucumber (130g), seeded, sliced thinly

1   Make thai pickle.
2   Meanwhile, place stock, juice, sauce and sugar in
large saucepan; bring to the boil. Add chicken and
garlic, reduce heat; simmer, stirring, about 5 minutes
or until chicken is cooked through. Cool 10 minutes.
Stir in shallot, herbs and chilli.
3   Serve larb with drained thai pickle on lettuce,
accompanied with steamed jasmine rice, if you like.

THAI PICKLE   Place sugar, vinegar, salt and the water
in small saucepan; bring to the boil. Cool 5 minutes.
Place capsicum, sprouts and cucumber in medium bowl;
pour vinegar mixture over capsicum mixture. Cover;
stand 30 minutes.

preparation time *15 minutes*
cooking time *15 minutes (plus standing time)* serves *4*
nutritional count per serving *10.5g total fat (3.1g
saturated fat); 1438kJ (344 cal); 34.1g carbohydrate;
26.7g protein; 2.9g fibre*

crisp hot and sweet beef with noodles

750g piece corned beef silverside
1kg fresh wide rice noodles
¼ cup (60ml) peanut oil
3 cloves garlic, crushed
3 fresh small red thai chillies, sliced thinly
4 spring onions, sliced thinly
2 tablespoons fish sauce
¼ cup (65g) grated palm sugar
1 cup firmly packed fresh coriander leaves

1 Place beef, in packaging, in large saucepan, cover with cold water; bring to the boil, uncovered. Reduce heat; simmer, covered, 1 hour 30 minutes. Remove from pan, discard packaging; drain beef on rack over tray for 15 minutes.
2 Meanwhile, place noodles in large heatproof bowl; cover with boiling water, separate with fork, drain.
3 Trim excess fat from beef; using two forks, shred beef finely. Heat oil in wok; stir-fry beef, in batches, until browned all over and crisp. Drain on absorbent paper.
4 Stir-fry garlic, chilli and onion in same wok until onion softens. Add sauce and sugar; stir-fry until sugar dissolves. Return beef to wok with noodles; stir-fry gently until heated through. Remove from heat; toss coriander leaves through stir-fry.

preparation time *20 minutes (plus standing time)*
cooking time *1 hour 45 minutes* serves *4*
nutritional count per serving *23.8g total fat (6.4g saturated fat); 2905kJ (695 cal); 70.8g carbohydrate; 47.4g protein; 2.3g fibre*

stir-fried asian greens in black bean sauce

2 cups (400g) jasmine rice
1 tablespoon peanut oil
150g sugar snap peas, trimmed
400g gai lan, chopped coarsely
200g snake beans, trimmed, cut into 5cm lengths
2 cloves garlic, sliced thinly
1 fresh small red thai chilli, chopped finely
2 medium zucchini (240g), sliced thickly
2 tablespoons black bean sauce
1 tablespoon kecap manis
1 teaspoon sesame oil
⅓ cup (50g) roasted unsalted cashews, chopped coarsely

1 Cook rice in large saucepan of boiling water, uncovered, until just tender; drain.
2 Meanwhile, heat peanut oil in wok; stir-fry peas, gai lan stems, beans, garlic, chilli and zucchini until stems are just tender.
3 Add sauces, sesame oil, gai lan leaves and nuts; stir-fry until leaves are just wilted. Serve stir-fry with rice.

preparation time *10 minutes*
cooking time *15 minutes* serves *4*
nutritional count per serving *13.3g total fat (2.6g saturated fat); 2274kJ (544 cal); 89.5g carbohydrate; 15.4g protein; 8.8g fibre*

sweet soy fried noodles

1kg fresh wide rice noodles
2 teaspoons sesame oil
2 cloves garlic, crushed
2 fresh small red thai chillies, sliced thinly
600g chicken thigh fillets, chopped coarsely
250g baby buk choy, quartered lengthways
4 green onions, sliced thinly
2 tablespoons kecap manis
1 tablespoon oyster sauce
1 tablespoon fish sauce
1 tablespoon grated palm sugar
¼ cup coarsely chopped fresh coriander
1 tablespoon fried onion

1   Place noodles in large heatproof bowl; cover with boiling water, separate with fork, drain.
2   Heat oil in wok; stir-fry garlic and chilli until fragrant. Add chicken; stir-fry until lightly browned. Add buk choy and green onion; stir-fry until green onion softens and chicken is cooked through.
3   Add noodles with kecap manis, sauces and sugar; stir-fry, tossing gently to combine. Remove from heat; add coriander, tossing gently to combine. Sprinkle with fried onion.

preparation time *15 minutes*
cooking time *15 minutes serves 4*
nutritional count per serving *10g total fat (2.2g saturated fat); 2057kJ (492 cal); 59.9g carbohydrate; 38.3g protein; 2.7g fibre*

pumpkin, basil and chilli stir-fry

⅓ cup (80ml) peanut oil
1 large brown onion (200g), sliced thinly
2 cloves garlic, sliced thinly
4 fresh small red thai chillies, sliced thinly
1kg pumpkin, chopped coarsely
250g sugar snap peas
1 teaspoon grated palm sugar
¼ cup (60ml) vegetable stock
2 tablespoons soy sauce
¾ cup loosely packed opal basil leaves
4 green onions, sliced thinly
½ cup (75g) roasted unsalted peanuts

1   Heat oil in wok; cook brown onion, in batches, until browned and crisp. Drain on absorbent paper.
2   Stir-fry garlic and chilli in wok until fragrant. Add pumpkin; stir-fry until browned all over and just tender. Add peas, sugar, stock and sauce; stir-fry until sauce thickens slightly.
3   Remove from heat; toss basil, green onion and nuts through stir-fry until well combined. Serve topped with cooked brown onion.

preparation time *10 minutes*
cooking time *15 minutes serves 4*
nutritional count per serving *28.1g total fat (5.3g saturated fat); 1672kJ (400 cal); 22g carbohydrate; 12.3g protein; 6.5g fibre*

nasi goreng

720g cooked medium king prawns
1 tablespoon peanut oil
175g dried chinese sausages, sliced thickly
1 medium brown onion (150g), sliced thinly
1 medium red capsicum (200g), sliced thinly
2 fresh long red chillies, sliced thinly
2 cloves garlic, crushed
2cm piece fresh ginger (10g), grated
1 teaspoon shrimp paste
4 cups cold cooked white long-grain rice
2 tablespoons kecap manis
1 tablespoon light soy sauce
4 green onions, sliced thinly
1 tablespoon peanut oil, extra
4 eggs

1   Shell and devein prawns.
2   Heat half the oil in wok; stir-fry sausage, in batches, until browned.
3   Heat remaining oil in wok; stir-fry onion, capsicum, chilli, garlic, ginger and paste, until vegetables soften. Add prawns and rice; stir-fry 2 minutes. Return sausage to wok with sauces and half the green onion; stir-fry until combined.
4   Heat extra oil in large frying pan; fry eggs, one side only, until just set. Divide nasi goreng among serving plates, top each with an egg; sprinkle with remaining green onion.

preparation time *25 minutes*
cooking time *15 minutes* serves *4*
nutritional count per serving *25.7g total fat (7.4g saturated fat); 2730kJ (653 cal); 48.5g carbohydrate; 54.7g protein; 3.3g fibre*

crab fried rice in omelette

¼ cup (60ml) peanut oil
4 green onions, chopped finely
2 fresh small red thai chillies, chopped finely
1 tablespoon red curry paste
2 cups cooked jasmine rice
250g fresh crab meat
2 tablespoons lime juice
2 tablespoons fish sauce
8 eggs
2 tablespoons water
1 lime, cut into wedges

1   Heat 1 tablespoon of the oil in wok; stir-fry onion and chopped chilli until onion softens. Add curry paste; stir-fry until mixture is fragrant.
2   Add rice; stir-fry until heated through. Remove from heat; place in large bowl. Add crab meat, juice and sauce; toss gently to combine.
3   Whisk eggs with the water in medium bowl. Heat about a quarter of the remaining oil in same cleaned wok; pour a quarter of the egg mixture into wok. Cook, tilting pan, over low heat until almost set. Spoon a quarter of the fried rice into centre of the omelette; using spatula, fold four sides of omelette over to enclose filling.
4   Press omelette firmly with spatula; turn carefully to brown other side. Remove omelette from wok; cover to keep warm. Repeat process with remaining oil, egg mixture and fried rice. Place omelettes on serving plate; serve with lime.

preparation time *15 minutes*
cooking time *25 minutes* serves *4*
nutritional count per serving *26.6g total fat (5.9g saturated fat); 1919kJ (459 cal); 29.4g carbohydrate; 24.9g protein; 2g fibre*

yellow coconut rice with serundeng

1¾ cups (350g) white long-grain rice
400ml can coconut cream
1¼ cups (310ml) water
1 teaspoon caster sugar
½ teaspoon ground turmeric
pinch saffron threads

SERUNDENG

2 tablespoons peanut oil
2 cloves garlic, crushed
4 green onions, chopped finely
3 cups (150g) flaked coconut
2 tablespoons brown sugar
½ cup (150g) tamarind concentrate
10cm stick fresh lemon grass (20g), chopped finely
1 cup (140g) roasted unsalted peanuts

1   Soak rice in large bowl of cold water 30 minutes. Pour rice into strainer; rinse under cold water until water runs clear. Drain.
2   Meanwhile, make serundeng.
3   Place rice and remaining ingredients in large heavy-based saucepan; cover, bring to the boil, stirring occasionally. Reduce heat; simmer, covered, about 15 minutes or until rice is tender.
4   Remove from heat; stand, covered, 5 minutes, before serving with serundeng.

SERUNDENG   Preheat oven to 150°C/130°C fan-forced. Heat oil in wok; stir-fry remaining ingredients, tossing constantly, about 15 minutes or until browned lightly. Transfer mixture to oven tray; cook, uncovered, about 20 minutes or until serundeng has dried.

preparation time *5 minutes (plus standing time)*
cooking time *25 minutes* serves *4*
nutritional count per serving *71.3g total fat (43.4g saturated fat); 4615kJ (1104 cal); 91.6g carbohydrate; 19.4g protein; 11.9g fibre*

chicken and thai basil fried rice

¼ cup (60ml) peanut oil
1 medium brown onion (150g), chopped finely
3 cloves garlic, crushed
2 fresh long green thai chillies, chopped finely
1 tablespoon brown sugar
500g chicken breast fillets, chopped coarsely
2 medium red capsicums (400g), sliced thinly
200g green beans, chopped coarsely
4 cups cooked jasmine rice
2 tablespoons fish sauce
2 tablespoons soy sauce
½ cup loosely packed fresh thai basil leaves

1   Heat oil in wok; stir-fry onion, garlic and chilli until onion softens. Add sugar; stir-fry until dissolved. Add chicken; stir-fry until lightly browned. Add capsicum and beans; stir-fry until vegetables are just tender and chicken is cooked through.
2   Add rice and sauces; stir-fry, tossing gently to combine. Remove from heat; add basil leaves, toss gently to combine.

preparation time *20 minutes*
cooking time *25 minutes* serves *4*
nutritional count per serving *19.7g total fat (4g saturated fat); 2445kJ (585 cal); 64g carbohydrate; 34.8g protein; 5g fibre*

classic pulao

1⅓ cups (265g) basmati rice, rinsed, drained
2½ cups (625ml) chicken stock
pinch saffron threads
50g butter
1 medium brown onion (150g), chopped finely
2 cloves garlic, crushed
1 cinnamon stick
6 cardamom pods
1 bay leaf
⅓ cup (55g) sultanas
½ cup (75g) roasted unsalted cashews

1   Place rice in medium bowl, cover with cold water; stand 20 minutes, drain.
2   Heat stock and saffron in small saucepan.
3   Meanwhile, melt butter in large saucepan; cook onion and garlic, stirring, until onion softens. Stir in cinnamon, cardamom and bay leaf; cook, stirring, 2 minutes.
4   Add rice; cook, stirring, 2 minutes. Add stock mixture and sultanas; simmer, covered, about 10 minutes or until rice is tender and liquid is absorbed.
5   Sprinkle pulao with nuts just before serving.

preparation time *10 minutes (plus standing time)*
cooking time *20 minutes* serves *4*
nutritional count per serving *20.6g total fat (8.8g saturated fat); 2128kJ (509 cal); 68.7g carbohydrate; 10.5g protein; 3g fibre*

teppanyaki

4 large uncooked prawns (200g)
2 cloves garlic, crushed
¼ cup (60ml) japanese soy sauce
1 fresh small red thai chilli, chopped finely
350g chicken breast fillets, skin on, cut into 5cm pieces
500g beef eye fillet, sliced thinly
4 shiitake mushrooms
1 medium brown onion (150g), sliced thinly
50g snow peas, trimmed
1 medium red capsicum (200g), chopped coarsely
4 green onions, sliced thinly

DIPPING SAUCE

½ cup (125ml) japanese soy sauce
1 tablespoon mirin
1 tablespoon brown sugar
1 tablespoon finely grated fresh ginger
½ teaspoon sesame oil

1   Shell and devein prawns, leaving tails intact. Combine garlic, soy sauce and chilli in medium bowl with prawns, chicken and beef; stand 20 minutes. Drain; discard marinade.
2   Remove and discard mushroom stems; cut a cross in the top of each cap. Arrange ingredients, except green onion, on serving platter.
3   Cook a selection of the ingredients on heated oiled grill plate (or grill or barbecue) until vegetables are just tender, prawns and beef are cooked as desired and chicken is cooked through.
4   Continue cooking remaining ingredients throughout the meal. Serve with green onion and individual bowls of dipping sauce.

DIPPING SAUCE Cook ingredients in medium saucepan, stirring, until sugar dissolves. Divide sauce among individual serving bowls.

preparation time *20 minutes (plus standing time)*
cooking time *20 minutes* serves *4*
nutritional count per serving *13.3g total fat (4.7g saturated fat); 1613kJ (386 cal); 9.6g carbohydrate; 55g protein; 2.1g fibre*

lamb biryani

1.5kg boneless lamb shoulder, cut into 2cm cubes
5cm piece fresh ginger (25g), grated finely
3 cloves garlic, crushed
2 fresh small red thai chillies, chopped finely
3 teaspoons garam masala
2 tablespoons chopped fresh coriander
large pinch ground turmeric
½ teaspoon ground chilli powder
1 teaspoon salt
1 cup (280g) thick yogurt
80g ghee
1 cup (140g) flaked almonds
⅓ cup (55g) sultanas
3 large (600g) brown onions, sliced thickly
1 cup (250ml) water
500g basmati rice, washed, drained
large pinch saffron threads
2 tablespoons hot milk
fresh coriander leaves, for serving

1 Combine lamb, ginger, garlic, chilli, garam masala, coriander, turmeric, chilli powder, salt and yogurt in medium bowl. Cover; refrigerate overnight.

2 Heat half the ghee in large, heavy-based saucepan; fry almonds and sultanas until browned lightly, remove from pan with a slotted spoon.

3 Heat remaining ghee in same pan; cook onion, covered, over medium heat for about 5 minutes or until onion is soft. Remove lid, cook for further 5 minutes or until onions are lightly browned. Remove half the onion mixture from pan.

4 Add lamb mixture to onion in pan, cook, stirring, until lamb is browned lightly. Add water; bring to the boil. Reduce heat; simmer, covered, over low heat, stirring occasionally, for 1 hour. Uncover, simmer, for further 30 minutes or until lamb is tender.

5 Meanwhile, cook rice in boiling water 5 minutes or until half-cooked; drain. Combine saffron and milk in small bowl; stand 15 minutes.

6 Preheat oven to 180°C/160°C fan-forced.

7 Spread half the lamb mixture in oiled 3.5-litre (14-cup) ovenproof dish, top with half the rice, then remaining lamb and rice. Drizzle saffron and milk mixture over rice; cover tightly with greased foil and lid.

8 Bake biryani about 40 minutes or until rice is tender. Serve topped with reheated reserved onions, almond mixture and extra coriander leaves.

preparation *35 minutes (plus refrigeration time)*
cooking time *2 hours 30 minutes* serves *8*
nutritional count per serving *38.2g total fat (15.9g saturated fat); 3281kJ (785 cal); 61.5g carbohydrate; 47g protein; 3.6g fibre*

chilli rice noodles with lamb

400g fresh thin rice noodles
1 tablespoon peanut oil
500g lamb mince
3 cloves garlic, crushed
2 fresh small red thai chillies, chopped finely
400g buk choy, sliced thinly
2 tablespoons tamari
1 tablespoon fish sauce
2 tablespoons kecap manis
4 green onions, sliced thinly
1 cup firmly packed fresh thai basil leaves
3 cups (240g) bean sprouts

1 Place noodles in medium heatproof bowl; cover with boiling water, separate with fork, drain.
2 Heat oil in wok; stir-fry lamb mince until browned. Add garlic and chilli; stir-fry until fragrant. Add noodles, buk choy, tamari, sauce and kecap manis; stir-fry until buk choy just wilts.
3 Remove from heat; stir in onion, basil and sprouts. Serve topped with sliced chilli, if you like.

preparation time *20 minutes*
cooking time *15 minutes* serves *4*
nutritional count per serving *14.4g total fat (4.7g saturated fat); 1877kJ (449 cal); 44.5g carbohydrate; 34.3g protein; 5.3g fibre*

lamb do piazz

5 cloves garlic, crushed
2 teaspoons grated fresh ginger
1 teaspoon cardamom seeds
1 teaspoon ground turmeric
1 teaspoon cayenne pepper
2 tablespoons water
5 large brown onions (1kg), sliced thickly
1kg diced lamb
⅓ cup (80ml) vegetable oil
1 teaspoon fennel seeds
2 teaspoons fenugreek seeds
¾ cup (210g) yogurt
4 small tomatoes (500g), seeded, diced
2 cups (500ml) beef stock
2 tablespoons lime juice
¼ cup finely chopped fresh coriander

1 Blend or process garlic, ginger, cardamom seeds, turmeric, cayenne pepper, the water and half of the onion until pureed; transfer to large non-reactive bowl. Add lamb; toss to coat in marinade. Cover; refrigerate 3 hours or until required.
2 Heat oil in large frying pan; cook remaining onion until browned lightly. Remove from pan; reserve.
3 Cook fennel seeds and fenugreek seeds in same pan, stirring, 1 minute or until seeds pop. Add lamb mixture; cook, stirring, until browned all over. Add yogurt, in four batches, stirring well between additions. Add tomato and stock; bring to the boil. Reduce heat; simmer, covered, about 1 hour or until lamb is tender.
4 Stir in reserved onion; simmer, uncovered, until heated through. Just before serving, stir in juice and coriander.

preparation time *20 minutes (plus refrigeration time)*
cooking time *1 hour 20 minutes* serves *6*
nutritional count per serving *28.6g total fat (9.1g saturated fat); 2002kJ (479 cal); 13.1g carbohydrate; 40.9g protein; 3.7g fibre*

mee krob

150g fresh silken firm tofu
vegetable oil, for deep-frying
125g rice vermicelli noodles
2 tablespoons peanut oil
2 eggs, beaten lightly
1 tablespoon water
2 cloves garlic, crushed
2 fresh small red thai chillies, chopped finely
1 fresh small green thai chilli, chopped finely
2 tablespoons grated palm sugar
2 tablespoons fish sauce
2 tablespoons tomato sauce
1 tablespoon rice wine vinegar
200g pork mince
200g shelled cooked small prawns, chopped coarsely
6 green onions, sliced thinly
¼ cup firmly packed fresh coriander leaves

1 Pat tofu all over with absorbent paper; cut into slices, then cut each slice into 1cm-wide matchsticks. Spread tofu on absorbent-paper-lined tray; cover tofu with more absorbent paper, stand at least 10 minutes.

2 Meanwhile, heat vegetable oil in wok; deep-fry vermicelli quickly, in batches, until puffed. Drain on absorbent paper.

3 Using same heated oil, deep-fry drained tofu, in batches, until lightly browned. Drain on absorbent paper. Cool oil; remove from wok and reserve for another use.

4 Heat 2 teaspoons of the peanut oil in cleaned wok; add half of the combined egg and water, swirl wok to make thin omelette. Cook, uncovered, until egg is just set. Remove from wok; roll omelette, cut into thin strips. Repeat with another 2 teaspoons of the peanut oil and remaining egg mixture.

5 Combine garlic, chillies, sugar, sauces and vinegar in small bowl; pour half of the chilli mixture into small jug, reserve.

6 Combine pork in bowl with remaining half of the chilli mixture.

7 Heat remaining peanut oil in same wok; stir-fry pork mixture about 5 minutes or until pork is cooked through. Add prawns; stir-fry 1 minute. Add tofu; stir-fry, tossing gently to combine.

8 Remove wok from heat; add reserved chilli mixture and half of the onion, toss to combine. Add vermicelli; toss gently to combine. Remove from heat; sprinkle with remaining onion, omelette strips and coriander leaves.

preparation time *35 minutes*
cooking time *20 minutes* serves *4*
nutritional count per serving *22.3g total fat (4.7g saturated fat); 1898kJ (454 cal); 30.9g carbohydrate; 31.3g protein; 2.2g fibre*

hainan chicken

4 single chicken breasts on bone (1kg)
1 teaspoon chinese rice wine
1 tablespoon light soy sauce
2cm-piece fresh ginger, sliced thinly
1 clove garlic, sliced thinly
2 green onions, chopped finely
2 litres (8 cups) water
1 teaspoon sesame oil
1 cup (200g) jasmine rice
1 lebanese cucumber (130g), sliced thinly
1 green onion, sliced thinly, extra

CHILLI GINGER SAMBAL

4 fresh small red thai chillies, chopped coarsely
1 clove garlic, chopped coarsely
2cm piece fresh ginger (10g), chopped coarsely
1 teaspoon sesame oil
1 teaspoon water
2 teaspoons lime juice

1 Rub chicken all over with combined rice wine and half of the sauce. Gently slide combined ginger, garlic and onion under chicken skin.

2 Bring the water to the boil in large saucepan. Place chicken in the water. Turn off heat; turn chicken pieces. Stand chicken in the water 20 minutes. Remove chicken from pan; return liquid to the boil. Return chicken to pan; stand 20 minutes. Repeat the boiling, turning and standing four times.

3 Remove chicken from pan; remove and discard skin. Brush chicken all over with combined oil and remaining sauce.

4 Return cooking liquid to the boil; boil, uncovered, until reduced by a half.

5 Meanwhile, rinse rice thoroughly under cold running water. Place rice in large saucepan; add enough water to cover rice by 2cm. Cover pan; bring to the boil. Stir several times to prevent rice sticking. When boiling, remove lid and continue to boil until tunnels appear in rice and all the water has evaporated or been absorbed; do not stir. Cover; stand rice 20 minutes. Stir with fork; stand, covered, further 10 minutes.

6 Meanwhile, make chilli ginger sambal.

7 Cut chicken into pieces; serve with rice, cucumber and chilli ginger sambal. Accompany with a bowl of cooking liquid sprinkled with extra onion.

CHILLI GINGER SAMBAL Blend ingredients (or grind in a mortar and pestle) until combined.

preparation time *25 minutes*
cooking time *1 hour 20 minutes (plus standing time)*
serves *4*
nutritional count per serving *12.5g total fat (3.6g saturated fat); 1965kJ (470 cal); 41.1g carbohydrate; 46.7g protein; 1.4g fibre*

gado gado

Gado gado translates roughly as 'mixed mixed', which helps explain the casual way Indonesians eat this salad. Each diner makes his or her personal selection from the assortment of vegetables, then mixes them together, dollops on the peanut sauce and mixes the salad again.

2 medium potatoes (400g), sliced thickly
2 medium carrots (240g), sliced thickly
150g green beans, chopped coarsely
600g green cabbage
vegetable oil, for deep-frying
300g firm tofu, cut into 2cm cubes
2 medium tomatoes (380g), cut into wedges
2 lebanese cucumbers (260g), sliced thickly
160g bean sprouts, tips trimmed
4 hard-boiled eggs, quartered

PEANUT SAUCE

1 cup (150g) unsalted roasted peanuts
1 tablespoon peanut oil
1 small brown onion (80g), chopped finely
1 clove garlic, crushed
3 fresh small red thai chillies, chopped finely
1cm piece fresh galangal (5g), grated finely
1 tablespoon lime juice
1 tablespoon brown sugar
½ teaspoon shrimp paste
1 cup (250ml) coconut milk
¼ teaspoon thick tamarind concentrate
1 tablespoon kecap manis

1 Make peanut sauce.

2 Meanwhile, boil, steam or microwave potato, carrot and beans, separately, until potato is cooked through and carrot and beans are just tender.

3 Drop cabbage leaves into large saucepan of boiling water; remove leaves and quickly plunge into cold water. Drain cabbage; slice thinly.

4 Heat oil in wok; deep-fry tofu, in batches, until browned. Drain on absorbent paper.

5 Place potato, carrot, beans, cabbage, tofu, tomato, cucumber, sprouts and egg in sections on serving plate; serve with peanut sauce in small bowl.

PEANUT SAUCE Blend or process nuts until chopped coarsely. Heat oil in small saucepan; cook onion, garlic and chilli, stirring, until onion is golden brown. Add nuts and remaining ingredients; bring to the boil. Reduce heat; simmer 5 minutes or until mixture thickens. Cool 10 minutes.

preparation time *1 hour (plus cooling time)*
cooking time *35 minutes* serves *4*
nutritional count per serving *52.4g total fat (18g saturated fat); 3273kJ (783 cal); 35.7g carbohydrate; 34.9g protein; 17.5g fibre*

chinese barbecued pork

1kg pork scotch fillet

MARINADE

2 star anise, crushed
2 tablespoons light soy sauce
2 tablespoons brown sugar
1½ tablespoons honey
1½ tablespoons dry sherry
2 teaspoons hoisin sauce
2cm piece fresh ginger (10g), grated
1 clove garlic, crushed
2 green onions, chopped finely
red food colouring

1   Cut pork into quarters lengthways.
2   Combine ingredients for marinade in large shallow dish; add pork, toss to combine. Cover; refrigerate 3 hours or overnight.
3   Preheat barbecue.
4   Drain pork; reserve marinade. Cook pork on heated oiled barbecue, uncovered, until browned and cooked through, brushing with reserved marinade during cooking.

preparation time *15 minutes (plus refrigeration time)*
cooking time *15 minutes* serves *6*
nutritional count per serving *13.5g total fat (4.5g saturated fat); 1321kJ (316 cal); 11.3g carbohydrate; 35.9g protein; 0.4g fibre*

asian-style braised pork neck

1 tablespoon peanut oil
1kg piece pork neck
2 cinnamon sticks
2 star anise
½ cup (125ml) soy sauce
½ cup (125ml) chinese rice wine
¼ cup (55g) firmly packed brown sugar
5cm piece fresh ginger (25g), sliced thinly
4 cloves garlic, quartered
1 medium brown onion (150g), chopped coarsely
1 cup (250ml) water

1   Preheat oven to 160°C/140°C fan-forced.
2   Heat oil in medium deep flameproof baking dish; cook pork, uncovered, until browned all over. Remove from heat.
3   Add combined spices, sauce, wine, sugar, ginger, garlic, onion and the water to pork; turn pork to coat in mixture. Cook, uncovered, in oven about 2 hours or until pork is tender, turning every 20 minutes. Remove pork; cover to keep warm.
4   Strain braising liquid through muslin-lined strainer over medium saucepan; bring to the boil. Reduce heat; simmer, uncovered, about 5 minutes or until sauce thickens slighly.
5   Serve pork drizzled with sauce; serve with steamed gai lan, if you like.

preparation time *10 minutes*
cooking time *2 hours* serves *4*
nutritional count per serving *18.7g total fat (5.6g saturated fat); 2040kJ (488 cal); 18.1g carbohydrate; 54.9g protein; 1.2g fibre*

barbecued pork in orange and tamarind broth

20g dried shiitake mushrooms
2 teaspoons vegetable oil
4 shallots (100g), chopped finely
1 clove garlic, crushed
2 fresh small red thai chillies, chopped finely
2 litres (8 cups) water
1 litre (4 cups) beef stock
2 teaspoons finely grated orange rind
¼ cup (60ml) orange juice
1 tablespoon tamarind concentrate
400g chinese barbecued pork, sliced thinly
100g swiss brown mushrooms, sliced thinly
4 green onions, sliced thinly

1   Place shiitake mushrooms in small bowl, cover with cold water; stand 1 hour. Drain; remove stems, slice thinly.
2   Heat oil in large saucepan; cook shallot, garlic and chilli, stirring, until shallot softens. Add the water, stock, rind, juice and tamarind; bring to the boil. Add pork, sliced shiitake mushrooms and swiss browns; reduce heat, simmer, covered, about 10 minutes or until soup is hot.
3   Serve bowls of soup sprinkled with onion.

preparation time *15 minutes (plus standing time)*
cooking time *30 minutes* serves *8*
nutritional count per serving *9.1g total fat (3.4g saturated fat); 648kJ (155 cal); 4.3g carbohydrate; 13.1g protein; 2.1g fibre*

barbecued pork neck with five-spice star-anise glaze

1kg piece pork neck
1 clove garlic, sliced thinly
4cm piece ginger (20g), sliced thinly
2 x 100g packets baby asian greens

FIVE-SPICE STAR-ANISE GLAZE

1 cup (220g) firmly packed brown sugar
1¼ cups (310ml) water
3 fresh long red chillies, chopped finely
1 star anise
1 teaspoon five-spice powder
⅓ cup (80ml) light soy sauce
¼ cup (60ml) rice vinegar

1   Make five-spice star-anise glaze; reserve 1 cup (250ml) of glaze.
2   Make several shallow cuts in pork. Press garlic and ginger into cuts; brush ¼ cup (60ml) of the remaining glaze over pork.
3   Cook pork on heated oiled barbecue flat plate, covered, over low heat, 30 minutes. Turn pork; cook, covered, 30 minutes. Increase heat to high; cook, uncovered, 5 minutes, turning and brushing with remaining glaze constantly. Remove pork from heat. Cover; stand 15 minutes, slice thickly.
4   Meanwhile, place reserved glaze in small saucepan; simmer about 5 minutes or until thickened slightly. Cool.
5   Combine greens with glaze in medium bowl; serve with pork.

FIVE-SPICE STAR-ANISE GLAZE Combine sugar and the water in medium saucepan; simmer about 10 minutes or until glaze thickens slightly. Remove from heat; stir in remaining ingredients.

preparation time *15 minutes*
cooking time *1 hour 20 minutes (plus standing time)*
serves *6*
nutritional count per serving *13.4g total fat (4.5g saturated fat); 1714kJ (410 cal); 36.4g carbohydrate; 36.5g protein; 0.6g fibre*

palak paneer

1 tablespoon vegetable oil
1 teaspoon cumin seeds
1 teaspoon fenugreek seeds
2 teaspoons garam masala
1 large brown onion (200g), chopped finely
1 clove garlic, crushed
1 tablespoon lemon juice
500g spinach, trimmed, chopped coarsely
¾ cup (180ml) cream
2 x 100g packets paneer cheese, cut into 2cm pieces

1 Heat oil in large frying pan; cook spices, onion and garlic, stirring, until onion softens.
2 Add juice and half of the spinach; cook, stirring, until spinach wilts. Add remaining spinach; cook, stirring, until wilted.
3 Blend or process spinach mixture until smooth; return to pan, stir in cream. Add cheese; cook over low heat, uncovered, stirring occasionally, about 5 minutes or until heated through.

preparation time *10 minutes*
cooking time *20 minutes* serves *6*
nutritional count per serving *24.2g total fat (14.1g saturated fat); 1124kJ (269 cal); 3g carbohydrate; 9g protein; 3.4g fibre*

sambal goreng telor

4 fresh long red chillies, chopped coarsely
4 medium brown onions (600g), chopped coarsely
4 cloves garlic, quartered
4cm piece fresh galangal (20g), chopped coarsely
2 teaspoons vegetable oil
2 teaspoons ground coriander
32 fresh curry leaves
1 tablespoon kecap asin
10 medium tomatoes (1.5kg), peeled, seeded, chopped finely
½ cup (140g) tomato paste
1½ cups (375ml) vegetable stock
12 hard-boiled eggs, halved

1 Blend or process chilli, onion, garlic and galangal until smooth.
2 Heat oil in large saucepan; cook chilli mixture with coriander, curry leaves and kecap asin, stirring, about 5 minutes or until fragrant.
3 Stir in tomato, tomato paste and stock; simmer, covered, 30 minutes.
4 Add egg; simmer, covered, until heated through.

preparation time *25 minutes*
cooking time *45 minutes* serves *6*
nutritional count per serving *13.5g total fat (3.8g saturated fat); 991kJ (237 cal); 9.4g carbohydrate; 17.9g protein; 3.9g fibre*

crisp-skinned thai chilli snapper

1 whole snapper (1.2 kg)
4 cloves garlic, crushed
¼ cup chopped fresh lemon grass
¼ cup chopped fresh coriander
2 fresh small red thai chillies, chopped finely
2 tablespoons mild sweet chilli sauce
4cm piece fresh ginger (20g), grated finely
1 tablespoon thai red curry paste
2 tablespoons lime juice
2 tablespoons mild sweet chilli sauce, extra
½ cup firmly packed fresh coriander leaves, extra

1 Make four deep slits diagonally across both sides of fish; place fish in shallow non-metallic ovenproof dish.
2 Combine remaining ingredients, except extra chilli sauce and extra coriander leaves, in medium bowl. Pour over fish; cover, refrigerate 3 hours or overnight.
3 Preheat oven to 180°C/160°C fan-forced.
4 Cover dish with foil; bake about 35 minutes or until fish is almost tender.
5 Preheat grill.
6 Brush fish with extra chilli sauce; place under grill about 10 minutes or until skin is browned and crisp. Serve topped with coriander leaves.

preparation time *15 minutes (plus refrigeration time)*
cooking time *45 minutes* serves *6*
nutritional count per serving *2.9g total fat (0.7g saturated fat); 447kJ (107 cal); 3.6g carbohydrate; 16.1g protein; 1.8g fibre*

steamed coconut fish

2 cups chopped fresh coriander
2 fresh small red thai chillies, chopped coarsely
2 cloves garlic, quartered
4cm piece fresh ginger (20g), peeled, chopped coarsely
1 tablespoon cumin seeds
⅔ cup (50g) shredded coconut
1 tablespoon peanut oil
4 x 450g medium whole snapper

1 Blend or process coriander, chilli, garlic, ginger and seeds until chopped finely.
2 Combine coriander mixture with coconut and oil in small bowl.
3 Score each fish three times both sides; place fish on large sheet of foil. Press coconut mixture onto fish; fold foil over to enclose fish.
4 Place fish in large bamboo steamer; steam fish, covered, over wok of simmering water 25 minutes or until cooked through.
5 Serve fish with lemon wedges, steamed long-grain white rice and stir-fried buk choy, if you like.

preparation time *10 minutes*
cooking time *25 minutes* serves *4*
nutritional count per serving *15.5g total fat (9g saturated fat); 1241kJ (297 cal); 1.9g carbohydrate; 36.3g protein; 2.9g fibre*

whole snapper wrapped in banana leaf

3 large banana leaves
⅓ cup (110g) thai chilli jam
2 tablespoons light soy sauce
1 tablespoon chinese rice wine
1 whole snapper (2kg)
6cm piece fresh ginger (30g), cut into matchsticks
1 small carrot (70g), cut into matchsticks
2 cloves garlic, crushed
227g can bamboo shoots, rinsed, cut into matchsticks
2 green onions, chopped coarsely
½ cup firmly packed fresh coriander leaves
2 limes, cut into wedges

1 Trim two banana leaves to make one 30cm x 50cm rectangle and two 15cm x 30cm rectangles. Using metal tongs, dip one piece at a time into large saucepan of boiling water; remove immediately. Rinse under cold water; pat dry. Trim remaining banana leaf to fit grill plate.
2 Combine jam, sauce and wine in small bowl.
3 Score fish both sides through thickest part of flesh; place on large tray, brush both sides with jam mixture.
4 Combine ginger, carrot, garlic, bamboo and onion in medium bowl.
5 Place 30cm x 50cm leaf on work surface. Place one 15cm x 30cm leaf in centre of larger leaf; top with fish. Pour over any remaining jam mixture. Top fish with ginger mixture and remaining 15cm x 30cm leaf. Fold corners of banana leaf into centre to enclose fish; tie parcel at 10cm intervals with kitchen string to secure.
6 Place remaining trimmed leaf onto heated grill plate (or grill or barbecue); place fish parcel on leaf. Cook, over medium heat, about 40 minutes or until fish is cooked, turning halfway through cooking time.
7 Serve fish sprinkled with coriander leaves and lime wedges.

preparation time *45 minutes*
cooking time *45 minutes* serves *10*
nutritional count per serving *2.1g total fat (0.7g saturated fat); 431kJ (103 cal); 3.7g carbohydrate; 16.2g protein; 0.7g fibre*

steamed fish with black bean and chilli sauce

500g gai lan, cut into 8cm lengths
4 x 180g snapper fillets
2 tablespoons black bean garlic sauce
1 tablespoon water
5cm piece fresh ginger (25g), sliced thinly
1 tablespoon peanut oil
2 fresh small thai red chillies, sliced thinly

1 Line bamboo steamer with plate large enough to just fit the steamer. Place gai lan stems in single layer on plate. Steam, covered tightly, over wok of boiling water 3 minutes.
2 Place gai lan leaves in steamer; top with fish. Spread fish with combined sauce and water; sprinkle with ginger. Cover, steam about 5 minutes or until fish is just cooked through.
3 Meanwhile, place oil and chilli in small microwave-safe jug; cook on HIGH (100%) 30 seconds or until hot.
4 Serve fish on gai lan; drizzle with hot oil mixture just before serving with steamed rice or noodles, if you like.

preparation time *5 minutes*
cooking time *8 minutes* serves *4*
nutritional count per serving *14.2g total fat (4.1g saturated fat); 1283kJ (307 cal); 3.7g carbohydrate; 38.8g protein; 5.1g fibre*

sweet and sour duck with broccolini

1kg chinese barbecued duck
2 small red onions (200g), cut into thin wedges
1 fresh small red thai chilli, chopped finely
250g broccolini, cut into 3cm pieces
¼ cup (60ml) chicken stock
¼ cup (90g) honey
¼ cup (60ml) rice vinegar
1 tablespoon light soy sauce
2 teaspoons pomegranate molasses
4 green onions, cut into 3cm lengths
1 tablespoon sesame seeds, toasted

1   Quarter duck; discard bones. Slice duck meat thickly, keeping skin intact. Heat oiled wok; stir-fry duck, in batches, until skin is crisp.
2   Heat oiled wok; stir-fry red onion and chilli until onion softens slightly. Add broccolini, stock, honey, vinegar, sauce and molasses; stir-fry until sauce thickens slightly.
3   Serve broccolini mixture with duck and green onion; sprinkle with seeds.

preparation time *25 minutes*
cooking time *10 minutes* serves *4*
nutritional count per serving *38.9g total fat (11.3g saturated fat); 2437kJ (583 cal); 24.7g carbohydrate; 33g protein; 3.7g fibre*

beef in satay sauce

1 tablespoon peanut oil
750g beef strips
1 fresh long red chilli, sliced thinly
1 medium brown onion (150g), sliced thinly
1 medium red capsicum (200g), sliced thinly
½ cup (140g) peanut butter
½ cup (125ml) coconut cream
¼ cup (60ml) sweet chilli sauce
1 tablespoon japanese soy sauce

1   Heat half the oil in wok; stir-fry beef, in batches, until cooked.
2   Heat remaining oil in wok; stir-fry chilli, onion and capsicum until soft. Remove from wok.
3   Combine peanut butter, coconut cream and sauces in wok; bring to the boil. Return beef and onion mixture to wok; stir-fry until hot.

preparation time *10 minutes*
cooking time *20 minutes* serves *4*
nutritional count per serving *42.2g total fat (15g saturated fat); 2629kJ (629 cal); 10.6g carbohydrate; 49.8g protein; 6.1g fibre*

1 SWEET AND SOUR DUCK WITH BROCCOLINI 2 BEEF IN SATAY SAUCE
3 CHIANG MAI PORK AND EGGPLANT [P 584] 4 CHIANG MAI NOODLES [P 584]

ASIAN NEIGHBOURS   583

chiang mai pork and eggplant

3 fresh small red thai chillies, halved
6 cloves garlic, quartered
1 medium brown onion (150g), chopped coarsely
500g baby eggplants
¼ cup (60ml) peanut oil
700g pork leg steaks, sliced thinly
1 tablespoon fish sauce
1 tablespoon dark soy sauce
1 tablespoon grated palm sugar
4 purple thai shallots (100g), sliced thinly
150g snake beans, cut into 5cm lengths
1 cup loosely packed thai basil leaves

1   Blend or process chilli, garlic and onion until mixture forms a paste.
2   Quarter eggplants lengthways; slice each piece into 5cm lengths. Cook eggplant in large saucepan of boiling water until just tender; drain, pat dry.
3   Heat half the oil in wok; stir-fry eggplant, in batches, until browned lightly. Drain.
4   Heat remaining oil in wok; stir-fry pork, in batches, until cooked.
5   Stir-fry garlic paste in wok about 3 minutes or until fragrant and browned lightly. Add sauces and sugar; stir-fry until sugar dissolves.
6   Add shallot and beans; stir-fry until beans are tender. Return eggplant and pork to wok; stir-fry until hot. Remove from heat; sprinkle with basil.

preparation time *20 minutes*
cooking time *25 minutes* serves *4*
nutritional count per serving *19.3g total fat (4.1g saturated fat); 1672kJ (400 cal); 10.1g carbohydrate; 43.6g protein; 5.8g fibre*

chiang mai noodles

vegetable oil, for deep-frying
500g fresh egg noodles
1 large brown onion (200g), sliced thinly
2 green onions, sliced thinly
¼ cup loosely packed fresh coriander leaves
¼ cup (75g) red curry paste
2 cloves garlic, crushed
¼ teaspoon ground turmeric
2 cups (500ml) water
400ml can coconut milk
500g chicken breast fillets, sliced thinly
¼ cup (60ml) fish sauce
1 tablespoon soy sauce
2 tablespoons grated palm sugar
2 teaspoons lime juice
2 tablespoons coarsely chopped fresh coriander
1 fresh long red thai chilli, seeded, sliced thinly

1   Heat oil in wok; deep-fry about 100g of the noodles, in batches, until crisp. Drain on absorbent paper.
2   Using same heated oil, deep-fry brown onion, in batches, until lightly browned and crisp. Drain on absorbent paper.
3   Combine fried noodles, fried onion, green onion and coriander leaves in small bowl. Cool oil; remove from wok and reserve for another use.
4   Place remaining noodles in large heatproof bowl, cover with boiling water; use fork to separate noodles, drain.
5   Cook paste, garlic and turmeric in cleaned wok, add the water and coconut milk; bring to the boil. Reduce heat; simmer, stirring, 2 minutes. Add chicken; cook, stirring, about 5 minutes or until chicken is cooked through. Add sauces, sugar and juice; cook, stirring, until sugar dissolves. Stir in chopped coriander.
6   Divide drained noodles among serving bowls; spoon chicken curry mixture into each bowl, then top with fried noodle mixture. Sprinkle chilli slices over each bowl.

preparation time *20 minutes*
cooking time *20 minutes* serves *4*
nutritional count per serving *34.7g total fat (20.8g saturated fat); 3436kJ (822 cal); 80.3g carbohydrate; 43.1g protein; 7.4g fibre*

sweet and sour pork

½ teaspoon five-spice powder
2 teaspoons rice wine (or sweet sherry)
1 tablespoon soy sauce
500g pork fillet, sliced thinly
1 tablespoon sesame oil
1 large red capsicum (350g), chopped coarsely
1 medium green capsicum (200g), chopped coarsely
1 medium red onion (170g), sliced thinly
1 small pineapple (900g), chopped coarsely

SWEET AND SOUR SAUCE

¼ cup (60ml) water
2 tablespoons caster sugar
2 tablespoons white wine vinegar
2 tablespoons salt-reduced soy sauce
2 tablespoons ketchup

1 Combine five spice, rice wine, soy sauce and pork in medium bowl. Cover; refrigerate 15 minutes.
2 Heat half the oil in wok; stir-fry capsicums and onion until onion softens. Remove from wok.
3 Heat remaining oil in wok; stir-fry pork, in batches, until browned and just cooked through. Remove from wok.
4 Meanwhile, make sweet and sour sauce.
5 Add sweet and sour sauce to wok; bring to the boil. Return capsicum mixture and pork; stir-fry until combined. Top stir-fry with pineapple; serve with steamed gai lan and white rice, if you like.

SWEET AND SOUR SAUCE Combine ingredients in small jug.

preparation time *10 minutes (plus refrigeration time)*
cooking time *15 minutes* serves *4*
nutritional count per serving *15g total fat (4g saturated fat); 1580kJ (378 cal); 26.9g carbohydrate; 31g protein; 4.4g fibre*

sang choy bow

2 teaspoons sesame oil
1 small brown onion (80g), chopped finely
2 cloves garlic, crushed
2cm piece fresh ginger (10g), grated
500g lean pork mince
2 tablespoons water
100g shiitake mushrooms, chopped finely
2 tablespoons light soy sauce
2 tablespoons oyster sauce
1 tablespoon lime juice
2 cups bean sprouts
4 green onions, sliced thinly
¼ cup coarsely chopped fresh coriander
12 large butter lettuce leaves

1 Heat oil in wok; stir-fry brown onion, garlic and ginger until onion softens. Add pork mince; stir-fry until mince is changed in colour.
2 Add the water, mushrooms, sauces and juice; stir-fry until mushrooms are tender. Remove from heat. Add sprouts, green onion and coriander; toss to combine.
3 Spoon sang choy bow into lettuce leaves to serve.

preparation time *15 minutes*
cooking time *15 minutes* serves *4*
nutritional count per serving *11.5g total fat (3.6g saturated fat); 1112kJ (266 cal); 8.9g carbohydrate; 29.3g protein; 4.1g fibre*

cucumber raita

2 teaspoons vegetable oil
¼ teaspoon black mustard seeds
¼ teaspoon cumin seeds
2 lebanese cucumbers (260g), seeded,
    chopped finely
500g yogurt

1   Heat oil in small frying pan; cook seeds, stirring,
over low heat, about 2 minutes or until seeds pop.
2   Combine seeds and remaining ingredients in
medium bowl.

preparation time *5 minutes*
cooking time *2 minutes* serves *6*
nutritional count per serve *4.4g total fat (2g
saturated fat); 314kJ (75 cal); 4.5g carbohydrate;
4.1g protein; 0.4g fibre*

date and tamarind chutney

2 cinnamon sticks
5 cardamom pods, bruised
2 teaspoons cloves
3½ cups (500g) seeded dried dates
1½ cups (375ml) white vinegar
½ cup (110g) firmly packed brown sugar
2 teaspoons coarse cooking salt
¼ cup (60ml) vegetable oil
2 tablespoons tamarind concentrate
2 teaspoons chilli powder

1   Place cinnamon, cardamom and cloves in centre of
20cm muslin square; tie tightly with kitchen string.
2   Place muslin bag in large saucepan with remaining
ingredients; bring to the boil, stirring constantly. Reduce
heat; simmer, partially covered, stirring occasionally,
about 40 minutes or until dates are soft.
3   Remove and discard spice bag before using.

preparation time *10 minutes*
cooking time *45 minutes* makes *2½ cups*
nutritional count per tablespoon *1.9g total fat (0.2g
saturated fat); 343kJ (82 cal); 15g carbohydrate;
0.4g protein; 1.7g fibre*

curry kapitan

2 tablespoons vegetable oil
2 medium brown onions (300g), sliced thinly
¼ cup (60ml) water
1.5kg chicken pieces
2¼ cups (560ml) coconut milk
1 cup (250ml) coconut cream

SPICE PASTE

10 fresh small red thai chillies
4 cloves garlic
3 teaspoons grated fresh turmeric
2 teaspoons grated fresh galangal
2 teaspoons finely chopped fresh lemon grass
10 candlenuts
1 tablespoon ground cumin

1   Make spice paste.
2   Heat oil in wok; stir-fry onion, until soft. Stir in spice paste and the water; stir-fry until fragrant.
3   Add chicken and coconut milk; simmer, covered, 20 minutes. Remove lid; simmer, uncovered, further 30 minutes, stirring occasionally, or until chicken is tender. Stir in coconut cream.

SPICE PASTE   Blend or process ingredients until smooth.

preparation time *30 minutes*
cooking time *45 minutes* serves *6*
nutritional count per serving *58.8g total fat (32.3g saturated fat); 2888kJ (691 cal); 8.3g carbohydrate; 32.1g protein; 3.6g fibre*

mussels with kaffir lime and thai basil

1.5kg small black mussels
1 tablespoon peanut oil
3cm piece fresh ginger (15g), sliced thinly
1 clove garlic, sliced thinly
2 shallots (50g), sliced thinly
2 fresh long red chillies, sliced thinly
½ teaspoon ground turmeric
¼ cup (60ml) kecap manis
¼ cup (60ml) fish stock
¼ cup (60ml) water
2 tablespoons lime juice
2 fresh kaffir lime leaves, shredded finely
½ cup firmly packed fresh coriander leaves
½ cup firmly packed thai basil leaves

1   Scrub mussels under cold water; remove beards.
2   Heat oil in wok; stir-fry ginger, garlic, shallot, chilli and turmeric until fragrant. Add kecap manis, stock and the water; bring to the boil. Add mussels; simmer, covered, about 5 minutes or until mussels open (discard any that do not).
3   Remove from heat, add remaining ingredients; toss gently to combine.

preparation time *30 minutes*
cooking time *10 minutes* serves *4*
nutritional count per serving *5.6g total fat (1.1g saturated fat); 414kJ (99 cal); 3.9g carbohydrate; 7.5g protein; 0.7g fibre*

burmese clam and mussel stir-fry

500g large black mussels
500g clams
2 teaspoons shrimp paste
1 small red onion (100g), quartered
2 x 10cm sticks fresh lemon grass (40g), chopped finely
4 fresh kaffir lime leaves
2cm piece fresh galangal (10g), sliced thinly
2 tablespoons sambal oelek
1 tablespoon grated palm sugar
2 tablespoons peanut oil
¼ cup (60ml) lime juice
1 tablespoon cornflour
¼ cup (60ml) water
2 green onions, sliced thickly
1 fresh long red chilli, sliced thinly

1   Scrub mussels; remove beards.
2   Rinse clams under cold water; place in large bowl, sprinkle with salt, cover with water. Soak 1½ hours; rinse, drain.
3   Meanwhile, wrap shrimp paste securely in small piece of foil. Heat wok; stir-fry shrimp paste parcel until fragrant. Discard foil; blend or process shrimp paste with red onion, lemon grass, lime leaves, galangal, sambal and sugar until mixture forms a smooth paste.
4   Heat oil in wok; stir-fry paste 5 minutes. Add clams, mussels and juice; stir-fry 2 minutes. Cover wok; cook about 5 minutes or until clams and mussels open (discard any that do not).
5   Uncover wok, stir in blended cornflour and the water; stir-fry until sauce boils and thickens. Sprinkle with green onion and chilli.

preparation time *20 minutes (plus standing time)*
cooking time *15 minutes* serves *4*
nutritional count per serving *10.5g total fat (1.8g saturated); 723kJ (173 cal); 12.2g carbohydrate; 6.9g protein; 0.9g fibre*

baked mussels infused with asian-flavours

1.5kg large black mussels
8cm piece fresh ginger (40g), cut into matchsticks
1 clove garlic, sliced thinly
2 fresh kaffir lime leaves, shredded finely
2 fresh long red chillies, sliced thinly
1 medium carrot (120g), cut into matchsticks
1 medium red capsicum (200g), cut into matchsticks
⅓ cup (80ml) water
¼ cup (60ml) kecap manis
¼ cup (60ml) lime juice
½ cup (40g) bean sprouts
⅔ cup loosely packed fresh coriander leaves

1   Preheat oven to 220°C/200°C fan-forced.
2   Scrub mussels; remove beards.
3   Place mussels in large baking dish with ginger, garlic, lime leaves, chilli, carrot, capsicum, the water, kecap manis and juice.
4   Bake mussels, covered, about 20 minutes or until mussels open (discard any that do not). Remove from oven; stir in sprouts and coriander.

preparation time *20 minutes*
cooking time *20 minutes* serves *4*
nutritional count per serving *1.6g total fat (0.4g saturated fat); 414kJ (99 cal); 8.2g carbohydrate; 11.2g protein; 2.1g fibre*

mixed dhal

60g ghee
2 medium brown onions (300g), chopped finely
2 cloves garlic, crushed
1 tablespoon grated fresh ginger
1½ tablespoons black mustard seeds
1½ tablespoons ground cumin
1½ tablespoons ground coriander
2 teaspoons ground turmeric
¾ cup (150g) brown lentils
¾ cup (150g) red lentils
¾ cup (150g) yellow mung beans
¾ cup (150g) green split peas
800g canned tomatoes
1 litre (4 cups) vegetable stock
⅔ cup (160ml) coconut cream
¼ cup coarsely chopped fresh coriander

1   Heat ghee in large heavy-based saucepan; cook onion, garlic and ginger, stirring, until onion is soft. Add seeds and spices; cook, stirring, until fragrant.
2   Add lentils, beans and peas to pan; stir to combine. Add undrained crushed tomatoes and stock; bring to the boil. Reduce heat; simmer, covered, about 1 hour, stirring occasionally, until lentils are tender and mixture thickens.
3   Just before serving, add coconut cream and coriander; stir over low heat until heated through.

preparation time *10 minutes*
cooking time *1 hour 10 minutes* serves *8*
nutritional count per serving *13.9g total fat (9g saturated fat); 1618kJ (387 cal); 38.7g carbohydrate; 21g protein; 11.2g fibre*

bombay potato masala

1.5kg potatoes
20g butter
1 large brown onion (200g), sliced thinly
3 cloves garlic, crushed
1 teaspoon yellow mustard seeds
3 teaspoons garam masala
2 teaspoons ground coriander
2 teaspoons ground cumin
½ teaspoon chilli powder
¼ teaspoon ground turmeric
400g canned tomatoes

1   Cut potatoes into wedges. Boil, steam or microwave potato until just tender; drain.
2   Heat butter in large frying pan; cook onion and garlic, stirring, until onion is soft. Add seeds and spices; cook, stirring, until fragrant.
3   Stir in undrained crushed tomatoes; cook, stirring, 2 minutes or until sauce thickens slightly. Add potato; gently stir until heated through.

preparation time *10 minutes*
cooking time *15 minutes* serves *6*
nutritional count per serving *3.1g total fat (1.8g saturated fat); 602kJ (144 cal); 22.6g carbohydrate; 4.5g protein; 3.8g fibre*

butter chicken

1 cup (150g) raw cashews
2 teaspoons garam masala
2 teaspoons ground coriander
¾ teaspoon chilli powder
3 cloves garlic, chopped coarsely
2 teaspoons grated fresh ginger
2 tablespoons white vinegar
⅓ cup (80g) tomato paste
½ cup (140g) yogurt
1kg chicken thigh fillets, halved
80g butter
1 large brown onion (200g), chopped finely
1 cinnamon stick
4 cardamom pods, bruised
1 teaspoon paprika
400g can tomato puree
¾ cup (180ml) chicken stock
1 cup (250ml) cream
2 cups (400g) white long-grain rice

1 Stir nuts, garam masala, coriander and chilli in heated small frying pan until nuts are browned lightly.
2 Blend or process nut mixture with garlic, ginger, vinegar, paste and half of the yogurt until just smooth. Transfer mixture to large bowl, add remaining yogurt and chicken; stir to combine. Cover; refrigerate 3 hours.
3 Melt butter in large saucepan; cook onion, cinnamon and cardamom, stirring, until onion is browned. Add chicken mixture; cook 10 minutes.
4 Add paprika, puree and stock; bring to the boil. Reduce heat; simmer, uncovered, 45 minutes, stirring occasionally. Remove and discard cinnamon and cardamom. Add cream; simmer 5 minutes.
5 Meanwhile, cook rice in large saucepan of boiling water until tender. Drain.
6 Serve butter chicken with rice.

preparation time *30 minutes (plus refrigeration time)* cooking time *1 hour* serves *6*
nutritional count per serving *54.7g total fat (25.6g saturated fat); 3958kJ (947 cal); 67.9g carbohydrate; 44.2g protein; 4.7g fibre*

green tea ice-cream with fruit

2 tablespoons green tea powder
2 tablespoons boiling water
1 tablespoon caster sugar
1 vanilla bean
1 cup (250ml) milk
2 egg yolks
¼ cup (55g) caster sugar, extra
300ml thickened cream, whipped
10 fresh lychees (250g), chopped finely
2 medium kiwifruits (170g), chopped finely
½ small papaya (325g), chopped finely
1 tablespoon finely chopped fresh mint

1 Combine tea, the water and sugar in small bowl; stand 10 minutes.
2 Split vanilla bean lengthways; scrape out seeds. Place pod, seeds and milk in small saucepan; bring to the boil. Stir in tea mixture; stand 5 minutes.
3 Meanwhile, whisk egg yolks and extra sugar in small bowl until creamy; gradually whisk into hot milk mixture. Stir over low heat, without boiling, until mixture thickens slightly.
4 Strain mixture into medium heatproof bowl; discard pod. Cover surface of custard with plastic wrap; cool. Refrigerate about 1 hour or until cold.
5 Fold whipped cream into cold custard. Pour mixture into ice-cream maker; churn according to manufacturer's instructions (or place custard in shallow container, cover with foil; freeze until almost firm). Place ice-cream in large bowl, chop coarsely then beat with electric mixer until smooth. Cover; freeze until firm. Repeat process twice more.
6 Combine fruit and mint in small bowl. Serve with green tea ice-cream.

preparation time *15 minutes (plus refrigeration and freezing time)* cooking time *10 minutes* serves *4*
nutritional count per serving *33.5g total fat (20.9g saturated fat); 2123kJ (508 cal); 43.7g carbohydrate; 6.9g protein; 3.3g fibre*

1

2

3

4

pistachio, honey and cardamom kulfi

2 x 375ml cans evaporated milk
¾ cup (180ml) cream
3 cardamom pods, bruised
2 tablespoons honey
⅓ cup (45g) finely chopped roasted pistachios
2 tablespoons coarsely chopped roasted pistachios

1 Combine milk, cream and cardamom in large heavy-based saucepan; bring to the boil. Reduce heat; simmer, uncovered, stirring occasionally, about 10 minutes or until reduced to about 3 cups. Stir in honey, remove from heat; cool 15 minutes.
2 Strain mixture into large bowl; discard cardamom. Divide kulfi mixture among four ¾-cup (180ml) moulds; sprinkle with finely chopped nuts. Cover with foil; freeze 3 hours or overnight.
3 Turn kulfi onto serving plates; sprinkle with coarsely chopped nuts to serve.

preparation time *10 minutes (plus cooling and freezing time)* cooking time *15 minutes* serves *4*
nutritional count per serving *45.1g total fat (25.6g saturated fat); 2621kJ (627 cal); 36.3g carbohydrate; 19.3g protein; 1.7g fibre*

almond and rosewater jelly

3 cups (750ml) milk
1½ cups (240g) blanched almonds
⅓ cup (75g) caster sugar
3½ teaspoons gelatine
1 teaspoon rosewater
2 passionfruit
1 medium mango (430g), chopped coarsely
1 starfruit (160g), sliced thinly
565g can lychees, rinsed, drained

1 Grease 8cm x 26cm bar cake pan.
2 Blend milk, nuts and sugar until mixture forms a smooth puree. Transfer to medium saucepan; heat until hot but not boiling. Remove from heat; stand 1 hour.
3 Pour mixture into large jug; strain through muslin-lined sieve into same cleaned pan; discard solids. Sprinkle gelatine over mixture; stir over heat, without boiling, until dissolved. Remove from heat, stir in rosewater; pour mixture into pan. Cover; refrigerate 3 hours or overnight.
4 Scoop pulp from passionfruit into medium bowl with remaining fruit; toss gently to combine.
5 Turn jelly onto chopping board, cut into 24 cubes. Serve jelly with fruit.

preparation time *20 minutes (plus standing and refrigeration time)* cooking time *15 minutes* serves *4*
nutritional count per serving *41.2g total fat (6.9g saturated fat); 2955kJ (707 cal); 56.1g carbohydrate; 23g protein; 11.2g fibre*

1 PISTACHIO, HONEY AND CARDAMOM KULFI 2 ALMOND AND ROSEWATER JELLY 3 BANANA LUMPIA WITH BROWN SUGAR SYRUP AND COCONUT ICE-CREAM [P 594] 4 GULAB JAMAN [P 594]

ASIAN NEIGHBOURS   593

banana lumpia with syrup and coconut ice-cream

1 cup (250ml) water
¼ cup (55g) brown sugar
¼ cup (55g) caster sugar
1 vanilla bean, split lengthways
2 star anise
2 tablespoons white sugar
2 teaspoons ground cinnamon
1 tablespoon cornflour
1 tablespoon water, extra
3 small ripe bananas (390g)
12 small (12.5cm x 12.5cm) spring roll wrappers
vegetable oil, for deep-frying
¾ cup (35g) toasted flaked coconut

COCONUT ICE-CREAM

1 cup (75g) toasted shredded coconut
¼ cup (60ml) coconut-flavoured liqueur
1 litre vanilla ice-cream, softened

1 Make coconut ice-cream.
2 Stir the water, brown sugar, caster sugar, vanilla bean and star anise in small saucepan over heat, without boiling, until sugar dissolves. Bring to the boil; boil, uncovered, without stirring, about 15 minutes or until syrup thickens. Remove and discard solids.
3 Meanwhile, combine white sugar and cinnamon in small bowl. Blend cornflour with the extra water in another small bowl.
4 Quarter each banana lengthways. Centre one piece of banana on each wrapper then sprinkle each with about ½ teaspoon cinnamon sugar. Fold wrapper over banana ends then roll wrapper to enclose filling. Brush edges with cornflour mixture to seal.
5 Heat oil in wok; deep-fry lumpia, in batches, until golden brown and crisp. Drain on absorbent paper. Sprinkle with combined remaining cinnamon sugar and coconut, drizzle with syrup; serve with ice-cream.

COCONUT ICE-CREAM Fold coconut and liqueur through slightly softened ice-cream. Cover; freeze about 3 hours or overnight.

preparation time *20 minutes (plus freezing time)* cooking time *15 minutes* makes *12*
nutritional count per lumpia and ⅓ cup ice-cream *9.9g total fat (6.9g saturated fat); 882kJ (211 cal); 24.8g carbohydrate; 2.4g protein; 1.5g fibre*

gulab jaman

2 cups (440g) caster sugar
2 cups (500ml) water
8 cardamom pods, bruised
2 cinnamon sticks
3 star anise
1 teaspoon rosewater
½ cup (75g) self-raising flour
¼ cup (25g) full-cream milk powder
125g spreadable cream cheese
24 raisins
vegetable oil, for deep-frying

1 Stir sugar, the water and spices in medium saucepan over heat, without boiling, until sugar dissolves. Bring to the boil; boil, uncovered, without stirring, 5 minutes. Remove from heat; stir in rosewater. Cool.
2 Combine flour, milk powder and cream cheese in medium bowl; mix to a soft dough. Knead dough on floured surface about 10 minutes. Roll 1 heaped teaspoon of dough around each raisin.
3 Heat oil in wok; deep-fry balls, in batches, until golden brown. Drain on absorbent paper. Place gulab jaman in syrup; stand 1 hour before serving.

preparation time *20 minutes (plus standing time)* cooking time *15 minutes* makes *24*
nutritional count per gulab jaman *2.5g total fat (1.4g saturated fat); 477kJ (144 cal); 21.4g carbohydrate; 1g protein; 0.1g fibre*

coconut sago pudding with caramelised banana

5cm strip fresh lime rind
1 cup (200g) sago
½ cup (135g) firmly packed grated palm sugar
¼ cup (60ml) water
140ml can coconut cream
4 unpeeled sugar bananas (520g), halved lengthways
1 tablespoon grated palm sugar, extra
½ teaspoon finely grated lime rind

1   Place rind strip in large saucepan of cold water; bring to the boil. Discard rind; add sago. Reduce heat; simmer, uncovered, about 15 minutes or until sago is almost transparent. Drain; rinse under cold water, drain.
2   Meanwhile, stir sugar and the water in small saucepan over heat, without boiling, until sugar dissolves. Bring to the boil; boil, uncovered, without stirring, about 10 minutes or until syrup is toffee coloured. Remove from heat; stir in coconut cream. Cool 10 minutes.
3   Sprinkle cut side of banana with extra sugar. Place, cut-side down, on heated greased grill plate (or grill or barbecue). Cook about 5 minutes or until tender.
4   Combine sago in medium bowl with coconut mixture and grated rind. Divide among serving bowls; serve with banana, and extra lime rind, if you like.

preparation time *10 minutes*
cooking time *25 minutes* serves *4*
nutritional count per serving *7.5g total fat (6.4g saturated fat); 2065kJ (494 cal); 101.3g carbohydrate; 2.1g protein; 4.1g fibre*

coconut custards with papaya

½ cup (135g) grated palm sugar
⅓ cup (80ml) water
3 eggs
⅔ cup (160ml) coconut cream
2 tablespoons milk
1 teaspoon vanilla extract
1 large red papaya (580g)
2 teaspoons grated lime rind
1 tablespoon lime juice
1 tablespoon grated palm sugar, extra

1   Stir sugar and the water in small saucepan over low heat until sugar is dissolved.
2   Using a balloon whisk, lightly beat eggs, coconut cream and milk until combined, but not frothy. Gradually whisk hot sugar syrup into egg mixture, then stir in extract. Strain custard into heatproof jug.
3   Pour custard into four ⅔-cup (160ml) heatproof dishes. Place dishes in bamboo steamer, cover dishes with a sheet of baking paper; place lid on steamer; gently steam about 15 minutes or until just set.
4   Meanwhile, peel and seed papaya; cut into quarters. Combine papaya in medium bowl with rind, juice and extra sugar.
5   Cool custards 5 minutes; serve with papaya mixture.

preparation time *15 minutes*
cooking time *20 minutes* serves *4*
nutritional count per serving *13.5g total fat (9.1g saturated fat); 1492kJ (357 cal); 54.4g carbohydrate; 7.3g protein; 3g fibre*

SWEET TREATS

sweet lime mangoes

4 small mangoes (1.2kg)
1 tablespoon grated lime rind
1 tablespoon lime juice
1 tablespoon brown sugar
½ cup (140g) yogurt

1 Preheat grill.
2 Slice cheeks from mangoes; score each in shallow criss-cross pattern. Combine rind and juice; drizzle over each cheek, sprinkle each with 1 teaspoon sugar.
3 Place mangoes under grill until sugar caramelises. Serve with yogurt.

preparation time *5 minutes*
cooking time *8 minutes* serves *4*
nutritional count per serving *1.7g total fat (0.7g saturated fat); 798kJ (191 cal); 35.8g carbohydrate; 4.1g protein; 4.1g fibre*

honey grilled figs

6 large figs (480g), halved lengthways
2 tablespoons caster sugar
¼ cup (90g) honey
1 teaspoon vanilla extract

1 Preheat grill.
2 Place figs, cut-side up, on oven tray; sprinkle with sugar. Place under grill about 5 minutes or until sugar melts and figs are browned lightly.
3 Meanwhile stir honey and extract in small saucepan over low heat, without boiling, until honey is very runny.
4 Serve warm figs drizzled with honey mixture; serve with mascarpone, if you like.

preparation time *5 minutes*
cooking time *5 minutes* serves *6*
nutritional count per serving *0.2g total fat (0g saturated fat); 45kJ (108 cal); 24.1g carbohydrate; 1.1g protein; 1.8g fibre*

plums with sour cream

825g can plums in syrup, drained
½ cup (120g) sour cream
½ cup (140g) honey-flavoured yogurt
⅓ cup (75g) firmly packed brown sugar

1 Preheat grill.
2 Halve plums; discard stones. Divide plums among four 1-cup (250ml) shallow flameproof serving dishes.
3 Combine sour cream, yogurt and 2 tablespoons of the sugar in small bowl. Spoon sour cream mixture over plums; sprinkle with remaining sugar.
4 Place plums under grill about 3 minutes or until sugar dissolves.

preparation time *5 minutes*
cooking time *5 minutes* serves *4*
nutritional count per serving *13.2g total fat (8.6g saturated fat); 1371kJ (328 cal); 48.4g carbohydrate; 2.9g protein; 1.4g fibre*

grilled nectarines with passionfruit swirl yogurt

8 medium nectarines (1.3kg), halved, seeded
2 tablespoons brown sugar
1 tablespoon Grand Marnier
1 cup (280g) natural yogurt
2 tablespoons icing sugar
2 tablespoons passionfruit pulp

1 Preheat grill.
2 Place nectarines, cut-side up, in baking tray; sprinkle with sugar and liqueur. Place under grill until browned.
3 Meanwhile, combine yogurt and sugar in medium bowl; spoon into serving bowl, swirl with passionfruit.
4 Serve nectarines with passionfruit yogurt.

preparation *10 minutes*
cooking *10 minutes* serves *4*
nutritional count per serving *2.7g total fat (1.5g saturated fat); 1012kJ (242 cal); 40.1g carbohydrate; 6.8g protein; 8.2g fibre*

plum cobbler

825g can plums in syrup
¾ cup (110g) self-raising flour
¼ cup (55g) caster sugar
1 teaspoon ground cinnamon
60g butter, chopped
1 egg yolk
¼ cup (60ml) buttermilk, approximately
2 tablespoons coarsely chopped roasted hazelnuts
2 tablespoons icing sugar

1 Preheat oven to 180°C/160°C fan-forced.
2 Drain plums over medium saucepan. Halve plums;
discard stones. Add plums to pan; bring to the boil.
Reduce heat; simmer, uncovered, about 5 minutes or
until plums soften.
3 Strain plums; reserve ½ cup liquid. Place plums
and reserved liquid in 1-litre (4-cup) ovenproof dish;
place dish on oven tray.
4 Sift flour, caster sugar and cinnamon into medium
bowl; rub in butter. Stir in egg yolk and enough of the
buttermilk to make a soft, sticky dough. Drop heaped
teaspoons of the mixture over hot plums; sprinkle with nuts.
5 Bake cobbler, uncovered, about 30 minutes or until
browned lightly. Serve dusted with sifted icing sugar.

preparation time *15 minutes*
cooking time *40 minutes* serves *4*
nutritional count per serving *17.8g total fat (8.9g
saturated fat); 2019kJ (483 cal); 72.1g carbohydrate;
5.9g protein; 3.7g fibre*

blackberry clafoutis

2 teaspoons caster sugar
1 cup (150g) frozen blackberries
⅓ cup (80ml) milk
⅔ cup (160ml) fresh cream
1 teaspoon vanilla extract
4 eggs
½ cup (110g) caster sugar, extra
1 tablespoon plain flour

1 Preheat oven to 180°C/160°C fan-forced. Grease
four ¾-cup (180ml) shallow oven-proof dishes; sprinkle
inside of dishes with caster sugar. Divide blackberries
evenly among dishes.
2 Bring milk, cream and extract to the boil in small
saucepan. Remove from heat.
3 Whisk eggs and extra caster sugar in small bowl
until creamy. Whisk in flour and strained milk mixture.
Pour over blackberries in dishes.
4 Place dishes on oven tray; bake 20 minutes or until
browned and just set. Serve warm dusted with sifted
icing sugar, if you like.

preparation time *10 minutes*
cooking time *25 minutes* serves *4*
nutritional count per serving *23.5g total fat (13.6g
saturated fat); 1664kJ (398 cal); 36.8g carbohydrate;
8.9g protein; 2.4g fibre*

1

2

3

4

passionfruit buttermilk cake

250g butter, softened
1 cup (220g) caster sugar
3 eggs, separated
2 cups (300g) self-raising flour
¾ cup (180ml) buttermilk
¼ cup (60ml) passionfruit pulp

PASSIONFRUIT ICING

1½ cups (240g) icing sugar
¼ cup (60ml) passionfruit pulp, approximately

1 Preheat oven to 180°C/160°C fan-forced. Grease and lightly flour 24cm bundt tin; tap out excess flour.
2 Beat butter and sugar in small bowl with electric mixer until light and fluffy. Add egg yolks, one at a time, beating until just combined between additions.
3 Transfer mixture to large bowl; stir in half the sifted flour and half the buttermilk, then stir in remaining flour, buttermilk and passionfruit pulp.
4 Beat egg whites in small bowl with electric mixer until soft peaks form. Fold into cake mixture, in two batches. Spread mixture into tin.
5 Bake cake about 40 minutes. Stand in pan 5 minutes; turn onto wire rack to cool.
6 Make passionfruit icing; drizzle icing over cold cake.

PASSIONFRUIT ICING Sift icing sugar into heatproof bowl; stir in enough passionfruit pulp to form a firm paste. Stand bowl over small saucepan of simmering water, stir until icing is a pouring consistency (do not overheat).

preparation time *20 minutes*
cooking time *45 minutes (plus cooling time)* serves *8*
nutritional count per serving *28.6g total fat (17.9g saturated fat); 2679kJ (641 cal); 86.2g carbohydrate; 7.8g protein; 3.5g fibre*

queen of puddings

2 cups (140g) stale breadcrumbs
1 tablespoon caster sugar
1 teaspoon vanilla extract
1 teaspoon finely grated lemon rind
2½ cups (625ml) milk
60g butter
4 eggs, separated
¼ cup (80g) raspberry jam, warmed
¾ cup (165g) caster sugar, extra

1 Preheat oven to 180°C/160°C fan-forced. Grease six ¾-cup (180ml) ovenproof dishes; place on oven tray.
2 Combine breadcrumbs, sugar, extract and rind in large bowl. Heat milk and butter in medium saucepan until almost boiling, pour over bread mixture; stand 10 minutes. Stir in yolks. Divide mixture among dishes.
3 Bake puddings about 30 minutes. Carefully spread top of hot puddings with jam.
4 Beat egg whites in small bowl with electric mixer until soft peaks form; gradually add extra sugar, beating until sugar dissolves. Spoon meringue over puddings; bake about 10 minutes.

preparation time *20 minutes*
cooking time *40 minutes* serves 6
nutritional count per serving *16.6g total fat (9.3g saturated fat); 1843kJ (441 cal); 60.5g carbohydrate; 11.4g protein; 1.2g fibre*

caramelised bananas

100g butter
⅓ cup (75g) firmly packed brown sugar
¾ cup (165g) caster sugar
2 tablespoons water
½ cup (125ml) cream
4 large ripe bananas (920g), sliced thickly

1 Heat butter in large frying pan, add sugars and
the water; stir over heat, without boiling, until sugar
dissolves. Stir in cream; bring to the boil. Add banana,
stir gently to coat in caramel.
2 Serve caramelised bananas with ice-cream or
cream, if you like.

preparation time *10 minutes*
cooking time *5 minutes* serves 4
nutritional count per serving *34.2g total fat (22.4g
saturated fat); 2893kJ (692 cal); 91.1g carbohydrate;
3.4g protein; 3.4g fibre*

orange cake

150g butter, softened
1 tablespoon finely grated orange rind
⅔ cup (150g) caster sugar
3 eggs
1½ cups (225g) self-raising flour
¼ cup (60ml) milk
¾ cup (120g) icing sugar
1½ tablespoons orange juice

1 Preheat oven to 180°C/160°C fan-forced. Grease
deep 20cm-round cake pan.
2 Beat butter, rind, caster sugar, eggs, flour and milk in
medium bowl with electric mixer on low speed until just
combined. Increase speed to medium, beat 3 minutes
or until mixture is smooth. Spread mixture into pan.
3 Bake cake about 40 minutes. Stand in pan 5 minutes;
turn, top-side up, onto wire rack to cool.
4 Combine sifted icing sugar and juice in small bowl;
spread over cake.

preparation time *10 minutes*
cooking time *40 minutes* serves *12*
nutritional count per serving *12g total fat (7.3g
saturated fat); 1129kJ (270 cal); 36.4g carbohydrate;
3.8g protein; 0.7g fibre*

grilled bananas with vanilla cream

4 medium bananas (800g), halved lengthways
¼ cup (55g) brown sugar
20g butter
2 tablespoons coconut-flavoured liqueur
1 vanilla bean
⅔ cup (160ml) thickened cream
1 tablespoon icing sugar

1 Preheat grill.
2 Sprinkle bananas with 1 tablespoon of the brown
sugar; place under grill until browned lightly.
3 Meanwhile, stir remaining brown sugar, butter and
liqueur in small saucepan over low heat until smooth.
4 Split vanilla bean in half lengthways, scrape seeds
into small bowl; discard pod. Add cream and icing
sugar; beat with electric mixer until soft peaks form.
5 Serve banana with vanilla cream; drizzle with sauce.

preparation time *10 minutes*
cooking time *10 minutes* serves *4*
nutritional count per serving *19.1g total fat (12.5g
saturated fat); 1446kJ (346 cal); 35.3g carbohydrate;
3.2g protein; 2.9g fibre*

mixed nut cake

125g butter, softened
1 teaspoon finely grated lemon rind
1¼ cups (275g) caster sugar
3 eggs
½ cup (75g) self-raising flour
1 cup (150g) plain flour
¼ teaspoon bicarbonate of soda
½ cup (125ml) milk
1 tablespoon lemon juice
2 tablespoons pistachios, chopped finely
2 tablespoons walnuts, chopped finely
2 tablespoons slivered almonds, chopped finely
2 teaspoons icing sugar

NUT TOPPING

2 tablespoons pistachios, chopped coarsely
2 tablespoons walnuts, chopped coarsely
2 tablespoons slivered almonds

1   Preheat oven to 180°C/160°C fan-forced. Line base and side of deep 22cm-round cake pan with baking paper.
2   Make nut topping.
3   Beat butter, rind and sugar in small bowl with electric mixer until light and fluffy. Beat in eggs. Using wooden spoon, stir in sifted dry ingredients and milk, in two batches; stir in juice and nuts. Spoon mixture into pan, level surface of cake; sprinkle with nut topping.
4   Bake cake 30 minutes. Cover cake loosely with foil; bake further 45 minutes. Stand in pan 5 minutes; turn, top-side up, onto wire rack. Dust with sifted icing sugar before serving.

NUT TOPPING   Combine ingredients in small bowl.

preparation time *25 minutes*
baking time *1 hour 15 minutes* serves *14*
nutritional count per serving *15.6g total fat (5.9g saturated fat); 1246kJ (298 cal); 32.9g carbohydrate; 5.7g protein; 1.6g fibre*

caramel butter cake

125g butter
1 teaspoon vanilla extract
1 cup (220g) firmly packed brown sugar
2 eggs
1 tablespoon golden syrup
1 cup (150g) plain flour
½ cup (75g) self-raising flour
1 teaspoon ground cinnamon
½ cup milk

CARAMEL ICING

1 cup (220g) firmly packed brown sugar
60g butter
2 tablespoons milk
¾ cup (120g) icing sugar
2 teaspoons milk, extra

1   Preheat oven to 180°C/160°C fan-forced. Grease deep 20cm-round cake pan; line base with paper.
2   Beat butter, extract and sugar in small bowl with electric mixer until light and fluffy. Beat in eggs and golden syrup. Transfer mixture to large bowl; fold in sifted dry ingredients and milk. Pour mixture into pan.
3   Bake cake about 50 minutes. Stand in pan 5 minutes; turn, top-side up, onto wire rack to cool.
4   Meanwhile, make caramel icing; spread over top of cake.

CARAMEL ICING   Place sugar, butter and milk in small saucepan; stir constantly over heat without boiling until sugar is dissolved. Bring to the boil, uncovered, without stirring. Stir in sifted icing sugar, then extra milk to make a spreadable consistency.

preparation time *20 minutes*
cooking time *55 minutes* serves *12*
nutritional count per serving *14.3g total fat (9g saturated fat); 1639kJ (392 cal); 61.4g carbohydrate; 3.7g protein; 0.7g fibre*

lemon curd, blueberry and meringue trifle

2 cups (500ml) grape juice
85g packet blueberry jelly crystals
200g sponge cake, cut into 3cm pieces
¼ cup (60ml) sweet sherry
2 teaspoons finely grated lemon rind
¾ cup (180ml) lemon juice
1 cup (220g) caster sugar
4 eggs
80g butter, chopped coarsely
1 teaspoon gelatine
1 tablespoon water
300ml thickened cream
50g meringue, chopped coarsely
2 cups (300g) fresh blueberries

1 Bring grape juice to the boil in small saucepan; stir in jelly crystals until dissolved. Pour jelly mixture into shallow container. Refrigerate about 20 minutes or until jelly is almost set.
2 Place cake in 3-litre (12-cup) bowl; sprinkle with sherry.
3 Combine rind, juice, sugar, eggs and butter in medium heatproof bowl. Place over medium saucepan of simmering water; cook, stirring, about 15 minutes or until curd coats the back of a spoon.
4 Sprinkle gelatine over the water in small heatproof jug. Stand jug in small saucepan of simmering water; stir until gelatine dissolves. Stir gelatine mixture into warm lemon curd. Cool to room temperature.
5 Pour jelly over cake; refrigerate 15 minutes. Top with lemon curd. Cover; refrigerate 3 hours or overnight.
6 Just before serving, beat cream in small bowl with electric mixer until soft peaks form; spread over curd. Sprinkle with meringue and berries.

preparation time *30 minutes (plus refrigeration and cooling time)* cooking time *20 minutes* serves 6 nutritional count per serving *34.7g total fat (21g saturated fat); 3168kJ (758 cal); 97.5g carbohydrate; 10.6g protein; 1.3g fibre*

passionfruit and coconut crème brûlèe

1 egg
2 egg yolks
2 tablespoons caster sugar
¼ cup (60ml) passionfruit pulp
280ml can coconut cream
½ cup (125ml) cream
1 tablespoon brown sugar

1 Preheat oven to 180°C/160°C fan-forced.
2 Combine egg, egg yolks, caster sugar and passionfruit in medium heatproof bowl.
3 Combine coconut cream and cream in small saucepan; bring to the boil. Gradually whisk hot cream mixture into egg mixture. Place bowl over medium saucepan of simmering water; stir over heat about 10 minutes or until custard thickens slightly.
4 Divide custard among four deep ½-cup (125ml) heatproof dishes. Place dishes in large baking dish; pour enough boiling water into baking dish to come halfway up sides of dishes.
5 Bake custards, uncovered, about 30 minutes or until set. Remove dishes from water; cool. Cover; refrigerate 3 hours or overnight.
6 Preheat grill.
7 Place dishes in shallow flameproof dish filled with ice cubes. Sprinkle each custard with 1 teaspoon brown sugar; using finger, gently smooth sugar over the surface of each custard. Place under grill until tops of crème brûlèe caramelise.

preparation time *15 minutes (plus refrigeration time)*
cooking time *50 minutes* serves *4*
nutritional count per serving *30.3g total fat (21.6g saturated fat); 1526kJ (365 cal); 16.7g carbohydrate; 5.7g protein; 3.3g fibre*

ginger crème caramels

¾ cup (165g) caster sugar
¾ cup (180ml) water
2 tablespoons finely chopped glacé ginger
4 eggs
1 teaspoon vanilla extract
¼ cup (55g) caster sugar, extra
1¼ cups (310ml) milk
¾ cup (180ml) thickened cream

1 Preheat oven to 180°C/160°C fan-forced.
2 Stir sugar, the water and ginger in medium saucepan over heat, without boiling, until sugar is dissolved. Bring to the boil; boil, uncovered, without stirring, 2 minutes. Strain sugar syrup. Return sugar syrup to same pan; bring back to the boil. Boil, uncovered, without stirring, about 3 minutes or until golden brown.
3 Pour caramel mixture into six ¾-cup (180ml) ovenproof dishes.
4 Whisk eggs, extract and extra sugar together in medium bowl. Combine milk and cream in medium saucepan, bring to boil, remove from heat, allow bubbles to subside; gradually whisk into egg mixture. Strain prepared custard into jug.
5 Place dishes in large baking dish; pour custard into dishes. Pour enough boiling water into baking dish to come half-way up sides of dishes.
6 Bake custards about 25 minutes or until just set. Remove dishes from water, cool to room temperature; refrigerate overnight.
7 Turn custards onto plates, serve with extra glacé ginger and strawberries, if you like.

preparation time *25 minutes (plus refrigeration time)*
cooking time *40 minutes* serves *6*
nutritional count per serving *16.7g total fat (9.7g saturated fat); 1509kJ (361 cal); 45.7g carbohydrate; 6.9g protein; 0g fibre*

coffee and walnut cake

30g butter

1 tablespoon brown sugar

2 teaspoons ground cinnamon

200g roasted walnuts

½ cup (125ml) milk

1 tablespoon instant coffee granules

185g butter, extra

1⅓ cups (300g) caster sugar

3 eggs

1 cup (150g) self-raising flour

¾ cup (110g) plain flour

TOFFEE

½ cup (110g) caster sugar

2 tablespoons water

3 teaspoons cream

1   Preheat oven to 160°C/140°C fan-forced. Grease and flour 22cm-baba cake pan; shake out excess flour.

2   Melt butter in small saucepan, add brown sugar, cinnamon and walnuts; stir well. Cool.

3   Stir milk and coffee in small bowl until coffee is dissolved.

4   Beat extra butter and caster sugar in small bowl with electric mixer until light and fluffy; beat in eggs. Fold in sifted flours, then milk mixture.

5   Spread one third of the cake mixture in base of pan, sprinkle with half walnut mixture, top with remaining cake mixture.

6   Bake cake about 45 minutes or until cooked when tested. Stand in pan 5 minutes; turn onto wire rack to cool.

7   Make toffee.

8   Place cake on wire rack over oven tray; drizzle some of the toffee on top of cake. Press on remaining walnut mixture; drizzle with remaining toffee.

TOFFEE Stir sugar and the water in small saucepan over low heat until sugar dissolves. Bring to the boil, simmer, uncovered, until sugar browns slightly. Add cream and stir 1 minute or until thickened slightly.

preparation time *20 minutes* cooking time *45 minutes (plus cooling and standing time)* serves *8*
nutritional count per serving *43.1g total fat (17.2g saturated fat); 3110kJ (744 cal); 77.8g carbohydrate; 10.2g protein; 2.9g fibre*

apple sponge

4 large apples (about 800g)

¼ cup (55g) caster sugar

¼ cup (60ml) water

SPONGE TOPPING

2 eggs

⅓ cup (75g) caster sugar

2 tablespoons cornflour

2 tablespoons plain flour

2 tablespoons self-raising flour

1   Preheat oven to 180°C/160°C fan-forced.

2   Peel, core, quarter and slice apples. Place in medium saucepan with sugar and the water; cook, covered, about 10 minutes or until apples are tender.

3   Meanwhile, make sponge topping.

4   Spoon hot apple mixture into deep 1.5-litre (6-cup) round ovenproof dish; spread sponge topping over hot apple mixture.

5   Bake sponge dessert about 25 minutes.

SPONGE TOPPING Beat eggs in small bowl with electric mixer about 7 minutes or until thick and creamy. Gradually add sugar, beating until dissolved between additions. Fold in sifted flours.

preparation time *15 minutes*
cooking time *40 minutes* serves *4*
nutritional count per serving *2.9g total fat (0.8g saturated fat); 1275kJ (305 cal); 62.1g carbohydrate; 5g protein; 3.3g fibre*

minted white chocolate mousse

This mixture will make 2 cups mousse; divide it among small glasses for serving – 40ml shot glasses will give you about 12 delicious mini servings.

30g butter
120g white eating chocolate
2 egg whites
⅔ cup (160ml) thickened cream, whipped
green food colouring
2 teaspoons mint-flavoured liqueur

1 Melt butter in small saucepan or in microwave oven; stand 2 minutes. Skim off and reserve clarified butter from the top, leaving milky solids; discard solids.
2 Melt chocolate in medium heatproof bowl over a medium saucepan of simmering water; stir in clarified butter.
3 Beat egg whites in small bowl with electric mixer until soft peaks form. Gently fold egg white, cream and colouring into white chocolate mixture; stir in liqueur.
4 Divide mousse among serving glasses; refrigerate about 3 hours or overnight.
5 Decorate mousse with sliced strawberries and fresh mint leaves, if you like.

preparation time *15 minutes (plus refrigeration and standing time)* cooking time *10 minutes* serves *12* nutritional count per serving *10.3g total fat (6.7g saturated fat); 523kJ (125 cal); 6.3g carbohydrate; 1.6g protein; 0g fibre*

polenta puddings with glazed oranges

125g butter, softened
1 tablespoon finely grated orange rind
1 cup (220g) caster sugar
2 eggs
1 cup (150g) self-raising flour
⅓ cup (50g) plain flour
¼ cup (40g) polenta
⅓ cup (80ml) orange juice
4 small oranges (720g), peeled, sliced

ORANGE SYRUP

1 cup (250ml) orange juice, strained
½ cup (125ml) water
¾ cup (165g) caster sugar

1 Preheat oven to 160°C/140°C fan-forced. Grease six ¾-cup (180ml) dariole moulds or ovenproof dishes; line bases with baking paper.
2 Beat butter, rind and sugar in small bowl with electric mixer until just combined. Beat in eggs. Stir in sifted flours, polenta and juice. Divide mixture among moulds; place on oven tray.
3 Bake puddings about 30 minutes.
4 Meanwhile, make orange syrup.
5 Turn puddings onto oven tray; brush each pudding all over with about 2 tablespoons of the hot syrup.
6 In medium frying pan, bring remaining syrup to the boil. Add orange slices, simmer 2 minutes or until oranges are heated through. Serve puddings with orange slices.

ORANGE SYRUP Stir ingredients in medium saucepan over medium heat until sugar dissolves. Boil, uncovered, about 3 minutes or until syrup thickens slightly.

preparation time *20 minutes*
cooking time *40 minutes* serves *6*
nutritional count per serving *19.5g total fat (11.9g saturated fat); 2633kJ (630 cal); 104g carbohydrate; 7.4g protein; 3.3g fibre*

fruit mince and brioche pudding

475g jar fruit mince
2 tablespoons brandy
300g brioche, sliced thickly
1 tablespoon demerara sugar

CUSTARD

2 cups (500ml) cream
1½ cups (375ml) milk
⅓ cup (75g) caster sugar
½ teaspoon vanilla extract
4 eggs

1 Preheat oven to 160°C/140°C fan-forced. Grease shallow 2-litre (8-cup) ovenproof dish.
2 Make custard.
3 Combine fruit mince and brandy in small bowl.
4 Layer brioche and half the fruit mixture, overlapping brioche slightly, in dish. Dollop spoonfuls of remaining fruit mixture over brioche. Pour custard over brioche; sprinkle with sugar.
5 Place dish in large baking dish; add enough boiling water to come halfway up sides of dish.
6 Bake pudding about 45 minutes or until set. Remove pudding from baking dish; stand 5 minutes before serving.

CUSTARD Bring cream, milk, sugar and extract to the boil in medium saucepan. Whisk eggs in large bowl; whisking constantly, gradually add hot cream mixture to egg mixture.

preparation time *20 minutes*
cooking time *50 minutes* serves *6*
nutritional count per serving *50.4g total fat (29.9g saturated fat); 3632kJ (869 cal); 85.6g carbohydrate; 13.4g protein; 3.5g fibre*

white chocolate and raspberry croissant pudding

5 croissants (300g), sliced thinly
⅓ cup (110g) raspberry jam
100g white eating chocolate, chopped coarsely
1 cup (135g) raspberries

CUSTARD

1½ cups (375ml) cream
1¼ cups (310ml) milk
⅓ cup (75g) caster sugar
1 teaspoon vanilla extract
4 eggs

1 Preheat oven to 160°C/140°C fan-forced. Grease shallow 2-litre (8-cup) ovenproof dish.
2 Make custard.
3 Layer croissant slices, overlapping slightly, in dish; dollop spoonfuls of jam over slices. Sprinkle with chocolate and berries. Pour custard over the top.
4 Place dish in large baking dish; add enough boiling water to come halfway up sides of ovenproof dish.
5 Bake pudding about 1 hour or until set. Remove pudding from baking dish; stand 5 minutes before serving.

CUSTARD Bring cream, milk, sugar and extract to the boil in medium saucepan. Whisk eggs in large bowl; whisking constantly, gradually add hot cream mixture to egg mixture.

preparation time *15 minutes*
cooking time *1 hour* serves *8*
nutritional count per serving *37.5g total fat (22.7g saturated fat); 2328kJ (557 cal); 44g carbohydrate; 10.4g protein; 2.2g fibre*

chocolate bread and butter pudding

2 small brioche (200g), sliced thickly
100g dark eating chocolate, chopped coarsely
⅓ cup (40g) coarsely chopped toasted pecans
CUSTARD
2 cups (500ml) cream
1½ cups (375ml) milk
⅓ cup (75g) caster sugar
1 vanilla bean
4 eggs

1 Preheat oven to 180°C/160°C fan-forced.
Grease shallow 2-litre (8-cup) ovenproof dish.
2 Make custard.
3 Layer brioche in dish with chocolate and nuts,
overlapping brioche slightly. Pour custard over brioche.
4 Place dish in large baking dish; add enough boiling
water to come halfway up sides of dish.
5 Bake pudding about 45 minutes or until set. Remove
pudding from baking dish; stand 5 minutes before serving.

CUSTARD Combine cream, milk and sugar in small
saucepan. Split vanilla bean in half lengthways; scrape
seeds into pan then add pod. Stir over heat until hot;
strain into large heatproof jug, discard pod. Whisk
eggs in large bowl; whisking constantly, pour hot cream
mixture into egg mxiture.

preparation time *20 minutes*
cooking time *50 minutes* serves *6*
nutritional count per serving *50.1g total fat (27.8g
saturated fat); 2796kJ (669 cal); 45g carbohydrate;
12.6g protein; 1.4g fibre*

rhubarb coconut cake

1½ cups (225g) self-raising flour
1¼ cups (275g) caster sugar
1¼ cups (110g) desiccated coconut
125g butter, melted
3 eggs, beaten lightly
½ cup (125ml) milk
1 teaspoon vanilla extract
¾ cup (90g) finely chopped rhubarb
2 stalks rhubarb (125g), extra
2 tablespoons demerara sugar

1 Preheat oven to 180°C/160°C fan-forced.
Grease deep 20cm-round cake pan; line base with
baking paper.
2 Combine flour, caster sugar and coconut in medium
bowl; stir in butter, egg, milk and extract until combined.
3 Spread half the mixture into pan; scatter chopped
rhubarb evenly over mixture. Spread remaining mixture
over rhubarb.
4 Cut extra rhubarb into 5cm lengths; arrange over
top of cake, sprinkle with demerara sugar.
5 Bake cake about 1¼ hours. Stand in pan 5 minutes;
turn onto wire rack to cool.

preparation time *25 minutes*
cooking time *1 hour 15 minutes (plus standing time)*
serves *10*
nutritional count per serving *19.8g total fat (13.9g
saturated fat); 1697kJ (406 cal); 48.8g carbohydrate;
6g protein; 3.8g fibre*

1 CHOCOLATE BREAD AND BUTTER PUDDING
2 RHUBARB COCONUT CAKE 3 APPLE PIE SLICE [P 612]
4 CHERRY AND SULTANA BUTTER CAKE WITH COCONUT FROSTING [P 612]

1

2

3

4

apple pie slice

1 cup (150g) self-raising flour
½ cup (75g) plain flour
80g cold butter, chopped coarsely
¼ cup (55g) caster sugar
1 egg, beaten lightly
¼ cup (60ml) milk, approximately
1 tablespoon milk, extra
1 tablespoon caster sugar, extra

APPLE FILLING

6 medium apples (900g), peeled, cored,
   cut into 1cm pieces
¼ cup (55g) caster sugar
¼ cup (60ml) water
¾ cup (120g) sultanas
1 teaspoon mixed spice
2 teaspoons finely grated lemon rind

1 Make apple filling.
2 Grease 20cm x 30cm lamington pan; line base with baking paper, extending paper 5cm over long sides.
3 Sift flours into medium bowl, rub in butter. Stir in sugar, egg and enough milk to make a firm dough. Knead on floured surface until smooth. Cover; refrigerate 30 minutes.
4 Preheat oven to 200°C/180°C fan-forced.
5 Divide dough in half. Roll one half large enough to cover base of pan; press firmly into pan. Spread apple filling over dough. Roll remaining dough large enough to cover filling and place over the top. Brush with extra milk; sprinkle with extra sugar.
6 Bake about 25 minutes; stand in pan 5 minutes.

APPLE FILLING Cook apple, sugar and the water in large saucepan, uncovered, stirring occasionally, about 10 minutes or until apple softens. Remove from heat; stir in sultanas, spice and rind. Cool.

preparation time *20 minutes (plus refrigeration time)*
cooking time *25 minutes* serves *8*
nutritional count per serving *9.7g total fat (5.9g saturated fat); 1463kJ (350 cal); 58.6g carbohydrate; 4.8g protein; 3.4g fibre*

cherry and sultana buttercake with coconut frosting

250g butter, softened
1 teaspoon vanilla extract
1 cup (220g) caster sugar
3 eggs
1¼ cups (185g) plain flour
1 cup (150g) self-raising flour
⅓ cup (80ml) milk
1 cup (160g) sultanas
¾ cup (150g) coarsely chopped red glacé cherries

COCONUT FROSTING

1 cup (160g) icing sugar
¾ cup (60g) desiccated coconut
1 egg white
pink food colouring

1 Preheat oven to 180°C/160°C fan-forced. Grease deep 22cm-round cake pan; line with baking paper.
2 Beat butter, extract and sugar in medium bowl with electric mixer until light and fluffy. Beat in eggs, one at a time. Stir in sifted flours and milk, in two batches. Stir in sultanas and cherries. Spread mixture into pan.
3 Bake cake about 1 hour. Stand in pan 5 minutes; turn, top-side up, onto wire rack to cool.
4 Meanwhile, make coconut frosting. Top cake with coconut frosting.

COCONUT FROSTING Sift icing sugar into medium bowl; stir in coconut and egg white until combined. Tint lightly with pink colouring.

preparation time *30 minutes*
cooking time *1 hour* serves *12*
nutritional count per serving *22.3g total fat (14.8g saturated fat); 2144kJ (513 cal); 70.7g carbohydrate; 5.9g protein; 2.5g fibre*

upside-down chocolate caramel nut cake

2 tablespoons chopped roasted unsalted macadamias
2 tablespoons chopped roasted unsalted pistachios
2 tablespoons chopped roasted unsalted walnuts
125g butter, chopped
1 cup (200g) firmly packed brown sugar
3 eggs
1 cup (150g) self-raising flour
¼ cup (35g) plain flour
¼ teaspoon bicarbonate of soda
⅓ cup (35g) cocoa powder
100g dark eating chocolate, melted
¾ cup (180ml) milk

CARAMEL TOPPING

40g butter
¼ cup (55g) brown sugar
2 tablespoons cream

1   Preheat oven to 160°C/140°C fan-forced. Grease deep 20cm-round cake pan; line base with baking paper.
2   Make caramel topping.
3   Pour topping over base of pan, sprinkle combined nuts over caramel; freeze while preparing cake mixture.
4   Beat butter and sugar in small bowl with electric mixer until light and fluffy. Beat in eggs, one at a time. Stir in sifted flours, soda and cocoa powder, then chocolate and milk. Spread mixture over caramel.
5   Bake cake about 1 hour 10 minutes. Stand in pan 15 minutes; turn onto a wire rack to cool.

CARAMEL TOPPING Stir butter, sugar and cream in small saucepan over low heat, without boiling, until sugar is dissolved. Bring to the boil; remove from heat.

preparation time *30 minutes*
cooking time *1 hour 15 minutes (plus standing time)*
serves *10*
nutritional count per serving *25g total fat (13.5g saturated fat); 1839kJ (440 cal); 46.5g carbohydrate; 6.7g protein; 1.4g fibre*

cardamom almond cake

185g butter
¾ cup (165g) firmly packed brown sugar
2 eggs
2 cups (300g) self-raising flour
2 teaspoons ground cardamom
¼ cup (30g) almond meal
½ cup (115g) golden syrup
½ cup (125ml) milk

1   Preheat oven to 180°C/160°C fan-forced. Grease a 20cm baba pan.
2   Beat butter and sugar in small bowl of electric mixer until light and fluffy. Beat in eggs. Transfer mixture to large bowl. Stir in sifted flour and cardamom and almond meal with combined syrup and milk, in two batches. Pour mixture into pan.
3   Bake cake about 50 minutes. Stand in pan 5 minutes; turn onto wire rack to cool. Dust with sifted icing sugar before serving, if you like.

preparation time *20 minutes*
cooking time *50 minutes* serves *10*
nutritional count per serving *18.7g total fat (10.8g saturated fat); 1588kJ (380 cal); 46.7g carbohydrate; 5.5g protein; 1.4g fibre*

almond pear flan

1¼ cups (185g) plain flour
90g butter
¼ cup (55g) caster sugar
2 egg yolks
3 firm ripe medium pears (690g), peeled,
    cored, quartered
2 tablespoons apricot jam, warmed, strained

ALMOND FILLING

125g butter
⅓ cup (75g) caster sugar
2 eggs
1 cup (120g) almond meal
1 tablespoon plain flour

1   Blend or process flour, butter, sugar and egg yolks
until just combined. Knead on floured surface until
smooth. Cover; refrigerate 30 minutes.
2   Meanwhile, make almond filling.
3   Preheat oven to 180°C/160°C fan-forced.
Grease 23cm-round loose-based flan tin.
4   Roll dough between sheets of baking paper until
large enough to line tin; ease dough evenly into base
and side of tin. Spread filling into pastry case; arrange
pears over filling.
5   Bake flan about 45 minutes. Brush top with jam.

ALMOND FILLING Beat butter and sugar in small bowl
with electric mixer until just combined. Add eggs, one
at a time; fold in meal and flour.

preparation time *30 minutes (plus refrigeration time)*
cooking time *45 minutes* serves *10*
nutritional count per serving *26.7g total fat (12.7g
saturated fat); 1785kJ (427 cal); 38.8g carbohydrate;
6.8g protein; 2.9g fibre*

vanilla pear almond cake

8 small corella pears (800g)
2½ cups (625ml) water
1 strip lemon rind
1¾ cups (385g) caster sugar
1 vanilla bean
125g butter, chopped
3 eggs
⅔ cup (160g) sour cream
⅔ cup (100g) plain flour
⅔ cup (100g) self-raising flour
¼ cup (40g) blanched almonds, roasted,
    chopped coarsely
40g dark eating chocolate, chopped coarsely
½ cup (60g) almond meal

1   Peel pears, leaving stems intact.
2   Place the water, rind and 1 cup of the sugar in
medium saucepan. Split vanilla bean in half lengthways;
scrape seeds into pan, then add pod. Stir over heat,
without boiling, until sugar dissolves. Add pears; bring
to the boil. Reduce heat; simmer, covered, 30 minutes
or until pears are just tender. Transfer pears to medium
bowl; bring syrup to the boil. Boil, uncovered, until
syrup reduces by half. Cool completely.
3   Preheat oven to 160°C/140°C fan-forced. Insert
base of 23cm springform tin upside-down in tin to
give a flat base; grease tin.
4   Beat butter and remaining sugar in medium bowl
with electric mixer until light and fluff. Beat in eggs.
Beat in sour cream until just combined (mixture may
curdle at this stage but will come together later). Stir in
2 tablespoons of the syrup, then flours, nuts, chocolate
and almond meal. Spread mixture into tin; place pears
upright around edge of tin, gently pushing to the base.
5   Bake cake, uncovered, about 1 hour 35 minutes.
Stand in pan 10 minutes; remove from tin. Serve warm,
brushed with remaining syrup.

preparation time *30 minutes*
cooking time *2 hours 15 minutes (plus cooling and
standing time)* serves *8*
nutritional count per serving *31.4g total fat (15.6g
saturated fat); 2675kJ (640 cal); 78.7g carbohydrate;
8.6g protein; 3.7g fibre*

date and butterscotch
self-saucing pudding

1 cup (150g) self-raising flour
½ cup (110g) firmly packed brown sugar
20g butter, melted
½ cup (125ml) milk
½ cup (70g) finely chopped dried seedless dates

CARAMEL SAUCE

½ cup (110g) firmly packed brown sugar
1¾ cups (430ml) boiling water
50g butter

1 Preheat oven to 180°C/160°C fan-forced.
Grease 2-litre (8-cup) shallow ovenproof dish.
2 Combine flour, sugar, butter, milk and dates in
medium bowl. Spread pudding mixture into dish.
3 Make caramel sauce; pour sauce slowly over
back of spoon onto mixture in dish.
4 Bake pudding about 45 minutes or until centre
is firm. Stand 5 minutes before serving.

CARAMEL SAUCE Stir ingredients in medium heatproof
jug until sugar is dissolved.

preparation time *20 minutes*
cooking time *45 minutes* serves *6*
nutritional count per serving *10.7g total fat (6.9g
saturated fat); 1526kJ (365 cal); 62.1g carbohydrate;
3.5g protein; 2.1g fibre*

orange and raspberry
self-saucing pudding

¼ cup (20g) flaked almonds
30g butter
¾ cup (110g) self-raising flour
⅓ cup (80ml) milk
⅔ cup (150g) firmly packed brown sugar
2 teaspoons finely grated orange rind
¾ cup (110g) frozen raspberries
¼ cup (60ml) orange juice
¾ cup (180ml) boiling water

1 Grease shallow 1.5-litre (6-cup) microwave-safe dish.
2 Place nuts in small microwave-safe bowl; cook,
uncovered, in microwave oven on HIGH (100%)
about 2 minutes or until browned lightly.
3 Place butter in medium microwave-safe bowl;
cook, uncovered, in microwave oven on HIGH (100%)
30 seconds. Add flour, milk and half of the sugar;
whisk until smooth. Stir in rind and raspberries; spread
into dish.
4 Sprinkle remaining sugar over raspberry mixture;
carefully pour over combined juice and boiling water.
5 Place pudding on microwave-safe rack; cook,
uncovered, in microwave oven on MEDIUM-HIGH
(70%-80%) about 12 minutes. Stand 5 minutes.
6 Sprinkle pudding with nuts. Serve with cream or
ice-cream, if you like.

preparation time *5 minutes*
cooking time *15 minutes* serves *4*
nutritional count per serving *10.2g total fat (4.8g
saturated fat); 1501kJ (359 cal); 60g carbohydrate;
4.9g protein; 3g fibre*

choc cherry self-saucing pudding

60g butter, chopped
1½ cups (225g) self-raising flour
1 cup (220g) caster sugar
⅓ cup (35g) cocoa powder
1¼ cups (310ml) milk
1 teaspoon vanilla extract
2 x 55g Cherry Ripe bars, chopped coarsely
½ cup (110g) firmly packed brown sugar
1 tablespoon cocoa powder, extra
2 cups (500ml) boiling water
50g butter, chopped, extra

1 Melt butter in deep 3-litre (12-cup) microwave-safe dish, uncovered, on HIGH (100%) in microwave oven about 1 minute or until butter has melted. Using oven mitts, remove dish from microwave oven.
2 Add sifted flour, caster sugar and cocoa to dish with milk and extract; whisk until smooth. Stir in Cherry Ripe.
3 Combine brown sugar and sifted extra cocoa in medium jug; gradually stir in the boiling water. Add extra butter; stir until butter melts. Carefully pour syrup mixture evenly over pudding mixture.
4 Cook, uncovered, on HIGH (100%) in microwave oven about 15 minutes or until just cooked in centre. Using oven mitts, remove dish from microwave oven; stand 5 minutes before serving with cream, if you like.

preparation time *10 minutes*
cooking time *15 minutes* serves *8*
nutritional count per serving *16.9g total fat (11.3g saturated fat); 1948kJ (466 cal); 71.1g carbohydrate; 5.8g protein; 2g fibre*

cherries jubilee

425g can seeded black cherries
1 tablespoon caster sugar
1 cinnamon stick
2 teaspoons arrowroot
1 tablespoon water
⅓ cup (80ml) brandy

1 Drain cherries, reserve syrup. Combine syrup, sugar and cinnamon in small saucepan; cook, stirring, until mixture boils. Reduce heat; simmer, uncovered, without stirring, 2 minutes. Strain syrup into small heatproof bowl; discard cinnamon.
2 Return syrup to pan; stir in blended arrowroot and the water. Cook, stirring, until mixture boils and thickens slightly. Add cherries; stir until heated through.
3 Heat brandy in small saucepan; stir into cherry mixture. Serve immediately, with thickened cream and macaroons, if you like.

preparation time *5 minutes*
cooking time *10 minutes* serves *4*
nutritional count per serving *0.1g total fat (0g saturated fat); 589kJ (141 cal); 22.5g carbohydrate; 1g protein; 1.8g fibre*

mini choc-chip friands

3 egg whites
90g butter, melted
½ cup (60g) almond meal
¾ cup (120g) icing sugar
¼ cup (35g) plain flour
100g dark eating chocolate, chopped finely
¼ cup (60ml) cream
100g dark eating chocolate, extra

1 Preheat oven to 180°C/160°C fan-forced.
Grease two 12-hole mini (2-tablespoon/40ml)
muffin pans.
2 Place egg whites in medium bowl; whisk lightly
with fork. Stir in butter, almond meal, sifted icing
sugar and flour and chopped chocolate. Spoon
mixture into pan holes.
3 Bake friands about 15 minutes or until browned
lightly and cooked through. Stand friands in pans
5 minutes; turn, top-side up, onto wire racks to cool.
4 Meanwhile, stir cream and extra chocolate in
medium heatproof bowl over medium saucepan
of simmering water until just melted. Stand until
thickened. Spoon chocolate mixture over tops
of friands.

preparation time *20 minutes*
cooking time *20 minutes (plus standing time)*
makes *24*
nutritional count per friand *7.9g total fat (4.2g
saturated fat); 518kJ (124 cal); 11.5g carbohydrate;
1.6g protein; 0.4g fibre*

berry cream roulade

3 eggs
½ cup (110g) caster sugar
½ cup (75g) wheaten cornflour
1 tablespoon custard powder
1 teaspoon cream of tartar
½ teaspoon bicarbonate of soda
1 tablespoon caster sugar, extra
1 tablespoon icing sugar

BERRY CREAM
¾ cup (180ml) thickened cream
1 teaspoon vanilla extract
1 tablespoon icing sugar
1 cup (150g) frozen blackberries, chopped coarsely

1 Preheat oven to 180°C/160°C fan-forced.
Grease 25cm x 30cm swiss roll pan; line base and
two long sides with baking paper, extending paper
5cm over long sides.
2 Beat eggs and caster sugar in small bowl with
electric mixer about 5 minutes or until sugar is dissolved
and mixture is thick and creamy; transfer to large bowl.
3 Sift cornflour, custard powder, cream of tartar and
soda together twice onto paper then sift over egg
mixture; gently fold dry ingredients into egg mixture.
Spread mixture into pan; bake about 12 minutes.
4 Meanwhile, place piece of baking paper cut the same
size as pan on bench; sprinkle with extra caster sugar.
5 Turn sponge onto sugared paper; peel lining paper
away. Cool; trim all sides of sponge. Cover with a
tea towel; cool.
6 Meanwhile, make berry cream; spread cream over
sponge. Using paper as a guide, roll sponge gently
from long side to enclose filling. Dust with icing sugar.

BERRY CREAM Beat cream, extract and icing sugar
in small bowl with electric mixer until soft peaks form;
fold in thawed berries.

preparation time *15 minutes*
cooking time *12 minutes* serves *8*
nutritional count per serving *10.4g total fat (6.1g
saturated fat); 957kJ (229 cal); 29.9g carbohydrate;
3.2g protein; 1.2g fibre*

tiramisu roulade

2 tablespoons coffee-flavoured liqueur
¼ cup (60ml) water
2 tablespoons caster sugar
1 tablespoon instant coffee granules
1 tablespoon boiling water
3 eggs
½ cup (110g) caster sugar, extra
½ cup (75g) plain flour
2 tablespoons flaked almonds

COFFEE LIQUEUR CREAM

1 cup (250g) mascarpone cheese
½ cup (125ml) thickened cream
2 tablespoons coffee-flavoured liqueur

1 Preheat oven to 220°C/200°C fan-forced. Grease
25cm x 30cm swiss roll pan; line base and two long
sides with baking paper, extending paper 5cm over
long sides.
2 Bring liqueur, the water and sugar to the boil in small
saucepan. Reduce heat; simmer, uncovered, without
stirring, about 5 minutes or until syrup thickens slightly.
Remove from heat, stir in half of the coffee; reserve syrup.
3 Dissolve remaining coffee in the boiling water.
4 Beat eggs and extra sugar in small bowl with electric
mixer about 5 minutes or until sugar is dissolved and
mixture is thick. Transfer mixture to large bowl; fold in
dissolved coffee.
5 Meanwhile, sift flour twice onto paper. Sift flour over
egg mixture then fold gently into mixture. Spread mixture
into pan; sprinkle with almonds. Bake about 15 minutes.
6 Meanwhile, place a piece of baking paper cut the
same size as pan on bench; sprinkle evenly with about
2 teaspoons of caster sugar. Turn sponge onto sugared
paper; peel away lining paper. Trim edges from all
sides of sponge. Roll sponge from long side, using
paper as guide; cool.
7 Meanwhile, beat ingredients for coffee liqueur cream
in small bowl with electric mixer until firm peaks form.
8 Unroll sponge, brush with reserved syrup. Spread
cream over sponge then re-roll sponge. Cover roulade
with plastic wrap; refrigerate 30 minutes before serving.

preparation time *35 minutes*
cooking time *20 minutes (plus refrigeration time)*
serves *8*
nutritional count per serving *26g total fat (15.1g
saturated fat); 1655kJ (396 cal); 30.4g carbohydrate;
6.6g protein; 1.1g fibre*

date and maple loaf

¾ cup (110g) finely chopped dates
⅓ cup (80ml) boiling water
½ teaspoon bicarbonate of soda
¼ cup (90g) maple syrup
90g butter, softened
⅓ cup (75g) firmly packed brown sugar
2 eggs
¾ cup (120g) wholemeal self-raising flour
½ cup (75g) plain flour

MAPLE BUTTER

125g butter, softened
2 tablespoons maple syrup

1 Preheat oven to 180°C/160°C fan-forced. Grease
14cm x 21cm loaf pan.
2 Combine dates and the water in small heatproof bowl.
Stir in soda; stand 5 minutes. Stir in maple syrup.
3 Meanwhile, beat butter and sugar in medium bowl
with electric mixer until light and fluffy. Add eggs, one
at a time, beating until just combined between additions
(mixture will curdle at this stage, but will come together
later). Add butter mixture to date mixture; stir in sifted
flours, in two batches. Spread mixture into pan.
4 Bake loaf about 50 minutes. Stand in pan 10 minutes;
turn, top-side up, onto wire rack to cool.
5 Meanwhile, whisk ingredients for maple butter in
small bowl until combined. Serve loaf warm or cold
with maple butter.

preparation time *20 minutes*
cooking time *50 minutes* serves *12*
nutritional count per serving *15.8g total fat (10g
saturated fat); 1191kJ (285 cal); 31.9g carbohydrate;
3.1g protein; 1.5g fibre*

toffee date and ginger puddings

½ cup (115g) finely chopped glacé ginger
½ cup (60g) finely chopped roasted walnuts
1 cup (140g) seeded dried dates
¾ cup (180ml) water
1 teaspoon bicarbonate of soda
50g butter, chopped coarsely
½ cup (110g) firmly packed brown sugar
2 eggs
¾ cup (110g) self-raising flour
1 teaspoon ground ginger

GINGER BUTTERSCOTCH SAUCE

½ cup (110g) firmly packed brown sugar
⅔ cup (160ml) cream
100g butter, chopped coarsely
½ teaspoon ground ginger

1 Preheat oven to 160°C/140°C fan-forced. Grease six-hole texas (¾-cup/180ml) muffin pan; line bases with baking paper.

2 Combine glacé ginger and nuts in small bowl; sprinkle mixture over base of pan holes.

3 Bring dates and the water to the boil in small saucepan. Remove from heat; stir in soda. Stand 5 minutes.

4 Blend or process date mixture with butter and sugar until smooth. Add eggs, flour and ground ginger; process until combined. Pour mixture into pan holes.

5 Bake puddings about 30 minutes. Stand in pan 5 minutes; turn onto wire rack to cool 5 minutes.

6 Meanwhile, make ginger butterscotch sauce.

7 Serve warm puddings drizzled with ginger butterscotch sauce.

GINGER BUTTERSCOTCH SAUCE Stir ingredients in small saucepan over low heat until smooth. Simmer, uncovered, 5 minutes.

preparation time *30 minutes*
cooking time *30 minutes* makes 6
nutritional count per pudding *41g total fat (22.1g saturated fat); 3035kJ (726 cal); 81.1g carbohydrate; 6.7g protein; 3.7g fibre*

chocolate crowned sticky date cakes

120g dark eating chocolate, melted
1¾ cups (250g) seeded dried dates
1 teaspoon bicarbonate of soda
1 cup (250ml) boiling water
60g butter, chopped
¾ cup (165g) firmly packed brown sugar
2 eggs
1 cup (150g) self-raising flour
80g dark eating chocolate, chopped coarsely

CHOCOLATE BUTTERSCOTCH SAUCE

½ cup (110g) firmly packed brown sugar
⅔ cup (160ml) cream
50g butter
1 tablespoon cocoa powder, sifted

1 Preheat oven to 180°C/160°C fan-forced.
Grease six-hole texas (¾-cup/180ml) muffin pan;
line bases with baking paper.
2 Spread melted chocolate over base of each pan
hole; refrigerate until set.
3 Meanwhile, place dates, soda and the water in a
food processor, put lid in position; stand for 5 minutes.
Process until smooth. Add butter and sugar; process until
combined. Add eggs and flour; pulse until combined.
Stir in chopped chocolate. Spoon mixture into pan holes.
4 Bake cakes about 15 minutes. Stand in pan
2 minutes; turn onto wire rack to cool slightly. Peel
away paper.
5 Meanwhile, make chocolate butterscotch sauce.
6 Serve warm cakes drizzled with sauce and whipped
cream, if you like.

CHOCOLATE BUTTERSCOTCH SAUCE Stir ingredients in
medium saucepan over heat, without boiling, until sugar
dissolves; bring to the boil. Remove from heat.

preparation time *25 minutes*
cooking time *30 minutes* makes *6*
nutritional count per cake *38.3g total fat (23.9g
saturated fat); 3398kJ (813 cal); 106g carbohydrate;
8g protein; 4.6g fibre*

pavlova with figs and turkish delight

6 egg whites
pinch cream of tartar
1½ cups (330g) caster sugar
1 tablespoon cornflour
1½ teaspoons white vinegar
2 teaspoons vanilla extract
3 fresh figs
1 pomegranate
1¾ cups (430ml) thickened cream, whipped softly
75g turkish delight, chopped

1 Preheat oven to 120°C/100°C fan-forced. Grease
a heatproof serving platter with soft butter; dust with
cornflour and shake away excess. (Or, mark a 16cm x
40cm rectangle, or a 22cm circle, on baking paper
and invert paper on a greased large oven tray.)
2 Beat egg whites and cream of tartar in medium bowl
with electric mixer until soft peaks form. Gradually add
sugar, beating until sugar dissolves between additions.
Quickly fold in cornflour, vinegar and vanilla.
3 Spoon meringue onto serving platter, allowing a few
centimetres around the edges for spreading. Flatten or
slightly hollow the top.
4 Bake meringue about 1½ hours or until dry to touch.
Turn off the oven; leave meringue to cool in the oven
with the door ajar.
5 Cut figs into eighths. Cut open pomegranate and
shake out the seeds. Before serving, spoon cream over
the pavlova, top with figs, pomegranate seeds and
turkish delight.

preparation time *25 minutes*
cooking time *1 hour 30 minutes (plus cooling time)*
serves *10*
nutritional count per serving *16.1g total fat (10.5g
saturated fat); 1450kJ (347 cal); 45.7g carbohydrate;
3.7g protein; 2.1g fibre*

coconut cream panna cotta

400ml can coconut milk
1 cup (250ml) cream
½ cup (110g) caster sugar
1½ teaspoons powdered gelatine
1 large mango (600g), peeled, chopped finely
¼ medium pineapple (320g), peeled, chopped finely
¼ medium papaya (250g), peeled, chopped finely

1 Stir milk, cream, sugar and gelatine in small saucepan over low heat until gelatine is dissolved; do not boil. Strain mixture into medium jug, cool to room temperature.
2 Pour coconut mixture into six serving glasses. Cover; refrigerate about 6 hours or until just set.
3 Meanwhile, combine the mango, pineapple and papaya in medium bowl.
4 Just before serving, spoon fruit mixture on top of panna cotta.

preparation time *20 minutes (plus refrigeration time)* cooking time *5 minutes (plus cooling time)* serves 6 nutritional count per serving *32g total fat (24g saturated fat); 1873kJ (448 cal); 35.2g carbohydrate; 3.9g protein; 3.5g fibre*

double chocolate mousse

100g dark eating chocolate, chopped coarsely
10g unsalted butter, chopped coarsely
1 egg, separated
½ cup (125ml) thickened cream, whipped
1 cup (250ml) thickened cream, whipped, extra

MILK CHOCOLATE MOUSSE

100g milk eating chocolate, chopped coarsely
10g unsalted butter, chopped coarsely
1 egg, separated
½ cup (125ml) thickened cream, whipped

1 Melt dark chocolate in small heatproof bowl over small saucepan of simmering water. Remove from heat; add butter, stir until smooth. Stir in egg yolk.
2 Beat egg white in small bowl with electric mixer until soft peaks form. Fold egg white and cream into chocolate mixture, in two batches.
3 Make milk chocolate mousse.
4 Divide dark chocolate mousse among six ¾-cup (180ml) serving glasses; top with milk chocolate mousse then extra whipped cream. Cover; refrigerate 3 hours or overnight.

MILK CHOCOLATE MOUSSE Melt milk chocolate in small heatproof bowl over small saucepan of simmering water. Remove from heat; add butter, stir until smooth. Stir in egg yolk. Beat egg white in small bowl with electric mixer until soft peaks form. Fold egg white and cream into chocolate mixture, in two batches.

preparation time *30 minutes (plus refrigeration time)* cooking time *15 minutes* serves 6 nutritional count per serving *43.9g total fat (28.1g saturated fat); 2128kJ (509 cal); 23.5g carbohydrate; 6.1g protein; 0.3g fibre*

divine chocolate and raspberry tarts

125g unsalted butter
½ cup (50g) cocoa powder
⅓ cup (110g) raspberry jam
⅔ cup (150g) caster sugar
2 eggs, beaten lightly
⅔ cup (100g) plain flour
pinch bicarbonate of soda
125g cream cheese, softened
1 egg yolk
½ cup (75g) frozen raspberries

1 Preheat oven to 160°C/140°C fan-forced. Grease six 10cm-round, loose-based flan tins; place on oven tray.
2 Melt butter in medium saucepan, add sifted cocoa; whisk over low heat until mixture boils. Remove from heat; whisk in jam and ½ cup of the sugar. Stir in eggs, then sifted flour and soda. Divide mixture among tins.
3 Beat cheese, remaining sugar and egg yolk in small bowl with electric mixer until smooth; stir in raspberries.
4 Drop spoonfuls of cheese mixture over chocolate mixture; pull a knife backwards and forwards several times through mixture for a marbled effect.
5 Bake tarts about 30 minutes. Serve warm or cold with whipped cream, if you like.

preparation time *15 minutes*
cooking time *40 minutes* makes 6
nutritional count per tart *28.1g total fat (17.2g saturated fat); 2090kJ (500 cal); 52.8g carbohydrate; 8.3g protein; 2g fibre*

chocolate pistachio tart

1¼ cups (185g) plain flour
½ cup (80g) icing sugar
125g cold unsalted butter, chopped coarsely
2 tablespoons iced water, approximately
½ cup (70g) roasted unsalted pistachios
100g unsalted butter, extra, softened
½ cup (110g) caster sugar
2 eggs
⅔ cup (100g) self-raising flour
⅓ cup (35g) cocoa powder
½ cup (160g) raspberry jam
12 roasted unsalted pistachios, extra
40g dark chocolate Melts, melted

1 Process sifted plain flour and icing sugar with butter until crumbly. Add enough of the water until ingredients just come together. Knead dough on floured surface until smooth. Cover; refrigerate for 30 minutes.
2 Grease a 12.5cm x 35cm loose-based fluted flan tin. Reserve one-quarter of the dough for making pastry rounds. Roll remaining dough between sheets of baking paper until large enough to line tin. Ease dough into tin; press into base and sides. Trim edges; prick base all over with a fork. Refrigerate 30 minutes.
3 Roll out reserved dough on a floured surface, cut out 12 x 2cm rounds from reserved dough; place on tray lined with baking paper. Refrigerate 30 minutes.
4 Preheat oven to 200°C/180°C fan-forced.
5 Blend or process nuts finely.
6 Beat extra butter and caster sugar in small bowl with electric mixer until light and fluffy. Beat in eggs, one at a time. Transfer mixture to medium bowl; stir in sifted self-raising flour and cocoa, and nuts. Spread jam over base of pastry case; top with pistachio filling. Top filling with pastry rounds. Bake 15 minutes.
7 Reduce oven to 180°C/160°C fan-forced; bake for 25 minutes. Cool. Dip extra nuts in chocolate; place on pastry rounds. Cool before slicing.

preparation *40 minutes (plus refrigeration time)*
cooking *40 minutes* serves *16*
nutritional count per serving *16.2g total fat (9.1g saturated fat); 1262kJ (302 cal); 34g carbohydrate; 4.4g protein; 1.5g fibre*

warm malt truffle muffins

1¼ cups (185g) self-raising flour
¼ cup (30g) malted milk powder
2 tablespoons cocoa powder
pinch bicarbonate of soda
¼ cup (55g) brown sugar
60g unsalted butter
⅓ cup (125g) barley malt syrup
½ cup (125ml) milk
1 egg
¾ cup (180ml) cream

MALT TRUFFLES

200g milk eating chocolate, chopped coarsely
¼ cup (60ml) cream
½ cup (60g) malted milk powder

1   Make malt truffles.
2   Preheat oven to 180°C/160°C fan-forced. Line a
12-hole (⅓-cup/80ml) muffin pan with paper cases.
3   Sift flour, malt powder, cocoa, soda and sugar into
medium bowl.
4   Stir butter and malt syrup in small saucepan over low
heat until smooth. Stir butter mixture into flour mixture
with milk and egg. Do not over-mix; mixture should be
lumpy. Divide half the mixture among cases. Place a
truffle into each case; top with remaining mixture.
5   Bake muffins about 20 minutes.
6   Meanwhile, stir reserved malt truffle mixture and
cream in small saucepan, over low heat, until smooth.
7   Serve warm muffins with warm sauce. Dust with
sifted cocoa powder, if you like.

MALT TRUFFLES Stir ingredients in small heatproof bowl
over small saucepan of simmering water until smooth.
Reserve ½ cup (125ml) mixture for malt sauce.
Refrigerate remaining mixture about 30 minutes or until
firm. Roll heaped teaspoons of mixture into balls; place
on baking-paper-lined tray. Freeze until firm.

preparation *15 minutes (plus refrigeration and freezing)*
cooking *30 minutes* makes *12*
nutritional count per muffin *19.1g total fat (12.1g
saturated fat); 1480kJ (354 cal); 39.6g carbohydrate;
5.7g protein; 0.8g fibre*

cosmopolitan granita

⅔ cup (150g) sugar
⅔ cup (160ml) water
2½ cups (625ml) cranberry juice
¼ cup (60ml) vodka
1 tablespoon Cointreau
1 tablespoon lime juice

1   Stir sugar and the water in small saucepan over
low heat, without boiling, until sugar dissolves. Remove
from heat; cool to room temperature.
2   Combine syrup with remaining ingredients in deep,
23cm-square cake pan. Freeze mixture until just firm.
Break up the mixture with a fork until flaky. Refreeze.
3   Just before serving, break up the mixture with a fork.
Scoop into chilled glasses.

preparation time *15 minutes (plus freezing time)*
cooking time *3 minutes (plus cooling time)*
serves *4*
nutritional count per serving *0g total fat (0g
saturated fat); 1208kJ (289 cal); 61.6g carbohydrate;
0.4g protein; 0g fibre*

fig and toffee cupcake crowns

125g butter, softened
½ teaspoon vanilla extract
⅔ cup (150g) caster sugar
2 eggs
¾ cup (150g) finely chopped dried figs
½ cup (60g) finely chopped walnuts
⅔ cup (100g) plain flour
⅓ cup (50g) self-raising flour
60g Mars bar, chopped finely
¼ cup (60ml) milk
6 medium fresh figs (360g), quartered

WHIPPED MILK CHOCOLATE GANACHE

⅓ cup (80ml) cream
200g milk eating chocolate

TOFFEE

½ cup (110g) caster sugar
¼ cup (60ml) water

1 Preheat oven to 180°C/160°C fan-forced. Line 12-hole (⅓-cup/80ml) muffin pan with paper cases.
2 Beat butter, extract, sugar and eggs in small bowl with electric mixer until light and fluffy. Stir in figs, nuts, sifted flours, Mars bar and milk. Divide mixture among cases; smooth surface.
3 Bake cupcakes about 30 minutes. Turn onto wire rack to cool.
4 Make whipped milk chocolate ganache.
5 Make toffee; drizzle stripes over rolling pin to make small rounds of stripes.
6 Spread cakes with ganache; decorate with fig quarters and toffee shapes.

WHIPPED MILK CHOCOLATE GANACHE Bring cream to the boil in small saucepan; pour over chocolate in small bowl of electric mixer, stir until smooth. Cover, refrigerate 30 minutes. Beat with electric mixer until light and fluffy.

TOFFEE Stir sugar and the water in small heavy-based saucepan over heat, without boiling, until sugar dissolves. Bring to the boil. Reduce heat; simmer, uncovered, without stirring, until mixture is golden brown. Remove from heat; stand until bubbles subside.

preparation time 30 minutes (plus refrigeration time)
cooking time 35 minutes makes 12
nutritional count per cupcake 21.7g total fat (11.5g saturated fat); 1848kJ (442 cal); 54g carbohydrate; 6g protein; 3.5g fibre

no-bake chocolate cups

5 x 60g Mars bars
50g butter
3½ cups (120g) Rice Bubbles
200g milk eating chocolate, melted

1 Line 12-hole (⅓-cup/80ml) muffin pan with paper cases. Chop four of the Mars bars coarsely; cut remaining bar into slices.
2 Stir chopped bars and butter in medium saucepan over low heat until smooth; stir in Rice Bubbles.
3 Press mixture into cases, spread with chocolate; top with sliced Mars bar. Refrigerate about 30 minutes or until set.

preparation time 15 minutes (plus refrigeration time)
cooking time 5 minutes makes 12
nutritional count per cup 12.4g total fat (7.6g saturated fat); 1099kJ (263 cal); 34.2g carbohydrate; 3.3g protein; 0.8g fibre

passionfruit curd cupcakes

90g butter, softened
½ cup (110g) caster sugar
2 eggs
1 cup (150g) self-raising flour
¼ cup (60ml) passionfruit pulp
85g packet passionfruit jelly
1 cup (250ml) boiling water
1 cup (80g) desiccated coconut
½ cup (125ml) thickened cream, whipped

PASSIONFRUIT CURD

2 eggs, beaten lightly
⅓ cup caster sugar
1 tablespoon lemon juice
¼ cup passionfruit pulp
60g butter, chopped coarsely

1 Make passionfruit curd.
2 Preheat oven to 180°C/160°C fan-forced. Line
12-hole (⅓-cup/80ml) muffin pan with paper cases.
3 Beat butter, sugar, eggs and flour in small bowl with
electric mixer on low speed until ingredients are just
combined. Increase speed to medium, beat until mixture
is changed to a paler colour. Stir in passionfruit pulp.
Divide mixture among cases; smooth surface.
4 Bake cupcakes about 20 minutes. Turn onto wire
rack to cool.
5 Dissolve jelly in the water. Refrigerate 30 minutes or
until set to the consistency of unbeaten egg white.
Remove cases from cakes. Roll cakes in jelly; stand in
jelly 15 minutes turning occasionally. Roll cakes in coconut;
place on wire rack over tray. Refrigerate 30 minutes.
6 Cut cakes in half; fill with curd and cream.

PASSIONFRUIT CURD Combine ingredients in small
heatproof bowl over small saucepan of simmering
water; stir constantly until mixture thickens slightly and
coats the back of a spoon. Remove from heat. Cover
tightly; refrigerate until cold.

preparation time *25 minutes (plus refrigeration time)*
cooking time *20 minutes* makes *12*
nutritional count per cupcake *20.4g total fat (13.7g
saturated fat); 1400kJ (335 cal); 31.7g carbohydrate;
5g protein; 2.9g fibre*

florentine cupcakes

60g dark eating chocolate, chopped coarsely
⅔ cup (160ml) water
90g butter, softened
1 cup (220g) firmly packed brown sugar
2 eggs
⅔ cup (100g) self-raising flour
2 tablespoons cocoa powder
⅓ cup (40g) almond meal
50g dark eating chocolate, melted

MILK CHOCOLATE GANACHE

¼ cup (60ml) cream
100g milk eating chocolate, chopped coarsely

FLORENTINE TOPPING

1 cup (80g) flaked almonds, toasted
½ cup (115g) coarsely chopped glacé ginger
1 cup (200g) red glacé cherries, halved

1 Preheat oven to 160°C/140°C fan-forced. Line
12-hole (⅓-cup/80ml) muffin pan with paper cases.
2 Stir chopped chocolate and the water in small
saucepan over low heat until smooth.
3 Beat butter, sugar and eggs in small bowl with
electric mixer until light and fluffy. Stir in sifted flour and
cocoa, almond meal and warm chocolate mixture.
Divide mixture among cases; smooth surface.
4 Bake cupcakes about 25 minutes. Turn onto wire
rack to cool.
5 Make milk chocolate ganache.
6 Make florentine topping.
7 Spread cakes with ganache, top with florentine
mixture; drizzle with melted chocolate.

MILK CHOCOLATE GANACHE Bring cream to the boil in
small saucepan, pour over chocolate in small bowl; stir
until smooth. Stand at room temperature until spreadable.

FLORENTINE TOPPING Combine ingredients in small bowl.

preparation time *25 minutes (plus standing time)*
cooking time *30 minutes* makes *12*
nutritional count per cupcake *19.9g total fat (9.2g
saturated fat); 1772kJ (424 cal); 54.5g carbohydrate;
5.7g protein; 1.6g fibre*

apple custard teacakes

90g butter
½ teaspoon vanilla extract
½ cup (110g) caster sugar
2 eggs
¾ cup (110g) self-raising flour
¼ cup (30g) custard powder
2 tablespoons milk
1 large unpeeled apple (200g), cored, sliced finely
30g butter, extra, melted
1 tablespoon caster sugar, extra
½ teaspoon ground cinnamon

CUSTARD

1 tablespoon custard powder
1 tablespoon caster sugar
½ cup (125ml) milk
¼ teaspoon vanilla extract

1 Make custard.
2 Preheat oven to 180°C/160°C fan-forced. Line 12-hole (⅓-cup/80ml) muffin pan with paper cases.
3 Beat butter, extract, sugar, eggs, flour, custard powder and milk in small bowl with electric mixer on low speed until ingredients are just combined. Increase speed to medium, beat until mixture is changed to a paler colour.
4 Divide half the mixture among cases. Top with custard, then remaining cake mixture; spread mixture to cover custard. Top with apple slices, pressing slightly into cake.
5 Bake cakes about 30 minutes. Brush hot cakes with extra butter, then sprinkle with combined extra sugar and cinnamon. Turn cakes onto wire rack. Serve warm or cold.

CUSTARD Blend custard powder and sugar with milk and extract in small saucepan; stir over heat until mixture boils and thickens. Remove from heat; cover surface with plastic wrap. Cool.

preparation time *25 minutes (plus cooling time)*
cooking time *40 minutes* makes *12*
nutritional count per cake *9.8g total fat (6g saturated fat); 815kJ (195 cal); 23.8g carbohydrate; 2.6g protein; 0.6g fibre*

lamington angel cupcakes

90g butter, softened
½ teaspoon vanilla extract
½ cup (110g) caster sugar
2 eggs
1 cup (150g) self-raising flour
2 tablespoons milk
1 cup (80g) desiccated coconut
¼ cup (100g) raspberry jam
½ cup (125ml) thickened cream, whipped

CHOCOLATE ICING

10g butter
⅓ cup (80ml) milk
2 cups (320g) icing sugar
¼ cup (25g) cocoa powder

1 Preheat oven to 180°C/160°C fan-forced. Line 12-hole (⅓-cup/80ml) muffin pan with paper cases.
2 Beat butter, extract, sugar, eggs, flour and milk in small bowl with electric mixer on low speed until ingredients are just combined. Increase speed to medium, beat until mixture is changed to a paler colour. Divide mixture among cases; smooth surface.
3 Bake cupcakes about 20 minutes. Turn cakes onto wire rack to cool.
4 Make chocolate icing.
5 Remove cases from cakes. Dip cakes in icing; drain off excess, toss cakes in coconut. Place cakes on wire rack to set.
6 Cut cakes as desired; fill with jam and cream.

CHOCOLATE ICING Melt butter in medium heatproof bowl over medium saucepan of simmering water. Stir in milk and sifted icing sugar and cocoa until icing is of a coating consistency.

preparation time *25 minutes*
cooking time *20 minutes* makes *12*
nutritional count per cupcake *16.8g total fat (11.6g saturated fat); 1538kJ (377 cal); 51.9g carbohydrate; 3.8g protein; 1.7g fibre*

chocolate rum and raisin slice

125g butter, chopped
200g dark eating chocolate, chopped
½ cup (110g) caster sugar
1 cup (170g) coarsely chopped raisins
2 eggs, beaten lightly
1½ cups (225g) plain flour
1 tablespoon dark rum

1   Preheat oven to 160°C/140°C fan-forced.
Grease 20cm x 30cm lamington pan.
2   Stir butter, chocolate, sugar and raisins in medium
saucepan over low heat until chocolate is melted. Cool
to room temperature. Stir in remaining ingredients until
well combined. Spread mixture into pan.
3   Bake slice about 30 minutes or until just firm; cool
in pan. Serve dusted with sifted icing sugar, if you like.

preparation time *15 minutes (plus cooling time)*
cooking time *30 minutes* makes *15*
nutritional count per piece *11.9g total fat (8.5g
saturated fat); 1087kJ (260 cal); 33.4g carbohydrate;
3.4g protein; 1.7g fibre*

maple caramel slice

200g packet plain un-iced chocolate biscuits,
    crushed finely
½ cup (45g) desiccated coconut
200g butter, melted
100g dark eating chocolate, melted
2 teaspoons vegetable oil

MAPLE CARAMEL

395g can sweetened condensed milk
60g butter
2 tablespoons maple-flavoured syrup

1   Grease 19cm x 29cm rectangular slice pan;
line base and two long sides with baking paper,
extending paper 2cm above edge of pan.
2   Combine biscuit crumbs, coconut and butter
in large bowl; press over base of pan. Cover;
refrigerate until firm.
3   Make maple caramel; spread hot maple caramel
over crumb layer. Cover; refrigerate until firm.
4   Spread combined chocolate and oil over slice;
leave to set.

MAPLE CARAMEL Whisk ingredients in medium
saucepan over heat until butter melts. Simmer, whisking
constantly, about 8 minutes or until mixture thickens and
is dark golden brown.

preparation time *15 minutes (plus refrigeration time)*
cooking time *10 minutes* makes *24*
nutritional count per piece *14.6g total fat (9.3g
saturated fat); 903kJ (216 cal); 18.8g carbohydrate;
2.3g protein; 0.5g fibre*

1 CHOCOLATE RUM AND RAISIN SLICE 2 MAPLE CARAMEL SLICE
3 FRUIT CHEWS [P 632] 4 PEPITA AND SESAME SLICE [P 632]

1

2

3

4

fruit chews

⅓ cup (75g) firmly packed brown sugar
90g butter
1¼ cups (185g) plain flour
1 egg yolk

TOPPING

2 eggs
1 cup (220g) firmly packed brown sugar
⅓ cup (50g) self-raising flour
½ cup (85g) raisins
¾ cup (120g) sultanas
1¼ cups (185g) roasted unsalted peanuts
1 cup (90g) desiccated coconut

1   Preheat oven to 180°C/160°C fan-forced.
Grease 20cm x 30cm lamington pan; line base
and two long sides with baking paper, extending
paper 2cm above edge of pan.
2   Stir sugar and butter in medium saucepan over
medium heat until butter is melted. Stir in sifted flour
and egg yolk. Press mixture over base of pan.
3   Bake slice about 10 minutes or until browned
lightly; cool.
4   Meanwhile, make topping.
5   Spread topping over cold base; bake slice further
30 minutes or until browned lightly. Cool in pan before
cutting into pieces.

TOPPING Beat eggs and sugar in small bowl with
electric mixer until changed to a lighter colour and
thickened slightly; fold in sifted flour. Transfer mixture to
large bowl; stir in remaining ingredients.

preparation time *20 minutes (plus refrigeration)*
cooking time *40 minutes* makes *18*
nutritional count per piece *13.3g total fat (6.6g
saturated fat); 1200kJ (287 cal); 34.9g carbohydrate;
5.5g protein; 2.6g fibre*

pepita and sesame slice

90g butter
1 teaspoon grated lemon rind
2 tablespoons caster sugar
1 egg
⅔ cup (100g) white plain flour
½ cup (80g) wholemeal plain flour
½ cup (80g) unsalted pepitas, chopped coarsely
¼ cup (80g) apricot jam
2 tablespoons sesame seeds, toasted

1   Preheat oven to 200°C/180°C fan-forced.
Grease 23cm-square slab pan; line base and two
opposite sides with baking paper, extending paper
2cm above edge of pan.
2   Beat butter, rind, sugar and egg in small bowl with
electric mixer until light and fluffy. Stir in sifted flours and
pepitas; press mixture evenly into pan. Spread base
with jam; sprinkle with seeds.
3   Bake slice about 20 minutes or until browned lightly.
Cool in pan before cutting into pieces.

preparation time *10 minutes*
cooking time *20 minutes* makes *16*
nutritional count per piece *7.8g total fat (3.7g
saturated fat); 564kJ (135 cal); 13.1g carbohydrate;
3.1g protein; 1.1g fibre*

berry, almond and coconut slice

2 cups (300g) frozen mixed berries
1 cup (220g) caster sugar
1 tablespoon lime juice
90g butter, softened
1 egg
⅔ cup (100g) plain flour
¼ cup (35g) self-raising flour
1 tablespoon custard powder

ALMOND COCONUT TOPPING

2 eggs, beaten lightly
1½ cups (75g) flaked coconut
1 cup (80g) flaked almonds
¼ cup (55g) caster sugar

1 Preheat oven to 180°C/160°C fan-forced. Grease
20cm x 30cm lamington pan; line base with baking
paper, extending paper 5cm over long sides.
2 Stir half the berries, half the sugar and the juice in
small saucepan over low heat until sugar dissolves;
bring to the boil. Reduce heat; simmer, uncovered,
stirring occasionally, about 20 minutes or until mixture
thickens. Cool 10 minutes. Stir in remaining berries.
3 Beat butter, egg and remaining sugar in small bowl
with electric mixer until light and fluffy; stir in sifted flours
and custard powder. Spread dough into pan; spread
with berry mixture.
4 Make almond coconut topping; sprinkle topping
over berry mixture.
5 Bake slice about 40 minutes. Cool in pan before
cutting into pieces.

ALMOND COCONUT TOPPING Combine ingredients in
small bowl.

preparation time *25 minutes (plus cooling time)*
cooking time *1 hour* makes 16
nutritional count per piece *11.6g total fat (6.2g
saturated fat); 932kJ (223 cal); 25g carbohydrate;
3.8g protein; 1.9g fibre*

hazelnut caramel slice

200g butter, chopped
½ cup (50g) cocoa powder
2 cups (440g) firmly packed brown sugar
1 teaspoon vanilla extract
2 eggs, beaten lightly
1½ cups (225g) plain flour
200g dark eating chocolate, melted, cooled
1 tablespoon vegetable oil

CARAMEL FILLING

180g butter, chopped
½ cup (110g) caster sugar
2 tablespoons golden syrup
¾ cup (180ml) sweetened condensed milk
1¼ cups (185g) whole hazelnuts, roasted

1 Preheat oven to 160°C/140°C fan-forced. Grease
20cm x 30cm lamington pan; line base with baking
paper, extending paper 5cm over long sides.
2 Stir butter and cocoa powder in medium saucepan
over low heat until smooth. Add sugar; stir until
dissolved. Remove from heat, add extract, egg and
sifted flour; mix well. Spread mixture into pan.
3 Bake base 20 minutes; cool.
4 Meanwhile, make caramel filling. Quickly spread
caramel filling evenly over base; refrigerate at least
30 minutes or until firm.
5 Combine chocolate and oil in small bowl; spread
over caramel filling. Refrigerate until set. Cut into pieces.

CARAMEL FILLING Stir butter, sugar, syrup and
condensed milk in medium saucepan over low heat
until butter is melted. Increase heat to medium; simmer,
stirring, about 13 minutes or until mixture is a dark
caramel colour. Remove from heat, stir in hazelnuts.

preparation time *25 minutes*
cooking time *45 minutes (plus cooling and
refrigeration time)* makes 30
nutritional count per piece *18.1g total fat (9g
saturated fat); 1317kJ (315 cal); 34g carbohydrate;
3.6g protein; 1.1g fibre*

nutty meringue sticks

3 egg whites
¾ cup (165g) caster sugar
1¼ cups (120g) hazelnut meal
1½ cups (185g) almond meal
¼ cup (35g) plain flour
100g dark eating chocolate, melted

1 Preheat oven to 160°C/140°C fan-forced.
Grease oven trays; line with baking paper.
2 Beat egg whites in small bowl with electric mixer
until foamy. Gradually beat in sugar, one tablespoon
at a time, until dissolved between additions. Transfer
mixture to large bowl; fold in nut meals and sifted flour.
3 Spoon mixture into large piping bag fitted with
1.5cm plain tube. Pipe 8cm sticks onto trays.
4 Bake meringue sticks about 15 minutes. Cool on
trays 5 minutes; place on wire racks to cool.
5 Drizzle sticks with melted chocolate, place on
baking-paper-lined trays to set.

preparation time *15 minutes*
cooking time *15 minutes* makes *34*
nutritional count per stick *6g total fat (0.8g
saturated fat); 401kJ (96 cal); 7.9g carbohydrate;
2.2g protein; 0.9g fibre*

choconut mint cookie stacks

125g butter, softened
¾ cup (165g) firmly packed brown sugar
1 egg
1½ cups (225g) plain flour
¼ cup (35g) self-raising flour
2 tablespoons desiccated coconut
½ teaspoon coconut essence
2 tablespoons cocoa powder
40 square after dinner mints

1 Beat butter, sugar and egg in small bowl with
electric mixer until combined. Stir in sifted flours,
in two batches. Place half the mixture into another
small bowl; stir in coconut and essence. Stir sifted
cocoa into the other bowl.
2 Knead each portion of dough on floured surface
until smooth. Roll between sheets of baking paper
until 3mm thick. Cover; refrigerate 30 minutes.
3 Preheat oven to 180°C/160°C fan-forced.
Grease oven trays; line with baking paper.
4 Using 6cm square cutter, cut 30 shapes from
each portion of dough. Place about 3cm apart
on oven trays.
5 Bake cookies about 8 minutes. While cookies
are still hot, sandwich three warm alternate-flavoured
cookies with after dinner mints; press down gently.
Cool on trays.

preparation time *25 minutes*
cooking time *10 minutes* makes *20*
nutritional count per stack *9.5g total fat (5.9g
saturated fat); 823kJ (197 cal); 25g carbohydrate;
2.6g protein; 0.9g fibre*

1 NUTTY MERINGUE STICKS 2 CHOCONUT MINT
COOKIE STACKS 3 CARAMEL GINGER CRUNCHIES [P 636]
4 ALMOND AND PLUM CRESCENTS [P 636]

SWEET TREATS   635

caramel ginger crunchies

2 cups (300g) plain flour
½ teaspoon bicarbonate of soda
1 teaspoon ground cinnamon
2 teaspoons ground ginger
1 cup (220g) caster sugar
125g cold butter, chopped
1 egg
1 teaspoon golden syrup
2 tablespoons finely chopped glacé ginger
45 wrapped hard caramels

1   Preheat oven to 160°C/140°C fan-forced.
Grease oven trays; line with baking paper.
2   Process sifted dry ingredients with butter until
mixture is crumbly; add egg, golden syrup and
ginger, process until ingredients come together.
Knead on floured surface until smooth.
3   Roll rounded teaspoons of mixture into balls;
flatten slightly. Place about 3cm apart on oven trays.
4   Bake cookies 13 minutes. Place one caramel on
top of each hot cookie; bake about 7 minutes or until
caramel begins to melt. Cool on trays.

preparation time *20 minutes*
cooking time *20 minutes* makes *45*
nutritional count per cookie *2.6g total fat (1.7g
saturated fat); 372kJ (89 cal); 15.1g carbohydrate;
0.9g protein; 0.3g fibre*

almond and plum crescents

1½ cups (225g) plain flour
½ cup (60g) almond meal
¼ cup (55g) caster sugar
2 teaspoons finely grated lemon rind
90g cream cheese, chopped
90g butter, chopped
2 tablespoons buttermilk
1 egg white
¼ cup (20g) flaked almonds, crushed lightly
FILLING
⅓ cup (60g) finely chopped prunes
¼ cup (80g) plum jam
¼ cup (55g) caster sugar
½ teaspoon ground cinnamon

1   Process flour, almond meal, sugar and rind until
combined. Add cream cheese and butter, pulse until
crumbly. Add buttermilk, process until ingredients come
together. Knead dough on floured surface until smooth.
2   Divide dough in half. Roll each half between sheets
of baking paper until large enough to be cut each
into a 22cm round; cut dough using 22cm cake pan
as a guide. Discard excess dough. Cover rounds;
refrigerate 30 minutes.
3   Preheat oven to 180°C/160°C fan-forced.
Grease oven trays; line with baking paper.
4   Make filling.
5   Cut each round into eight wedges, spread each
wedge with a little filling mixture; roll from the wide
end into a crescent shape. Place on oven trays, brush
with egg white, sprinkle with flaked almonds.
6   Bake crescents about 25 minutes. Cool on trays.

FILLING Combine ingredients in small bowl.

preparation time *25 minutes (plus refrigeration time)*
cooking time *25 minutes* makes *16*
nutritional count per crescent *9.5g total fat (4.5g
saturated fat); 782kJ (187 cal); 21.2g carbohydrate;
3.5g protein; 1.3g fibre*

butterscotch ginger dumplings

1 cup (150g) self-raising flour
2 tablespoons caster sugar
60g butter, chopped
⅓ cup (80ml) water
2 tablespoons finely chopped glacé ginger
¼ cup (20g) flaked almonds

BUTTERSCOTCH SAUCE

30g butter
½ cup (100g) firmly packed brown sugar
2 tablespoons golden syrup
1½ cups (375ml) water

1 Preheat oven to 180°C/160°C fan-forced.
2 Sift flour into large bowl, add sugar; rub in butter.
Add the water and ginger; mix to a soft dough.
3 Divide dough into eight equal portions, shape
into oval dumplings. Place dumplings in shallow
1.5-litre (6-cup) ovenproof dish.
4 Make butterscotch sauce; pour over dumplings.
5 Bake dumplings 20 minutes. Spoon sauce in dish
over dumplings; sprinkle with almonds. Bake a further
10 minutes or until dumplings are browned.

BUTTERSCOTCH SAUCE Stir ingredients in small
saucepan over low heat until sugar dissolves.
Bring to the boil; remove from heat.

preparation *15 minutes*
cooking *35 minutes* serves *4*
nutritional count per serving *21.2g total fat (12.1g
saturated fat); 2211kJ (529 cal); 78.3g carbohydrate;
4.9g protein; 1.9g fibre*

choc-mint brownies

200g dark eating chocolate, melted
125g butter, chopped coarsely
200g dark eating chocolate, chopped coarsely
½ cup (110g) caster sugar
2 eggs
1¼ cups (185g) plain flour
6 mint patties (120g), chopped coarsely

1 Preheat oven to 180°C/160°C fan-forced.
Grease deep 19cm-square cake pan; line base
with baking paper, extending paper 5cm over sides.
Line base with foil.
2 Spread melted chocolate evenly over base of pan;
cover, refrigerate until set.
3 Meanwhile, stir butter and chopped chocolate
in medium saucepan over low heat until smooth.
Remove from heat; stir in sugar. Cool 10 minutes.
4 Stir in eggs, then sifted flour and mint patties.
Spread mixture over chocolate in pan.
5 Bake brownies about 30 minutes. Cool in pan;
refrigerate about 30 minutes to set chocolate again.
6 Turn brownie, chocolate-side up, onto board;
carefully peel foil from chocolate topping. Cut into
nine squares; cut squares in half diagonally.

preparation time *15 minutes (plus refrigeration time)*
cooking time *30 minutes* makes *18*
nutritional count per brownie *14.1g total fat (8.8g
saturated fat); 1116kJ (267 cal); 31.4g carbohydrate;
3.3g protein; 0.7g fibre*

white chocolate, cranberry and pistachio hedgehog slice

¾ cup (180ml) sweetened condensed milk
60g butter, chopped
180g white eating chocolate, chopped coarsely
150g plain sweet biscuits
½ cup (65g) dried cranberries
⅓ cup (45g) roasted unsalted pistachios

1 Grease 8cm x 26cm bar pan; line base with baking paper, extending paper 5cm over long sides.
2 Stir condensed milk and butter in small saucepan over low heat until smooth. Remove from heat; add chocolate, stir until smooth.
3 Break biscuits into small pieces; place in large bowl with cranberries and nuts. Stir in chocolate mixture.
4 Spread mixture into pan, cover; refrigerate about 3 hours or overnight until firm. Cut into 12 slices.

preparation time *10 minutes (plus refrigeration time)* cooking time *5 minutes* makes *12 slices*
nutritional count per slice *14.9g total fat (8.2g saturated fat); 1179kJ (282 cal); 32.3g carbohydrate; 4.4g protein; 0.9g fibre*

rhubarb custard melting moments

You need to cook 1 large stem chopped rhubarb with about 1 tablespoon sugar (or to taste) and 1 tablespoon water over low heat, until rhubarb is pulpy. Drain, cool.

250g butter, softened
½ teaspoon vanilla extract
½ cup (80g) icing sugar
1 cup (125g) custard powder
1 cup (150g) plain flour
1 tablespoon icing sugar, extra

RHUBARB CUSTARD

1 tablespoon custard powder
1 tablespoon caster sugar
½ cup (125ml) milk
⅓ cup stewed rhubarb

1 Preheat oven to 160°C/140°C fan-forced. Grease oven trays; line with baking paper.
2 Make rhubarb custard.
3 Beat butter, extract and sifted icing sugar in small bowl with electric mixer until light and fluffy. Stir in sifted custard powder and flour, in two batches.
4 With floured hands, roll rounded teaspoons of mixture into balls. Place about 5cm apart on oven trays; flatten slightly with a floured fork.
5 Bake biscuits about 15 minutes. Stand on trays 5 minutes; cool on wire racks.
6 Sandwich biscuits with a little rhubarb custard.

RHUBARB CUSTARD Blend custard powder and sugar with milk in small saucepan; stir over heat until mixture boils and thickens. Remove from heat, stir in rhubarb. Cover surface of custard with plastic wrap; refrigerate until cold.

preparation time *25 minutes (plus refrigeration time)* cooking time *25 minutes* makes *25*
nutritional count per melting moment *8.5g total fat (5.5g saturated fat); 564kJ (135 cal); 13.6g carbohydrate; 0.9g protein; 0.3g fibre*

lemon polenta biscuits

250g butter, softened
1 teaspoon vanilla extract
1¼ cups (200g) icing sugar
2 tablespoons finely grated lemon rind
½ cup (85g) polenta
2½ cups (375g) plain flour
1 tablespoon lemon juice

1 Beat butter, extract, icing sugar and 1 teaspoon of the rind in small bowl with electric mixer until combined. Stir in polenta, flour and juice, in two batches.
2 Knead dough on floured surface until smooth. Divide dough in half; shape pieces into two 20cm-long logs. Cover; refrigerate 2 hours or until firm.
3 Preheat oven to 200°C/180°C fan-forced. Grease two oven trays.
4 Cut logs into 1cm slices; place slices about 2cm apart on trays, sprinkle tops with remaining rind.
5 Bake biscuits about 15 minutes. Stand on trays 5 minutes; turn onto wire rack to cool.

preparation time *20 minutes (plus refrigeration time)* cooking time *15 minutes* makes *40* nutritional count per biscuit *5.3g total fat (3.4g saturated fat); 364kJ (87 cal); 8.4g carbohydrate; 1.2g protein; 0.4g fibre*

date and walnut scrolls

125g butter, softened
⅓ cup (75g) caster sugar
1 teaspoon ground cardamom
1 egg
1½ cups (225g) plain flour
1 cup (100g) walnuts, roasted, ground finely
2 cups (280g) dried dates, chopped coarsely
¼ cup (55g) caster sugar, extra
2 teaspoons finely grated lemon rind
⅓ cup (80ml) lemon juice
¼ teaspoon ground cardamom, extra
½ cup (125ml) water

1 Beat butter, sugar, cardamom and egg in small bowl with electric mixer until combined. Stir in sifted flour and walnuts. Knead dough on floured surface until smooth; divide into two portions. Roll each portion between sheets of baking paper to 15cm x 30cm rectangles; refrigerate 20 minutes.
2 Meanwhile, stir dates, extra sugar, rind, juice, extra cardamom and the water in medium saucepan over heat, without boiling, until sugar is dissolved; bring to the boil. Reduce heat, simmer, uncovered, stirring occasionally, about 5 minutes or until mixture is thick and pulpy. Transfer to large bowl; refrigerate 10 minutes.
3 Spread filling evenly over each rectangle, leaving 1cm border. Using paper as a guide, roll rectangles tightly from short side to enclose filling. Wrap rolls in baking paper; refrigerate 30 minutes.
4 Preheat oven to 180°C/160°C fan-forced. Grease oven trays; line with baking paper.
5 Trim edges of roll; cut each roll into 1cm slices. Place slices, cut-side up, on oven trays; bake about 20 minutes.

preparation time *20 minutes (plus refrigeration time)* cooking time *20 minutes* makes *28* nutritional count per scroll *6.4g total fat (2.6g saturated fat); 577kJ (138 cal); 17.4g carbohydrate; 1.9g protein; 1.5g fibre*

passionfruit gems

1 cup (150g) plain flour
½ cup (75g) self-raising flour
2 tablespoons custard powder
⅔ cup (110g) icing sugar
90g cold butter, chopped
1 egg yolk
¼ cup (60ml) passionfruit pulp
BUTTER ICING
125g unsalted butter, softened
1½ cups (240g) icing sugar
2 tablespoons milk

1 Process dry ingredients and butter together until crumbly; add egg yolk and passionfruit pulp, pulse until ingredients come together. Knead dough on floured surface until smooth. Roll between sheets of baking paper until 5mm thick; refrigerate 30 minutes.
2 Preheat oven to 180°C/160°C fan-forced. Grease oven trays; line with baking paper.
3 Using 4cm round flower-shaped cutter, cut rounds from dough. Place about 3cm apart on oven trays.
4 Bake cookies about 10 minutes. Cool on wire racks.
5 Make butter icing; spoon into piping bag fitted with a small fluted tube. Pipe stars onto cookies.

BUTTER ICING Beat butter in small bowl with electric mixer until as white as possible. Gradually beat in half the sifted icing sugar, milk, then remaining icing sugar.

preparation time *20 minutes (plus refrigeration time)* cooking time *10 minutes* makes *70* nutritional count per gem *2.7g total fat (1.7g saturated fat); 237kJ (56.8 cal); 7.6g carbohydrate; 0.4g protein; 0.2g fibre*

choc-mallow wheels

125g butter, softened
¾ cup (165g) firmly packed brown sugar
1 egg
1½ cups (225g) plain flour
¼ cup (35g) self-raising flour
¼ cup (25g) cocoa powder
28 marshmallows
375g dark chocolate Melts
1 tablespoon vegetable oil
¼ cup (80g) raspberry jam

1 Beat butter, sugar and egg in small bowl with electric mixer until combined. Stir in sifted flours and cocoa, in two batches. Knead dough on floured surface until smooth. Roll between sheets of baking paper until 3mm thick. Cover; refrigerate 30 minutes.
2 Preheat oven to 180°C/160°C fan-forced. Grease oven trays; line with baking paper.
3 Using 7cm round fluted cutter, cut 28 rounds from dough. Place about 3cm apart on trays.
4 Bake cookies about 12 minutes. Cool on wire racks.
5 Place half the cookies, base-side up, on oven tray. Use scissors to cut marshmallows in half horizontally; press four marshmallow halves, cut-side down, onto biscuit bases on tray. Bake 2 minutes.
6 Melt chocolate in medium heatproof bowl over medium saucepan of simmering water. Remove from heat; stir in oil.
7 Spread jam over bases of remaining cookies; press onto softened marshmallow. Stand 20 minutes or until marshmallow is firm. Dip wheels into chocolate; smooth away excess chocolate using metal spatula. Place on baking-paper-lined trays to set.

preparation time *25 minutes (plus refrigeration and standing time)* cooking time *15 minutes* makes *14* nutritional count per wheel *17.6g total fat (12.7g saturated fat); 1613kJ (386 cal); 51.3g carbohydrate; 4.3g protein; 2.1g fibre*

checkerboard cookies

200g butter, softened
¾ cup (165g) caster sugar
½ teaspoon vanilla extract
1 egg
2 cups (300g) plain flour
1 tablespoon cocoa powder
1 teaspoon finely grated orange rind
¼ cup (40g) finely chopped dried cranberries
1 egg white, beaten lightly

1   Beat butter, sugar, extract and egg in small bowl with electric mixer until light and fluffy. Stir in sifted flour in two batches.
2   Divide dough in half, knead sifted cocoa into one half; knead rind and cranberries into the other half. Using ruler, shape each batch of dough into 4.5cm x 4.5cm x 15cm rectangular bars. Wrap each in baking paper; refrigerate 30 minutes.
3   Cut each bar lengthways equally into three slices. Cut each slice lengthways equally into three; you will have nine 1.5cm x 1.5cm x 1.5cm slices of each dough.
4   Brush each slice of dough with egg white, stack alternate flavours together in threes. Stick three stacks together to recreate the log; repeat with second log. Refrigerate 30 minutes.
5   Preheat oven to 180°C/160°C fan-forced. Grease oven trays; line with baking paper.
6   Using a sharp knife, cut each log into 1cm slices. Place, cut-side up, on oven trays about 3cm apart.
7   Bake cookies about 15 minutes. Stand on trays 5 minutes; transfer to wire racks to cool.

preparation time *30 minutes (plus refrigeration time)*
cooking time *15 minutes* makes *30*
nutritional count per cookie *5.8g total fat (3.7g saturated fat); 481kJ (115 cal); 13.8g carbohydrate; 1.5g protein; 0.5g fibre*

pink macaroons

3 egg whites
2 tablespoons caster sugar
pink food colouring
1¼ cups (200g) icing sugar
1 cup (120g) almond meal
2 tablespoons icing sugar, extra

WHITE CHOCOLATE GANACHE

100g white eating chocolate, chopped coarsely
2 tablespoons thickened cream

1   Make white chocolate ganache.
2   Grease oven trays; line with baking paper.
3   Beat egg whites in small bowl with electric mixer until soft peaks form. Add sugar and food colouring, beat until sugar dissolves. Transfer mixture to large bowl; fold in sifted icing sugar and almond meal, in two batches.
4   Spoon mixture into large piping bag fitted with 1.5cm plain tube. Pipe 36 x 4cm rounds, 2cm apart, onto trays. Tap trays on bench top to allow macaroons to spread slightly. Dust with sifted extra icing sugar; stand 15 minutes.
5   Preheat oven to 150°C/130°C fan-forced.
6   Bake macaroons about 20 minutes. Stand on trays 5 minutes; transfer to wire rack to cool.
7   Sandwich macaroons with ganache. Dust with a little sifted icing sugar, if you like.

WHITE CHOCOLATE GANACHE Stir chocolate and cream in small saucepan over low heat until smooth. Transfer mixture to small bowl. Cover; refrigerate until mixture is spreadable.

preparation time *15 minutes (plus standing time)*
cooking time *20 minutes* makes *18*
nutritional count per macaroon *6.4g total fat (1.9g saturated fat); 581kJ (139 cal); 17.7g carbohydrate; 2.4g protein; 0.6g fibre*

peanut brittle cookies

125g butter, softened
¼ cup (70g) crunchy peanut butter
½ cup (100g) firmly packed brown sugar
1 egg
1½ cups (225g) plain flour
½ teaspoon bicarbonate of soda

PEANUT BRITTLE

¾ cup (100g) roasted unsalted peanuts
½ cup (110g) caster sugar
2 tablespoons water

1 Preheat oven to 160°C/140°C fan-forced.
Grease oven trays; line with baking paper.
2 Make peanut brittle.
3 Beat butter, peanut butter, sugar and egg in small
bowl with electric mixer until combined. Stir in sifted
dry ingredients and crushed peanut brittle.
4 Roll heaped teaspoons of mixture into balls with
floured hands. Place about 5cm apart on oven trays;
flatten slightly with hand.
5 Bake cookies about 12 minutes. Cool on trays.

PEANUT BRITTLE Place nuts on baking-paper-lined oven
tray. Stir sugar and the water in small frying pan over
heat, without boiling, until sugar is dissolved. Bring to
the boil; boil, uncovered, without stirring, until golden
brown. Pour mixture over nuts; leave until set. Crush
coarsely in food processor.

preparation time *20 minutes*
cooking time *18 minutes* makes *42*
nutritional count per cookie *4.6g total fat (1.9g
saturated fat); 364kJ (87 cal); 10g carbohydrate;
1.3g protein; 0.5g fibre*

macadamia anzac biscuits

125g butter, chopped
2 tablespoons golden syrup
½ teaspoon bicarbonate of soda
2 tablespoons boiling water
1 cup (90g) rolled oats
1 cup (150g) plain flour
1 cup (220g) firmly packed brown sugar
¾ cup (60g) desiccated coconut
½ cup (65g) finely chopped macadamias
¼ cup (45g) finely chopped glacé ginger

1 Preheat oven to 180°C/160°C fan-forced.
Grease oven trays; line with baking paper.
2 Stir butter and golden syrup in medium saucepan
over low heat until smooth. Stir in combined soda
and the water; stir in remaining ingredients.
3 Roll level tablespoons of mixture into balls. Place
about 5cm apart on oven trays; flatten slightly.
4 Bake biscuits about 15 minutes. Cool on trays.

preparation time *15 minutes*
cooking time *18 minutes* makes *32*
nutritional count per biscuit *6.3g total fat (3.5g
saturated fat); 422kJ (101 cal); 9.4g carbohydrate;
1.3g protein; 0.9g fibre*

fudgy chocolate, cherry and coconut cookies

125g butter, softened
¾ cup (165g) firmly packed brown sugar
1 egg
1 teaspoon vanilla extract
1 cup (150g) plain flour
¼ cup (35g) self-raising flour
⅓ cup (35g) cocoa powder
½ teaspoon bicarbonate of soda
½ cup (125ml) milk
4 x 55g Cherry Ripe chocolate bars,
    cut into 1cm pieces
100g dark eating chocolate, cut into 1cm pieces

1 Preheat oven to 180°C/160°C fan-forced.
Grease three oven trays; line with baking paper.
2 Beat butter, sugar, egg and extract in medium
bowl with electric mixer until smooth. Stir in sifted
flours, cocoa and soda with milk, in two batches;
stir in Cherry Ripe pieces.
3 Drop level tablespoons of mixture, about 5cm
apart, on trays; press with fork to flatten slightly.
4 Bake cookies about 10 minutes. Stand on trays
5 minutes; transfer to wire rack to cool.

preparation time *20 minutes*
cooking time *10 minutes* makes *36*
nutritional count per cookie *5.5g total fat (3.6g
saturated fat); 460kJ (110 cal); 13.5g carbohydrate;
1.5g protein; 0.6g fibre*

wholemeal rosemary butter cookies

125g butter, softened
2 teaspoons finely grated orange rind
1 cup (220g) firmly packed brown sugar
1⅓ cups (200g) wholemeal self-raising flour
1 cup (100g) walnuts, roasted, chopped coarsely
⅔ cup (100g) raisins, halved
2 teaspoons dried rosemary
⅓ cup (80ml) orange juice
⅔ cup (50g) desiccated coconut
⅔ cup (60g) rolled oats

1 Preheat oven to 180°C/160°C fan-forced.
Grease oven trays; line with baking paper.
2 Beat butter, rind and sugar in small bowl with
electric mixer until combined. Transfer to medium
bowl; stir in flour, then remaining ingredients.
3 Roll rounded tablespoons of mixture into balls,
place about 5cm apart on trays; flatten slightly.
4 Bake cookies about 15 minutes. Cool on trays.

preparation time *15 minutes*
cooking time *15 minutes* makes *28*
nutritional count per cookie *7.7g total fat (3.7g
saturated fat); 934kJ (142 cal); 15.7g carbohydrate;
1.9g protein; 1.6g fibre*

double-choc freckle cookies

125g butter, softened
¾ cup (165g) firmly packed brown sugar
1 egg
1½ cups (225g) plain flour
¼ cup (35g) self-raising flour
¼ cup (35g) cocoa powder
200g dark eating chocolate, melted
⅓ cup (85g) hundreds and thousands

1 Beat butter, sugar and egg in small bowl with electric mixer until combined. Stir in sifted dry ingredients, in two batches. Knead dough on floured surface until smooth. Roll dough between sheets of baking paper until 5mm thick. Cover; refrigerate 30 minutes.
2 Preheat oven to 180°C/160°C fan-forced. Grease oven trays; line with baking paper.
3 Using 3cm, 5cm and 6.5cm round cutters, cut 14 rounds from dough using each cutter. Place 3cm rounds on one oven tray; place remainder on other oven trays.
4 Bake small cookies about 10 minutes; bake larger cookies about 12 minutes. Cool on wire racks.
5 Spread tops of cookies with chocolate; sprinkle with hundreds and thousands. Set at room temperature.

preparation time *25 minutes (plus refrigeration time)* cooking time *10 minutes* makes *42*
nutritional count per cookie *4.1g total fat (2.5g saturated fat); 405kJ (97 cal); 13.4g carbohydrate; 1.3g protein; 0.3g fibre*

snickerdoodles

250g butter, softened
1 teaspoon vanilla extract
½ cup (110g) firmly packed brown sugar
1 cup (220g) caster sugar
2 eggs
2¾ cups (410g) plain flour
1 teaspoon bicarbonate of soda
½ teaspoon ground nutmeg
1 tablespoon caster sugar, extra
2 teaspoons ground cinnamon

1 Beat butter, extract and sugars in small bowl with electric mixer until light and fluffy. Add eggs, one at a time, beating until combined. Transfer to large bowl; stir in sifted flour, soda and nutmeg, in two batches. Cover; refrigerate 30 minutes.
2 Preheat oven to 180°C/160°C fan-forced. Grease oven trays; line with baking paper.
3 Combine extra caster sugar and cinnamon in small shallow bowl. Roll level tablespoons of the dough into balls; roll balls in cinnamon sugar. Place balls about 7cm apart on oven trays.
4 Bake biscuits about 12 minutes. Cool on trays.

preparation time *20 minutes (plus refrigeration time)* cooking time *12 minutes* makes *42*
nutritional count per biscuit *5.2g total fat (3.3g saturated fat); 481kJ (115 cal); 15.3g carbohydrate; 1.4g protein; 0.4g fibre*

passionfruit butter biscuits

250g butter, softened
1⅓ cups (220g) icing sugar mixture
2 cups (300g) plain flour
½ cup (75g) cornflour
⅓ cup (50g) rice flour
2 tablespoons passionfruit pulp

1 Process butter, sugar and flours 2 minutes or until mixture is combined. Add passionfruit; process until mixture clings together. Knead dough on floured surface until smooth. Divide dough in half; roll each half into 26cm log. Wrap in plastic wrap; refrigerate 1 hour.
2 Preheat oven to 180°C/160°C fan-forced. Grease oven trays.
3 Cut logs into 1cm slices. Place slices about 3cm apart on trays.
4 Bake biscuits about 20 minutes or until pale golden colour. Cool on wire rack.

preparation time *25 minutes (plus refrigeration time)* cooking time *20 minutes (plus cooling time)* makes *40*
nutritional count per biscuit *5.2g total fat (3.4g saturated fat); 447kJ (107 cal); 13.7g carbohydrate; 1g protein; 0.5g fibre*

christmas pudding cookies

1⅔ cups (250g) plain flour
⅓ cup (40g) almond meal
⅓ cup (75g) caster sugar
1 teaspoon mixed spice
1 teaspoon vanilla extract
125g cold butter, chopped
2 tablespoons water
700g rich dark fruit cake
⅓ cup (80ml) brandy
1 egg white
400g dark eating chocolate, melted
½ cup (75g) white chocolate Melts, melted
30 red glacé cherries

1   Process flour, almond meal, sugar, spice, extract and butter until crumbly. Add the water, process until ingredients come together. Knead dough on floured surface until smooth. Roll dough between sheets of baking paper until 5mm thick. Cover; refrigerate 30 minutes.
2   Preheat oven to 180°C/160°C fan-forced. Grease oven trays; line with baking paper.
3   Using 5.5cm round cutter, cut 30 rounds from dough. Place about 3cm apart on oven trays.
4   Bake cookies about 10 minutes.
5   Meanwhile, crumble fruit cake into a medium bowl; add brandy. Press mixture firmly into round metal tablespoon measures. Brush partially baked cookies with egg white, top with cake domes; bake further 5 minutes. Cool on wire racks.
6   Place wire racks over oven tray, coat cookies with dark chocolate; set at room temperature. Spoon white chocolate over cookies; top with cherries.

preparation time *30 minutes (plus refrigeration time)* cooking time *10 minutes* makes *30* nutritional count per cookie *8.2g total fat (4g saturated fat); 803kJ (192 cal); 24.7g carbohydrate; 2.8g protein; 1.3g fibre*

choc-cherry macaroon heart cookies

100g butter, softened
½ cup (150g) caster sugar
1 egg
2 cups (300g) plain flour
1 tablespoon cocoa powder
100g dark eating chocolate, melted

MACAROON FILLING

1 egg white
¼ cup (55g) caster sugar
½ teaspoon vanilla extract
¾ cup (60g) desiccated coconut
1 teaspoon plain flour
2 tablespoons finely chopped red glacé cherries

1   Make macaroon filling.
2   Beat butter, sugar and egg in small bowl with electric mixer until light and fluffy; stir in sifted dry ingredients, in two batches. Stir in chocolate. Knead dough on floured surface until smooth. Roll dough between sheets of baking paper until 7mm thick.
3   Preheat oven to 180°C/160°C fan-forced. Grease oven trays; line with baking paper.
4   Using 8cm heart-shaped cutter, cut hearts from dough. Place about 2cm apart, on oven trays. Using 4cm heart-shaped cutter, cut out centres from hearts.
5   Bake cookies about 7 minutes; remove from oven. Reduce oven temperature to 150°C/130°C fan-forced.
6   Divide filling among centres of cookies; smooth surface. Cover with foil (like a tent so foil does not touch surface of filling). Bake 15 minutes or until filling is firm. Cool on trays 5 minutes; transfer to wire racks to cool.

MACAROON FILLING Beat egg white in small bowl with electric mixer until soft peaks form. Gradually add sugar 1 tablespoon at a time, beating until dissolved between additions. Fold in extract, coconut, flour and cherries.

preparation time *30 minutes (plus refrigeration time)* cooking time *22 minutes* makes *22* nutritional count per cookie *7.3g total fat (4.9g saturated fat); 715kJ (171 cal); 23.4g carbohydrate; 2.5g protein; 1g fibre*

Conversion Charts

One Australian metric measuring cup or jug holds approximately 250ml; one Australian metric tablespoon holds 20ml; one Australian metric teaspoon holds 5ml.

The difference between one country's measuring cups and another's is within a two- or three-teaspoon variance, which is only 10 or 15ml and will not affect your cooking results. Most countries, including the US, the UK and New Zealand, use a 15ml tablespoon.

All cup and spoon measurements are level. The most accurate way of measuring dry ingredients is to weigh them. When measuring liquids, use a clear glass or plastic jug with metric markings at eye level.

In this book we used large eggs with an average weight of 60g each.

Please note that those who might be at risk from the effects of salmonella poisoning (such as pregnant women, the elderly or young children) should consult their doctor before eating raw eggs.

OVEN TEMPERATURES

These oven temperatures are only a guide for conventional ovens. For fan-forced ovens, check the manufacturer's manual.

	°C (Celsius)	°F (Fahrenheit)	Gas Mark
Very slow	120	250	½
Slow	150	275-300	1-2
Moderately slow	160	325	3
Moderate	180	350-375	4-5
Moderately hot	200	400	6
Hot	220	425-450	7-8
Very hot	240	475	9

LIQUID MEASURES

metric	imperial
30ml	1 fluid oz
60ml	2 fluid oz
100ml	3 fluid oz
125ml	4 fluid oz
150ml	5 fluid oz (¼ pint/1 gill)
190ml	6 fluid oz
250ml	8 fluid oz
300ml	10 fluid oz (½ pint)
500ml	16 fluid oz
600ml	20 fluid oz (1 pint)
1000ml (1 litre)	1¾ pints

DRY MEASURES

metric	imperial
15g	½oz
30g	1oz
60g	2oz
90g	3oz
125g	4oz (¼lb)
155g	5oz
185g	6oz
220g	7oz
250g	8oz (½lb)
280g	9oz
315g	10oz
345g	11oz
375g	12oz (¾lb)
410g	13oz
440g	14oz
470g	15oz
500g	16oz (1lb)
750g	24oz (1½lb)
1kg	32oz (2lb)

LENGTH MEASURES

metric	imperial
3mm	⅛in
6mm	¼in
1cm	½in
2cm	¾in
2.5cm	1in
5cm	2in
6cm	2½in
8cm	3in
10cm	4in
13cm	5in
15cm	6in
18cm	7in
20cm	8in
23cm	9in
25cm	10in
28cm	11in
30cm	12in (1ft)

GLOSSARY & INDEX

glossary

ALL-BRAN a low-fat, high-fibre breakfast cereal based on wheat bran.

ALLSPICE also called pimento or jamaican pepper; tastes like a combination of nutmeg, cumin, clove and cinnamon. Available whole or ground.

ALMONDS
blanched brown skins removed.
flaked paper-thin slices.
meal also known as ground almonds.
slivered small pieces cut lengthways.
vienna toffee-coated almonds.

ARROWROOT a starch made from the rhizome of a Central American plant, used mostly as a thickening agent.

ARTICHOKE HEARTS tender centre of the globe artichoke; can be harvested from the plant after the prickly choke is removed. Cooked hearts can be bought from delicatessens or canned in brine.

BACON RASHERS also known as bacon slices.

BAHARAT an aromatic spice blend, includes some or all of the following: mixed spice, black pepper, allspice, dried chilli flakes, paprika, coriander seeds, cinnamon, clove, sumac, nutmeg, cumin seeds and cardamom seeds. It is used through the Middle East; here, it is often sold as Lebanese seven-spice, and can be found in Middle-Eastern food stores, some delicatessens and specialist food stores.

BAKING POWDER a raising agent consisting mainly of two parts cream of tartar to one part bicarbonate of soda. *see also gluten-free baking powder*

BANANA LEAVES used to line steamers and wrap food; sold in bundles in Asian food shops, greengrocers and supermarkets. Cut leaves, on both sides of centre stem, into required sized pieces then immerse in hot water or hold over a flame until pliable enough to wrap or fold over food; secure with kitchen string, toothpicks or skewers.

BARLEY a nutritious grain used in soups and stews. Hulled barley, the least processed, is high in fibre. Pearl barley has had the husk removed then been steamed and polished so that only the "pearl" of the original grain remains, much the same as white rice.

BASIL
holy also called kra pao or hot basil; different from thai and sweet basil, having an almost hot, spicy flavour similar to clove. Used in many Thai dishes, especially curries; distinguished from thai basil by tiny "hairs" on its leaves and stems.
sweet the most common type of basil; used extensively in Italian dishes and one of the main ingredients in pesto.
thai also known as horapa; different from holy basil and sweet basil in both look and taste, having smaller leaves and purplish stems. It has a slight aniseed taste and is one of the identifying flavours of Thai food.

BAY LEAVES aromatic leaves from the bay tree available fresh or dried; adds a strong, slightly peppery flavour.

BEAN SPROUTS tender new growths of assorted beans and seeds germinated for consumption as sprouts.

BEANS
black also called turtle beans or black kidney beans; an earthy-flavoured dried bean completely different from the better-known Chinese black beans (fermented soybeans). Used mostly in Mexican and South American cooking.
borlotti also called roman beans or pink beans, can be eaten fresh or dried. Interchangeable with pinto beans due to their similarity in appearance – pale pink or beige with dark red streaks.
broad also called fava, windsor and horse beans; available dried, fresh, canned and frozen. Fresh should be peeled twice (discarding both the outer long green pod and the beige-green tough inner shell); the frozen beans

have had their pods removed but the beige shell still needs removal.
butter cans labelled butter beans are, in fact, cannellini beans. Confusingly butter is also another name for lima beans, sold both dried and canned; a large beige bean having a mealy texture and mild taste.
cannellini small white bean similar in appearance and flavour to other *phaseolus vulgaris* varieties (great northern, navy or haricot). Available dried or canned.
kidney medium-size red bean, slightly floury in texture yet sweet in flavour; sold dried or canned, it's found in bean mixes and is used in chilli con carne.
lima large, flat kidney-shaped, beige dried and canned beans. Also known as butter beans.
snake long (about 40cm), thin, round, fresh green beans, Asian in origin, with a taste similar to green or french beans. Used most frequently in stir-fries, they are also known as yard-long beans because of their (pre-metric) length.
soy the most nutritious of all legumes; high in protein and low in carbohydrate and the source of products such as tofu, soy milk, soy sauce, tamari and miso. Sometimes sold fresh as edamame; also available dried and canned.
white a generic term we use for canned or dried cannellini, haricot, navy or great northern beans belonging to the same family, *phaseolus vulgaris*.

BEEF
chuck inexpensive cut from the neck and shoulder area; good minced and slow-cooked.
corned beef also called corned silverside; little fat, cut from the upper leg and cured. Sold cryovac-packed in brine.
eye-fillet tenderloin, fillet; fine texture, most expensive and extremely tender.
gravy boneless stewing beef from shin; slow-cooked, imbues stocks, soups and casseroles with a gelatine richness. Cut crossways, with bone in, is osso buco.
minced also known as ground beef.

new-york cut boneless striploin steak.
oxtail a flavourful cut originally from the ox but today more likely to be from any beef cattle; requires long, slow cooking so it is perfect for curries and stews.
rump boneless tender cut taken from the upper part of the round (hindquarter). Cut into steaks, good for barbecuing; as one piece, great as a roast.
scotch fillet cut from the muscle running behind the shoulder along the spine. Also known as cube roll, cuts include standing rib roast and rib-eye.
silverside also called topside roast; the actual cut used for making corned beef.
skirt steak lean, flavourful coarse-grained cut from the inner thigh. Needs slow-cooking; good for stews or casseroles.
T-bone sirloin steak with bone in and fillet eye attached.

BEETROOT also known as red beets; firm, round root vegetable.

BESAN see flour

BICARBONATE OF SODA also known as baking soda.

BLACK BEAN SAUCE an Asian cooking sauce made from salted and fermented soybeans, spices and wheat flour; used most often in stir-fries.

BLOOD ORANGE a virtually seedless citrus fruit with blood-red-streaked rind and flesh; sweet, non-acidic, salmon-coloured pulp and juice having slight strawberry or raspberry overtones. The juice can be drunk straight or used in cocktails, sauces, sorbets and jellies; can be frozen for use in cooking when the growing season finishes. The rind is not as bitter as an ordinary orange.

BREADCRUMBS
fresh bread, usually white, processed into crumbs.
japanese also called ponko; available in two kinds: larger pieces and fine crumbs; have a lighter texture than Western-style ones. Available from Asian food stores and some supermarkets.

packaged prepared fine-textured but crunchy white breadcrumbs; good for coating foods that are to be fried.
stale crumbs made by grating, blending or processing 1- or 2-day-old bread.

BRIOCHE French in origin; a rich, yeast-leavened, cake-like bread made with butter and eggs. Available from cake or specialty bread shops.

BROCCOLINI a cross between broccoli and Chinese kale; long asparagus-like stems with a long loose floret, both completely edible. Resembles broccoli but is milder and sweeter in taste.

BRUISING a cooking term to describe the slight crushing given to aromatic ingredients, particularly herbs, with the flat side of a heavy knife or cleaver to release flavour and aroma.

BUCKWHEAT a herb in the same plant family as rhubarb; not a cereal so it is gluten-free. Available as flour; ground (cracked) into coarse, medium or fine granules (kasha) and used similarly to polenta; or groats, the whole kernel sold roasted as a cereal product.

BUK CHOY also known as bok choy, pak choi, Chinese white cabbage or Chinese chard; has a fresh, mild mustard taste. Use stems and leaves, stir-fried or braised. Baby buk choy, also known as pak kat farang or shanghai bok choy, is much smaller and more tender. Its mildly acrid, distinctively appealing taste has made it one of the most commonly used Asian greens.

BURGHUL also called bulghur wheat; hulled steamed wheat kernels that, once dried, are crushed into various sized grains. Used in Middle Eastern dishes such as felafel, kibbeh and tabbouleh. Is not the same as cracked wheat.

BUTTER we use salted butter unless stated otherwise; 125g is equal to 1 stick (4 ounces).

BUTTERMILK see milk

CACHOUS also called dragées in some countries; minuscule metallic-looking-but-edible confectionery balls used in cake decorating; available in silver, gold or various colours.

CANDLENUTS a hard nut, used to thicken curries in Malaysia and Indonesia. Almonds, brazil nuts or macadamias can be substituted.

CAPERBERRIES olive-sized fruit formed after the buds of the caper bush have flowered; they are usually sold pickled in a vinegar brine with stalks intact.

CAPERS the grey-green buds of a warm climate (usually Mediterranean) shrub, sold either dried and salted or pickled in a vinegar brine; tiny young ones, called baby capers, are also available both in brine or dried in salt. Their pungent taste adds piquancy to a tapenade, sauces and condiments.

CAPSICUM also called pepper or bell pepper. Discard seeds and membranes before use.

CARAWAY SEEDS the small, half-moon-shaped dried seed from a member of the parsley family; adds a sharp anise flavour when used in both sweet and savoury dishes. Used widely, in foods such as rye bread, harissa and the classic Hungarian fresh cheese, liptauer.

CARDAMOM a spice native to India and used extensively in its cuisine; can be purchased in pod, seed or ground form. Has a distinctive aromatic, sweetly rich flavour and is one of the world's most expensive spices.

CASHEWS plump, kidney-shaped, golden-brown nuts having a distinctive sweet, buttery flavour and containing about 48 per cent fat. Because of this high fat content, they should be kept, sealed tightly, under refrigeration to avoid becoming rancid. We use roasted unsalted cashews in this book, unless otherwise stated; they're available from health-food stores and most supermarkets. Roasting cashews brings out their intense nutty flavour.

CAYENNE PEPPER *see chilli*

CELERIAC tuberous root with knobbly brown skin, white flesh and a celery-like flavour. Keep peeled celeriac in acidulated water to stop it discolouring. It can be grated and eaten raw in salads; used in soups and stews; boiled and mashed like potatoes; or sliced thinly and deep-fried as chips.

CHAR SIU also called Chinese barbecue sauce; a paste-like ingredient dark-red-brown in colour with a sharp sweet and spicy flavour. Made with fermented soybeans, honey and various spices; can be diluted and used as a marinade or brushed onto grilling meat.

CHEESE
blue mould-treated cheeses mottled with blue veining. Varieties include firm and crumbly stilton types and mild, creamy brie-like cheeses.
bocconcini from the diminutive of "boccone", meaning mouthful in Italian; walnut-sized, baby mozzarella, a delicate, semi-soft, white cheese traditionally made from buffalo milk. Sold fresh, it spoils rapidly so will only keep, refrigerated in brine, for 1 or 2 days at the most.
brie soft-ripened cow-milk cheese with a delicate, creamy texture and a rich, sweet taste that varies from buttery to mushroomy. Best served at room temperature after a brief period of ageing, brie should have a bloomy white rind and creamy, voluptuous centre which becomes runny with ripening.
cream commonly called philadelphia or philly; a soft cow-milk cheese, its fat content ranges from 14 to 33 per cent.
fetta Greek in origin; a crumbly textured goat- or sheep-milk cheese having a sharp, salty taste. Ripened and stored in salted whey; particularly good cubed and tossed into salads.

fontina a smooth, firm Italian cow-milk cheese with a creamy, nutty taste and brown or red rind; an ideal melting or grilling cheese.
goats made from goat milk, has an earthy, strong taste. Available in soft, crumbly and firm textures, in various shapes and sizes, and sometimes rolled in ash or herbs.
gorgonzola a creamy Italian blue cheese with a mild, sweet taste; good as an accompaniment to fruit or used to flavour sauces (especially pasta).
gruyere a hard-rind Swiss cheese with small holes and a nutty, slightly salty flavour. A popular cheese for soufflés.
haloumi a Greek Cypriot cheese with a semi-firm, spongy texture and very salty sweet flavour. Ripened and stored in salted whey; best grilled or fried, and holds its shape well on being heated. Eat while still warm as it becomes tough and rubbery on cooling.
mascarpone an Italian fresh cultured-cream product made in much the same way as yogurt. Whiteish to creamy yellow in colour, with a buttery-rich, luscious texture. Soft, creamy and spreadable, it is used in Italian desserts and as an accompaniment to fresh fruit.
mozzarella soft, spun-curd cheese; originating in southern Italy where it was traditionally made from water-buffalo milk. Now generally made from cow milk, it is the most popular pizza cheese because of its low melting point and elasticity when heated.
parmesan also called parmigiano; is a hard, grainy cow-milk cheese originating in the Parma region of Italy. The curd for this cheese is salted in brine for a month, then aged for up to 2 years in humid conditions. Reggiano is the best parmesan, aged for a minimum 2 years and made only in the Italian region of Emilia-Romagna.
pecorino the Italian generic name for cheeses made from sheep milk. This family of hard, white to pale-yellow cheeses, traditionally made in the Italian winter and spring when sheep graze on

natural pastures, have been matured for 8 to 12 months. They are classified according to the area in which they were produced – romano from Rome, sardo from Sardinia, siciliano from Sicily and toscano from Tuscany. If you can't find it, use parmesan.
pizza cheese a commercial blend of varying proportions of processed grated mozzarella, cheddar and parmesan.
provolone a mild stretched-curd cheese similar to mozzarella when young, becoming hard, spicy and grainy the longer it's aged. Golden yellow in colour, with a smooth waxy rind, provolone is a good all-purpose cheese used in cooking, for dessert with cheese, and shredded or flaked.
ricotta a soft, sweet, moist, white cow-milk cheese with a low fat content (8.5 per cent) and a slightly grainy texture. The name roughly translates as "cooked again" and refers to ricotta's manufacture from a whey that is itself a by-product of other cheese making.
roquefort considered the "king of cheeses", this is a blue cheese with a singularly pungent taste; made only from the milk of specially bred sheep and ripened in the damp limestone caves found under the village of Roquefort-sur-Soulzon in France. Has a sticky, bone-coloured rind and, when ripe, the sharp, almost metallic-tasting interior is creamy and almost shiny.

CHERVIL also known as cicily; mildly fennel-flavoured member of the parsley family with curly dark-green leaves. Available both fresh and dried but, like all herbs, is best used fresh; like coriander and parsley, its delicate flavour diminishes the longer it's cooked.

CHICKEN
barbecued we use cooked whole barbecued chickens weighing about 900g apiece in our recipes. Skin discarded and bones removed, this size chicken provides 4 cups (400g) shredded meat or about 3 cups (400g) coarsely chopped meat.

breast fillet breast halved, skinned and boned.

drumette small fleshy part of the wing between shoulder and elbow, trimmed to resemble a drumstick.

drumstick leg with skin and bone intact.

maryland leg and thigh still connected in a single piece; bones and skin intact.

small chicken also known as spatchcock or poussin; no more than 6 weeks old, weighing a maximum of 500g. Also a cooking term to describe splitting a small chicken open, flattening then grilling.

tenderloin thin strip of meat lying just under the breast; good for stir-frying.

thigh skin and bone intact.

thigh cutlet thigh with skin and centre bone intact; sometimes found skinned with bone intact.

thigh fillet thigh with skin and centre bone removed.

CHICKPEAS also called garbanzos, hummus or channa; an irregularly round, sandy-coloured legume used extensively in Mediterranean, Indian and Hispanic cooking. Firm texture even after cooking, a floury mouth-feel and robust nutty flavour; available canned or dried (reconstitute for several hours in cold water before use).

CHILLI use rubber gloves when seeding and chopping fresh chillies as they can burn your skin. We use unseeded chillies because the seeds contain the heat; use fewer chillies rather than seeding the lot.

ancho mild, dried chillies commonly used in Mexican cooking.

cayenne pepper a thin-fleshed, long, extremely hot dried red chilli, usually purchased ground.

chipotle pronounced cheh-pote-lay. The name used for jalapeño chillies once they've been dried and smoked. Having a deep, intensely smokey flavour, rather than a searing heat, chipotles are dark brown, almost black in colour and wrinkled in appearance.

flakes also sold as crushed chilli; dehydrated deep-red extremely fine slices and whole seeds.

green any unripened chilli; also some particular varieties that are ripe when green, such as jalapeño, habanero, poblano or serrano.

jalapeño pronounced hah-lah-pain-yo. Fairly hot, medium-sized, plump, dark green chilli; available pickled, sold canned or bottled, and fresh, from greengrocers.

long red available both fresh and dried; a generic term used for any moderately hot, long, thin chilli (about 6cm to 8cm long).

powder the Asian variety is the hottest, made from dried ground thai chillies; can be used instead of fresh in the proportion of ½ teaspoon chilli powder to 1 medium chopped fresh red chilli.

sauce, sweet comparatively mild, fairly sticky and runny bottled sauce made from red chillies, sugar, garlic and white vinegar; used in Thai cooking.

thai also known as "scuds"; tiny, very hot and bright red in colour.

CHINESE BARBECUED DUCK *see duck*

CHINESE BARBECUED PORK *see pork*

CHINESE COOKING WINE also called hao hsing or chinese rice wine; made from fermented rice, wheat, sugar and salt with a 13.5 per cent alcohol content. Inexpensive and found in Asian food shops; if you can't find it, replace with mirin or sherry.

CHIVES related to the onion and leek; has a subtle onion flavour. Used more for flavour than as an ingredient; chopped finely, they're good in sauces, dressings, omelettes or as a garnish.

CHOCOLATE

Choc Bits also known as chocolate chips or chocolate morsels; available in milk, white and dark chocolate. Made of cocoa liquor, cocoa butter, sugar and an emulsifier, these hold their shape in baking and are ideal for decorating.

Melts small discs of compounded milk, white or dark chocolate ideal for melting and moulding.

couverture a term used to describe a fine quality, very rich chocolate high in both cocoa butter and cocoa liquor. Requires tempering when used to coat but not if used in baking, mousses or fillings.

dark cooking also called compounded chocolate; good for cooking as it doesn't require tempering and sets at room temperature. Made with vegetable fat instead of cocoa butter so it lacks the rich, buttery flavour of eating chocolate. Cocoa butter is the most expensive component in chocolate, so the substitution of a vegetable fat means that compounded chocolate is much cheaper to produce.

dark eating also known as semi-sweet or luxury chocolate; made of a high percentage of cocoa liquor and cocoa butter, and little added sugar. Unless stated otherwise, we use dark eating chocolate in this book as it's ideal for use in desserts and cakes.

milk most popular eating chocolate, mild and very sweet; similar in make-up to dark with the difference being the addition of milk solids.

white contains no cocoa solids but derives its sweet flavour from cocoa butter. Very sensitive to heat.

CHOCOLATE HAZELNUT SPREAD also known as Nutella; made of cocoa powder, hazelnuts, sugar and milk.

CHORIZO sausage of Spanish origin, made of coarsely ground pork and highly seasoned with garlic and chilli.

CHOY SUM also known as pakaukeo or flowering cabbage, a member of the buk choy family; easy to identify with its long stems, light green leaves and yellow flowers. Stems and leaves are both edible, steamed or stir-fried.

CIABATTA in Italian, the word means slipper, the traditional shape of this popular crisp-crusted, open-textured white sourdough bread. A good bread to use for bruschetta.

CINNAMON available both in the piece (called sticks or quills) and ground into powder; one of the world's most common spices, used universally as a sweet, fragrant flavouring for both sweet and savoury foods. The dried inner bark of the shoots of the Sri Lankan native cinnamon tree; much of what is sold as the real thing is in fact cassia, Chinese cinnamon, from the bark of the cassia tree. Less expensive to process than true cinnamon, it is often blended with Sri Lankan cinnamon to produce the type of "cinnamon" most commonly found in supermarkets.

CLOVES dried flower buds of a tropical tree; can be used whole or in ground form. They have a strong scent and taste so should be used sparingly.

COCOA POWDER also known as unsweetened cocoa; cocoa beans (cacao seeds) that have been fermented, roasted, shelled, ground into powder then cleared of most of the fat content.

COCONUT
cream obtained commercially from the first pressing of the coconut flesh alone, without the addition of water; the second pressing (less rich) is sold as coconut milk. Available in cans and cartons at most supermarkets.
desiccated concentrated, dried, unsweetened and finely shredded coconut flesh.
essence synthetically produced from flavouring, oil and alcohol.
flaked dried flaked coconut flesh.
milk not the liquid found inside the fruit, which is called coconut water, but the diluted liquid from the second pressing of the white flesh of a mature coconut (the first pressing produces coconut cream). Available in cans and cartons at most supermarkets.
shredded unsweetened thin strips of dried coconut flesh.

COINTREAU see liqueurs

COOKING-OIL SPRAY see oil

COPPA salted and dried sausage made from the neck or shoulder of pork. It is deep red in colour and is available mild and spicy; it is more marbled with fat so it's less expensive.

CORELLA PEARS miniature dessert pear up to 10cm long.

CORIANDER also called cilantro, pak chee or chinese parsley; bright-green-leafed herb having both pungent aroma and taste. Used as an ingredient in a wide variety of cuisines. Often stirred into or sprinkled over a dish just before serving for maximum impact as, like other leafy herbs, its characteristics diminish with cooking. Both the stems and roots of coriander are used in Thai cooking: wash well before chopping. Coriander seeds are dried and sold either whole or ground, and neither form tastes remotely like the fresh leaf.

CORN FLAKES commercially manufactured cereal made of dehydrated then baked crisp flakes of corn. Also available is a prepared finely ground mixture used for coating or crumbing food before frying or baking, sold as "crushed corn flakes" in 300g packages in most supermarkets.

CORNFLOUR also known as cornstarch. Available made from corn or wheat (wheaten cornflour, gluten-free, gives a lighter texture in cakes); used as a thickening agent in cooking.

CORNICHON French for gherkin, a very small variety of cucumber. Pickled, they are a traditional accompaniment to pâté; the Swiss always serve them with fondue (or raclette).

COS LETTUCE see lettuce

COUSCOUS a fine, grain-like cereal product made from semolina; from the countries of North Africa. A semolina flour and water dough is sieved then dehydrated to produce minuscule even-sized pellets of couscous; it is

rehydrated by steaming or with the addition of a warm liquid and swells to three or four times its original size; eaten like rice with a tagine, as a side dish or salad ingredient.

CRANBERRIES available dried and frozen; have a rich, astringent flavour and can be used in cooking sweet and savoury dishes. The dried version can usually be substituted for or with other dried fruit.

CREAM OF TARTAR the acid ingredient in baking powder; added to confectionery mixtures to help prevent sugar from crystallising. Keeps frostings creamy and improves volume when beating egg whites.

CREME FRAICHE a mature, naturally fermented cream (minimum fat content 35 per cent) having a velvety texture and slightly tangy, nutty flavour. Crème fraîche, a French variation of sour cream, can boil without curdling and be used in sweet and savoury dishes.

CUMIN also known as zeera or comino; resembling caraway in size, cumin is the dried seed of a plant related to the parsley family. Its spicy, almost curry-like flavour is essential to the traditional foods of Mexico, India, North Africa and the Middle East. Available dried as seeds or ground. Black cumin seeds are smaller than standard cumin, and dark brown rather than true black; they are mistakenly confused with kalonji.

CURRY POWDER a blend of ground spices used for making Indian and some South-East Asian dishes. Consists of some of the following spices: dried chilli, cinnamon, coriander, cumin, fennel, fenugreek, mace, cardamom and turmeric. Available mild or hot.

CUSTARD POWDER instant mixture used to make pouring custard; similar to North American instant pudding mixes.

DAIKON also called white radish; an everyday fixture at the Japanese table, this long, white horseradish has a wonderful, sweet flavour. After peeling, eat it raw in salads or shredded as a garnish; also great when sliced or cubed and cooked in stir-fries and casseroles. The flesh is white but the skin can be either white or black; buy those that are firm and unwrinkled from Asian food shops.

DASHI the basic fish and seaweed stock that accounts for the distinctive flavour of many Japanese dishes, such as soups and various casserole dishes. Made from dried bonito (a type of tuna) flakes and kombu (kelp); instant dashi (dashi-no-moto) is available in powder, granules and liquid concentrate from Asian food shops.

DEGLAZE a cooking term to describe making the base for a sauce by heating a small amount of wine, stock or water in a pan in which meat or poultry has been cooked (with most of the excess fat removed) then stirring to loosen the browned bits of food adhering to the bottom. After "deglazing" a pan, it is used as part of the sauce accompanying that food cooked earlier in the pan.

DILL also known as dill weed; used fresh or dried, in seed form or ground. Its anise/celery sweetness flavours the food of the Scandinavian countries, and Germany and Greece. Its feathery, frond-like fresh leaves are grassier and more subtle than the dried version or the seeds (which slightly resemble caraway in flavour). Use dill leaves with smoked salmon and sour cream, poached fish or roast chicken; use the seeds with simply cooked vegetables, or home-baked dark breads.

DRIED CHINESE SAUSAGE also called lap cheong; highly spiced, bright red, thin pork sausages. The meat is preserved by the high spice content and can be kept at room temperature.

DRIED CURRANTS tiny, almost black raisins so-named after a grape variety that originated in Corinth, Greece.

DUCK we use whole ducks in some recipes; available from specialty chicken shops, open-air markets and some supermarkets.
breast fillets boneless whole breasts, with the skin on.
chinese barbecued traditionally cooked in special ovens in China; dipped into and brushed during roasting with a sticky sweet coating made from soy sauce, sherry, ginger, five-spice, star anise and hoisin sauce. Available from Asian food shops as well as dedicated Chinese barbecued meat shops.

DUKKAH an Egyptian specialty spice mixture made up of roasted nuts, seeds and an array of aromatic spices.

EGGPLANT also called aubergine. Ranging in size from tiny to very large and in colour from pale green to deep purple. Can also be purchased char-grilled, packed in oil, in jars.
baby also called finger or japanese eggplant; very small and slender so can be used without disgorging.
pea tiny, about the size of peas; sometimes known by their thai name, "makeua puang". Sold in clusters of 10 to 15 eggplants, similar to vine-ripened cherry tomatoes; very bitter in flavour, a quality suited to balance rich, sweet coconut-sauced Thai curries. Available in Asian greengrocers and food shops, fresh or pickled.
thai found in a variety of different sizes and colours, from a long, thin, purplish-green one to a hard, round, golf-ball size having a white-streaked pale-green skin. This last looks like a small unripe tomato and is the most popular eggplant used in Thai and Vietnamese curries and stir-fries.

EGGS we use large chicken eggs weighing an average of 60g unless stated otherwise in the recipes in this book. If a recipe calls for raw or barely cooked eggs, exercise caution if there is a salmonella problem in your area, particularly in food eaten by children and pregnant women.

ESSENCE/EXTRACT an essence is either a distilled concentration of a food quality or an artificial creation of it. Coconut and almond essences are synthetically produced substances used in small amounts to impart their respective flavours to foods. An extract is made by actually extracting the flavour from a food product. In the case of vanilla, pods are soaked, usually in alcohol, to capture the authentic flavour. Essences and extracts keep indefinitely if stored in a cool dark place.

FENNEL also called finocchio or anise; a crunchy green vegetable slightly resembling celery that's eaten raw in salads; fried as an accompaniment; or used as an ingredient in soups and sauces. Also the name given to the dried seeds of the plant which have a stronger licorice flavour.

FENUGREEK hard, dried seed usually sold ground as an astringent spice powder. Good with seafood and in chutneys, fenugreek helps mask unpleasant odours.

FISH SAUCE called naam pla on the label if Thai-made, nuoc naam if Vietnamese; the two are almost identical. Made from pulverised salted fermented fish (most often anchovies); has a pungent smell and strong taste. Available in varying degrees of intensity, so use according to your taste.

FIVE-SPICE POWDER although the ingredients vary from country to country, five-spice is usually a fragrant mixture of ground cinnamon, cloves, star anise, sichuan pepper and fennel seeds. Used in Chinese and other Asian cooking; available from most supermarkets or Asian food shops.

FLOUR

besan also known as chickpea flour or gram; made from ground chickpeas so is gluten-free and high in protein. Used in Indian cooking to make dumplings, noodles and chapati; for a batter coating for deep-frying; and as a sauce thickener.

buckwheat *see buckwheat*

cornflour *see cornflour*

plain also known as all-purpose; unbleached wheat flour is the best for baking: the gluten content ensures a strong dough, which produces a light result.

rice very fine, almost powdery, gluten-free flour; made from ground white rice. Used in baking, as a thickener, and in some Asian noodles and desserts. Another variety, made from glutinous sweet rice, is used for chinese dumplings and rice paper.

self-raising all-purpose plain or wholemeal flour with baking powder and salt added; make yourself with plain or wholemeal flour sifted with baking powder in the proportion of 1 cup flour to 2 teaspoons baking powder.

wholemeal also known as wholewheat flour; milled with the wheat germ so is higher in fibre and more nutritional than plain flour.

FROMAGE FRAIS a light, fresh French cheese that has the consistency of thick yogurt with a refreshing, slightly tart taste. Low fat varieties are available.

GAI LAN also known as gai larn, chinese broccoli and chinese kale; green vegetable appreciated more for its stems than its coarse leaves. Can be served steamed and stir-fried, in soups and noodle dishes. One of the most popular Asian greens, best known for its appearance on a yum cha trolley, where it's steamed then sprinkled with a mixture of oyster sauce and sesame oil.

GALANGAL also known as ka or lengkaus if fresh and laos if dried and powdered; a root, similar to ginger in its use. It has a hot-sour ginger-citrusy flavour; used in fish curries and soups.

GARAM MASALA literally meaning blended spices in its northern Indian place of origin; based on varying proportions of cardamom, cinnamon, cloves, coriander, fennel and cumin, roasted and ground together. Black pepper and chilli can be added for a hotter version.

GELATINE we use dried (powdered) gelatine in this book; it's also available in sheet form known as leaf gelatine. A thickening agent made from either collagen, a protein found in animal connective tissue and bones, or certain algae (agar-agar). Three teaspoons of dried gelatine (8g or one sachet) is about the same as four gelatine leaves. The two types are interchangable but leaf gelatine gives a much clearer mixture than dried gelatine; it's perfect in dishes where appearance matters.

GHEE clarified butter; with the milk solids removed, this fat has a high smoking point so can be heated to a high temperature without burning. Used as a cooking medium in Indian recipes.

GINGER

fresh also called green or root ginger; the thick gnarled root of a tropical plant. Can be kept, peeled, covered with dry sherry in a jar and refrigerated, or frozen in an airtight container.

glacé fresh ginger root preserved in sugar syrup; crystallised ginger (sweetened with cane sugar) can be substituted if rinsed with warm water and dried before using.

ground also called powdered ginger; used as a flavouring in baking but cannot be substituted for fresh ginger.

pickled pink or red coloured; available, packaged, from Asian food shops. Pickled paper-thin shavings of ginger in a mixture of vinegar, sugar and natural colouring; used in Japanese cooking.

GLACE CHERRIES also called candied cherries; boiled in heavy sugar syrup and then dried.

GLACE FRUIT fruit such as peaches, pineapple and orange cooked in heavy sugar syrup then dried.

GLUCOSE SYRUP also known as liquid glucose, made from wheat starch; used in jam and confectionery making. Available at health-food stores and supermarkets.

GLUTEN-FREE BAKING POWDER used as a leavening agent in bread, cake, pastry or pudding mixtures. Suitable for people with an allergic response to glutens or seeking an alternative to everyday baking powder. *see also baking powder*

GOLDEN SYRUP a by-product of refined sugarcane; pure maple syrup or honey can be substituted. Golden syrup and treacle (a thicker, darker syrup not unlike molasses), also known as flavour syrups, are similar sugar products made by partly breaking down sugar into its component parts and adding water. Treacle is more viscous, and has a stronger flavour and aroma than golden syrup (which has been refined further and contains fewer impurities, so is lighter in colour and more fluid). Both can be use in baking and for making certain confectionery items.

GOW GEE WRAPPERS *see wonton wrappers*

GRAND MARNIER *see liqueurs*

GRAPEVINE LEAVES from early spring, fresh grapevine leaves can be found in most specialist greengrocers. Alternatively, cryovac-packages containing about 60 leaves in brine can be found in Middle Eastern food shops and some delicatessens; these must be rinsed well and dried before using. Used as wrappers for savoury fillings in Mediterranean cuisines.

HARISSA a North African paste made from dried red chillies, garlic, olive oil and caraway seeds; can be used as a rub for meat, an ingredient in sauces and dressings, or eaten as a condiment. It is available from Middle Eastern food shops and some supermarkets.

HAZELNUTS also known as filberts; plump, grape-sized, rich, sweet nut having a brown skin that is removed by rubbing heated nuts together vigorously in a tea-towel.
meal is made by grounding the hazelnuts to a coarse flour texture for use in baking or as a thickening agent.
oil a mono-unsaturated oil, made in France, extracted from crushed hazelnuts.

HOISIN SAUCE a thick, sweet and spicy Chinese barbecue sauce made from salted fermented soybeans, onions and garlic; used as a marinade or baste, or to accent stir-fries and barbecued or roasted foods. From Asian food shops and supermarkets.

HONEY the variety sold in a squeezable container is not suitable for the recipes in this book.

HORSERADISH a vegetable with edible green leaves but mainly grown for its long, pungent white root. Occasionally found fresh in specialty greengrocers and some Asian food shops, but commonly purchased in bottles at the supermarket in two forms: prepared horseradish and horseradish cream. These cannot be substituted one for the other in cooking but both can be used as table condiments. Horseradish cream is a commercially prepared creamy paste consisting of grated horseradish, vinegar, oil and sugar, while prepared horseradish is the preserved grated root.

HUMMUS a Middle Eastern salad or dip made from softened dried chickpeas, garlic, lemon juice and tahini; can be purchased ready-made from most delicatessens and supermarkets. Also the Arabic word for chickpeas.

HUNDREDS AND THOUSANDS tiny sugar-syrup-coated sugar crystals that come in a variety of colours.

IRISH CREAM see liqueurs

JELLY CRYSTALS a combination of sugar, gelatine, colours and flavours; when dissolved in water, the solution sets as firm jelly.

JUNIPER BERRIES dried berries of an evergreen tree; it is the main flavouring ingredient in gin.

KAFFIR LIME also known as magrood, leech lime or jeruk purut. The wrinkled, bumpy-skinned green fruit of a small citrus tree originally grown in South Africa and South-East Asia. As a rule, only the rind and leaves are used.

KAFFIR LIME LEAVES also known as bai magrood and looks like two glossy dark green leaves joined end to end, forming a rounded hourglass shape. Used fresh or dried in many South-East Asian dishes, they are used like bay leaves or curry leaves, especially in Thai cooking. Sold fresh, dried or frozen, the dried leaves are less potent so double the number if using them as a substitute for fresh; a strip of fresh lime peel may be substituted for each kaffir lime leaf.

KAHLUA see liqueurs

KALONJI also called nigella or black onion seeds. Tiny, angular seeds, black on the outside and creamy within, with a sharp nutty flavour that is enhanced by frying briefly in a dry hot pan before use. Typically sprinkled over Turkish bread immediately after baking or as an important spice in Indian cooking, kalonji can be found in most Asian and Middle Eastern food shops. Often erroneously called black cumin seeds.

KASHA see buckwheat

KECAP ASIN a thick, dark, salty Indonesian soy sauce.

KECAP MANIS a dark, thick sweet soy sauce used in most South-East Asian cuisines. Depending on the manufacturer, the sauces's sweetness is derived from the addition of either molasses or palm sugar when brewed.

KIRSCH see liqueurs

KIWIFRUIT also known as Chinese gooseberry; having a brown, somewhat hairy skin and bright-green flesh with a unique sweet-tart flavour. Used in fruit salads, desserts and eaten as is.

KUMARA the polynesian name of an orange-fleshed sweet potato often confused with yam; good baked, boiled, mashed or fried similarly to other potatoes.

LAMB
backstrap also known as eye of loin; the larger fillet from a row of loin chops or cutlets. Tender, best cooked rapidly: barbecued or pan-fried.
cutlet small, tender rib chop; sometimes sold french-trimmed, with all the fat and gristle at the narrow end of the bone removed.
fillets fine texture, most expensive and extremely tender.
leg cut from the hindquarter; can be boned, butterflied, rolled and tied, or cut into dice.
minced ground lamb.
rolled shoulder boneless section of the forequarter, rolled and secured with string or netting.
shank forequarter leg; sometimes sold as drumsticks or frenched shanks if the gristle and narrow end of the bone are discarded and the remaining meat trimmed.
shoulder large, tasty piece having much connective tissue so is best pot-roasted or braised. Makes the best mince.

LEEKS a member of the onion family, the leek resembles a green onion but is much larger and more subtle in flavour. Tender baby or pencil leeks can be eaten whole with minimal cooking but adult leeks are usually trimmed of most of the green tops then chopped or sliced and cooked as an ingredient in stews, casseroles and soups.

LEMON GRASS also known as takrai, serai or serah. A tall, clumping, lemon-smelling and tasting, sharp-edged aromatic tropical grass; the white lower part of the stem is used, finely chopped, in much of the cooking of South-East Asia. Can be found, fresh, dried, powdered and frozen, in supermarkets, greengrocers and Asian food shops.

LENTILS (red, brown, yellow) dried pulses often identified by and named after their colour. Eaten by cultures all over the world, most famously perhaps in the dhals of India, lentils have high food value.
french green lentils are a local cousin to the famous (and very expensive) French lentils du puy; green-blue, tiny lentils with a nutty, earthy flavour and a hardy nature that allows them to be rapidly cooked without disintegrating.

LETTUCE
butter small, round, loosely formed heads with a sweet flavour; soft, buttery-textured leaves range from pale green on the outer leaves to pale yellow-green inner leaves.
cos also known as romaine lettuce; the traditional caesar salad lettuce. Long, with leaves ranging from dark green on the outside to almost white near the core; the leaves have a stiff centre rib giving a slight cupping effect to the leaf on either side.
iceberg a heavy, firm round lettuce with tightly packed leaves and crisp texture.
mesclun pronounced mess-kluhn; also known as mixed greens or spring salad mix. A commercial blend of assorted young lettuce and other green leaves, including baby spinach leaves, mizuna and curly endive.
mizuna Japanese in origin; the frizzy green salad leaves have a delicate mustard flavour.

radicchio Italian in origin; a member of the chicory family. The dark burgundy leaves and strong, bitter flavour can be cooked or eaten raw in salads.

LIQUEURS
cointreau citrus-flavoured liqueur.
Grand Marnier orange liqueur based on cognac-brandy.
irish cream we used Baileys, a smooth and creamy natural blend of fresh Irish cream, the finest Irish spirits, Irish whiskey, cocoa and vanilla.
kahlua coffee-flavoured liqueur.
kirsch cherry-flavoured liqueur.
limoncello Italian lemon-flavoured liqueur; originally made from the juice and peel of lemons grown along the Amalfi coast.
rum we use a dark underproof rum (not overproof) for a more subtle flavour in cooking. White rum is almost colourless, sweet and used mostly in mixed drinks.
Tia Maria coffee-flavoured liqueur.

LIMENCELLO see liqueurs

LYCHEES a small fruit from China with a hard shell and sweet, juicy flesh. The white flesh has a gelatinous texture and musky, perfumed taste. Discard the rough skin and seed before using in salads or as a dessert fruit. Also available canned in a sugar syrup.

MACADAMIAS native to Australia; fairly large, slightly soft, buttery rich nut. Used to make oil and macadamia butter; equally good in salads or cakes and pastries; delicious eaten on their own. Should always be stored in the fridge to prevent their high oil content turning them rancid.

MANGO tropical fruit originally from India and South-East Asia. With skin colour ranging from green to yellow and deep red; fragrant, deep yellow flesh surrounds a large flat seed. Slicing off the cheeks, cross-hatching them with a knife then turning them inside out shows the sweet, juicy flesh at its best.

Mangoes can also be used in curries and salsas, or pureed for ice-cream, smoothies or mousse. Mango cheeks in light syrup are available canned. Sour and crunchy, green mangoes are just the immature fruit that is used as a vegetable in salads, salsas and curries.

MAPLE-FLAVOURED SYRUP is made from sugar cane and is also known as golden or pancake syrup. It is not a substitute for pure maple syrup.

MAPLE SYRUP distilled from the sap of sugar maple trees found only in Canada and about ten states in the USA. Most often eaten with pancakes or waffles, but also used as an ingredient in baking or in preparing desserts. Maple-flavoured syrup or pancake syrup is not an adequate substitute for the real thing.

MARINARA MIX a mixture of uncooked, chopped seafood available from fishmarkets and fishmongers.

MARSALA a fortified Italian wine produced in the region surrounding the Sicilian city of Marsala; recognisable by its intense amber colour and complex aroma. Often used in cooking.

MAYONNAISE, WHOLE-EGG commercial mayonnaise of high quality made with whole eggs and labelled as such; some prepared mayonnaises substitute emulsifiers such as food starch, cellulose gel or other thickeners to achieve the same thick and creamy consistency but never achieve the same rich flavour. Must be refrigerated once opened.

MERGUEZ a small, spicy sausage believed to have originated in Tunisia but eaten throughout North Africa, France and Spain; is traditionally made with lamb meat and is easily recognised because of its chilli-red colour. Can be fried, grilled or roasted; available from many butchers, delicatessens and specialty sausage stores.

MILK we use full-cream homogenised milk unless otherwise specified.
buttermilk in spite of its name, buttermilk is actually low in fat, varying between 0.6 per cent and 2.0 per cent per 100ml. Originally the term given to the slightly sour liquid left after butter was churned from cream, today it is intentionally made from no-fat or low-fat milk to which specific bacterial cultures have been added during the manufacturing process. It is readily available from the dairy department in supermarkets. Because it is low in fat, it's a good substitute for dairy products such as cream or sour cream in some baking and salad dressings.
evaporated unsweetened canned milk from which water has been extracted by evaporation. Evaporated skim or low-fat milk has 0.3 per cent fat content.
full-cream powder instant powdered milk made from whole cow milk with liquid removed and emulsifiers added.
sweetened condensed a canned milk product consisting of milk with more than half the water content removed and sugar added to the remaining milk.

MIRIN a Japanese champagne-coloured cooking wine, made of glutinous rice and alcohol. It is used expressly for cooking and should not be confused with sake. A seasoned sweet mirin, manjo mirin, made of water, rice, corn syrup and alcohol, is used in various Japanese dipping sauces.

MISO fermented soybean paste. There are many types of miso, each with its own aroma, flavour, colour and texture; it can be kept, airtight, for up to a year in the fridge. Generally, the darker the miso, the saltier the taste and denser the texture. Salt-reduced miso is available. Buy in tubs or plastic packs.

MIXED DRIED FRUIT a combination of sultanas, raisins, currants, mixed peel and cherries.

MIXED SPICE a classic spice mixture generally containing caraway, allspice, coriander, cumin, nutmeg and ginger, although cinnamon and other spices can be added. It is used with fruit and in cakes.

MUSHROOMS
button small, cultivated white mushrooms with a mild flavour. When a recipe in this book calls for an unspecified type of mushroom, use button.
dried porcini the richest-flavoured mushrooms, also known as cèpes. Expensive but, because they are so strongly flavoured, only a small amount is required for any particular dish.
flat large, flat mushrooms with a rich earthy flavour, ideal for filling and barbecuing. They are sometimes misnamed field mushrooms which are wild mushrooms.
oyster also known as abalone; grey-white mushrooms shaped like a fan. Prized for their smooth texture and subtle, oyster-like flavour.
shiitake fresh, are also known as Chinese black, forest or golden oak mushrooms. Although cultivated, they have the earthiness and taste of wild mushrooms. Large and meaty, they can be used as a substitute for meat in some Asian vegetarian dishes. dried also called donko or dried Chinese mushrooms; have a unique meaty flavour. Sold dried; rehydrate before use.
swiss brown also known as roman or cremini. Light to dark brown mushrooms with full-bodied flavour; suited for use in casseroles or being stuffed and baked.

MUSLIN inexpensive, undyed, finely woven cotton fabric called for in cooking to strain stocks and sauces; if unavailable, use disposable coffee filter papers.

MUSTARD
american-style bright yellow in colour, a sweet mustard containing mustard seeds, sugar, salt, spices and garlic. Serve with hot dogs and hamburgers.

dijon also called french. Pale brown, creamy, distinctively flavoured, fairly mild French mustard.
english traditional hot, pungent, deep yellow mustard. Serve with roast beef and ham; wonderful with hard cheeses.
japanese hot mustard available in ready-to-use paste in tubes or powder form from Asian food shops.
wholegrain also known as seeded. A French-style coarse-grain mustard made from crushed mustard seeds and dijon-style french mustard. Works well with cold meats and sausages.

MUSTARD SEEDS
black also known as brown mustard seeds; more pungent than the white variety; used frequently in curries.
white also known as yellow mustard seeds; used ground for mustard powder and in most prepared mustards.

NAAN the rather thick, leavened bread associated with the tandoori dishes of northern India, where it is baked pressed against the inside wall of a heated tandoor (clay oven). Now available prepared by commercial bakeries and sold in most supermarkets.

NOODLES
dried rice noodles also known as rice stick noodles. Made from rice flour and water, available flat and wide or very thin (vermicelli). Must be soaked in boiling water to soften.
fresh egg also called ba mee or yellow noodles; made from wheat flour and eggs, sold fresh or dried. Range in size from very fine strands to wide, spaghetti-like pieces as thick as a shoelace.
fresh rice also called ho fun, khao pun, sen yau, pho or kway tiau, depending on the country of manufacture; the most common form of noodle used in Thailand. Can be purchased in strands of various widths or large sheets weighing about 500g which are to be cut into the desired noodle size. Chewy and pure white, they do not need pre-cooking before use.

hokkien also known as stir-fry noodles; fresh wheat noodles resembling thick, yellow-brown spaghetti needing no pre-cooking before use.

rice stick also known assen lek, ho fun or kway teow; especially popular South-East Asian dried rice noodles. They come in different widths (thin used in soups, wide in stir-fries), but all should be soaked in hot water to soften. The traditional noodle used in pad thai which, before soaking, measures about 5mm in width.

rice vermicelli also known as sen mee, mei fun or bee hoon. Used throughout Asia in spring rolls and cold salads; similar to bean threads, only longer and made with rice flour instead of mung bean starch. Before using, soak the dried noodles in hot water until softened, boil them briefly then rinse with hot water. Vermicelli can also be deep-fried until crunchy and used in salad or as a garnish or bed for sauces.

soba thin, pale-brown noodle originally from Japan; made from buckwheat and varying proportions of wheat flour. Available dried and fresh, and in flavoured (for instance, green tea) varieties; eaten in soups, stir-fries and, chilled, on their own.

udon available fresh and dried, these broad, white, wheat Japanese noodles are similar to the ones in home-made chicken noodle soup.

NORI a type of dried seaweed used in Japanese cooking as a flavouring, garnish or for sushi. Sold in thin sheets, plain or toasted (yaki-nori).

NUTMEG a strong and pungent spice ground from the dried nut of an evergreen tree native to Indonesia. Usually found ground but the flavour is more intense from a whole nut, available from spice shops, so it's best to grate your own. Used most often in baking and milk-based desserts, but also works nicely in savoury dishes. Found in mixed spice mixtures.

OATMEAL also sold as oatmeal flour, is made from milled oat kernels; not the same product as rolled oats or oat bran. It is available at health food stores.

OIL
cooking spray we use a cholesterol-free cooking spray made from canola oil.

grapeseed comes from grape seeds; available from supermarkets.

hazelnut oil see hazelnuts

macadamia oil see macadamias

olive made from ripened olives. Extra virgin and virgin are the first and second press, respectively, of the olives and are therefore considered the best; the "extra light" or "light" name on other types refers to taste not fat levels.

peanut pressed from ground peanuts; the most commonly used oil in Asian cooking because of its high smoke point (capacity to handle high heat without burning).

sesame made from roasted, crushed, white sesame seeds; a flavouring rather than a cooking medium.

vegetable any of a number of oils sourced from plant rather than animal fats.

OKRA also known as bamia or lady fingers. A green, ridged, oblong pod with a furry skin. Native to Africa, this vegetable is used in Indian, Middle Eastern and South American cooking. Can be eaten on its own; as part of a casserole, curry or gumbo; used to thicken stews or gravies.

ONIONS
fried onion served as a condiment on Asian tables to be sprinkled over just-cooked food. Found in cellophane bags or jars at all Asian grocery shops; once opened, they will keep for months if stored tightly seeled. Make your own by frying thinly sliced peeled baby onions until golden and crisp. see also shallots

green also known as scallion or (incorrectly) shallot; an immature onion picked before the bulb has formed, having a long, bright-green edible stalk.

red also known as spanish, red spanish or bermuda onion; a sweet-flavoured, large, purple-red onion.

spring crisp, narrow green-leafed tops and a round sweet white bulb larger than green onions.

ORANGE FLOWER WATER concentrated flavouring made from orange blossoms.

OYSTER SAUCE Asian in origin, this thick, richly flavoured brown sauce is made from oysters and their brine, cooked with salt and soy sauce, and thickened with starches. Use as a condiment.

PANCETTA an Italian unsmoked bacon, pork belly cured in salt and spices then rolled into a sausage shape and dried for several weeks. Used, sliced or chopped, as an ingredient rather than eaten on its own; can also be used to add taste and moisture to tough or dry cuts of meat.

PAPRIKA ground dried sweet red capsicum (bell pepper); there are many grades and types available, including sweet, hot, mild and smoked.

PASTA
farfalle bow-tie shaped short pasta; sometimes known as butterfly pasta.

fettuccine fresh or dried ribbon pasta made from durum wheat, semolina and egg. Also available plain or flavoured.

fresh lasagne sheets thinly rolled wide sheets of plain or flavoured pasta; they do not requiring par-boiling prior to being used in cooking.

gnocchi Italian 'dumplings' made of potatoes, semolina or flour; can be cooked in boiling water or baked with sauce.

macaroni tube-shaped pasta available in various sizes; made from semolina and water, and does not contain eggs.

risoni small rice-shape pasta; very similar to another small pasta, orzo.

spaghetti long, thin solid strands of pasta.

spiral pasta corkscrew-shaped pasta available in various flavours and sizes.

tagliatelle long, flat strips of wheat pasta, slightly narrower and thinner than fettuccine.

tortellini circles of fresh plain pasta that are stuffed with a meat or cheese filling, and then folded into little hats.

PEANUTS also known as groundnut, not in fact a nut but the pod of a legume. We mainly use raw (unroasted) or unsalted roasted peanuts.

PEARL BARLEY see barley

PECANS native to the US and now grown locally; pecans are golden brown, buttery and rich. Good in savoury as well as sweet dishes; walnuts are a good substitute.

PEPITAS are the pale green kernels of dried pumpkin seeds; they can be bought plain or salted.

PINE NUTS also known as pignoli; not a nut but a small, cream-coloured kernel from pine cones. They are best roasted before use to bring out the flavour.

PIRI PIRI SAUCE a Portuguese chilli sauce made from red chillies, ginger, garlic, oil and various herbs.

PISTACHIOS green, delicately flavoured nuts inside hard off-white shells. Available salted or unsalted in their shells; you can also get them shelled.

PLUM SAUCE a thick, sweet and sour dipping sauce made from plums, vinegar, sugar, chillies and spices.

POLENTA also known as cornmeal; a flour-like cereal made of dried corn (maize). Also the dish made from it.

POMEGRANATE dark-red, leathery-skinned fresh fruit about the size of an orange filled with hundreds of seeds, each wrapped in an edible lucent-crimson pulp having a unique tangy sweet-sour flavour.

POMEGRANATE MOLASSES not to be confused with pomegranate syrup or grenadine (used in cocktails); pomegranate molasses is thicker, browner, and more concentrated in flavour — tart and sharp, slightly sweet and fruity. Brush over grilling or roasting meat, seafood or poultry, add to salad dressings or sauces. Buy from Middle Eastern food stores or specialty food shops.

POPPY SEEDS small, dried, bluish-grey seeds of the poppy plant, with a crunchy texture and a nutty flavour. Can be purchased whole or ground in delicatessens and most supermarkets.

PORK
american-style spareribs well-trimmed mid-loin ribs.
belly fatty cut sold in rashers or in a piece, with or without rind or bone.
chinese barbecued roasted pork fillet with a sweet, sticky coating. Available from Asian food shops or specialty stores.
cutlets cut from ribs.
fillet skinless, boneless eye-fillet cut from the loin.
minced ground lean pork.
neck sometimes called pork scotch, boneless cut from the foreloin.
shoulder joint sold with bone in or out.

POTATOES
bintje oval, creamy skin, yellow flesh; good all-purpose potato, great baked and fried, good in salads.
coliban round, smooth white skin and flesh; good for baking and mashing.
desiree oval, smooth and pink-skinned, waxy yellow flesh; good in salads, boiled and roasted.
idaho also known as russet burbank; russet in colour, fabulous baked.
king edward slightly plump and rosy; great mashed.
kipfler small, finger-shaped, nutty flavour; great baked and in salads.
lasoda round, red skin with deep eyes, white flesh; good for mashing or roasting.

new potatoes also known as chats; not a separate variety but an early harvest with very thin skin. Good unpeeled steamed, eaten hot or cold in salads.
pontiac large, red skin, deep eyes, white flesh; good grated, boiled and baked.
russet burbank long and oval, rough white skin with shallow eyes, white flesh; good for baking and frying.
sebago white skin, oval; good fried, mashed and baked.

PRESERVED LEMON whole or quartered salted lemons preserved in a mixture of olive oil and lemon juice and occasionally spices such as cinnamon, clove and coriander. A North African specialty, they are usually added to casseroles and tagines to impart a rich, salty-sour acidic flavour; also added to salad dressings or chopped and stirred into yogurt. Available from delicatessens and specialty food shops. Use the rind only and rise well under cold water before using.

PRESERVED TURNIP also called hua chai po or cu cai muoi, or dried radish because of its similarity to daikon. Sold packaged whole or sliced, is very salty and must be rinsed and dried before use.

PROSCIUTTO a kind of unsmoked Italian ham; salted, air-cured and aged, it is usually eaten uncooked. There are many styles of prosciutto, one of the best being Parma ham, from Italy's Emilia Romagna region, traditionally lightly salted, dried then eaten raw.

QUAIL related to the pheasant and partridge; a small, delicate-flavoured farmed game bird ranging in weight from 250g to 300g.

QUINCE yellow-skinned fruit with hard texture and astringent, tart taste; eaten cooked or as a preserve. Long, slow cooking makes the flesh a deep rose pink.

RADICCHIO see lettuce

RAISINS dried sweet grapes (traditionally muscatel grapes).

RAITA yogurt that is whipped and seasoned with salt, pepper and one or two piquant spices; often has mint stirred in. Served as a condiment, it possesses cooling properties to help temper the heat of a curry.

READY-MADE WHITE ICING also known as soft icing, ready-to-roll and prepared fondant.

READY-ROLLED PUFF PASTRY packaged sheets of frozen puff pastry, available from supermarkets.

READY-ROLLED SHORTCRUST PASTRY packaged sheets of frozen shortcrust pastry, available from supermarkets.

REDCURRANT JELLY a preserve made from redcurrants used as a glaze for desserts and meats or in sauces.

RHUBARB a plant with long, green-red stalks; becomes sweet and edible when cooked.

RICE
arborio small, round grain rice well-suited to absorb a large amount of liquid; the high level of starch makes it especially suitable for risottos, giving the dish its classic creaminess.
basmati a white, fragrant long-grained rice; the grains fluff up beautifully when cooked. It should be washed several times before cooking.
doongara a white rice with a lower glycaemic index (GI) than most other rices, so it is more slowly absorbed into the blood stream, providing sustained energy release for endurance. Cooks to a firm, fluffy rice, even if it is overcooked
jasmine or Thai jasmine, is a long-grained white rice recognised around the world as having a perfumed aromatic quality; moist in texture, it clings together after cooking. Sometimes substituted for basmati rice.

koshihikari small, round-grain white rice. Substitute white short-grain rice and cook by the absorption method.
long-grain elongated grains that remain separate when cooked; this is the most popular steaming rice in Asia.
short-grain fat, almost round grain with a high starch content; tends to clump together when cooked.
white is hulled and polished rice, can be short-or long-grained.

RISONI see pasta

ROCKET also called arugula, rugula and rucola; peppery green leaf eaten raw in salads or used in cooking. Baby rocket leaves are smaller and less peppery.

ROLLED OATS flattened oat grain rolled into flakes and traditionally used for porridge. Instant oats are also available, but use traditional oats for baking.

ROLLED RICE flattened rice grain rolled into flakes; looks similar to rolled oats.

ROLLED RYE flattened rye grain rolled into flakes and similar in appearance to rolled oats.

ROSEWATER extract made from crushed rose petals, called gulab in India; used for its aromatic quality in many sweetmeats and desserts.

ROSEMARY pungent herb with long, thin pointy leaves; use large and small sprigs, and the leaves are usually chopped finely.

RUM see liqueurs

SAFFRON stigma of a member of the crocus family, available ground or in strands; imparts a yellow-orange colour to food once infused. The quality can vary greatly; the best is the most expensive spice in the world.

SAGE pungent herb with narrow, grey-green leaves; slightly bitter with a slightly musty mint aroma. Refrigerate fresh sage wrapped in a paper towel

and sealed in a plastic bag for up to 4 days. Dried sage comes whole, crumbled or ground. Store in a cool, dark place no more than three months.

SAKE Japan's favourite wine, made from fermented rice, is used for marinating, cooking and as part of dipping sauces. If sake is unavailable, dry sherry, vermouth or brandy can be substituted. If drinking sake, stand it first in a container in hot water for 20 minutes to warm it through.

SAMBAL OELEK also ulek or olek; an Indonesian salty paste made from ground chillies and vinegar.

SASHIMI fish sold as sashimi has to meet stringent guidelines regarding its handling. We suggest you seek local advice from authorities before easting any raw seafood.

SAVOY CABBAGE large, heavy head with crinkled dark-green outer leaves; a fairly mild tasting cabbage.

SEAFOOD
blue swimmer crab also known as sand crab, blue manna crab, bluey, sand crab or sandy. Substitute with lobster, balmain or moreton bay bugs.
blue-eye also known as deep sea trevalla or trevally and blue-eye cod; thick, moist white-fleshed fish.
bream (yellowfin) also known as silver or black bream, seabream or surf bream; soft, moist white flesh. Substitute with snapper or ocean perch.
clams also called vongole; we use a small ridge-shelled variety of this bivalve mollusc.
fish fillet use your favourite firm-fleshed white fish fillet.
mussels should only be bought from a reliable fish market: they must be tightly closed when bought, indicating they are alive. Before cooking, scrub shells with a strong brush and remove the beards; do not eat any that do not open after cooking. Varieties include black and green-lip.

ocean trout a farmed fish with pink, soft flesh. It is from the same family as the atlantic salmon; one can be substituted for the other.

octopus usually tenderised before you buy them; both octopus and squid require either long slow cooking (usually for the large molluscs) or quick cooking over high heat (usually for the small molluscs) — anything in between will make the octopus tough and rubbery.

oysters available in many varieties, including pacific, bay/blacklip, and Sydney or New Zealand rock oyster.

prawns also known as shrimp. Varieties include, school, king, royal red, Sydney harbour, tiger. Can be bought uncooked (green) or cooked, with or without shells.

salmon red-pink firm flesh with few bones; moist delicate flavour.

squid also known as calamari; a type of mollusc. Buy squid hoods to make preparation and cooking faster.

swordfish also known as broadbill. Substitute with yellowfin or bluefin tuna or mahi mahi.

tuna reddish, firm flesh; slightly dry. Varieties include bluefin, yellowfin, skipjack or albacore; substitute with swordfish.

white fish means non-oily fish; includes bream, flathead, whiting, snapper, dhufish, redfish and ling.

SEMOLINA coarsely ground flour milled from durum wheat; the flour used in making gnocchi, pasta and couscous.

SESAME SEEDS black and white are the most common of this small oval seed, however there are also red and brown varieties. The seeds are used as an ingredient and as a condiment. Roast the seeds in a heavy-based frying pan over low heat.

SEVEN-SPICE MIX (shichimi togarashi) a Japanese blend of seven ground spices, seeds and seaweed. The mixture varies but includes some hot and aromatic flavours. Used as a seasoning with noodles and cooked meats and fish.

SHALLOTS also called french shallots, golden shallots or eschalots. Small and elongated, with a brown-skin, they grow in tight clusters similar to garlic.
fried can be purchased at Asian grocery stores; once opened, fried shallots will keep for months if stored in a tightly sealed glass jar. see also onion
purple also known as Asian shallots; related to the onion but resembling garlic (they grow in bulbs of multiple cloves). Thin-layered and intensely flavoured, they are used in cooking throughout South-East Asia.

SHRIMP PASTE also known as kapi, trasi and blanchan; a strong-scented, very firm preserved paste made of salted dried shrimp. Used sparingly as a pungent flavouring in many South-East Asian soups, sauces and rice dishes. It should be chopped or sliced thinly then wrapped in foil and roasted before use.

SICHUAN PEPPERCORNS also called szechuan or Chinese pepper, native to the Sichuan province of China. A mildly hot spice that comes from the prickly ash tree. Although it is not related to the peppercorn family, small, red-brown aromatic sichuan berries look like black peppercorns and have a distinctive peppery-lemon flavour and aroma.

SILVER BEET also known as Swiss chard and incorrectly, spinach; has fleshy stalks and large leaves, both of which can be prepared as for spinach.

SKEWERS metal or bamboo skewers can be used. Rub oil onto metal skewers to stop meat sticking; soak bamboo skewers in water for at least 1 hour or overnight to prevent them splintering or scorching during cooking.

SNOW PEAS also called mangetout; a variety of garden pea, eaten pod and all (although you may need to string them). Used in stir-fries or eaten raw in salads. Snow pea sprouts are available from supermarkets or greengrocers and are usually eaten raw in salads or sandwiches.

SOPRESSA a salami from the north of Italy, can be found in both mild and chilli-flavoured varieties. If you can't find it easily, you can use any hot salami, but the taste won't be exactly the same.

SOY SAUCE also known as sieu; made from fermented soybeans. Several variations are available in supermarkets and Asian food stores; we use Japanese soy sauce unless indicated otherwise.
dark deep brown, almost black in colour; rich, with a thicker consistency than other types. Pungent but not particularly salty; good for marinating.
japanese an all-purpose low-sodium soy sauce made with more wheat content than its Chinese counterparts; fermented in barrels and aged. Possibly the best table soy and the one to choose if you only want one variety.
light fairly thin in consistency and, while paler than the others, the saltiest tasting; used in dishes in which the natural colour of the ingredients is to be maintained. Not to be confused with salt-reduced or low-sodium soy sauces.

SPECK smoked pork.

SPINACH also known as english spinach and incorrectly, silver beet. Baby spinach leaves are best eaten raw in salads; the larger leaves should be added last to soups, stews and stir-fries, and should be cooked until barely wilted.

SPONGE FINGER BISCUITS also known as savoiardi, savoy biscuits or lady's fingers, they are Italian-style crisp fingers made from sponge cake mixture.

SPRING ROLL WRAPPERS also known as egg roll wrappers; they come in various sizes and can be purchased fresh or frozen. Made from a delicate wheat-based pastry, they can be used for making gow gee and samosas as well as spring rolls.

STAR ANISE a dried star-shaped pod whose seeds have an astringent aniseed flavour; commonly used to flavour stocks and marinades.

STARFRUIT also known as carambola, five-corner fruit or Chinese star fruit; pale green or yellow colour, it has a clean, crisp texture. Flavour may be either sweet or sour, depending on the variety and when it was picked. There is no need to peel or seed it and they're slow to discolour.

SUGAR we use coarse, granulated table sugar, also known as crystal sugar, unless otherwise specified.
brown a soft, finely granulated sugar retaining molasses for its characteristic colour and flavour.
caster also known as superfine or finely granulated table sugar.
demerara small-grained golden-coloured crystal sugar.
icing also known as confectioners' sugar or powdered sugar; pulverised granulated sugar crushed together with a small amount of cornflour.
muscovado a fine-grained, moist sugar that comes in two types, light and dark. Light muscovado has a light toffee flavour and is good for sticky toffee sauce and caramel ice-cream. Dark muscovado is used in sweet and spicy sauces.
palm also called nam tan pip, jaggery, jawa or gula melaka; made from the sap of the sugar palm tree. Light brown to black in colour and usually sold in rock-hard cakes; use with brown sugar if unavailable.
pure icing also known as confectioners' sugar or powdered sugar.
raw natural brown granulated sugar.

SUGAR SNAP PEAS also called honey snap peas; fresh small pea which can be eaten whole, pod and all.

SUMAC a purple-red, astringent spice ground from berries growing on shrubs that flourish wild around the Mediterranean; adds a tart, lemony flavour to dips and dressings and goes well with barbecued meat. Can be found in Middle Eastern food stores.

SUNFLOWER SEEDS grey-green, slightly soft, oily kernels; a nutritious snack.

SWEET CHILLI SAUCE see chilli

TACO SEASONING MIX a packaged seasoning meant to duplicate the Mexican sauce made from oregano, cumin, chillies and other spices.

TAHINI sesame seed paste available from Middle Eastern food stores.

TAMARI similar to but thicker than japanese soy; very dark in colour with a distinctively mellow flavour. Good used as a dipping sauce or for basting.

TAMARIND the tamarind tree produces clusters of hairy brown pods, each of which is filled with seeds and a viscous pulp, that are dried and pressed into the blocks of tamarind found in Asian food shops. Gives a sweet-sour, slightly astringent taste to marinades, pastes, sauces and dressings.

TAMARIND CONCENTRATE (or paste) the commercial result of the distillation of tamarind juice into a condensed, compacted paste.

TIA MARIA see liqueurs

THYME a member of the mint family; the "household" variety, simply called thyme in most shops, is French thyme; it has tiny grey-green leaves that give off a pungent minty, light-lemon aroma. Dried thyme comes in both leaf and powdered form. Lemon thyme's scent is due to the high level of citral in its leaves, an oil also found in lemon, orange, verbena and lemon grass. The citrus scent is enhanced by crushing the leaves in your hands before using the herb.

TOFU also known as soybean curd or bean curd; an off-white, custard-like product made from the "milk" of crushed soybeans. Comes fresh as soft or firm, and processed as fried or pressed dried sheets. Fresh tofu can be refrigerated in water (changed daily) for up to 4 days.
firm made by compressing bean curd to remove most of the water. Good used in stir-fries as it can be tossed without disintegrating. Can also be flavoured, preserved in rice wine or brine.
silken not a type of tofu but reference to the manufacturing process of straining soybean liquid through silk; this denotes best quality.
soft delicate texture; does not hold its shape when overhandled. Can also be used as a dairy substitute in ice-cream or cheesecakes.

TOMATOES
canned whole peeled tomatoes in natural juices; available crushed, chopped or diced, sometimes unsalted or reduced salt. Use undrained.
cherry also known as tiny tim or tom thumb tomatoes; small and round.
egg also called plum or roma, these are smallish, oval-shaped tomatoes much used in Italian cooking or salads.
paste triple-concentrated tomato puree used to flavour soups, stews, sauces and casseroles.
puree canned pureed tomatoes (not tomato paste); substitute with fresh peeled and pureed tomatoes.
semi-dried partially dried tomato pieces in olive oil; softer and juicier than sun-dried, these are not a preserve thus do not keep as long as sun-dried.
sun-dried tomato pieces that have been dried with salt; this dehydrates the tomato and concentrates the flavour. We use sun-dried tomatoes packaged in oil, unless otherwise specified.
truss small vine-ripened tomatoes with vine still attached.

TURKISH BREAD also known as pide. Sold in long (about 45cm) flat loaves as well as individual rounds; made from wheat flour and sprinkled with black onion seeds.

TURMERIC also called kamin; is a rhizome related to galangal and ginger. Must be grated or pounded to release its acrid aroma and pungent flavour. Known for the golden colour it imparts, fresh turmeric can be substituted with the more commonly found dried powder.

VANILLA

bean dried, long, thin pod from a tropical golden orchid; the minuscule black seeds inside the bean are used to impart a luscious vanilla flavour in baking and desserts. Place a whole bean in a jar of sugar to make the vanilla sugar often called for in recipes; a bean can be used three or four times.
extract obtained from vanilla beans infused in water; a non-alcoholic version of essence.

VEAL

osso buco another name butchers use for veal shin, usually cut into 3cm to 5cm thick slices and used in the famous Italian slow-cooked casserole of the same name.
rack row of small chops or cutlets.
scaloppine a piece of lean steak hammered with a meat mallet until almost see-through; cook over high heat for as little time as possible.
schnitzel thinly sliced steak.

VIETNAMESE MINT not a mint at all, but a pungent and peppery narrow-leafed member of the buckwheat family. Not confined to Vietnam, it is also known as Cambodian mint, pak pai (Thailand), laksa leaf (Indonesia), daun kesom (Singapore) and rau ram in Vietnam. A common ingredient in Thai foods such as soups, salads and stir-fries.

VINEGAR

balsamic originally from Modena, Italy, there are now many balsamic vinegars on the market ranging in pungency and quality depending on how, and for how long, they have been aged. Quality can be determined up to a point by price; use the most expensive sparingly.

brown malt made from fermented malt and beech shavings.
cider made from fermented apples.
rice a colourless vinegar made from fermented rice and flavoured with sugar and salt. Also known as seasoned rice vinegar; sherry can be substituted.
white made from distilled grain alcohol.

WALNUTS as well as being a good source of fibre and healthy oils, nuts contain a range of vitamins, minerals and other beneficial plant components called phytochemicals. Each type of nut has a special make-up and walnuts contain the beneficial omega-3 fatty acids.

WASABI also called wasabe; an Asian horseradish used to make the pungent, green-coloured sauce traditionally served with Japanese raw fish dishes; sold in powdered or paste form.

WATER CHESTNUTS resemble true chestnuts in appearance, hence the English name. Small brown tubers with a crisp, white, nutty-tasting flesh. Their crunchy texture is best experienced fresh; however, canned water chestnuts are more easily obtained and can be kept for about a month in the fridge, once opened. Used, rinsed and drained, in salads and stir-fries.

WATERCRESS one of the cress family, a large group of peppery greens used raw in salads, dips and sandwiches, or cooked in soups. Highly perishable, so it must be used as soon as possible after purchase.

WITLOF also known as belgian endive; related to and confused with chicory. A versatile vegetable, it tastes as good cooked as it does eaten raw. Grown in darkness like white asparagus to prevent it becoming green; looks somewhat like a tightly furled, cream to very light-green cigar. The leaves can be removed and used to hold a canapé filling; the whole vegetable can be opened up, stuffed then baked or

casseroled; and the leaves can be tossed in a salad with other vegetables.

WOMBOK also known as Chinese cabbage, peking or napa cabbage; elongated in shape with pale green, crinkly leaves, this is the most common cabbage in South-East Asia. Can be shredded or chopped and eaten raw or braised, steamed or stir-fried.

WONTON WRAPPERS and gow gee or spring roll pastry sheets, made of flour, egg and water, are found in the refrigerated or freezer section of Asian food shops and many supermarkets. These come in different thicknesses and shapes. Thin wrappers work best in soups, while the thicker ones are best for frying; and the choice of round or square, small or large is dependent on the recipe.

WORCESTERSHIRE SAUCE thin, dark-brown spicy sauce developed by the British when in India; used as a seasoning for meat, gravies and cocktails, and as a condiment.
japanese there are two types available, one similar to normal worcestershire and the other somewhat blander; both are made from varying proportions of vinegar, tomatoes, onions, carrots, garlic and spices.

YEAST (dried and fresh), a raising agent used in dough making. Granular (7g sachets) and fresh compressed (20g blocks) yeast can almost always be substituted one for the other when yeast is called for.

YOGURT we use plain full-cream yogurt in our recipes unless specifically noted otherwise. If a recipe in this book calls for low-fat yogurt, we use one with a fat content of less than 0.2 per cent.

ZUCCHINI also called courgette; small, pale- or dark-green or yellow vegetable of the squash family. Harvested when young, its edible flowers can be stuffed with a mild cheese and deep-fried.

index

General manager Christine Whiston
Editorial director Susan Tomnay
Creative director and designer Hieu Chi Nguyen
Senior editor Stephanie Kistner
Design assistant Melissa Deare
Food director Pamela Clark
Food editor Cathie Lonnie
Nutritional information Belinda Farlow

Director of sales Brian Cearnes
Marketing manager Bridget Cody
Business analyst Rebecca Varela
Operations manager David Scotto
Production manager Victoria Jefferys
International rights enquiries Laura Bamford lbamford@acpuk.com

ACP Books are published by ACP Magazines a division of PBL Media Pty Limited

Group publisher, Women's lifestyle Pat Ingram
Director of sales, Women's lifestyle Lynette Phillips
Commercial manager, Women's lifestyle Seymour Cohen
Marketing director, Women's lifestyle Matthew Dominello
Public relations manager, Women's lifestyle Hannah Deveraux
Creative director, Events, Women's lifestyle Luke Bonnano
Research Director, Women's lifestyle Justin Stone
ACP Magazines, Chief Executive officer Scott Lorson
PBL Media, Chief Executive officer Ian Law

Photographers Alan Benson, Luke Burgess, Joshua Dasey, Ben Dearnley, Joe Filshie, Louise Lister, Andre Martin, Rob Palmer, Con Poulos, Prue Roscoe, Rob Reichenfeld, Brett Stevens, John Paul Urizar, Ian Wallace, Dean Wilmot, Andrew Young, Gorta Yuuki, Tanya Zouev.
Stylists Wendy Berecry, Julz Beresford, Kristin Beusing, Janelle Bloom, Margot Braddon, Kate Brown, Marie-Helene Clauzon, Jane Hann, Trish Heagerty, Amber Keller, Opel Khan, Michaela Le Compte, Vicki Liley, David Morgan, Kate Murdoch, Hieu Chi Nguyen, Sarah O'Brien, Justine Osborne, Louise Pickford, Christine Rouke, Stephanie Souvlis.

Produced by ACP Books, Sydney. Published by ACP Books, a division of ACP Magazines Ltd.
54 Park St, Sydney NSW Australia 2000. GPO Box 4088, Sydney, NSW 2001.
Phone +61 2 9282 8618 Fax +61 2 9267 9438 acpbooks@acpmagazines.com.au www.acpbooks.com.au

Printed by C&C Offset Printing, China.

Australia Distributed by Network Services,
GPO Box 4088, Sydney, NSW 2001.
Phone +61 2 9282 8777 Fax +61 2 9264 3278 networkweb@networkservicescompany.com.au
United Kingdom Distributed by Australian Consolidated Press (UK),
10 Scirocco Close, Moulton Park Office Village, Northampton, NN3 6AP.
Phone +44 1604 642 200 Fax +44 1604 642 300 books@acpuk.com www.acpuk.com
Canada Distributed by Publishers Group Cananda,
Order Desk & Customer Service, 9050 Shaughnessy Street, Vancouver, BC V6P 6E5
Phone (800) 663 5714 Fax (800) 565 3770 service@raincoast.com
New Zealand Distributed by Southern Publishers Group,
21 Newton Road, Auckland, NZ.
Phone +64 9 360 0692 Fax +64 9 360 0695 hub@spg.co.nz
South Africa Distributed by PSD Promotions,
30 Diesel Road Isando, Gauteng Johannesburg. PO Box 1175, Isando 1600, Gauteng Johannesburg.
Phone +27 11 392 6065/6/7 Fax +27 11 392 6079/80 orders@psdprom.co.za

Title: 1000 best-ever recipes from the AWW: the Australian women's weekly/editor, Pamela Clark.
Publisher: Sydney: ACP Books, 2008.
ISBN: 978-1-86396-847-8
Notes: Includes index.
Subjects: Cookery.
Other authors: Clark, Pamela.
Also titled: One thousand best-ever recipes from the AWW;
Thousand best-ever recipes from the AWW; Australian women's weekly.
Dewey number: 641.5

To order books, phone 136 116 (within Australia).
Send recipe enquiries to: askpamela@acpmagazines.com.au